CRIMINOLOGY TODAY

AN INTEGRATIVE INTRODUCTION

CRIMINOLOGY TODAY

AN INTEGRATIVE INTRODUCTION

❖

S E C O N D   E D I T I O N

FRANK SCHMALLEGER, Ph.D.

The Justice Research Association

Pearson
Education

PRENTICE HALL, UPPER SADDLE RIVER, NEW JERSEY 07458

Library of Congress Cataloging-in-Publication Data

Schmalleger, Frank.
    Criminology today : an integrative introduction / Frank
Schmalleger. — 2nd ed.
        p.   cm.
    Includes bibliographical references and indexes.
    ISBN 0-13-848268-3
    1. Criminology.   2. Criminology—United States.   I. Title.
HV6025.S346 1999   99-17310
364—dc21   CIP

Acquisitions Editor: *Neil Marquardt*
Director of Manufacturing & Production: *Bruce Johnson*
Managing Editor: *Mary Carnis*
Manufacturing Buyer: *Ed O'Dougherty*
Editorial Assistant: *Jean Auman*
Production Liaison: *Denise Brown*
Full Service Production/Formatting: *Lori Harvey/Carlisle Communications*
Printer/Binder: *RR Donnelley & Sons/Willard*
Creative Director: *Marianne Frasco*
Electronic Art: *Mark La Salle/Carlisle Communications*
Cover Photo: *Sam Kittner*
Cover Design: *Joe Sengotta*
Interior Design: *Patrice Sheridan*
Director, Image Resource Center: *Lori Morris-Nantz*
Photo Research Supervisor: *Melinda Lee Reo*
Image Permission Supervisor: *Kay Dellosa*
Photo Research: *Beth Boyd*
Marketing Manager: *Frank Mortimer, Jr.*

Chapter Opening Photo Credits: 1—Bob Riha, Gamma-Liaison, Inc.; 2—USA Today; 3—Bohdan Hyrnewych, Stock Boston; 4—The Granger Collection; 5—Ian Turner/Spooner, Gamma-Liaison, Inc.; 6—Photofest; 7—Springer, Gamma-Liaison, Inc.; 8—Ken Hawkins, Stock South/Uniphoto/PNI; 9—AP/Wide World Photos; 10—Photofest; 11—Joel Stettenheim, SABA Press Photos, Inc.; 12—Illustration, Marc Yankus; 13—NcNamee, Corbis-Bettmann; 14—Photofest

Printed in the United States of America

10 9 8 7 6 5 4 3 2 1

ISBN 0-13-848268-3

Prentice-Hall International (UK) Limited, *London*
Prentice-Hall of Australia Pty. Limited, *Sydney*
Prentice-Hall Canada Inc., *Toronto*
Prentice-Hall Hispanoamericana, S.A., *Mexico*
Prentice-Hall of India Private Limited, *New Delhi*
Prentice-Hall of Japan, Inc., *Tokyo*
Simon & Schuster Asia Pte. Ltd., *Singapore*
Editora Prentice-Hall do Brasil, Ltda., *Rio de Janeiro*

To my wife, Harmonie,

whose loving spirit and close friendship

have been my constant inspiration.

And to my daughter, Nicole, whom I will always cherish.

CONTENTS

FOREWORD

The United States is currently witnessing an unprecedented level of violent crime. Not only do the rates of criminal violence exceed anything in our history, but the acts have become more random, more brutal, and targeted toward more vulnerable victims, for example, children and innocent bystanders.

Unfortunately, experts predict another crime wave by the year 2000 because of a projected increase in the number of teenagers in America, who are twice as violent as adults. The next generation of children is also more likely to be born to a single mother, to experience poverty, and to be unemployed than previous generations—all factors known to relate to later criminality. When James Q. Wilson, a foremost authority on crime, wrote recently about what advice he would give to Americans struggling with the crime problem, he offered only two words: "Get ready."[1]

It is this sense of urgency that creates a daunting challenge for today's criminology students, who must, above all, learn criminology so that they can contribute to its solutions. In short, *criminology students must seek to become relevant*. We have become too detached from applied criminology, and as a result, current crime policies are overly bureaucratic and highly political. We must strive to change the perception that "criminologists . . . are insular and detached types who fiddle with equations while the cities burn."[2]

Criminology is the only academic discipline devoted exclusively to the scientific study of crime causation and control. When the public puts pressure on government officials to "do something" about the crime problem, surely criminologists have an obligation to assist in identifying key issues, proposing policy and program solutions, and evaluating the consequences.

But learning criminology is not easy. In fact, it is hard to imagine a more difficult subject matter than criminology. At its core, criminology requires an understanding of the vagaries of human behavior, with an appreciation of their biological, cultural, and sociological foundations. Each contributes a partial explanation for crime, but none is comprehensive and all are fraught with controversy. Understanding crime is made even more complex because the behavior is defined and controlled by a justice system that consists of many diverse organizations, such as the police and corrections, and each is governed by a separate system of complex laws and philosophies. How can a person make sense of all these competing theories and contradictory data?

Thank goodness for Frank Schmalleger's book, *Criminology Today!* In writing it, he has done most of the hard work for us. He succeeds in making this complex social problem clearly understandable. He begins by describing, in an easy-to-understand manner, the nature and diversity of the crime problem today. He critically reviews the nation's divergent crime indicators and suggests what recent patterns portend about the crime problem—ever changing, ever more threatening. He then advances our understanding of the causes of crime by synthesizing criminology's most salient theories, grounding his review in current as well as historical traditions. Students can flounder in crime data and theory without a good and objective guide. Dr. Schmalleger serves as an authoritative and compassionate guide.

The uniqueness of this book and its biggest strength derives from Schmalleger's orientation: it is always practical and socially relevant. He teaches the student how to relate criminology facts and theories to the everyday world. Discussions of the death penalty, for example, are illustrated with newspaper stories of recent executions; and the material covered in the text is particularly up-to-date. Events such as the use of DNA evidence in O.J. Simpson's criminal and civil trial, the recent federal crime bill, and the Oklahoma City bombing are all discussed. Including such material not only makes the connection between academic criminology and real-world practice patently obvious, it provides an immediate attention getter for students, who are more likely to become fully engaged by such timely material. In a sense, it makes criminology come alive.

This book synthesizes and interprets the best available evidence on crime and crime control, but it goes still further. In his final chapter, Schmalleger encourages us to consider our future and work toward promoting better crime prevention and control practices. In the end, mastering the material in *Criminology Today* should enable us to do much more than simply sit passively and "get ready" for the next crime wave. For what we understand, we can often change. Schmalleger's text provides an excellent road map for increasing that understanding.

Joan Petersilia, Ph.D.
Professor of Criminology, Law & Society
University of California, Irvine
and former President
The American Society of Criminology

1. James Q. Wilson and Joan Petersilia, *Crime* (Institute for Contemporary Studies, San Francisco, 1995).
2. Elliott Currie, "Shifting the Balance: On Social Action and the Future of Criminological Research," *Journal Research in Crime and Delinquency,* vol. 30, no. 4 (1993).

PREFACE

More than a quarter century ago the great criminologist Austin Turk began the preface to his book *Criminality and Legal Order* with these words:[1]

> Embarrassment provided much of the initial push that led to the writing of this book. I was embarrassed at my lack of good answers when confronted by students who wondered, somewhat irreverently, why criminology is 'such a confused mish-mash.' . . . Some of these students were especially bothered by the 'unreality' of criminological studies, by which they meant the lack of sustained attention to connections between the theories and statistics about crime, and what they heard every day about relations among social conflicts, political maneuvers, and law violation and enforcement.

Much has changed since Turk's time, yet much remains the same. Far more criminological studies have been proposed and conducted. The Law Enforcement Assistance Administration, funded under President Johnson, which made many millions of dollars available in the fight against crime, has come and gone. The Clinton administration's $30-billion crime bill was signed into law in 1994, with agencies everywhere continuing to scramble for a part of the financial pie it represents.

Yet crime is still with us as we enter the twenty-first century—and although crime statistics are actually showing some decline, fear of crime continues to run high among wide segments of the American population. Recent public opinion polls conducted by *USA Today*, CNN, and Gallup interviewers all show that crime outranks the economy, health care, foreign policy, and other social issues as one of the primary concerns of the American public today.

Such heightening of concern, although new to many of today's students, appears to follow something of a cyclical pattern. For a long while concerns over individual rights have swung the proverbial social and legislative pendulum in what has now come to be seen by many as an overly permissive direction—one in which criminal offenders are coddled and shielded from accountability. Contemporary policymakers of the late twentieth century found themselves awash in calls to reverse the pendulum's direction by those intent on protecting the law-abiding public, by those wanting to ensure the swift and certain punishment of criminal predators, and by still others wishing to unshackle agents of law enforcement to make certain that individual offenders were held firmly responsible for their actions.

Because of the ever increasing interest in crime and its causation, today's textbook market is flooded with introductory criminology books. What makes *Criminology Today* different from all the other available texts which deal with the same subject matter? The following list highlights what I see as the important differences:

- *Criminology Today* acknowledges the current primacy of the sociological perspective in studying crime and criminal activity.
- *Criminology Today* also emphasizes the wide and interdisciplinary variety of academic perspectives which contribute to a thorough and well-informed understanding of the crime problem; hence the book's subtitle: *An Integrative Introduction.*
- *Criminology Today* is up-to-date. It addresses the latest social issues and discusses innovative criminological perspectives within a well-grounded and traditional theoretical framework.
- *Criminology Today* is socially relevant. It contrasts contemporary issues of crime and social order with existing and proposed crime-control policies.
- *Criminology Today* is interesting and easy to read. It is written for today's student and makes use of attention-getting stories, news briefs, images, and graphical outlines to capture student attention.
- *Criminology Today* is policy oriented. Unlike most existing texts, *Criminology Today* stresses the consequences of criminological thought for social policy and describes the practical issues associated with understanding and controlling crime. Social policies focusing on prevention, treatment, rehabilitation, and victim restoration are all discussed.
- *Criminology Today* is thematic. It builds upon the divergence between the social problems viewpoint and the social responsibility perspective. In so doing, it highlights the central issue facing criminologists today: whether crime should be addressed as a matter of individual responsibility and accountability, or treated as a symptom of a dysfunctional society.
- *Criminology Today* provides instructors and students with a wealth of resources for studying crime and society's response to it, including an award-winning World Wide Web site (*http://www.prenhall.com/cjcentral*), a video library, full-color transparencies, and an excellent student study guide.

The thematic approach of *Criminology Today* is dualistic. On the one hand, it presents a social problems framework, which holds that crime may be a manifestation of underlying cultural issues such as poverty, discrimination, and the breakdown of traditional social institutions. It contrasts the social problems approach, on the other hand, with a social responsibility perspective, which claims that individuals are fundamentally responsible for their own behavior and maintains that they choose crime over other, more law-abiding, courses of action. The thematic contrast is an important one, for it provides students with a useful framework for integrating the voluminous material contained within the field of criminology. Contrasting the two perspectives, as this book does, provides fertile ground for a dialectical process whereby readers can better understand the central issues defining contemporary criminology and come to their own conclusions about the value of criminological theorizing.

As an author I have tried to ensure that today's students will find *Criminology Today* relevant, interesting, and informative. It is my fondest hope that this book will assist them in drawing their own conclusions about the American crime problem, that it will help prepare them for the future, and that it will allow them to make informed decisions about public policy in the crime-control area. For one day it is they who will forge public policy, and it is they who will soon be writing books like this one.

1. Austin Turk, *Criminality and Legal Order* (Chicago: Rand McNally, 1969), p. vii.

ACKNOWLEDGMENTS

A book like *Criminology Today* draws upon the talents and resources of many people, and is the end result of much previous effort. This text could not have been written without the groundwork laid by previous criminologists, academicians, and researchers; hence, a hearty "thank you" is due everyone who has contributed to the development of the field of criminology throughout the years, and especially those theorists, authors, and social commentators who are cited in this book. Without their work the field would be that much poorer. I would like to thank, as well, all the adopters—professors and students alike—of my previous textbooks, for they have given me the encouragement and fostered the steadfastness required to write this new edition of *Criminology Today*.

The Prentice-Hall team whom I have come to know so well, and who have worked so professionally with me on this and other projects deserves a special thanks. The team includes Neil Marquardt, Denise Brown, Frank Mortimer, Jr., Marianne Frasco, and Jean Auman. My thanks also to cover designer Joe Sengotta, and interior designer Patrice Sheridan, whose efforts have helped make *Criminology Today* both attractive and visually appealing. In addition, I would like to thank Lori Harvey and the rest of the Carlisle Publishers Services team for their commitment and attention to this project.

Manuscript reviewers Michael P. Brown, Ball State University; Dianne Carmody, Western Washington University; Ellen G. Cohn, Florida International University; Mark L. Dantzker, Loyola University; Taylor Davis, Georgia Southern University; Patrick G. Donnelly, The University of Dayton; Martin E. Heischmidt, Rend Lake College; Ronald D. Hunter, Jacksonville State University; Debra Kelley, Longwood College; Joan Luxenburg, University of Central Oklahoma; Robert Mutchnick, Indiana University of Pennsylvania; Glen E. Sapp, Central Carolina Community College; and Anthony W. Zumpetta, West Chester University are due a special "thank you" for helping me stick to important themes when I might otherwise have strayed, and for their guidance in matters of detail. I am especially thankful to supplements author Gordon Armstrong for the quality products he has created, and for his exceptional ability to intuitively build upon concepts in the text. Thanks also to Bob Winslow at California State University–San Diego for insight and encouragement on a number of important issues; and to Richard Guymon at Maplewoods Community College, to Debra Kelley at Virginia's Longwood College, and Stephen J. Schoenthaler for their valuable suggestions in the preparation of this new edition.

This book has benefited greatly from the quick availability of information and other resources which are available through online services such as America Online, and in various locations on the Internet's World Wide Web. I am grateful to the many information providers who, although they are too numerous to list, have helped establish such useful resources.

I am thankful as well for the assistance of Bill Tafoya and Nancy Carnes, both with the FBI (Bill is now retired); David Beatty, Director of Public Affairs with the National Victim Center; Kris Rose at the National Criminal Justice Reference Service; Marilyn Marbrook and Michael Rand at the Office of Justice Programs; Mark Reading at DEA; and Barbara Maxwell at *USA Today*.

Last, but by no means least, I wish to thank my family—my wife, Harmonie; daughter, Nicole; son, Jason; and mother, Margaret—for their personal help and encouragement.

ABOUT THE AUTHOR

Frank Schmalleger, Ph.D., Director
The Justice Research Association

Frank Schmalleger, Ph.D., is director of The Justice Research Association (JRA), a private consulting firm and "think-tank" focusing on issues of crime and justice. The Justice Research Association, which is based in Hilton Head Island, South Carolina, serves the needs of the nation's civil and criminal justice planners and administrators through workshops, conferences, and grant writing and program evaluation support. JRA also supports the Criminal Justice Distance Learning Consortium (CJDLC), which can be found on the web at *http://cjentral.com/cjdlc.*

Dr. Schmalleger holds degrees from the University of Notre Dame and the Ohio State University, having earned both a master's (1970) and a doctorate in sociology (1974) from Ohio State University with a special emphasis in criminology. From 1976 to 1994 he taught criminal justice courses at the University of North Carolina at Pembroke. For the last sixteen of those years he chaired the university's Department of Sociology, Social Work, and Criminal Justice. As an adjunct professor with Webster University in St. Louis, Missouri, Schmalleger helped develop the university's graduate program in security administration and loss prevention. He taught courses in that curriculum for more than a decade. Schmalleger has also taught in the New School for Social Research's online graduate program, helping to build the world's first electronic classrooms in support of distance learning through computer telecommunications. An avid Web surfer, Schmalleger is also the creator of award-winning World Wide Web sites, including one which supports this textbook (*http://www.prenhall.com/cjcentral*).

Frank Schmalleger is the author of numerous articles and many books, including the widely used *Criminal Justice Today: An Introductory Text for the 21st Century* (Prentice-Hall), now in its fifth edition; *Criminal Justice: A Brief Introduction* (Prentice-Hall, 1999); *Crime and the Justice System in America: An Encyclopedia* (Greenwood Publishing Group, 1997); *Trial of the Century: People of the State of California vs. Orenthal James Simpsons* (Prentice-Hall, 1996); *Computers in Criminal Justice* (Wyndham Hall Press, 1991); *Career Paths: A Guide to Jobs in Federal Law Enforcement* (Regents/Prentice-Hall, 1994); *Criminal Justice Ethics* (Greenwood Press, 1991); *Finding Criminal Justice in the Library* (Wyndham Hall Press, 1991); *Ethics in Criminal Justice* (Wyndham Hall Press, 1990); *A History of Corrections* (Foundations Press of Notre Dame, 1983); and *The Social Basis of Criminal Justice* (University Press of America, 1981). Schmalleger is also founding editor of the journal *The Justice Professional.*

Schmalleger's philosophy of both teaching and writing can be summed up in these words: "In order to communicate knowledge we must first catch, then hold, a person's interest—be it student, colleague, or policy-maker. Our writing, our speaking, and our teaching must be relevant to the problems facing people today, and they must—in some way—help solve those problems."

CRIMINOLOGY
TODAY

AN INTEGRATIVE INTRODUCTION

PART ONE

THE CRIME PICTURE

I'm the big man, I got the gun. Why does she have this attitude?

—*Statement made to police by a 16-year-old boy charged with killing 38-year-old Christine Schweiger with a sawed-off shotgun while her 10-year-old daughter watched. Ms. Schweiger told the boy she had no money.*

. . . if you wish to make a big difference in crime, you must make fundamental changes in society.

—*James Q. Wilson*[1]

WHAT IS CRIMINOLOGY?

Crime is the only way to get ahead, Duke—You'll never have anything if you live your life within the law.

—DIALOG FROM THE NBC-TV MOVIE *BEYOND SUSPICION*[2]

Violence is tearing the heart out of our country.

—PRESIDENT CLINTON

Much is already known about the phenomenon of crime. Further development in theoretical criminology will result primarily from making sense out of what we already know.

—GEORGE B. VOLD AND THOMAS J. BERNARD[3]

❖ CHAPTER OUTLINE ❖

⟸ IMPORTANT TERMS ⟹

crime	common law	unicausal
civil law	statutory law	integrated theory
criminal law	deviance	social policies
felony	criminologist	social problems perspective
misdemeanor	criminology	social responsibility perspective
offense	criminality	social relativity
administrative law	criminal justice	criminal justice system
statute	theory	socialization
criminalize	general theory	phenomenology

❖ INTRODUCTION

Senseless murder is the type of crime that everyone fears. On April 19, 1997, fear became reality for Georgio Gallara, 24, and Jeremy Giordano, 22, as they answered a call to deliver a pizza to a deserted location in rural Sussex County, New Jersey. Both met gruesome deaths—shot repeatedly in the face, neck, and chest, allegedly by two mean-spirited teenagers out to prove that they could kill.[4]

    Charged in the murders of Gallara and Giordano are 17-year-old Jason Vreeland and 18-year-old Thomas Koskovich. Police say that Vreeland and Koskovich killed the deliverymen just for kicks. The teenagers allegedly called five pizzerias before they found one willing to deliver to the desolate address they had chosen for murder. When they called Tony's Pizza and Pasta, owner Georgio Gallara agreed to send deliveryman Giordano. Gallara had only recently opened the business and was trying hard to please customers. Because the call came from an area known for trouble, Gallara told Giordano that he would accompany him on the run.

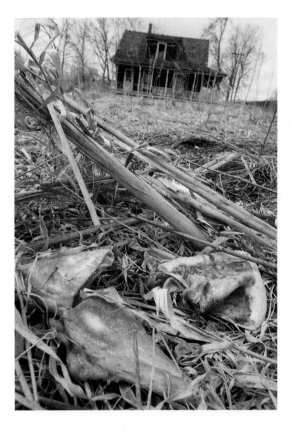

The abandoned house where Georgio Gallara, 24, and Jeremy Giordano, 22, were killed. The two young men were shot repeatedly as they answered a call to deliver a pizza to a deserted location in rural Sussex County, N.J. What do killings like these have to say about the condition of American society today? *New Jersey Newsphotos.*

According to police, the two young men arrived at the ramshackle abandoned house whose address they had been given at approximately 10:30 P.M. Koskovich and Vreeland stepped out of the dark as Gallara rolled down his window and attempted to hand over the pizza. Vreeland opened fire with a .22-caliber handgun at point-blank range, shooting the manager in the head. On the other side of the car, Koskovich began firing his .45-caliber revolver through the closed window at Giordano.

As he was dying Giordano must have hit the gas, for the car lurched forward thirty yards and pitched nose down into a swamp. The killers ran after the vehicle, dragged the victims out of the car, and shot each again in the back of the head execution style—apparently to make sure that they were dead. Neither man's wallet was taken, and the pizza was never touched. "They just wanted to see what it would be like to kill somebody," said one police investigator.

Two days after the killings, Koskovich and Vreeland were arrested and charged with the murders. A tip from a neighbor who said Koskovich had bragged about stealing guns led police to the teenagers. Two pistols, .45-caliber and .22-caliber handguns, were recovered in a duffel bag at Koskovich's home. Both weapons had been taken during a sporting goods store burglary two weeks earlier. Other witnesses said that they had seen Koskovich and Vreeland placing calls from a pay phone inside of a Dunkin' Donuts shop on Route 23, near the site of the killings, on the night of the crime. Telephone tracking systems showed that five pizzerias were called from that location, and a security camera at the donut shop appeared to show Koskovich and Vreeland borrowing a phone book from a store employee.

As profiles of the two defendants emerged, they painted a portrait of young men trying to impress others with their level of violence. Koskovich, who had been in constant trouble at vocational college, finally quit the school after bringing a sawed-off shotgun into the building. "He would bring shotguns in all the time," said Buddy Duziak, a junior at Sussex County Vocational-Technical School. "We all thought he was trying to be tough." Friends said that Koskovich had been telling them for months that he wanted to be a hitman and that he planned to kill someone.

Vreeland, the younger of the two accused killers, looked intimidating. He wore eight earrings in one ear, three in the other, and proudly displayed a silver stud worn through his tongue. He was known in his neighborhood for vandalizing cars and destroying mail in streetside deliveryboxes. Neighbors said that he had been arrested a month before the killings for firing a pellet gun at cars. Classmates at the vocational school said that Vreeland would threaten people in the halls, saying that he was going to kill them.

In sharp contrast to the profiles of the suspects, friends and relatives of Giordano and Gallara said that both victims were hardworking, well-meaning, and friendly young men. Neighbors recounted stories of how the two men helped them in countless small ways. "Jeremy was always volunteering to help me, shoveling snow or chopping ice outside my store in winter," said Donna Rockafellow, the owner of Donna's Boutique, which is located a few doors down from Tony's Pizza. Gallara, she said, "walked with a bounce. He was a sweet man. He was always giving us extra treats, powdered pastries, appetizers, and never charged for them."

As this book goes to press, Koskovich and Vreeland remain in custody—Vreeland in a juvenile facility and Koskovich in jail in lieu of a $1-million bond set by Judge Lorraine Parker in the Newton, New Jersey, Superior Court. Both have yet to be tried, and it is likely that Vreeland will be bound over for trial in adult criminal court.

The troubling aspect about the deaths of Giordano and Gallara, however, is not so much *how* they were killed, but *why* they died. Richard Giuriceo, who had once employed Koskovich at his own pizza parlor, tried to determine a motive for the killings. "What we're all afraid of," he concluded, "is that there was no reason."

▓ WHAT IS CRIME?

Americans and the American mass media display an unabashed penchant for closely following gruesome and spectacular crimes such as the pizza killings described here, and for thoroughly documenting the violent deaths of celebrities and other well-known individuals. The 1997 murders of fashion designer Gianni Versace and Ennis Cosby (son of entertainer Bill Cosby), the 1996 killing of 6-year-old starlet JonBenet Ramsey, and the 1993 murder of basketball great Michael Jordan's father (James Jordan) on a North Carolina roadside, for example, all received much press coverage. The alleged misdeeds of other celebrities such as O.J. Simpson, Michael Jackson, Snoop Doggy Dogg (see Chapter 13), and Michael Tyson seem to attract even more attention.

Crime human conduct in violation of the criminal laws of a state, the federal government, or a local jurisdiction that has the power to make such laws.

Of course, not all misdeeds are crimes. **Crime,** simply defined, is human conduct in violation of the criminal laws of a state, the federal government, or a local jurisdiction that has the power to make such laws. Without a law that circumscribes a particular form of behavior, there can be no crime, no matter how deviant or socially repugnant the behavior in question may be.

A recent case from Down Under well illustrates the principle that without a law defining an activity as illegal, there can be no crime. In 1997 an Australian court acquitted Aboriginal activist John Kelly of "making a demand with menaces"—an offense under Australian law that is similar to the crime of extortion. Kelly was charged by prosecutors with trying to extort $10,000 (Australian) by threatening to "point the bone," or place a death curse, on a well-known Australian comedian. Northern Territory Supreme Court Judge Steven Bailey directed a jury to acquit Kelly after a three-day trial, saying that "there was no evidence of unlawful conduct" in the Aboriginal activity of "pointing the bone," and that any threat made on the basis of such activity was essentially meaningless.[5] Had Kelly threatened to kill the comedian with a gun, the judge would have probably found otherwise. As in this case, however, the laws of most states would make it difficult or impossible to convict someone of assault charges for putting a voodoo curse on another person, or for burning an effigy of the person in a "black magic" ritual.

The notion of crime as behavior[6] that violates the law derives from earlier work by criminologists, such as Paul Tappan,[7] who defined crime as "an intentional act in violation of the criminal law . . . committed without defense or excuse, and penalized by the state as a felony or misdemeanor." Edwin Sutherland,[8] regarded by many as a founding figure in American criminology, said of crime that its "essential characteristic . . . is that it is behavior which is prohibited by the State as an injury to the State and against which the State may react . . . by punishment."

In the study of criminology three major forms of the law must be distinguished: civil, criminal, and administrative. **Civil law** deals with arrangements between individuals, such as contracts and claims to property. Civil law exists primarily for the purpose of enforcing private rights. In contrast, **criminal law** regulates actions which have the potential to harm interests of the state or the federal government. Because the state is made up of citizens, acts that are harmful to citizens of the state are fundamentally criminal in nature. Hence, although serious crimes with identifiable victims such as murder and rape are clearly criminal, offenses that have no obvious victims such as drug use, gambling, and prostitution may be regulated by the criminal law because they detract from the quality of life or decrease social order. Serious criminal offenses are referred to as **felonies,** whereas other, less serious crimes are termed **misdemeanors.** A third category of criminal law violation, the "ticketable" **offense,** includes a variety of minor regulated behaviors including jaywalking, some motor vehicle law violations, and—in a few jurisdictions—minor incursions of the law regulating the use and possession of controlled substances. In addition to civil and criminal laws, a third category of law—administrative law—can be identified. **Administrative law** regulates many daily business activities, and violations of such regulations generally result in warnings or fines, depending on their adjudged severity.

Although the legalistic approach to crime—which sees crime solely as conduct in violation of the criminal law—is useful in the study of criminology, it is also limiting. Those who adhere to a legalistic perspective insist that the nature of crime cannot be separated from the nature of law, as the one explicitly defines the other.

Civil law body of law that regulates arrangements between individuals, such as contracts and claims to property.

Criminal law body of law that regulates actions which have the potential to harm interests of the state or the federal government.

Felony a serious criminal offense; specifically one punishable by death or by incarceration in a prison facility for a year or more.

Misdemeanor a criminal offense which is less serious than a felony; one punishable by incarceration, usually in a local confinement facility, typically for a year or less.

Offense (1) a violation of the criminal law or, in some jurisdictions, (2) a minor crime, such as jaywalking, sometimes described as "ticketable."

Administrative law regulates many daily business activities, and violations of such regulations generally result in warnings or fines, depending upon their adjudged severity.

The Crime Picture

Statute a formal written enactment of a legislative body.

Not recognized by any legalistic definition of crime, however, is the social, moral, and individual significance of fundamentally immoral forms of behavior. Simply put, some activities not contravened by **statute** nonetheless call out for a societal response, sometimes leading commentators to proclaim "that ought to be a crime!" or "there ought to be a law against that!" Ron Claassen, for example, suggests that "crime is primarily an offense against human relationships, and secondarily a violation of a law—since laws are written to protect safety and fairness in human relationships."[9]

Practically speaking, however, the legalistic perspective is persuasive. In most places, no one can be arrested for any particular conduct, no matter how atrocious, unless a law on the books criminalizes that particular activity.[10] Similarly, according to American judicial principles, a new law cannot retroactively apply to past behavior. Only those prohibited acts that are committed after the effective date of any new statute can be prosecuted as crimes. Hence, if the manufacture and sale of tobacco products should one day be declared criminal, individuals who are today engaged in the "tobacco trade" could not be prosecuted under it. Only if they continued their (now illegal) behavior, would they be subject to lawful sanction.

A serious shortcoming of the legalistic approach to crime is that it yields the moral high ground to powerful individuals who are able to influence the making of laws and the imposition of criminal definitions on lawbreakers. By making their own laws, powerful but immoral individuals may escape the label "criminal." Although democratic societies such as the United States would seem to be immune from such abuses of the legislative process, history demonstrates otherwise. In a later chapter we will explore this issue further and focus on the process of criminalization, which is the method used to **criminalize** some forms of behavior— or make them illegal—while other forms remain legitimate.

Criminalize to make illegal.

The legalistic definition of crime also suffers from its seeming lack of recognition of the fact that formalized laws have not always existed. Undoubtedly, much immoral behavior occurred even in dimly remembered historical epochs, and contemporary laws probably now regulate most such behavior. English **common law,** for example, upon which much American **statutory law** is based, judged behavior in terms of usage and custom rather than against written statutes. Although all American jurisdictions have enacted comprehensive legal codes, many states still adhere to a common law tradition. In such "common law states" individuals may be prosecuted for violating traditional notions of right and wrong, even though no violation of statutory law occurred. Needless to say, such prosecutions rarely occur, and when they do they are not often successful.[11] Common law is discussed in more detail in Chapter 4.

Common law law originating from usage and custom rather than from written statutes. The term refers to nonstatutory customs, traditions, and precedents that help guide judicial decision making.

Statutory law law in the form of statutes or formal written strictures, made by a legislature or governing body with the power to make law.

Changes in the law will undoubtedly continue to occur, perhaps even legitimizing former so-called crimes or recognizing that fundamentally moral forms of behavior have been unduly criminalized. Over the last decade, for example, state legislatures along with members of the general public have debated the virtues of euthanasia. Dr. Jack Kevorkian, perhaps the best known pro-euthanasia activist of modern times, has been waging a crusade to legalize doctor-assisted suicide for terminally ill individuals. In mid-1997 Kevorkian publicly acknowledged having helped a total of forty-five people kill themselves.[12] Kevorkian has been tried and acquitted three times on charges related to the deaths of five people in Michigan.

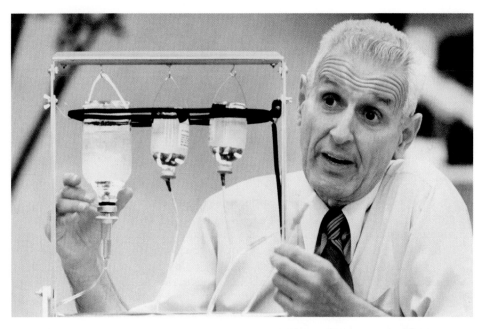

The debate over assisted suicide highlights the changing nature of criminal activity. Although never convicted, Dr. Jack Kevorkian, a proponent of euthanasia, has been repeatedly charged with crimes such as assisting a suicide, conspiracy to commit a felony, representing himself as a physician while engaging in unlawful conduct, possessing controlled substances, removing bodies without permission of the medical examiner, and attempting to assist in suicide. Do you think that doctor-assisted suicide should be a crime? *Detroit News/Gary Porter/Gamma-Liaison, Inc.*

Recognizing the difficulties that attend euthanasia, Kevorkian recently said publicly that "the whole controversy" over assisted suicides could be resolved by certifying doctors to perform assisted suicides. "All we have to do to solve the whole controversy is have the medical profession come forward [and] lay the guidelines down,"[13] Kevorkian said on *Larry King Live.* "The guidelines [should] say only certain doctors can do it, and if you don't, we're going to punish you."

Practical considerations can also force reevaluation of existing laws. A few years ago, for example, former U.S. Surgeon General Joycelyn Elders suggested that drug legalization could reduce the rate of other crimes. "I do think it would likely reduce the crime rate if drugs were legalized,"[14] Elders remarked in a 1993 speech to the National Press Club. Other countries that have legalized drugs, Elders said, have seen a drop in violence. She suggested that studies are needed to determine whether the legalization in the United States of controlled substances such as heroin, cocaine, and marijuana could reduce the incidence of criminal violence.[15] The politically insensitive remark cost Elders her job.

■■ CRIME AND DEVIANCE

From a broader point of view, most crimes can be regarded as deviant forms of behavior, that is, as behaviors which are in some way abnormal. Abnormality, **deviance,** and crime, however, are concepts that do not always easily mesh. Some

Deviance behavior that violates social norms or is statistically different from the "average."

T H E O R Y   V E R S U S   R E A L I T Y

Should Doctor-Assisted Suicide Remain Illegal?

On June 26, 1997, the U.S. Supreme Court upheld the constitutionality of two laws prohibiting assisted suicide. In *Vacco* v. *Quill*,[16] plaintiffs claimed that a New York law banning physician-assisted suicide violated the Fourteenth Amendment's equal protection clause because state law allows persons wishing to hasten their own deaths to do so by directing the removal of life-support systems, but does not permit terminally ill persons to self-administer prescribed lethal drugs to end their lives. The Court disagreed and upheld the New York ban.

The other 1997 case was that of *Washington* v. *Glucksberg*.[17] In *Glucksberg*, the Court upheld a Washington State law that makes "[p]romoting a suicide attempt" a felony, and provides: "A person is guilty of [that crime] when he knowingly causes or aids another person to attempt suicide." Respondents in the case were four Washington physicians who occasionally treated terminally ill, suffering patients. The physicians declared that they would assist such patients in ending their lives were it not for the state's assisted suicide ban. They, along with three gravely ill plaintiffs and a nonprofit organization that counsels people considering physician-assisted suicide, filed suit against the state of Washington seeking a declaration that the ban is unconstitutional. The basis of their action resided in the claim that the Fourteenth Amendment's due process clause establishes a liberty interest which extends to a personal choice by a mentally competent, terminally ill adult to commit physician-assisted suicide. The Supreme Court disagreed, ruling that Washington's prohibition against causing or aiding a suicide does not violate the due process clause. In the words of the Court:

> "An examination of our Nation's history, legal traditions, and practices demonstrates that Anglo-American common law has punished or otherwise disapproved of assisting suicide for over 700 years; that rendering such assistance is still a crime in almost every State; that such prohibitions have never contained exceptions for those who were near death; that the prohibitions have in recent years been reexamined and, for the most part, reaffirmed in a number of States; and that the President recently signed the Federal Assisted Suicide Funding Restriction Act of 1997, which prohibits the use of federal funds in support of physician assisted suicide." The Court concluded that: "In light of that history, this Court's decisions lead to the conclusion that respondents' asserted 'right' to assistance in committing suicide is not a fundamental liberty interest protected by the Due Process Clause."

Although the Court ruled that terminally ill people do not have a constitutionally protected right to doctor-assisted suicide, it did nothing to bar states from legalizing the process. Now, inspired by a growing right-to-die movement, some jurisdictions appear ready to lift the traditional ban on such activity.

In 1994 Oregon became the first state to legalize doctor-assisted suicide under prescribed conditions. Although a state judge later blocked the Oregon law from taking immediate effect,[18] the new statute represented a complete about-face in the legal status of medically assisted suicide. In 1997 the United States Ninth Circuit Court of Appeals reversed the lower court's ruling and reinstated the law. The Oregon law allows a terminally ill patient, defined as a person having no more than six months to live, to request a prescription for a fatal dose of medication. The patient must make the request three times—both in writing and verbally. A fifteen-day waiting period is mandated before the second request can be made. Moreover, two doctors must agree that the patient is terminally ill, and witnesses have to attest that the patient's desire to die is voluntary. If the patient appears depressed, a psychologist must be called, and the patient, not the doctor, must self-administer the lethal medication. Lethal injections are prohibited.[19]

Oregon's assisted suicide law continues to face many challenges. As of this writing, opponents of the law are attempting to gain a hearing before the U.S. Supreme Court, and state legislators have promised to bring the measure up for a public vote before it can go into effect. Although the Oregon law remains on the books, it provides an example of the fact that what may be a crime in one jurisdiction or location may not be criminal in another.[20]

DISCUSSION QUESTIONS

1. What is crime? Is doctor-assisted suicide a crime? Why or why not?
2. Who is Dr. Jack Kevorkian (discussed elsewhere in this chapter)? Is he a criminal? Why or why not?
3. Are there any activities that are not against the law which you think should be criminal? If so, what are they?
4. Are there any activities that are against the law, but which you think should not be illegal? If so, what are they?

forms of deviance are not criminal, and the reverse is equally true. Deviant styles of dress, for example, although perhaps outlandish to the majority, are not circumscribed by criminal law unless (perhaps) decency statutes are violated by a lack of clothing. Even in such cases, laws are subject to interpretation and may be modified as social norms change over time.

In November 1991, for example, Patricia Marks, a New York State county judge, overturned the convictions of ten women who had been arrested for publicly displaying their breasts. The women, known as the Topfree Ten, had originally been arrested in 1989 after baring their chests during a picnic in a city park. New York law forbids women from displaying their breasts in public—unless they are breastfeeding or performing on stage. Judge Marks, in reversing the convictions, ruled that the New York law was sexist and gender biased because "male and female breasts are physiologically similar except for lactation capability."[21] The judge relied in part on the testimony of experts who articulated their belief "that community standards

Deviance is relevant to the social context within which it occurs, as these bathers on an Italian nude beach show. Why is public nudity against the law in most American jurisdictions? *Lucas/The Image Works.*

have changed and women's breasts are no longer considered a private or intimate part of the body."

This case holds special interest for students of criminology because it highlights the role that societal interpretation plays in defining a criminal offense. Even if Judge Marks is right, and no noteworthy physiological difference exists between the breasts of men and women, American society nonetheless appears to have turned relatively minor differences of size and shape into a major distinguishing factor between the sexes. In other words, a relatively insignificant biological difference has been endowed with great social significance—and laws have evolved based on subjective perceptions rather than objective considerations.

Some forms of behavior, although quite common, are still against the law. Speeding on interstate highways, for example, although probably something that most motorists engage in at least one time, is illegal. Complicating matters still further is the fact that some forms of behavior are illegal in some jurisdictions but not so in others. Adult homosexual behavior, for example, is regarded as a matter of personal choice in many states, but is considered a criminal offense in others.

IN MINNESOTA, A CRIME OF COVER-UP

POLICE SAY MUSLIM'S DRESS BREAKS THE LAW

Can a mode of dress be against the law in the United States even when it almost completely covers the body? As the story in this box shows, styles of dress may be more than simply a matter of individual choice.

Minneapolis—As a Muslim, Tayyibah Amatullah chooses to cover her entire body with layers of clothing, leaving only her eyes visible to the outside world.

To her, it's a matter of religious freedom.

To St. Paul police, it's breaking the law.

Amatullah, 21, of Minneapolis says she was shopping in a downtown St. Paul mall when five police officers ticketed her for concealing her identity.

Because of three bank robberies, thefts and other mall crimes, police have stepped up enforcement of a seldom-used law that prevents people from hiding their identity "by means of a robe, mask or other disguise."

Police say they've ticketed people wearing ski masks and gang members wearing bandannas over their faces.

Police say Amatullah didn't look like the traditional Muslim women they've seen.

Her clothes were dirty and tattered. She wore gloves. Her face was hidden. When they asked her to remove her veil, she refused.

The citation upsets Muslims here—about 25,000 live in the Twin Cities area. They say the case is an infringement of their religious and human rights.

"We're angry," says Magda Saikali, an activist who organized protests over Amatullah's treatment. "We are harassed all the time because of our clothes. . . . But this is really too much."

Across the USA, religious groups are increasingly winning the battle for rights. A federal bill enacted last November made it more difficult for officials to interfere with religious practices.

"We're Angry": From left, Magda Saikali, Adrianna Sutherland, and Amatullah Bantely protest the ticketing of Tayyibah Amatullah. The women spoke at the University of Minnesota. Do these women have a right to dress the way they want? *Cheryl Meyer/Star Tribune.*

"It's not for [St. Paul police] to define what they think a Muslim should dress like," says Ibrahim Hooper of the Council on American-Islamic Relations in Washington, D.C. The group is considering legal action, including a discrimination claim, against the police department.

"We have to make it possible for a Muslim woman who wants to wear a face veil to walk the streets of Minnesota," Hooper says.

Police spokesman Paul Adelmann says, "Procedure is not to tag everybody." But when officers stopped Amatullah to question her, she "was belligerent" and refused to show her face. "They didn't know if it was a man or a woman or what."

Amatullah denies her clothes were tattered. She says the officers told her "you can't run around dressed like that in public."

She also says she was told to either leave the mall or take off the veil. When she refused, she says she was taken to a room where police forced her to remove it.

"I felt degraded," says Amatullah, who converted to Islam two years ago. "It's just like somebody pulling down your underwear in public."

To add to the controversy, police released reports that Amatullah had been arrested three years ago for shoplifting and again nine months ago, in similar dress, for writing a bad check.

Amatullah says she was caught shoplifting on her 18th birthday, but says that was before she converted to Islam. She says the charge was eventually reduced in court.

She denies writing bad checks but says she was arrested on an outstanding ticket for not having car insurance.

She says she is still paying off the $550 fine.

For Saikali and other Twin Cities Muslims, Amatullah's record is irrelevant.

Amatullah is scheduled to appear in court on Monday.

St. Paul's assistant city attorney, Theodore Leon, is reviewing the charge, which could bring a maximum $700 fine and 90 days in jail.

"I didn't do anything to hurt anybody," says Amatullah. "Why is it that people can walk around half naked and nobody will say anything? I choose to cover up and people have a problem with it."

Religion versus Local Laws—

- School officials in Livingston, California, banned Sikh students from wearing *kirpans,* sheathed blades worn next to the skin that are considered sacred, citing a no-weapons policy. A federal appeals court ruled the policy violates religious freedom.

- The Supreme Court upheld Oregon's refusal to pay unemployment to a Native American fired for using peyote, a drug outlawed as hallucinogenic but part of tribal religious rituals since before Columbus.

- Amish leaders persuaded Minnesota's Supreme Court to overturn a requirement that they affix orange warning signals to their slow-moving black vehicles. They objected to the bright color on religious grounds.

- Cubans in Florida ran into a law banning the ritual sacrifice of chickens required by Santeria, a religion with African roots. The Supreme Court overturned it.

- A Rhode Island medical examiner performed an autopsy on a Laotian immigrant, overriding Hmong refugees who say autopsies mutilate the body and prevent the spirit from being set free.

—Gary Fields

Questions

1. What is the difference between crime and deviance? Why might certain modes of dress be considered deviant? How can deviant modes of dress be criminalized?
2. Should the way in which a person dresses be controlled by law? If so, what limits should the law specify?
3. Do you believe that religious dress codes should be especially protected by the courts? Why or why not?

Source: Carolyn Pesce, "In Minn., A Crime of Cover-up," *USA Today,* October 5, 1994, p. 3A. Copyright 1994, *USA Today.* Reprinted with permission.

WHAT DO CRIMINOLOGISTS DO?

A typical dictionary definition of a **criminologist** is "one who studies crime, criminals, and criminal behavior."[22] People who have a doctoral degree (Ph.D.) in the field of criminology or criminal justice from an accredited university often refer to themselves as criminologists. Some criminologists hold degrees in related fields such as sociology and political science, and have specialized in the study and control of crime and deviance. Most Ph.D. criminologists either teach criminology or criminology-related subjects in institutions of higher learning, including universities and two- and four-year colleges. Nearly all criminology professors are involved in research or writing projects by which they strive to advance criminological knowledge. Some Ph.D. criminologists are strictly researchers and work for federal agencies such as the National Institute of Justice and the National Criminal Justice Reference Service, or for private (albeit often government funded) organizations with such names as the RAND Corporation and the Search Group, Inc.

The results of criminological research in the United States are generally published in journals such as *Criminology* (the official publication of the American Society of Criminology), *Theoretical Criminology, Justice Quarterly* (the Academy of Criminal Justice Sciences), *Crime and Delinquency,* the *American Journal of Criminal Justice* (the Southern Criminal Justice Association), the *Journal of Qualitative Criminology, Social Problems,* and *Victimology.*[23] International English-language journals are numerous and include the *Canadian Journal of Criminology,* the *Australian and New Zealand Journal of Criminology,* and the *British Journal of Criminology.*

The term *criminologist* may also be applied to persons who have earned master's of arts, master's of science, and bachelor's degrees in the field. Degrees such as these may provide entree into police investigative or support work, probation and parole

Criminologist one who is trained in the field of criminology; also, one who studies crime, criminals, and criminal behavior.

agencies, court-support activities, and correctional (prison) work. Forensics laboratory technicians, ballistics experts, computer crime investigators, polygraph operators, crime scene photographers, and prison program directors provide examples of the kinds of jobs available to criminologists. Criminologists also work for government agencies interested in the development of effective social policies intended to deter or combat crime. Many criminologists with master's degrees also teach at two- and four-year colleges and schools.

Private security provides another career track for individuals interested in criminology. The number of personnel employed by private security agencies today is twice that of public law enforcement agencies, and the gap is widening. Many upper and middle level private managers working for private security firms hold criminology or criminal justice degrees. The same will soon be true of the majority of law enforcement personnel.

Of course, individuals as criminologists have various alternatives. Many with undergraduate degrees in criminology or criminal justice go on to law school. Some teach high school while others become private investigators. Many criminologists provide civic organizations (such as victims' assistance and justice advocacy groups) with much needed expertise, a few work for politicians and legislative bodies, and some appear on talk shows to debate the pros and cons of various kinds of social policies designed to "fight" crime. Some criminologists even write books such as this one!

▚ WHAT IS CRIMINOLOGY?

The attempt to understand crime predates written history. Prehistoric evidence, including skeletal remains showing signs of primitive cranial surgery, seem to indicate that preliterate people explained deviant behavior via reference to spirit possession. Primitive "surgery" was an attempt to release unwanted spiritual influences. In the thousands of years since, many other theoretical perspectives on crime have been advanced. This book describes various criminological theories and covers some of the more popular ones in detail.

Before beginning any earnest discussion, however, it is necessary to define the term *criminology*. As our earlier discussion of the nature of crime and deviance indicates, criminologists must not only deal with a complex subject matter—consisting of a broad range of illegal behaviors committed by frequently unknown or uncooperative individuals—they must also manage their work under changing conditions mandated by ongoing revisions of the law and fluctuating social policy. All this leads to considerable difficulties in defining the subject matter under study. Nonetheless, definitions of criminology abound.

Edwin Sutherland, one of the best-known American criminologists of the twentieth century, suggested that criminology consists of three "principal divisions": (1) the sociology of law, (2) scientific analysis of the causes of crime, and (3) crime control.[24] Another well-known criminologist, Clarence Ray Jeffery, similarly sees three components of the field: (1) detection (of the offender), (2) treatment, and (3) explaining crime and criminal behavior.[25] In like manner, the contemporary criminologist Gregg Barak writes that criminology is "an interdisciplinary study of

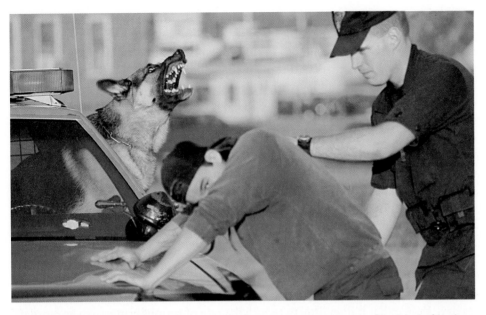

Criminology examines the causes of crime and seeks ways to prevent or control it. Criminal justice examines the criminal justice system, including police, courts, and corrections. How do the two disciplines complement one another? *D. Greco/The Image Works.*

the various bodies of knowledge, which focuses on the etiology of crime, the behavior of criminals, and the policies and practices of crime control."[26]

For our purposes we will use a definition that brings together the works of previous writers, but which also recognizes the increasingly professional status of the criminological enterprise. Throughout this book, then, we will view **criminology** as an interdisciplinary profession built around the scientific study of crime and criminal behavior, including their manifestations, causes, legal aspects, and control. As this definition indicates, criminology includes consideration of possible solutions to the problem of crime. Hence, this text (in later chapters) describes treatment strategies and social policy initiatives that have grown out of the existing array of theoretical explanations for crime.

Our definition is in keeping with the work of Jack Gibbs, an outstanding criminologist of the twentieth century, who has written that the purpose of criminology is to offer well-researched and objective answers to four basic questions: (1) "Why do crime rates vary?" (2) "Why do individuals differ as to **criminality**?" (3) "Why is there variation in reactions to crime?" and (4) "What are the possible means of controlling criminality?"[27]

As a field of study, criminology in its present form is primarily a social scientific discipline. Contemporary criminologists generally recognize, however, that their field is interdisciplinary; that is, it draws upon other disciplines to provide an integrated approach to understanding the problem of crime in contemporary society and to advance solutions to the problems crime creates. Hence, biology, sociology, political science, psychology, economics, medicine, psychiatry, law, philosophy, and numerous other fields all have something to offer the student of criminology, as do the tools provided by statistics, computer science, and other forms of scientific and data analysis.

Criminology an interdisciplinary profession built around the scientific study of crime and criminal behavior, including their form, causes, legal aspects, and control.

Criminality a behavioral predisposition that disproportionately favors criminal activity.

It is, however, important to note that although criminology may be interdisciplinary in its approach to the subject matter of crime, few existing explanations for criminal behavior have been successfully integrated. Just as physicists today are seeking a unified field theory to explain the wide variety of observable forms of matter and energy, criminologists have yet to develop a generally accepted integrated approach to crime and criminal behavior that can explain the many diverse forms of criminality while also leading to effective social policies in the area of crime control. The attempt to construct criminological theories of relevance is made all the more difficult because, as discussed earlier, the phenomenon under study—crime—is subject to arbitrary and sometimes unpredictable legalistic and definitional changes.

Not only must a successfully integrated criminology bring together the contributions of various theoretical perspectives and disciplines, it must also—if it is to have any relevance—blend the practical requirements of our nation's judicial system with emotional and rational calls for morality and justice. Is the death penalty, for example, justified? If so, on what basis? Is it because it is a type of vengeance, and therefore deserved? Can we say that it is unjustified because many sociological studies have shown that it does little to reduce the rate of serious crime such as murder? Just what do we mean by *justice,* and what can criminological studies tell us—if anything—about what is just and what is unjust?

The editors of the relatively new journal, *Theoretical Criminology,*[28] which began publication in 1997, tell us in their inaugural issue that "criminology has always been somewhat of a haphazardly-assembled umbrella-like structure which nevertheless usefully shelters a variety of theoretical interests that are espoused and employed by different disciplinary, methodological and political traditions." Such a structure, they say, "has obvious advantages, notably that it facilitates an interdisciplinary and inclusivist formation rather than supposing an exclusive but contentious 'core.' But one of its weaknesses is that its inhabitants, many of whom shuttle backwards and forwards between it and their parent disciplines, tend to communicate honestly and meaningfully only with those who speak the same theoretical language."[29] In other words, while the field of criminology can benefit from the wide variety of ideas available via a multiplicity of perspectives, all of which seek to understand the phenomenon we call "crime," cross-discipline collaboration can be quite difficult.

As the earlier definition of *criminology* indicates, however, it is more than a field of study or a collection of theories—it is also a profession.[30] In his 1996 presidential address to the American Society of Criminology, Charles F. Wellford identified the "primary purposes" of the criminology profession. Wellford said: "Controlling crime through prevention, rehabilitation, and deterrence and ensuring that the criminal justice system reflects the high aspiration we have as a society of 'justice for all,' characterize the principal goals that in my judgment motivate the work of our field."[31]

Notably, criminology also contributes to the discipline of **criminal justice,** which emphasizes application of the criminal law and study of the components of the justice system, especially the police, courts, and corrections. As one author stated, "criminology gives prominence to questions about the *causes of criminality,* while the *control of lawbreaking* is at the heart of criminal justice."[32]

Criminal justice the scientific study of crime, the criminal law, and components of the criminal justice system, including the police, courts, and corrections.

THEORETICAL CRIMINOLOGY

Theoretical criminology, a subfield of general criminology, is the variety of criminology most often found in colleges and universities. Theoretical criminology, rather than simply describing crime and its occurrence, posits explanations for criminal behavior. As Edwin Sutherland stated, "[t]he problem in criminology is to explain the criminality of behavior. . . . However, an explanation of criminal behavior should be a specific part of [a] general theory of behavior and its task should be to differentiate criminal from noncriminal behavior."[33]

To explain and understand crime, criminologists have developed many theories. A **theory,** at least in its ideal form, is made up of clearly stated propositions that posit relationships, often of a causal sort, between events and things under study. An old Roman theory, for example, proposed that insanity is caused by the influence of the moon, and may even follow its cycles—hence the term *lunacy.*

Theories attempt to provide us with explanatory power and help us to understand the phenomenon under study. The more applicable a theory is found to be, the more generalizable it is from one specific instance to others—in other words, the more it can be applied to other situations. A **general theory** of crime is one that attempts to explain all (or at least most) forms of criminal conduct through a single, overarching approach. Unfortunately, as Don Gottfredson observes, "[t]heories in criminology tend to be unclear and lacking in justifiable generality."[34] When we consider the wide range of behaviors regarded as criminal—from murder, through drug use, to white-collar and computer crime—it seems difficult to imagine one theory that can explain them all, or which might even explain the same type of behavior under varying circumstances. Still, many past theoretical approaches to crime causation were **unicausal** while attempting to be all-inclusive. That is, the approaches posited a single, identifiable source for all serious deviant and criminal behavior.

An **integrated theory,** in contrast to a general theory, does not necessarily attempt to explain all criminality, but is distinguishable by the fact that it merges (or attempts to merge) concepts drawn from different sources. As Gregg Barak states: "An integrative criminology . . . seeks to bring together the diverse bodies of knowledge that represent the full array of disciplines that study crime."[35] Hence, integrated theories provide potentially wider explanatory power than narrower formulations. Don C. Gibbons notes: "The basic idea of theoretical integration is straightforward; it concerns the combinations of single theories or elements of those theories into a more comprehensive argument. At the same time, it would be well to note that in practice, integration is a matter of degree: some theorists have combined or integrated more concepts or theoretical elements than have others."[36]

Both theoretical integration and the general applicability of criminological theories to a wide variety of law-violating behavior are intuitively appealing concepts. Even far more limited attempts at criminological theorizing, however, often face daunting challenges. "As we shall see . . ." notes Gibbons, "criminologists have not managed to articulate a large collection of relatively formalized arguments in a general or integrated form."[37] Hence, although we will use the word *theory* in describing the many explanations for crime covered by this book, it should be

Theory a series of interrelated propositions that attempt to describe, explain, predict, and ultimately to control some class of events. A theory gains explanatory power from inherent logical consistency and is "tested" by how well it describes and predicts reality.

General theory one that attempts to explain all (or at least most) forms of criminal conduct through a single, overarching approach.

Unicausal having one cause. Unicausal theories posit only one source for all that they attempt to explain.

Integrated theory an explanatory perspective that merges (or attempts to merge) concepts drawn from different sources.

recognized that the word is only loosely applicable to some of the perspectives we will discuss.

As we shall learn in Chapter 3, many social scientists insist that to be considered *theories,* explanations must consist of sets of clearly stated, logically interrelated, and measurable propositions. The fact that only a few of the theories described in this book rise above the level of organized conjecture—and those offer only limited generalizability and have rarely been integrated—is one of the greatest failures of criminology today.

■■ CRIMINOLOGY AND SOCIAL POLICY

Social policies
government initiatives, programs, and plans intended to address problems in society. The "War on Crime," for example, is a kind of generic (large-scale) social policy—one consisting of many smaller programs.

Of potentially broader importance than theory testing are **social policies** based on research findings. Approximately one year ago, for example, the U.S. Senate heard testimony from Attorney General Janet Reno, Senator Paul Simon, and television studio executives over the claim that television is responsible for encouraging violent acts among young people. The hearing grew, in part, from an Ohio mother's claim that the Music Television (MTV) cartoon, *Beavis and Butt-Head* led her 5-year-old son to set a fire that killed his 2-year-old sister. The show had featured a lead character chanting "fire is good." As the investigation revealed, experts who study televised cartoons have found that violent episodes average nearly one every two minutes.[38]

In a report[39] presented to Attorney General Reno, the Citizens Task Force on TV Violence recommended, among other things, restricting violence on television between 6 A.M. and 10 P.M.—the time when children are most likely to be watching. The task force told Reno that networks and cable companies should voluntarily agree to the restrictive period or face regulation through government action.

Copycat violence has also been attributed to films. Touchstone Pictures, for example, reedited the movie *The Program,* cutting scenes in which drunken football players test their nerve by lying end to end in the middle of a highway. Several young men who apparently copied the stunt were either killed or critically injured. Commenting on the incidents, a Touchstone spokesperson said, "[w]hile the scene in the movie in no way advocates this irresponsible activity, it is impossible for us to ignore that someone may have recklessly chosen to imitate it. . . ."[40] Although the jury (and the Senate) is still out on TV violence, legislation can soon be expected to regulate programming if the television industry does not do more to regulate itself. In the words of Senator Simon, "TV is a powerful sales medium, and too often what it sells is violence."[41]

Professional criminologists are themselves acutely aware of the need to link sound social policy to the objective findings of well-conducted criminological research. A recent meeting of the American Society of Criminology (ASC), for example, focused on the need to forge just such a link. At the meeting, ASC president Alfred Blumstein, of Carnegie Mellon University, told criminologists gathered there that "an important mission of the ASC and its members involves the generation of knowledge that is useful in dealing with crime and the operation of the criminal justice system, and then helping public officials to use that knowledge intelligently and effectively."[42] Blumstein added that "[s]o little is known about the causes of crime and about the effects of criminal justice policy on crime that new insights about the criminal justice system can often be extremely revealing and can eventually change the way people think about the crime problem or about the criminal justice system."[43]

SOCIAL POLICY AND THE FEAR OF CRIME

Fear of crime remains pervasive in contemporary America. Two decades ago crime was the number one concern of Americans voicing opinions in public polls. In the interim, concern over crime came to be replaced with cold war and, later, economic worries. Following a spate of seemingly random violence, however, including well-publicized shootings of foreign tourists in Florida, cult-based violence in Texas and elsewhere, gang-related drive-by shootings, terrorist bombings, and highly visible inner-city violence, fear of crime once again moved to the forefront of national concerns.

A recent CNN/*USA Today*/Gallup poll[44] found that 38 percent of people polled often worry about being sexually assaulted, 35 percent often worry about being burglarized, and 90 percent of all respondents felt safe when alone at night only by staying home. Almost half of those polled have had special locks installed for residential security, and nearly a third have purchased guns. In some areas guns have proliferated to the extent that citizens who do not carry them may be in the minority. Fear of crime appears to be greatest in inner-city areas. In the CNN poll, only 33 percent of respondents reported feeling safe when using public transportation by themselves at night, and nearly the same percentage admitted to carrying a weapon for personal protection. Another 10 percent carried whistles to attract attention in the event of attack.

More telling than the statistics alone is the fact that respondents in every category reported greater fear today than a generation ago (in 1981). Nearly twice as many people (19 percent) reported frequently fearing for their lives than did so a generation ago. The survey also revealed fast-growing concern over personal and sexual assault.

According to pollsters, fear of crime is the American public's top concern. Given recent statistics showing falling crime rates, is such fear realistic? *H. Darr Beisner/USA Today.*

Another survey of American voters[45] found that crime topped the list of citizens' concerns. In the words of the pollsters, "Americans say crime is the No. 1 problem facing the country today...."[46] Crime was reported to be the respondents' "top concern" by 26 percent of those participating in the survey—easily outdistancing reported concerns over the economy (9 percent), jobs (7 percent), unemployment (7 percent), and drugs (6 percent). Interestingly, survey respondents appeared to separate drug-related crimes from the threat of more personal crimes such as murder, rape, and robbery. An independent *Washington Post* poll confirmed the survey's findings, showing that 21 percent of Americans are more concerned about crime than about any other issue.[47]

A final study conducted at about the same time as the CNN survey found that workplace homicide is the fastest-growing type of murder in the United States today, and that it is the leading cause of workplace death for women.[48] Experts explained the rise in on-the-job homicides as the outgrowth of the recession years of the early 1990s which led to corporate downsizing and increased job-related stresses.[49] Substance abuse and the ready availability of guns were cited as other contributing factors. Robbery is another. Of all workers, taxi drivers are most at risk of being murdered on the job. A recent National Institute for Occupational Safety and Health study showed that, during the past decade, 26.9 of every 100,000 taxi drivers and dispatchers were murdered on the job—nearly 40 times the overall 0.7 per 100,000 job-related homicide rate for all workers.[50]

Fear of crime is not necessarily related to the actual incidence of crime, however, as crime rates (discussed in detail in Chapter 2) have actually declined in recent years. Harry E. Allen, past president of the Academy of Criminal Justice Sciences, notes that "fear of crime is unreasonably high and is increasing...."[51] Even if fear of crime has reached "unreasonable" levels when objectively compared with the actual incidence of criminal activity, however, fear remains an important determinant of public policy. Hence, government agendas promising to lower crime rates, and which call for changes in the conditions that produce crime, can be quite successful politically for those who promote them in an environment where fear of crime is high.[52]

CRIME FIGHTERS ON THE MARCH

NEIGHBORS TAKING BACK THEIR STREETS

When government crime control policies fail, citizens sometimes take matters into their own hands. As this story describes, Jackson, Tennessee, residents have decided to take their streets back from criminals and drug dealers, and are not waiting for police or government intervention.

For Shirlene Mercer, it was the empty feeling of watching young boys die that drove her to the streets.

A year later, the Jackson, Tenn., woman has rallied a town into action. And her weekly anticrime marches—

leading between 50 and 350 residents into crime-battered neighborhoods—are credited in part for murders in Jackson falling from 19 in 1993 to only four so far this year.

"What we have come to understand is when the community comes together, black and white, rich and poor, everybody gets together and unites to speak out against the violence, drug dealing and all the things destroying our community," she says. "I think it could work anywhere."

Crime experts say it is.

Across the country, grass-roots efforts to stop the violence are blooming into a national attack on crime.

Marches and vigils lead to petition drives, tougher laws and community policing programs with bite:

- Grieving wife in Flint, Mich., leads thousands in a fight that brings about state-wide sentencing reform.
- A councilman who watches gang members buy arm-loads of ammunition fights to ban bullet sales in Chicago.
- A Dallas woman who lost her son to a gang bullet leads marches to counter the Southern state's pro-gun mentality.
- A Seattle computer consultant leads volunteers in planting 10,000 daffodils to remember a slain Japanese student.
- Pittsburgh police hunt for illegal guns based on anonymous tips to a new hot line set up by local businesses.
- Angry Milwaukee residents, scared by soaring murder rates, go door-to-door seeking to ban handguns.

"It's the only way" to fight crime, says Andrew Chisom, director of a Uni-versity of South Carolina anti-violence program that helps 10 Southern states design prevention programs. "We still think federal bucks can do away with these problems. They cannot."

He says the efforts "have certainly proven volunteerism is the best interdiction policy we could have in America because it recruits average Joe Blow citizens."

An estimated 100 million Americans have been affected by violent crime. Some suffer silently—others want to act.

"It's therapeutic, but it's also exhausting," says Julia Cooper, whose son was pulled from his car and fatally shot in the head by a gang member two years ago. Cooper, of Texans Against Violence, says going against gun owners in the Lone Star State often leaves her "so tired and emotionally drained."

But "it can only do good," she says. "People say we're not changing the world, and we're not. But one small step at a time is a step in the right direction. I think this is the way we start." Crime fighters agree.

Attorney General Janet Reno urged local residents to find their own solutions—create their own battle plans against crime—when she detailed how the Justice Department will enact the new, sweeping federal crime laws.

Pittsburgh Police Chief Earl Buford says everyone can help.

"It's absolutely critical that the extra eyes and ears are out there to help," says Buford. "If there is one thing we've learned in law enforcement, it's that we can't do the job by ourselves. We all have a stake in this."

Dave Brown, 34, of Boise, Idaho, once walked across the country to raise awareness of crimes against children. Now he has launched a national magazine called

Wanted by the Law: America's Monthly Crime Report! The magazine tells stories of heroics by both citizens and police officers. And it's filled with pictures of the nation's most wanted. "People want to know who their neighbors are now," Brown says. "Crimes are so heinous." And, he says, people across the nation are linked by a need to stop violence. "People are just fed up, but they don't know where to begin."

Next month, people from across the nation will gather at a Washington, D.C., conference to learn how to mount grass-roots attacks on gun violence.

The toughest part of the fight, some activists say, is battling the gun lobby. "On any level, once you get going you're going to run up against the NRA," says Desmond Riley of the Educational Fund to End Handgun Violence.

"People don't want to be boycotted by gun owners," Riley says. "They don't want massive mailings sent to them."

But the National Rifle Association promises not to quit fighting to protect gun owners.

"It's finally very clear that this fight is about them wanting to take every gun from every American," says NRA chief Wayne LaPierre. "We're not going to let that happen." He says cities where guns are banned are not safer.

And, he echoes the NRA call to reform the criminal justice system in an attempt to keep violent offenders off the streets.

The NRA's goals are similar to Linda Clark's, who often finds people unwilling to help out of fear of the gun lobby.

"A lot of times there are doors that are closed, but you just have to turn and go the other way," says Clark, a Flint, Mich., woman who worked for sentencing reform after her husband was killed in a convenience store holdup. Kevin Clark had stopped to buy treats for his two children.

"We sometimes forget that we the people are the government," his wife says. "We have a mandate to say how it's run."

Chisom says programs that work key on kids not much younger than the people accused of killing Clark's husband. "I don't want to sound mushy, but when youngsters see that people care, they respond to that care," he says.

Shirlene Mercer says involving kids made Jackson safer. "That's why we put the children on the front line of our marches," says Jackson.

"We have to teach children that they have to be sensitive about what's going on around them. As a mama, you care about your children."

Questions

1. Do you believe that citizens should take an active role in crime prevention, such as that described in this article? Why or why not?
2. What kinds of citizen involvement in crime prevention can you envision that are not discussed in this article?
3. What kinds of government policies might further the role of citizen involvement in crime prevention? How might such policies be crafted so as to ensure meaningful cooperation between citizen volunteers and formal agencies of justice?

Source: Robert Davis, "Crime Fighters on the March," *USA Today*, September 30, 1994, p. 9A. Copyright 1994, *USA Today*. Reprinted with permission.

▚ THE THEME OF THIS BOOK

This book builds on a social policy theme by contrasting two perspectives now popular in American society and in much of the rest of the world (see Figure 1.1). One point of view, termed the **social problems perspective,** holds that crime is a manifestation of underlying social problems such as poverty, discrimination, the breakdown of traditional social institutions, the poor quality of formal education available to some, pervasive family violence experienced during the formative years, and inadequate socialization practices that leave young people without the fundamental values necessary to contribute meaningfully to the society in which they live. Advocates of the social problems perspective, while generally agreeing that crime and violence have reached frightening levels, advance solutions based on what is, in effect, a public health model which says that crime needs to be addressed much like a public health concern.

Proponents of this perspective typically foresee solutions to the crime problem as coming in the form of large-scale government expenditures in support of social programs designed to address the issues that lie at the root of crime. A few years ago, for example, Health and Human Services Secretary Donna Shalala, commenting on a shooting rampage that occurred on a Long Island, New York, commuter train, told a gathering of the nation's mayors that "[v]iolence affects all of us. It must be thought of as a public health crisis that requires public health solutions like polio in the 1950s and AIDS today."[53] Shalala called violence "not just a criminal justice but also a public health problem because it's preventable."

Those who advocate a social problems perspective often look to legislatively enhanced social, educational, occupational, and other opportunities as offering programmatic solutions to ameliorate most causes of crime. The social problems approach to crime is characteristic of what social scientists term a *macro* approach because it portrays instances of individual behavior (crimes) as arising out of wide-

Social problems perspective the belief that crime is a manifestation of underlying social problems such as poverty, discrimination, pervasive family violence, inadequate socialization practices, and the breakdown of traditional social institutions.

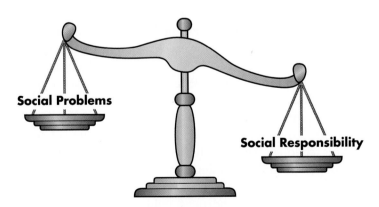

FIGURE 1.1   The Theme of This Book: Social Problems versus Social Responsibility. At the core of today's thinking about crime exists a crucial distinction between those who believe that *crime is a matter of individual responsibility* (the social responsibility perspective), and those who emphasize that *crime is a manifestation of underlying social problems* beyond the control of individuals (the social problems viewpoint).

Social responsibility
perspective the belief
that individuals are
fundamentally responsible
for their own behavior
and that they choose
crime over other, more
law-abiding, courses of
action.

spread and contributory social conditions which enmesh unwitting individuals in a causal nexus of uncontrollable social forces. In 1993, in response to growing national concerns about crime and violence, President Clinton appointed a federal task force to study the issues involved. Commenting on the president's initiative, Shalala concluded, "[r]ebuilding civil society is very much a part of what we need to talk about. It's a complex issue that requires a very comprehensive solution. . . . We're going to see what the government can do. It may be laws. It may simply be inspiring different parts of our society to take their own responsibilities. In the end, it will be communities organizing, community by community, neighborhood by neighborhood."[54]

A contrasting perspective lays the cause of crime squarely at the feet of individual perpetrators. This point of view holds that individuals are fundamentally responsible for their own behavior and maintains that they choose crime over other, more law-abiding courses of action. Perpetrators may choose crime, advocates of this perspective say, because it is exciting, it offers illicit pleasures and the companionship of like-minded thrill seekers, or because it is simply less demanding than conformity. This viewpoint, which we shall call the **social responsibility perspective,** tends to become increasingly popular in times when the fear of crime rises. Advocates of the social responsibility perspective, with their emphasis on individual choice, tend to believe that social programs do little to solve the problem of crime because, they say, a certain number of crime-prone individuals, for a variety of personalized reasons, will always make irresponsible choices. Hence, advocates of the social responsibility approach suggest crime reduction strategies based on firm punishments, imprisonment, individualized rehabilitation, increased security, and a wider use of police powers. The social responsibility perspective characteristically emphasizes a form of *micro* analysis that tends to focus on individual offenders and their unique biology, psychology, background, and immediate life experiences. A note about wording is in order: although this perspective might also be termed the *individual responsibility perspective,* because it stresses individual responsibility above all else, we've chosen to use the term *social responsibility perspective* instead, as it holds that individuals must be ultimately responsible to the social group of which they are a part, and that they should be held accountable by group standards if they are not. In short, this perspective is one characterized by societal demands for the exercise of individual responsibility.

The contrast between the social problems and the social responsibility perspectives came to the fore in the 1997 trial of Jesse Timmendequas, a previously convicted sex offender and admitted killer of 7-year-old Megan Kanka.[55] The defense for Timmendequas centered on his claims of repeated sexual abuse by his father as he was growing up—an experience his attorneys said left him helplessly attracted sexually to young children. The jury hearing the case rejected Timmendequas' abuse defense, found him guilty of killing Kanka, and recommended that he be sentenced to die. In summing up the feelings of many of those present, prosecutor Kathryn Flicker noted that "Timmendequas' childhood was not a bed of roses." But, she asked, "where does individual responsibility fit into the whole scheme? He was responsible as an adult, as we all are."[56]

In recent years the social responsibility perspective has come to the forefront of national thinking. Examples of a new conservatism in our nation's approach to criminals abound. The Violent Crime Control and Law Enforcement Act of 1994, for example, which is discussed in detail in Chapter 13, expanded the number of capital crimes under federal law from a handful of offenses to fifty-two.[57] The law also made $8.8 billion available to municipalities to put 100,000 new police officers on the streets, and allocated $7.9 billion for states to build and operate prisons and incarceration alternatives such as boot camps. Prison funding was intended to ensure that additional prison cells would be available to put—and keep—violent offenders behind bars. A subchapter of the 1994 Violent Crime Control Act created a federal "Three Strikes and You're Out" law, mandating life imprisonment for criminals convicted of three violent federal felonies or drug offenses. Similarly, the law increased or created new penalties for over seventy federal criminal offenses, primarily covering violent crimes, drug trafficking, and gun crimes.

Since the 1994 federal legislation was passed, many states have moved to toughen their own laws against violent criminals. Violent juveniles and repeat offenders have been especially targeted. Legislatures in a number of states have also moved to reduce inmate privileges, such as removing television sets, exercise equipment, and free magazines and reducing the number of hours of visitation and recreation permitted inmates. The growing strength of belief in the social responsibility perspective among today's voting public could be heard in the cries of Barbara Devlin, a neighbor of the Kankas, reacting to Timmendequas' death sentence. "Yes!" she exploded, as she heard the verdict. "I'm sorry," she added. "May God forgive me . . . he deserves it!"[58]

THEORY VERSUS REALITY

A Public Health Model of Crime Control

This book builds upon a theme that contrasts the social problems perspective on crime with another approach called social responsibility. An example of the social problems perspective can be had in the growing popularity of the public health model of crime control. According to the National Institute of Justice (NIJ): "Looking at violence only as a criminal justice issue has limited crime prevention strategies." But now, says NIJ, "policymakers are recognizing that violence is a health issue as well." Excerpts from a recent NIJ report, which are contained in this box, detail how the public health approach can be applied to the study of crime and justice.

Treating violence as a major problem in criminal justice and health suggests some new strategies for prevention. Public health campaigns to induce people to take responsibility for avoiding illness have led many to change their daily behavior. Safer sex practices are a dramatic and widespread personal response to the AIDS epidemic. Although it is decidedly harder to protect oneself against violence than against a virus, the public health approach offers useful lessons in preventing and controlling violence. Three public health concepts especially germane to preventing violence are public education, control of contagion, and early detection.

PUBLIC EDUCATION

Education forms the backbone of public health efforts. Over the past twenty years, full-scale public education campaigns have increased the use of seat belts and reduced the use of tobacco. Antismoking education has been successful not only in getting a large part of the smoking population to quit but also in preventing many young people from starting to smoke. An antiviolence campaign even half as effective as the antismoking campaign would dramatically reduce violent behavior. Such a campaign could target youth and could get at the roots of violent behavior (such as a lack of respect for women, in cases of sexual and domestic assault) and teach alternative ways to solve disputes (e.g., conflict resolution and communication skills).

CONTROLLING CONTAGION

The health care model stresses control of epidemics by targeting persons at risk for disease, such as those living in crowded or unsanitary conditions. Who is at risk for violence? Through new research and anecdotal evidence, some profiles of at-risk populations are emerging. For instance, increasing evidence suggests that a predilection toward violence can be transmitted from generation to generation. One research study found that youths who have been abused or neglected are 38 percent more likely to be arrested for a violent crime by the time they are adults than those who have not been mistreated.

In addition, data indicate that a person who has been shot is more likely to be victimized again than someone who has not. And yet another recent study found that women who were raped or were victims of attempted rape as adolescents were more than twice as likely as other women to be the victim of rape or attempted rape during their first year in college.

How do we inoculate those at risk? Counseling can provide victims of violence support and constructive ways to channel their rage, which would reduce the likelihood they would lash out at someone else, seek retribution, or continue to feel vulnerable. Counseling can also provide new coping and crime prevention skills to reduce fear as well as the chance of a repeat victimization. When a person comes to the emergency room with a gunshot or knife wound, the hospital staff must report the incident to the police so that the criminal justice system can intervene. Funding is needed for counseling to help victims prevent repeat victimization and guide them from becoming victimizers themselves.

EARLY DETECTION

To treat people at risk for violence, the system must identify who they are. The public health model teaches that the earlier an ailment can be detected, the better the chance of curing it. In cases of violence between strangers, detection is usually straightforward: the victim turns to the criminal justice system. When the victim and offender have a prior relationship, the criminal justice system may not be involved until the violence escalates into serious assault or murder. In these cases, early detection and intervention can be especially important.

PROMISE FOR THE FUTURE

An opportunity exists to screen for violence by a medical community that increasingly emphasizes prevention and the family doctor approach to health care. Family doctors are well positioned to notice patterns that suggest a patient is at risk of violence. Twenty years ago doctors rarely asked patients about their sexual and drinking habits, but now most doctors routinely ask such questions. Asking, "Do you have trouble controlling your temper? What happens when you lose it?" could be just as routine. If a patient replies that he occasionally "takes a swipe" at his partner or "breaks furniture," the physician could tell him that this is a health problem and that the patient needs help.

Treating violence as both a health and a criminal justice issue opens the door to more resources. Researchers sponsored by the National Institute of Justice (NIJ) are studying violence, but vast amounts of information still need to be collected. Computerized records of reasons for injuries and sophisticated studies about prevalence will offer a better grasp of patterns. With data in hand, stronger arguments can be made for increased allocation of limited resources. A better balance is needed: the federal government spends on research about $794 per year per life lost because of cancer, but only $31 per year per life lost to violence.

The value of the public health approach is that investing in detection, education, and counseling is cost effective. It is less expensive to incorporate early identification into the health care system and provide services than to face the burden of escalating emergency room, law enforcement, court, child welfare, and prison costs. But what is truly unbearable is the cost in human lives that the nation will pay if efforts to prevent violence fail. Ultimately, early intervention and treatment by the health care system, combined with criminal justice efforts, will start giving the victims of violence what they deserve: for the crime not to have happened.

DISCUSSION QUESTIONS

1. What are the major differences between the social problems and the social responsibility perspectives on crime?
2. Which perspective do you find personally most appealing? Why?
3. Which perspective is closest to the medical model of crime prevention discussed here?
4. Do you believe that the public health model is applicable to the crime problem? Can crime be effectively prevented or reduced using a public health model? Why or why not?

Source: Lucy N. Friedman, "Adopting the Health Care Model to Prevent Victimization," *National Institute of Justice Journal,* November 1994.

▚ THE SOCIAL CONTEXT OF CRIME

Crime does not occur in a vacuum. Every crime has a quasi-unique set of causes, consequences, and participants. Crime affects some people more than others, having a special impact on those who are direct participants in the act itself—offenders, victims, police officers, bystanders, and so on. Crime, in general, provokes reactions from the individuals it victimizes, from concerned groups of citizens, from the criminal justice system, and sometimes from society as a whole, which manifests its concerns via the creation of social policy. Reactions to crime, from the everyday to the precedent setting, may color the course of future criminal events.[59]

In this book we shall attempt to identify and examine some of the many social, psychological, economic, biological, and other causes of crime, while simultaneously expounding on the many differing perspectives that have been advanced to explain both crime and criminality. An example of differing perspectives can be found in an upcoming box in this chapter entitled "The Murder of John Lennon." The box provides insight into the motivation of Mark David Chapman (Lennon's killer) and shows that the assumptions we, as outsiders to the event itself, make about the genesis of criminal purpose are not always correct. As the box reveals, popular conceptions of criminal motivation are typically shaped by media portrayals of offender motivation, which often fail to take into consideration the felt experiences of the law violator. By identifying and studying this diversity of perspectives on criminality, we will discover the characteristic disjuncture among victims, offenders, the justice system, and society as to the significance that each assigns to the behavior in question—and, often, to its motivation. It will not be unusual to find, for example, that sociological or psychological initiatives are assigned to offenders by theorists and others, with which the offenders themselves do not identify.

Another example of misattribution can be seen in the case of Damian Williams, the black man sentenced in December 1993 to ten years in prison for beating white truck driver Reginald Denny during the Los Angeles riots. Most reporters and many attorneys assumed that Williams was motivated during the beating by his knowledge of verdicts of innocence that had been returned earlier that same day in the state trial of California police officers accused of beating black motorist Rodney King—an incident whose capture on videotape galvanized the nation. An infuriated Williams, the media supposed (and reported), attacked Denny in response to frustrations he felt at a justice system that seemed to protect whites at the expense of blacks. Williams, however, told a reporter at his sentencing that he knew nothing about the verdicts, and was just caught up in the riots. "Maybe other people knew about [the King verdict], but I wasn't aware of it until later . . . I was just caught up in the rapture," Williams said.[60]

MAKING SENSE OF CRIME: THE CAUSES AND CONSEQUENCES OF THE CRIMINAL EVENT

This book is built around the fact that criminal activity is diversely created and variously interpreted. In other words, *crime, like other social events and experiences, is fundamentally a social construction.*[61] To say that crime is a social construction is not

THEORY VERSUS REALITY

The Murder of John Lennon

At 10:50 P.M. on December 8, 1980, Mark David Chapman, 25, killed famous musician and former Beatle John Lennon. Lennon, who was returning home from a recording session with his wife, Yoko Ono, died in a hail of bullets fired from Chapman's .38-caliber pistol. As a musical luminary, John Lennon was well known to the world. Even his private life—from his residence in the exclusive Dakota Apartments in New York City to his dietary preferences and investment portfolios—was the subject of popular news stories and media exposés.

Following Lennon's death, the public generally assumed that Chapman had chosen his murderous course of action due to innate, albeit perverted, needs fed by a twisted rationale—specifically, to become famous by killing a celebrity. In similar assassination attempts involving Gerald Ford, Ronald Reagan, and others, the media has assumed much the same type of motivation. News stories have communicated to the public the image of would-be assassins sparked by the desire to make headlines and see their names become household words. To assign such motivation to the killers of famous people is understandable from the media perspective. Many of the people encountered by newscasters and writers in daily work have an obvious interest in seeing their names in print. Constant experiences with such people do much to convince byline authors and narrators that the drive for glory is a major motivator of human behavior.

Such "pop psychology," however, probably does not provide an accurate assessment of the motivation of most assassins. We know from recent conversations with Chapman that he, at least, was driven by a different mind-set. In an interview ten years after the killing (the first one he gave since the shooting), Chapman related a story of twisted emotions and evil whisperings inside his own head. Just before the shooting, the unemployed Chapman, living in Hawaii, had gotten married. Faced with a difficult financial situation and rising debts, he became enraged by what he perceived as Lennon's "phoniness." Lennon, he reasoned, had become rich singing about the virtues of the common person, yet Lennon himself lived in luxury made possible by wealth far beyond the reach of Chapman and others like him. According to Chapman, "He [Lennon] had told us to imagine. . . . He had told us not to be greedy. And I had believed!" In effect, Chapman shifted responsibility for his own failure onto Lennon. For that, he reasoned, Lennon must pay. In preparation for the killing, Chapman would record his own voice over Lennon's songs, screaming such things as, "John Lennon must die! John Lennon is a phony." Once a born-again Christian, Chapman turned to Satanism and prayed for demons to enter his body so that he could have the strength to carry out the mission he had set for himself.

Today, says Chapman, he has changed. Much of his time behind bars is spent writing religious tracts and other stories, with inspiration drawn from verses Lennon made famous. Chapman will be eligible for parole in the year 2000.

DISCUSSION QUESTIONS

1. Why did Chapman kill Lennon? Will we ever be sure of his true motivation? How can we be certain we have uncovered it?
2. Was Chapman insane at the time of the killing? What does *insanity* mean in this context? How can it be determined?
3. Should Chapman be released from custody? Why or why not?

Source: Jack Jones, "Decade Later, Killer Prays to be Forgiven," *USA Today,* December 3, 1990, p. 1A.

to lessen the impact of the victimization experiences which all too many people undergo in our society every day. Nor does such a statement trivialize the significance of crime prevention efforts or the activities of members of the criminal justice system. Likewise, it does not underplay the costs of crime to individual victims and to society as a whole. It does, however, recognize that although a given instance of criminal behavior may have many causes, it also carries with it many different kinds of meaning—at least one for offenders, another (generally quite different meaning, of course) for victims, and still another for agents of the criminal justice system. Similarly, a plethora of social interest groups, from victims' advocates, through prisoner "rights" and gun control organizations, all interpret the significance of lawbreaking behavior from unique points of view—and each arrives at different conclusions as to what should be done about the so-called crime problem.

For these reasons, we have chosen to apply the concept of **social relativity** to the study of criminality.[62] Social relativity refers to the fact that social events are differently interpreted according to the cultural experiences and personal interests of the initiator, the observer, or the recipient of that behavior. Hence, as a social phenomenon, crime means different things to the offender, to the criminologist who studies it, to the policeman or policewoman who investigates it, and to the victim who experiences it firsthand.

Figure 1.2 illustrates both the causes and consequences of crime in rudimentary diagrammatic form. The figure consists of a foreground, describing those features which immediately determine the nature of the criminal event (including responses to the event as it is transpiring); and a background, in which generic contributions to crime can be seen with interpretations of the event after it has taken place. We call the background causes of crime "contributions," and use the word "inputs" to signify the more immediate propensities and predispositions of the actors involved in the situation. Inputs also include the physical features of the setting in which a specific crime takes place. Both background contributions and immediate inputs contribute to and shape the criminal event. The more or less immediate results or

Social relativity the notion that social events are differently interpreted according to the cultural experiences and personal interests of the initiator, the observer, or the recipient of that behavior.

FIGURE 1.2   The Causes and Consequences of Crime.

consequences of crime are termed "outputs;" while the term "interpretations" appears in the diagram to indicate that any crime has a lasting impact both on surviving participants and on society.

As Figure 1.2 shows, the criminal event is ultimately a result of the coming together of inputs provided by the:

- offender
- victim
- society
- justice system

Offenders bring with them certain background features, such as personal life experiences, a peculiar biology (insofar as they are unique organisms), a distinct personality, personal values and beliefs, and various kinds of skills and knowledge (some of which may be useful in the commission of crime). Background contributions to crime can be vitally important. Recent research, for example, tends to cement the existence of a link between child-rearing practices and criminality in later life. Joan McCord,[63] reporting on a thirty-year study of family relationships and crime, found that self-confident, nonpunitive, and affectionate mothers tend to insulate their male children from delinquency and, consequently, later criminal activity. Difficulties associated with the birthing process have also been linked to crime in adulthood.[64] Birth trauma and negative familial relationships are but two of the literally thousands of kinds of experiences individuals may have. Whether individuals who undergo trauma at birth and are deprived of positive maternal experiences will turn to crime depends on many other things, including their own mixture of other experiences and characteristics, the appearance of a suitable victim, failure of the justice system to prevent crime, and the evolution of a social environment in which criminal behavior is somehow encouraged or valued.

Immediate inputs are contributed to the criminal event by each of the parties identified in Figure 1.2. Foreground contributions by the offender may consist of a particular motivation, a specific intent (in many cases), or a drug-induced state of mind.

Some crimes are especially difficult to understand, no matter how they are viewed. In 1995, for example, the town of Union, South Carolina, was devastated by the trial of Susan Smith. Smith, who originally claimed a carjacker had forced her from her car and drove off with her two young sons still in the vehicle, confessed to the murders of both Alex, 1, and Michael, 3. Smith admitted she drove the car, with her sons still strapped into child safety seats, off a pier and into a nearby lake. An exhaustive ten-day nationwide search for the boys had failed to turn up any significant leads, and the case might have gone unsolved until investigators discovered a letter from Smith's lover saying that he felt unable to accept both her and the children. An autopsy revealed that the children were still alive as the car went into the lake, but that both drowned as the car flipped onto its roof and sunk.

Criminal justice system the various agencies of justice, especially police, courts, and corrections, whose goal it is to apprehend, convict, punish, and rehabilitate law violators.

Like the offender, the **criminal justice system** also contributes to the criminal event, albeit unwillingly, through its failure to (1) prevent criminal activity, (2) adequately identify specific offenders prior to their involvement in crime, and (3) prevent the early release of convicted criminals who later become repeat offenders. Such background contributions can be seen in prisons (a central component of the justice system) that serve as "schools for crime," fostering anger against society and building a propensity for continued criminality in inmates who have been "turned out." Similarly, the failure of system-sponsored crime prevention programs—ranging from the patrol activities of local police departments to educational and diversionary programs intended to redirect budding offenders—helps to set the stage for the criminal event. On the other hand, proper system response may reduce crime. A recent study by Carol W. Kohfeld and John Sprague, for example, found that police response (especially arrest) could, under certain demographic conditions, dramatically reduce the incidence of criminal behavior.[65] Additionally, Kohfeld and Sprague found that arrest "constitutes communication to criminals in general. . .," further supporting the notion that inputs provided by the justice system have the power to either enhance or reduce the likelihood of criminal occurrences. Immediate inputs provided by the justice system typically consist of features of the situation such as the presence or absence of police officers, the ready availability (or lack thereof) of official assistance, the willingness of police officers to intervene in pre-crime situations, and the response time required for officers to arrive at a crime scene.

Few crimes can occur without a victim. Sometimes the victim is a passive participant in the crime, for example, an innocent person killed on the street outside of his or her home by random gunfire from a drive-by shooting. In such cases, the victim is simply in the proverbial wrong place at the wrong time. Even then, however, merely by being present the victim contributes his or her person to the event, thereby increasing the severity of the incident (i.e., the random shooting that injures no one may still be against the law, but it is a far less serious crime than a sim-

Some crimes are especially difficult to understand. Susan Smith, of Union, South Carolina, confessed to drowning her two young sons Alex, 1, and Michael, 3, in 1994. The boys are shown in happier times in the photo on the left. *Spartan Herald Journal/Sygma and American Fast Photo/SABA Press Photos, Inc.*

ilar incident in which somebody is killed). Sometimes, however, victims more actively contribute to their own victimization through the appearance of defenselessness (perhaps because of old age, drunkenness, or disability), by failing to take appropriate defensive measures (leaving doors unlocked or forgetting to remove keys from a car's ignition), through an unwise display of wealth (flashing large-denomination bills in a public place), or simply by making other unwise choices (walking down a dark alley off of Times Square at 2 or 3 A.M., for example). In a recent study of Canadian victimization, Leslie W. Kennedy and David R. Forde found that violent personal victimization ". . . is contingent on the exposure that comes from following certain lifestyles."[66] This was especially true, they found, "for certain demographic groups, particularly young males."

Although lifestyles may provide the background that fosters victimization, a more active form of victimization characterizes "victims" who initiate criminal activity—such as the barroom brawler who picks a fight, but ends up on the receiving end of the ensuing physical violence. Victim-precipitated offenses are those that involve active victim participation in the initial stages of a criminal event and that take place when the soon-to-be victim instigates the chain of events which ultimately results in the victimization.

Finally, the general public (termed *society* in Figure 1.2) contributes to the criminal event both formally and informally. Society's formal contributions sometimes take the form of legislation, whereby crime itself is defined. Hence, as we shall discuss in considerable detail in Chapter 13, society structures the criminal event in a most fundamental way by delineating (through legislation and via statute) what forms of activity are to be thought of as criminal.

Society's less formal contributions to crime arise out of generic social practices and conditions such as poverty, poor and informal education, various forms of discrimination by which pathways to success are blocked, and the **socialization** process. The process of socialization has an especially important impact on crime causation because it provides the interpretative foundation used to define and understand the significance of particular situations in which we find ourselves, and it is upon those interpretations that we may (or may not) decide to act. Date rape, for example, can occur when a man concludes that his date "owes" him something for the money he has spent on her. That feeling, however inappropriate from the point of view of the victim and the justice system, probably has its roots in early learned experiences—including values communicated from television, the movies, and popular music—about gender-related roles under such circumstances. In other words, society, through the divergent values and expectations it places upon people, property, and behavior under particular conditions, may provide the motivational basis for many offenses.

The contributions society makes to the backgrounds of both offender and victim, and to the structure of the justice system, and the influences each in turn have upon the general social order, provide for a kind of "feedback loop" in our vision of crime (even though the loop is not shown in Figure 1.2 for fear of unnecessarily complicating it). Through socialization, for example, individuals learn about the dangers of criminal victimization; but when victimization occurs and is publicized it reinforces the socialization process, leading to an increased wariness of others, and so on. An example can be seen in the fact that children throughout the United States are routinely taught to avoid strangers and to be suspicious of people they do not know. A few decades ago, stranger avoidance was not ordinarily communicated to children, but entered cultural awareness following a number of horrendous and well-publicized crimes involving child victims. It is now a shared part of the socialization process experienced by countless children every day throughout the United States.

Socialization the lifelong process of social experience whereby individuals acquire the cultural patterns of their society.

The contributions made by society to crime are complex and far reaching. Some say that the content of the mass media (television, newspapers, popular music, etc.) can lead to crime by exposing young people to inappropriate role models and to the kinds of activity—violence and unbridled sexuality, for example—that encourage criminality.

Society's foreground contributions to crime largely emanate from the distribution of resources and the accessibility of services, which are often the direct result of economic conditions. In a study of the availability of medical resources (especially quality hospital emergency services), William G. Doerner[67] found that serious assaults may "become" homicides when such resources are lacking, but that homicides can be prevented via the effective utilization of capable medical technology. Hence, societal decisions leading to the distribution and placement of advanced medical support equipment and personnel can effectively lower homicide rates in selected geographic areas. Of course, homicide rates will be higher in areas where such equipment is not readily available. In Doerner's words, "the causes of homicide transcend the mere social world of the combatants."[68]

The moments that immediately precede any crime are ripe with possibilities. When all the inputs brought to the situation by all those present coalesce into activity which violates the criminal law, a crime occurs. Together, the elements, experiences, and propensities brought to the situation by the offender and the victim, and those that are contributed to the pending event by society and the justice system, precipitate and decide the nature, course, and eventual outcome of the criminal event. It is important to note that some of the inputs brought to the situation may be inhibiting; that is, they may tend to reduce the likelihood or severity of criminal behavior.

As mentioned earlier, the causes of crime, however well documented, tell only half the criminological story. Each and every crime has consequences. Although the immediate consequences of crime may be relatively obvious for those parties directly involved (e.g., the offender and the victim), crime also indirectly impacts society and the justice system. Figure 1.2 terms the immediate effects of crime *outputs.* As with the causes of crime, however, the real impact of such outputs is mediated by perceptual filters, resulting in what the figure terms *interpretations.* Boxes in the figure labeled with the word *interpretation* indicate that after a crime has taken place each party to the event must make sense out of what has transpired. Such interpretations consist of cognitive, emotional, and (ultimately) behavioral reactions to the criminal event.

Interpretations are ongoing. They happen before, during, and after the criminal event, and are undertaken by all those associated with it. In an interesting and detailed study of the interpretive activity of criminal justice system personnel, James F. Gilsinan has documented what happens when callers reach the 911 dispatcher on police emergency lines.[69] Because many prank calls and calls for information are made to 911 operators, the operator must judge the seriousness of every call that comes through. What the caller says was found to be only a small part of the informational cues that the dispatcher seeks to interpret prior to assigning the call to a particular response (or nonresponse) category. Honest calls for help may go unanswered if the operator misinterprets the call. Hence, quite early on in the criminal event, the potential exists for a crucial representative of the justice system to misinterpret important cues and conclude that no crime is taking place.

Other interpretative activities are at least as significant. The justice system, taken as a whole, must decide guilt or innocence and attempt to deal effectively with convicted offenders. Victims must attempt to make sense of their victimizations in such a way as to allow them to testify in court (if need be) and to pick up the pieces of crime-shattered lives. The offender must come to terms with oneself and decide whether to avoid prosecution (if escape, for example, is possible), accept blame, or deny responsibility. Whatever the outcome of these more narrowly focused interpretative activities, society—because of the cumulative impact of individual instances of criminal behavior—will also face tough decisions through its courts and lawmaking agencies. Societal-level decision making may revolve around the implementation of policies designed to stem future instances of criminal behavior, the revision of criminal codes, or the elimination of unpopular laws.

Our perspective takes a double-barreled view of the social event called *crime*. We will (1) consistently attempt to identify the multiplicity of causes which give rise to criminal behavior, and (2) highlight the processes involved in the continual and ongoing interpretation and redefinition of the crime phenomenon. Such a perspective has been variously termed *interpretive sociology, phenomenological psychology,* or *symbolic interactionism,* depending not only on the subject matter to which it has been applied, but also to the scholarly era in which it has predominated. From this perspective, crime can be viewed as an emergent phenomenon—one that arises out of the complex interrelationships between victim, offender, and the social order. The advantages of a **phenomenological** perspective come in accurately assessing and communicating the personal and social underpinnings, as well as the consequences, of crime. As one criminologist recently explained, "An understanding of crime and criminality as constructed from the immediate interactions of criminals, control agents, victims, and others, and therefore as emerging from a tangled experiential web of situated dangers and situated pleasures, certainly refocuses theories of criminal causality on the criminal moment."[70] The chapters that follow employ the integrative perspective advocated here to analyze criminal events and to show how various theoretical approaches can be woven into a consistent explanation of crime.

Phenomenology the study of the contents of human consciousness without regard to external conventions or prior assumptions.

❖ THE PRIMACY OF SOCIOLOGY

Like many other criminology texts, this book recognizes the contributions made by numerous disciplines to the study of crime and crime causation including biology, psychology, and political science. It is important to recognize, however, that the primary perspective from which most contemporary criminologists operate is a sociological one. Today's dominant theoretical understandings of criminal behavior are routinely couched in the language of social science, especially within the framework of sociological theory. The social problems versus social responsibility theme, around which this book is built, is in keeping with such a tradition. The phenomenological perspective, discussed in the last few paragraphs, also falls squarely within a sociological framework and, as mentioned earlier, is frequently referred to as *phenomenological sociology.*

The primacy of the sociological perspective in today's criminological enterprise recognizes the fact that crime, as a subject of study, is a social phenomenon. Central to any study of crime must be the social context of the criminal event, which brings victims and criminals together.[71] Hence, contemporary criminology rests upon a sound tradition of social scientific investigation into the nature of crime and criminal behavior that is rooted in European and American sociological traditions that are now well over 200 years old.[72] Although sociological explanations for crime will be discussed throughout this text—and especially in Chapters 7, 8, and 9—it is important for today's students to realize at the outset that the sociological perspective forms the contemporary foundation of the discipline of criminology.

One of sociology's problems, however, has been its seeming inability to conclusively demonstrate effective means of controlling violent crime. As Diana Fishbein, professor of criminology at the University of Baltimore, says: "Sociological factors play a role. But they have not been able to explain why one person becomes violent and another doesn't."[73]

While sociological theories continue to develop, new and emerging perspectives ask to be recognized. The role of biology in explaining criminal tendencies, for example, appears to be gaining strength as investigations into the mapping of human DNA continues with apace. Charles F. Wellford, past president of the American Society of Criminology, explained the current state of affairs, saying: "I strongly believe that the future development of causal theory is dependent upon our movement toward integrated theories that involve biological, social, and cultural dimensions. Our failure to achieve much in the way of understanding the causal sequences of crime is in part a reflection of our slowness in moving toward multidisciplinary, integrated theoretical structures. The fact is that for two-thirds of this century, as criminology developed, we remained committed to a small number of sociological models for which there is extensive proof of their important but limited value. Fortunately in the last 20 years, this has begun to change. Today we see under way substantial research efforts that are based upon models of explanation that far exceed the traditional sociological approaches."[74]

Nonetheless, whatever new insights may develop over the coming years, it is likely that the sociological perspective will continue to dominate the field of criminology for decades to come. Such dominance is rooted in the fact that crime—regardless of all the causative nuances that may be identified in its development—occurs within the context of the social world. As such, the primary significance of crime and of criminal behavior is fundamentally social in nature, and any control over crime must stem from effective social policy.

SUMMARY

At the start of this chapter, the term *crime* was simply defined as a violation of the criminal law. Near the end of this chapter we recognized the complexity of crime, calling it an "emergent phenomenon." In the process, crime was effectively redefined as a lawbreaking event whose significance arises out of an intricate social nexus involving a rather wide variety of participants. As we enter the twenty-first century, contemporary criminologists face the daunting task of reconciling an extensive and diverse collection of theoretical explanations for criminal behavior. All these perspectives aim to assist in understanding the social phenomenon of crime—a phenomenon that is itself open to interpretation and runs the gamut from petty offenses to major infractions of the criminal law. At the very least, we should recognize that explanations for criminal behavior rest on shaky ground insofar as the subject matter they seek to interpret contains many different forms of behavior, each of which is subject to personal, political, and definitional vagaries.

WEB WATCH

Access the *Criminology Today* home page on the World Wide Web by pointing your browser at www.prenhall.com/cjcentral. Once there, click on *Criminology Today* in order to access the wealth of electronic resources supporting this text.

On-site resources include (1) "Chapter Links," which provides succinct overviews of critical ideas from the textbook and links selected materials from around the Web to concepts found in the text; (2) "General Reference—Law and Justice Links," which is organized by chapter and leads to other useful resources on the World Wide Web such as libraries, electronic discussion lists, and electronic journals; (3) "Criminology Sites on the Web," which lists links to organizations such as the American Society of Criminology and the National Organization for Victims Assistance (NOVA), as well as crime prevention links and statistics on crime and justice. Many other Web-based resources can be accessed via the *Criminology Today* site, including the federal Justice Information Center, the Bureau of Justice Statistics, the FBI, the RAND Corporation, the Vera Institute of Justice, PAVNET (an online "Partnership Against Violence," run by seven different federal agencies), and the National White Collar Crime Center.

Still another feature of the *Criminology Today* Web site is e-mail homework. Homework can be composed on-site and submitted to instructors using the instructor's e-mail address. To use the e-mail homework feature, click on "E-Mail Homework" on the opening page, and then type answers to the questions that appear in the spaces provided. Use your instructor's e-mail address to submit homework answers. The *Criminology Today* Web site also provides links to powerful Web-based search engines that can help you find topics of interest to you as you progress through your course of study. Search engines can be found under the home page heading "Criminology Sites on the Web."

DISCUSSION QUESTIONS

1. This book emphasizes a social problems versus social responsibility theme. Describe both perspectives. How might social policy decisions based on these perspectives vary?

2. What is *crime?* What is the difference between crime and deviance? How might the notion of crime change over time? What impact does the changing nature of crime hold for criminology?

3. Do you believe that doctor-assisted suicide should be legalized? Why or why not? What do such crimes as doctor-assisted suicide have to tell us about the nature of the law and about crime in general?

4. Do you think that policymakers should address crime as a matter of individual responsibility and accountability, or do you think that crime is truly a symptom of a dysfunctional society? Why?

5. Describe the various participants in a criminal event. How does each contribute to a definition of the event?

6. What do criminologists do? Do you think you might want to become a criminologist? Why or why not?

7. This chapter recognizes the primacy of the sociological perspective in today's criminological thought. Why is the sociological perspective especially important in studying crime? What other perspectives might be relevant? Why?

NOTES

[1] James Q. Wilson, *Thinking About Crime* (New York: Basic Books, 1983), p. 251.

[2] Air date: November 22, 1993.

[3] George B. Vold and Thomas J. Bernard, *Theoretical Criminology,* 3rd ed. (New York: Oxford University Press, 1986).

[4] Narrative materials in this section derive from Marc Peywer and T. Trent Gegax, "A Deadly Late-Night Delivery," *Newsweek,* May 5, 1997, p. 65; Robert Hanley, "Woman Led Police to Suspect in Pizza Murders, Court Papers Say," *New York Times* news service, via Simon and Schuster NewsLink, April 26, 1997; and Robert D. McFadden, "2 Youths Held in Thrill-Killings of Pizza Deliverymen," *New York Times* news service, via Simon and Schuster NewsLink, April 23, 1997.

[5] "Aborigine Cleared of Death Curse Extortion," Reuters wire service, February 20, 1997.

[6] From the standpoint of the law, the proper word is *conduct* rather than *behavior,* because the term *conduct* implies intentional and willful activity, whereas *behavior* refers to any human activity—even that which occurs while a person is unconscious, as well as that which is unintended.

[7] Paul W. Tappan, "Who Is the Criminal?" in Gilbert Geis and Robert F. Meier, eds., *White Collar Crime* (New York: Free Press, 1947), p. 277.

[8] Edwin Sutherland, *Principles of Criminology,* 4th ed. (New York: J. B. Lippincott, 1947).

[9] Ron Claassen, "Restorative Justice: Fundamental Principles," web posted at http://www.fresno.edu/pacs/rjprinc.htm.

[10] This is not entirely true. In common law jurisdictions, which are discussed shortly, a person can be arrested for serious violations of community standards even without an existing statute criminalizing the behavior in question.

[11] In 1996, for example, euthanasia advocate Dr. Jack Kevorkian was arrested and

unsuccessfully prosecuted in Michigan on charges of violating the state's common law against suicide.

[12]"Kevorkian Gets Green Light in Libel Suit Against AMA," CNN online, May 28, 1997, http://cnn.com/US/9705/28/briefs/kevorkian/index.html.

[13]"Kevorkian Suggests Guidelines for Suicides," CNN Interactive online, January 14, 1997, http://cnn.com/US/9701/14/kevorkian/index.html.

[14]"Elders Says Drug Legalization Could Cut Violence," Reuters wire service, December 7, 1993.

[15]Elders was fired by President Clinton amidst the controversy raised by her comments.

[16]*Vacco* v. *Quill*, U.S. Supreme Court. No. 95-1858. Decided June 26, 1997.

[17]*Washington* v. *Glucksberg*, U.S. Supreme Court. No. 96-110. Decided June 26, 1997.

[18]Carrie Dowling, "Assisted-Suicide Law Blocked," *USA Today*, December 8, 1994, p. 3A.

[19]Carey Goldberg, "Oregon Braces for New Fight on Helping the Dying to Die," *New York Times*, June 17, 1997, p. 1A.

[20]See William McCall, "Oregon Assisted Suicide Law in Limbo," Associated Press wire service, June 27, 1997.

[21]"Topless Standard," *Fayetteville Observer-Times*, November 14, 1991, p. 7A.

[22]*The American Heritage Dictionary* on CD-ROM.

[23]This list is not meant to be exclusive. There are many other journals in the field, too numerous to list here.

[24]Sutherland, *Principles of Criminology*, p. 1.

[25]Clarence Ray Jeffery, "The Historical Development of Criminology," in Herman Mannheim, ed., *Pioneers in Criminology* (Montclair, N.J., Paterson Smith, 1972), p. 458.

[26]Gregg Barak, *Integrating Criminologies* (Boston: Allyn and Bacon, 1998), p. 303.

[27]Jack P. Gibbs, "The State of Criminological Theory," *Criminology*, vol. 25, no. 4 (November 1987), pp. 822–823.

[28]Available through Sage Publications, Thousand Oaks, Calif.

[29]Piers Beirne and Colin Sumner, "Editorial Statement," *Theoretical Criminology: An International Journal*, vol. 1, no. 1 (February 1997), pp. 5–11.

[30]There are, however, those who deny that criminology is deserving of the name "discipline." See, for example, Don C. Gibbons, *Talking about Crime and Criminals: Problems and Issues in Theory Development in Criminology* (Englewood Cliffs, N.J.: Prentice Hall, 1994), p. 3.

[31]Charles F. Wellford, "Controlling Crime and Achieving Justice: The American Society of Criminology 1996 Presidential Address," *Criminology*, vol. 35, no. 1 (1997), p. 1.

[32]Gibbons, *Talking about Crime and Criminals: Problems and Issues in Theory Development in Criminology*, p. 4.

[33]Sutherland, *Principles of Criminology*.

[34]Don M. Gottfredson, "Criminological Theories: The Truth as Told by Mark Twain," in William S. Laufer and Freda Adler, eds., *Advances in Criminological Theory*, vol. 1 (New Brunswick, N.J.: Transaction, 1989), p. 1.

[35]Barak, *Integrating Criminologies*, p. 5.

[36]Don G. Gibbons, "Talking About Crime: Observations on the Prospects for Causal Theory in Criminology," *Criminal Justice Research Bulletin*, vol. 7, no. 6 (Sam Houston State University, 1992).

[37]Ibid.

[38]"Fanning the Fire over Beavis, *USA Today*, October 15, 1993, p. D1.

[39]"Networks Turn Thumbs Down on TV-Violence Report," United Press wire service, Northeastern edition, December 17, 1993.

[40]"Film Scene to Be Cut After Fatal Imitation," *USA Today*, October 20, 1993, p. 1A.

[41]"Fanning the Fire over Bevis."

[42]Alfred Blumstein, "Making Rationality Relevant: The American Society of Criminology 1992 Presidential Address," *Criminology*, vol. 31, no. 1 (February 1993), p. 1.

[43]Ibid.

[44]"Poll: More Fear Being Murdered," *USA Today*, November 26–28, 1993, pp. A1 and A8.

[45]"Job Worries Persist, Poll Shows," *USA Today*, December 15, 1993, p. 4A, reporting on the 1994 Battleground Survey by the Tarrance Group and Mellman-Lazarus-Lake.

[46]Ibid., p. 4A.

[47]*Washington Post* wire service, December 20, 1993.

[48]Northwestern National Life Company, *Fear and Violence in the Workplace*, research report, October 18, 1993.

[49]"Survey: Homicides at Work on the Rise," *USA Today*, October 18, 1993, p. 3B.

[50]"Cab Drivers Face High Death Risk," *Fayetteville Observer-Times*, October 31, 1993, p. 8A.

[51]Harry E. Allen, "The American Dream and Crime in the Twenty-First Century: Presidential Address to the Academy of Criminal Justice Sciences," *Justice Quarterly*, vol. 12, no. 3 (September 1995), p. 433.

[52]For an especially good discussion of this issue, see Theodore Sasson, *Crime Talk: How Citizens Construct a Social Problem* (Hawthorne, N.Y.: Aldine de Gruyter, 1995).

[53]"Clinton—Crime," Associated Press wire service, December 9, 1993.

[54]"Clinton Task Force to Act Against Violence," Reuters wire service, December 9, 1993.

[55]Megan's death led most states and the federal government to pass "Megan's Laws," requiring community notification when released sex offenders move into an area.

[56]Melanie Burney, "Megan's Law," Associated Press wire service, June 21, 1997.

[57]Nat Hentoff, "Justice Blackmun Reconsiders the Death Penalty," *Washington Post* wire service, December 11, 1993.

[58]"Megan's Law," op. cit.

[59]For a good overview of this issue, see Wesley G. Skogan, ed., *Reactions to Crime and Violence*, The Annals of the American Academy of Political and Social Science (Thousand Oaks, Calif.: Sage, 1995).

[60]"Denny Beating," Associated Press wire service, December 8, 1993.

[61]For a good discussion of the social construction of crime, see Leslie T. Wilkins, "On Crime and its Social Construction: Observations on the Social Construction of Crime," *Social Pathology*, vol. 1, no. 1 (January 1995), pp. 1–11.

[62]For a parallel approach, see Terance D. Miethe and Robert F. Meier, *Crime and Its Social Context: Toward an Integrated Theory of Offenders, Victims, and Situations* (Albany, N.Y.: State University of New York Press, 1995).

[63]Joan McCord, "Family Relationships, Juvenile Delinquency, and Adult Criminality," *Criminology*, vol. 29, no. 3 (August 1991), pp. 397–417.

[64]Elizabeth Candle and Sarnoff A. Mednick, "Perinatal Complications Predict Violent Offending," *Criminology*, vol. 29, no. 3 (August 1991), pp. 519–529.

[65]Carol W. Kohfeld and John Sprague, "Demography, Police Behavior, and Deterrence," *Criminology*, vol. 28, no. 1 (February 1990). pp. 111–136.

[66]Leslie W. Kennedy and David R. Forde, "Routine Activities and Crime: An Analysis of Victimization in Canada," *Criminology*, vol. 28, no. 1 (February 1990), pp. 137–152.

[67]William G. Doerner, "The Impact of Medical Resources on Criminally Induced Lethality: A Further Examination," *Criminology*, vol. 26, no. 1 (February 1988), pp. 171–177.

[68]Ibid, p. 177.

[69]James F. Gilsinan, "They is Clowning Tough: 911 and the Social Construction of Reality," *Criminology*, vol. 27, no. 2 (May 1989), pp. 329–344.

[70]Jeff Ferrell, "Criminological *Verstehen:* Inside the Immediacy of Crime," *Justice Quarterly*, vol. 14, no. 1 (1997), p. 11.

[71]See, for example, Terance D. Miethe and Robert F. Meier, *Crime and Its Social Context: Toward an Integrated Theory of Offenders, Victims, and Situations* (Albany, N.Y.: State University of New York Press, 1995).

[72]For a good discussion of the historical development of criminology, see Don C. Gibbons, *Talking About Crime and Criminals: Problems and Issues in Theory Development in Criminology* (Englewood Cliffs, N.J.: Prentice Hall, 1994); Don C. Gibbons, *The Criminological Enterprise* (Englewood Cliffs, N.J.: Prentice Hall, 1979); and Leon Radzinowicz, *In Search of Criminology* (Cambridge, Mass.: Harvard University Press, 1962).

[73]As quoted in W. Wayt Gibbs, "Trends in Behavioral Science: Seeking the Criminal Element," *Scientific American*, vol. 272, no. 3 (March 1995), pp. 100–107.

[74]Charles F. Wellford, "Controlling Crime and Achieving Justice: The American Society of Criminology 1996 Presidential Address," *Criminology*, vol. 35, no. 1 (1997), p. 4.

PATTERNS OF CRIME

The statistics are staggering: a person murdered an average of every 22 minutes, a rape every four minutes, a robbery every 26 seconds. You're right to be afraid.

—THE ASSOCIATED PRESS[1]

First, we must recognize that most violent crimes are committed by a small percentage of criminals who too often break the laws even when they are on parole. Now those who commit crimes should be punished, and those who commit repeated violent crimes should be told when you commit a third violent crime, you will be put away and put away for good. Three strikes and you are out.

—PRESIDENT CLINTON, 1994 STATE OF THE UNION ADDRESS

✛ CHAPTER OUTLINE ✛

INTRODUCTION
A HISTORY OF CRIME STATISTICS
    Adolphe Quételet and André Michel Guerry
CRIME STATISTICS TODAY
    The UCR Program
    Data Gathering Under the NCVS
    Criminal Homicide
    Forcible Rape
    Robbery
    Aggravated Assault
    Burglary
    Larceny
    Motor Vehicle Theft
    Arson
    Part II Offenses
    Unreported Crimes
THE SOCIAL DIMENSIONS OF CRIME
    What are "Social Dimensions"?
    Age and Crime
    Gender and Crime
    Ethnicity and Crime
    Social Class and Crime
THE COSTS OF CRIME
SUMMARY

⬅ IMPORTANT NAMES ⬅

Adolphe Quételet	André Michel Guerry	Thomas Robert Malthus
John J. DiIulio, Jr.	Alfred Blumstein	Joan Petersilia
William Wilbanks	Coramae Richey Mann	John Braithwaite

⬅ IMPORTANT TERMS ⬅

demographics	household crimes	robbery
statistical school	criminal homicide	aggravated assault
National Crime Victimization Survey (NCVS)	first-degree murder	simple assault
	second-degree murder	burglary
Uniform Crime Report (UCR)	negligent homicide	larceny-theft
	serial murder	motor vehicle theft
Part I offenses	mass murder	carjacking
clearance rate	felony murder	arson
National Incident-Based Reporting System (NIBRS)	forcible rape	correlation
	date rape	superpredators
		cohort

:::: INTRODUCTION

Wesley "Pop" Honeywood, 94, knows little about statistics—but he is familiar with crime. Over the years Honeywood, who lives in Jacksonville, Florida, has been arrested forty-six times. Five of those arrests were for felonies. Honeywood has been imprisoned on eight occasions since 1946, serving sentences in Philadelphia, Baltimore, Tampa, Orlando, and Jacksonville.

Honeywood's troubles with the law began at the close of World War II when he and a couple of friends stole a bomber and flew it over Italy for fun. After landing, Honeywood was arrested by military police, did a brief stint in jail, and received a dishonorable discharge from the army.

Not long ago, the geriatric career criminal stood before a Florida judge, awaiting sentencing after pleading guilty to charges of armed assault and possession of a firearm by a convicted felon. The incident grew out of Honeywood's liking for grapes, which he had watched ripen in his neighbor's yard at the end of the summer. Finally, unable to resist the temptation any longer, Honeywood helped himself to bunches of the fruit. When confronted by the neighbor, Honeywood pulled a gun and threatened the man.

Because of all the crimes he's committed, Honeywood now faces sentencing as a habitual offender and could be sent to prison for sixty years. Making matters worse is the fact that Honeywood was on probation for the attempted sexual battery of a 7-year-old girl when he was arrested for the grape theft. And age hasn't mellowed him. Honeywood admits shooting a man in the buttocks in 1989, but claims self-defense. The case never went to trial.

Honeywood says he is not afraid of a prison sentence. "I can do it," he smiles. "I've been locked up a whole lot of times here, but they turn me loose every time."

Circuit Judge R. Hudson Olliff, who will soon sentence Honeywood, worries about his age and the fact that he probably won't survive a long prison stay. But, he says, "[t]he first duty is to protect the public. If he is a 94-year-old that is a danger to the public and he has to go to jail, so be it."

Honeywood, however, wishes he would have plea bargained. "I wish they would give me house arrest," he says. "I don't go nowhere, but stay home. My lawyer says he [the judge] might put me in an old folks home." Even if he goes to prison, Honeywood figures he may beat the odds. His father lived to be 113.

:::: A HISTORY OF CRIME STATISTICS

Pop Honeywood is a statistical anomaly. Few people are involved in crime past middle age. Fewer still ever reach Honeywood's stage in life. Statistical data from the *Sourcebook of Criminal Justice Statistics*[2] show that the likelihood of crime commission declines with age. Persons 65 years of age and older, for example, commit fewer than 1 percent of all crimes, and the proportion of crimes committed by those over age 90 is so small that it cannot be meaningfully expressed as a percentage of total crime.

Although the gathering of crime statistics is a relatively new phenomenon, population statistics have been collected periodically since pre-Roman times. Old Testament accounts of enumerations of the Hebrews, for example, provide evidence of Middle Eastern census-taking thousands of years ago. In like manner, The New Testament describes how the family of Jesus had to return home to be counted during an official census—providing evidence of routine census-taking during the time of Christ. The lustrum, which was a ceremonial purification of the entire ancient Roman population after census-taking, leads historians to conclude that Roman population counts were made every five years. Centuries later, the *Doomsday Book,* created by order of William the Conqueror in 1085 to 1086, provided a written survey of English landowners and their property. Other evidence shows that primitive societies around the world also took periodic counts of their members. The Incas, for example, a pre-Columbian Indian empire in western South America, required successive census reports to be recorded on knotted strings called *quipas.*

Demographics the characteristics of population groups, usually expressed in statistical form

Although census-taking has occurred throughout history, inferences based on statistical **demographics** appear to be a product of the last 200 years. In 1798 the English economist **Thomas Robert Malthus** (1766–1834) published his *Essay on the Principle of Population as It Affects the Future Improvement of Society,* in which he described a worldwide future of warfare, crime, and starvation. The human population, Malthus predicted, would grow exponentially over the following decades or centuries, leading to a shortage of needed resources, especially food. Conflict on both the interpersonal and international levels would be the result, Malthus claimed, as individuals and groups competed for survival.

ADOLPHE QUÉTELET AND ANDRÉ MICHEL GUERRY

As a direct result of Malthusian thought, investigators throughout Europe began to gather "moral statistics," or social enumerations which they thought may prove useful in measuring the degree to which crime and conflict existed in societies of the period. Such statistics were scrutinized in hopes of gauging "the moral health of nations"—a phrase commonly used throughout the period. One of the first such investigators was **André Michel Guerry** (1802–1866), who calculated per capita crime rates throughout various French provinces in the early 1800s.

In 1835 the Belgian astronomer and mathematician **Adolphe Quételet** (1796–1864) published a statistical analysis of crime in a number of European countries, including Belgium, France, and Holland. Quételet set for himself the goal of assessing the degree to which crime rates vary with climate, sex, and age. He noticed what is still obvious to criminal statisticians today—that crime changes with the seasons, with many violent crimes showing an increase during the hot summer months and property crimes increasing in frequency during colder parts of the year. As a consequence of these observations, Quételet proposed what he called the "thermic law." According to thermic law, Quételet claimed, morality undergoes seasonal variation—a proposal that stimulated widespread debate in its day.[3]

The first officially published crime statistics appeared in London's *Gazette* beginning in 1828 and France's 1825 *Compte generale.* Soon comparisons (or what contemporary statisticians call *correlations*) began to be calculated between economic conditions and the rates of various types of crime. From a study of English statistical data covering the years 1810 to 1847, Joseph Fletcher concluded that prison commitments increased as the price of wheat rose. In like fashion, the German writer Gerog von Mayr, whose data covered the years 1836 to 1861, discovered that the rate of theft increased with the price of rye in Bavaria.

The work of statisticians such as Guerry and Quételet formed the historical basis for what has been called the **statistical school** of criminology. The statistical school foreshadowed the development of both sociological criminology and the ecological school, perspectives which are discussed in considerable detail later in this book.

CRIME STATISTICS TODAY

The gathering of crime statistics has continued apace ever since crime-related data collection began over a century ago. Crime statistics in the United States are reported in two major surveys: the **National Crime Victimization Survey (NCVS)** published yearly by the Bureau of Justice Statistics (BJS) and the Federal Bureau of Investigation's **Uniform Crime Report (UCR).**

NCVS data appear in a number of annual reports, the most significant of which are *Criminal Victimization in the United States* and *Crime and the Nation's Households.* FBI data take the form of the annual publication *Crime in the United States.* Numerous other surveys and reports are made available through the Bureau of Justice Statistics. Such surveys cover not only the incidence of crime and criminal activity in the United States, but also extend to many other aspects of the criminal justice profession, including justice system expenditures, prisons and correctional data, probation and parole populations, jail inmate information, statistics on law enforcement agencies and personnel, and information on the activities of state and federal courts. These and other reports are generally made available free of charge to interested parties through the National Criminal Justice Reference Service (NCJRS), which is located in Rockville, Maryland.[4]

The largest single annual statistical compilation of printed data on crime and criminal justice in one source is BJS's *Sourcebook of Criminal Justice Statistics,* which is stocked yearly by the U.S. Government Printing Office. The *Sourcebook* consists of approximately 800 tables covering all aspects of criminal justice in the United States. Sourcebook information is a compilation of statistics from many different sources, and includes much of the data found in the aforementioned *Crime in the United States* and *Criminal Victimization in the United States.* Available on the World Wide Web,[5] as well as in print, the Web-posted *Sourcebook* is continually updated.

Other sources of crime-related and criminal justice information include the National Archive of Criminal Justice Data, operated by the Interuniversity Consortium for Political and Social Research (ICPSR) at Ann Arbor, Michigan; the Justice Statistics Clearinghouse (part of BJS); the Justice Research and Statistics Association in Washington, D.C.; the Bureau of Justice Assistance Clearinghouse; the Police Executive Research Forum (PERF); the Police Foundation; the Data Resources Program of the National Criminal Justice Reference Service; and the SEARCH Group, Inc. The SEARCH Group, located in Sacramento, California, is one of a number of agencies and organizations providing online access to statistical

Statistical school a criminological perspective with roots in the early 1800s which seeks to uncover correlations between crime rates and other types of demographic data.

National Crime Victimization Survey (NCVS) conducted annually by the Bureau of Justice Statistics (BJS); provides data on surveyed households that report they were affected by crime.

Uniform Crime Report (UCR) a summation of crime statistics tallied annually by the Federal Bureau of Investigation (FBI) and consisting primarily of data on crimes reported to the police and of arrests.

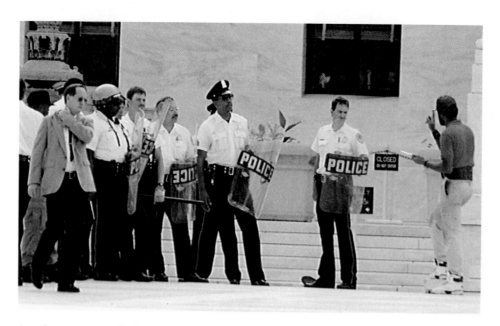

Americans are especially fearful of violent crimes. Here a man with a knife threatens Washington, D.C., police outside the U.S. Supreme Court building. How might rates of violence be lowered? *Dennis Cook/AP/Wide World Photos.*

information. Links to these sites are available at the *Criminology Today* Web site (see the Web Watch section at the end of this chapter for details).

This chapter will describe crime in the United States, or what some authors call "the crime picture" in America, using information derived from the latest available NCVS report and the UCR. It is important to realize at the outset, however, that the two surveys differ significantly in both purpose and methodology. A recent UCR release, for example, begins with these words: "Data users are cautioned against comparisons of crime trends presented in this report and those estimated by the National Crime Victimization Survey (NCVS), administered by the Bureau of Justice Statistics. Because of differences in methodology and crime coverage, the two programs examine the Nation's crime problem from somewhat different perspectives, and their results are not strictly comparable. The definitional and procedural differences can account for many of the apparent discrepancies in results from the two programs."[6] The next few paragraphs highlight the key features of UCR and NCVS survey data.

THE UCR PROGRAM

The Uniform Crime Reporting Program was begun by the FBI in 1929 in response to a national initiative undertaken by the International Association of Chiefs of Police (IACP). The IACP goal was to develop a set of uniform crime statistics for use by police agencies and policymakers throughout the country. In 1930 the U.S. Congress enacted Title 28, Section 534 of the United States Code, which authorized the attorney general of the United States to begin gathering crime information. The attorney general designated the FBI to serve as a national clearinghouse on crime

⚏

TABLE 2.1

MAJOR CRIMES KNOWN TO THE POLICE, 1996
(UCR PART I OFFENSES)

Offense	Number	Rate per 100,000	Clearance Rate
Personal/Violent Crimes			
Murder	19,645	7.4	67%
Forcible rape	957,679	36.1	53
Robbery	537,050	202.4	27
Aggravated assault	1,029,814	388	58
Property Crimes			
Burglary	2,501,524	943	14
Larceny	7,894,620	2,975.9	20
Motor vehicle theft	1,395,192	525.9	14
Arson	88,887	44.3	16
U.S. total	13,562,501	5,078.9	22

Source: Federal Bureau of Investigation, *Crime in the United States, 1996* (Washington, D.C.: U.S. Government Printing Office, 1997).

statistics, and police agencies around the country began submitting data under the UCR Program. In its initial year of operation, 400 police departments representing cities and towns in forty-three states participated in the program.

Initial UCR data were structured in terms of seven major offense categories: murder, rape, robbery, aggravated assault, burglary, larceny, and motor vehicle theft. These crimes, called **Part I offenses,** when averaged together and compared with the country's population formed a crime index. The *crime index* provides a crime rate that can be compared over time and from one geographic location to another. Rates of crime under the UCR Program are generally expressed as "x-number of offenses per 100,000 persons." The 1996 rate of criminal homicide, for example, was 7.4 people murdered for every 100,000 persons in the American population.

In 1979 Congress mandated that arson be added to the list of index offenses. Unfortunately, the inclusion of arson as an eighth index offense has made it more difficult to compare pre- and post-1979 crime indexes. Such comparisons now often require a separate tabulation whereby arson is factored out of the index.

Part I offenses are subdivided into two categories: violent personal crimes—consisting of murder, rape, robbery, and aggravated assault—and property crimes—consisting of burglary, larceny, motor vehicle theft, and arson. Part I offenses, showing the number of crimes reported to the police in 1996 are listed in Table 2.1 and diagrammatically represented in Figure 2.1, the FBI's "Crime Clock."

When the FBI issues the annual UCR, it includes information within each Part I offense category on the percentage of crimes that have been cleared. *Cleared crimes* are those for which an arrest has been made or for which the perpetrator is known but an arrest is not possible (as when the offender is deceased or out of the country).

Part I offenses that group of offenses, also called "major offenses" or "index offenses," for which the UCR publishes counts of reported instances, and which consist of murder, rape, robbery, aggravated assault, burglary, larceny, auto theft, and arson.

While crime clocks provide a useful visual representation of the extent of crime, caution must be used in viewing them because they imply a regularity of crime commission which does not exist.

FIGURE 2.1   The FBI's "Crime Clock" for 1996. *Source:* FBI, *Crime in the United States, 1996* (Washington, D.C.: U.S. Government Printing Office 1997).

Cleared crimes are also referred to as "solved," although clearances as counted by the FBI have nothing to do with successful in-court prosecution. Hence, those charged with a crime that is scored as cleared by the FBI may not yet have been adjudicated.

In official UCR terminology, a Part I offense is regarded as cleared or solved when (1) "a law enforcement agency has charged at least one person with the offense" or (2) "a suspect has been identified and located and an arrest is justified, but action is prevented by circumstances outside law enforcement control." Clearance rates are reported in the UCR for each Part I crime category. A **clearance rate** refers to the proportion of reported or discovered crimes within a given offense category that are solved.

Clearance rate the proportion of reported or discovered crimes within a given offense category that are solved.

Programmatic Problems with Available Data

The most significant methodological feature of the Uniform Crime Reporting Program is indicated by its name. It is a "reporting" program. In other words, only crimes that are reported to the police (or which are discovered by them, or by someone else who then reports them) are included in the statistics compiled by the program. Unless someone complains to the police about a criminal incident, it will go unreported and will not appear in the UCR. Most complaints, of course, are made by victims.

Because UCR data are based on *reported* crime, the program has been criticized for seriously underestimating the true incidence of criminal activity within the United States—a measurement that would also include unreported crimes. Unreported and underreported criminal activity has been called the "hidden figure" of crime. Some experts say, for example, that rape is the most underreported crime in the UCR, with four to five times as many rapes occurring each year as are reported. Reasons for not reporting a crime such as rape are numerous and include (1) fear of the perpetrator; (2) shame, which may carry over from traditional attitudes about sexual behavior and a woman's role in sexual encounters; (3) fears the victim may have of not being believed; and (4) fear of further participation in the justice system, such as the possibility of the victim's being required to go to court and testify against the offender, thereby exposing herself to potentially embarrassing cross-examination and public scrutiny.

Many other crimes are underreported as well. Although rape is indeed seriously underreported (a conclusion drawn from comparison of NCVS and UCR rape statistics), the most seriously underreported crime may in fact be larceny, because the theft of small items may never make it into official police reports and may even be forgotten by victims during interviews with NCVS surveyors.

Another problem with the UCR (and with the NCVS) lies in the specialized definitions it employs in deciding which events should be scored as crimes, and in the difficulties this creates in assigning reported crimes to specific offense categories. UCR definitions of criminal activity rarely correspond precisely with statutory definitions of federal and state crimes, making comparisons with other state and federal crime tabulations difficult. Contrast, for example, the following four definitions of rape, one of which represents the standard UCR definition, another the NCVS definition, whereas a third is taken from the United States Code, and a fourth is quoted verbatim from California criminal law:

Forcible Rape (UCR)

Forcible rape, as defined in the Program, is the carnal knowledge of a female forcibly and against her will. Included are rapes by force and attempts or assaults to rape. Statutory offenses (where no force is used but the victim is under the age of legal consent) are excluded.

Rape (NCVS)

Carnal knowledge through the use of force or the threat of force, including attempts. Statutory rape (without force) is excluded. Both heterosexual and homosexual rape are included.

Aggravated Sexual Abuse (U.S. Code): Title 18, Chapter 109A, Section 2241

(a) By force or threat. Whoever, in the special maritime and territorial jurisdiction of the United States or in a Federal prison, knowingly causes another person to engage in a sexual act—

(1) by using force against that other person; or

(2) by threatening or placing that other person in fear that any person will be subjected to death, serious bodily injury, or kidnapping; or attempts to so, shall be fined under this title, imprisoned for term of years or life, or both.

Rape (California Penal Code)

Rape is an act of sexual intercourse accomplished with a person not the spouse of the perpetrator, under any of the following circumstances:

(a) Where a person is incapable, because of mental disorder or development or physical disability, of giving legal consent . . .

(b) Where it is accomplished against a person's will by means of force, violence, duress, menace, or fear of immediate and unlawful bodily injury on the person of another.

(c) Where a person is prevented from resisting by any intoxicating or anesthetic substance, or any controlled substance . . .

(d) Where a person is at the time unconscious of the nature of the act . . .

(e) Where a person submits under the belief that the person committing the act is the victim's spouse . . .

(f) Where the act is accomplished against the victim's will by threatening to retaliate in the future against the victim or any other person . . .

(g) Where the act is accomplished against the victim's will by threatening to use the authority of a public official to incarcerate, arrest, or deport the victim or another . . .

As the definitions reveal, the UCR only counts as rape the forced "carnal knowledge" of a *female* individual and excludes homosexual rape. Even more significantly, the UCR Program counts attempts to commit rape as though the crime had actually been accomplished—even though a woman may have fought off her assailant. The NCVS, on the other hand, counts homosexual rape (the rape of a person by another person of the same gender) within its tally of rape statistics but, as discussed in more detail shortly, does not include rapes perpetrated on individuals under the age of 12. California law defines rape exclusively in terms of sexual intercourse, although it does not define that term other than to say that "penetration however slight" is sufficient for the crime of rape to have occurred. Likewise, the California law does not specifically exclude the rape of male individuals from consideration for prosecution under the law, but it does preclude from prosecution the rape of one's spouse (although a separate California statute, entitled "Spousal Rape," does not). Federal law is the most inclusive of all, since a 1986 law against "sexual abuse" replaced previous federal rape statutes. Under the new federal statute, which avoids use of the term *rape* entirely, the crime of "sexual abuse" encompasses both hetero- and homosexual forms of rape, as well as rape within marriage and many other forms of forced sexual activity.

The New UCR

National Incident-Based Reporting System (NIBRS) a new form of the UCR that will collect data on each single incident and arrest within twenty-two crime categories.

Recently the UCR has undergone a number of significant changes, and more are scheduled to be implemented shortly as a new enhanced UCR Program is phased in. The new program will revise the definitions of a number of index offenses and will be incident driven. "Incident driven" means that in the future the UCR Program, now officially called the **National Incident-Based Reporting System (NIBRS),** will "collect data on each single incident and arrest within 22 crime categories," with incident, victim, property, offender, and arrestee information being gathered when available. The goal of NIBRS is to make data on reported crime more useful by relating it more completely than the old system did to other available information such as victim and offender characteristics. Although the FBI began accepting crime incident data in NIBRS format in 1989, the transition process is not moving as quickly as planned. NIBRS was scheduled to be fully in place by 1999. However, delays continue to occur in some areas. According to the FBI, NIBRS will be implemented "at a pace commensurate with the resources, abilities, and limitations of the contributing law enforcement agencies."

Another recent change in the UCR Program involves the collection of hate crime statistics, which was mandated by the U.S. Congress with passage of the 1990 Hate Crime Statistics Act. The law established a five-year period during which the FBI was required to serve as a repository for data collected on crimes motivated by religious, ethnic, racial, or sexual orientation and prejudice. Hate crimes data collection began in 1990. The Violent Crime Control and Law Enforcement Act of 1994 mandated the addition to the hate crimes category of crimes motivated by biases against persons with disabilities, and the UCR Program began reporting such crimes in 1997.

DATA GATHERING UNDER THE NCVS

The NCVS differs from the UCR in one especially significant way: rather than depending on reports of crimes to the police, the data contained in the NCVS consist of information elicited through interviews with members of randomly selected households throughout the nation. Hence, the NCVS uncovers a large number of crimes that may not have been reported, and it is therefore regarded by many researchers as a more accurate measure of the actual incidence of crime in the United States than is the UCR. NCVS data are gathered by U.S. Census Bureau personnel who survey approximately 49,000 households consisting of about 101,000 persons. Interviews are conducted at six-month intervals, with individual households rotating out of the sample every three years. New households are continually added to the sample to replace those which have been dropped.

NCVS interviewers collect individual and household victimization data from anyone 12 years old or older at residences within the sample. Questions are about the incidence of rape, personal robbery, aggravated and simple assault, household burglary, personal and household theft, and motor vehicle theft as they have affected household members during the past six months. Information is gathered on victims (including sex, age, race, ethnicity, marital status, income, and educational level), offenders (sex, age, race, and relationship to the victim), and crimes (time and place of occurrence, use of weapons, nature of injury, and economic consequences of the criminal activity for the victim). Questions also cover self-protective measures employed by victims, the possibility of substance abuse by offenders, and the level of previous experience victims may have had with the criminal justice system. Finally, interviewed victims are asked to describe and assess law enforcement response to victimizations that were reported to the police. Unlike the UCR, the NCVS does not measure criminal homicide, arson, or crimes against businesses (such as shoplifting,

HATE CRIMES: CHURCH FIRES

INVESTIGATORS ARE FRUSTRATED

Hate crimes are now being closely tracked by the FBI. As this story describes, some of the most heinous of such crimes involve burnings of churches with predominately black congregations.

In Hale County, Ala., investigators rushed so quickly into the glowing embers of a black church fire that their rubber-soled shoes melted. In neighboring Greene County, Ala., 1,000 of the 3,000 residents have been interviewed by federal agents. Some federal agents have even attended services at the churches to show they care, to show they are there.

But as hard as federal agents try, they're still struggling to gain the confidence of the black community. "Nobody expects the frustration in the community to be allayed until everyone of these is solved," says Deval Patrick, chief of the Justice Department's Civil Rights Division and head of a new task force on the church fires. "That's a frustration I share."

But Patrick says he won't let frustration lead to weak prosecutions. "My job is not to make quick arrests in order to serve the public relations interest of this investigation," he says. "My job is to get to the bottom of these incidents and the question of whether these incidents are connected."

In what is believed to be the largest federal investigation now under way, 200 agents are trying to solve the 32 arsons at black churches since January 1995. Hundreds of state and local authorities also are on the streets.

The Bureau of Alcohol, Tobacco and Firearms (ATF), in particular, has launched an all-out effort to solve the fires and repair a reputation harmed by agents who attended a racism-tainted gathering, the Good O' Boys Roundup. To do that, the ATF rushed 24 agents to the June 3 fire in Greensboro, Alabama, while the Justice Department and FBI sent eight people there. In Effingham, S.C., federal, state and local investigators interviewed nearly every gas station attendant and convenience store worker who may have sold the kerosene used in the fire.

Tron Brekke, the FBI's Civil Rights section chief, says even he's frustrated that more cases aren't solved. Federal agents offered rewards in Greene County, one of the nation's poorest. "We basically got nothing," he says.

Nationwide, nearly $200,000 in rewards has been offered by groups ranging from law enforcement to the Christian Coalition. The ATF has opened a hot line—1-888-ATF-FIRE—that is staffed 24 hours a day, seven days a week to receive tips.

For the ATF, the 100 agents participating make up nearly 6% of its force. The ATF is spending $180,000 a week on the investigation, the fifth largest in its 23-year history. It has agents working 12- to 14-hour days. Agents are extensively using lie detector tests and so-phisticated crime labs. They're also checking financial records and insur-ance policies, a necessary but touchy task; some pastors feel unfairly targeted.

But even with these aggressive tac-tics, church arsons are difficult to solve because the evidence burns in the crime and, since the churches are rural, there usually are no witnesses other than the arsonists. The cases are circumstantial.

Jim Cavanaugh, the agent in charge of the investigations in Alabama and Mississippi, says the investigations in Boligee, Ala.—where three churches burned—have been "really tough" be-cause the churches were "burned to the slab," leaving little evidence.

Investigators say only 16% of church arsons are solved. Proving the more serious charge of civil rights vio-lations and conspiracy is even tougher.

There have been arrests in five church fires and convictions in two of those cases. Convicted were three drunken white racists who burned Friendship Baptist Church and Canaan African Methodist Episcopal Church, both in rural Tennessee.

"We are absolutely, positively and to our soul committed to solving these crimes," said Patrick. "Those who are out there who are perpetrating these crimes and have not yet been caught, rest assured: We will catch you."

Questions

1. Why have churches with predominately black congregations come under attack by arsonists? What purpose might such arsons serve in the minds of the fire setters?
2. Investigators say that only 16 percent of church arsons are solved. Why do you think the figure is so low?
3. What percentage of black church fires do you think are caused by criminal activity? Of those, what percentage would you suspect qualify as "hate crimes"?

Source: Gary Fields, "Frustration Over Church Fires," *USA Today,* June 10, 1996, p. 3A. Copyright 1996, *USA Today.* Reprinted with permission.

burglaries of stores, robberies of gas stations and convenience stores, and credit card and commercial fraud). Similarly, the NCVS does not attempt to uncover, nor does it report, crimes against children under 12 years of age.

The NCVS survey instrument is well designed, and data gatherers are thor-oughly schooled in interviewing techniques. NCVS interviewers are trained, for ex-ample, to not inadvertently lead or "coach" respondents into supplying doubtful in-formation, or to spend an excess amount of time making small talk with respondents. Questions used by the survey, however, are designed to elicit informa-tion about crimes that may not be in the forefront of respondents' minds. Following are a few typical survey questions.

Myrlie Evers-Williams, chairperson of the NAACP's Board of Directors (right) surveys the charred remains of the Matthews-Murkland Presbyterian Church in Charlotte, NC. The 1996 fire in the all-black church was determined to have been the result of arson. What is the central feature of "hate crime?"
Peter A. Harris/AP/Wide World Photos.

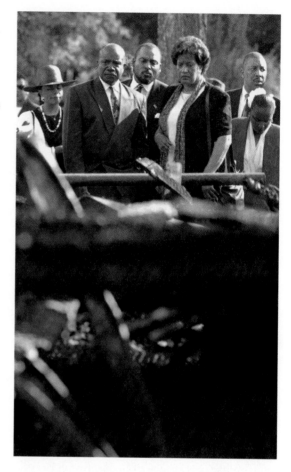

CRIME AND JUSTICE INFORMATION ON THE WORLD WIDE WEB

A rich repository of crime and justice information on the World Wide Web can be found at the Justice Information Center (JIC), a service of the National Criminal Justice Reference Service (NCJRS). Through JIC and at its offices in Rockville, Maryland, NCJRS maintains one of the most extensive sources of information on crime statistics, crime prevention, and research and evaluation in the area of crime control. Its database of criminological literature is easily searchable, and much of it is directly available through the Web.

The Justice Information Center makes an excellent starting point for Web exploration in the field of criminology because it is essentially a collection of clearinghouses supporting all bureaus of the U.S. Department of Justice (DOJ), Office of Justice Programs (OJP), the National Institute of Justice (NIJ), the Office of Juvenile Justice and Delinquency Prevention (OJJDP), the Bureau of Justice Statistics (BJS), the Bureau of Justice Assistance (BJA), the

Office for Victims of Crime (OVC), and OJP Program offices. It also supports the Office of National Drug Control Policy (ONDCP), home of our nation's cabinet-level "Drug Czar."

When you arrive at the JIC home page you will find it arranged by topical areas, each of which is "clickable." The JIC site contains links organized under the following headings:

Corrections
Courts
Crime Prevention
Criminal Justice Statistics
Drugs and Crime
International
Juvenile Justice
Law Enforcement
Research and Evaluation
Victims
New This Week
Current Highlights

Headings along the bottom of the main page allow for a "Keyword Search" of all topics on the site, and permit users to review NCJRS catalogs, see a listing of upcoming conferences in the crime and justice area, review currently available crime and justice grants, and see a list of government sponsors who have made the JIC site possible.

JIC provides a wealth of services to an international community of policymakers and professionals in the field of criminology. You can be among them by pointing your browser at the JIC home page: http://www.ncjrs.org. If you require technical assistance or have specific questions on topics in the field of criminology and criminal justice, you can send an e-mail message to askncjrs@ncjrs.org. For additional information on NCJRS or the JIC, and for updated links to NCRJS-related sites, visit the *Criminology Today* home page at http://www.prenhall.com/cjcentral.

Source: National Criminal Justice Reference Center home page on the World Wide Web, May 27, 1998.

51. Was anything stolen from you while you were away from home, for instance at work, in a theater or restaurant, or while traveling? (If "yes," how many times?)

52. (Other than any incidents you've already mentioned) was anything (else) at all stolen from you during the last 6 months? (If "yes," how many times?)

53. Did you find any evidence that someone ATTEMPTED to steal something that belonged to you? (other than any incidents already mentioned) (If "yes," how many times?)

54. Did you call the police during the last 6 months to report something that happened to YOU which you thought was a crime? (Do not count any calls made to the police concerning the incidents you have just told me about.) (If "yes," what happened?)

55. Did anything happen to YOU during the last 6 months which you thought was a crime, but did NOT report to the police? (other than incidents already mentioned) (If "yes," what happened?)

The number of victimizations counted by the NCVS for any single reported criminal occurrence is based on the number of persons victimized by the event. Hence, a robbery may have more than one victim, and will be so reported in NCVS data. Although this distinction is applied to personal crimes, households are treated as individual units and all household crimes are counted only once no matter how many members the household contains.

NCVS Findings

The next few sections of this chapter present both UCR and NCVS data in narrative form. Some of the more general findings from NCVS reports for the 1990s, however, reveal a number of consistent and interesting patterns. They include

- Nearly 35 million victimizations are reported to the NCVS annually.
- Approximately 23 million American households (25 percent of the total) report being touched by crime in any given year.
- City residents are twice as likely as rural residents to be criminally victimized.
- About one-half of all violent crimes, two-fifths of all **household crimes,** and slightly more than one-quarter of all personal thefts are reported to the police.
- Men are more likely to be victimized than are women.
- Young people are more likely to be victimized than are older people.
- Blacks are more likely than members of any other racial group to be victimized.
- Members of lower-income families are more likely to become victims of violent crimes than are members of middle- and upper-income families.
- Young men display the greatest likelihood of violent victimization, whereas elderly women display the lowest.
- The chance of violent criminal victimization is much higher among young black men than among any other segment of the population.

Household crimes (NCVS) attempted and completed crimes that do not involve personal confrontation (such as burglary, motor vehicle theft, and household larceny).

Finally, it must be noted that victimization rates reported by the NCVS are declining in all categories except crimes of violence. Rates of criminal victimization for index crimes, crimes of violence, and property crimes throughout the United States for the years 1975 through 1996 are shown in Figure 2.2.[7] The decline in observed rates of victimization since 1990 is especially significant because it contrasts with an otherwise heightened fear of crime, as reported in Chapter 1. Increased levels of crime fear may, however, be explained by three events: (1) increases in the *absolute number* of violent crimes that have been significant (although the *rate* of such

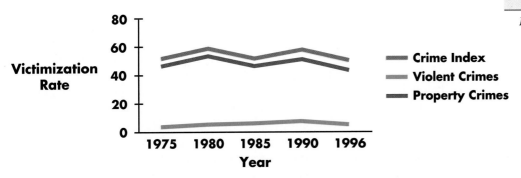

FIGURE 2.2   Rates of criminal victimization in the United States, 1975–1996. *Source:* Federal Bureau of Investigation, *Crime in the United States* (Washington, D.C.: U.S. Department of Justice, various years).

crimes has held constant or decreased due to growth in the American population); (2) increased reporting of all crimes, especially crimes of violence, which has led to the sense that crime is on the increase throughout America; and (3) an ever grow-ing media focus on violent crime, especially as it characterizes America's cities, and on drug abuse.

Increased reporting, in turn, may be the result of a growth in crime awareness. In 1973, for example, only about 33 percent of all crimes were reported to the po-lice.[8] Today nearly 40 percent of all crimes which occur are so reported. Similarly, while approximately 20 percent of personal thefts were reported to the police in 1973, the rate of reporting for such crimes now stands at approximately 30 percent.[9]

Critique of the NCVS

Just as the UCR has been criticized for underestimating the actual incidence of criminal activity within the United States, the NCVS can be criticized for possible overreporting. No attempt is made to verify the actual occurrence of any of the crimes reported to NCVS interviewers. Hence, no measure exists as to the number of crimes falsely reported, or of the number of crimes that might be underreported in NCVS data. Although the proportion is not known, it is likely that some indi-viduals, when approached by NCVS interviewers, may be unable to resist embell-ishing crime reports pertaining to their households, and may even concoct crimi-nal incidence data for purposes of self-aggrandizement or because of attempts to please interviewers via the provision of copious amounts of data.

NCVS data-gathering efforts began in 1972. Hence, the program is much newer than the FBI's UCR Program, and comparisons of officially reported crimes with levels of self-reported victimization are unavailable for the years prior to 1973. As with the UCR, definitions of crimes measured by the NCVS do not necessarily cor-respond to any federal or state statutes or definitions used for other purposes—making comparisons with other state and federal crime records difficult. Complicating matters still further, recent changes in NCVS categories have resulted in the inability to easily compare NCVS findings of even a few years ago with cur-rent NCVS data.[10]

CRIMINAL HOMICIDE

A few years ago, in a dispute turned violent over grades, Charles R. Mize, Jr., 24, repeatedly knifed and killed his father, a popular Georgia high school football coach, and then stabbed his mother twelve times before she persuaded him to call police.[11] Mize, a student at Georgia State University, who was described as a stable, fun-loving young man by friends and neighbors, pled guilty under Georgia law to "murder with malice." As a result of his cooperation, prosecutors dropped their plans to seek the death penalty, and Mize was sentenced to life in prison plus five years. Mize's mother recovered and has indicated that, in time, she may be able to forgive her son for what he did. Charles Mize will be eligible for parole in as few as seven years.

The terms *homicide* and *murder* are often used interchangeably, although they are not the same. **Homicide** refers to the willful killing of one human being by another, whereas **murder** is an unlawful homicide. Some homicides, such as those committed in defense of one's self or family, may be justifiable and therefore legal. The term used by most courts and law enforcement agencies to describe murder is **criminal homicide.** In legal parlance criminal homicide means the causing of the death of another person without legal justification or excuse.

Jurisdictions generally distinguish between various types of murder. Among the distinctions made are **first-degree murder,** also called premeditated murder, **second-degree murder,** and third-degree murder, or **negligent homicide.** First-degree murder differs from the other two types of murder in that it is planned. It involves what some statutes call "malice aforethought," which may become evident by someone "lying in wait" for the victim, but can also be proven by a murderer's simple action of going into an adjacent room to find a weapon and returning with it to kill. In effect, any activity in preparation to kill that demonstrates the passage of time, however brief, between formation of the intent to kill and the act of killing itself is technically sufficient to establish the legal requirements needed for a first-degree murder prosecution.

Second-degree murder, on the other hand, is legally regarded as a true crime of passion. It is an unlawful killing in which the intent to kill and the killing itself arise almost simultaneously. Hence, a person who kills in a fit of anger is likely to be charged with second-degree murder, as is one who is provoked into killing by insults, physical abuse, and the like. For a murder to be second degree, however, the killing must follow immediately upon the abuse. Time that elapses between abuse or insults and the murder itself allows the opportunity for thought to occur and, hence, for premeditation.

Both first- and second-degree murderers intend to kill. Third-degree murder is different. It is a term that varies in meaning between jurisdictions, but often refers to homicides that are the result of some other action which is unlawful or negligent. Hence, it is frequently called negligent homicide, negligent manslaughter, manslaughter, or involuntary manslaughter. Under negligent homicide statutes, for example, a drunk driver whose driving results in a fatal accident may be charged with third-degree murder, even though that person had not the slightest intent to kill.

Serial murder and **mass murder** are two varieties of what is usually first-degree murder.[12] Although most murderers only kill once in their lives, serial and mass murderers kill more than one person. Serial killers murder their victims over a long

Criminal homicide the causing of the death of another person without legal justification or excuse. Also, the illegal killing of one human being by another.

First-degree murder criminal homicide that is planned or involves premeditation.

Second-degree murder criminal homicide that is unplanned and is often described as a "crime of passion."

Negligent homicide (UCR) causing death of another by recklessness or gross negligence.

Serial murder criminal homicide which involves the killing of several victims in three or more separate events.

Mass murder the illegal killing of four or more victims at one location, within one event.

time, perhaps even years.[13] The serial killer John Wayne Gacy, for example, who was put to death in Illinois in 1994, and whose execution is described in a box in this chapter, was the highly publicized killer of thirty-three young men and boys. Gacy's sale of prison paintings to curious collectors earned him thousands of dollars.[14]

Jeffrey Dahmer, another serial killer, was convicted a decade ago of the homosexual dismemberment slayings of fifteen young men and sentenced to 936 years in prison. Dahmer was himself murdered in prison in 1994. Other serial killers of the past few years include David Berkowitz, better known as the infamous "Son of Sam" who killed young men and women in New York; Charles Manson who ordered his followers to kill seven Californians, including famed actress Sharon Tate; Henry Lee Lucas, the Texas killer convicted of eleven murders, but linked to as many as 140 more;[15] Ted Bundy, who killed many college-age women; and the female serial killer Aileen Carol Wuornos, charged with the murders of six men who picked her up as she hitchhiked through Florida. For record-keeping purposes, serial murder has been defined as criminal homicide that "involves the killing of several victims in three or more separate events."[16]

Similar to the serial killer is the spree killer, who kills a number of victims over a relatively short time—in what has often been called a "killing spree." Andrew Cunanan, who killed fashion designer Gianni Versace and others in 1997, provides an example of a spree killer. Cunanan's killing spree lasted three months and claimed five victims.[17] He was put on the FBI's "Ten Most Wanted" list before committing suicide aboard a Miami yacht where he had hidden.

Mass murderers are different. They kill a number of people at one time. Mass murder has been defined by the Bureau of Justice Statistics as "the killing of four or more victims at one location, within one event."[18] Terrorist actions, as in the 1993 World Trade Center bombing in which five people died, sometimes result in mass murder. Robberies may result in numerous homicide victims, and revenge-seeking gunmen sometimes claim many lives. There have been many mass killings in the United States in recent years. The worst probably occurred in 1990 at the Happy Land social club in the Bronx, New York, when eighty-seven people were burned to death by an arsonist upset that his girlfriend, who worked as a hat checker at the club, had left him. Other instances of mass murder include thirty-one people killed in 1991 when a gunman smashed a pickup truck through the front window of a Kileen, Texas, cafeteria and shot lunchgoers to death; twenty-one killed at a McDonald's restaurant in San Ysidro, California, in 1984 by an out-of-work security guard named James Huberty; and thirteen killed at the University of Texas by sniper Charles Whitman who was holed up in a clock tower.

Some jurisdictions have created a special category of **felony murder,** whereby an offender who commits a crime during which someone dies (or which causes someone to die) can be found guilty of first-degree murder, even though the person committing the crime had no intention of killing anyone. Bank robberies in which one of the robbers is shot to death by police, for example, or in which a bank patron succumbs to a fear-induced heart attack, may leave a surviving robber subject to the death penalty under the felony murder rule. Hence, felony murder is a special class of criminal homicide whereby an offender may be charged with first-degree murder when that person's criminal activity results in another person's death.

Felony murder a special class of criminal homicide whereby an offender may be charged with first-degree murder when that person's criminal activity results in another person's death.

THEORY VERSUS REALITY

Serial Killer John Wayne Gacy's Execution

On May 10, 1994, serial killer John Wayne Gacy was put to death by lethal injection at Statesville Correctional Center, a maximum-security facility in Joliet, Illinois. Gacy, once known as an affable remodeling contractor, had been convicted a decade and a half earlier of the sex-linked slayings of thirty-three young men and boys. His execution was originally set for June 1980, but dozens of appeals kept him alive on death row for fourteen years.

According to prosecutors, Gacy often dressed as a clown, handcuffing his victims and looping a rope around their necks on the pretext that he was about to perform a clever stunt. Others may have participated willingly in the sexual sadism that preceded their deaths. Most ended up being horribly tortured and mutilated before dying. Bodies of some of Gacy's victims were discovered in the muddy basement crawl space of his home near O'Hare International Airport. Others were dumped into a nearby river.

As Gacy was strapped to a gurney in preparation for execution, revelers outside shouted "Kill the clown!" Others yelled, "John-nee, the devil's waiting for you!" Vendors sold $10 T-shirts bearing slogans that read "No Tears for the Clown." Death penalty opponents, however, continued to file appeals and seek clemency for Gacy right up until the time of execution. Seth Donnelly, executive director of the Illinois Coalition Against the Death Penalty, explained his group's delaying tactics this way: "The crimes for which he [Gacy] has been convicted are heinous. But, we're opposed to the death penalty as an institution, not on the basis of who may be scheduled to be executed."

Following the procedure, relatives of Gacy's victims expressed relief that he was dead. "I don't think anything he has gone through has been the smallest part of what he has put us and our families through. He got off easy," said Vito Mazzara, whose 20-year-old brother, James, was killed by Gacy. "He got a much easier death than any of his victims," said William Kunkle, who prosecuted Gacy and witnessed the execution.

According to State Corrections Director Howard Peters, Gacy's last statement was that "taking his life would not compensate for the loss of the others and that this was the state murdering him."

DISCUSSION QUESTIONS

1. What is the difference between mass murder and serial killing? Between first- and second-degree murder? Which categories best fit Gacy? Why?
2. Why would someone such as Gacy kill? What might have motivated him? How could you investigate such a question so that you could have confidence that your answers would reflect Gacy's true motivation?
3. Are you in favor of the death penalty or opposed to it? Defend your position.

Sources: Lindsey Tanner, "Gacy Execution," the Associated Press on-line, May 10, 1994; and "State Team Preparing for Gacy Killing," United Press on-line, Central edition, April 11, 1994.

Murder Statistics

Statistics discussed in this section are derived from the UCR, because the NCVS does not gather information on criminal homicide. UCR statistics count only the number of murders committed, not attempts to murder, because attempts are scored as aggravated assaults. Likewise, the UCR program does not count cases of negligent manslaughter among murder statistics.

According to the UCR, 19,645 murders were committed throughout the United States in 1996.[19] The 1996 rate of criminal homicide was 7.4 persons murdered for every 100,000 individuals in the American population.

Age is no barrier to murder. In 1996, for example, 247 murder victims were under the age of 1, while 320 were 75 years old or older. Eighty-three murders were committed by offenders over 75, while three murders were committed by those aged 5 to 8. Of the murder victims in 1996, 77 percent were male and 48 percent were black (48 percent were white, and the remainder were of other races).

The most populous region of the country, the southern states, accounted for the most murders—43 percent of the total. However, although the UCR divides the country into four regions (the Northeast, South, Midwest, and West), each region varies significantly by population. Hence cross-regional comparisons, other than rates or changes in reported rates, must be interpreted with caution. While all regions of the country showed a decrease in the murder rate of 9 percent from 1995 to 1996, the nation's cities showed a 10 percent decrease. Metropolitan murder rates were twice that of rural areas—approximately 8 per every 100,000 city residents.

Serial killer John Wayne Gacy sometimes dressed as a clown to disarm his victims. This painting by Gacy shows his fascination with clowns. Do you agree that Gacy should have been executed? *Brad Elterman/SIPA Press.*

As in other recent years, the typical murder offender (arrestee) in 1996 was a young black man. Of all those arrested for murder in 1996, 79 percent were male, 69 percent were between the ages of 17 and 34 years old, and 55 percent were black. Significantly, although blacks comprise only 13 percent of the American population, they account for more than half of all persons arrested for murder.

FBI statistics reveal a plethora of other information about the crime of murder. Approximately one-half of all murder victims in 1996, for example, were either related to (13 percent) or acquainted with (38 percent) their assailants. Only 15 percent of murders were committed by strangers, and the relationship between killer and victim was undetermined for 35 percent of all reported murders.

Murder is primarily an intraracial crime. In 1996, 85 percent of white victims were killed by other whites, whereas 93 percent of black victims died at the hands of black killers. As in other years, handguns were the weapon of choice in most murders, with 54 percent of all murder victims dying of handgun-inflicted injuries. Another 4 percent were killed with shotguns and 3 percent with rifles. Knives (or other sharp instruments) were used in 14 percent of murders, and blunt instruments (clubs, hammers, etc.) in 5 percent. Hands, feet, and fists were listed as murder weapons in those 6 percent of all murder cases in which victims were kicked and punched to death.

Various circumstances lead to murder, although in 1996 arguments were the most common cause of such crime. Thirty percent of all murders resulted from arguments, and 19 percent were the consequence of other felonious activity such as robbery, rape, and arson. Murderous arguments may arise over sexual claims, jealousy, money, personal honor, or about anything else that may lead to anger or bring offense.

Of all reported or discovered criminal homicides in 1996, 67 percent were cleared—the highest rate of clearance for any of the index offenses. Small cities and towns (those with populations under 10,000) reported the highest clearance rates (79 percent), while large cities had the lowest rates of clearance (66 percent).

FORCIBLE RAPE

Forcible rape (UCR) the carnal knowledge of a female forcibly and against her will. Assaults or attempts to commit rape by force or threat of force are also included in the UCR definition; however, statutory rape (without force) and other sex offenses are excluded.

Former world heavyweight boxing champion Mike Tyson may be the most famous person to have recently served prison time for **forcible rape.** In 1991 Tyson was convicted of the hotel room rape of 18-year-old Desiree Washington and sentenced to six years in prison. Ms. Washington was participating in the 1991 Miss Black America pageant when she met Tyson and accompanied him to his room. Tyson was released from prison in 1995 and reentered the world of professional boxing—only to be banned from the sport by the Nevada State Athletic Commission, after he bit off part of Evander Holyfield's ear during a World Boxing Association heavyweight title rematch in Las Vegas in 1997.

The UCR distinguishes between three categories of rape: (1) forcible rape, (2) statutory rape, and (3) attempted forcible rape. Some jurisdictions draw a distinction between forcible rape with the use of a weapon and forcible rape without the use of a weapon. Although the UCR does not make such a distinction, it does, however, record statistics on the use of weapons associated with the crime of rape.

Other types of rape include spousal rape, gang rape, date rape, and homosexual rape. Spousal rape, or the rape of one's spouse, is a relatively new concept, having only entered the law of many state jurisdictions in recent years. Prior to modern times it was believed that a woman entering into marriage implicitly gave her consent to sexual intercourse at the behest of her husband. In today's more enlightened times, wives may prosecute their spouses under rape statutes if their husbands force them to have nonconsensual intercourse.

Date rape, which is often defined as unlawful forced sexual intercourse with a woman against her will that occurs within the context of a dating relationship, has also received much attention in recent times, although it is undoubtedly a phenomenon that has existed as long as the institution of dating. According to recent studies, date rape is much more common than previously believed. Some authors suggest that date rape may occur when the male partner concludes that his date "owes" him something for the money he has spent on her.[20] Many women apparently do not report the crime, and their hesitancy exists for a variety of reasons. Sometimes they feel responsible for some aspect of the social relationship which led to the rape, or in other instances they may feel some concern for the offender and not wish to have him become the target of a criminal prosecution—even one that is deserved.

Homosexual rape, although not punishable as rape in all jurisdictions, is coming to be more widely recognized. Many states and a number of foreign countries now provide for the prosecution of men who force other men to have sex with them, as especially happens in prison. In 1994 the English House of Lords, for example, passed an amendment to the British Criminal Justice Bill[21] replacing the offense of "non-consensual buggery of men," which carried a ten-year sentence, with the crime of "male rape," which is punishable by life imprisonment.

Although rape statutes have evolved to the point where many jurisdictions prosecute cases of homosexual rape, gender bias still characterizes most rape laws. No jurisdictions, for example, effectively prosecute husbands raped by their wives, and lesbian rape (the rape of one woman by another) is never prosecuted as such. On very rare occasions, however, a female individual may be charged with the rape of a male individual. In 1993, for example, Jean-Michelle Whitiak, 24, a Fairfax County, Virginia, swimming coach, pled guilty to one count of statutory rape resulting from an affair with a 13-year-old boy.[22] Whitiak also admitted to having sex with two of the boy's friends.

The motivation of rapists has been the subject of frequent study. Contemporary social scientific wisdom, supported by the research of scholars such as A. Nicholas Groth,[23] holds that rape is primarily a crime of power, and that most rapists seek self-aggrandizement via the degradation of another human being. Rapists, this school of thought maintains, demean their victims in order to feel important and powerful. Hence, the rape of elderly and physically unattractive women by virile and powerful young men can be explained as a crime of power rather than one of sex. Some scholars, however, have recently begun to cast doubt on power as the primary motivation of rapists, returning to an emphasis on sexual gratification as the root cause of sexual assault.[24]

Date rape unlawful forced sexual intercourse with a woman against her will which occurs within the context of a dating relationship.

Rape Statistics

UCR statistics on rape include both forcible rape and attempted forcible rape. Statutory rape and other sex offenses are excluded from the count of rape crimes. In 1996, 95,796 rapes were reported nationwide under the UCR program, a decrease of 1.7 percent over the previous year. The rate of reported forcible rape was officially put at 36.1 rapes per 100,000 persons. However, the rape rate for females is effectively twice that figure, because any realistic tally of such crimes should compare the number of women raped with the number of female individuals in the overall population (rather than to a count of the entire population, which includes men). When such a comparison is made, the rate of reported rape for women in large cities is 75 per 100,000, 68 per 100,000 for women in small towns, and 47 per 100,000 women in rural counties. The hot summer months generally show the highest rate of reported forcible rape. The year 1996 was no exception, with the month of July showing the largest number of reports.

Substantial regional variation exists in UCR statistics on forcible rape. In 1996 the highest rape rate was recorded at 79 victims per 100,000 females in the southern states, with 73 per 100,000 in the western states, 75 per 100,000 in the Midwest, and a low of 49 per 100,000 in the Northeast. Although the FBI reports that rapes in the southern part of the United States occur with almost twice the frequency of such crimes in the northeastern part of the nation, it makes no attempt to explain the observed variation.

Forcible rapes show the highest rate from among all reported crimes to be "unfounded." Unfounded crime reports are those determined by police investigation to be false. In the case of rape, false reports may be made (1) out of anger, (2) from a felt need for revenge, (3) as a tool of blackmail, (4) because of personal disappointment in the course of a love relationship, and (5) because of numerous other causes. In 1996 police departments across the country determined that 8 percent of forcible rape complaints were unfounded (versus a 2 percent average for other reported index offenses).

In 1996, 53 percent of all reported forcible rapes were cleared by arrest or exceptional means, with rural and suburban county law enforcement agencies reporting slightly higher clearance rates than city law enforcement agencies. The nationwide number of reported rapes decreased slightly over the previous year, and the proportion of clearances decreased slightly (by 2 percent).

NCVS data paint a somewhat different picture of rape than the UCR statistics. According to the NCVS, 98,000 rapes occurred in 1996 while 99,000 were attempted—giving a total rape count of 197,000 cases.[25] The NCVS calculates a rape rate of 180 per 100,000 females—a rate substantially higher than that found in the UCR.

The NCVS reports that rapes by strangers are almost twice as common as those by nonstrangers. Of rapes involving strangers, 50 percent occur between 6 P.M. and midnight, while only 38 percent of nonstranger rape occurs during those hours. The NCVS also records the location of criminal events to include parking lots or garages, commercial buildings, school property, school buildings, apartments, yards and parks, public transportation, and so forth. Most rapes (17.9 percent) are described as occurring "on the street not near own or friend's home." However, of the rapes involving nonstrangers, 50 percent occur within the victim's home. Only 17.2 percent of rapes recorded by the NCVS involved the use of weapons, although weapons were employed in 34.6 percent of all rapes committed by strangers.

The NCVS also collects data on self-protective measures taken by victims. Of the rape victims responding to NCVS interviewers, 80 percent reported the use of some type of self-protective measure. Self-protective measures included "resisting" (20.8 percent of all such measures reported), persuading or appeasing the offender (18.7 percent), running away or hiding (13 percent), scaring or warning the offender (13 percent), raising an alarm (11 percent), and screaming (8.9 percent). Only 6 percent of rape victims reported attacking their victimizers, and fewer than one of 100 attacked the offender with weapons.

Many rape victims (51 percent) reported that self-protective measures that were taken helped the situation, although 17 percent believed the measures made their situation worse. Another 14 percent said such measures had no effect on the situation. Twenty percent of rape victims reported economic costs due to time lost from work as a result of victimization.

As mentioned earlier, NCVS data score only victimizations of household residents who are 12 years of age or older. Recent Bureau of Justice Statistics studies, however, have found that many victims of rape are quite young. A 1994 study,[26] for example, of eleven states and the District of Columbia, found that 10,000 female individuals under the age of 18 were raped in reporting jurisdictions—about half of all the rapes that were reported in those areas. Investigators found that at least 3,800 victims were children under the age of 12. As a result of these figures, the study's authors concluded that "the rape of young girls is alarmingly commonplace." When young women and girls are raped, however, the crimes often go unreported because they frequently involve family members or friends. The survey found that although girls under the age of 18 comprise 25 percent of the nation's female population, they account for 51 percent of all rape victims.

Even researchers were surprised by the number of young girls who reported having been raped. As Patrick A. Langan, one of the report's authors, said, "The [finding] that one in six of the reported rapes were girls under 12 was startling. You would think that the number would have been minute. But it's not tiny. . . . It's a substantial part of the picture."

Earlier studies of rape had found that 20 percent of female victims under the age of 12 had been raped by their fathers, 26 percent were attacked by other relatives, and 50 percent were assaulted by friends and acquaintances. Only 4 percent of rape victims under 12 were attacked by strangers, such studies found.

ROBBERY

The crime of robbery is regarded as a personal crime because it is committed in the presence of the victim. **Robbery** is defined by the UCR Program as "the unlawful taking or attempted taking of property that is in the immediate possession of another by force or threat of force or violence and/or by putting the victim in fear." The NCVS definition is similar, and also involves *attempts*. Although some individuals mistakenly use the terms *robbery* and *burglary* interchangeably

Robbery (UCR) the unlawful taking or attempted taking of property that is in the immediate possession of another by force or threat of force or violence and/or by putting the victim in fear.

(as in the phrase "my house was robbed"), it should be remembered that robbery is a personal crime and that individuals are robbed, not houses (which are burglarized).[27]

A number of terms are used to describe subtypes of robbery. *Highway robbery,* for example, simply refers to any robbery that occurs in a public place, generally out of doors. It is also called "street robbery" by the FBI. *Strong-armed robbery* means that the robber or robbers were unarmed and took the victim's possessions through intimidation or brute physical force. Strong-armed robbery is often perpetrated by a group of robbers working in consort, as when a gang preys upon one or two unwary victims. The term *armed robbery* signifies that a weapon was used—most often a gun. Armed robberies usually occur when banks, service stations, convenience stores, and other commercial establishments are robbed.

Robbery Statistics

The 1996 UCR reports that 537,050 robberies came to the attention of authorities across the nation that year, meaning that the rate of robbery was 202 per every 100,000 people in the United States. Cities are the places where most robberies occur, with metropolitan areas recording a robbery rate of 244 per 100,000 inhabitants in 1996. Small towns reported a robbery rate of only 72 per 100,000, and rural areas a mere 18 per 100,000.

In 1996, according to the UCR, 39 percent of robberies were committed using strong-arm tactics, and firearms were the weapons of choice in 41 percent more. Knives were used in 9 percent, and a variety of other dangerous weapons in the remainder.

Robberies occur most frequently in December, probably reflecting an increased need for money and other goods around the holiday season. Most robbery (approximately 51 percent) takes the form of highway robbery, while robberies of businesses account for approximately 24 percent of all such crimes. Less than 2 percent of robberies are bank robberies, and in 1996, over 10,000 bank robberies were reported. According to the FBI, the average amount lost per robbery incident in 1996 was $929, with a per incident bank robbery loss of $4,207 increasing the average.

Estimated losses due to robberies throughout the United States in 1996 totaled $500 million. However, as the FBI concludes, "[t]he impact of this violent crime on its victims cannot be measured in terms of monetary loss alone. While the object of a robbery is to obtain money or property, the crime always involves force or threat of force, and many victims suffer serious personal injury."[28] In addition to monetary loss and possible physical injury, many robbery victims suffer lasting psychological trauma.

The nationwide clearance rate for robberies reported by the UCR in 1996 was 27 percent. The highest clearance rate was 42 percent in rural counties, and the lowest rate of clearance for robberies was found in the nation's cities. Persons under the age of 18 accounted for offenders arrested in 18 percent of all robberies counted as cleared, and 65 percent of all persons apprehended for robbery were under 25 years of age. The offenders were males in 90 percent of all robberies, whereas blacks accounted for 58 percent of those arrested. Of the arrestees, 40 percent were white and the remainder were members of other racial groups.

NCVS statistics show a much higher number of robberies than UCR data. NCVS surveyors uncovered approximately 1,134,000 robberies in 1996, which the BJS report broke down as 757,000 completed and 377,000 attempted. NCVS data show that 1 in every 3 attempted or completed robberies resulted in injuries to the victim. By far the most robbery-prone segment of the population is the 12- to 15-year-old age group, and males are robbed almost twice as frequently as females. Blacks report a robbery victimization rate three times higher than that of whites, and the incidence of robbery declines as family income rises. Members of the poorest families interviewed by NCVS field researchers (those with family incomes of less than $7,500) were the most frequently robbed (9.9 per 1,000 persons), while members of families with yearly incomes above $75,000 reported the lowest incidence of robbery (2.0 per 1,000 persons). Of course, income and educational levels tend to be correlated. Hence, as the NCVS report concluded, the more educated a person is, the less their chance of being robbed.

NCVS data reveal that victims took some type of protective action in 63 percent of all robberies, and that "a robbery . . . committed by an offender who was known to the victim was significantly more likely to result in physical injury than a robbery . . . that was committed by a stranger."[29] Eleven percent of all robbery victims incurred medical expenses as a direct result of victimization, and 12 percent of all robberies resulted in victims missing time at work.

NCVS survey data reveal that only 50.1 percent of all robberies are reported to the police. Women are far more likely to report robberies (64 percent) than are men (42 percent), although men are only slightly more likely to resist robbery than are women.

AGGRAVATED ASSAULT

On May 12, 1994, rapper Luther Campbell of the group 2 Live Crew was arrested and charged in Miami, Florida, with aggravated assault for allegedly aiming a gun at a woman and threatening to kill her.[30] The woman, Tina Barnett, was variously identified as Campbell's wife or as a former live-in girlfriend. According to police spokesperson Patrick Brickman, "They were having a verbal altercation over their relationship and the altercation escalated to Mr. Campbell pointing a gun at her and saying 'I swear I will kill you and dump you in a lake somewhere.'" Campbell was later released on $7,500 bond.

The UCR Program defines **aggravated assault** as "the unlawful attack by one person upon another for the purpose of inflicting severe or aggravated bodily injury." If a weapon is used, or if serious bodily injury requiring hospitalization results, the UCR is likely to count the offense as one of aggravated assault. The NCVS definition of aggravated assault is essentially the same, although the NCVS also reports on the crime of **simple assault,** which it defines as an "attack without a weapon resulting either in minor injury or in undetermined injury requiring less than two days of hospitalization." Hence, under both programs an assault with a deadly weapon would be scored as aggravated assault, although UCR data are far more likely to score any assault that results in hospitalization as "aggravated." Under both programs, assaults that cause serious bodily injury are also scored as

Aggravated assault (UCR) the unlawful attack by one person upon another for the purpose of inflicting severe or aggravated bodily injury.

Simple assault (NCVS) an attack without a weapon resulting either in minor injury or in undetermined injury requiring less than two days of hospitalization.

aggravated assaults, even without the use of a weapon. If an assault results in death, however, the offense would become a homicide rather than an assault, for statistical reporting purposes.

Assault Statistics

According to the UCR, 1,029,814 aggravated assaults were reported to police agencies across the nation in 1996, producing an aggravated assault rate of 388.2 for every 100,000 people in the country. A total of 1,910,000 aggravated assaults were reported to NCVS interviewers in 1996, which translates into an aggravated assault rate of 880 per every 100,000 persons aged 12 or over. Rates of aggravated assault were highest in metropolitan areas and lowest in rural areas.

The greatest number of aggravated assaults are usually recorded during the hot summer months, and 1996 was no exception, with July showing the highest incidence of such crimes. When cross-regional comparisons are made (always difficult as populations vary between regions), the southern states accounted for the most aggravated assaults (41 percent), the western states provided 24 percent of the total, the Midwestern region 20 percent, and the Northeast 15 percent. Assault rates were higher in the South than elsewhere in the country.

During 1996, 34 percent of aggravated assaults reported to the police were committed with blunt objects, meaning that the offender probably grabbed whatever was at hand to commence or continue the attack. Hands, feet, and fists were used in 26 percent of all aggravated assaults, while firearms were employed in 22 percent, and knives or other cutting or stabbing instruments in 18 percent. Like most other index offenses, aggravated assault has shown a steady yearly decrease. The number of aggravated assaults reported nationwide has decreased by 12 percent over the past five years.

Because victims often know the people who assault them, the clearance rate for aggravated assault (which stood at 58 percent in 1996) is relatively high. As with most crimes, city police agencies report a lower rate of clearances for aggravated assault than other law enforcement departments, while rural areas have the highest rate of clearances.

BURGLARY

Burglary is a property crime, although it can have tragic consequences. In January 1994, Paxton, Massachusetts, police chief Robert Mortell, 38, was shot in the chest and died while involved in a foot chase with burglary suspects. A small town of only 4,100 residents, Paxton is unaccustomed to violence. Chief Mortell, a husband and father of three children, who were at the time aged 7 to 12, was quite popular with townspeople. "He was more than an authority figure. He was a security figure. When you lose a security figure, it sends shock waves through the community," said Joseph W. McKay, Paxton's chief selectman.[31]

Burglary (UCR) the unlawful entry of a structure to commit a felony or a theft.

The UCR defines **burglary** as "the unlawful entry of a structure to commit a felony or a theft." The definition goes on to say that "the use of force to gain entry is not required to classify an offense as burglary." Burglaries, as scored by both the NCVS and the UCR, generally fall into three subclassifications: (1) forcible entry, (2) attempted forcible entry, and (3) unlawful entry where no force is used. Forcible entries are those burglaries in which some evidence of breakage, prying, or other evidence of forceful entry is found. Hence, a broken window, a jimmied door, a loosened air-conditioning duct—all may provide evidence of forcible entry. Attempted forcible entries (i.e., attempted burglaries) are another form of burglary reported by the UCR. Attempted forcible entry also shows evidence of force, although no actual entry may have been achieved by the perpetrator. The third type of burglary, unlawful entry when no force is used, refers to the fact that some burglars enter unlocked residences uninvited, stealing items found there.

Although most burglaries are, strictly speaking, property crimes, the potential for personal violence is inherent in many such crimes. Nighttime burglary, for example, which is more severely punished in some jurisdictions than daytime burglary, holds the possibility of violent confrontation between offender and homeowner. Assault, rape, and even murder may be the outcome of such encounters. On the other hand, sometimes burglars themselves are injured or killed by irate residents.

According to the laws of most jurisdictions and UCR and NCVS definitional categories, burglary has not occurred unless it was the intent of the unlawful entrant to commit a felony or theft once inside the burglarized location. Other forms of illegal entry may simply be counted as trespass.

Burglary Statistics

The UCR recorded 2,501,524 reported burglaries in 1996, a decrease of almost 4 percent over the previous year. Burglary is a crime that has shown a steady decrease over the past decade, with today's burglary rate standing approximately 20 percent lower than five years ago. The UCR rate of reported burglary in 1996 was 943 per 100,000 inhabitants. As with most other Part I offenses, cities had the highest rate of burglary (993 per 100,000), whereas rural areas had the lowest (620 per 100,000).

Of reported burglaries in 1996, 69 percent involved forcible entry, 23 percent were the result of unlawful entries in which no force was used, and 8 percent were attempts. Two of every three reported burglaries were of residences (the remainder were commercial burglaries, or burglaries committed on government property).

The average amount lost per burglary in 1996 was set at $1,332 by the FBI, although the loss was slightly higher for residential property (on average $1,350 per incident) than for nonresidential property ($1,296 per incident). The total loss suffered by all burglary victims in 1996 was estimated at approximately $3.3 billion.

Of all persons arrested for the crime of burglary in 1996, 89 percent were men, 64 percent were under the age of 25, and 68 percent were white. Blacks accounted for 30 percent of burglary arrestees and members of other races made up the remaining 2 percent.

Because burglaries are typically property crimes, the clearance rate for burglaries is quite low. Only 14 percent of all burglaries were cleared in 1996. As with other crimes, rural law enforcement agencies cleared a higher proportion of burglaries (18 percent) than city departments (13 percent).

CRIME AND JUSTICE—IN THE NEWS

WANTED: THE TRUE CRIME RATE

Winston Churchill once said, "We have nothing to fear but fear itself." He was, of course, referring to British involvement in World War II. Americans, it seems, are now involved in a war of their own—the highly touted "war on crime." As in any war, fears run high. Some researchers, however, question whether our nationwide fear of crime is more the result of media hype and national hysteria than it is the logical consequence of any real rise in crime rates. What follows is an article written by Associated Press staffer Arlene Levinson that raises just such questions.

If ever a mystery persisted in the annals of American crime, it's the magnitude of crime itself. Anxiety about crime grips the land but, looking at federal statistics, you have to wonder why. The FBI reports crime is merely crawling upward. Victim surveys show crime actually falling. Yet for many people, an evening stroll, an unlocked car or going alone to the mall hint at lunacy. After tucking in their children, many parents bolt the doors, check the alarms and pat the guns under their beds goodnight.

Measuring the dimensions of crime in the United States is a statistical nightmare: This is a vast, populous country in which crime rates vary sharply, even from police precinct to neighboring police precinct. Try to draw a picture of crime besetting 250 million people and you lose the detail. Polls indicate people feel more vulnerable, to violent crime especially. This fear fuels the "three strikes, you're out" efforts occupying Congress and close to 30 states this year, the avid prison building and the pervasive unease. Are perceptions wildly out of sync with statistics? First, some numbers:

- Crime reported by police the past 20 years climbed 36 percent, FBI Uniform Crime Reports figures show. The overwhelming majority of crime reported—85 percent—was property crime. But the largest jump in any category came in the area of violent crime, which shot up 81 percent, driven mainly by juveniles with guns settling drug scores.
- The two-decade federal victims survey indicated a 29 percent drop in crime nationwide since 1975. The National Crime Victimization Survey counts one in four households visited by crime each year, down from about one in three in 1975. The survey also found the rate of violent crime basically unchanged, except for a sharp increase in teenage and black victims.
- Last year, about 24,500 murders were reported in the United States. That's much as it's been for the past several decades.

"The best scientific evidence we have clearly shows there is no increase in crime or violent crime in the last 20 years," said William Chambliss, a sociologist at George Washington University. "The fact is, even if the crime rate was going up, the victims who were the victims remain the victims," said Chambliss, who also is a past president of the American Society of Criminology. "The most dangerous place you can go is to your home with your boyfriend or girlfriend, family members and acquaintances. They account for most of the violent crimes that take place."

Forget the statistics, you might say. Everyone knows crime is America's biggest worry nowadays. National polls show not only that, but that many people think it is increasing in their own communities—and even more think it is increasing nationally. An Associated Press poll of 1,004 Americans last month found 52 percent of men and 68 percent of women personally worried about becoming crime victims. Even among those who said there was nowhere within a mile of their homes they would be afraid to walk at night, half still worried about being victimized.

One reason crime gets the spotlight is that it's moved up on the charts, ahead of foreign crises and the economy. Crime always ranks high on polls evaluating the country's most important problems, said Tom W. Smith, director of the General Social Survey at the National Opinion Research Center, based at the University of Chicago. And with the Cold War over and the economy brightening, politicians took note of Americans' intensified outrage against crime, adding their own spin. "For good political reasons, the Congress and the president have found crime is something politically attractive to be against," Smith said.

Other influences are at work. Crime stories permeate American life—witness their popularity as a topic of news and entertainment. Last year, crime news reported on the three major television networks more than doubled, and coverage of murders tripled, compared with 1992, according to a survey by the Center for Media and Public Affairs in Washington. Another recent survey indicates this coverage rings familiar alarm bells. In a *Times Mirror* poll released April 6, 63 percent of respondents said the media accurately depicts the amount of crime in this country, while 29 percent said it exaggerates. Half the people surveyed also said they were very concerned about becoming a crime victim, up from 36 percent in 1988.

Some criminologists suggest another reason the fear of crime might be greater than statistics warrant is the extra attention paid to crimes occurring in unusual spots. The highway sniper, the post office massacre, the tourist mugged and killed, the bank machine holdup, gunfire in a schoolroom—these are the crimes that dominate headlines. But exceptional bloodshed doesn't even ripple the crime graph line, even though it shocks. "You only hear about a very small number [of crimes] and that is the impression that everybody carries around," said Malcolm Young, who runs The Sentencing Project in Washington, which promotes criminal justice. "We've accepted the 19,000 [other killings] or whatever threshold we don't hear about."

Questions
1. Why is it so difficult for criminologists to agree on the true rate of crime? How does our definition of crime affect the rate of measured crime?
2. Do you agree with the author of this article that the fear of crime is out of proportion to the rate of crime? How can the two be so disjointed?

Source: Arlene Levinson, "America Behind Bars—Crime, Wanted: the True Crime Rate," Associated Press Newswire, Northern edition, May 8, 1994. Reprinted with permission.

In contrast to the UCR, NCVS statistics on burglary paint quite a different picture. In 1996, the NCVS reported 4,845,000 household burglaries and attempted burglaries—nearly 100 percent more than UCR estimates.[32] Rates of burglary were generally higher for black households than for whites, regardless of family income levels (although wealthy black families had far lower burglary rates than did low-income white families). The same was true for locality. Hence, black persons living in cities were more likely than whites to have their houses burglarized, while blacks living in rural areas were also more likely than their white neighbors to become burglary victims, although wealthy blacks in either locale were less likely than poor whites to experience burglary. NCVS data also show that the longer a respondent lives at a particular residence, the less likely that person will be to report having been burglarized. Hence, a residence of six months or less was associated with a burglary rate of 151 (per 1,000 households) versus a rate of only 38 (per 1,000 households) when those living at the reporting address had been there for five years or more.

LARCENY

Larceny-theft (UCR) the unlawful taking, carrying, leading, or riding away by stealth of property, other than a motor vehicle, from the possession or constructive possession of another, including attempts.

Larceny is another name for theft. Sometimes the word *larceny* is used by itself in published crime reports, and at other times *larceny-theft* is used. Both mean the same thing. The UCR definition of **larceny-theft** reads: "the unlawful taking, carrying, leading, or riding away by stealth of property, other than a motor vehicle, from the possession or constructive possession of another, including attempts." The NCVS definition is similar, except that it further subdivides larceny into categories of "household larceny" and "personal larceny." Crimes of larceny do not involve force, nor do those who commit larceny intentionally put their victims in fear as do robbers.

Differences exist between the NCVS and UCR in the way subtypes of larceny are categorized. The UCR, for example, scores both purse-snatching and pocket-picking as larceny-theft, whereas the NCVS calls such crimes "personal larceny with contact." Similarly, the UCR scores shoplifting and thefts from coin-operated machines as larceny, but the NCVS does not gather data on commercial thefts and so excludes all such incidents from larceny counts. With these provisos in mind, larceny data in the NCVS and UCR can be compared.

Larceny Statistics

The UCR Program counted 7,894,620 reports of larceny in 1996, for a rate of 2,976 such crimes per every 100,000 persons in the population. The larceny rate decreased slightly (1.3 percent) from the previous year but, as in other years, reported larcenies were most common during July and August 1996. Most items reported stolen had been taken from motor vehicles (25 percent), meaning that packages, money, and other goods were stolen from parked cars. Of all larcenies reported, 11 percent were of motor vehicle accessories such as tires, "mag" wheels, cellular phones, CD players, radar detectors, etc. Another 13 percent of the total reported number of larcenies were from buildings, 15 percent were due to shoplifting, and 6 percent were of bicycles. Purse-snatching, pocket-picking, and thefts from coin-operated machines each accounted for less than 1 percent of the total number of larcenies reported to the police in 1996.

The average reported value of property stolen per larceny incident was $532 in 1996. This figure, however, is open to interpretation because reports to the police which estimate the value (in dollar terms) of stolen or destroyed property are likely to be exaggerated. Oftentimes victims hope to receive a high return from insurance companies for stolen goods (even though such hope may be unfounded), sometimes they are unsure of the value of missing items, whereas at other times they honestly overestimate the worth of lost goods because they do not realistically allow for depreciation. In addition, false claims are sometimes filed by persons seeking to bilk insurance companies. Hence, in instances of larceny, burglary, auto theft, and arson, it is difficult to know with certainty what the true value of lost or stolen items might be.

NCVS data on larceny estimate 21,120,000 cases of larceny in 1996, with the majority (7,580,000 cases) involving the theft of items worth less than $50. NCVS estimates put the figure for larceny far above the number of thefts officially reported to the police and recorded by the UCR. NCVS trend data, however, show that all forms of larceny have been on the decline since peaking around 1978 and 1979.

MOTOR VEHICLE THEFT

Motor vehicle theft is defined by the UCR simply as "the theft or attempted theft of a motor vehicle." The FBI adds that "this offense category includes the stealing of automobiles, trucks, buses, motorcycles, motorscooters, snowmobiles, etc." Excluded from the UCR count of motor vehicle theft is the stealing of vehicles such as airplanes, boats, trains, and spacecraft (which would be counted as larcenies), and the taking of a motor vehicle by a person having lawful access to that vehicle is similarly excluded. The designation of persons who have lawful access to a vehicle often includes spouses, who are sometimes reported as having stolen a vehicle owned by their marriage partners. In most jurisdictions, however, married persons effectively own most types of property jointly even though titles, deeds, receipts, and so forth may not specifically list both parties. Hence, a wife who tells her husband that he may not drive her car will not be taken seriously when she calls the police if he disobeys.

Carjacking, a much more serious crime than motor vehicle theft, involves the stealing of a car while it is occupied. Hence, although carjacking involves theft, it is

Motor vehicle theft (UCR) the theft or attempted theft of a motor vehicle. According to the FBI, this offense category includes the stealing of automobiles, trucks, buses, motorcycles, motorscooters, snowmobiles, etc.

Carjacking the stealing of a car while it is occupied.

akin to robbery or kidnapping. Often the theft occurs at gunpoint, and in many carjacking cases, the victim is either injured or killed. Carjacking, almost unheard of a decade ago, increased rapidly in the early 1990s when thieves targeted vehicles that could be easily sold for valuable parts.

The NCVS definition of a motor vehicle is quite concise, and reads: "an automobile, truck, motorcycle, or any other motorized vehicle legally allowed on public roads and highways." Both the NCVS and UCR include attempts in counts of motor vehicle theft. Because of the similarity of definitions, and because most motor vehicle thefts are reported for insurance purposes, NCVS and UCR statistics on motor vehicle theft are in close agreement. A total of 1,395,192 vehicles were reported stolen in 1996 by the FBI, while NCVS data estimate that 1,387,000 were illegally taken. The rate of motor vehicle theft in 1996 was 526 vehicles per 100,000 people according to the FBI, and the value of motor vehicles stolen that year totaled $7.5 billion nationwide.

August is usually the prime month for motor vehicle thefts, and most thefts in any given month occur in the nation's cities. As a result, the UCR calls motor vehicle theft "primarily a large-city problem."

Law enforcement agencies reported a 14 percent clearance rate for motor vehicle thefts nationwide in 1996, although 68 percent of all stolen vehicles were recovered. Hence, although many stolen vehicles were eventually returned to their rightful owners, relatively few arrests of car thieves were made.

ARSON

A few years ago William Krause and Kenneth Hayward were convicted under a federal antiarson statute of burning two large wooden crosses in the yard of a home owned by a white couple who had entertained black guests over the Labor Day weekend in 1989. Each was sentenced to a number of years in prison, but appealed to the U.S. Supreme Court, claiming that their cross-burning conviction violated their constitutional right of freedom of expression. In 1994, however, the Supreme Court upheld both convictions without comment.[33]

Arson (UCR) any willful or malicious burning or attempt to burn, with or without intent to defraud, a dwelling house, public building, motor vehicle or aircraft, personal property of another, etc.

The UCR defines **arson** as "any willful or malicious burning or attempt to burn, with or without intent to defraud, a dwelling house, public building, motor vehicle or aircraft, personal property of another, etc." The FBI adds that "only fires determined through investigation to have been willfully or maliciously set are classified as arsons." The NCVS does not report arson statistics.

Arson may occur for a variety of reasons. Some arsonists are thrill seekers and set fires for the excitement it brings. Others are vandals, wanting only to accomplish a random sort of destruction. Such people, sometimes called *pyromaniacs,* may suffer from psychological problems which contribute to their firesetting activities. Sometimes arson is a vengeful act, in which a former employee may strike back at an employer, or an aggrieved former spouse may attempt to settle past scores. A few arsonists are called *vanity pyromaniacs.* They are persons, often in some official or responsible role, who place themselves in position to take credit for putting out fires which they secretly start. A handful of security guards, firemen, and others in similar positions of trust have been involved in this kind of behavior.

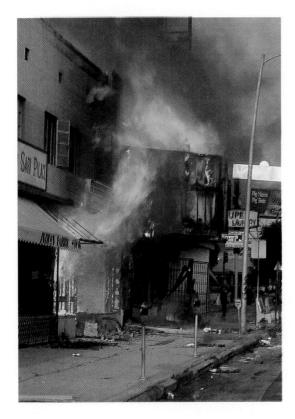

An arson fire. Arson causes millions of dollars' worth of property damage yearly. Are UCR statistics on arson accurate? *Lester Sloan/Woodfin Camp & Associates.*

In many other instances arson is used to disguise other felonies such as murder or burglary. Buildings containing the bodies of murder victims, for example, may be burned to cover the evidence of homicide or to make the victim's death appear to have been caused by the fire itself. Most instances of arson, however, appear intended to defraud insurance companies into paying for property that owners no longer want but which they haven't been able to dispose of legally (through sale, transfer, etc.).

Arson Statistics

Although nearly 16,000 law enforcement agencies contributed data to the FBI for use in 1996 UCR tabulations, only 11,453 agencies forwarded any kind of arson information. Much of the arson data received by the FBI during 1996 was incomplete, consisting of less than 12 months of information or lacking in the kind of detail needed for FBI composites. Only 11,250 agencies provided complete arson information for any part of the year, and 8,325 agencies reported such data for all 12 months of 1996. Hence, UCR arson data remain incomplete. As the FBI warns, "Caution is recommended when viewing arson trend information. The percent change figures may have been influenced by improved arson reporting procedures during the collection's relatively limited timespan. It is expected that year-to-year statistical comparability will improve as collection continues."[34]

With these provisos in mind, it is safe to say that 88,887 instances of arson were reported under the UCR Program in 1996, with an average property loss per instance of approximately $10,280. Of the total number of arsons reported, 59 percent involved residences, 27 percent were of motor vehicles, 6 percent were of commercial buildings, and nearly 5 percent involved storage facilities of one sort or another. Public buildings were targeted by approximately 5 percent of all reported arsons.

Nationally, the clearance rate for arson was only 16 percent, with the highest rates of clearance being reported in small towns (those with populations of less than 10,000). Of all arson arrests in 1996, 53 percent involved juveniles—a higher percentage than for any other index crime. Seventy-four percent of arson arrestees were white and 85 percent were men.

PART II OFFENSES

The UCR also contains a report on arrests made by police for various crimes which are referred to as Part II offenses. *Part II offenses* are generally less serious than Part I offenses, and some of them are classified as misdemeanors in many jurisdictions. Only arrests are recorded because many Part II offenses, by virtue of both their semisecret nature (some might be regarded as victimless or social order offenses) and lesser degree of seriousness, are not reported to the police—and are discovered only when an arrest occurs.

A list of Part II offenses and the 1996 incidence of each is provided in Table 2.2. Total arrests for Part II offenses in 1996 were estimated at 8.6 million, with arrests for driving under the influence (1.5 million), simple assault (1.3 million), and drug abuse violations (1.5 million) leading the list. When Part I offenses are added to the total, the overall arrest rate for the United States in 1996 was measured at 5,838 arrests per 100,000 persons, with arrests of city residents (7,700 per 100,000) showing the highest rate.

Part II offenses reported in the UCR do not identify arrestees and make no attempt to distinguish offenders arrested once from those who are arrested many times. Hence, some frequently arrested individuals may have contributed significantly to the overall incidence of Part II crime statistics.

UNREPORTED CRIMES

Although differences between the UCR and NCVS abound, the greatest distinction between the two has to do with the ability of the NCVS to ferret out crimes which are not reported to the police (and that therefore do not appear in UCR statistics). According to NCVS analysts, "the majority of crimes measured by the NCVS (recently) were not reported to the police."[35] More specifically, according to the NCVS:[36]

- Only 38 percent of all victimizations, 48 percent of violent victimizations, 29 percent of personal thefts, and 41 percent of all household crimes were reported to the police. In fact, household crimes and personal thefts were more likely to not be reported to the police than to be reported.

⚏

TABLE 2.2

UCR PART II OFFENSES, 1996

Offense Category	Number of Arrests
Simple assault	1,329,000
Forgery and counterfeiting	121,600
Fraud	465,000
Embezzlement	15,700
Stolen property (receiving)	151,100
Vandalism	320,900
Weapons (carrying)	216,200
Prostitution and related offenses	99,000
Sex offenses (statutory rape, etc.)	95,800
Drug law violations	1,506,200
Gambling	21,000
Offenses against the family (nonsupport, etc.)	149,800
Driving under the influence	1,467,300
Liquor law violations	677,400
Public drunkenness	718,700
Disorderly conduct	842,600
Vagrancy	27,800
Curfew/loitering	185,100
Runaways	195,700
All other violations of state and local laws (except traffic law violations)	3,743,200
Total	8,605,900

Source: Federal Bureau of Investigation, *Crime in the United States, 1996* (Washington, D.C.: U.S. Government Printing Office, 1997).

- Of the three major crime categories, violent crimes were most likely to be reported to the police, followed by household crimes. Personal thefts were the least likely crimes to be reported.
- Three of four motor vehicle thefts were reported to the police, making this the most highly reported of crimes. Personal larcenies without contact between victim and offender and household larcenies were least likely to be reported (at 28 and 27 percent, respectively).
- Women were more likely to report violent victimizations to the police than were men, and some evidence points that this was also the case for crimes of theft.
- White victims were somewhat more likely than black victims to report thefts to the police. The reporting rates for violent crimes committed against whites and blacks were similar.
- Violent crimes committed by strangers were no more likely to be reported to the police than violent crimes committed by someone who was known to the victim.

- The youngest victims of violent crimes and thefts—those between 12 and 19 years of age—were less likely than persons in any other age group to report crimes to the police.
- Homeowners were significantly more likely than those who rented to report household crimes to the police (44 percent versus 38 percent).
- Families with an annual income of $25,000 a year or more were more likely to report victimizations of their households than those earning under $10,000 a year.
- Generally, as the value of loss increased, so did the likelihood that a household crime would be reported.

Reasons for reporting and for not reporting varied somewhat by race, sex, and age. The most common reason given for reporting violent crime was to prevent future victimization by the same offender. An interest in recovering property or in receiving insurance payments motivated most victims of property crimes who reported their victimization to the police. The two most common reasons for not reporting violent victimizations were that the crime was a personal or private matter (20 percent) or that the offender was unsuccessful and the crime was only attempted (17 percent).

▦ THE SOCIAL DIMENSIONS OF CRIME

WHAT ARE "SOCIAL DIMENSIONS"?

Crime does not occur in a vacuum. It involves real people—human perpetrators and victims, just like you and me. Because society defines certain personal characteristics as especially important, however, it is possible to speak of the "social dimensions of crime," that is, aspects of crime and victimization as they relate to socially significant attributes by which groups are defined, and according to which individuals are assigned group membership. Socially significant attributes include gender, ethnicity or race, age, income or wealth, profession, and social class or standing within society. Such personal characteristics provide criteria by which individuals can be assigned to groups such as "the rich," "the poor," "male," "female," "young," "old," "black," "white," "white-collar worker," "manual laborer," and so on.[37]

We have already alluded briefly to the fact that both the UCR and NCVS structure the data they gather in ways that reflect socially significant characteristics. The UCR, for example, provides information on reported crimes which reveals the sex, age, and race of both the offenders and the perpetrators. NCVS statistics document the race, age, and sex of crime victims and the incomes of households reporting victimizations.

The social dimensions of crime are said by statisticians to reveal relationships or correlations. A **correlation** is simply a connection or association which is observed to exist between two measurable variables.

Correlations are of two types: positive and negative. If one measurement increases when another, with which it is correlated, does the same, then a positive correlation or positive relationship is said to exist between the two. When one mea-

Correlation a causal, complementary, or reciprocal relationship between two measurable variables.

surement decreases in value as another rises, a negative or inverse correlation has been discovered. NCVS data, for example, show a negative relationship between age and victimization. As people age, victimization rates decline. Hence, although some elderly people do become crime victims, older people as a group tend to be less victimized than younger people. UCR data, on the other hand, show a positive relationship between youth and likelihood of arrest—specifically, between young adulthood and arrest. Young adults, it appears, commit most crimes. Hence, as people age, they tend to be both less likely to be victimized and less likely to become involved in criminal activity.

A word of caution is in order, however. Correlation does not necessarily imply causation. Because two variables appear to be correlated does not mean that they have any influence on one another, or that one causes another to either increase or decrease. Correlations that involve no causal relationship are said to be *spurious*. A study of crime rates, for example, shows that many crimes seem to occur with greater frequency in the summer. Similarly, industry groups tell us that food retailers sell more ice cream in the summer than at any other time. Are we to conclude, then, from the observed correlation between crime rates and ice cream sales, that one in some way causes the other? To do so on the basis of an observed correlation alone would obviously be foolish.

Even if two variables appear to be related, it may be difficult to determine the actual nature of the relationship. Some criminologists have observed, for example, that as the number of prison cells increase, so does the crime rate—the implication being that building more prison cells will somehow cause more crime. Others have noted how the rather remarkable growth in the number of criminal defense attorneys over the past three or four decades has almost precisely paralleled the observed rate of increase in violent crime—with similar implications. Of course, it would seem logical to conclude that swelling crime rates have led to increases in both the number of attorneys and prison cells.

Some observed correlations do appear to shed at least some light on either the root causes of crime or the nature of criminal activity. It is to these that our discussion now turns.

AGE AND CRIME

If arrest records are any guide, criminal activity is associated more with youth than with any other stage of life. Every year the UCR consistently shows that young persons, from their late teens to their early and mid-twenties account for the bulk of street, property, and predatory crime (i.e., Part I offenses) reported in this country. Recent writings by a number of well-known criminologists, among them **Alfred Blumstein,**[38] **John J. DiIulio, Jr.,**[39] **James A. Fox,**[40] **Joan Petersilia,**[41] and **James Q. Wilson**[42] have alerted policymakers to the fact that a coming demographic shift will combine with an increased tendency toward violence to lead to a substantial increase in crime, especially violent predatory crime, throughout the United States over the next decade or two. Shifting demographics will soon result in an increase in the percentage of the American population that is made up of young people in what has been called the "crime prone years."

James A. Fox, for example, notes that, "[b]y the year 2005, the number of teens, ages 14–17, will increase by 20 percent, with a larger increase among blacks in this age group (26 percent)." Such an observation, says Fox, is especially worrisome because over the past ten years, "the rate of murder committed by teens, ages 14–17, [has] increased 172 percent." Indicative of a significant trend, says Fox, "black males aged 14–24," although comprising only 1 percent of the population, "now constitute 17 percent of the victims of homicide and over 30 percent of the perpetrators." Also, says Fox, "the differential trends by age of offender observed for homicide generalize to other violent offenses." During the last five years, for example, "the arrest rate for violent crimes (murder, rape, robbery and aggravated assault) rose over 46% among teenagers, but only 12% among adults."

Echoing Fox, John J. DiIulio, Jr., warns of a coming generation of **superpredators**—young violent offenders bereft of any moral sense, and steeped in violent traditions. Superpredators, according to DiIulio, are juveniles "who are coming of age in actual and 'moral poverty' without the benefits of parents, teachers, coaches and clergy to teach them right from wrong and show them 'unconditional love.'" Moral poverty, says DiIulio, consists of conditions in which children grow "up surrounded by deviant, delinquent, and criminal adults in chaotic, dysfunctional, fatherless, godless and jobless settings...." Superpredators are most often seen as emerging from within poverty-stricken and violent inner-city subcultures, where the conditions necessary to produce them exist.

Like other writers warning of a coming crime wave, Alfred Blumstein, past president of the American Society of Criminology (ASC), notes that "[p]articularly relevant to future crime, and to consideration of prevention and intervention strategies, is the size of the current teenage population. The age cohort responsible for much of the recent youth violence is the smallest it has been in recent years. By contrast, the **cohort** of children ages 5 to 15, who will be moving into the crime-prone ages in the near future, is larger. This suggests that if current age-specific rates do not decline, planning needs to begin now to address the increase in crime likely to occur as this group grows older."

As Joan Petersilia, another former ASC president, notes in the forward of this textbook, many scholars believe that an avalanche of youth-spawned violence will soon inundate American society, and that there is little that anyone can do to avert it. Petersilia cites James Q. Wilson's sage advice: "Get ready." Many criminologists continue to hold to this belief, although FBI statistics show that violent juvenile crime declined 3% in 1995, and an additional 5.8% in 1996—prompting some to charge that anyone warning of a coming surge in juvenile crime is an alarmist. James Fox, however, says the problem is far from solved. The recent drop in juvenile crime, says Fox, is good news, but "it hardly means the problem [has been] solved. It's like a 500-pound man losing 50 pounds. It doesn't mean he's thin."

Crime waves, however, come and go—and no one stays young forever. Involvement in crime appears to decrease consistently, beginning at approximately age 25. The same is true for Part II offenses, with the exception of vagrancy, public drunkenness, gambling, and certain sex crimes—when declines in criminal involvement are more likely to begin at approximately age 30.

Although most forms of criminality may decrease with age, even old age is no bar to criminal involvement. According to UCR statistics, more than 500,000 per-

Superpredators a new generation of juveniles "who are coming of age in actual and 'moral poverty' without the benefits of parents, teachers, coaches and clergy to teach them right from wrong and show them unconditional love"[39] The term is often applied to those inner-city youths who meet the criteria.

Cohort a group of individuals sharing certain significant social characteristics in common, such as gender, time, and place of birth.

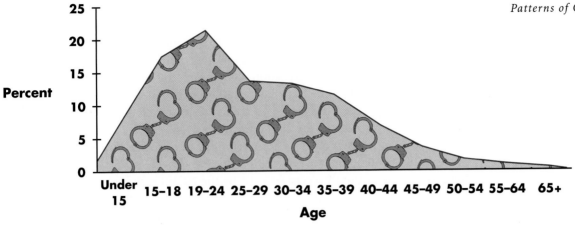

FIGURE 2.3   Arrests of Persons by Age: Part I Offenses, 1996. *Source:* Federal Bureau of Investigation, *Crime in the United States 1996* (Washington, D.C.: U.S. Government Printing Office, 1997).

sons aged 50 or over are arrested every year throughout the country. Of those, nearly 73,000 are past the age of 65. Figure 2.3 provides a graphical comparison of persons arrested by age for all reported Part I offenses.

Recently, crimes of the elderly, or geriatric criminality, have sparked much interest among criminologists and the popular media. Movies such as *The Over the Hill Gang* have depicted the exploits of aged criminals. Although in the minority, real-life elderly criminals are not hard to find. The case of Edward Cook, 68, who still remains a fugitive, is illustrative. Cook usually works with an elderly female companion and the two are known for showing up in swank jewelry stores, posing as casually dressed tourists. The couple travels with a video camera casually slung over Cook's shoulder. Cook, however, keeps the camera running—recording security devices and showcased valuables throughout the targeted stores. Cook returns after closing hours, deactivates store alarms, and helps himself to the choicest jewels.

Why do older people commit crimes? One author explains it this way: "The reasons older people turn to crime are varied. Some people never retire—from trouble. Others find that retirement gets them into trouble. Boredom and unstructured leisure, fear of the future, frustration over limited finances, family neglect or stress—the same conditions that contribute to teenage crime—can lead seniors to commit desperate or foolish acts."[43]

Some older criminals use their age to advantage. Few people, for example, suspect older people of criminal intent. Hence, potential victims are less likely to be on their guard against crime in the presence of an older offender. Similarly, experience gained from previous criminality, and from life in general, can be turned into assets in the criminal arena. As the old adage goes, "knowledge is power," and whereas social convention holds that wisdom comes with age, so does increased criminal opportunity for those so inclined.

Although street crime may be the bailiwick of the young, the indications are that older offenders are over represented in other forms of crime, including those that require special skills and knowledge for their commission. Many of these crimes are job related and involve fraud, deception, or business activities which are criminal. Such crimes are discussed in detail in a later chapter.

Although the elderly are less likely to be victimized than other groups, statistics show many more elderly victims than geriatric criminals. The NCVS defines *elderly* to include all persons aged 65 or older living in the United States.[44] NCVS data show that "[p]ersons age 65 or older are the least likely of all age groups in the nation to experience crime,"[45] and victimization rates among the elderly have been declining since 1974—about the time NCVS data gathering began. According to the NCVS, "[t]he rates for personal theft and household crime among the elderly in 1996 were the lowest ever recorded in the 20 year history of NCVS."[46]

Even so, approximately 2 million criminal victimizations of elderly persons occur in the United States every year.[47] Table 2.3 shows NCVS victimization rates for various age groups. A recent report[48] by the NCVS makes the following observations about elderly crime victims.

- The violent crime rate is nearly sixteen times higher for persons under 25 than for persons over age 65 (64.6 versus 4 victimizations per 1,000 persons in each age group).
- As with personal crime victimizations, persons over the age of 65 are significantly less likely to become victims of all forms of household crime than members of younger age groups.
- Personal larceny with contact (purse-snatching and pocket-picking) is an exception. Those who are 65 or older were about as likely as those under age 65 to be victims of personal larceny with contact.
- Injured elderly victims of violent crime are more likely than younger victims to suffer a serious injury.
- Elderly violent crime victims are more likely than younger victims to face assailants who are strangers.
- Elderly victims of violent crime are almost twice as likely as younger victims to be raped, robbed, or assaulted at or near their home.
- Elderly victims less often than younger victims act to protect themselves during a violent crime.
- Elderly victims of robbery and personal theft are more likely than younger victims to report those crimes to the police.

■■

TABLE 2.3

NUMBER OF VICTIMIZATIONS BY AGE
(PER 1,000 PERSONS)

Age	Violent Crime	Personal Theft
12–24	64.6	112.7
25–49	27.2	71.2
50–64	8.5	38.3
65 and over	4.0	19.5

Source: U.S. Department of Justice, *Elderly Crime Victims* (Washington, D.C.: Bureau of Justice Statistics, March 1994); and BJS, *Age Patterns of Victims of Serious Violent Crime* (Washington, D.C.: BJS, September 1997).

One crime against the elderly which is often not reported is elder abuse. The physical and emotional abuse of elderly persons by family members, caregivers, and others has been called a "national tragedy,"[49] involving as it does an estimated 1.5 million cases per year. Recent hearings before the House Subcommittee on Human Services, Select Committee on Aging revealed that one of every twenty-five Americans over the age of 65 suffers from some form of abuse, neglect, or exploitation.[50] Subcommittee members also concluded that elder abuse is increasing. Unfortunately, however, cases of elder abuse rarely come to the attention of authorities. The desire shared by many elderly citizens for privacy, fear of embarrassment at having abuse at the hands of loved ones revealed, and the relatively limited ability of elderly citizens to access law enforcement services all contribute to the problem.

To address the concerns of the elderly the 1994 Violent Crime Control and Law Enforcement Act provides, under Title 24, Protections for the Elderly, monies for the development of local community partnerships between senior citizen groups and law enforcement agencies designed to combat crimes against older Americans.

The act also provides monies to assist with funding a Missing Alzheimer's Disease Patient Alert Program which, in the words of the legislation, "shall be a locally based, proactive program to protect and locate missing patients with Alzheimer's disease and related dementias." Finally, the act increases penalties for telemarketing fraud directed against the elderly and requires criminal justice agencies to assist in providing background information on caregivers with felony convictions who are being considered for employment in nursing homes and long-term care facilities.

GENDER AND CRIME

Gender appears so closely linked to most forms of criminal activity that it has been called "the best single predictor of criminality . . ."[51] Table 2.4 shows degree of involvement in each of the major crimes by gender. Columns in the table do not show the total number of crimes reported, but rather represent the proportion of male–female involvement in each Part I offense. For example, of all murders in this country in a given year, approximately 90 percent are committed by men and 10 percent by women.

The apparently low rate of female criminality has been explained by some as primarily due to cultural factors, including early socialization, role expectations, and a reluctance among criminal justice officials to arrest and prosecute women. Others have assumed a biological propensity toward crime and aggression among men which may be lacking in women. Although these and other issues are addressed in later chapters, it is important here to note that the rate of female criminality has changed very little over time—a fact much in contrast to assumptions made years ago by some criminologists who insisted that the degree of female involvement in crime would increase as women assumed more powerful roles in society.

Even when women commit crimes, they are more often followers than leaders. A 1996 study[52] of women in correctional settings, for example, found that women are far more likely to assume "secondary follower rules during criminal events," than "dominant leadership roles." Only 14 percent of women surveyed played

⁙

TABLE 2.4

MALE–FEMALE INVOLVEMENT IN CRIME

| | Percentage of Arrests by Gender | |
UCR Index Crimes	*Males*	*Females*
Murder and nonnegligent manslaughter	89.7%	10.3%
Rape	98.8	1.2
Robbery	90.3	9.7
Aggravated assault	82.1	17.2
Burglary	88.7	11.3
Larceny-theft	66.2	33.8
Motor vehicle theft	86.4	13.6
Arson	85.1	14.9
Average, all major crimes	85.9	14.1

Source: Federal Bureau of Investigation, *Crime in the United States, 1996* (Washington, D.C.: U.S. Government Printing Office, 1997).

primary roles, but those that did "felt that men had little influence in initiating or leading them into crime." African-American women, however, were found to be more likely to play "primary and equal crime roles" with men or with women accomplices, than were white or Hispanic women. Statistics such as these dispel the myth that the female criminal in America has taken her place alongside male offenders—either in terms of leadership roles or the absolute number of crimes committed.

Turning to victimization as it is associated with gender, women are victimized far less frequently than men in most crime categories. NCVS data show that crimes of violence reported by American women reflect victimization rates of 34.6 per 1,000 female individuals aged 12 or older, versus 49.9 for men; while rates of personal theft among women stand at 1.6 versus 1.3 for men. As with the population in general, the rate of female victimization for all crimes decreases with age, leading NCVS authors to conclude that (1) white women age 65 or older have the lowest violent crime rates and (2) black women age 65 or older have the lowest personal theft rates.[53]

Two significant exceptions are rape and spousal abuse. Rape is a crime of special concern to many people because official reports to the police of rape have generally continued to increase even as reports of many other types of crimes have decreased.[54] Figure 2.4 illustrates the growth in the number of reported rape cases over the past twenty years along with a recent 3-year decline. Recognizing some of the problems facing women today, federal policymakers—through the 1994 Violent Crime Control and Law Enforcement Act—provided more than $1 billion in funding to support a special "violence against women" initiative. The initiative

- Includes funds (1) to increase and train police, prosecutors, and judges in the area of spousal abuse, (2) to encourage pro-arrest policies when abuse is encountered, (3) to provide victim services and victim's advocates, (4) to sup-

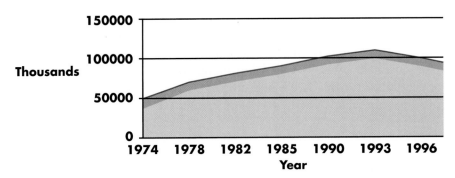

FIGURE 2.4 Female Rape (Number of Reported Cases by Year), 1974–1996. *Source:* Federal Bureau of Investigation, *Crime in the United States* (Washington, D.C.: U.S. Government Printing Office, various years).

port battered women's shelters, (5) to fund rape education and community prevention programs, (6) to establish a national family violence hotline, and (7) to increase security in public places.
- Provides first-ever civil rights remedies for victims of felonies motivated by gender bias.
- Extends "rape shield law" protections to civil cases and to all criminal cases to bar irrelevant inquiries into a rape victim's sexual history.
- Requires all states to honor "stay-away orders" issued by courts in other states.
- Requires confidentiality for the addresses of family violence shelters and abused persons.

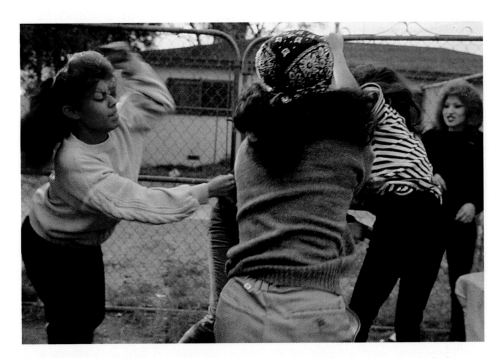

Female gang members fighting. Although much female criminality has long been overlooked, criminologists are now increasingly aware of gender issues. How does the criminality of men and women appear to differ? *Copaken/Gamma-Liaison, Inc.*

The 1994 act provides crime prevention block grants for the creation of battered women's shelters through a competitive funding program to be administered by the Department of Health and Human Services. It also creates supervised centers for divorced or separated parents to visit their children in "safe havens" when a history of risk of physical or sexual abuse is indicated.

THEORY VERSUS REALITY

Adolescent Motherhood and Crime

A 1997 study by the Office of Juvenile Delinquency and Prevention identified a significant relationship between adolescent motherhood and crime. The study found that children born to teenage mothers had a considerably higher likelihood of turning to crime than those born to older mothers. Following are edited excerpts from the study.

Nearly 1 million American teenagers (about 10 percent of all 15- to 19-year-old girls) become pregnant each year. About 33 percent abort their pregnancies, 14 percent miscarry, and 52 percent bear children—72 percent of them out of wedlock. Of the half million teens who give birth, approximately 75 percent are first-time mothers. More than 175,000 are 17 years old or younger.

These young mothers and their offspring are especially vulnerable to severe adverse social and economic consequences. More than 80 percent of these young mothers end up in poverty and on welfare, many for the majority of their children's critically important developmental years.

One recent study looked at the higher engagement in crime by male children of adolescent mothers and found that the sons of adolescent mothers are 2.7 times more likely to be incarcerated than the sons of mothers who delay childbearing until their early twenties. Nationally, about 5 percent of all young men were found behind bars over a thirteen-year period. This is well below the 10.3 percent rate of observed incarceration for young men born to adolescent mothers and slightly above the 3.8 percent rate for young men born to mothers who began their families at age 20 or 21.

Roughly half of the observed difference for young men born to adolescent versus older childbearers is accounted for by observable differences in the demographic and background characteristics of offspring of both groups of mothers. Still, if these adolescents postponed childbearing until age 20 or 21, it would, by itself, reduce the incarceration rate for the affected children by 13 percent (from 10.3 percent to 9.1 percent).

Even the relatively small fraction of the higher incarceration rate that is directly attributable to adolescent childbearing costs society dearly. A delay in childbearing until the age of 20.5 would reduce the national average incarceration rate by 3.5 percent, for an annual savings of about $1 billion in correctional costs and a potential savings of nearly $3 billion in total law enforcement costs. These results are, of course, long range. Even if all prospective adolescent mothers were to delay their childbearing as of tomorrow, the incarceration rates would not fall as predicted for approximately twenty years—the earliest age at which young offenders start going to jail in any substantial numbers.

Thus, policies that successfully address adolescent childbearing and these other factors could lead to additional cost savings for the nation.

Source: Rebecca A. Maynard, Ph.D. and Eileen M. Garry, *Adolescent Motherhood: Implications for the Juvenile Justice System* (Washington, D.C.: Office of Juvenile Delinquency and Prevention, January 1997), citing "Crime: The Influence of Early Childbearing on the Cost of Incarceration," in Rebecca A. Maynard, ed., *Kids Having Kids: Economic Costs and Social Consequences of Teen Pregnancy* (Washington, D.C.: Urban Institute Press, 1996).

ETHNICITY AND CRIME

A few years ago, Professor Lani Guinier of the University of Pennsylvania School of Law was interviewed on *Think Tank,* a PBS show. Guinier was asked by Ben Wattenberg, the program's moderator, "When we talk about crime, crime, crime, are we really using a code for black, black, black?" Guinier responded this way: "To a great extent, yes, and I think that's a problem, not because we shouldn't deal with the disproportionate number of crimes that young black men may be committing, but because if we can't talk about race, then when we talk about crime, we're really talking about other things, and it means that we're not being honest in terms of acknowledging what the problem is and then trying to deal with it. It's a way of distancing ourselves from the real problem, which is the terrible rise in urban violence."[55]

Crimes, of course, are committed by individuals of all races. The link between crime—especially violent, street, and predatory crimes—and race, however, shows a pattern that is striking in terms of its ethnic dimensions. In some crime categories arrests of black offenders equal or exceed arrests of whites. In 1996, for example, 55 percent of all murder arrestees in the United States were black and 43 percent were white. Although these simple numbers may be surprising to some, more significant still are crime rates based on ethnicity. Such rates, which take into consideration the relative proportion of ethnic groups in the American population and calculate the extent to which criminal activity is associated with each, are quite revealing. The U.S. Bureau of Census, for example, says that 12.4 percent of the American population consists of individuals identifying themselves as black, and 84.1 percent count themselves as white. Hispanic-Americans make up most of the remainder of the population. Arrest rates by ethnicity are shown in Figure 2.5. The figure shows, for example, that although black persons are arrested for approximately 55 percent of all murders committed in a given year, the murder rate among blacks is nine times that of whites, because blacks account for only one-eighth of the population. Similar rate comparisons are shown in Figure 2.5 for a few other crimes. The chart diagrammatically represents relative rates of arrest by race that are numerically presented in Table 2.5.

FIGURE 2.5 Relative Arrest Rates by Race and Type of Crime, Selected Offenses, 1996. *Source:* Derived from FBI, *Crime in the United States, 1996* (Washington, D.C.: U.S. Government Printing Office, 1997), and U.S. Census Bureau, January 1, 1998 official census estimates.

TABLE 2.5

ARREST RATES BY RACE (PER 1,000 PERSONS) AND RELATIVE RATES OF ARREST—SELECTED OFFENSES, 1996

	Blacks	Whites	Rate of Arrest, Black vs. White
Murder	.036	.004	9.0:1
Rape	.052	.010	5.2:1
Robbery	.664	.101	6.6:1
Larceny	2.78	1.17	2.4:1
Weapons	.40	.11	3.6:1
Drug abuse	1.68	.44	3.8:1

Source: Derived from FBI, *Crime in the United States 1996* (Washington, D.C.: U.S. Government Printing Office, 1997), and U.S. Census Bureau, January 1, 1998 census estimates.

Some authors maintain that racial differences in arrest and imprisonment rates are due to the differential treatment of blacks at the hands of a discriminatory criminal justice system.[56] In a recent book, for example, Marvin D. Free, Jr.[57] claims that the fact that blacks are underrepresented as criminal justice professionals results in their being overrepresented in arrest statistics. Some police officers, according to Free, may be more prone to arrest blacks than whites, may frequently arrest blacks without sufficient evidence to support criminal charges, and may overcharge in criminal cases involving black defendants, which may lead to unfair and misleading statistical tabulations that depict blacks as responsible for a greater proportion of crime than is in fact the case.

Other writers disagree. In *The Myth of a Racist Criminal Justice System*,[58] for example, **William Wilbanks** claims that although the practice of American criminal justice may have been significantly racist in the past, and while some vestiges of racism may indeed remain, the system is today by and large objective in its processing of criminal defendants. Using statistical data, Wilbanks shows that "[a]t every point from arrest to parole there is little or no evidence of an overall racial effect, in that the percentage outcomes for blacks and whites are not very different."[59] Wilbanks claims to have reviewed "all the available studies that have examined the possible existence of racial discrimination from arrest to parole." In essence, he says, "this examination of the available evidence indicates that support for the 'discrimination thesis' is sparse, inconsistent, and frequently contradictory."[60]

Practically speaking, a nonracist criminal justice system is not necessarily the result of a total absence of racism, because some individual actors within the system will inevitably act in racially biased fashion. Rather, it may be the result of a series of actions, some of which may be racially motivated, but, when taken together, collectively balance. Hence, says Wilbanks, the net result is a system that is today not observably racist in its results.

Wilbanks is careful to counter arguments advanced by those who continue to suggest the system is racist. He writes, for example, ". . . perhaps the black/white gap at arrest is a product of racial bias by the police in that the police are more likely to select and arrest black than white offenders. The best evidence on this question comes from the National Crime Survey which interviews 130,000 Americans each year about crime victimization. . . . The percent of offenders described by victims as being black is generally consistent with the percent of offenders who are black according to arrest figures."[61] Such data are supported by annual surveys conducted by the Centers for Disease Control and Prevention (CDC), which consistently find that people treated at hospital emergency rooms for nonfatal gunshot wounds related to crime are mainly male, black, and young. The most recent CDC study, for example, found that men comprise almost 90 percent of those treated for firearm injuries connected to crimes, and that 59 percent of those treated are black. According to the CDC, "[t]he racial breakdown for crime-related [gunshot] wounds [is] 59% black, 19% white and 14% Hispanic . . ."[62]

However, observes Wilbanks, "[t]he assertion that the criminal justice system is not racist does not address the reasons why blacks appear to offend at higher rates than whites before coming into contact with the criminal justice system. . . . It may be," he suggests, "that racial discrimination in American society has been responsible for conditions (e.g., discrimination in employment, housing, and education) that lead to higher rates of offending by blacks, but that possibility does not bear on the question of whether the criminal justice system discriminates against blacks."[63] Marvin Free, Jr., agrees, suggesting that blacks are still systematically denied equal access to societal resources which would allow for full participation in American society—resulting in a higher rate of law violation. In an even more recent work that considers such issues in great detail, John Hagan and Ruth D. Peterson attribute higher crime rates among ethnic minorities to (1) concentrated poverty, (2) joblessness, (3) family disruption, and (4) racial segregation.[64]

A more fundamental critique of Wilbanks' thesis comes from **Coramae Richey Mann,**[65] who says that his overreliance on quantitative or statistical data fails to capture the reality of racial discrimination within the justice system. White victims, says Mann, tend to overreport being victimized by black offenders because they often misperceive Hispanic and other minority offenders as black. Similarly, says Mann, black victims are sometimes reluctant to report victimization—especially at the hands of whites. Moreover, says Mann, statistics on specific crimes such as rape may include false accusations by white women to hide their involvement with black lovers. And, says Mann, a greater integration of black neighborhoods (in the sense that whites are less reluctant to enter such neighborhoods than blacks are to enter white neighborhoods) may result in a disproportionate but misleading number of reports of white victims. Finally, the fact that far more whites than blacks live in the United States means that they will naturally account for a greater percentage of victims, which explains the seeming overvictimization of whites by blacks.

Although Mann cites the need for the greater use of qualitative measures, most available data on race and crime are statistical. And so speaking, African-Americans not only appear to commit street crimes at a rate disproportionate to their representation in the population, but they are also disproportionately victimized by such crimes. One author recently asserted that "black-on-black crime is the true face of crime in America."[66] No less a figure than the American civil rights leader Jesse Jackson has identified black-on-black crime as "the most important issue of the civil rights movement today."[67] If such assertions are even partially correct, although unpopular, then it is incumbent upon policymakers to admit and realistically assess the degree of overinvolvement in street crime that characterizes a disproportionately large segment of the black population in America today—for such an admission is the first step toward realistically addressing the problem.

Indeed, such overinvolvement may be a sign of a more sinister form of racism. U.S. District Judge Robert L. Carter points out that although American society seems prepared to tolerate the conditions that produce high crime rates among blacks, it is unlikely that it would if whites were committing as many crimes. During a recent speech Judge Carter said that two of every three black men in the United States aged 20 to 29 are either in prison, awaiting trial, or on probation—but noted that "everyone in this room knows that if white men were in this situation or in danger of being so placed, there would be a nationwide howl of protest."[68] The fact that no such protest can be heard, said Carter, "is outrageous and constitutes unmitigated racism. Instead of seeking remedies," observed the judge, "the nation is spending billions of dollars for new prison facilities, apparently gearing up to be able to soon house half the 20 to 29-year-old black men."

High rates of crime and of criminal victimization within the black community have led to a heightened fear of crime among black Americans. A recent report by the Bureau of Justice Statistics, which was based on data from the American Housing Survey (conducted by the Department of Housing and Urban Development), found that "black households are nearly three times more likely than white ones to fear crime in their neighborhoods and that black fear is growing faster than white fear....."[69] The survey shows that fear of neighborhood crime has risen almost twice as much among blacks as whites since the mid-1980s. In black central-city households, neighborhood crime was cited as residents' primary concern. Study findings are said to "mirror the incidence of violent crime, which victimizes blacks more than whites and central city residents more than those in suburbs or rural areas."[70] The BJS report noted that a separate survey of state prison inmates found that 43 percent were serving time for crimes committed in their own neighborhoods.

SOCIAL CLASS AND CRIME

Prior to 1960, criminologists generally assumed that a correlation existed between social class and crime. They believed that members of lower social classes were more prone to commit crime, and they thought that that propensity applied to all types of criminal activity. In the early 1960s, however, studies of the relationship between social class and crime, which made use of offender self-reports, seemed to show that the relationship between social class and criminality was an artifact of discretionary practices within the criminal justice system.[71] Such studies, especially of teenagers, found that rates of self-reported delinquency and criminality were fairly consistent across various social classes within American society. Similar studies of white-collar criminality (which is discussed in more detail in Chapter 10) seemed to show that although the nature of criminal activity may vary between classes, members of all social classes had nearly equal tendencies toward criminality. Hence, the apparent penchant for crime among members of the lower social classes was explained away as a consequence of discretionary decisions by police officers, prosecutors, and judges—decisions that discriminated against those with lower social status, and which resulted in such individuals being arrested, found guilty, and sentenced to imprisonment, much more frequently than members of other classes.

In 1978 a comprehensive reevaluation of thirty-five previous studies of the relationship between social class and crime concluded that previously claimed links were nonexistent.[72] Publication of the 1978 report fueled further study of the relationship between social class and crime, and in 1981 a seminal article by Australian criminologist **John Braithwaite**—which summarized the results of 224 previous studies on the subject—concluded rather convincingly that members of lower social classes were indeed more prone to commit crime.[73] In contrast to earlier studies, Braithwaite found that "socioeconomic status is one of the very few correlates of criminality which can be taken, on balance, as persuasively supported by a large body of empirical evidence."

Many of the difficulties surrounding research into the relationship between social class and crime appear to stem from a lack of definitional clarity. In the many different studies evaluated by Braithwaite, for example, neither *crime* nor *class* were uniformly defined. Margaret Farnworth, Terence P. Thornberry, Marvin D. Krohn,[74] and others have similarly suggested that earlier studies may have been seriously flawed by their near-exclusive focus on young people and by their conceptualization of crime in terms of relatively minor offenses (truancy, vandalism, etc.). Hence, a lack of concise definitions of the subject matter, combined with inadequate measurement techniques, may have led to misleading results.

More recent data, provided by the National Youth Survey (NYS),[75] and analytical techniques which define *class* based on a status attainment model using indicators of sustained underclass status,[76] and which define *delinquency* as repeated involvement in more serious street crimes,[77] conclude that a fairly significant correlation between criminality and social class exists.[78] Therefore—although it would be grossly unfair to conclude that all, or even most, members of lower social classes are criminals—careful statistical analysis of available information appears to show that street crimes, including crimes of violence, theft, and drug abuse, are more likely to be perpetrated by individuals with low socioeconomic status.[79] Such findings have led to introduction of the "underclass" concept as a way of helping to explain the criminality of those with low social standing.

‚ THE COSTS OF CRIME

Fear of crime and the changes it forces us to make in our lives are important aspects of the overall cost of crime. The total impact of crime on American society, however, is difficult to measure because crime can affect its victims in many ways. Some victims are physically injured and may require medical treatment or hospitalization. Others suffer the loss of valued property or are psychologically traumatized. Still others will miss time from work as they strive to repair lives shattered by crime. The Bureau of Justice Statistics, using NCVS data, attempts to measure the economic costs of crime by assessing two dimensions of total cost: the value of property lost to criminal activity and medical expenses associated with victimization. As BJS points out, however, such data are not all-inclusive. "Medical costs may continue to accumulate for months or years after a victimization,"[80] says the bureau. "The victim is not specifically asked about psychological counseling, although some victims may have included this as a medical cost. Increases to insurance premiums as a result of filing claims, decreased productivity at work, moving costs incurred when moving as a result of victimization, intangible costs of pain and suffering, and other similar costs are also not included."[81]

According to BJS, victims of major crime (rape, robbery, assault, personal and household theft, burglary, and motor vehicle theft) lost $17.6 billion in direct costs in 1992. These costs included "losses from property theft or damage, cash losses, medical expenses, and amount of pay lost because of injury or activities related to . . . crime." Estimated economic losses for crimes recorded by the NCVS in 1992 are shown in Table 2.6. A more comprehensive review of the costs associated with all types of crime was conducted by the National Institute of Justice and reported in 1996.[82] According to NIJ, "victimizations generate $105 billion annually in property and productivity losses and outlays for medical expenses. This amounts to an annual 'crime tax' of roughly $425 per man, woman, and child in the United States." When the values of pain, long-term emotional trauma, disability, and risk of death are put in dollar terms, the costs rise to $450 billion annually (or $1,800 per person).

❖

TABLE 2.6

ESTIMATED ECONOMIC LOSSES DUE TO CRIME

	Average Loss per Incident	*Total Losses all Incidents*
Personal crimes	*$218*	*$4,110,000,000*
Rape	234	33,000,000
Robbery	555	680,000,000
Assault	124	649,000,000
Personal larceny	N.A.	2,748,000,000
Household crimes	*914*	*13,536,000,000*
Household larceny	221	1,750,000,000
Burglary	834	3,970,000,000
Motor vehicle theft	3,990	7,816,000,000
Mean loss, all crimes	*$524*	*$17,646,000,000*

N.A.—Not available.
Source: Patsy A. Klaus, "The Costs of Crime to Victims of Crime," *Bureau of Justice Statistics Crime Data Brief,* February 1994.

The bureau also notes that:

- Economic loss of some type occurs in 71 percent of all personal crimes, which include rape, robbery, assault, and personal theft.
- In crimes of violence (rape, robbery, assault), economic losses occur in 23 percent of victimizations.
- Household crimes of burglary, theft, and motor vehicle theft involve economic loss in 91 percent of all victimizations.
- Lost property is not recovered in 89 percent of personal crimes and 85 percent of household crimes.
- Approximately 31 percent of all victims of crimes of violence (robbery and assault) sustain some physical injury.
- For crimes of violence involving injuries in which medical expenses are known, 65 percent involve costs of $250 or more.
- 1.8 million victims lose 6.1 million days from work each year as a result of crime, which translates into an average of 3.4 days of lost work per victimization.

SUMMARY

❖

Crime statistics have been gathered in one form or another for at least 150 years. Although early data about crime may have been used to assess the moral health of nations, modern-day criminal statistics programs provide a fairly objective picture of crime in the United States and elsewhere. Statistics often form the basis for social policy, and innovative strategies such as the "three strikes and you're out" initiative of recent years are frequently based on an understanding of crime provided by such information.

Today, two large-scale government programs collect crime data in the United States. One, the National Crime Victimization Survey, is run by the Bureau of Justice Statistics and provides yearly reports on the criminal victimization of households and individuals. The other, the Uniform Crime Reporting Program, is administered by the Federal Bureau of Investigation and annually collects information on crimes reported to the police and on arrests throughout the country.

As discussed, the social correlates of crime in America include age, sex, race, and social class. Although crime statistics do not tell the whole story and other forms of crime need to be recognized, it appears from the best information available that young black men are especially overrepresented in American street crime statistics. Recognizing the reality of such involvement should help our society secure a safer future for all its citizens and enhance effective crime prevention efforts.

Other than gender, age, and ethnicity, social class can be a significant indicator of the likelihood of criminal involvement. Suffice it here to say that crimes are committed by members of all social classes. As we will recognize in later chapters, however, powerful classes make the laws and are therefore less apt to have need of breaking them and are probably more committed to preservation of the status quo. Hence, many offenders, especially those arrested for street, property, and predatory crimes, come from the lower social classes.

Some people argue that crime statistics do not justify the degree of fear Americans express about crime. Others suggest that statistics are misleading and that they do not provide a true picture of crime in America. Even though the actual incidence of crime is difficult to measure, crime statistics do provide us with an appreciation for the extent of the problems facing victims of crime, social policymakers, and law enforcement personnel today.

DISCUSSION QUESTIONS

1. This book emphasizes a social problems versus social responsibility theme. Which perspective, if any, is best supported by a realistic appraisal of the "social dimensions" of crime discussed in this chapter?
2. What are the major differences between the NCVS and the UCR? Can useful comparisons be made between these two crime indices? If so, of what might such comparisons consist?
3. What is a crime *rate*? How are rates useful? How might both the NCVS and UCR make better use of rates?
4. What are the reasons victims don't report crimes to the police? Which crimes appear to be the most underreported? Why are those crimes so infrequently reported? Which crimes appear to be the most frequently reported? Why are they so often reported?
5. From a study of the incidence of crimes and crime rates discussed in this chapter, do you feel that the seemingly widespread fear of crime among Americans is justified? Why or why not?

6. This chapter discusses losses due to crime. Can you think of any ways in which "losses due to crime" might be measured other than those discussed here? If so, what might they be?

7. This chapter seems to say that black people appear to be overrepresented in many categories of criminal activity. Do you believe that the statistics cited in this chapter accurately reflect the degree of black–white involvement in crime? Why or why not? How might they be inaccurate?

 WEB WATCH

Access the *Criminology Today* home page on the World Wide Web by pointing your browser at www.prenhall.com/cjcentral. Once there, click on *Criminology Today* in order to access the wealth of electronic resources supporting this text.

Onsite resources include (1) "Chapter Links," which provides succinct overviews of critical ideas from the textbook and links selected materials from around the Web to concepts found in the text; (2) "General Reference—Law and Justice Links." Organized by chapter, these links lead to other useful resources on the World Wide Web, such as libraries, electronic discussion lists, and electronic journals; (3) "Criminology Sites on the Web," which lists links to organizations such as the American Society of Criminology and the National Organization for Victims Assistance (NOVA), as well as crime prevention links and statistics on crime and justice. Many other Web-based resources can be accessed via the *Criminology Today* site, including the federal Justice Information Center, the Bureau of Justice Statistics, the FBI, the RAND Corporation, the Vera Institute of Justice, PAVNET (an online "Partnership Against Violence," run by seven different federal agencies), and the National White Collar Crime Center.

Still another feature of the *Criminology Today* Web site is e-mail homework. Homework can be composed onsite and submitted to instructors using the instructor's e-mail address. To use the e-mail homework feature, click on "E-Mail Homework" on the opening page, and then type answers to the questions that appear in the spaces provided. Use your instructor's e-mail address to submit homework answers. The *Criminology Today* Web site also provides links to powerful Web-based search engines that can help you find topics of interest to you as you progress through your course of study. Search engines can be found under the home page heading "Criminology Sites on the Web."

One feature of the *Criminology Today* web site which is especially relevant to this chapter is its link to the official site of the *Sourcebook of Criminal Justice Statistics*. The *Sourcebook* is a data-rich resource published by the U.S. Department of Justice, Bureau of Justice Statistics, which brings together data and statistics on all aspects of criminology and criminal justice agencies within the United States. The online version of the *Sourcebook*, which is presented in Adobe Acrobat® format, makes available more than 650 tables and figures from over 100 different sources. The site is regularly updated to reflect new data as they become available.

NOTES

⬛

[1]"Safety Fears," Associated press, May 20, 1994.

[2]Kathleen Maguire and Ann L. Pastore, *Sourcebook of Criminal Justice Statistics* (Washington, D.C.: U.S. Government Printing Office, 1997).

[3]A number of contemporary criminologists continue to study the effect of weather on crime. See, for example, Ellen G. Cohn, "The Effect of Weather and Temporal Variations on Calls for Police Service," *American Journal of Police,* vol. 15, no. 1 (1996), pp. 23–43; Ellen G. Cohn, "The Prediction of Police Calls for Service: The Influence of Weather and Temporal Variables on Rape and Domestic Violence," *Environmental Psychology,* vol. 13 (1993), pp. 71–83; Ellen G. Cohn, "Weather and Crime," *British Journal of Criminology,* vol. 30, no. 1 (1990), pp. 51–64; and Derral Cheatwood, "Is There a Season for Homicide?" *Criminology,* vol. 26, no. 2 (May 1988), pp. 287-306.

[4]NCJRS may be reached at 800-851-3420 or write to National Institute of Justice, National Criminal Justice Reference Service, Box 6000, Rockville, MD 20850.

[5]http://www.albany.edu/sourcebook.

[6]Federal Bureau of Investigation, *Crime in the United States, 1992* (Washington, D.C.: U.S. Government Printing Office, 1993), p. vi.

[7]Recent redesign of the NCVS make previous years difficult to compare and necessitated use of FBI crime statistics.

[8]Bureau of Justice Statistics, *Criminal Victimization in the United States, 1973–92 Trends* (Washington, D.C.: U.S. Department of Justice, 1994), p. 5.

[9]Ibid.

[10]For further information, see Ronet Bachman and Bruce Taylor, "The Measurement of Family Violence and Rape by the Redesigned National Crime Victimization Survey," *Justice Quarterly,* vol. 11, no. 3 (September 1994); Bureau of Justice Statistics, "National Crime Victimization Survey Redesign," *BJS Fact Sheet* (October 19, 1994); and BJS, "Questions and Answers About the Redesign" (October 30, 1994).

[11]"Son Pleads Guilty to Killing Father, Wounding Mother," United Press wire service, Northern edition, February 21, 1994.

[12]Although, technically speaking, mass murder could be classified as second-degree murder depending on the circumstances under which it occurs, no cases of second-degree mass murder are documented.

[13]For excellent coverage of serial killers, see Steven Egger, *The Killers Among Us: An Examination of Serial Murder and its Investigation* (Upper Saddle River, N.J.: Prentice Hall, 1998); Steven A. Egger, *Serial Murder: An Elusive Phenomenon* (Westport, C.T.: Praeger, 1990); Stephen J. Giannangelo, *The Psychopathology of Serial Murder: A Theory of Violence* (New York: Praeger Publishers, 1996); and Philip Jenkins, *Using Murder: The Social Construction of Serial Homicide* (Hawthorne, N.Y.: Aldine de Gruyter, 1994).

[14]The state of Illinois later sued Gacy's estate to recoup the money made on his paintings. For additional information, see "State Wants Gacy's Money, Even If He's Dead," United Press wire service, Southeast edition, May 18, 1994.

[15]A few years ago Lucas recanted all of his confessions, saying he never killed anyone—except possibly his mother (a killing which he said he didn't remember). See "Condemned Killer Admits Lying, Denies Slayings," *The Washington Post,* October 1, 1995.

[16]Bureau of Justice Statistics, *Report to the Nation on Crime and Justice,* 2nd ed. (Washington, D.C.: U.S. Government Printing Office, 1988), p. 4.

[17]There is no definitive "cutoff" between serial killing and spree killing in terms of time. Cunanan's three-month spree may quality him as a serial killer in the minds of some criminologists. Nonetheless, renowned homicide investigators Robert Ressler (a former FBI criminal profiler) and Vernon Geberth (a retired New York commander of homicide investigations and noted forensic expert) both classify him as a spree killer. (See Michael Grunwald, "Cunanan Leaves Experts at Loss," *The Boston Globe* via Simon and Schuster Newslink, July 28, 1997.

[18]Ibid.

[19]This and other UCR statistics in this chapter are taken from Federal Bureau of Investigation,

Crime in the United States, 1996 (Washington, D.C.: U.S. Government Printing Office, 1997).

[20]Frank Schmalleger and Ted Alleman, "The Collective Reality of Crime: An Integrative Approach to the Causes and Consequences of the Criminal Event," in Gregg Barak, *Varieties of Criminology: Readings from a Dynamic Discipline* (New York: Praeger Publishers, 1994).

[21]"British Law Lords Recognize Male Rape," United Press wire service, Northern edition, July 12, 1994.

[22]"Swim Coach Guilty of Statutory Rape," *USA Today,* August 13, 1993, p. 3A.

[23]A. Nicholas Groth, *Men Who Rape: The Psychology of the Offender* (New York: Plenum Press, 1979).

[24]See, for example, Frank Schmalleger and Ted Alleman, "The Collective Reality of Crime: An Integrative Approach to the Causes and Consequences of the Criminal Event."

[25]This and most other NCVS data are taken from the Bureau of Justice Statistics, *Criminal Victimization, 1996* (Washington, D.C.: BJS, 1997).

[26]Patrick A. Langan and Caroline Wolf Harlow, "Child Rape Victims, 1992" (Washington, D.C.: Bureau of Justice Statistics, 1994); and Pierre Thomas, "Rape of Girls Too Common, Study Finds; Half of All Victims Are Under Age 18," *The Washington Post* wire service, June 23, 1994.

[27]The occupants of houses may be robbed, of course, by someone who comes to their door. Hence, household robbery is a crime distinguishable from household burglary.

[28]FBI, *Crime in the United States, 1992,* p. 27.

[29]BJS, *Criminal Victimization in the United States, 1990,* p. 68.

[30]"Rapper Arrested," Associated Press wire service, Northern edition, May 17, 1994.

[31]Trudy Tynan, "Chief Killed," Associated Press wire service, February 2, 1994.

[32]This is true even though the NCVS does not record burglaries of businesses or commercial properties.

[33]Richard Carelli, "Scotus-Cross Burning," Associated Press wire service, March 28, 1994.

[34]FBI, *Crime in the United States, 1992,* p. 54.

[35]BJS, *Criminal Victimization in the United States, 1990,* p. 100.

[36]Ibid., pp. 100–101.

[37]For an excellent overview of the social dimensions of crime, see John Hagan and Ruth D. Peterson, *Crime and Inequality* (Stanford, Calif.: Stanford University Press, 1995); and James W. Messerschmidt, *Crime as Structured Action: Gender, Race, Class and Crime in the Making* (Thousand Oaks, Calif.: Sage, 1997).

[38]Alfred Blumstein, "Violence by Young People: Why the Deadly Nexus?" *National Institute of Justice Journal,* no. 229 (August 1995).

[39]John J. Dilulio, Jr., "The Question of Black Crime," *The Public Interest,* Fall 1994, pp. 3–12.

[40]James Alan Fox, *Trends in Juvenile Violence: A Report to the United States Attorney General on Current and Future Rates of Juvenile Offending* (Washington, D.C.: Bureau of Justice Statistics, 1996); and Gary Fields, "Youth Violent Crime Falls 9.2%," *USA Today,* October 3-5, 1997, p. 1A (quoting James Fox).

[41]James Q. Wilson and Joan Petersilia, *Crime* (San Francisco, Calif.: Institute of Contemporary Studies, 1995).

[42]Ibid.

[43]Edna Buchanan, "You're Under Arrest," *New Choices for Retirement Living,* June 1994, p. 61.

[44]U.S. Department of Justice, *Elderly Crime Victims* (Washington, D.C.: Bureau of Justice Statistics, March 1994).

[45]Ibid.

[46]BJS, *Age Patterns of Serious Violent Crime* (Washington, D.C.: September 1997).

[47]For an excellent review of homicide and the elderly, see James Alan Fox and Jack Levin, "Homicide Against the Elderly: A Research Note," *Criminology,* vol. 29, no. 2 (May 1994), pp. 317–327.

[48]U.S. Department of Justice, *Elderly Crime Victims.*

[49]Mel E. Weith, "Elder Abuse: A National Tragedy," *FBI Law Enforcement Bulletin,* February 1994, pp. 24–26.

[50]U.S. Congress, House Subcommittee on Human Services, Select Committee on Aging, *Elder Abuse: An Assessment of the Federal Response,* 101st Congress, 1st Session, June 7, 1989.

[51]Stephen E. Brown, Finn-Aage Esbensen, and Gilbert Geis, *Criminology: Explaining Crime and Its Context,* 2nd ed. (Cincinnati, Ohio: Anderson, 1996), p. 198.

[52]Leanne Fiftal Alarid, James W. Marquart, Velmer S. Burton, Jr., Francis T. Cullen, and

Steven J. Cuvelier, "Women's Roles in Serious Offenses: A Study of Adult Felons," *Justice Quarterly,* vol. 13, no. 3 (September 1996), pp. 432–454.

[53]U.S. Department of Justice, *Elderly Crime Victims,* p. 4.

[54]NCVS data show that the rate of rape has dropped somewhat over the past two decades even though the number of such crimes reported to the police has increased. Generally UCR data are probably more reliable than NCVS data where rape is concerned, because NCVS use of a redesigned questionnaire has thrown the reliability of NCVS rape data into question. In fact, for 1992, the number of rapes reported to the police (UCR data) exceeded the number of estimated rape victimizations (NCVS data) for the first time since record keeping began. See Maguire and Pastore, *Sourcebook of Criminal Justice Statistics, 1993* (Washington, D.C.: U.S. Superintendent of Documents, 1994), Table 3.26, for additional information.

[55]Reprinted in "For the Record," *Washington Post* wire service, March 3, 1994.

[56]For a good overview of the issues, see Dee Cook and Barbara Hudson, *Racism and Criminology* (Thousand Oaks, Calif.: Sage, 1993).

[57]Marvin D. Free, Jr., *African-Americans and the Criminal Justice System* (New York: Garland, 1996).

[58]William Wilbanks, *The Myth of a Racist Criminal Justice System* (Monterey, Calif.: Brooks/Cole, 1987).

[59]William Wilbanks, "The Myth of a Racist Criminal Justice System," *Criminal Justice Research Bulletin,* vol. 3, no. 5 (Huntsville, Texas: Sam Houston State University, 1987), p. 2.

[60]Ibid., p. 5.

[61]Ibid., p. 3.

[62]Jim Abrams, "Gun Crimes," Associated Press wire service, April 12, 1997.

[63]Wilbanks, "The Myth of a Racist Criminal Justice System," p. 2.

[64]John Hagan and Ruth D. Peterson, *Crime and Inequality* (Stanford, Calif.: Stanford University Press, 1995).

[65]Coramae Richey Mann, "The Reality of a Racist Criminal Justice System," in Barry W. Hancock

and Paul M. Sharp, *Criminal Justice in America: Theory, Practice and Policy* (Upper Saddle River, N.J.: Prentice Hall, 1996), pp. 51–59.

[66]Paul Glastris and Jeannye Thornton, "A New Civil Rights Frontier: After His Own Home and Neighborhood Were Invaded by Street Punks, Jesse Jackson Dedicated Himself to Battling Black-on-Black Crime," *U.S. News & World Report,* January 17, 1994, p. 38.

[67]Ibid.

[68]Robert L. Carter, "The Criminal Justice System is Infected with Racism," *Vital Speeches of the Day,* vol. 62, no. 10 (March 1, 1996), pp. 290–293.

[69]Michael J. Sniffen, "Crime Fear," Associated Press wire service, Northern edition, June 20, 1994.

[70]Ibid.

[71]For a good review of the issues involved, see John Hagan, *Structural Criminology* (New Brunswick, N.J.: Rutgers University Press, 1989).

[72]Charles R. Tittle, Wayne Villemez, and Douglas Smith, "The Myth of Social Class and Criminality: An Empirical Assessment of the Empirical Evidence," *American Sociological Review,* vol. 43, no. 5 (1978), pp. 643–656; see also Charles R. Tittle, "Social Class and Criminality," *Social Forces,* vol. 56, no. 2 (1977), pp. 474–502.

[73]John Braithwaite, "The Myth of Social Class and Criminality Reconsidered," *American Sociological Review,* vol. 46, no. 1 (1981), pp. 36–57.

[74]Margaret Farnworth, Terence P. Thornberry, and Marvin D. Krohn, "Measurement in the Study of Class and Delinquency: Integrating Theory and Research," *Journal of Research in Crime and Delinquency,"* vol. 31, no. 1 (1994), pp. 32–61.

[75]The National Youth Survey (NYS) began in 1977 and is headquartered at the University of Colorado.

[76]See, for example, Delbert S. Elliott, "Serious Violent Offenders: Onset, Developmental Course, and Termination—The American Society of Criminology 1993 Presidential Address," *Criminology,* vol. 32, no. 1 (1994), pp. 1–21; and Delbert S. Elliott and Suzanne S. Ageton, "Reconciling Race and Class Differences

in Self-Reported and Official Estimates of Delinquency," *American Sociological Review,* vol. 45, no. 1 (1980), pp. 95–100.

[77]Such as that conducted by Farnworth, Thornberry, and Krohn, op. cit.

[78]International studies are similarly supportive. See, for example, Per Olof H. Wikstrom, "Housing Tenure, Social Class and Offending: The Individual-Level Relationship in Childhood and Youth," *Criminal Behaviour and Mental Health,* vol. 1, no. 1 (1991), pp. 69–89; and William R. Smith, *Social Structure, Family Structure, Child Rearing, and Delinquency: Another Look* (Stockholm: University of Stockholm, 1991).

[79]See also Nicole H. Rafter, "Crime and the Family," *Women and Criminal Justice,* vol. 1, no. 2 (1990), pp. 73–86; and Margaret Farnworth, *Social Background and the Early Onset of Delinquency: Exploring the Utility of Various Indicators of Social Class Background* (Albany, N.Y.: Hindelang Criminal Justice Research Center, 1990).

[80]Patsy A. Klaus, Bureau of Justice Statistics Crime Data Brief, "The Costs of Crime to Victims of Crime," February 1994.

[81]Ibid.

[82]National Institute of Justice, "The Extent and Costs of Crime Victimization: A New Look," January 1996.

RESEARCH METHODS

AND THEORY DEVELOPMENT

Criminological research is most frequently concerned with the discovery of the causes of crime and the effect of various methods of treatment.

—HERMANN MANNHEIM[1]

Researchers always say that more money is needed for research. But let me point out that the nation's budget for research on violence is considerably less than one-half what the federal government will spend this year on mohair price subsidies. Nothing against goats, but a shortage of fuzzy sweaters is not what is keeping people behind locked doors at night.

—JOHN MONAHAN[2]

The cardinal principle of experimentation is that we must accept the outcome whether or not it is to our liking.

—ABRAHAM KAPLAN[3]

⊞ CHAPTER OUTLINE ⊞

⇐ IMPORTANT TERMS ⇒

theory	hypothesis	research
randomization	operationalization	research designs
variable	controlled experiments	internal validity
confounding effects	control group	intersubjectivity
external validity	quantitative methods	applied research
replicability	*verstehen*	data confidentiality
qualitative methods	pure research	primary research
informed consent	secondary analysis	survey research
secondary research	inferential statistics	tests of significance
descriptive statistics	quasi-experimental designs	meta-analysis
participant observation		

⊞ INTRODUCTION

Years ago, I taught my first criminology class at a small southern college in the heart of what was then referred to as the "Bible belt." Many of my students were devoutly religious and thoroughly churched in such hallowed concepts as good and evil, sin, salvation, and redemption. When the 3½-month course was nearly over, and a detailed discussion of biological, psychological, and sociological theories of crime causation had ended, I decided to take a survey. I wanted to see which of the theories we had discussed most appealed to the majority of my students. On the last day of class I took a brief survey. After explaining what I was about to do, I started with the question: "How many of you think that most criminal behavior can be explained by the biological theories of crime causation we've studied?" Only one or two students raised their hands. This was a very small number, for the class, a popular one, held 131 students and was taught in a small auditorium. "How many of you," I continued, "think psychological theories explain most crime?" Again, only a handful of students responded. "Well, then, how many of you feel sociological theories offer the best explanation for crime?" I asked. A few more hands went up. Still, the majority of students had not voted one way or the other. Fearing that my teaching had been for naught, and not knowing what else to ask, I blurted out: "How many of you believe that 'the devil made him do it' is the best explanation for crime that we can offer?" At that, almost all the students raised their hands.

I realized then that an entire semester spent trying to communicate the best thoughts of generations of criminologists had had little impact on most students in the class. They had listened to what I had to say, they had considered each of the theories I presented, and then they had dismissed all of them out of hand as so much idle conjecture—assigning them the status of ruminations sadly out of touch with the true character of human nature and lacking in appreciation for the true cosmic temper of human activity.

That class held a lesson for me greater than any which the students had learned. It taught me that criminological theory could not be fully appreciated until and unless its fundamental assumptions were comprehended. Until students could be brought to see the value of criminological theorizing, unless they could be shown why criminologists think and believe the way they do, it would be impossible to ever convince future students that the criminological enterprise was worthy of serious attention.

This chapter, which concerns itself with criminological research methods and theory development, is my way of showing to those now embarking upon the study of criminology why modern-day criminology has both validity and purpose—that is, to show how it is applicable to social life in today's world. Were it not, criminological study would be pointless, and criminological theorizing fruitless. Happily, because it is built on a scientific approach to the subject matter of crime, criminology has much to offer as we attempt to grapple with the crime problems now facing us. For criminology to bear the fruit of which it is capable, however, more than mere scientific acceptance is necessary. To realize its ultimate promise, criminology must become accepted as a policymaking tool, consulted by lawmakers and social planners alike, and respected for what it can tell us about both crime and its prevention.

THE SCIENCE OF CRIMINOLOGY

Over the past century, criminologists have undertaken the task of building a "scientific criminology" as distinguished from what had been the "armchair criminology" of earlier years. Armchair criminologists offered their ideas to one another as conjecture—fascinating "theories" that could be debated (and sometimes were) ad nauseam. Although the ruminations of armchair criminologists may have achieved a considerable degree of popular acclaim through (1) the involvement of distinguished lecturers, (2) the association of such ideas with celebrated bastions of higher learning, and (3) their publication in prestigious essays, they were rarely founded on anything other than mere speculation.

The ideas of armchair criminologists followed in the intellectual tradition of Christian apologists who busied themselves with debates over questions such as how many angels could fit on the head of a pin, or whether Noah had forgotten to take certain types of insects aboard the ark, but which had made the famous journey by happenstance (Why, for example, would anyone take two mosquitoes?). They were the kinds of things one could probably never know with certainty, no matter how much the ideas were debated. Under such circumstances, one person's theory was another's fact, and still another's wishful thinking.[4]

Although it is easy to dispense of armchair criminology as the relaxed musings of carefree intellectuals undertaken almost as sport, it is far more difficult to agree on the criteria necessary to move any undertaking into the realm of serious scientific endeavor. Present-day criminology is decidedly more scientific, however, than its intellectual predecessor—which means that it is amenable to objective scrutiny and systematic testing. In fact, the drive to make criminology "scientific" has been a conscious one, beginning with many of the approaches discussed in Chapter 5.

A variety of criteria have been advanced for declaring any endeavor "scientific." Among them are[5]

- The systematic collection of related facts (as in the building of a database).
- An emphasis on the availability and application of the scientific method.
- "The existence of general laws, a field for experiment or observation . . . and control of academic discourse by practical application."
- "The fact that it has been . . . accepted into the scientific tradition."
- An "emphasis on a worthwhile subject in need of independent study even if adequate techniques of study are not yet available" (as in the investigation of paranormal phenomena).

Probably all the forgoing could be said of criminology. For one thing, criminologists do gather facts. The mere gathering of facts, however, although it may lead to a descriptive criminology, falls short of offering satisfactory explanations for crime. Hence, most contemporary criminologists are concerned with identifying relationships among the facts they observe, and with attempting to understand the many and diverse causes of crime. This emphasis on unveiling causality moves criminology beyond the merely descriptive into the realm of conjecture and theory building. A further emphasis on measurement and objectivity gives contemporary criminology its scientific flavor.

THE DEVIL MADE HER DO IT!

DEMONIC POSSESSION TRIAL IN DALLAS

Scientific criminology generally scoffs at claims of supernatural influences in crime commission. As the story that follows shows, however, not everyone is convinced.

Dallas—Doretha Crawford insists she and her sister didn't gouge out their sister's eyeballs with their fingers. But when a prosecutor asked her Tuesday if her sister had been possessed, she didn't hesitate.

"It wasn't her," Crawford said, describing how her sister, Myra Obasi, 30, while seemingly possessed by a demon, drove wildly, swerved toward huge trucks and tried to run off the road.

"Her whole features changed. Her eyes were big . . . She spoke in a man's voice. Mist came out of her mouth. Her teeth were black and scattered. It said it got her, and it was going to get us, too."

In one of the most bizarre cases in recent Texas history, Crawford and her sister, Beverly Johnson, testified in their own defense, saying they didn't blind Obasi in Dallas last March.

Instead, they insist, they fled demons for two days, prayed and sought out ministers, all trying to save their sister.

Obasi, stunning courtroom observers, said she agrees.

A Shreveport, La., schoolteacher who is now totally blind, Obasi testified in a near-whisper, crying occasionally, that she has no idea how she lost her eyeballs. But she insisted her sisters had nothing to do with it.

All three sisters were in the house of Mattye Bradfield, an elderly preacher in southern Dallas, when Obasi was horribly blinded.

But Crawford, 34, and Johnson, 35, testified that they couldn't remember the critical period—a claim prosecutor George West mocked as "stereo memory loss."

Police and prosecutors have said Obasi at first told them the sisters blinded her while trying to "beat the devil" out of her. The tale, by any measure, is a truly hellish one.

Last spring Johnson began having headaches that a doctor could not cure, according to her father, Chester Crawford. Crawford reluctantly told jurors he then took Johnson to see Benny Morgan, a practitioner of "hoodoo," a Christianized version of voodoo.

Prosecutors and police have said the diagnosis was that the family was under attack by demons. Johnson said her father told them later that one of their sisters, living in Houston, was trying to kill them. So when someone wrote the words "BLOOD ROOM" on Obasi's car last March, they fled from Arcadia, La., where the two defendants lived, to Dallas. They turned their five children over to a stranger along the way.

All three sisters say they are firm Christian believers. But prosecutors, who expect to finish the trial today, say they will convince jurors otherwise.

Both women face two to 10 years for aggravated assault.

Questions

1. Do you believe that the devil plays a role in modern-day crime causation? If so, describe the nature of that role.
2. How might we research whether the devil, or some other supernatural force, is active in influencing crime rates today?

Source: Mark Potok, "Demonic Possession Trial Has Dallas Under Its Spell, *USA Today*, September 21, 1994, p. 8A. Copyright 1994, *USA Today*. Reprinted with permission.

◼ THEORY BUILDING

Ultimately, the goal of research within criminology is the construction of theories or models that allow for a better understanding of criminal behavior and that permit the development of strategies intended to address the problem of crime. A theory consists of a set of interrelated propositions which provide a relatively complete form of understanding. Hence, even if we find that crime is higher when the moon is full, we must still ask, "Why?" Is it because the light from full moons makes it possible for those interested in crime commission to see better at night? If so, then we would expect crime to be higher on full moon nights in areas where there is no cloud cover than in areas where clouds obliterate the moon's light. Likewise, cities should show less of a rise in crime during full moons than rural areas and small towns, as city lights effectively minimize the impact of the light of the moon. In any event, a complete lunar theory of crime causation would contain specific propositions about the causal nature of the phenomena involved.

There are many ways to define the word *theory*. One cogent definition comes from Don M. Gottfredson, a well-known criminologist of modern times, who writes that "[t]heories consist of postulates" (i.e., assumptions), "theoretical constructs, logically derived hypotheses, and definitions. Theories," says Gottfredson, "can be improved steadily through **hypothesis** testing, examination of evidence from observations, revisions of the theory, and repetitions of the cycle, repeatedly modifying the theory in light of the evidence."[6] Another well-known methodologist describes theories this way: ". . . a theory is a set of related propositions that suggest why events occur in the manner that they do. The propositions that make up theories are of the same form as hypotheses: they consist of concepts and the linkages or relationships between them."[7]

These definitions all have something to offer; however, the definition of the term *theory* that we choose to use in this book combines aspects of them all. For our purposes, then, a **theory** consists of a series of interrelated propositions which attempt to describe, explain, predict, and ultimately control some class of events. Theories gain explanatory power from inherent logical consistency and are "tested" by how well they describe and predict reality. In other words, a good theory provides relatively complete understanding at the same time that it is supported by observations and stands up to continued scrutiny.

Theories serve a number of purposes. For one thing, they give meaning to observations. They explain what we see in a particular setting by relating those observations to other things already understood. Hence, a simple example of a theory of physics explains the behavior of light by saying that light has the properties of both waves and particles. Such a theory is immediately useful, for although we may have trouble conceptualizing the light's essence, we can easily grasp ideas such as "wave" and "particle," both of which we experience in everyday living.

Theories within criminology serve the same purpose as those in the physical sciences, although they are often more difficult to test. Few people, for example, can intuitively understand the motivation of "lust murderers" (a term developed by the FBI and popularized by some recent movies) or men who sexually abuse and kill women, often sadistically. Most people, after all, are not lust murderers, and therefore lack an intellectual starting point in striving to understand what goes on in the

Hypothesis 1. an explanation that accounts for a set of facts and that can be tested by further investigation . . .
2. something that is taken to be true for the purpose of argument or investigation.

Theory a series of interrelated propositions that attempt to describe, explain, predict, and ultimately to control some class of events. A theory gains explanatory power from inherent logical consistency and is "tested" by how well it describes and predicts reality.

minds of those who are. Some psychiatric theories (discussed in Chapter 6) suggest that lust murderers kill because of a deep-seated hatred of women. Hate is something that most minds can grasp, and a vision of lust murder as an extreme example of the age-old battle between the sexes provides an intellectual "handle" that many can appreciate. Hence, theory building dispenses of the old adage that "it takes one to know one," instead bringing at least the possibility of understanding within the reach of all. Note, however, that although such limited explanations as the one discussed here may provide a degree of understanding, they must still be tested to determine whether they are true.

Theories provide understanding in a number of ways. Kenneth R. Hoover identifies four "uses of theory in social scientific thinking."[8] They are

- Theories provide *patterns* for the interpretation of data. Population density, for example, tends to be associated with high crime rates, and maps showing high population density tend to be closely associated with diagrams that reflect rates of crime. Hence, some theorists are quick to suggest, overcrowding increases aggression and therefore crime. "People," says Hoover, "like to think in terms of images, analogies, and patterns; this helps to simplify complex realities and to lighten the burden of thought."
- Theories *link* one study with another. Some years ago, for example, a case study of women's prisons in California found the existence of artificially constructed "families," around which women's lives centered. A similar, but later, study of a Chinese prison also found that familylike groups had been created by female inmates there—prompting some theorists to suggest that women felt a need to nurture and to be nurtured by aspects of social structure, and that they carried such a need with them into prison. The fact that cross-cultural support was found for the suggestion provided a linkage between the two studies which tended to lend further support to the suggestion itself.
- Theories supply frameworks within which concepts and variables acquire *special significance*. The death penalty, for example, although especially significant to individuals condemned to die, acquires special significance when seen as a tool employed by the powerful to keep the powerless under their control.
- Theories allow us to interpret the larger meaning of our findings for ourselves and for others. Hence, the death penalty has become a moral issue for many Americans today, shrouded as it is in ethical considerations and images of national identity and ultimate justice.

❖ THE ROLE OF RESEARCH

More important than the claims made by theories and by the theorists who create them are findings of fact that either support those claims or leave them without foundation. Hence, theories, once proposed, need to be tested against the real world via a variety of research strategies, including experimentation and case studies.

Any theory gains credence if activity based on it produces results in keeping with what that theory would predict. Bernard P. Cohen, a seminal thinker on the subject of social scientific theory construction, tells us that "scientific knowledge is

Research the use of standardized, systematic procedures in the search for knowledge.

Applied research scientific inquiry that is designed and carried out with practical application in mind.

Pure research research undertaken simply for the sake of advancing scientific knowledge.

theoretical knowledge, and the purpose of methods in science is to enable us to choose among alternative theories."[9]

Knowledge is inevitably built on experience and observation. Hence, the crux of scientific research is data collection. Data collection occurs through a variety of techniques, including direct observation, the use of surveys and interviews, participant observation, and the analysis of existing data sets—all of which will be discussed shortly.

Research can be defined as the use of standardized, systematic procedures in the search for knowledge.[10] Some researchers distinguish between applied research and nonapplied or pure research. **Applied research** "consists of scientific inquiry that is designed and carried out with practical application in mind."[11] In applied research the researcher is working toward some more or less practical goal. It may be the reduction of crime, the efficient compensation of victims of crime, or an evaluation of the effectiveness of policies implemented to solve some specific aspect of the crime problem. **Pure research,** on the other hand, is undertaken simply for the sake

Sisters: Doretha Crawford, center, and Beverly Johnson, left, were tried for gouging out Myra Obasi's eyes. Obasi (shown in photo on right) says her sisters had nothing to do with it. Is a spiritual influence active in certain forms of criminality? *(a) Pat Sullivan/AP/Wide World Photos; (b and c) Ariane Kadoch/The Dallas Morning News.*

of advancing scientific knowledge. Pure research "does not carry the promise or expectation of immediate, direct relevance."

Another type of research is called secondary research or secondary analysis, and can be distinguished from primary research.[12] **Primary research** "is characterized by original and direct investigation,"[13] whereas **secondary research** consists of new evaluations of existing information which has already been collected by other researchers.

Scientific research generally proceeds in stages, which can be divided conceptually among (1) problem identification, (2) the development of a research design, (3) a choice of data-gathering techniques, and (4) a review of findings, which often includes statistical analysis.

PROBLEM IDENTIFICATION

Problem identification, the first step in any research, consists of the naming of a problem or choice of an issue to be studied. Topics may be selected for a variety of reasons. Larry S. Miller and John T. Whitehead, for example, say that "the choice of what criminologists study is influenced by political decisions,"[14] meaning that the availability of government grant monies frequently determines the focus of much contemporary research in the area of crime. It may also be that private foundation monies have become available to support studies in a specific area, perhaps the researcher has a personal interest in a particular issue and wants to learn more, or maybe a professor or teacher has assigned a research project as part of the requirements for successful class completion. Whatever the reason for beginning research, however, the way in which a research problem is stated will help narrow the research focus and serve as a guide to the formulation of data-gathering strategies.

Although some criminological research undertaken today is purely descriptive, the bulk of such research is intended to explore issues of causality—especially the claims made by theories purporting to explain criminal behavior. As such, much contemporary research in criminology is involved with the testing of hypotheses.

The *American Heritage Dictionary* defines the word *hypothesis* in two ways:

1. "[a]n explanation that accounts for a set of facts and that can be tested by further investigation . . .
2. [s]omething that is taken to be true for the purpose of argument or investigation . . ."

Within the modern scientific tradition, a hypothesis serves both purposes. Some criminologists, as mentioned earlier, have observed what appears to be a correlation, or relationship, between phases of the moon and the rate of crime commission. Such observers may propose the following hypothesis: "The moon causes crime." Although this is a useful starting hypothesis, it needs to be further refined before it can be tested. Specifically, the concepts contained within the hypothesis must be translated into measurable variables. A **variable** is simply a concept that can undergo measurable changes.

Primary research
research characterized by original and direct investigation.

Secondary research new evaluations of existing information which has already been collected by other researchers.

Variable a concept that can undergo measurable changes.

Operationalization the process by which concepts are made measurable.

Scientific precedent holds that only measurable items can be satisfactorily tested. The process of turning a simple hypothesis into one that is testable is called **operationalization.** An operationalized hypothesis is one that is stated in such a way as to facilitate measurement. It is specific in its terms and in the linkages it proposes. We might, for example, move a step further toward both measurability and specificity in our hypothesis about the relationship between the moon and crime by restating it as follows: "Rates of murder, rape, robbery, and assault rise when the moon's fullness increases, and are highest when the moon is fullest." Now we have specified what we mean by crime (i.e., murder, rape, robbery, and assault), rates of which can be calculated. The degree of the moon's fullness can also be measured. Once we have operationalized a hypothesis and made the concepts it contains measurable, those concepts have, in effect, become variables.

Now that the concepts within our hypothesis are measurable, we can test the hypothesis itself. That is to say, we can observe what happens to crime rates as the moon approaches fullness, as well as what happens when the moon is full, and see whether our observations support our hypothesis. As our dictionary definition tells us, once a hypothesis has been operationalized it is assumed to be true for purposes of testing. It is accepted, for study purposes, until observation proves it untrue, at which point it is said to be rejected. As one renowned researcher stated, "[t]he task of theory-testing . . . is predominantly one of rejecting inadequate hypotheses."[15]

RESEARCH DESIGNS

Research design the logic and structure inherent in an approach to data gathering.

Research designs structure the research process. They provide a kind of road map to the logic inherent in one's approach to a research problem. They also serve as guides to the systematic collection of data. **Research designs** consist of the logic and structure inherent in any particular approach to data gathering.

A simple study, for example, might be designed to test the assertion that the consumption of refined white sugar promotes aggressive or violent tendencies among men. One could imagine researchers approaching prison officials with the proposal that inmate diets should be altered to exclude all refined sugar. Under the plan cafeteria cooks would be instructed to prepare meals without the use of sugar. Noncaloric sweeteners would be substituted for sugar in recipes calling for sugar, and Kool Aid, sweetened iced tea, and carbonated beverages containing sugar would be banned. Likewise the prison canteen would be prohibited from selling items containing sugar for the duration of the experiment.

To determine whether the forced reduction in sugar consumption actually impacted inmates' behavior, researchers might look at the recorded frequency of aggressive incidents (sometimes called "write-ups" in prison jargon) occurring within the confines of the prison before the experiment was initiated and compare such data with similar information on such incidents following the introduction of dietary changes. A research design employing this kind of logic can be diagrammed as follows:

$$O_1 \times O_2$$

Here "O_1" (termed a *pretest*) refers to the information gathered on inmate aggressiveness prior to the introduction of dietary changes (which themselves are shown as "X," also called the *experimental intervention*), and "O_2" (termed the *posttest*) signifies a second set of observations—that occurring after dietary changes have been implemented. Researchers employing a strategy of this type, which is known as a "one-group pretest-posttest" design, would likely examine differences between the two sets of observations, one made before introduction of the experimental intervention, and the other after. The difference, they may assume, would show changes in behavior resulting from changes in diet—in this case the exclusion of refined white sugar.

Although this basic research design well illustrates the logic behind naive experiments, it does not lend good structure to a research undertaking, because it does not eliminate other possible explanations of behavioral change. For example, during the time between the first and second observations inmates may have been exposed to some other influence which reduced their level of aggression. A new minister may have begun preaching effective sermons filled with messages of love and peace to the prison congregation; television cable service to the prison may have been disrupted, lowering the exposure inmates received to violent programming; a new warden may have taken control of the facility, relaxing prison rules and reducing tensions; a transfer or release of especially troublesome inmates, scheduled at some earlier time, may have occurred; a new program of conjugal visitation may have been initiated, creating newfound sexual outlets and reducing inmate tensions; and so on. In fact, the possibilities for rival explanations (i.e., those that rival the explanatory power of the hypothesis under study) are nearly limitless. Rival explanations such as these, called by some researchers competing hypotheses and by others **confounding effects,** make the results of any single series of observations uncertain.

Achieving Validity in Research Designs

Confounding effects, which may invalidate the results of research, are of two general types: those that affect the **internal validity** of research findings and those that limit the ability of researchers to generalize the research findings to other settings—called **external validity.** Often, when external validity is threatened, researchers do not feel confident that interventions that "worked" under laboratorylike or other special conditions will still be effective when employed in the field. Hence, researchers achieving internal validity may be able to demonstrate that diets low in refined white sugar lower the number of instances of overt displays of aggressiveness in a single prison under study. They may not feel confident (for reasons discussed in the paragraphs that follow), however, that similar changes in diet, if implemented in the general nonprison population, would have a similar effect. Most researchers consider internal validity, or the certainty that experimental interventions did indeed cause the changes observed in the study group, the most vital component of any planned research. Without it, considerations of external validity become irrelevant. Factors that routinely threaten the internal validity of a design for research are said to include[16]

Confounding effects
rival explanations, also called competing hypotheses, which are threats to the internal or external validity of any research design.

Internal validity the certainty that experimental interventions did indeed cause the changes observed in the study group; also the control over confounding factors which tend to invalidate the results of an experiment.

External validity the ability to generalize research findings to other settings.

- *History:* Specific events that occur between the first and second observations, which may impact measurement. The examples given in the prison study described earlier (the arrival of a new minister or new warden, etc.) are all applicable here.
- *Maturation:* Processes occurring within the respondents or subjects that operate as a result of the passage of time. Fatigue and decreases in response time due to age are examples.
- *Testing:* The effects of taking a test upon the scores of a later testing. When respondents are measured in some way that requires them to respond, they tend to do better (i.e., their scores increase) the next time they are tested. In effect, they have learned how to take the test, or how to be measured, even though they may not have acquired more knowledge about the subject matter which the test intends to measure.
- *Instrumentation:* Changes in measuring instruments, or in survey takers, which occur as a result of time. Batteries wear down, instruments need to be recalibrated, interviewers grow tired or are replaced with others, and so on—all of which can change the nature of the observations made.
- *Statistical regression:* When respondents have been selected for study on the basis of extreme scores (as may be the case with personality inventories), later testing will tend to show a "regression toward the mean," or a return to more average scores, because some extreme scores are inevitably more the result of accident or luck rather than anything else.
- *Differential selection:* Built-in biases result when more than one group of subjects is involved in a study and when the groups being tested are initially somehow different. The random assignment of subjects to test groups greatly reduces the chances that such significant differences will exist.
- *Experimental mortality:* A differential loss of respondents from comparison groups, which may occur when more than one group is being tested (i.e., one group loses members at a greater rate than another group, or certain kinds of members are lost from one group, but not from another).

Threats to external validity include

- *Reactive effects of testing:* A pretest may sensitize subjects in such a way that they especially respond to the experimental intervention when it is introduced. Nonpretested subjects (such as those in other locations) may not respond in the same way.
- *Self-selection:* A process whereby subjects are allowed to decide whether they want to participate in a study. Self-selected subjects may be more interested in participation than others, and they may respond more readily to the experimental intervention or treatment.
- *Reactive effects of experimental arrangements:* Persons being surveyed or tested may know that they are part of an experiment and therefore react differently than if they were in more natural settings. Even if they are not aware of their participation in a study, some investigative paraphernalia (such as observers, cameras, and tape recorders) that may be present might change the way in which they behave.

- *Multiple-treatment interference:* Sometimes more than one study is simultaneously conducted on the same persons or group of persons. Under such circumstances "treatments" to which subjects are exposed may interact, changing what would otherwise be the study's results. Multiple-treatment interference may also result from delayed effects, as when a current study is affected by the impact of one which has already been completed.

Experimental and Quasi-Experimental Research Designs

To amass greater confidence that the changes intentionally introduced into a situation are the real cause of observed variations, it is necessary to achieve some degree of control over factors that threaten internal validity. In the physical sciences, controlled experiments often provide the needed guarantees. **Controlled experiments** are those that attempt to hold conditions (other than the intentionally introduced experimental intervention) constant. In fact, some researchers have defined the word *experiment* simply as controlled observation.

Whereas constancy of conditions may be possible to achieve within laboratory settings, it is far more difficult to come by in the social world—which by its very nature is in an ongoing state of flux. Hence, although criminologists sometimes employ true experimental designs in the conduct of their research, they are more likely to find it necessary to use quasi-experimental designs or approaches to research which "are deemed worthy of use where better designs are not feasible."[17] **Quasi-experimental designs** are especially valuable when aspects of the social setting are beyond the control of the researcher. The crucial defining feature of quasi-experimental designs is that they give researchers control over *the when and to whom of measurement,* even though others decide the "when and to whom" of exposure to the experimental intervention.

Sometimes, for example, legislators enact new laws intended to address some aspect of the crime problem, specifying the kinds of crime preventative measures to be employed and what segment of the population is to receive them. Midnight basketball, intended to keep young people off the streets at night, is an example of such legislatively sponsored intervention. During debate on the 1994 Violent Crime Control and Law Enforcement Act, midnight basketball became a point of contention, with senators asking whether money spent in support of such an activity would actually reduce the incidence of serious street crime in our nation's inner cities. Unfortunately, no good research data that could answer the question were available to legislators at the time. Now, however, federally funded midnight basketball programs might be studied by researchers. Hence, although criminologists were not politically situated so as to be able to enact midnight basketball legislation, they are able to study the effects of such legislation after it has been enacted.

Whether criminologists decide on experimental or quasi-experimental designs to guide their research, they depend upon well-considered research strategies to eliminate rival explanations for the effects they observe. One relatively powerful research design frequently employed by criminologists is diagrammed as follows:

Controlled experiments those that attempt to hold conditions (other than the intentionally introduced experimental intervention) constant.

Quasi-experimental designs approaches to research which, although less powerful than experimental designs, are deemed worthy of use when better designs are not feasible.

experimental group	O_1	$\times$	O_2
control group	O_3		O_4

The meaning of the notation used here is similar to that of the one-shot case study design discussed earlier. This approach, however, called the "pretest–posttest control group design," gains considerable power from the addition of a second group. The second group is called a **control group,** because it is not exposed to the experimental intervention.

Critical to the success of a research design such as this is the use of randomization in the assignment of subjects to both experimental and control groups. **Randomization** is the process whereby individuals are assigned to study groups without biases or differences resulting from selection. Self-selection is not permitted (when some individuals volunteer for membership in either the experimental or control group), nor are researchers allowed to use personal judgment in assigning subjects to groups.

Control over potential threats to internal validity is achieved by the introduction of a properly selected control group, because it is assumed that both experimental and control groups are essentially the same at the start, and that any threats to internal validity will affect both groups equally as the experiment progresses— effectively canceling out when final differences between the two groups are measured. If some particular historical event, for example, affects the experimental group and modifies the measurable characteristics of that group, that event should have the same impact on the control group. Hence, in the previous design, when O_4 is subtracted from O_2, the remaining observable *net effects* are assumed to be attributable to the experimental intervention.

In the prison study discussed earlier, randomization would require that *all* inmates be systematically but randomly divided into two groups. Random assignments are typically made by using a table of random numbers. In this simple study, however, something as easy as the flip of a coin should suffice. One group, the experimental group, would no longer receive refined white sugar in their diets, while the other (the control group) would continue eating as before. Because, with this one exception in diet, both groups would continue to be exposed to the same environment, it can be assumed that any other influences on the level of violence within the prison will cancel out when final measurements are taken, and that measurable differences in violence between the two groups can be attributed solely to the effects of the experimental variable (in this case, of course, removal of sugar from the diet).

Control group a group of experimental subjects which, although the subject of measurement and observation, are not exposed to the experimental intervention.

Randomization the process whereby individuals are assigned to study groups without biases or differences resulting from selection.

TECHNIQUES OF DATA COLLECTION

It is the combination of (1) hypothesis building, (2) operationalization, and (3) systematic observation in the service of hypothesis testing that has made modern-day criminology scientific, and which has facilitated scientific theory building within the field. Hence, once a research problem has been identified, concepts made measurable, and a design for the conduct of the research selected, investigators must then decide on the type of data to be gathered and the techniques of data gathering they wish to employ. Ultimately, all research depends on the use of techniques to

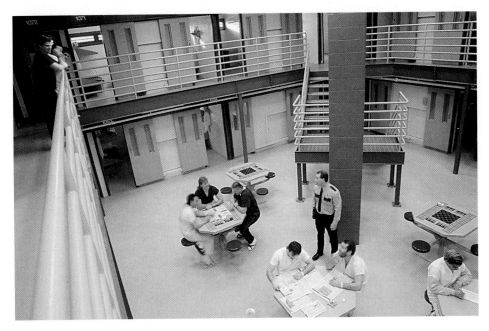

Social science research within a correctional setting. Inmate surveys may increase our knowledge of crime causation. Specifically, what might such surveys tell us? *Rick Friedman/Black Star.*

gather information, or data, for eventual analysis. Like research designs, which structure a researcher's approach to a problem, data-gathering strategies provide approaches to the accumulation of information needed for analysis to occur.

Many first-time researchers select data-gathering techniques on the basis of ease or simplicity. Some choose according to cost or the amount of time required by the techniques themselves. The most important question to consider, however, when beginning to gather information is *whether the data-gathering strategy selected will produce information in a form usable to the researcher.* The kind of information needed depends, of course, on the questions to be answered. Surveys of public opinion as to the desirability of the death penalty, for example, cannot address issues of the punishment's effectiveness as a crime control strategy.

Five major data-gathering strategies typify research in the field of criminology:

Surveys: **Survey research** typically involves the use of questionnaires. Respondents may be interviewed in person, over the telephone, or queried via e-mail or fax. Mail surveys are common, although they tend to have a lower response rate than other types of social surveys. The information produced through the use of questionnaires is referred to as *survey data.* Survey data provide the lifeblood of pollsters such as Gallup, CNN, and Roper who gather data on public opinion, voting preferences, and so forth. Similarly, U.S. Census Bureau data are gathered by survey takers who are trained periodically for that purpose. Survey data also inform the National Crime Victimization Survey and result in such publications as *Crime and the Nation's Households, Criminal Victimization in the United States,* and other NCVS-related reports produced by the Bureau of Justice Statistics. Surveys have also been used in criminology to assess fear of crime and attitudes toward the police, and to discover the extent of unreported crime.

Survey research a social science data-gathering technique which involves the use of questionnaires.

Case studies: Case studies are built around in-depth investigations into individual cases. The study of one (perhaps notorious) offender, scrutiny of a particular criminal organization, analysis of a prison camp, and others may all qualify as case studies. Case studies are useful for what they can tell us to expect about other, similar cases. If study of a street gang, for example, reveals the central role of a few leaders, then we would expect to find a similar organizational style among other gangs of the same kind.

When one individual (termed a *single subject*) is the focus of a case study, the investigation may take the form of a life history. *Life histories* involve gathering as much historical data as possible about a given individual and his or her experiences during early socialization and adulthood. Most life histories are quite subjective due to the fact that they consist primarily of recounts of events by the participants themselves. Life histories may also be gathered on groups of individuals, and similarities in life experience which are thereby discovered may provide researchers with clues to current behavior, or with points at which to begin further investigations.

Case studies, although they may suffer from high levels of subjectivity in which feelings cannot be easily separated from fact, provide the opportunity to investigate individual cases—an element that is lacking in both survey research and participant observation.

Participant observation: **Participant observation** "involves a variety of strategies in data gathering in which the researcher observes a group by participating, to varying degrees, in the activities of the group."[18] Some participant researchers operate undercover, without revealing their identity as researchers to those whom they are studying, whereas others make their identity and purpose known from the outset of the research endeavor. As one criminologist states, participation observation "means that criminologists must venture inside the immediacy of crime."[19]

One of the earliest and best-known participant observers in the field of criminology was William Foote Whyte, who described his 1943 study of criminal subcultures in a slum district that he called "Cornerville" this way: "My aim was to gain an intimate view of Cornerville life. My first problem, therefore, was to establish myself as a participant in the society so that I would have a position from which to observe. I began by going to live in Cornerville, finding a room with an Italian family. . . . It was not enough simply to make the acquaintance of various groups of people. The sort of information that I sought required that I establish intimate social relations. . . . This active participation gave me something in common with them so that we had other things to talk about besides the weather. It broke down the social barriers and made it possible for me to be taken into the intimate life of the group."[20]

It is possible to distinguish between at least two additional kinds of participant observation: (1) the participant as observer and (2) the observer as complete participant. When researchers make their presence known to those whom they are observing, without attempting to influence the outcome of their observations or the activities of the group, they fit the category of participants who are observers. When they become complete participants in the group they are observing, however, researchers run the risk of influencing the group's direction. As Whyte explains, "I made it a rule that I should try to avoid influencing the actions of the group. I wanted to observe what the men did under ordinary circumstances; I did not want to lead them into different activities."[21] Even researchers who make their presence

Participant observation a variety of strategies in data gathering in which the researcher observes a group by participating, to varying degrees, in the activities of the group.

known, however, may inadvertently influence the nature and direction of social interaction because people tend to act differently if they know they are being watched.

Another problem facing the participant observer is that of "going native," or of assuming too close an identification with the subjects or the behavior under study. Like undercover police officers who may at times be tempted to participate in the illegalities they are supposed to be monitoring, participant researchers may begin to experience feelings of kinship with their subjects. When that happens, all sense of the research perspective may be lost, and serious ethical problems can arise.

On the other hand, some researchers may feel disgust for the subjects of their research. Data gatherers with a particular dislike of drug abuse, for example, may be hard put to maintain their objectivity when working as participant observers within the drug subculture. Hence, as Frank Hagan observes, "[t]he researcher must avoid not only overidentification with the study group, but also aversion to it."[22]

Self-reporting: Another subjective data-gathering technique is one that uses self-reports to investigate aspects of a problem not otherwise amenable to study. When official records are lacking, for example, research subjects may be asked to record and report rates of otherwise secretive behavior. Self-reports may prove especially valuable in providing checks on official reports consisting of statistical tabulations gathered through channels such as police departments, hospitals, and social services agencies.

Self-reports may also be requested of subjects in survey research, and it is for that reason that self-reporting is sometimes considered simply another form of survey research. However, many self-reporting techniques require the maintenance of a diary or personal journal and request vigilant and ongoing observations of one's own behavior by the subject under study. Hence, sex researchers may ask subjects to maintain an ongoing record of their frequency of intercourse, the variety of sexual techniques employed, and their preference in partners—items of information that are not easy to come by through other means or that cannot be accurately reconstructed from memory.

Self-reporting enters the realm of the purely subjective when it consists of introspection, or personal reflection. Introspective techniques, or those intended to gather data on secretive feelings and felt motivation, are often used by psychologists seeking to assess the mental status of patients. Criminologists, however, have at times used introspective techniques to categorize criminal offenders into types and to initiate the process of developing concepts more amenable to objective study.

Secondary analysis: Not all data-gathering techniques are intended to generate new information. **Secondary analysis** entails the reanalysis of existing data, that is, secondhand analysis of data that were gathered for another purpose. The secondary analysis of existing data and the use of previously acquired information describe strategies that can save researchers a considerable amount of time and expense.

One important source of data for secondary analysis is the National Archive of Criminal Justice Data located in the Institute for Social Research at the University of Michigan. In the words of the U.S. Department of Justice, the archive's sponsoring agency, "[t]he Archive continually processes the most relevant criminal justice data sets for the research community,"[23] maintaining information on victimization, various aspects of the criminal justice system, and juvenile delinquency. Access to archive data is by request, and data sets are for sale to individual researchers.

Secondary analysis the reanalysis of existing data.

Many other important sources of existing information useful in criminological research can be found in the National Institute of Justice's publication, *Directory of Criminal Justice Information Sources,*[24] available in a new edition every few years from NIJ. The latest edition contains a summary of information services offered, contact persons, phone numbers, addresses, a listing of publications produced, and more for 159 criminology-related information sources.

⬛

THE NATIONAL ARCHIVE OF CRIMINAL JUSTICE DATA

In 1978 the National Archive of Criminal Justice Data began operating under the joint auspices of the Bureau of Justice Statistics, an arm of the U.S. Department of Justice, and the Interuniversity Consortium for Political and Social Research (ICPSR) based at the Institute for Social Research at the University of Michigan. The three goals of ICPSR are to

- Provide computer-readable data for the quantitative study of crime and the criminal justice system through the development of a central data archive that disseminates computer-readable data.
- Supply technical assistance in selecting data collections and the computer hardware and software for analyzing data efficiently and effectively.
- Offer training in quantitative methods of social science research to facilitate secondary analysis of criminal justice data.

ICPSR brings together the data collections of over 370 member colleges and universities in the United States and abroad. It also routinely receives data from BJS, NIJ, the Office for Juvenile Justice and Delinquency Prevention (OJJDP), and the FBI. As a consequence, the Consortium, which maintains the world's largest repository of computer-based research data in the area of the social sciences, has access to voluminous amounts of information. UCR and NCVS data are available through ICPSR, as is information on capital punishment, adult and juvenile correctional facilities, jails, state and federal court statistics, expenditure and employment data for the criminal justice system, and surveys of law enforcement and other criminal justice agencies.

Much of the information available through ICPSR takes the form of data sets which are ready for analysis through software packages such as the Statistical Package for the Social Sciences (SPSS) and SPSS PC-plus. A link to the National Archive of Criminal Justice Data is available on the *Criminology Today* home page. It can be accessed directly at http://www.icpsr.umich.edu/index.html.

Sources: ICPSR home page on the World Wide Web, May 27, 1998; National Institute of Justice, *Data Resources Program of the National Institute of Justice* (Washington, D.C.: NIJ, 1994); and NIJ, *National Archive of Criminal Justice Data* (no date).

The use of secondary data rarely alerts research subjects to the fact that they (or the data they have provided) are being studied, although they may have been so aware when data were first gathered. Hence, secondary analysis, which constitutes one form of unobtrusive research, is said to be nonreactive. Although unobtrusive measures include other forms of data collection, the use of archival records in data analysis constitutes a virtual "goldmine of information waiting to be exploited."[25] Nonetheless, it is important to keep in mind that secondary data usually involve the use of information that was collected for a purpose outside of the interests of the current researcher.

Problems in Data Collection

Scientific data gathering builds on observations of one sort or another. Observation is, of course, not unique to science. Individuals often make personal observations, and draw a plethora of intimate conclusions based on what they see or hear. Scientific observation, however, generally occurs under controlled conditions, and must meet the criteria of intersubjectivity and replicability. **Intersubjectivity** requires that, for observations to be valid, independent observers must report seeing the same thing under the same circumstances. "Do you see what I see?" is a question that highlights the central role of intersubjectivity in scientific observation. If observers cannot agree on what they saw, then the raw data necessary for scientific analysis have not been acquired. **Replicability** of observations means that, at least in the field of scientific experimentation, when the same conditions exist, the same results can be expected to follow. Hence, valid experiments can be replicated. The same observations made at one time can be had again at a later time if all other conditions are the same.

In the physical sciences, replicability is easy to achieve. Water at sea level, for example, will always boil at 100 degrees Celsius. Anyone can replicate the conditions needed to test such a contention. When replicability cannot be achieved, it casts the validity of observations into doubt. Some years ago, for example, a few scientists claimed to have achieved nuclear fusion at room temperature. Their supposed accomplishment was dubbed "cold fusion" and hailed as a major breakthrough in the production of nuclear energy. When scientists elsewhere, however, attempted to replicate the conditions under which cold fusion was said to occur, they could find no evidence that the initial experimenters were correct. Replicability and intersubjectivity are critical to the scientific enterprise for, as one researcher states, "[s]cience rests its claim to authority upon its firm basis in observable evidence . . ."[26]

It is important to recognize, however, that some observations—even those which stand up to the tests of intersubjectivity and replicability—can lead to unwarranted conclusions. For example, spirit possession, an explanation for deviance that was apparently widely held in primitive times, must have appeared well validated by the positive behavioral changes which became apparent in those who submitted to the surgery called for by the theory—a craniotomy intended to release offending spirits from the head of the afflicted party. The actual cause of behavioral reformation may have been brain infections resulting from unsanitary surgical conditions, slips of the stone knife, or the intensity of pain endured by those undergoing the

Intersubjectivity a scientific principle which requires that independent observers see the same thing under the same circumstances for observations to be regarded as valid.

Replicability (experimental) a scientific principle which holds that the same observations made at one time can be had again at a later time if all other conditions are the same.

procedure without anesthetics. To the uncritical observer, however, the theory of spirit possession as a cause of deviance, and cranial surgery as a treatment technique, would probably appear to have been supported by the evidence of induced behavioral change.

Some methodologists note that "[t]heories are as much involved in the determination of fact as facts are in establishing a theory."[27] Theories are intimately involved in the process of data collection. They determine what kinds of data we choose to gather, what we look for in the data itself, and how we interpret the information we have gathered. In short, theories determine what we see, as well as what we ignore. In the late 1700s, for example, when a meteorite shower was reported to the French Academy of Sciences, observers reported that some fragments had struck the ground, causing tremendous explosions. The learned scientists of the academy quickly dismissed these accounts, however, calling them "a superstition unworthy of these enlightened times."[28] Anyone, they said, knows that stones don't fall from the sky.

Data Analysis

Some data, once collected, are simply archived or stored. Most data, however, are subject to some form of analysis. Data analysis generally involves the use of mathematical techniques intended to uncover correlations between variables, and to assess the likelihood that research findings can be generalized to other settings. Such techniques are called *statistics,* and their use in analyzing data is called *statistical analysis.* Some theorists, for example, posit a link between poverty and crime. Hence, we might suspect that low-income areas would be high-crime areas. Once we specify what we mean by "low income" and "crime," so that they become measurable variables, and gather data on income levels and the incidence of crime in various locales, we are ready to begin the job of data analysis.

Statistical techniques provide tools for summarizing data. They also provide quantitative means for identifying patterns within the data and for determining the degree of correlation that exists between variables. Statistical methods can be divided into two types: descriptive and inferential. **Descriptive statistics** are those that (1) describe, (2) summarize, or (3) highlight the relationships within the data which have been gathered. **Inferential statistics,** on the other hand, attempt to generalize findings by specifying how likely they are to be true for other populations, or in other locales.

Descriptive statistics include measures of central tendency, commonly called the mean, median, and mode. The *mode* refers to the most frequently occurring score or value in any series of observations. If, for example, we measure the age of all juvenile offenders held in a state training facility, it may be that they range in age from 12 to 16, with 15 being the most commonly found age. Fifteen, then, would be the modal age for the population under study.

The *median* defines the midpoint of a data series. Half of the scores will be above the mean and the other half will be below. It may be, for example, that in our study of juveniles, we find equal numbers in each age category. The median age for those held might then be 14.

Descriptive statistics describe, summarize, or highlight the relationships within data which have been gathered.

Inferential statistics specify how likely findings are to be true for other populations, or in other locales.

The mathematical average of all scores within a given population is referred to as the *mean*. The mean is the most commonly used measure of central tendency. It is calculated by simply adding together all the scores (or ages, in our example) and dividing by the total number of observations. Although calculations of the mean, median, and mode will often yield similar results, such will not be the case with populations that are skewed in a particular direction. If our population of juveniles under study, for example, consisted almost entirely of 16-year-olds, then the mode for that population would inevitably be 16, while other measures of central tendency would yield somewhat lower figures.

Other descriptive statistics provide measures of the standard deviation of a population (i.e., the degree of dispersion of scores about the mean) and the degree of correlation or interdependence between variables (i.e., the extent of variation in one that can be expected to follow from a measured change in another). As discussed in Chapter 2 (where the term *correlation* is defined), although the degree of correlation may vary, the direction of correlation can also be described. We say, for example, that if one variable increases whenever another, upon which it is dependent, does the same, a positive correlation or positive relationship exists between the two. When one variable decreases in value as another rises, a negative or inverse correlation exists.

Another statistical technique, one which provides a measure of the likelihood that a study's findings are the results of chance, is commonly found in criminological literature. **Tests of significance** are designed to provide researchers with confidence that their results are in fact true, and not the result of sampling error. We may, for example, set out to measure degree of gun ownership. Let's say that the extent of gun ownership in the area under study is actually 50 percent. We have no way of knowing that, of course, until our study is complete. We may decide to use door-to-door surveys of randomly selected households, because cost prohibits us from canvassing all households in the study area. Even if we have made our best survey effort, however, some slight probability remains that the households we have chosen to interview may all be populated by gun owners. Although it is very unlikely, we may, by chance, have excluded those without guns. Assuming that everyone interviewed answers truthfully, we would come away with the mistaken impression that 100 percent of the population in the study area are armed!

The likelihood of faulty findings increases as sample size decreases. Were we to sample only one or two households we would have little likelihood of determining the actual incidence of gun ownership. The larger the sample size, however, the greater the confidence we can have in our findings. Hence a positive correlation exists between sample size and the degree of confidence we can have in our results. Even so, in most criminological research, it is not possible to study all members of a given population, and so samples must be taken. Statistical tests of significance, expressed as a percentage, assess the likelihood that our study findings are due to chance. Hence, a study that reflects a 95 percent confidence level can be interpreted as having a 5 percent likelihood that the results it reports are mere happenstance. In other words, for every hundred such studies, five yield misleading results. The problem, of course, is that it would be impossible to know (without further research) which five that would be!

Tests of significance statistical techniques intended to provide researchers with confidence that their results are in fact true, and not the result of sampling error.

"I had," said he, "come to an entirely erroneous conclusion which shows, my dear Watson, how dangerous it always is to reason from insufficient data."
—ARTHUR CONAN DOYLE, THE ADVENTURE OF THE SPECKLED BAND

QUANTITATIVE VERSUS QUALITATIVE METHODS

A few years ago, U.S. Attorney General Janet Reno addressed researchers, criminologists, and professors gathered at the annual meeting of the American Society of Criminology in Miami, Florida. "Let's stop talking about numbers," Reno exhorted the crowd, "and start talking about crime in human terms." In her admonition Reno placed herself squarely on the side of those who feel that there has been a tendency in American criminology over the past half century to overemphasize **quantitative methods** or techniques—that is, those that produce measurable results which can be analyzed statistically. To be sure, as such critics would be quick to admit, a considerable degree of intellectual comfort must be achieved in feeling that one is able to reduce complex forms of behavior and interaction to something countable (as, say, the frequency of an offense). Intellectual comfort of this sort derives from the notion that anything expressible in numbers must be somehow more meaningful than that which is not.

> **Quantitative methods** research techniques that produce measurable results.

It is crucial to realize, however, that numerical expression is mostly a result of how researchers structure their approach to the subject matter and is rarely inherent in the subject matter itself. Such is especially true in the social sciences, where attitudes, feelings, behaviors, and perceptions of all sorts are subject to quantification by researchers who impose upon such subjective phenomena artificial techniques for their quantification.

One recent highly quantitative study, for example,[29] reprinted in the journal *Criminology,* reported on the relationship between personality and crime. The study found that "greater delinquent participation was associated with a personality configuration characterized by high Negative Emotionality and Weak Constraint." Although it may seem easy to quantify "delinquent participation" by measuring official arrest statistics (even here, however, official statistics may not be a good measure of delinquent behavior, as many law violations go undiscovered), imagine the conceptual nightmares associated with trying to make measurable concepts such as "negative emotionality" and "weak constraint." In such studies, even those replete with numerical data derived through the use of carefully constructed questionnaires, questions still remain of precisely what it is that has been measured.

Not everyone who engages in social science research labors under the delusion that everything can and must be quantified. Those who do, however, are said to suffer from the mystique of quantity. As some critics point out, "[t]he failure to recognize this instrumentality of measurement makes for a kind of *mystique of quantity,* which responds to numbers as though they were repositories of occult powers. . . . The mystique of quantity is an exaggerated regard for the significance of measurement, just because it is quantitative, without regard either to what has been measured or to what can subsequently be done with the measure."[30] The mystique of quantity treats numbers as having intrinsic scientific value. Unfortunately, this kind of thinking has been popular in the social sciences where researchers, seeking to make clear their intellectual kinship with physical scientists, have been less than cautious in their enthusiasm for quantification.

It is . . . pathetic to observe how many statistical refinements are wasted on utterly inadequate basic material.

— HERMANN MANNHEIM [31]

Qualitative methods, in contrast to those that are quantitative, produce subjective results or results which are difficult to quantify. Even though their findings are not expressed numerically, qualitative methods provide yet another set of potentially useful criminological research tools. Qualitative methods are important for the insight they provide into the subjective workings of the criminal mind and the processes by which meaning is accorded to human experience. Introspection, life histories, case studies, and participant observation all contain the potential to yield highly qualitative data.[32]

Consider, for example, how the following personal account[33] of homicidal motivation conveys subjective insights into the life of a Los Angeles gang member that would otherwise be difficult to express.

Wearing my fresh Pendleton shirt, beige khakis, and biscuits [old men's comfort shoes, the first shoe officially dubbed "Crip shoe"], I threw on my black bomber jacket and stepped out into the warm summer night. I walked up Sixty-Ninth Street to Western Avenue and took a car at gunpoint. Still in a state of indecision, I drove toward the hospital.

I intentionally drove through Sixties'hood. Actually, I was hoping to see one of them before I had made it through, and what luck did I have. There was Bank Robber, slippin' [not paying attention, not being vigilant] hard on a side street. I continued past him and turned at the next corner, parked and waited. He would walk right to me.

Sitting in the car alone, waiting to push yet another enemy out of this existence, I reflected deeply about my place in this world, about things that were totally outside the grasp of my comprehension. Thoughts abounded I never knew I could conjure up. In retrospect, I can honestly say that in those moments before Bank Robber got to the car, I felt free. Free, I guess, because I had made a decision about my future.

"Hey," I called out to Robber, leaning over to the passenger side, "got a light?"

"Yeah," he replied, reaching into his pants pocket for a match or lighter. I never found out which.

I guess he felt insecure, because he dipped his head down to window level to see who was asking for a light.

"Say your prayers, muthaf. . . ."

Before he could mount a response I blasted him thrice in the chest, started the car, and drove home to watch 'Benny Hill.' Bangin' was my life. That was my decision.

The passage was written by Sanyika Shakur, once known as "Monster Kody" to fellow South Central Los Angeles Crips members. Monster, named for his readiness

An 18-year-old Los Angeles gang member. Some researchers doubt that quantitative methods can adequately assess the subjective experiences of certain kinds of offenders. What is the nature of such "subjective experiences"? *Jim Tynan/Impact Visuals Photo & Graphics, Inc.*

to commit acts of brutality so extreme that they repulsed even other gang members, joined the Crips at age 11. Sent to a maximum security prison while still in his teens, Monster learned to write, took on the name Sanyika Shakur, and joined the black nationalist New Afrikan Independence Movement. Shakur's prison-inspired autobiography, Monster, provides a soul-searching account of the life of an L.A. gang member. The purpose of the book, says Shakur, is "to allow my readers the first ever glimpse at South Central from my side of the gun, street, fence, and wall."

Although Shakur's book is a purely personal account, and may hold questions of generalizability for researchers, imagine the difficulties inherent in acquiring this kind of data through the use of survey instruments or other traditional research techniques. Autobiographical accounts, introspection, and many forms of participant observation amount to a kind of phenomenological reporting, in which description leads to understanding and intuition is a better guide to theory building than volumes of quantifiable data.

Verstehen the kind of subjective understanding that can be achieved by criminologists who immerse themselves into the everyday world of the criminals they study.

In a seminal 1997 article, Jeff Ferrell uses the term **verstehen** to describe the kind of subjective understanding that can be achieved by criminologists who immerse themselves into the everyday world of the criminals they study. Criminological *verstehen*, a term derived from the early writings of sociologist Max Weber, means, says Ferrell, "a researcher's subjective understandings of crime's situational meanings and emotions—its moments of pleasure and pain, its emergent logic and excitement—within the larger process of research." Ferrell adds, "[i]t further implies that a researcher, through attentiveness and participation, at least can begin to apprehend and appreciate the specific roles and experiences of criminals, crime victims, crime control agents, and others caught up in the day-to-day reality of crime."[34]

A growing number of criminologists believe that qualitative data-gathering strategies represent the future of criminological research. Martin D. Schwartz and David O. Friedrichs say that this initiative is central to postmodern criminology. As discussed in Chapter 14, postmodern criminology builds upon:

1. a method that can reveal starkly how knowledge is constituted, and can uncover pretensions and contradictions of traditional scholarship in the field.

2. a highlighting of the significance of language and signs in the realm of crime and criminal justice.
3. a source of metaphors and concepts (e.g., "hyperreality") that capture elements of an emerging reality, and the new context and set of conditions in which crime occurs.[35]

"The guiding premise here," say Schwartz and Friedrichs, "is that a postmodernist approach enables us to comprehend at a more appropriate level" than do the more traditional techniques of quantitative criminology, "our knowledge of a dynamic and complex human environment."

⬛ VALUES AND ETHICS IN THE CONDUCT OF RESEARCH

Research, especially that conducted within the social sciences, does not occur in a vacuum. Values enter into all stages of the research process, from the selection of the problem to be studied, to the choice of strategies to address it. In short, research is never entirely free from preconceptions and biases, although much can be done to limit the impact such biases have on the results of research.

The most effective way of controlling the effects of biases is to be aware of them at the outset of the research. If, for example, researchers know that the project they are working on elicits strong personal feelings but necessitates the use of interviewers, then it would be beneficial to strive to hire interviewers who are relatively free of biases or can control the expression of their feelings. Potential data gatherers might themselves be interviewed to determine their values and the likelihood that they might be tempted to interpret the data they gather, or to report it in ways that are biased. Similarly, data gatherers who are prejudiced against subgroups of potential respondents can represent a threat to the validity of the research results. The use of such interviewers may "turn off" some respondents, perhaps through racial innuendo, personal style, mannerisms, and so forth.

Of similar importance are ethical issues which, although they may not affect the validity of research results, can have a significant impact on the lives of both researchers and research subjects. The protection of human subjects, privacy, and **data confidentiality**—in which research data are not shared outside of the research environment—are the most important ethical issues facing researchers today. **Informed consent** is a strategy used by researchers to overcome many of the ethical issues inherent in criminological research. Informed consent means that research subjects will be informed as to the nature of the research about to be conducted, their anticipated role in it, and the uses that will be made of the data they provide. Ethics may also require that data derived from personal interviews or the testing of research subjects be anonymous (not associated with the names of individual subjects) and that raw (unanalyzed) data be destroyed after a specified time interval (often at the completion of the research project).

Federal regulations require a plan for the protection of sensitive information as part of grant proposals submitted to federal agencies. The National Institute of Justice, for example, a major source of grant support for researchers in the area of criminology, has this to say:[36]

Data confidentiality an ethical requirement of social scientific research which stipulates that research data not be shared outside of the research environment.

Informed consent an ethical requirement of social scientific research which specifies that research subjects will be informed as to the nature of the research about to be conducted, their anticipated role in it, and the uses to which the data they provide will be put.

Research that examines individuals' traits and experiences plays a vital part in expanding our knowledge about criminal behavior. It is essential, however, that researchers protect subjects from needless risk of harm or embarrassment and proceed with willing and informed cooperation.

NIJ requires that investigators protect information identifiable to research participants. When information is safeguarded, it is protected by statute from being used in legal proceedings: "[S]uch information and copies thereof shall be immune from legal process, and shall not, without the consent of the person furnishing such information, be admitted as evidence or used for any purpose in any action, suit, or other judicial, legislative, or administrative proceedings" (42 United States Code 3789g).

Some universities, research organizations, and government agencies have established institutional review boards tasked with examining research proposals before they are submitted to funding organizations to determine whether expectations of ethical conduct have been met. Institutional review boards often consist of other researchers with special knowledge of the kinds of ethical issues involved in criminological research.

Participant observation sometimes entails an especially thorny ethical issue. In other words, should researchers themselves violate the law if their research participation appears to require it? The very nature of participant observation is such that researchers of adult criminal activity may at times find themselves placed in situations where they are expected to "go along with the group" in violating the law. Those researching gang activity, for example, have sometimes been asked to transmit potentially incriminating information to other gang members, to act as drug couriers, and even to commit crimes of violence to help establish territorial claims important to members of the gang. Researchers who refuse may endanger not only their research, but themselves. Compliance with the expectations of criminal groups, of course, evokes other kinds of dangers, including the danger of apprehension and prosecution for violations of the criminal law. As one criminologist explains, "criminological (and other) field researchers cannot conveniently distance themselves from their subjects of study, or from the legally uncertain situations in which the subjects may reside, in order to construct safe and 'objective' studies. Instead criminological field research unavoidably entangles those who practice it in complex and ambiguous relations to the subjects and situations of study, to issues of personal and social responsibility, and to law and legality."[37]

Although the dilemma of a participant observer, especially one secretly engaged in research, is a difficult one, some of the best advice on the subject is offered by Frank E. Hagan, who says: "In self-mediating the potential conflicting roles of the criminal justice researcher, it is incumbent on the investigator to enter the setting with eyes wide open. A decision must be made beforehand on the level of commitment to the research endeavor and the analyst's ability to negotiate the likely role conflicts. Although there are no hard and fast rules . . . *the researcher's primary role is that of a scientist.*"[38]

Hagan also suggests that a code of ethics should guide all professional criminologists in their research undertakings. This code, says Hagan, would require the researcher to take the following personal responsibilities.[39]

- Avoid procedures that may harm respondents.
- Honor commitments to respondents and respect reciprocity.
- Exercise objectivity and professional integrity in performing and reporting research.
- Protect confidentiality and privacy of respondents.

▰ WRITING THE RESEARCH REPORT

Following the research and the analysis of data, findings are typically presented in the form of a report or paper in which suggestions for further study may be made. Policy issues, or strategies for addressing the problems identified by the researcher, are also frequently discussed. Charts, graphs, and tables may be included in the body of a research report. Most reports are professional-looking documents prepared on a word processor with a grammar and spell checker, and printed on a laser or ink-jet printer. Some are eventually published in professional journals and a few become staples of the field—frequently cited works that serve to illustrate fundamental criminological or methodological principles.

Most research reports follow a traditional format which has been developed over the years as a generally acceptable way of presenting research results. Following are the component features of professional reports.

- *Title page:* The title page contains information about the report's authors, their institutional or professional affiliations, the date of the report, and, of course, its title. Many report titles consist of a main title and a subtitle. Subtitles generally give more information about the report's subject matter. Although some report titles seem all-inclusive, such as

"The Impact of Family Structure and Quality on Delinquency: A Comparative Assessment of Structural and Functional Factors,"[40]

others are relatively straightforward and to the point, such as

"Comparing Criminal Career Models."[41]

- *Acknowledgments:* Often the author wishes to express appreciation to individuals and/or organizations that facilitated the study or without whose help the study would not have been possible. Sources of grant support, including funding agencies and foundations; individuals and organizations who either participated in the study or were themselves studied; and personnel who facilitated various aspects of the study or production of the report are all frequently acknowledged.
- *Table of contents:* Reports of any length (say, beyond ten or twelve pages) often contain a table of contents. Tables of contents help readers quickly find the needed material and provide structure to the report itself. Any good table of contents will reflect section headings within the body of the report.

- *Preface* (if desired): The purpose of a preface is to allow the author to make observations, often of a personal nature, which might not be appropriate within the body of the report. Reasons for choosing the subject of study, observations about the promise held by the field of study, and wide-ranging statements about the future of criminological research are all frequent topics of prefaces found in research reports.
- *Abstract:* An abstract is a brief (usually one paragraph) summation of the report's findings, allowing readers to gauge, without reading the entire report, whether the subject matter will be of interest to them. In this day of modern electronic information retrieval, abstracts serve the additional function of providing a quick synopsis that can readily be made available to those searching large databases containing many research articles. Reproduced here is a concise and well-written abstract from John M. Hagedorn's study entitled "Homeboys, Dope Fiends, Legits, and New Jacks" that appeared in the May 1994 issue of *Criminology.*[42] Note that this abstract concludes with a one-sentence policy observation.

Milwaukee research finds that most young male adult gang members cannot be described accurately as "committed long-term participants" in the drug economy. Rather, most adult gang members are involved sporadically with drug sales, moving in and out of conventional labor markets at irregular intervals. Four types of male adult gang members are described; only one type has rejected conventional values. Despite relatively high average earnings from drug sales, most gang members would accept full-time jobs with modest wages. This suggests that severe and mandatory penalties for cocaine use and sales should be ended.

- *Introduction:* Most authors write an introductory section as part of their research report. The introduction describes the aim and purpose of the study and provides a general statement of the problem studied. It also furnishes a general conceptual framework for the remainder of the report. The introduction may outline issues related to the problem under study and those which could benefit from further investigation.
- *Review of existing literature:* Most research builds on existing knowledge and makes use of previous findings. To cite a few proverbial observations, although it is not true that "there is nothing new under the sun," when conducting research, it is also "not necessary to reinvent the wheel." In other words, the relevant works of other researchers should be discussed in any report, and the bearing previous studies have upon the present one should be explained. Sometimes researchers who are engaged in literature reviews discover that the questions they wish to study have already been answered, or that someone else has found a more concise way of stating their concerns. Hence, concept development that is merely repetitive, and even data gathering that has already been undertaken, can be avoided by new investigators.
- *Description of existing situation:* Sometimes a description of the existing situation is combined with a report's introduction. If not, then it is appropriate

to elaborate on the problem under study by providing details which describe the conditions existing at the beginning of the study.

- *Statement of the hypotheses:* Research etiquette in criminology frequently requires the statement of a hypothesis to be tested. Most researchers have an idea of what they expect to find. Often they have set out to test a theory or a proposition derived from a theory. Researchers may, for example, wish to test whether the Brady law, which limits handgun sales, has effectively met its goal of reduced deaths by firearms. Any hypothesis should be a clear and concise statement of what the study purports to test. As mentioned previously, hypotheses useful in guiding research are always operationalized, or expressed in terms that are in some way measurable. Descriptive studies, on the other hand, are not designed to prove or disprove assumptions (although they may not be free of them), and such studies may not contain hypotheses.

- *Description of the research plan:* The research design, data-gathering strategies, and plans for statistical analysis should all be described here. This section, although it may be elaborate and lengthy, simply provides an overview of the methodology employed by the researcher, and explains how the problem was investigated and why particular research strategies were chosen.

- *Disclaimers and limitations:* Any research is subject to limitations. Shortages of money, time, personnel, and other resources impose limitations on research undertakings, as do shortcomings in statistical techniques and restrictions on the availability of data. Limitations should be honestly appraised and presented in the research report so that readers will be able to assess their impact on the results that are reported.

- *Findings or results:* Along with an overview of the research as it was actually conducted, the "findings" section provides a statement of research results. Many regard it as the heart of the report. The manner in which results are presented can be crucial for ease of understanding. Some researchers choose to employ tables containing raw numbers, when pictorial forms of representation such as charts and graphs may better facilitate comprehension. Bar charts and pie charts are probably the most commonly employed types of diagrams, although the type of data collected will determine the appropriate format for its presentation.

- *Analysis and discussion:* Once findings have been presented, they should be discussed and analyzed. Not all analysis need be of a quantitative sort. However, much of today's criminological literature is replete with statistical analyses, some of it quite sophisticated. Unfortunately, however, poorly conceptualized research cannot be helped by later analysis, no matter how sophisticated it may be. It is therefore of crucial importance to the success of any research endeavor that early planning—including conceptual development, strategies for data collection, and research designs—be undertaken with an eye toward producing data that will lend themselves to meaningful analysis after data gathering has been completed. The analysis section should also focus on whether the data, as analyzed, support the study's guiding hypotheses.

- *Summary and conclusions:* The summation section encapsulates the study's purpose and findings in a few paragraphs. It may also contain discussion of suggested improvements or recommended solutions to the problem studied based on the evidence produced by the report. Policy implications are also discussed (if at all) in the conclusion of the report, because they are simply broad-based solutions to problems which have been identified.

- *Appendices:* Not all reports contain appendices. Those that do may place sample questionnaires, accompanying cover letters, concise exhibits from literature reviews, detailed statistical tables, copies of letters of support, detailed interview information, and so forth near the end of the document. Appendices should only be used if they serve the purpose of further explicating the report's purpose, methods, or findings. Otherwise appendices may appear to "pad" the report and can discredit the researcher's efforts in the eyes of readers.

- *List of references:* No report is complete without a bibliography or other list of references used in planning the study and in document preparation. Although all items listed in the bibliography may not be referenced within the body of the report, source material should still be listed if it was reviewed and served some purpose in study development. Literature that was examined, for example, may guide the researcher to other material or provide useful insights during the study's overall conceptual formation.

- *Endnotes:* Either endnotes or footnotes may be used to reference quoted sources or to refer readers to supporting documents. Sometimes a combination of footnotes and endnotes is employed. Endnotes, as their name implies, appear at the conclusion of a report (often after the summary but before the appendices), whereas footnotes are found at the bottom of the pages containing the referenced material.

WRITING FOR PUBLICATION

Criminologists often seek to publish the results of their research to share them with others working in the field. The primary medium for such publication consists of refereed professional journals. *Refereed journals* are those that employ the services of peer reviewers to gauge the quality of the manuscripts submitted to them. Although the review process can be time consuming, it is believed to result in the publication of manuscripts that make worthwhile contributions to the field of criminology and in the rejection of those of lesser quality.

Perhaps the best-known professional journals in the field of criminology today are the *American Journal of Criminal Justice, Crime and Delinquency, Crime and Social Justice,* the *Crime Control Digest, Criminal Justice and Behavior, Criminal Justice Ethics,* the *Criminal Justice Policy Review,* the *Criminal Justice Review, Criminology,* the *Journal of Contemporary Criminal Justice,* the *Journal of Crime and Justice,* the *Journal of Criminal Law and Criminology,* the *Journal of Criminal Justice Education,* the *Journal of Research in Crime and Delinquency,* the *Justice Professional, Justice Quarterly,* and *Theoretical Criminology.*

Each journal has its own requirements for manuscript submission. Some require a single copy of a manuscript; others ask for multiple copies. A few journals request manuscript files on disk along with hard copies, and still others are moving toward electronic submission via the Internet. An increasing number of journals have established submission fees, usually in the $10 to $20 range to help defray the costs associated with the review process.

Submission etiquette within the field of criminology demands that an article be sent to only one journal at a time. Simultaneous submissions are disliked and create real difficulties for both authors and editors when articles are accepted by more than one publication. Given the complexities of the review and publications processes, it is probably best to write the editor of any journal to which submission is being contemplated to inquire as to that journal's particular expectations.

Most journals require that manuscripts be prepared according to a particular style, meaning that citations, capitalization, footnoting, abstracts, notes, headings, and subheadings are all expected to conform to the style of other articles published in the same journal. Two of the most prevalent styles are the APA style (the style promulgated by the American Psychological Association) and the ASA or American Sociological Association style.

Most criminological journals, however, utilize a modification of one of these styles. When considering the submission of a manuscript for publication review, it is advisable to write to the editor of the journal in question requesting a style sheet or general stylistic guidelines. Style guides are also available from the American Psychological Association[43] and the American Sociological Association, with third-party publishers making style guides available through university and special-purpose bookstores.

If a research report is not intended for publication, then other styles may be acceptable. Answers to general questions about report writing and style can be found in publications such as Strunk and White's *The Elements of Style*[44] and Mary-Claire van Leunen's *A Handbook for Scholars.*[45]

STUDY CRITICAL OF D.A.R.E. REJECTED

The interplay between politics and research is well demonstrated by the following story, which shows what can happen when research results don't support the interests of influential groups. Although the research discussed here was originally reported in 1993, a comprehensive review of repeated evaluations of the same program found that it was generally ineffective in reducing drug use.[1]

The federal government has decided not to publish a new study that concludes D.A.R.E., the nation's largest drug education effort, is not effective at reducing youth drug use.

The Justice Department says it rejected the federally funded study because the government disagrees with conclusions that D.A.R.E. has no statistically significant effect on drug use and was less effective than other programs.

"We're not trying to hide the study," says the National Institute of Justice's Ann Voit. "We just do not agree with one of the major findings."

Project D.A.R.E. participants. In the real world few studies are value free. Studies of Project D.A.R.E. have questioned its effectiveness, but government sponsors decided not to publish the results. How can the objectivity of social scientific research be ensured? *Mark Burnett/Stock Boston.*

D.A.R.E. spokeswoman Roberta Silverman faulted the study as "old data from old studies about a curriculum that's not taught any more." She says D.A.R.E. is now more interactive with students, who are taught D.A.R.E.'s antidrug message in just over half the USA's school systems.

D.A.R.E. has attacked the study since early results were revealed at a conference in March 1993.

"We're proud to have the support of the Department of Justice," says D.A.R.E. America executive director Glenn Levant in a statement.

The government's decision not to publish was criticized by scientists, including the head of D.A.R.E.'s scientific advisory board.

"As a scientist, I'm much happier having the data out so we can debate it," says Herb Kleber, head of the D.A.R.E. scientific board.

Tom Colthurst, head of drug studies at the University of California–San Diego, also says the study should be published. "Science loses something when this happens," he says.

D.A.R.E.—Drug Abuse Resistance Education—gets $700 million a year from the Justice Department, Education Department, local governments, and private donors.

But the eleven-year-old program has been haunted by studies that have found it ineffective.

In 1991, the National Institute of Justice hired the Research Triangle Institute, a respected research firm in North Carolina, to do an extensive study of D.A.R.E., including a statistical analysis of all D.A.R.E. studies.

D.A.R.E. originally supported the study. A 1992 letter to state coordinators urged cooperation: "The review of the D.A.R.E. evaluation literature will give us ammunition to respond to critics who charge that D.A.R.E. has not proven its effectiveness."

But D.A.R.E. began to criticize the study after researchers failed to find statistical evidence that D.A.R.E. had an effect on drug use.

Research Triangle Institute researcher Susan Ennett says the report, which analyzed eight studies involving 9,300 children, is valid. It should help decide how to spend drug education money, she says.

Today, in contrast to the National Institute of Justice, the most prestigious academic journal in the field will publish the study's results. The *American Journal of Public Health* says the D.A.R.E. study passed rigorous scrutiny by its academic experts.

And it criticized D.A.R.E. for pressuring it to withdraw the study from its September issue.

"D.A.R.E. has tried to interfere with the publication of this," says the journal's Sabine Beisler. "They tried to intimidate us."

D.A.R.E.'s Silverman says she asked that the article be pulled because "we felt it was highly inappropriate for the broad study to come out before NIJ released its findings."

After learning the journal planned to publish the results, the National Institute of Justice on Thursday released a two-page summary of the study, focusing on D.A.R.E.'s popularity. It briefly mentioned D.A.R.E.'s failure to reduce drug use but gave no details.

National Institute of Justice director Jeremy Travis, a police department lawyer until last month, says he did not succumb to pressure from D.A.R.E. He says his group won't publish the report because its independent reviewers unanimously recommended against it.

But reviewer William DeJong says he never advised against publishing the study. "They may be misremembering what I said," says DeJong, a Harvard lecturer.

He says the study should have been more careful in choosing drug education programs to compare with D.A.R.E. Also, he says drug use among adolescents, some in the fifth grade, is so low it's hard to measure.

Questions

1. Government spokespersons cited here say they "disagree with findings" of the D.A.R.E. study. How might they arrive at such a conclusion independent of other studies?
2. Do you believe it would be more productive for critics to challenge a study's findings, or its methods? Why?
3. Do you believe that quality research should be published regardless of the findings it reports, or do you believe that political considerations should play a role in deciding which studies will be published? Give reasons for your position.

1. See Office of Justice Programs, *Preventing Crime: What Works, What Doesn't, What's Promising* (Washington, D.C.: U.S. Dept. of Justice, 1997).
Source: Dennis Cauchon, "Study Critical of D.A.R.E. Rejected," *USA Today,* October 4, 1994, p. 2A. Copyright 1994, *USA Today.* Reprinted with permission.

▓ SOCIAL POLICY AND CRIMINOLOGICAL RESEARCH

A few years ago Joan Petersilia, then-president of the American Society of Criminology, used the occasion of her 1990 presidential address to identify how research funded by the National Institute of Justice had impacted social policy. Petersilia identified five such areas. Research, she said,[46] has

1. shaped the way police respond to calls for service and how they are deployed;
2. helped to identify career criminals and has provided information about their behavior, along with suggestions on how best to deal with such people;
3. improved the ability of judges, correctional officials, and others to classify offenders and to predict recidivism;
4. provided useful information about the relationship between drug use and crime; and
5. confirmed that no particular rehabilitation program "necessarily" reduces recidivism.

Although research in the area of criminology may have much to offer policymakers, publicly elected officials are often either ignorant of current research or do not heed the advice of professional criminologists, seeking instead to create politically expedient policies. Even when excellent research is available to guide policy creation, a realistic appraisal must recognize that criminologists are as much to blame for counterproductive policies as anyone.

As Robert Bohm explained in his 1993 presidential address to the Academy of Criminal Justice Sciences: "Besides powerful critiquing of both existing and proposed policies, many of us have the capability of producing reasoned analyses and proposals based on historical, theoretical, and cross-cultural understanding. Yet . . . much of our work is simply ignored because it is not politically expedient or does not serve the dominant ideology. At the same time, others among us are more than willing to do the bidding of politicians and criminal justice officials in order to feed at the trough of political largess. I don't know whether these people actually believe in what they are doing, or maybe they still believe in the myth that their work is objective or value-neutral. In either case, these apologists for the status quo legitimize and perpetuate . . . short-sighted, counterproductive, detrimental policies . . . and do a disservice to our discipline."[47]

"Three-strikes" laws, which became popular with legislatures across the country over the last decade, provide an example of the kind of dilemma facing criminologists who would influence social policy on the basis of statistical evidence. Three-strikes laws require that three-time felons receive lengthy prison sentences (often life without the possibility of parole) following their third conviction. Such laws are built on the commonsense notion that "getting tough" on repeat offenders by putting them in prison for long periods should reduce the crime rate. Logic seems to say that lengthy prison sentences for recidivists will reduce crime by removing the most dangerous offenders from society.

A 1997 study of the three-strikes laws in twenty-two states, however, concluded that such legislation typically results in clogged court systems and crowded correctional facilities, and encourages three-time felons to take dramatic risks to avoid capture.[48] A wider-based study,[49] dubbed "the most comprehensive study ever of crime prevention,"[50] found that "much of the research on prisons was inadequate or flawed, making it impossible to measure how much crime was actually prevented or deterred by locking up more criminals." More significantly, the central finding of the massive 1997 study, which was sponsored by the federal Office of Justice Programs and carried out by researchers at the University of Maryland's Department of Criminology and Criminal Justice, was that current government-sponsored crime prevention initiatives—totaling over $3 billion annually—are often poorly evaluated, leading to uncertainty over whether funded programs actually "work." The study, a **meta-analysis** (i.e., a study of other studies), reviewed more than 500 impact evaluations of local crime prevention programs and practices throughout the nation. Researchers concluded that due to largely ineffective evaluation efforts which are often only loosely tied to funded programs, "the current [government-sponsored research] plan does not . . . provide effective guidance to the nation about what works to prevent crime." Hence, although the three-strikes laws remain popular with the voting public, and lawmakers have been quick to seize upon get-tough crime prevention policies in the interest of vote-getting, solid and consistent research support showing the efficacy of such laws continues to be elusive.

Meta-analysis a study of other studies about a particular topic of interest.

⸭

THE AMERICAN SOCIETY OF CRIMINOLOGY TASK FORCE REPORTS

At the 1994 annual meeting of the American Society of Criminology (ASC), Attorney General Janet Reno appealed to the nation's assembled criminologists for urgent assistance in dealing with some of the major crime and criminal justice issues facing the country. Her address to conventioneers identified 12 important problem areas, and she challenged Society members to translate existing research findings into useful recommendations that could benefit practitioners and policymakers throughout the nation who routinely confront issues of crime and justice.

Following her presentation, the ASC National Policy Committee formed 12 task forces—one to investigate each issue identified by the Attorney General. Task Force members were asked to distill research findings into policy recommendations that could meaningfully contribute to public debates which were then raging (and are still continuing) over how best to deal with problems of crime, juvenile delinquency, prison overcrowding, and so on.

In 1997, after all 12 Task Forces had submitted final reports to the Attorney General, each report was published by the National Institute of Justice (NIJ), and made available through the National Criminal Justice Reference Service. At the time of publication Freda Adler, former ASC president, noted: "Many of the[se] findings have already found their way into the policymaking process; others are likely to follow the same path." Jeremy Travis, Director of the National Institute of Justice, termed the reports a "remarkable contribution to improving our understanding of the issues of crime and the challenge of justice."

Titles of the Task Force reports are:

- Early Prevention of and Intervention for Delinquency and Related Problem Behavior
- Youth Violence
- A New Vision for Inner-City Schools
- Drug Policy Options: Lessons From Three Epidemics
- Drugs and the Community
- Violence Against Women
- Domestic and International Organized Crime
- Designing Out Crime
- The State of the Police
- A Crime Control Rationale for Reinvesting in Community Corrections
- Three-Strikes Legislation: Prevalence and Definitions
- American Crime Problems From a Global Perspective

Task force reports are available in their entirety in text-only format from the National Criminal Justice Reference Service's World Wide Web site (http://www.ncjrs.org), or may be viewed at the Criminology Today web site (where they are available in both html and Adobe Acrobat® format).

Source: National Institute of Justice, *Critical Criminal Justice Issues: Task Force Reports From the American Society of Criminology* (Washington, D.C.: NIJ, May 1997).

SUMMARY

Criminology—like its sister disciplines of sociology, psychology, geography, and political science—is a social science which endeavors to apply the techniques of data collection and hypothesis testing through observation and experimentation. Successful hypothesis testing can lead to theory building and to a more complete understanding of the nature of crime and crime causation. Although the scientific framework and its techniques have largely been inherited from the physical sciences—such as chemistry, astronomy, and physics—in which they have been well established for centuries, criminology has been accepted into the scientific tradition by all but the most hard-nosed purists. Even so, criminologists are still game to study aspects of the field which are "in need of study" even where adequate resources (funding) or techniques (for example, the complete mapping of all human chromosomes) are not yet available.

Another component of scientific criminology, the detailed description of crime and related phenomena even where meaningful hypotheses are lacking, is also very much with us. In one descriptive area alone, that of crime statistics (discussed in

WEB WATCH

Access the *Criminology Today* home page on the World Wide Web by pointing your browser at www.prenhall.com/cjcentral. Once there, click on *Criminology Today* in order to access the wealth of electronic resources supporting this text.

Onsite resources include (1) "Chapter Links," which provides succinct overviews of critical ideas from the textbook and links selected materials from around the Web to concepts found in the text; (2) "General Reference—Law and Justice Links." Organized by chapter, these links lead to other useful resources on the World Wide Web, such as libraries, electronic discussion lists, and electronic journals; (3) "Criminology Sites on the Web," which lists links to organizations such as the American Society of Criminology and the National Organization for Victims Assistance (NOVA), as well as crime prevention links and statistics on crime and justice. Many other Web-based resources can be accessed via the *Criminology Today* site, including the federal Justice Information Center, the Bureau of Justice Statistics, the FBI, the RAND Corporation, the Vera Institute of Justice, PAVNET (an online "Partnership Against Violence," run by seven different federal agencies), and the National White Collar Crime Center.

Still another feature of the *Criminology Today* Web site is e-mail homework. Homework can be composed onsite and submitted to instructors using the instructor's e-mail address. To use the e-mail homework feature, click on "E-Mail Homework" on the opening page, and then type answers to the questions that appear in the spaces provided. Use your instructor's e-mail address to submit homework answers. The *Criminology Today* Web site also provides links to powerful Web-based search engines that can help you find topics of interest to you as you progress through your course of study. Search engines can be found under the home page heading "Criminology Sites on the Web."

Of special interest to this chapter, you may read or download the study conducted by the University of Maryland's Department of Criminology and Criminal Justice which is referred to at the conclusion of this chapter by visiting the site and clicking on "What Works." The complete study, called "Preventing Crime: What Works, What Doesn't, What's Promising," is available in HTML format but is over 500 pages in length. A summary version of the study is also available at the *Criminology Today* Web site.

Chapter 2), so much data have already been gathered that it is unlikely they will ever be completely analyzed.

The fondest hope of many criminologists today is that effective research into the causes of crime, coupled with meaningful evaluations of crime prevention efforts, will one day significantly influence social policy mandates, resulting in legislation and government-sponsored initiatives built on programs demonstrated to be effective.

DISCUSSION QUESTIONS

⊞

1. This book emphasizes a social problems versus social responsibility theme. How might a thorough research agenda allow us to decide which perspective is the most fruitful in combating crime?
2. What is a *hypothesis?* What does it mean to operationalize a hypothesis? Why is operationalization necessary?
3. What is a *theory?* Why is the task of criminological theory construction so demanding? How do we know if a theory is any good?
4. Explain experimental research. How might a good research design be diagrammed? What kinds of threats to the validity of research designs can you identify? How can such threats be controlled or eliminated?
5. List and describe the various types of data-gathering strategies discussed in this chapter. Is any one technique "better" than another? Why or why not? Under what kinds of conditions might certain types of data-gathering strategies be most appropriate?
6. What is the difference between qualitative and quantitative research? What are the advantages and disadvantages of each?

NOTES

⊞

[1] Hermann Mannheim, *Comparative Criminology* (Boston: Houghton Mifflin, 1967), p. 73.

[2] John Monahan, "The Causes of Violence," *FBI Law Enforcement Bulletin,* January 1994, p. 14.

[3] Abraham Kaplan, *The Conduct of Inquiry: Methodology for Behavioral Science* (San Francisco: Chandler, 1964), p. 145.

[4] As discussed by Piers Beirne and Colin Sumner, "Editorial Statement," *Theoretical Criminology: An International Journal,* vol. 1, no. 1 (February 1997), pp. 5–11.

[5] Mannheim, *Comparative Criminology,* p. 20.

[6] Don M. Gottfredson, "Criminology Theories: The Truth as Told by Mark Twain," in William S. Laufer and Freda Adler, eds., *Advances in Criminological Theory,* vol. 1 (New Brunswick, N.J.: Transaction, 1989), p. 3.

[7] Kenneth R. Hoover, *The Elements of Social Scientific Thinking,* 5th ed. (New York: St. Martin's, 1992).

[8] Ibid., p. 35.

[9] Bernard P. Cohen, *Developing Sociological Knowledge: Theory and Method,* 2nd ed. (Chicago: Nelson-Hall, 1989), p. 13.

[10] Ibid., p. 71.

[11] Susette M. Talarico, *Criminal Justice Research: Approaches, Problems and Policy* (Cincinnati: Anderson, 1980), p. 3.

[12] For a good review of secondary research, see J. H. Laub, R. J. Sampson, and K. Kiger, "Assessing the Potential of Secondary Data Analysis: A New Look at the Glueck's Unraveling Juvenile Delinquency Data," in Kimberly L. Kempf, ed., *Measurement Issues in Criminology* (New York: Springer-Verlag, 1990), pp. 241–257; and Robert J. Sampson and John H. Laub, *Crime in the Making* (Cambridge, Mass.: Harvard University Press, 1993).

[13] Ibid., p. 3.

[14] Larry S. Miller and John T. Whitehead, *Introduction to Criminal Justice Research and Methods* (Cincinnati: Anderson, 1996).

[15] Donald T. Campbell and Julian C. Stanley, *Experimental and Quasi-Experimental Designs for Research* (Chicago: Rand McNally, 1966), p. 35.

[16] As identified in Donald T. Campbell and Julian C. Stanley, *Experimental and Quasi-Experimental Designs for Research* (Chicago: Rand McNally, 1966), p. 5, from which many of the descriptions that follow are taken.

[17]Ibid., p. 34.

[18]Frank E. Hagan, *Research Methods in Criminal Justice and Criminology* (New York: Macmillan, 1993), p. 103.

[19]Jeff Ferrell, "Criminological *Verstehen:* Inside the Immediacy of Crime," *Justice Quarterly,* vol. 14, no. 1 (1997), p. 11.

[20]William Foote Whyte, *Street Corner Society: The Social Structure of an Italian Slum* (Chicago: University of Chicago Press, 1943), pp. v–vii.

[21]Ibid., p. vii.

[22]Hagan, *Research Methods in Criminal Justice and Criminology,* p. 192.

[23]Nicole Vanden Heuvel, *Directory of Criminal Justice Information Sources,* 8th ed. (Washington, D.C.: National Institute of Justice, 1992), p. 145.

[24]Joyce Hutchinson, *Directory of Criminal Justice Information Sources,* 9th ed. (Washington, D.C.: National Institute of Justice, 1994).

[25]Hagan, *Research Methods in Criminal Justice and Criminology,* p. 218.

[26]Hoover, *The Elements of Social Scientific Thinking,* p. 34.

[27]Kaplan, *The Conduct of Inquiry,* p. 134.

[28]As reported in ibid.

[29]Avshalom Caspim, Terrie E. Moffitt, Phil A. Silva, Magda Stouthamer-Loeber, Robert F. Krueger, and Pamela S. Schmutte, "Are Some People Crime-Prone? Replications of the Personality-Crime Relationship Across Countries, Genders, Races, and Methods," *Criminology,* vol. 32, no. 2 (May 1994), pp. 163–195.

[30]Kaplan, *The Conduct of Inquiry,* p. 172.

[31]Mannheim, *Comparative Criminology,* p. 87.

[32]Of course, as with almost anything else, qualitative data can be assigned to categories and the categories numbered. Hence qualitative data can be quantified, although the worth of such effort is subject to debate.

[33]Sanyika Shakur, *Monster: The Autobiography of an L.A. Gang Member* (New York: Penguin Books, 1993), pp. 45–46.

[34]Jeff Ferrell, "Criminological *Verstehen:* Inside the Immediacy of Crime," *Justice Quarterly,* vol. 14, no. 1 (1997), p. 10.

[35]Martin D. Schwartz and David O. Friedrichs, "Postmodern Thought and Criminological Discontent: New Metaphors for Understanding Violence," *Criminology,* vol. 32, no. 2 (May 1994), pp. 221–246.

[36]National Institute of Justice, 1994–95 NIJ Program Plan (Washington, D.C.: NIJ, 1993), p. 21.

[37]Jeff Ferrell, "Criminological *Verstehen:* Inside the Immediacy of Crime," *Justice Quarterly,* vol. 14, no. 1 (1997), p. 8.

[38]Hagan, *Research Methods in Criminal Justice and Criminology,* pp. 31–32.

[39]Ibid., p. 42.

[40]Patricia Van Voorhis, Francis T. Cullin, Richard A. Mathers, and Connie Chenoweth Garner, "The Impact of Family Structure and Quality on Delinquency: A Comparative Assessment of Structural and Functional Factors," *Criminology,* vol. 26, no. 2 (May 1988), pp. 235–261.

[41]David F. Greenberg, "Comparing Criminal Career Methods," *Criminology,* vol. 30, no. 1 (February 1992), pp. 133–140.

[42]John M. Hagedorn, "Homeboys, Dope Fiends, Legits, and New Jacks," *Criminology,* vol. 32, no. 2 (May 1994), p. 197.

[43]American Psychological Association, *Publication Manual of the American Psychological Association* (Washington, D.C.: APA, 1994).

[44]William Strunk, Jr., and E. B. White, *The Elements of Style,* 3rd ed. (New York: Macmillan, 1979, and later editions).

[45]Mary-Claire van Leunen, *A Handbook for Scholars,* rev. ed. (Oxford: Oxford University Press, 1992).

[46]Joan Petersilia, "Policy Relevance and the Future of Criminology—The American Society of Criminology, 1990 Presidential Address," *Criminology,* vol. 29, no. 1, 1991, pp. 1–15.

[47]Robert M. Bohm, "On the State of Criminal Justice: 1993 Presidential Address to the Academy of Criminal Justice Sciences," *Justice Quarterly,* vol. 10, no. 4 (December 1993), p. 537.

[48]The Campaign for an Effective Crime Policy, *The Impact of Three Strikes and You're Out Laws: What Have We Learned?* (Washington, D.C.: CECP, 1997).

[49]Lawrence W. Sherman, Denise Gottfredson, Doris MacKenzie, John Eck, Peter Reuter, Shawn Bushway, et al., *Preventing Crime: What Works, What Doesn't, What's Promising* (Washington, D.C.: National Institute of Justice, 1997).

[50]Fox Butterfield, no headline, *New York Times News Service* online, April 16, 1997, 7:06 EST.

PART TWO

CRIME CAUSATION

The only way to get out is to die.

—*Eleven-year-old Eric Norah, after attending the funeral of his classmate Robert Sandifer,*
killed in a gang shooting in Chicago as police sought him on murder charges.

G.pe Rossi dis.   G.pe Benaglia inc.

THE CLASSICAL THINKERS

What we don't see is that freedom is not a concept in which people can do anything they want, be anything they can be. Freedom is about authority. Freedom is about the willingness of every single human being to cede to lawful authority a great deal of discretion about what you do.

—NYC MAYOR RUDOLPH W. GIULIANI

Nature has placed mankind under the governance of two sovereign masters, pain and pleasure.

—JEREMY BENTHAM[1]

The more promptly and the more closely punishment follows upon the commission of a crime, the more just and useful will it be.

—CESARE BECCARIA[2]

❖ CHAPTER OUTLINE ❖

⟽ IMPORTANT NAMES ⟾

Jean-Jacques Rousseau	Thomas Hobbes	John Locke
Montesquieu	Cesare Beccaria	Jeremy Bentham
Thomas Paine	William Graham Sumner	

⟽ IMPORTANT TERMS ⟾

social contract	natural law	natural rights
the Enlightenment	trephination	folkways
mores	*mala in se*	*mala prohibita*
Code of Hammurabi	Twelve Tables	common law
deterrence	hedonistic calculus	utilitarianism
Panopticon	retribution	just deserts model
specific deterrence	general deterrence	recidivism
incapacitation	classical school	dangerousness
recidivism rate	neoclassical criminology	capital punishment
law and order	individual rights	
advocates	advocates	

❖ INTRODUCTION

A few years ago, at a conference sponsored by The *New York Post,* New York City Mayor Rudolph W. Giuliani confronted issues of crime and social responsibility head on. In his speech, Giuliani laid the crux of the crime problem at the feet of what he called the tension between personal freedoms and individual responsibilities. We mistakenly look to government and elected officials, Giuliani said, to take on responsibility for solving the problem of crime when, instead, it is each individual citizen who must become accountable for fixing what is wrong with society today. In the mayor's words, "We only see the oppressive side of authority. . . . What we don't see is that freedom is not a concept in which people can do anything they want, be anything they can be. Freedom is about authority. Freedom is about the willingness of every single human being to cede to lawful authority a great deal of discretion about what you do."

"The fact is," the mayor continued, "that we're fooling people if we suggest to them the solutions to these very, very deep-seated problems are going to be found in government. . . . The solutions are going to be found when we figure out as a society what our families are going to be like in the next century, and how maybe they are going to be different. They are going to have to be just as solid and just as strong in teaching every single youngster their responsibility for citizenship. We're going to find the answer when schools once again train citizens. . . . If we don't do that, it's very hard to hold us together as a country, because it's shared values that hold us together. We're going to come through this when we realize that it's all about, ultimately, individual responsibility. That, in fact, the criminal act is about individual responsibility and the building of respect for law and ethics is also a matter of individual responsibility."

Many of the problems facing Guiliani's administration, including rampant crime, and what the mayor sees as an overemphasis on individual rights at the expense of group responsibility, have roots that go back centuries to the time of the Enlightenment and to the American and French Revolutions. We shall discuss that era shortly, following some additional introductory comments.

◼️ MAJOR PRINCIPLES OF THE CLASSICAL SCHOOL

This brief section serves to summarize the central features of the classical school of criminological thought. Each of the points listed in this discussion can be found elsewhere in this chapter, where they are discussed in more detail. The present cursory overview, however, is intended to provide more than a summation—it is meant to be a guide to the rest of this chapter.

Most classical theories of crime causation make the following basic assumptions.

- Human beings are fundamentally rational, and most human behavior is the result of free will coupled with rational choice.
- Pain and pleasure are the two central determinants of human behavior.
- Punishment, a necessary evil, is sometimes required to deter law violators and to serve as an example to others who would also violate the law.
- Root principles of right and wrong are inherent in the nature of things, and cannot be denied.
- Society exists to provide benefits to individuals which they would not receive in isolation.

- When men and women band together for the protection offered by society, they forfeit some of the benefits which accrue from living in isolation.
- Certain key rights of individuals are inherent in the nature of things, and governments that contravene those rights should be disbanded.
- Crime disparages the quality of the bond that exists between individuals and society, and is therefore an immoral form of behavior.

▪▪ FORERUNNERS OF CLASSICAL THOUGHT

The notion of crime as a violation of established law did not exist in the most primitive of preliterate societies. The lack of lawmaking bodies, the paucity of formal written laws, and loose social bonds precluded the concept of crime as law violation. All human societies, however, from the simplest to the most advanced, evidence their own widely held notions of right and wrong. Sociologists term such fundamental concepts of morality and propriety as mores and folkways. Mores, folkways, and laws were terms used by **William Graham Sumner**[3] near the start of the twentieth century to describe the three basic forms of behavioral strictures imposed by social groups upon their members. According to Sumner, mores and folkways govern behavior in relatively small primitive societies, whereas in large, complex societies, they are reinforced and formalized through written laws.

Mores consist of proscriptions covering potentially serious violations of a group's values. Murder, rape, and robbery, for example, would probably be repugnant to the mores of any social group. **Folkways,** on the other hand, are simply time-honored customs, and although they carry the force of tradition, their violation is less likely to threaten the survival of the social group. The fact that American men have traditionally worn little jewelry illustrates a folkway which has given way in recent years to various types of male adornment, including earrings, gold chains, and even makeup. Mores and folkways, although they may be powerful determinants of behavior, are nonetheless informal, because only laws, from among Sumner's trinity, have been codified into formal strictures wielded by institutions and created specifically for enforcement purposes.

Another method of categorizing socially proscriptive rules is provided by some criminologists who divide crimes into the dual categories of *mala in se* and *mala prohibita*. Acts that are **mala in se** are said to be fundamentally wrong, regardless of the time or place in which they occur. Forcing someone to have sex against his or her will and the intentional killing of children are sometimes given as examples of behavior thought to be *mala in se*. Those who argue for the existence of *mala in se* offenses as a useful heuristic category usually point to some fundamental rule, such as religious teachings (the Ten Commandments, the Koran, etc.), to support their belief that some acts are inherently wrong. Such a perspective assumes that uncompromisable standards for human behavior rest within the very fabric of lived experience.

Mala prohibita offenses are those acts that are said to be wrong for the simple reason that they are prohibited. So-called victimless or social order offenses such as prostitution, gambling, drug use, and premarital sexual behavior provide examples

Mores behavioral proscriptions covering potentially serious violations of a group's values. Examples might include strictures against murder, rape, and robbery.

Folkways time-honored customs. Although folkways carry the force of tradition, their violation is unlikely to threaten the survival of the social group.

Mala in se acts that are thought to be wrong in and of themselves.

Mala prohibita acts that are wrong only because they are prohibited.

of *mala prohibita* offenses. The status of such behaviors as *mala prohibita* is further supported by the fact that they are not necessarily crimes in every jurisdiction. Prostitution, for example, is legal in parts of Nevada, as is gambling. Gambling, mainly because of the huge revenue potential it holds, is being rapidly legalized in many areas while it remains illegal in others.

THE DEMONIC ERA

Since time began humankind has been preoccupied with what appears to be an ongoing war between good and evil. Oftentimes evil has appeared in impersonal guise, as when the great bubonic plague, also known as the Black Death, ravaged Europe and Asia in the fourteenth century, leaving as much as three-quarters of the population dead in a mere span of twenty years. At other times evil has seemed to wear a human face, as when the Nazi Holocaust claimed millions of Jewish lives during World War II.

Whatever its manifestation, the very presence of evil in the world has begged for interpretation, and sage minds throughout human history have advanced many explanations for the evil conditions that individuals and social groups have at times been forced to endure. Some forms of evil, such as the plague and the Holocaust, appear cosmically based whereas others—including personal victimization, criminality, and singular instances of deviance—are the undeniable result of individual behavior. Cosmic-level evil has been explained by ideas as diverse as divine punishment, karma, fate, and the vengeful activities of offended gods. Early explanations of personal deviance ranged from demonic possession to spiritual influences to temptation by fallen angels—and even led to the positing of commerce between supernatural entities such as demons, werewolves, vampires, and ghosts and human beings.

Archeologists have unearthed skeletal remains which provide evidence that some early human societies believed outlandish behavior among individuals was a consequence of spirit possession. Carefully unearthed skulls, dated by various techniques to approximately 40,000 years ago, show signs of early cranial surgery, or **trephination,** apparently intended to release evil spirits thought to be residing within the heads of offenders. Such surgical interventions were undoubtedly crude, and probably involved fermented anesthesia along with flint cutting implements.

As discussed in Chapter 3, any theory gains credence if activity based on it produces results in keeping with what that theory would predict. Hence, spirit possession, as an explanation for deviance, probably appeared well validated by positive behavioral changes in those "patients" who submitted to the surgery called for by the theory. The actual cause of such observed reformation, however, may have been brain infections resulting from unsanitary conditions, accidental slips of the stone knife, or the deterrent power of the pain endured by those undergoing the procedure. Nonetheless, to the uncritical observer the theory of spirit possession as a cause of deviance, and cranial surgery as a treatment technique, might have appeared to be supported by the "evidence" of low rates of future crime.

Trephination a form of surgery, typically involving bone and especially the skull. Early instances of cranial trephination have been taken as evidence for primitive beliefs in spirit possession.

EARLY SOURCES OF THE CRIMINAL LAW

The Code of Hammurabi

Code of Hammurabi an early set of laws established by the Babylonian King Hammurabi, who ruled the ancient city from 1792 to 1750 B.C.

Modern criminal law is the result of a long evolution of legal principles. The **Code of Hammurabi** is one of the first known bodies of law to survive and be available for study today. King Hammurabi ruled the ancient city of Babylon from 1792 to 1750 B.C. and created a legal code consisting of a set of strictures engraved on stone tablets. The Hammurabi laws were originally intended to establish property and other rights and were crucial to the continued growth of Babylon as a significant commercial center. Hammurabi law spoke to issues of theft, property ownership, sexual relationships, and interpersonal violence. As Marvin Wolfgang has observed, "In its day, 1700 B.C., the Hammurabi Code, with its emphasis on **retribution,** amounted to a brilliant advance in penal philosophy mainly because it represented an attempt to keep cruelty within bounds."[4] Prior to the code, captured offenders often faced the most barbarous of punishments, frequently at the hands of revenge-seeking victims, no matter how minor their transgressions had been.

Retribution the act of taking revenge upon a criminal perpetrator.

Early Roman Law

Of considerable significance for our own legal tradition is early Roman law. Roman legions under Emperor Claudius I (10 B.C.–54 A.D.) conquered England in the mid-first century, and Roman authority over "Britannia" was further consolidated by later Roman rulers who built walls and fortifications to keep out the still-hostile Scots. Roman customs, law, and language were forced upon the English population during the succeeding three centuries under the Pax Romana—a peace imposed by the military might of Rome.[5]

Twelve Tables early Roman laws written circa 450 B.C. which regulated family, religious, and economic life.

Early Roman law derived from the **Twelve Tables,** which were written circa 450 B.C. The tables were a collection of basic rules regulating family, religious, and economic life. They appear to have been based on common and fair practices generally accepted among early tribes which existed prior to the establishment of the Roman Republic. Unfortunately, only fragments of the tables survive today.

The best known legal period in Roman history occurred during the reign of Emperor Justinian I (527–565 A.D.). By the end of the sixth century, the Roman Empire had declined substantially in size and influence and was near the end of its life. In what may have been an effort to preserve Roman values and traditions, Justinian undertook the laborious process of distilling Roman laws into a set of writings. The Justinian Code, as these writings came to be known, actually consisted of three lengthy legal documents: (1) the Institutes, (2) the Digest, and (3) the Code itself. Justinian's code distinguished between two major legal categories: public and private laws. Public laws dealt with the organization of the Roman state, its Senate, and governmental offices. Private law concerned itself with contracts, personal possessions, the legal status of various types of persons (citizens, free persons, slaves, freedmen, guardians, husbands and wives, and so forth), and injuries to citizens. It contained elements of both our modern civil and criminal law and influenced Western legal thought through the Middle Ages.

Common Law

Common law forms the basis for much of our modern statutory and case law. It has often been called *the* major source of modern criminal law. **Common law** refers to a traditional body of unwritten legal precedents created through everyday practice and supported by court decisions during the Middle Ages in English society. Common law is so called because it was based on shared traditions and standards, rather than on those that varied from one locale to another. As novel situations arose and were handled by British justices, their declarations became the start for any similar future deliberation. These decisions generally incorporated the customs of society as it operated at the time.

Common law was given considerable legitimacy upon the official declaration that it was the law of the land by the English King Edward the Confessor (ruled 1042–1066) in the eleventh century. The authority of common law was further reinforced by the decision of William the Conqueror to use popular customs as the basis for judicial action following his subjugation of Britain in 1066 A.D.

Eventually, court decisions were recorded and made available to *barristers* (the English word for trial lawyers) and judges. As Howard Abadinsky wrote, "Common law involved the transformation of community rules into a national legal system. The controlling element (was) precedent."[6] Today common law forms the basis of many of the laws on the books in English-speaking countries around the world.

Common law a body of unwritten judicial opinion originally based on customary social practices of Anglo-Saxon society during the Middle Ages. (Also discussed in Chapter 1.)

The Magna Carta, an important source of modern Western laws and legal procedure. What are some other important sources of modern criminal law? *Corbis-Bettmann.*

The Magna Carta

The Magna Carta (literally, "great charter") is another important source of modern laws and legal procedure. The Magna Carta was signed on June 15, 1215, by King John of England at Runnymede, under pressure from British barons who took advantage of John's military defeats at the hands of Pope Innocent III and King Philip Augustus of France. The barons demanded a pledge from the king to respect their traditional rights and forced the king to agree to be bound by law.

At the time of its signing, the Magna Carta, although sixty-three chapters in length, was little more than a feudal document[7] listing specific royal concessions. Its original purpose was to ensure feudal rights and to guarantee that the king could not encroach on the privileges claimed by landowning barons. Additionally, the Magna Carta guaranteed the freedom of the church and ensured respect for the customs of towns. Its wording, however, was later interpreted during a judicial revolt in 1613 to support individual rights and jury trials. Sir Edward Coke, chief justice under James I, held that the Magna Carta guaranteed basic liberties for all British citizens and ruled that any acts of Parliament which contravened common law would be void. Some evidence suggests that this famous ruling became the basis for the rise of the U.S. Supreme Court, with its power to nullify laws enacted by Congress.[8] Similarly, one specific provision of the Magna Carta, designed originally to prohibit the king from prosecuting the barons without just cause, was expanded into the concept of "due process of law," a fundamental cornerstone of modern legal procedure. Because of these later interpretations, the Magna Carta has been called "the foundation stone of our present liberties."[9]

THE ENLIGHTENMENT

Enlightenment, (the) also known as the Age of Reason. A social movement that arose during the eighteenth century, and built upon ideas such as empiricism, rationality, free will, humanism, and natural law.

Social contract the Enlightenment-era concept that human beings abandon their natural state of individual freedom to join together and form society. Although, in the process of forming a social contract, individuals surrender some freedoms to society as a whole, government, once formed, is obligated to assume responsibilities toward its citizens and to provide for their protection and welfare.

The Enlightenment, also called the Age of Reason, was a highly significant social movement which occurred during the eighteenth century. The Enlightenment built upon ideas developed by seventeenth-century thinkers such as Francis Bacon (1561–1626), Thomas Hobbes (1588–1679), John Locke (1632–1704), René Descartes (1596–1650), Jean-Jacques Rousseau (1712–1778), Baruch Spinoza (1632–1677), and others. Because of their indirect contributions to classical criminological thought, it will be worthwhile to spend a few paragraphs discussing the writings of a few of these important historical figures.

Thomas Hobbes (1588–1679)

The English philosopher **Thomas Hobbes** developed what many writers regard as an extremely negative view of human nature and social life which he described in his momentous work, *Leviathan* (1651). Hobbes described the natural state of men and women as one that is "nasty, brutish, and short." Fear of violent death, he said, forces human beings into a **social contract** with one another to create a state. The state, according to Hobbes, demands the surrender of certain natural rights and submission to the absolute authority of a sovereign, while offering protection and succor to its citizens in return. Although the social contract concept significantly influenced many of Hobbes's contemporaries, much of his writing was condemned for assuming an overly pessimistic view of both human nature and existing governments.

John Locke (1632–1704)

In 1690 the English philosopher **John Locke** published his *Essay Concerning Human Understanding* (1690), in which he put forth the idea that the natural human condition at birth is akin to that of a blank slate upon which interpersonal encounters and other experiences indelibly inscribe the traits of personality. In contrast to earlier thinkers, who assumed that people are born with certain innate propensities and even rudimentary intellectual concepts and ideas, Locke ascribed the bulk of adult human qualities to life experiences.

In the area of social and political thought, Locke further developed the Hobbesian notion of the social contract. Locke contended that human beings, through a social contract, abandon their natural state of individual freedom and lack of interpersonal responsibility to join together and form society. Although individuals surrender some freedoms to society, government, once formed, is obligated to assume responsibilities toward its citizens and to provide for their protection and welfare. According to Locke and other writers, governments should be required to guarantee certain inalienable rights to their citizens, including the right to life, health, liberty, and possessions. A product of his times, during which the dictatorial nature of monarchies and the Roman church were being much disparaged, Locke stressed the duties which governments have toward their citizens, while paying very little attention to the inverse—the responsibilities of individuals to the societies of which they are a part. As a natural consequence of such an emphasis, Locke argued that political revolutions, under some circumstances, might become an obligation incumbent upon citizens.

Locke also developed the notion of checks and balances between divisions of government, a doctrine that was elaborated by the French jurist and political philosopher Charles Louis de Secondat **Montesquieu** (1689–1755). In *The Spirit of Laws* (1748), Montesquieu wove Locke's notions into the concept of a separation of powers between divisions of government. Both ideas later found a home in the United States Constitution.

Jean-Jacques Rousseau (1712–1778)

The Swiss-French philosopher and political theorist **Jean-Jacques Rousseau** further advanced the notion of the social contract in his treatise of that name (*Social Contract*, 1762). According to Rousseau, human beings are basically good and fair in their natural state, but historically were corrupted by the introduction of shared concepts and joint activities such as property, agriculture, science, and commerce. As a result, the social contract emerged when civilized people agreed to establish governments and systems of education to correct the problems and inequalities brought on by the rise of civilization.

Rousseau also contributed to the notion of **natural law,** a concept originally formulated by St. Thomas Aquinas (1225–1274), Baruch Spinoza (1632–1677), and

Natural law the philosophical perspective that certain immutable laws are fundamental to human nature and can be readily ascertained through reason. Man-made laws, in contrast, are said to derive from human experience and history—both of which are subject to continual change.

others to provide an intuitive basis for the defense of ethical principles and morality. Natural law was used by early Christian church leaders as a powerful argument in support of their interests. Submissive to the authority of the church, secular rulers were pressed to reinforce church doctrine in any laws they decreed. Thomas Aquinas, a well-known supporter of natural law, wrote in his *Summa Theologica* that any man-made law which contradicts natural law is corrupt in the eyes of God. Religious practice, which strongly reflected natural law conceptions, was central to the life of early British society. Hence, natural law, as it was understood at the time, was incorporated into English common law throughout the Middle Ages.

Rousseau agreed with earlier writers that certain immutable laws are fundamental to human nature and can be readily ascertained through reason. Man-made law, in contrast, he claimed, derives from human experience and history—both of which are subject to continual change. Hence man-made law, also termed *positive law,* changes from time to time, and from epoch to epoch. Rousseau expanded the concept of natural law to support emerging democratic principles, and claimed that certain fundamental human and personal rights were inalienable because they were based on the natural order of things.

Natural rights the rights which, according to natural law theorists, individuals retain in the face of government action and interests.

Thomas Paine (1737–1809), the English-American political theorist and author of *The Rights of Man* (1791 and 1792), defended the French Revolution, arguing that only democratic institutions could guarantee the **natural rights** of individuals. At the Second Continental Congress, Thomas Jefferson (1743–1826) and other congressional representatives—many of whom were well versed in the writ-

Thomas Paine (1737–1809) was an important contributor to the concept of natural law. What are the central tenants of natural law? *Corbis-Bettmann.*

ings of Locke and Rousseau—built the Constitution of the United States around an understanding of natural law as they perceived it. Hence, when Jefferson wrote of inalienable rights to "life, liberty, property," he was following in the footsteps of his intellectual forebearers, and meant that such rights were the natural due of all men and women because they were inherent in the social contract between citizens and their government.

Natural law and natural rights have a long intellectual history and are with us today in a number of guises. In a *National Review* article[10] subtitled "If natural law does not permit us to distinguish between men and hogs, what does?" Harry V. Jaffa, director of the Claremont Institute's Center for the Study of the Natural Law, called an 1854 speech given by Abraham Lincoln "the most moving and compelling exhibition of natural-law reasoning in all political history." In that speech Lincoln argued in favor of freedom for slaves by succinctly pointing out that there is no difference between people whatever their color. In Lincoln's words: "Equal justice to the South, it is said, requires us to consent to the extending of slavery to new countries. That is to say, inasmuch as you do not object to my taking my hog to Nebraska, therefore I must not object to your taking your slave. Now, I admit this is perfectly logical, if there is no difference between hogs and Negroes." Lincoln's point, of course, was that there is a huge difference between human beings and animals by virtue of their nature, and that such a difference cannot be denied by logic.

Other commentators have cited the "crimes against humanity" committed by Nazis during World War II as indicative of natural law principles. The chilling testimony of Rudolf Hess,[11] Hitler's deputy, during the 1945 war crimes trial in Nuremberg, Germany, as he recalled the "Fuehrer's" order to exterminate millions of Jews indicates the extent of the planned "final solution." Hess testified: "In the summer of 1941 I was summoned to Berlin to Reichsfuehrer SS Himmler to receive personal orders. He told me something to the effect—I do not remember the exact words—that the Fuehrer had given the order for a final solution of the Jewish question. We, the SS, must carry out that order. If it is not carried out now then the Jews will later on destroy the German people. He had chosen Auschwitz on account of its easy access by rail and also because the extensive site offered space for measures ensuring isolation."[12] Who could argue against the premise, natural law supporters ask, that Hitler's final solution to the Jewish "problem" was inherently wrong?

Although the concept of natural law has waned somewhat in influence over the past half century, many people today still hold that the basis for various existing criminal laws can be found in immutable moral principles, or in some other identifiable aspect of the natural order. The Ten Commandments, "inborn tendencies," the idea of sin, and perceptions of various forms of order in the universe and in the social world have all provided a basis for the assertion that natural law exists. Modern-day advocates of natural law still claim that it comes from outside the social group and that it is knowable through some form of revelation, intuition, or prophecy.

The present debate over abortion is an example of modern-day use of natural law arguments to support both sides in the dispute. Antiabortion forces, frequently called "pro-lifers," claim that an unborn fetus is a person and that he or she is entitled to all the protection that we would give to any other living human being. Such protection, they suggest, is basic and humane and lies in the natural relationship of one human being to another, and within the relationship of a society to its children.

Right-to-lifers are striving for passage of a law, or a reinterpretation of past Supreme Court precedent, that would support their position. Advocates of the present law (which allows abortion upon request under certain conditions) maintain that abortion is a "right" of any pregnant woman because she is the only one who should be in control of her body. Such "pro-choice" groups also claim that the legal system must address the abortion question, but only by way of offering protection to this "natural right" of women.

Perhaps the best known modern instance of natural law debate occurred during confirmation hearings for U.S. Supreme Court Justice Clarence Thomas. Thomas, who was confirmed in 1991, once wrote an opinion in which he argued from a natural law point of view. That opinion was later challenged by Senate Judiciary Committee members who felt that it reflected an unbending judicial attitude.

⬛ THE CLASSICAL SCHOOL

As many authors have pointed out, the Enlightenment fueled the fires of social change, leading eventually to the French and American Revolutions and providing many of the intellectual underpinnings of the U.S. Constitution. The Enlightenment—one of the most powerful intellectual initiatives of the last millennium—also inspired other social movements and freed innovative thinkers from the chains of convention. As a direct consequence of Enlightenment thinking, superstitious beliefs were discarded and men and women began to be perceived, for the first time, as self-determining entities possessing a fundamental freedom of choice. Following the Enlightenment, many supernatural explanations for human behavior fell by the wayside and free will and rational thought came to be recognized as the linchpins of all significant human activity. In effect, the Enlightenment inspired the reexamination of existing doctrines of human behavior from the point of view of rationalism.

Within criminology the Enlightenment led to the development of the **classical school** of criminological thought. Crime and deviance, which had been previously explained by reference to mythological influences and spiritual shortcomings, took their place in Enlightenment thought alongside other forms of human activity as products of the exercise of free will. Once man was seen as self-determining, crime came to be explained as a particularly individualized form of evil, or moral wrongdoing fed by personal choice.

CESARE BECCARIA (1738–1794)

Cesare Beccaria (whose Italian name was Cesare Bonesana, but who held the title Marchese di Beccaria) was born in Milan, Italy. The eldest of four children, he was trained at Catholic schools and earned a doctor of laws degree by the time he was 20.

In 1764 Beccaria published his *Essay on Crimes and Punishments*.[13] Although the work appeared originally in Italian, it was translated in London into English in 1767. Beccaria's *Essay* consisted of forty-two short chapters covering only a few major themes. Beccaria's purpose in penning the *Essay* was not to set forth a theory of

Classical school a criminological perspective operative in the late 1700s and early 1800s which had its roots in the Enlightenment, and which held that men and women are rational beings, that crime is the result of the exercise of free will, and that punishment can be effective in reducing the incidence of crime, as it negates the pleasure to be derived from crime commission.

crime, but to communicate his observations on the laws and justice system of his time. In the *Essay,* Beccaria distilled the notion of the social contract into the idea that "[l]aws are the conditions under which independent and isolated men united to form a society." More than anything else, however, his writings consisted of a philosophy of punishment. Beccaria claimed, for example, that although most criminals are punished based on an assessment of their criminal intent, they should be punished instead based on the degree of injury they cause. The purpose of punishment, he said, should be **deterrence** rather than retribution, and punishment should be imposed to prevent offenders from committing additional crimes. Beccaria saw punishment as a tool to an end and not an end in itself, and crime prevention was more important to him than revenge.

Deterrence the prevention of crime.

To help prevent crimes, Beccaria argued, adjudication and punishment should both be swift, and once punishment is decreed, it should be certain. In his words: "[t]he more promptly and the more closely punishment follows upon the commission of a crime, the more just and useful it will be." Punishment that is imposed immediately following crime commission, claimed Beccaria, is connected with the wrongfulness of the offense, both in the mind of the offender and in the minds of others who might see the punishment imposed and thereby learn of the consequences of involvement in criminal activity.

Beccaria concluded that punishment should be only severe enough to outweigh the personal benefits to be derived from crime commission. Any additional punishment, he argued, would be superfluous. Beccaria's concluding words on punishment are telling. "In order," he said, "for punishment not to be, in every instance, an act of violence of one or of many against a private citizen, it must be essentially public, prompt, necessary, the least possible in the given circumstances, proportionate to the crimes, [and] dictated by the laws."

Beccaria distinguished between three types of crimes—those that threatened the security of the state, those that injured citizens or their property, and those that ran contrary to the social order. Punishment should fit the crime, Beccaria wrote, declaring that theft should be punished through fines, personal injury through corporeal punishment, and serious crimes against the state (such as inciting revolution) via application of the death penalty. Beccaria, however, was opposed to the death penalty in most other circumstances, seeing it as a kind of warfare waged by society against its citizens.

Beccaria condemned the torture of suspects, a practice still used in the eighteenth century, saying that it was a device which ensured that weak suspects would incriminate themselves, while strong ones would be found innocent. Torture, he argued, was also unjust, because it punished individuals before they had been found guilty in a court of law. In Beccaria's words, "No man can be called guilty before a judge has sentenced him, nor can society deprive him of public protection before it has been decided that he has in fact violated the conditions under which such protection was accorded him. What right is it then, if not simply that of might, which empowers a judge to inflict punishment on a citizen while doubt still remains as to his guilt or innocence?"

Beccaria's *Essay* also touched upon a variety of other topics. He distinguished, for example, between two types of proof—that which he called perfect proof in which there was no possibility of innocence and imperfect proof, where some possibility of innocence remained. Beccaria also believed in the efficacy of a jury of one's peers, but recommended that half of any jury panel should consist of peers of the victim, whereas the other half should be made up of peers of the accused. Finally, Beccaria wrote that oaths were useless in a court of law, because accused individuals will naturally deny their guilt even if they know themselves to be fully culpable.

Beccaria's ideas were widely recognized as progressive by his contemporaries. His principles were incorporated into the French penal code of 1791, and significantly influenced the justice-related activities of European leaders such as Catherine the Great of Russia, Frederick the Great of Prussia, and the Austrian Emperor Joseph II. Evidence suggests that Beccaria's *Essay* influenced framers of the American Constitution, and some scholars claim that the first ten amendments to the Constitution, known as the Bill of Rights, might not have existed were it not for Beccaria's emphasis on the rights of individuals in the face of state power. Perhaps more than anyone else, Beccaria is responsible for the contemporary belief that criminals have control over their behavior, that they choose to commit crimes, and that they can be deterred by the threat of punishment.

Jeremy Bentham (1748–1832)

Jeremy Bentham,[14] another founding personality of the classical school, wrote in his *Introduction to the Principles of Morals and Legislation* (1789) that "nature has placed mankind under the governance of two sovereign masters, pain and pleasure." To reduce crime or, as Bentham put it, "to prevent the happening of mischief," the pain of crime commission must outweigh the pleasure to be derived from criminal activity. Bentham's claim rested upon his belief, spawned by Enlightenment thought, that human beings are fundamentally rational and that criminals will weigh in their minds the pain of punishment against any pleasures thought likely to be derived from crime commission.

Bentham advocated neither extreme nor cruel punishment—only punishment sufficiently distasteful to the offender that the discomfort experienced would outweigh the pleasure to be derived from criminal activity. Generally, Bentham argued, the more serious the offense the more reward it holds for its perpetrator and, therefore, the more weighty the official response must be. "Pain and pleasure," said Bentham, "are the instruments the legislator has to work with" in controlling antisocial and criminal behavior.

Hedonistic calculus or **utilitarianism** the belief, first proposed by Jeremy Bentham, that behavior holds value to any individual undertaking it according to the amount of pleasure or pain that it can be expected to produce for that person.

Bentham's approach has been termed **hedonistic calculus** or **utilitarianism** because of its emphasis on the worth any action holds for an individual undertaking it. As Bentham stated, "[b]y the principle of utility is meant that principle which approves or disapproves of every action whatsoever, according to the tendency which it appears to have to augment or diminish the happiness of the party whose interest is in question; or, what is the same thing . . . to promote or to oppose that happiness." In other words, Bentham believed that individuals could be expected to weigh, at least intuitively, the consequences of their behavior before acting so as to maximize their own pleasure and minimize pain. The value of any pleasure, or the inhibitory tendency of any pain, according to Bentham, could be calculated by its intensity, duration, certainty, and immediacy (or remoteness in time).

Jeremy Bentham (1748–1832) whose work is closely associated with the classical school of criminology. What are the key features of the classical school? *Corbis-Bettmann.*

Bentham claimed that nothing was really new in his pleasure-pain perspective. "Nor is this a novel and unwarranted, any more than it is a useless theory," he wrote. "In all this there is nothing but what the practice of mankind, wheresoever they have a clear view of their own interest, is perfectly comfortable to. An article of property, an estate in land, for instance, is valuable, on what account? On account of the pleasures of all kinds which it enables a man to produce, and what comes to the same thing the pains of all kinds which it enables him to avert." In fact, Bentham's ideas were not new, but their application to criminology was. In 1739 David Hume distilled the notion of utilitarianism into a philosophical perspective in his book *A Treatise of Human Nature.* Although Hume's central concern was not to explain crime, scholars who followed Hume observed that human behavior is typically motivated more by self-interest than by anything else.

Like Beccaria, Bentham focused on the potential held by punishment to prevent crime and to act as a deterrent for those considering criminal activity. In any criminal legislation, he wrote, "[t]he evils of punishment must . . . be made to exceed the advantage of the offence." Bentham distinguished between eleven different types of punishment, as follows:

- *capital punishment* or death.
- *afflictive punishment,* which includes whipping and starvation.
- *indelible punishment* such as branding, amputation, and mutilation.
- *ignominious punishment,* such as public punishment involving use of the stocks or pillory.
- *penitential punishment,* whereby an offender might be censured by his or her community.

- *chronic punishment* such as banishment, exile, and imprisonment.
- *restrictive punishment* such as license revocation or administrative sanction.
- *compulsive punishment* which requires an offender to perform a certain action such as to make restitution or keep in touch with a probation officer.
- *pecuniary punishment* involving the use of fines.
- *quasi-pecuniary punishment* in which the offender is denied services which would otherwise be available to him or her.
- *characteristic punishment* such as mandating that prison uniforms be worn by incarcerated offenders.

Utilitarianism is a practical philosophy, and Bentham was quite practical in his suggestions about crime prevention. Every citizen, he said, should have their first and last names tattooed on their wrists for the purpose of facilitating police identification. He also recommended creation of a centralized police force focused on crime prevention and control—a recommendation which found life in the English Metropolitan Police Act of 1829 when it established London's New Police under the direction of Sir Robert Peel.

Panopticon a prison designed by Jeremy Bentham which was to be a circular building with cells along the circumference, each clearly visible from a central location staffed by guards.

Bentham's other major contribution to criminology was his suggestion that prisons be designed along the lines of what he called a Panopticon House. The **Panopticon,** as Bentham envisioned it, was to be a circular building with cells along the circumference, each clearly visible from a central location staffed by guards. Bentham recommended that Panopticons should be constructed near or within cities so that they might serve as examples to others of what would happen to them should they commit crimes. He also wrote that prisons should be managed by contractors who could profit from the labor of prisoners, and that the contractor should "be bound to insure the lives and safe custody of those entrusted to him." Although a Panopticon was never built in Bentham's England, French officials funded a modified version of such a prison which was eventually built at Lyons, and three prisons modeled after the Panopticon concept were constructed in the United States.

Bentham's critics have been quick to point out that punishments seem often not to work. Even punishments as severe as death appear not to have any effect on the incidence of crimes such as murder (a point which we will discuss in greater detail later in this chapter). Such critics forget Bentham's second tenant, however, which is that for punishment to be effective, "it must be swift and certain." For any punishment to have teeth, Bentham said, it must not only mandate a certain degree of displeasure, but must follow almost immediately upon its being decided, and there must be no way of avoiding it.

HERITAGE OF THE CLASSICAL SCHOOL

The classical school was to influence criminological thinking for a long time to come. From the French Revolution and the U.S. Constitution to today's emphasis on deterrence and crime prevention, the classical school has molded the way in which thinkers on the subject of crime have viewed the topic for more than 200 years. The heritage left by the classical school is still operative today in the following five principles, each of which is a fundamental constituent of modern-day perspectives on crime and human behavior:

- *The Principle of Rationality:* Human beings have free will and the actions they undertake are the result of choice.
- *The Principle of Hedonism:* Pleasure and pain, or reward and punishment, are the major determinants of choice.
- *The Principle of Punishment:* Criminal punishment is a deterrent to unlawful behavior, and deterrence is the best justification for punishment.
- *The Human Rights Principle:* Society is made possible by individuals cooperating together. Hence, society owes to its citizens respect for their rights in the face of government action, and for their autonomy insofar as such autonomy can be secured without endangering others or menacing the greater good.
- *The Due Process Principle:* An accused should be presumed innocent until proven otherwise, and an accused should not be subject to punishment prior to guilt being lawfully established.

⋮⋮ NEOCLASSICAL CRIMINOLOGY

As some writers have observed, "[t]here appeared to be a tentative resurgence of the Classical School in the 1970s demonstrated in part by the adoption of determinate sentencing tactics and the reduction of emphasis on rehabilitation."[15] Determinate sentencing is a strategy which mandates a specified and fixed amount of time to be served for every offense category. Under determinate sentencing schemes, for example, judges in affected jurisdictions might be required to impose a seven-year sentence on armed robbers, but only one-year sentences upon strong-arm robbers (who use no weapon). Determinate sentencing schemes build upon the twin notions of classical thought that (1) the pleasure of a given crime can be somewhat accurately assessed, and (2) a fixed amount of punishment necessary for deterrence can be calculated and specified.

Although some writers have loudly proclaimed the death of classical and neoclassical thought, their demise is greatly exaggerated. Two **neoclassical criminology** schools of thought continue to exist today. The first neoclassical school continues to build upon ideas inherent in the notion of a social contract and places an emphasis on individual rights and due process. A second takes the form of three ideas that extend well beyond the calculus of determinate sentencing. Those three ideas are (1) criminal behavior is the result of free choice; (2) criminal behavior is rewarding and crime holds a number of attractions, from sensuality to monetary gain to fame; and (3) criminal punishment is necessary for deterrence. In its modern guise this second type of classical thinking has taken the form of a **just deserts model** of criminal sentencing, with a society-wide emphasis on both deterrence and retribution as the twin goals of criminal punishment. If a person is attracted to crime and chooses to violate the law, modern neoclassical thinkers argue, he or she *deserves* to be punished because the consequences of crime were known to the offender before the crime was committed. Moreover, the criminal *must* be punished, such thinkers propose, so that future criminal behavior can be curtailed. It is the second school of neoclassical thought that is now in ascendancy, and it is to this mode of thought that we turn our attention throughout much of the remainder of this chapter.

Neoclassical criminology a contemporary version of classical criminology which emphasizes deterrence and retribution with reduced emphasis on rehabilitation.

Just deserts model the notion that criminal offenders deserve the punishment they receive at the hands of the law, and that punishments should be appropriate to the type and severity of crime committed.

NOT ALL URGING MERCY
FOR TEEN FACING FLOGGING

The 1994 "caning" of an American teenager in Singapore provided an example of the continuing popularity of the just deserts philosophy in America—as the following story from *USA Today* illustrates.

Michael Fay's father pleaded Sunday for the International Red Cross to intervene. Fay's mother begged for leniency. President Clinton said the penalty outweighs the crime.

But when it comes to the case of the Dayton, Ohio, man who may be flogged—six lashes—for spray-painting cars in Singapore, some Americans have no sympathy, and have written Singapore officials to say so.

The punishment—meted out with a 4-foot-long, half-inch-thick split-bamboo rod called a rotan—is "hardly a spanking," says lawyer Theodore Simon, who represents Fay, 18.

When a prisoner is struck, "pieces of skin and flesh fly at each stroke of the rotan," says Simon. If the prisoner faints, he's revived by a doctor so the flogging can continue.

"This is mutilation, basically," says the father, George Fay of Dayton.

The elder Fay said he thinks his son's confession was coerced and he'll ask Singapore President Ong Teng Cheong for clemency. He also intends to get the International Red Cross to attend and monitor the flogging.

Michael Fay was singled out because he's an American, his father says. Fay's mother, Randy Chan, with whom he lives in Singapore, has lobbied for leniency.

Also:

- A worldwide association of meeting planners is threatening to boycott Singapore unless it grants Fay clemency. "We'll hit Singapore in its pocketbook" if Fay is caned, said Troy Johnson of the Arizona-based International Society of Meeting Planners.
- Clinton has called the punishment extreme and has urged Singapore to reconsider.
- Although the sentence has outraged Fay's parents, more than 100 letters and 200 phone calls in support of the punishment have come from Americans, says Chin Hock Seng of the Singapore Embassy.
- "America should be taking lessons from Singapore on how to prevent crime. Hold the line—don't give in," said a letter from Huntington Beach, Calif.
- "Punish hooligans and enjoy the benefits of a safe, clean society!" said a writer from Fresno, Calif.
- "I urge you to . . . vigorously apply Singapore law to the criminal's rear end," said a writer from Silver Spring, Md.

Chicago Tribune columnist Mike Royko wrote that he had received letters "several inches high," and 99% wrote that "yes, hooray, [Fay] should be flogged."

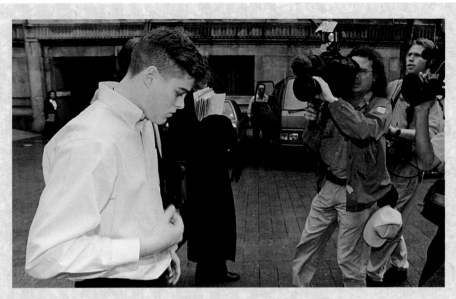

Michael Fay, the 18-year-old American teenager who was caned in Singapore in 1994 for spray-painting cars, makes the "sign of the cross" before entering Singapore's High Court. Should Fay have been caned? *Jonathan Drake/Corbis-Bettman.*

The Dayton *Daily News,* Fay's hometown newspaper, also is getting mail in support of the flogging.

The ordeal began last month when Michael Fay pleaded guilty to a 10-day spree in which he and other foreign students spray-painted and threw eggs, bricks and flower pots at 18 cars. Fay was sentenced to four months in prison, a $2,230 fine and flogging with the split-bamboo cane.

A State Department human-rights report last year criticized caning, and Amnesty International has called it a form of torture.

Michael Fay remained in jail in Singapore, awaiting the outcome of his appeal. No date has been set for the punishment.

As most readers will recall, Fay did not receive clemency and was flogged— a punishment referred to as "caning" in Singapore. Due to American outcry over the event, however, the number of lashes he received was reduced to four. Fay then spent an additional month imprisoned in Singapore before being released and returning to the United States.

Questions

1. Do you believe that corporeal punishments can be an effective response to crime? Why or why not?
2. Do you believe that the caning of Michael Fay was deserved? Why or why not?
3. Do you believe that independent nations, such as Singapore, should be permitted to implement their own sense of justice without American interference? Why or why not?

Source: Carol J. Castaneda, "Not All Urging Mercy for Teen Facing Flogging," *USA Today,* April 4, 1994, p. 3A. Copyright 1994, *USA Today.* Reprinted with permission.

FREE WILL IN NEOCLASSICAL THOUGHT

Representative of today's neoclassical scholars who emphasize the rewards of crime is Jack Katz, whose book *Seductions of Crime*[16] explains crime as the result of what Katz calls the "often wonderful attractions within the lived experience of criminality." Crime, Katz says, is often pleasurable for those committing it and pleasure of one sort or another is the major motivation behind crime. Sometimes, however, the kind of pleasure to be derived from crime is not immediately obvious. Unfortunately, as Katz points out in the following paragraph, few criminologists have been interested in understanding just how crime *feels* to those who commit it.

> The social science literature contains only scattered evidence of what it means, feels, sounds, tastes, or looks like to commit a particular crime. Readers of research on homicide and assault do not hear the slaps and curses, see the pushes and shoves, or feel the humiliation and rage that may build toward the attack, sometimes persisting after the victim's death. . . . How adolescents manage to make the shoplifting or vandalism of cheap and commonplace things a thrilling experience has not been intriguing to many students of delinquency. . . . The description of "cold-blooded, senseless murders" has been left to writers outside the social sciences. Neither academic methods nor academic theories seem to be able to grasp . . . how it makes sense to them to kill when only petty cash is at stake. Sociological and psychological studies of robbery rarely focus on the distinctive attractions of robbery, even though research has now clearly documented that alternative forms of criminality are available and familiar to many career robbers. . . .[17]

For criminal offenders, crime is indeed rewarding, Katz says. It feels good, he tells his readers. "The particular seductions and compulsions [which criminals] experience may be unique to crime," he says, "but the sense of being seduced and compelled is not. To grasp the magic in the criminal's sensuality, we must acknowledge our own." Katz describes the almost sexual attraction shoplifting held for one young offender. As the thief said, "the experience was almost orgasmic for me. There was a buildup of tension as I contemplated the danger of a forbidden act, then a rush of excitement at the moment of committing the crime, and finally a delicious sense of release."[18]

Katz's approach, which stresses the sensual dynamics of criminality, provides a novel explanation for crime—one which says that, for many people, crime is sensually compelling. As one writer states, "Jack Katz argues for a redirection of the criminological gaze—from the traditional focus on background factors such as age, gender, and material conditions to foreground or situational factors that directly precipitate criminal acts and reflect crimes' sensuality."[19]

Another contemporary incarnation of classical thought can be had in "rational choice theory," which is discussed in Chapter 14. Willful (and often calculated) participation in forbidden activity, be it as simple as shoplifting or as felonious as murder, marks the offender in the minds of today's neoclassical thinkers as a candidate for punishment.

PUNISHMENT AND NEOCLASSICAL THOUGHT

Deterrence

True to its historical roots, deterrence is a hallmark of modern neoclassical thought. In contrast to early thinkers, however, today's neoclassical writers distinguish between deterrence that is specific and that which is general. **Specific deterrence** is a goal of criminal sentencing that seeks to prevent a particular offender from engaging in repeat criminality. **General deterrence,** in contrast, works by way of example and seeks to prevent others from committing crimes similar to the one for which a particular offender is being sentenced.

Following their classical counterparts, modern-day advocates of general deterrence frequently stress that for punishment to be an effective impediment to crime it must be swift, certain, and severe enough to outweigh the rewards which flow from criminal activity. Unfortunately, those who advocate punishment as a deterrent are often frustrated by the complexity of today's criminal justice system and the slow and circuitous manner in which cases are handled and punishments are meted out. Punishments today, even when imposed by a court, are rarely swift in their imposition. Swift punishments would follow quickly after sentencing. The wheels of modern criminal justice, however, are relatively slow to grind to a conclusion given the many delays inherent in judicial proceedings and the numerous opportunities for delay and appeal available to defense counsel. Similarly, certainty of punishment is anything but a reality. Certain punishments are those which cannot be easily avoided. However, even when punishments are ordered, they are frequently not carried out—at least not fully. In contemporary America, offenders sentenced to death, for example, are unlikely to ever have their sentences finalized. For those who do, an average of nearly eight years passes between the time a sentence of death is imposed and the time it is carried out.[20] Death row inmates and their lawyers typically barrage any court that will hear them with a plethora of appeals designed to delay or derail the process of justice. Often they win new trials. If they are able to wait long enough, most inmates will find their sentences overturned by blanket U.S. Supreme Court rulings that find fault with some obscure aspect of a state's trial process. Those who are able to delay even longer may die of natural causes before the machinery of the state grinds its way to a conclusion.

If the neoclassicists are correct, ideally criminal punishments should prevent a repetition of crime. Unfortunately, as high rates of contemporary recidivism indicate, punishments in America rarely accomplish that goal. **Recidivism** means, quite simply, the repetition of criminal behavior by those already involved in crime. Recidivism can also be used to measure the success of a given approach to the problem of crime. When so employed it is referred to as a **recidivism rate,** expressed as the percentage of convicted offenders who have been released from prison and who are later rearrested for a new crime, generally within five years following release. Studies show that recidivism rates are high indeed, reaching levels of 80 to 90 percent in some instances, meaning that eight or nine of every ten criminal offenders released from confinement are rearrested for new lawbreaking activity within five years of being set free. Such studies, however, do not measure the numbers of released offenders who return to crime but who are not caught, or who return to

Specific deterrence a goal of criminal sentencing which seeks to prevent a particular offender from engaging in repeat criminality.

General deterrence a goal of criminal sentencing which seeks to prevent others from committing crimes similar to the one for which a particular offender is being sentenced.

Recidivism the repetition of criminal behavior.

Recidivism rate the percentage of convicted offenders who have been released from prison and who are later rearrested for a new crime, generally within five years following release.

crime later than five years after release from prison. Were such numbers available, recidivism rates would likely be even higher.

One reason why American criminal justice seems so ineffectual at preventing crime and reducing recidivism may be that the punishments provided for by contemporary criminal law are rarely applied to the majority of offenders. Statistics show that few lawbreakers are ever arrested, and of those who are, fewer still are convicted of the crimes with which they have been charged. After a lengthy court process, most offenders processed by the justice system are released, fined, or placed on probation. Relatively few are sent to prison, although short of capital punishment, prison is the most severe form of punishment available to authorities today. To represent this situation, criminal justice experts often utilize a diagram known as a "crime funnel." Figure 4.1 shows the crime funnel for 1996. As the figure shows, fewer than 1 percent of criminal law violators in America can be expected to spend time in prison as punishment for their crimes.

Exacerbating the situation further is the fact that few persons sent to prison ever serve anything close to the sentences that have been imposed on them. Many inmates serve only a small fraction of their sentences due to early release made possible by time off for good behavior, mandated reentry training, and the practical considerations necessitated by prison overcrowding.

Neoclassical perspectives are experiencing a contemporary resurgence through a newfound emphasis on the wider use of punishment as a criminal deterrent. A recent *Washington Post* article, for example, unwittingly headlined the modern-day survival of classical notions of crime and punishment when it proclaimed "Failure to Punish Misdemeanors Fuels Violence."[21] The *Post* article was reporting on the fact that more than three of every hundred St. Louis, Missouri, residents are victimized violently every year. In analyzing the data on St. Louis, Thomas Edsall, the article's author, concluded that "the real failing of the criminal justice system is in dealing with the seemingly minor crime and deviant behavior that disrupts communities and is the first step toward violent crime."

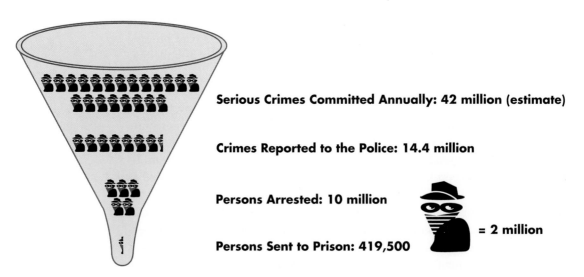

Serious Crimes Committed Annually: 42 million (estimate)

Crimes Reported to the Police: 14.4 million

Persons Arrested: 10 million

= 2 million

Persons Sent to Prison: 419,500

FIGURE 4.1 The Crime Funnel. *Source:* Statistics derived from The Bureau of Justice Statistics, *Sourcebook of Criminal Justice Statistics, 1996* (Washington, D.C.: National Institute of Justice, 1997).

Supporting Edsall's claims were numerous justice systems experts such as St. Louis District Attorney Dee Joyce Hayes. Hayes, reacting to the crime wave which has swept St. Louis for the past few decades, claimed that the real "fraud" in the criminal justice system is that almost "no one convicted of a misdemeanor does jail time" because the nation's prisons and jails are so overcrowded. As a result of this situation, according to the implication, misdemeanants never have the opportunity to learn that criminal behavior can carry with it serious negative consequences. David Barber, Alabama's Jefferson County district attorney, believes Hayes is right. "The hammer doesn't come down on anybody until it's too late," said Barber. "We've reinforced their activity." Such thinking, frequently found among contemporary criminal justice professionals, is part of the heritage left by the classical school.

Just Deserts

The old adages, "he got what was coming to him" or "she got her due," well summarize the thinking behind the just deserts model of criminal sentencing. Just deserts, as discussed earlier in the chapter, refers to the notion that criminal offenders deserve the punishment they receive at the hands of the law, and that any punishment which is imposed should be appropriate to the type and severity of crime committed. The idea of just deserts has long been a part of Western thought, dating back at least to Old Testament times. The Old Testament dictum of "an eye for an eye, and a tooth for a tooth" has been cited by many as divine justification for strict punishments. Some scholars believe, however, that in reality the notion of "an eye for an eye" was intended to reduce the barbarism of existing penalties whereby an aggrieved party might exact the severest of punishments for only minor offenses. Even petty offenses were often punished by whipping, torture, and sometimes death.

One famous modern-day advocate of the just deserts philosophy was the Christian apologist C. S. Lewis, who wrote:

> The concept of desert is the only connecting link between punishment and justice. It is only as deserved or undeserved that a sentence can be just or unjust. I do not here contend that the question: "is it deserved?" is the only one we can reasonably ask about a punishment. We may very properly ask whether it is likely to deter others and to reform the criminal. But neither of these two last questions is a question about justice. There is no sense in talking about a "just deterrent" or a "just cure"—we demand of a deterrent not whether it is just but whether it will deter. We demand of a cure not whether it is just but whether it succeeds. Thus when we cease to consider what the criminal deserves and consider only what will cure him or deter others, we have tacitly removed him from the sphere of justice altogether.[22]

According to the neoclassical perspective, doing justice ultimately comes down to an official meting out of what is deserved. Justice for an individual is nothing more nor less than what that individual deserves when all the circumstances surrounding that person's situation and behavior are taken into account.

Punishment is a central feature of both classical and neoclassical thought. Whereas punishment served the ends of deterrence in classical thought, its role in neoclassical thinking has been expanded. It is, for example, but a small step from the concept of just deserts to the concept of retribution. Those who advocate retribution see the primary utility of punishment in its ability to provide revenge.

Notions of just deserts and retribution are morally based. They build on a sense of indignation at criminal behavior and on the sense of righteousness inherent in Judeo-Christian notions of morality and propriety. Both philosophies of punishment turn a blind eye to the mundane and practical consequences of any particular form of punishment. Hence, advocates of the just deserts or retributive philosophies of punishment easily dismiss critics of, say, the death penalty, who frequently challenge the efficacy of court-ordered capital punishment on the basis that such sentences do little to deter others. Wider issues, including general deterrence, become irrelevant when a person focuses narrowly on the emotions which crime and victimization engender in a given instance. Simply put, from the neoclassical perspective some crimes cry out for vengeance, while others demand little more than a slap on the wrist or an apology from the offender.

The Death Penalty

Capital punishment the legal imposition of a sentence of death upon a convicted offender. Another term for the death penalty.

Notions of deterrence, retribution, and just deserts all come together in **capital punishment.** Given the many different philosophies of punishment represented by the death penalty it is not surprising that so much disagreement exists as to the efficacy of death as a form of criminal sanction.

The extent to which the death penalty acts as a general deterrent has been widely studied. As mentioned earlier in this chapter, some researchers[23] have compared murder rates between states which have eliminated the death penalty and those which retain it, finding little variation in the rate at which murders are committed. Others have looked at variations in murder rates over time in jurisdictions which have eliminated capital punishment, with similar results.[24] A 1988 Texas study provided a comprehensive review of capital punishment by correlating homicide rates with the rate of executions within the state between 1930 and 1986.[25] The study, which was especially important because Texas has been quite active in the capital punishment arena, failed to find any support for the use of death as a deterrent. Opponents of capital punishment frequently cite such studies to claim that the death penalty is ineffective as a deterrent and should be abolished.

Other abolitionist rationales include claims that (1) the death penalty has, at times, been imposed on innocent people, (2) human life is sacred and state-imposed death lowers society to the same moral (or amoral) level as the individual murderer, (3) the death penalty has been (and may still be) imposed in haphazard and discriminatory fashion, and (4) the death penalty is imposed disproportionately upon ethnic minorities.

Advocates of capital punishment generally discount each of these claims, countering with the notion that death is *deserved* by those who commit especially heinous acts, and that anything short of capital punishment under certain circumstances is an injustice in itself. Some people, the claim is made, deserve to die for what they have done. Such arguments evolve from a natural law perspective, and are based on the notion of just deserts as discussed earlier.

THEORY IN PERSPECTIVE

The Classical School and Neoclassical Thinkers

THE CLASSICAL SCHOOL

a criminological perspective operative in the late 1700s and early 1800s which had its roots in the Enlightenment, and which held that men and women are rational beings, that crime is the result of the exercise of free will, and that punishment can be effective in reducing the incidence of crime because it negates the pleasure to be derived from crime commission.

CLASSICAL CRIMINOLOGY.

The application of classical school principles to problems of crime and justice.

PERIOD: 1700s–1880

THEORISTS: Cesare Beccaria, Jeremy Bentham, others

CONCEPTS: Free will, deterrence through punishment, social contract, natural law, natural rights, due process, Panopticon

NEOCLASSICAL CRIMINOLOGY, TYPE I: THE LAW AND ORDER SCHOOL.

Involves modern-day application of classical principles to problems of crime and crime control in contemporary society in the guise of "get-tough" social policies.

PERIOD: 1970s–Present

THEORISTS: Jack Katz, many others

CONCEPTS: Determinate sentencing, just deserts, specific deterrence, general deterrence

NEOCLASSICAL CRIMINOLOGY, TYPE II: INDIVIDUAL RIGHTS ADVOCACY.

Involves modern-day application of the classical principles of due process and natural rights to problems of crime in contemporary society.

PERIOD: 1960s–Present

THEORISTS: Many

CONCEPTS: Due process, constitutional rights, incapacitation, dangerousness

Many death penalty advocates are also not convinced that the sanction cannot be an effective deterrent. As with other punishments, a death penalty that is swift and certain, they point out, is likely to deter others. Modern-day capital punishment, however, rarely meets these requirements. In contemporary America, offenders sentenced to death are unlikely to ever have their sentences finalized. For those who do, years often pass between the time their sentence of death is imposed and the time it is carried out.[26] Even if the threat of death does not effectively deter others, advocates of capital punishment say, it will ensure that those people who are put to death will never commit another crime.

Capital Punishment and Race

According to the Washington-based Death Penalty Information Center,[27] the death penalty has been imposed disproportionately on racial minorities throughout American history. Statistics maintained by the center show that, "since 1930 nearly 90% of those executed for the crime of rape in this country were African-Americans. Currently, about 50% of those on the nation's death rows are from minority populations representing 20% of the country's population." The center, a fervent anti–capital punishment organization, claims that "evidence of racial discrimination in the application of capital punishment continues. Nearly 40% of those executed since 1976 have been black, even though blacks constitute only 12% of the population. And in almost every death penalty case, the race of the victim is white." In 1996 alone, according to the center, "89% of the death sentences carried out involved white victims, even though 50% of the homicides in this country have black victims. Of the 229 executions that have occurred since the death penalty was reinstated [in 1972]," says the center, "only one has involved a white defendant for the murder of a black person."

A 1994 congressional report by the Subcommittee on Civil and Constitutional Rights[28] reached much the same conclusion. The report, entitled "Racial Disparities in Federal Death Penalty Prosecutions 1988–1994," had this to say about race and capital punishment under federal law: "Racial minorities are being prosecuted under federal death penalty law far beyond their proportion in the general population or the population of criminal offenders. Analysis of prosecutions under the federal death penalty provisions of the Anti-Drug Abuse Act of 1988 reveals that 89% of the defendants selected for capital prosecution have been either African-American or Mexican-American. Moreover, the number of prosecutions under this Act has been increasing over the past two years with no decline in racial disparities. All ten of the recently approved federal capital prosecutions have been against black defendants. This pattern of inequality adds to the mounting evidence that race continues to play an unacceptable part in the application of capital punishment in America today." The report was prepared with the assistance of the Death Penalty Information Center.

On the other hand, capital punishment advocates say that the real question is not whether ethnic differences exist in the rate of imposition of the death penalty, but whether the penalty is *fairly* imposed. They argue, for example, that if 50 percent of all capital punishment–eligible crimes are committed by members of a particular, but small, ethnic group, then anyone anticipating fairness in imposition of the death penalty would expect to see 50 percent of death row populations composed of members of that particular ethnic group. In like manner, one would also expect to see the same relative ethnicity among those executed. In short, they say, if fairness is to be any guide, those committing capital crimes should be the ones sentenced to death—regardless of race, ethnicity, gender, or other similar social characteristics.

The claim that the death penalty is or is not discriminatory is difficult to investigate. Although evidence may suggest that blacks and other minorities in the United States have in the past been unfairly sentenced to die,[29] the present evidence is not so clear. For an accurate appraisal to be made, any claims of disproportionality must go beyond simple comparisons with racial representation in the larger population, and must somehow measure both frequency and seriousness of capital crimes between and within racial groups. Following that line of reasoning, the Supreme Court, in the 1987 case of *McCleskey* v. *Kemp*,[30] held that a simple showing of racial discrepancies in the application of the death penalty does not amount to a constitutional violation.

REHABILITATION ON A SMALL SCALE

INTENSIVE PROGRAMS SAVE SOME YOUNGSTERS

Can criminal offenders be changed if caught early enough? Does the process of change take strict discipline? As the following story shows, innovative programs may be demonstrating that change is possible.

Marriottsville, Md.—John Yates was 15 and abandoned by his parents when he started prowling the streets, breaking into cars and homes.

So 30 years later, he has no trouble relating to the young offenders he supervises at the Thomas O'Farrell Youth Center here.

"They're 'tough guys' but they're really kids," says Yates, called "Colonel" to 38 teen-age boys whose crimes range from drug dealing and car theft to armed robbery and assault.

Juvenile justice experts name the center as one of a number of programs that help turn criminal kids around.

Through strict regimens of education, discipline and counseling, these small, intensive facilities show that some young offenders can, indeed, be reformed.

"We've come a long way from a few years ago when the claim was 'nothing works,' " says John Wilson, acting chief of the federal Office of Juvenile Justice and Delinquency Prevention. "A lot of programs work."

Critics say those programs are all too rare—but they count O'Farrell among them.

Barry Krisberg, president of the National Council on Crime and Delinquency, declares O'Farrell "wonderful—a national model."

Not every bad kid can be saved: overall, six of 10 O'Farrell residents avoid further trouble with the law— much better than the 70% recidivism in some correction programs.

O'Farrell does not admit murderers or rapists because of an agreement with the local community.

The campus-like center is nestled in Maryland's rolling horse country. It's a far cry from traditional juvenile correctional facilities where a hundred or more young criminals may be held in aging institutional buildings.

Key to O'Farrell's program: 8–10 months of intensive counseling, schooling and discipline, followed by six months of supervision and support.

"We give them a vision . . . hope," says Yates, who oversees the operation of O'Farrell and two other programs.

A case in point: Neal, 17, came to O'Farrell in May after three years of crime. For him, lawbreaking began with selling crack and smoking pot.

He armed himself with a TEC-9—a semiautomatic pistol—to protect against "stick-up boys" who rob drug dealers. But he found that selling drugs "wasn't interesting enough," so he began stealing cars, too.

When that lost its thrill, Neal became an armed robber.

"It made me feel very powerful, in total control," he says. "It makes your heart pump . . . keeps you on the edge. I didn't care about my life anymore."

Since his arrest, Neal is trying to earn a high school equivalency diploma. He works at the center's kitchen and hopes to become an architect.

What would Neal say to people who are skeptical that criminals like him can be reformed?

"I would take them to a facility just like this one," he says. "They would see a bunch of changed young men." Other successful programs:

- South Carolina's Family and Neighborhood Services program relies on master's degree–level therapists working with juvenile offenders and their families on a daily basis. After more than a year, only 20% of those in the program are incarcerated for some other charge, compared with 68% of juvenile offenders who are simply placed on probation.
- The Florida Environmental Institute—a program in a remote part of the Everglades and known as "The Last Chance Ranch"—exposes some of the state's most serious juvenile offenders to school, hard work and adult role models. After three years, only one-third have a new conviction.
- Alternative Rehabilitative Communities, a non-profit group that runs 10 facilities in Pennsylvania, including a secure facility for murderers and other seriously violent boys ages to 18. Courts often send kids to ARC as the last stop before transferring them to the adult criminal system.

ARC students follow strict schedules of classes, chores, physical exercise, and intensive counseling to root out causes of their violent acts.

Of the 13 "students" at the Chambersburg facility on a recent day, two had attempted murder; yet even with the hardest cases, ARC reports about two-thirds of students who graduate don't re-offend.

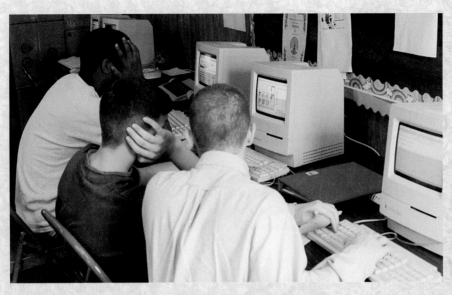

Juvenile offenders train on computers at Thomas O'Farrell Youth Center in Marriottsville, a facility that has been successful in turning young criminals around. Could similar programs work with older offenders? *Tim Dillon/USA Today.*

The "nasty kid who wants to take on the whole world is the one we work with best," says ARC director Dan Elby.

Heather, 16, argued with her stepfather and stabbed him four times with a kitchen knife: "He about died, but he didn't."

First she went to a detention facility where, she says, "You just watch TV." Then she came to ARC for a year where she studied, got a culinary degree and was released this month to a foster home.

Ruben, 18, came to ARC's Chambersburg facility eight months ago, after his life of drug deals and drive-by shootings ended with the wounding of an 8-year-old boy. He'll be out early next year.

Ruben says ARC taught him a sense of discipline and morality, and "to talk about my problems. Before, I just reacted."

Even in the best programs, not all juvenile offenders will reform. But rehabilitation efforts are still in the public's best interest, Wilson says.

"If all you've done is warehouse them, they're going to come out as monsters."

Frustration Setting In

USA Today's "Crackdown on Kids" coverage describes a nation panicked at the rising violence of youth crime, and frustrated with a juvenile justice system that often fails either to protect or rehabilitate.

• The juvenile justice system spends $20 billion a year to arrest and jail kids—and as many as 70% commit crimes again.

- Rehabilitation programs seem costly and slow to a public panicked by ever-deadlier youth crime: In 10 years, the share of murders juveniles committed rose 125%.
- Stiff penalties have popular appeal. In a *USA Today*/CNN/Gallup poll, 60% favor executing teen murderers. And at least 19 states plan get-tough changes in juvenile codes.
- But critics say most get-tough, punitive programs only lock up kids for a while, then send them back as more vicious, proficient criminals.

Questions
1. Can criminal offenders be changed if caught early enough?
2. Does it take strict discipline to bring about change, or will other strategies work equally well? Describe other possible strategies.

Source: Sam Vincent Meddis and Patricia Edmonds, "Rehabilitation on a Small Scale—Intensive Programs Save Some Youngsters," *USA Today,* September 29, 1994, p. 10A. Copyright 1994, *USA Today.* Reprinted with permission.

▚ POLICY IMPLICATIONS OF THE CLASSICAL SCHOOL

Much of the practice of criminal justice in America today is built around a conceptual basis provided by classical school theorists. Programs designed to prevent crime have their philosophical roots in the classical axiom of deterrence, and punishment—in the modern guise of probation, fines, and especially imprisonment—remains a central tenant of modern-day criminal justice practice. The emphasis on punishment, however, as an appropriate response to crime, whether founded on principles of just deserts, revenge, or deterrence, has left many contemporary criminal justice initiatives foundering on overcrowded prisons and courtrooms packed into near paralysis.

There can be little denying that prisons today are dramatically overcrowded. By the beginning of 1997 the nation's state and federal prison population (excluding jails) stood at 1,182,169 inmates, a figure that represented an increase of 5 percent over the previous year.[31] Overcrowding in federal institutions exceeded 25 percent, while state prisons were between 16 and 24 percent over capacity depending on the state in question. Drug offenses have accounted for almost half of the growth in prison populations since 1980, according to a Bureau of Justice Statistics report. Increases in the number of parole and probation violators returned to prison, and heightened rates of imprisonment for crimes such as sexual assault, robbery, aggravated assault, and burglary, explain the remainder of the increase.

According to the Bureau of Justice Statistics, 3.2 percent of all black men in the United States are in prison, compared with less than one-half of 1 percent of all white men.[32] In other words, black men today are approximately seven times as likely as white men to be imprisoned.

Among the states, Texas had the highest incarceration rate at 686 inmates per 100,000 residents, followed by Louisiana at 615 per 100,000, and Oklahoma at 591 per 100,000. States with the largest inmate population included California, with 147,712; Texas, with 132,383; and New York, with 69,709 inmates. Figure 4.2 shows the total U.S. prison population projected through the year 2000.

The social policy position of today's classical school heirs is complex and anything but clear. On the one hand, those heirs of the classical school who see punishment as the central tenant of criminal justice policy believe it to be a natural and deserved consequence of criminal activity. Such thinkers call for greater prison capacity and new prison construction. They use evidence such as the crime funnel (Figure 4.1) to argue that although punishment is theoretically an effective crime preventative, in today's society few criminals are ever effectively punished. These proponents of neoclassical theory, often called **law and order advocates,** frequently seek stiffer criminal laws and enhanced penalties for criminal activity. They insist on the importance of individual responsibility and claim that law violators should be held unfailingly responsible for their actions. Law and order advocates generally want to ensure that sentences imposed by criminal courts are the sentences served by offenders, and they argue against reduced prison time for whatever reason. Finally, many such neoclassical thinkers of today rally around the death penalty because they believe it is either justified as a natural consequence of specific forms of abhorrent behavior or because they believe that it will deter others from committing similar crimes in the future. They answer critics who claim that evidence does

Law and order advocates those who suggest that, under certain circumstances involving criminal threats to public safety, the interests of society should take precedence over individual rights.

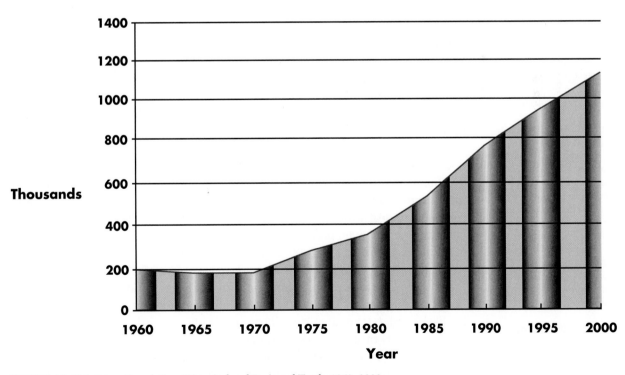

FIGURE 4.2 U.S. Prison Population, Historical and Projected Totals, 1960–2000.
Source: Christopher J. Mumola and Allen J. Beck, *Prisoners in 1996* (Annapolis Junction, Maryland: Bureau of Justice Statistics, 1997); and "Bureau of Prisons Cites Need to Expand Prison Industries," *Criminal Justice Newsletter,* May 16, 1994, pp. 4–5.

Rahway (New Jersey) State Prison. Today's "law and order" approach has led to dramatically overcrowded prisons. How can overcrowding be reduced? *J.P. Laffont/Sygma.*

Individual rights advocates those who seek to protect personal freedoms in the face of criminal prosecution.

Dangerousness the likelihood that a given individual will later harm society or others; it is often measured in terms of **recidivism,** or as the likelihood of new crime commission or rearrest for a new crime within a five-year period following arrest or release from confinement. (Dangerousness is discussed in more detail in Chapter 6.)

Incapacitation the use of imprisonment or other means to reduce the likelihood that an offender will be capable of committing future offenses.

not support a belief in capital punishment as a deterrent by pointing out that death is at least a specific deterrent, if not a general one. As previously discussed, they add that the efficacy of the death penalty as a deterrent is impossible to accurately assess, because capital punishment today is so mired in procedural restrictions that it is anything but certain and swift.

On the other hand, a second school of today's neoclassical thinkers emphasizes individual rights, rather than punishment. **Individual rights advocates** intuitively defend the prerogatives of individuals against potential government excesses inherent in the social contract. Citing correctional overcrowding, high rates of recidivism, and increased criminal activity in many areas of society, this second school of neoclassical thinkers points out that an increasing emphasis on imprisonment has done little to stem the tide of rising crime. They call for renewed recognition of individual rights in the face of criminal prosecution, and for reduction in the use of imprisonment as a criminal sanction—suggesting that it be employed as a kind of last resort to deal with only the most dangerous offenders. **Dangerousness,** or the likelihood that a given individual will later harm society or others, should be the major determining criterion for government action against the freedom of its citizens, individual rights advocates argue. Dangerousness, they suggest, should form the standard against which any need for incapacitation might be judged. **Incapacitation,** simply put, is the use of imprisonment or other means to reduce the likelihood that an offender will be capable of committing future offenses.

Proponents of modern-day incapacitation often distinguish between selective incapacitation, in which crime is controlled via the imprisonment of specific individuals, and collective incapacitation, whereby changes in legislation and/or sentencing patterns lead to the removal from society of entire groups of individuals judged to be dangerous. Advocates of selective incapacitation as a crime-control strategy point to studies which show that the majority of crimes are perpetrated by a small number of hard-core repeat offenders. The most famous of those studies was conducted by University of Pennsylvania Professor Marvin Wolfgang and focused on 9,000 male individuals born in Philadelphia in 1945. By the time this cohort of men had reached age 18, Wolfgang was able to determine that 627 "chronic recidivists" were responsible for the large majority of all serious violent crimes committed by the group. Other, more recent, studies have similarly shown that a small hard core of criminal perpetrators is probably responsible for most criminal activity in the United States.

Such thinking has led to the development of incapacitation as a modern-day treatment philosophy, and to the creation of innovative forms of incapacitation that do not require imprisonment—such as home confinement, the use of halfway houses or career training centers for convicted felons, and psychological and/or chemical treatments designed to reduce the likelihood of future crime commissions. Similarly, such thinkers argue, the decriminalization of many offenses and the enhancement of social programs designed to combat what they see as the root causes of crime—including poverty, low educational levels, a general lack of skills, and inherent or active discrimination—will lead to a much reduced incidence of crime in the future, making high rates of imprisonment unnecessary.

Although both the law and order and the individual rights perspectives have much to recommend them, it appears that advocates of law and order have the upper hand in today's political arena. The country is rife with fear of crime; calls for "get-tough-on-crime" policies are well received by most political constituencies.

Responses have not been slow in coming. In 1994 the U.S. Congress passed the Violent Crime Control and Enforcement Act, one of the most far-reaching get-tough-on-crime measures ever seen on Capitol Hill. The law (which is discussed in greater detail in Chapter 13) contains a "three-strikes-and-you're-out" provision that provides for mandatory life sentences after a third felony conviction. It also allocates massive amounts of money ($22 billion) for new prison construction and mandates long prison sentences for violent offenders and for those who use guns during the commission of crimes. Get-tough comments characteristic of many lawmakers on the eve of the bill's passage were made by Texas Republican Phil Gramm, who said, "We want ten years in prison without parole for possessing a firearm during commission of a violent crime; twenty years for discharging it. We want life imprisonment for murder, and the death penalty in aggravated cases."[33] The new law also bans many types of semiautomatic assault weapons and authorizes the hiring of 20,000 additional police officers across the country. Typical of the current nationwide resurgence of interest in the death penalty, it expands the federal death penalty to nearly sixty offenses.

Many of today's new get-tough policies directly impact incarcerated offenders. A few years ago, for example, Texas Governor Ann Richards, in a fashion characteristic of her gubernatorial counterparts across the nation, unveiled a plan to put prisoners to work on community service projects throughout the state. "We want the work done by these inmates to serve as payment to the citizens of this state," she said. "We're putting prisoners to work where it benefits our communities."[34] Richards also devised a method whereby Texas inmates would pay for all phone calls they make, with a portion of fees paid returned to the state. "Every time a prisoner makes a call home," Richards said, "he or she will be making a payment to the state." Texas Comptroller John Sharp estimated that the phone plan would generate up to $43 million in additional revenues over a five-year period, but Richards said the figure would be higher because the state is building more prisons, which will allow inmates to serve longer sentences.

Other get-tough policies include truth-in-sentencing initiatives which require judges to assess and make public the actual time an offender is likely to serve once sentenced to prison. Over the years, time off for good behavior and early release because of prison overcrowding have dramatically reduced the time a sentenced offender can be expected to spend behind bars. A few years ago, for example, in support of a growing national initiative, the Supreme Court for the state of New Jersey imposed a truth-in-sentencing rule on judges throughout the state, requiring them to disclose how much time a convicted defendant is likely to spend behind bars.[35] New Jersey Governor Christie Whitman had pushed for truth-in-sentencing as part of her anticrime platform. Other states have since joined the truth-in-sentencing bandwagon, requiring convicted violent offenders to serve at least 85 percent of their sentences before being eligible for any form of release.

■ A CRITIQUE OF CLASSICAL THEORIES

The classical school of thought represents more a philosophy of justice than it does a theory of crime causation. As Randy Martin, Robert Mutchnick, and Timothy Austin have observed, however, "[t]he true test of Beccaria's essay can be judged by the influence it has had over time on our justice system."[36] The influence of Beccaria, the Enlightenment, and classical thinkers remains today in the U.S. Constitution, in the get-tough approaches to crime, and in the emphasis on individual rights. Martin and colleagues conclude that the classical school "has left behind a legacy that we see in almost every aspect of our present-day justice system."[37]

Critics charge, however, that the classical school lacks explanatory power over criminal motivation—other than to advance the simple claim that crime is the result of free will and individual choice. Such critics point out that classical theory is bereft of meaningful explanations as to how a choice for or against criminal activity is made. Similarly, classical theory lacks any appreciation for the deeper fonts of personal motivation, including those represented by aspects of human biology, psychology, and the social environment. Moreover, the classical school, as originally detailed in the writings of Beccaria and Bentham, lacked any scientific basis for the claims it made. Although neoclassical writers have advanced the scientific foundation of classical claims (via studies such as those showing the effectiveness of particular forms of deterrence), many still defend their way of thinking by reference to philosophical ideals (such as just deserts).

In a world grown accustomed to measuring the success of an idea in terms of its measurable consequences, neoclassical theorists are hard put to defend their philosophies. Citing the fact that boot camp prisons, for example, have not measured up to the claims of reduced recidivism touted by get-tough neoclassical politicians, some writers have called for a return to programs already shown to work. As the pragmatic editorialist Colman McCarthy recently pointed out in an article criticizing the Clinton administration's plan to increase funding for boot camp prisons, "If helping nonviolent first offenders get their lives and values together is the goal, then the $3 billion for boot camps needs to be redirected to such proven programs as drug counseling, alternative sentences, work furloughs, literacy courses and well-supervised probation."[38]

THEORY VERSUS REALITY

Assessing Dangerousness

Dangerousness is a difficult concept to comprehend. Indicators of dangerousness have yet to be well defined in the social scientific literature, and legislators who attempt to codify any assessment of future dangerousness often find themselves frustrated. On the individual level, however, dangerousness might be more easily assessed. What follows is a description of the criteria one judge, Lois G. Forer, used in deciding whether an offender needed to spend a long time away from society.

I had my own criteria or guidelines—very different from those established by most states and the federal government—for deciding on a punishment. My primary concern was public safety. The most important question I asked myself was whether the offender could be deterred from committing other crimes. No one can predict with certainty who will or will not commit a crime, but there are indicators most sensible people recognize as danger signals:

- First, was this an irrational crime? If an arsonist sets a fire to collect insurance, that is a crime but also a rational act. Such a person can be deterred by being made to pay for the harm done and the costs to the fire department. However, if the arsonist sets fires just because he likes to see them, it is highly unlikely that he can be stopped from setting others, no matter how high the fine. Imprisonment is advisable even though it may be a first offense.
- Second, was there wanton cruelty? If a robber maims or slashes the victim, there is little likelihood that he can safely be left in the community. If a robber simply displays a gun but does not fire it or harm the victim, then one should consider his life history, provocation, and other circumstances in deciding whether probation is appropriate.
- Third, is this a hostile person? Was his crime one of hatred, and does he show any genuine remorse? Most rapes are acts of hostility, and the vast majority of rapists have a record of numerous sexual assaults. I remember one man who raped his mother. I gave him the maximum sentence under the law—20 years—but with

good behavior, he got out fairly quickly. He immediately raped another elderly woman.

- Fourth, is this a person who knows he is doing wrong but cannot control himself? Typical of such offenders are pedophiles. One child abuser who appeared before me had already been convicted of abusing his first wife's child. I got him on the second wife's child and sentenced him to the maximum. Still, he'll get out with good behavior, and I shudder to think about the children around him when he does. This is one case in which justice is not tough enough.

By contrast, some people who have committed homicide present very little danger of further violence—although many more do. Once a young man came before me because he had taken aim at a person half a block away and then shot him in the back, killing him. Why did he do it? "I wanted to get me a body." He should never get out.

DISCUSSION QUESTIONS

1. How are public safety and criminal punishment related?
2. Do you agree that the criteria used by Judge Forer to identify dangerousness are useful? Why or why not?
3. Do you believe that offenders who are identified as "dangerous" should be treated differently from other offenders? If so, how?

Source: Lois G. Forer, "Justice by the Numbers; Mandatory Sentencing Drove Me from the Bench," *The Washington Monthly,* April 1992, pp. 12–18. Reprinted with permission from *The Washington Monthly.* Copyright by *The Washington Monthly Company,* 1611 Connecticut Ave., N.W., Washington, D.C. 20009 (202) 462-0128.

SUMMARY

The Enlightenment, a social and cultural renaissance which occurred throughout the late seventeenth and early eighteenth centuries, proved to be a highly liberating force in the Western world. Enlightenment thinkers established many of the democratic principles that formed the conceptual foundations of the American and French Revolutions. Their ideas are still alive today, and significantly shape our understanding of human nature and human behavior. The twin conceptual prongs around which this textbook is built—social responsibility and individual rights—both have their roots in Enlightenment thought, and in the belief in free will which it engendered. Notions of deterrence as a goal of justice system intervention, and of punishment as a worthy consequence of crime, owe much of their contemporary influence to the classical school of criminology. As we begin the twenty-first century we carry with us an intellectual heritage far older than we may realize.

WEB WATCH

Access the *Criminology Today* home page on the World Wide Web by pointing your browser at www.prenhall.com/cjcentral. Once there, click on *Criminology Today* in order to access the wealth of electronic resources supporting this text.

Onsite resources include (1) "Chapter Links," which provides succinct overviews of critical ideas from the textbook and links selected materials from around the Web to concepts found in the text; (2) "General Reference—Law and Justice Links." Organized by chapter, these links lead to other useful resources on the World Wide Web, such as libraries, electronic discussion lists, and electronic journals; (3) "Criminology Sites on the Web," which lists links to organizations such as the American Society of Criminology and the National Organization for Victims Assistance (NOVA), as well as crime prevention links and statistics on crime and justice. Many other Web-based resources can be accessed via the *Criminology Today* site, including the federal Justice Information Center, the Bureau of Justice Statistics, the FBI, the RAND Corporation, the Vera Institute of Justice, PAVNET (an online "Partnership Against Violence," run by seven different federal agencies), and the National White Collar Crime Center.

Still another feature of the *Criminology Today* Web site is e-mail homework. Homework can be composed onsite and submitted to instructors using the instructor's e-mail address. To use the e-mail homework feature, click on "E-Mail Homework" on the opening page, and then type answers to the questions that appear in the spaces provided. Use your instructor's e-mail address to submit homework answers. The *Criminology Today* Web site also provides links to powerful Web-based search engines that can help you find topics of interest to you as you progress through your course of study. Search engines can be found under the home page heading "Criminology Sites on the Web."

DISCUSSION QUESTIONS

1. This book emphasizes a social problems versus social responsibility theme. Which perspective is most supported by classical and neoclassical thought? Why?
2. Name the various pre-classical thinkers identified by this chapter. What ideas did each contribute to Enlightenment philosophy? What form did those ideas take in classical criminological thought?
3. Define *natural law.* Do you believe that natural law exists? If so, what types of behavior would be contravened by natural law? If not, why not?

4. What is meant by the idea of a "social contract"? How does the concept of social contract relate to natural law?

5. What were the central concepts that defined the classical school of criminological thought? Which of those concepts are still alive? Where do you see evidence for the survival of those concepts?

6. What are the various philosophies of punishment identified by this chapter? Which philosophy of punishment appeals most to you? Why? Which is the least attractive? Why?

7. Define *recidivism*. What is a recidivism rate? Why are recidivism rates so high today? What can be done to lower them?

NOTES

1. Jeremy Bentham, *An Introduction to the Principles of Morals and Legislation* (1789).

2. Cesare Beccaria, *Essay on Crimes and Punishments,* translated by Henry Paolucci (New York: Bobbs-Merrill, 1963).

3. William Graham Sumner, *Folkways* (New York: Dover, 1906).

4. Marvin Wolfgang, "The Key Reporter," *Phi Beta Kappa,* vol. 52, no. 1.

5. Roman influence in England had ended by 442 A.D., according to Crane Brinton, John B. Christopher, and Robert L. Wolff, *A History of Civilization,* 3rd ed., vol. 1 (Englewood Cliffs, N.J.: Prentice Hall, 1967), p. 180.

6. Howard Abadinsky, *Law and Justice* (Chicago: Nelson-Hall, 1988), p. 6.

7. Edward McNall Burns, *Western Civilization,* 7th ed. (New York: W. W. Norton, 1969), p. 339.

8. Ibid., p. 533.

9. Brinton, Christopher, and Wolff, *A History of Civilization,* p. 274.

10. Harry V. Jaffa and Ernest van den Haag, "Of Men, Hogs, and Law: If Natural Law Does Not Permit Us to Distinguish Between Men and Hogs, What Does?" *National Review,* February 3, 1992, p. 40.

11. Referred to in official transcripts as Rudolf Franz Ferdinand Hoess.

12. International Military Tribunal, "One Hundred and Eighth Day, Monday, 4/15/1946, Part 03," in *Trial of the Major War Criminals Before the International Military Tribunal, Volume XI.*

Proceedings: 4/8/1946–4/17/1946 (Nuremberg: IMT, 1943), pp. 398–400.

13. Beccaria, *Essay on Crimes and Punishments.*

14. Bentham, *An Introduction to the Principles of Morals and Legislation.*

15. Randy Martin, Robert J. Mutchnick, and W. Timothy Austin, *Criminological Thought: Pioneers Past and Present* (New York: Macmillan, 1990), p. 18.

16. Jack Katz, *Seductions of Crime: Moral and Sensual Attractions in Doing Evil* (New York: Basic Books, 1988).

17. Ibid., p. 3.

18. Ibid., p. 71.

19. Bill McCarthy, "Not Just 'For the Thrill of It': An Instrumentalist Elaboration of Katz's Explanation of Sneaky Thrill Property Crimes," *Criminology,* vol. 33, no. 4 (1995), pp. 519–538.

20. Lawrence A. Greenfeld, *Capital Punishment 1989* (Washington, D.C.: Bureau of Justice Statistics, 1990), p. 1.

21. "Failure to Punish Misdemeanors Fuels Violence," *Washington Post* wire service, April 11, 1994.

22. C. S. Lewis, "The Humanitarian Theory of Punishment," *Res Judicatae,* vol. 6 (1953), pp. 224–225.

23. See, for example, W. C. Bailey, "Deterrence and the Death Penalty for Murders in Utah: A Time Series Analysis," *Journal of Contemporary Law,* vol. 5, no. 1 (1978), pp. 1–20; and "An Analysis

of the Deterrent Effect of the Death Penalty for Murder in California," *Southern California Law Review,* vol. 52, no. 3 (1979), pp. 743–764.

[24]See, for example, B. E. Forst, "The Deterrent Effect of Capital Punishment: A Cross-State Analysis of the 1960s," *Minnesota Law Review,* vol. 61 (1977), pp. 743–764.

[25]Scott H. Decker and Carol W. Kohfeld, "Capital Punishment and Executions in the Lone Star State: A Deterrence Study," *Criminal Justice Research Bulletin* (Criminal Justice Center, Sam Houston State University), vol. 3, no. 12 (1988).

[26]Lawrence A. Greenfeld, *Capital Punishment 1989* (Washington, D.C.: Bureau of Justice Statistics, 1990), p. 1.

[27]From the Death Penalty Information Center's site on the World Wide Web: http://www.essential.org/dpic/dpicrace.html.

[28]A subcommittee of the Committee on the Judiciary.

[29]As some of the evidence presented before the Supreme Court in *Furman* v. *Georgia* (408 U.S. 238, 1972) suggested.

[30]*McCleskey* v. *Kemp,* 481 U.S. 279, 107 S.Ct. 1756, 95 L. Ed. 2d 262 (1987).

[31]Christopher J. Mumola and Allen J. Beck, *Prisoners in 1996* (Annapolis Junction, Maryland: Bureau of Justice Statistics, June 1997).

[32]Ibid.

[33]"Senate Reaffirms Tough Stand Against Crime," Reuters wire service, May 19, 1994.

[34]"Richards: Inmates Must Pay for Calls," United Press wire service, Southwest edition, June 27, 1994.

[35]Thomas Martello, "Truth in Sentencing," Associated Press wire service, April 26, 1994.

[36]Martin, Mutchnick, and Austin, *Criminological Thought,* p. 17.

[37]Ibid., p. 18.

[38]Colman McCarthy, "Give the Boot to Boot Camps," *Washington Post* wire service, March 26, 1994.

BIOLOGICAL ROOTS

OF BEHAVIOR

The evidence is very firm that there is a genetic factor involved in crime.

—SARNOFF A. MEDNICK[1]

Investigators of the link between biology and crime find themselves caught in one of the most bitter controversies to hit the scientific community in years.

—*TIME*[2]

Men have always loved to fight. If they didn't love to fight, they wouldn't be men.

—GENERAL GEORGE S. PATTON, JR.[3]

⠿ CHAPTER OUTLINE ⠿

INTRODUCTION
MAJOR PRINCIPLES OF BIOLOGICAL THEORIES
BIOLOGICAL ROOTS OF HUMAN AGGRESSION
    Early Biological Theories
    Body Types
    Chemical and Environmental Precursors of Crime
    Hormones and Criminality
GENETICS AND CRIME
    Criminal Families
    The XYY "Supermale"
    Chromosomes and Modern-Day Criminal Families
    Twin Studies
    Male–Female Differences in Criminality
    Sociobiology
CRIME AND HUMAN NATURE: A CONTEMPORARY SYNTHESIS
POLICY ISSUES
CRITIQUES OF BIOLOGICAL THEORIES
SUMMARY

⠿ IMPORTANT NAMES AND CASES ⠿

Konrad Lorenz	Cesare Lombroso	Charles Darwin
Franz Joseph Gall	C. Ray Jeffery	Johann Gaspar Spurzheim
Ernst Kretschmer	William H. Sheldon	Charles Buckman Goring
Earnest A. Hooton	Richard L. Dugdale	Henry H. Goddard
Edward O. Wilson	James Q. Wilson	Richard J. Herrnstein
Buck v. *Bell*	Arthur H. Estabrook	

⠿ IMPORTANT TERMS ⠿

biological theories	criminaloids	atavism
born criminals	cycloid	positivism
phrenology	somatotyping	ectomorph
testosterone	mesomorph	endomorph
hypoglycemia	supermale	monozygotic (MZ) twins
Juke family	eugenics	Kallikak family
sociobiology	constitutional theories	criminal anthropology
paradigm		

⣳ INTRODUCTION

One of the most vicious murders ever to occur in Arizona was the 1984 mutilation killing of Maude Moormann by her 36-year-old adoptive son, Robert Henry Moormann.[4] Moormann's biological mother drowned shortly after his birth in 1948, and he lived with his grandparents for a short while before being turned over to a Catholic social services agency for adoption. At age 2½, a childless couple, Henry and Maude Moormann, adopted the boy. According to popular accounts, Maude was overly protective of her new son, leaving him ill prepared for encounters with other children. Robert became a notoriously poor student, frequently failing classes and often running away from home. At age 13 he was sent to the Sun School in Phoenix, a shelter for troubled boys, after having been accused of molesting a little girl. While home for Christmas holidays he hid a .22-caliber pistol under his pillow and shot his mother in the stomach when she sat by his bed to talk with him. The bullet lodged in her liver and surgeons feared to remove it. Though she recovered, Maude Moormann always insisted that the shooting had been an accident. Afterward, Robert was in and out of juvenile facilities for a variety of offenses—most centered on sexual maladjustment and the molestation of young girls. By the time he was 18, Moormann had been arrested for accosting yet another girl and had been placed on the drug Mellaril to limit his sexual appetites.

As an adult, Moormann was finally sent to prison for kidnapping and molesting an 8-year-old neighbor girl in 1972. In 1979 he was paroled, but soon went back to prison for a parole violation. By 1984 Moorman had entered the prison's furlough program and, on January 12 of that year, was released to visit with his mother in a local motel. On that fateful night, Moormann demanded that his mother sign papers that would leave him sole heir to her estate. After she refused, Moormann beat her, tied her to the motel room bed, and suffocated her with a pillow. He then made a brief trip to a convenience store where he bought household cleansers and a variety of knives. Upon returning to the motel room he cut his mother's body into many pieces, stuffing some in a local trash dumpster and flushing her severed fingers down the toilet so that her remains couldn't be easily identified. Then he meticulously cleaned the room to hide any signs of the murder. He was arrested, however, after arousing the suspicions of a prison guard to whom he had offered a box of flesh-covered raw bones for the guard's dogs. It took a jury only two hours to convict him and he was sentenced to death.

Robert Moormann was a poor physical specimen who had been judged unfit for the military draft. He had poor vision and flat feet, and suffered from low reading skills and learning disabilities. One physician, to whom he had been taken as a boy, diagnosed him as suffering from brain-stem trauma—the result of two traffic accidents in which he had been involved when young.

Did Moormann's crimes have a biological basis? Of that we may never be sure, although many biological theories have been advanced to explain criminality. Abnormalities of the brain, genetic predispositions, vitamin deficiencies, an excess of hormones such as testosterone, hypoglycemia (low blood sugar), an overabundance of neurotransmitters such as serotonin, and blood abnormalities are among the many biological explanations of crime available today.

The field of criminology has been slow to give credence to biological theories of human behavior. One reason for this, as noted in Chapter 1, is the fact that criminology's academic roots are firmly grounded in the social sciences. As the well-known biocriminologist **C. Ray Jeffery,** commenting on the historical development of the field, observes, "[t]he term *criminology* was given to a social science approach to crime as developed in sociology. . . . Sutherland's (1924) text *Criminology* was pure sociology without any biology or psychology; beginning with publication of that text, criminology was offered in sociology departments as a part of sociology separate from biology, psychology, psychiatry and law. . . . Many of the academicians who call themselves criminologists are sociologists."[5]

Even today, little doubt exists that biological understandings of criminality are out of vogue. In 1992, for example, a National Institutes of Health–sponsored conference[6] that was intended to focus on the biological roots of crime was canceled after critics charged that the meeting would, by virtue of its biological focus, be racist and might intentionally exclude sociological perspectives on the subject. Dr. Peter Breggin, director of the Center for the Study of Psychiatry in Bethesda, Maryland, and leader of the opposition to the conference, argued that "[t]he primary problems that afflict human beings are not due to their bodies or brains, they are due to the environment. Redefining social problems as public health problems is exactly what was done in Nazi Germany."[7] Three years later, when the conference was finally held at a site selected to discourage demonstrations, C. Ray Jeffery pointed out that "[w]hen ideology replaces rational thought there is little hope for a better understanding of human problems."[8]

"One reason why most criminologists are skeptical about genetic influences on criminal behavior is that it seems improbable that behavior that is defined differently in every society could have a genetic foundation."[9] "In other words," say Lee Ellis and Anthony Walsh, "why would genes affect behavior that is circumscribed by laws that vary from one society to another?" The answer, say Ellis and Walsh, "lies in the fact that in nearly all societies with written criminal statutes, there are a fairly standard set of 'core behavior patterns' that are criminalized."[10] Hence, they conclude, "it is possible to maintain that there is little variation from one society to another in what constitutes criminal behavior."

Unfortunately for the field of criminology, critics of biological investigation into the root causes of crime fail to recognize that the advance of science has never been impeded by objective consideration of alternative points of view. Narrow-minded criticism, made before all the facts are in, does little to advance human understanding. Open inquiry, as C. Ray Jeffery notes, requires objective consideration of all points of view, and an unbiased examination of each for their ability to shed light upon the subject under study. Hence, for an adequate consideration of biological theories as they may relate to crime and crime causation, we need to turn to literature outside of the sociological and psychological mainstream.

Biological theories (of criminology) maintain that the basic determinants of human behavior, including criminality, are constitutionally or physiologically based and often inherited.

▰▰ MAJOR PRINCIPLES OF BIOLOGICAL THEORIES

This brief section serves to summarize the central features of **biological theories** of crime causation. Each of these points can be found elsewhere in this chapter, where they are discussed in more detail. This cursory overview, however, is intended to provide more than a summary—it is meant to be a guide to the rest of this chapter.

Biological theories of crime causation make certain fundamental assumptions. Among them are

- The brain is the organ of the mind and the locus of personality. In the words of the well-known biocriminologist Clarence Ray Jeffery, "The brain is the organ of behavior; no theory of behavior can ignore neurology and neurochemistry."[11]
- The basic determinants of human behavior, including criminal tendencies, are, to a considerable degree, constitutionally or genetically based.
- Observed gender and racial differences in rates and types of criminality may be at least partially the result of biological differences between the sexes and/or between racially distinct groups.
- The basic determinants of human behavior, including criminality, may be passed on from generation to generation. In other words, a penchant for crime may be inherited.
- Much of human conduct is fundamentally rooted in instinctive behavioral responses characteristic of biological organisms everywhere. Territoriality, condemnation of adultery, and acquisitiveness are but three examples of behavior which may be instinctual to human beings.
- The biological roots of human conduct have become increasingly disguised, as modern symbolic forms of indirect expressive behavior have replaced more primitive and direct ones.
- At least some human behavior is the result of biological propensities inherited from more primitive developmental stages in the evolutionary process. In other words, some human beings may be further along the evolutionary ladder than others, and their behavior may reflect that fact.
- The interplay between heredity, biology, and the social environment provides the nexus for any realistic consideration of crime causation.

▪▪ BIOLOGICAL ROOTS OF HUMAN AGGRESSION

In 1966 **Konrad Lorenz** published his now famous work *On Aggression.*[12] It was an English-language translation of a 1963 book entitled *Das Sogenannte Bose: Zur Naturgeschichte der Aggression (The Nature of Aggression)* which had originally appeared in German. In his writing, Lorenz described how aggression permeates the animal kingdom, and asked "What is the value of all this fighting?" "In nature," he said, "fighting is such an ever-present process, its behavior mechanisms and weapons are so highly developed and have so obviously arisen under the . . . pressure of a species-preserving function, that it is our duty to ask this . . . question."[13]

Lorenz accepted the evolutionary thesis of the nineteenth-century biologist **Charles Darwin** that intraspecies aggression favored the strongest and best animals in the reproductive process, but he concluded that aggression served a variety of other purposes as well. Aggression, said Lorenz, ensures an "even distribution of animals of a particular species over an inhabitable area . . ."[14] and provides for a

The brain is indeed "the organ of the mind" as modern researchers are continuing to discover. Here a computer-enhanced image shows areas of activity within the brain. Do you think biology may play a role in crime? *Scott Camazsine/Photo Researchers, Inc.*

defense of the species from predators. Human aggression, he claimed, meets many of the same purposes, but can take on covert forms. The drive to acquire wealth and power, for example, that was so characteristic of Western men at the time of his writing, was described by Lorenz as part of the human mating ritual whereby a man might "win" a prized woman through displays of more civilized forms of what could otherwise be understood as intraspecies aggression.

In today's enlightened times such observations may seem to many like mere foolishness. Lorenz's greatest contribution to the study of human behavior, however, may have been his claim that all human behavior is, at least to some degree, "adapted instinctive behavior." In other words, much of human conduct, according to Lorenz, is fundamentally rooted in instinctive behavioral responses characteristic of biological organisms everywhere, and present within each of us in the form of a biological inheritance from more primitive times. Even rational human thought, claimed Lorenz, derives its motivation and direction from instinctual aspects of human biology. The highest human virtues, such as the value placed on human life, "could not have been achieved," said Lorenz, "without an instinctive appreciation of life and death."[15]

Building upon the root functions of aggression, Lorenz concluded that much of what we today call crime is the result of overcrowded living conditions, such as those experienced by city dwellers, combined with a lack of legitimate opportunity for the effective expression of aggression. Crowding, from this perspective, increases the likelihood of aggression, while contemporary socialization simultaneously works to inhibit it. In the words of Lorenz, ". . . in one sense we are all psychopaths, for each of us suffers from the necessity of self-imposed control for the good of the community."[16] When people break down, said Lorenz, they become neurotic or

Charles Darwin (1809–1882), founder
of modern evolutionary theory. *Julia
Cameron/Corbis-Bettmann.*

delinquent, and crime may be the result of stresses that have been found to typically
produce aggression throughout the animal kingdom.

At first blush, Lorenz's explanations, like many of the biologically based theories we will encounter in this chapter, appear more applicable to violent crime than
to other forms of criminal offense. However, it is important to recognize that modern frustrations and concomitant manifestations of aggression may be symbolically, rather than directly, expressed. Hence, the stockbroker who embezzles a
client's money, spurred on by the need to provide material goods for an overly acquisitive family, may be just as criminal as the robber who beats his victim and steals
her purse to have money to buy liquor.

EARLY BIOLOGICAL THEORIES

Numerous perspectives on criminal biology predate Lorenz's work. Some of the perspectives fall into the category of criminal anthropology. **Criminal anthropology** is
the scientific study of the relationship between human physical characteristics and
criminality. One of the earliest criminological anthropologists was **Franz Joseph
Gall** (1758–1828). Gall hypothesized, in his theory of **phrenology** (also called *cran-
iology*), that the shape of the human skull was indicative of the personality and could
be used to predict criminality. Gall's approach contained four themes:

- The brain is the organ of the mind.
- Particular aspects of personality are associated with specific locations in the
  brain.

Criminal anthropology
the scientific study of the
relationship between
human physical character-
istics and criminality.

Phrenology the study of
the shape of the head to
determine anatomical
correlates of human
behavior.

THEORY IN PERSPECTIVE

Types of Biological Theories

BIOLOGICAL THEORIES

adhere to the principle that the basic determinants of human behavior, including criminality, are constitutionally or physiologically based and inherited.

EARLY POSITIVISM. These biological approaches built upon evolutionary principles and were the first to apply scientific techniques to the study of crime and criminals. Early positivistic theories saw criminals as throwbacks to earlier evolutionary epochs.

PERIOD: 1880s–1930

THEORISTS: Franz Joseph Gall, Johann Gaspar Spurzheim, Cesare Lombroso, Charles Goring, and Earnest Hooton

CONCEPTS: Phrenology, atavism, born criminals, criminaloids

CONSTITUTIONAL THEORIES. Such biological theories explain criminality by reference to offenders' body types, inheritance, genetics, and/or external observable physical characteristics.

PERIOD: Modern constitutional theories 1960s–Present, Classical constitutional theories 1930s–1940s

THEORISTS: Ernst Kretschmer, William H. Sheldon, Richard Dugdale, Arthur H. Estabrook, Henry H. Goddard

CONCEPTS: Somatotyping, mesomorph, ectomorph, endomorph, XYY supermale, twin studies

BODY CHEMISTRY. Such biological theories utilize chemical influences, including hormones, food additives, allergies, vitamins, and other chemical substances to explain criminal behavior.

PERIOD: 1940s–Present

THEORISTS: Various

CONCEPTS: Hypoglycemia, vitamins, food allergies, seratonin, PMS, MAOA

SOCIOBIOLOGY. A theoretical perspective developed by Edward O. Wilson to include "the systematic study of the biological basis of all social behavior," which is "a branch of evolutionary biology and particularly of modern population biology."

PERIOD: 1975–Present

THEORISTS: Edward O. Wilson

CONCEPTS: Altruism, tribalism, survival of the gene pool

- Portions of the brain that are well developed will cause personality character-istics associated with them to be more prominent in the individual under study, whereas poorly developed brain areas lead to a lack of associated per-sonality characteristics.
- The shape of a person's skull corresponds to the shape of the underlying brain and is therefore indicative of the personality.

Gall was one of the first Western writers to firmly locate the roots of personal-ity in the brain. Prior to his time it was thought that aspects of personality resided in various organs throughout the body—a fact reflected in linguistic anachronisms which survive into the present day (as, for example, when someone is described as "hard hearted," or as having "a lot of gall," or as thinking with some organ other than the brain). The Greek philosopher Aristotle was said to believe that the brain served no function other than to radiate excess heat from the body. Hence, Gall's perspective, although relatively primitive by today's standards, did much to advance physiological understandings of the mind–body connection in Western thought.

Although Gall never tested his theory, it was widely accepted by many of his contemporaries because it represented something of a shift away from theological perspectives prevalent at the time and a move toward scientific understanding—a trend that was well underway by the time of his writings. Phrenology also provided for systematic evaluation of suspected offenders and was intriguing for its ease of use. One of Gall's students, **Johann Gaspar Spurzheim** (1776–1853), brought phrenological theory to America and, through a series of lectures and publications on the subject, helped to spread its influence. Phrenology's prestige in America ex-tended into the twentieth century, finding a place in classification schemes used to evaluate newly admitted prisoners. Even Arthur Conan Doyle's fictional character Sherlock Holmes was described as using phrenology to solve a number of crimes. It is still popular today among palm readers and fortune tellers, some of whom of-fer phrenological "readings"—although a few states have outlawed such activities.

The Positivist School

One of the best known, early scientific biological theorists—nineteenth-century Italian physician **Cesare Lombroso** (1836–1909)—coined the term *atavism* to sug-gest that criminality was the result of primitive urges which, in modern-day human throwbacks, survived the evolutionary process. He described "the nature of the criminal" as "an atavistic being who reproduces in his person the ferocious instincts of primitive humanity and the inferior animals."[17]

At about this time, Charles Darwin was making a substantial impact on the sci-entific world with his theory of biological evolution. Darwin proposed that human beings and other contemporary living organisms were the end products of a long evolutionary process governed by rules such as natural selection, survival of the fittest, and so on. Lombroso adapted elements of Darwin's theory to suggest that primitive traits survived in present-day human populations and led to heightened criminal tendencies among individuals who harbored them. Darwin himself had proposed this idea when he wrote: "[w]ith mankind some of the worst dispositions

Atavism a concept used by Cesare Lombroso to suggest that criminals are physiological throwbacks to earlier stages of human evolution. The term is derived from the Latin term *atavus,* which means "ancestor."

which occasionally without any assignable cause make their appearance in families, may perhaps be reversions to a savage state, from which we are not removed by very many generations."[18]

The atavistic individual, said Lombroso in his now classic work *L'Uomo delinquente* (1876), was essentially a throwback to a more primitive biological state. According to Lombroso, such an individual, by virtue of possessing a relatively undeveloped brain, is incapable of conforming his behavior to the rules and expectations of modern complex society. Lombroso has been called the father of modern criminology because he was the first criminologist of note to employ the scientific method—particularly measurement, observation, and attempts at generalization—in his work. Other writers, more specific in their pronouncements, have referred to him as the "father of the Italian School" of criminology.

Lombroso's scientific work consisted of postmortem studies of the bodies of executed offenders, which he conducted with assistants, measuring the bodies in many different ways. The body of one such well-known criminal, named Vilella, provided Lombroso with many of his findings and reinforced his belief that most offenders were genetically predisposed toward criminality. Study of another offender, an Italian soldier whom Lombroso calls "Misdea" in his writings[19] and who "attacked and killed eight of his superior officers and comrades," supported such conclusions. The use of science and scientific techniques in the service of criminology has been termed ***positivism.***[20] C. Ray Jeffery, offering a somewhat limited definition of the term, but one which applies well to Lombroso's work, has said that "the main characteristic of Positivism is its attempt to answer the riddle of criminality by means of scientific studies of the individual offender."[21]

Positivism the application of scientific techniques to the study of crime and criminals.

Lombroso claimed to have found a wide variety of bodily features predictive of criminal behavior. Among them were exceptionally long arms, an index finger as long as the middle finger, fleshy pouches in the cheeks "like those in rodents," eyes that were either abnormally close together or too far apart, large teeth, ears which lacked lobes, prominent cheekbones, a crooked nose, a large amount of body hair, protruding chin, large lips, a nonstandard number of ribs, and eyes of differing colors or hues. Lombroso went so far as to enumerate characteristics of particular types of offenders. Murderers, whom he called "habitual homicides," have, in Lombroso's words, "cold, glassy eyes, immobile and sometimes sanguine and inflamed; the nose, always large, is frequently aquiline or, rather, hooked; the jaws are strong, the cheekbones large, the hair curly, dark, and abundant; the beard is frequently thin, the canine teeth well developed and the lips delicate . . . ."[22]

Atavism implies the notion that criminals are born that way. Lombroso was continuously reassessing his estimates of the proportion, from among all offenders, of the born criminal population. At one point he asserted that fully 90 percent of offenders committed crimes because of atavistic influences. He later revised the figure downward to 70 percent, admitting that normal individuals might be pulled into lives of crime. In addition to the category of the born criminal, Lombroso described other categories of offenders, including the insane, criminaloids, and criminals incited by passion. The insane were said to include mental and moral degenerates, alcoholics, drug addicts, and so forth. **Criminaloids,** also termed occasional criminals, were described as persons who were pulled into breaking the law by virtue of environmental influences. Nevertheless, most criminaloids were seen by

Criminaloids a term used by Cesare Lombroso to describe occasional criminals who were pulled into criminality primarily by environmental influences.

Lombroso as exhibiting some degree of atavism and hence were said to "differ from **born criminals** in degree, not in kind." Those who became criminals by virtue of passion were said to have surrendered to intense emotions, including love, jealousy, hatred, or an injured sense of honor.

Although he focused on physical features, Lombroso was not insensitive to behavioral indicators of criminality. In his later writings he claimed that criminals exhibited acute sight, hearing abilities that were below the norm, an insensitivity to pain, a lack of moral sensibility, cruelty, vindictiveness, impulsiveness, a love of gambling, and a tendency to be tattooed.

In 1893 Lombroso published *The Female Offender.*[23] In that book he expressed his belief that women exhibit far less anatomical variation than do men, but insisted that criminal behavior among women, as among men, derived from atavistic foundations. Lombroso saw the quintessential female offender, the prostitute, as "the genuine typical representative of criminality . . . ."[24] Prostitutes, he said, are acting out atavistic yearnings and returning to a form of behavior characteristic of humankind's primitive past.

Evaluations of Atavism

Following in Lombroso's positivistic footsteps, at approximately the turn of the twentieth century the English physician **Charles Buckman Goring** (1870–1919) conducted a well-controlled statistical study of Lombroso's thesis of atavism. Using newly developed but advanced mathematical techniques to measure the degree of correlation between physiological features and criminal history, Goring examined nearly 3,000 inmates at Turin prison beginning in 1901 and enlisted the aid of London's Biometric Laboratory to conclude that "the whole fabric of Lombrosian doctrine, judged by the standards of science, is fundamentally unsound."[25] Goring compared the prisoners with students at Oxford and Cambridge Universities, British soldiers, and noncriminal hospital patients, and published his findings in 1913 in his lengthy treatise *The English Convict: A Statistical Study.*[26] The foreword to Goring's book was written by Karl Pearson, who praised Goring for having no particular perspective of his own to advance and who could, he said, therefore objectively evaluate the ideas of others such as Lombroso.

A similar study was conducted between 1927 and 1939 by **Earnest A. Hooton,** a professor of anthropology at Harvard University. In 1939 Hooton published *Crime and the Man,*[27] in which he reported having evaluated 13,873 inmates from ten states, comparing them along 107 physiological dimensions with 3,203 nonincarcerated individuals who formed a control group. His sample consisted of 10,953 prison inmates, 2,004 county jail prisoners, 743 criminally insane, 173 "defective delinquents," 1,227 "insane civilians," and 1,976 "sane civilians."

Hooton distinguished between regions of the country, saying that "states have favorite crimes, just as they have favorite sons." He reported finding physiological features characteristic of specific criminal types in individual states. For example, "Massachusetts criminals," he said, "are notable for thick beards, red-brown hair, dark brown, green-brown and blue-gray eyes, whites of eyes discolored with yellow or brown pigment flecks, rayed pattern of the iris of the eye, external and median folds of the upper eyelids, broad, high nasal roots and bridges, concave nasal profiles, thick nasal tips, right deflections of the nasal septum, thin integumental lips, thin upper membranous lip and thick lower lip, absence of lip seam, some . . . protrusion of the jaws, pointed or median chins, much dental decay but few teeth lost, small and soldered or attached ear lobes, and right facial asymmetries."[28] He went on to say that, through a sufficient degree of statistical manipulation, "[w]e finally emerge with differences between the offense groups which are not due to accidents of sampling, are not due to state variations, and are independent of differences between the ages of the offense groups. Thus, in the case of first-degree murder we find the members of that offense group deficient in persons with abundant head hair, deficient in individuals with narrow nasal bridges, presenting an excess of persons with pointed or median chins, and with compressed cheek bones."[29] He also found that first-degree murderers were more "square-shouldered" than other criminals and had larger ear lobes. From findings such as these, he was drawn to the conclusion that "crime is not an exclusively sociological phenomenon, but is also biological."[30]

In writing "it is impossible to improve and correct environment to a point at which these flawed and degenerate human beings will be able to succeed in honest social competition,"[31] Hooton made it clear that he did not believe that rehabilitation programs could have much effect upon most offenders and suggested banishing them to a remote location. Hooton concluded that criminals showed an overall physiological inferiority to the general population, and that crime was the result of "the impact of environment upon low grade human organisms."[32]

Hooton, an example of whose work is provided in Figure 5.1, was quickly criticized along a number of dimensions. Stephen Schafer, the well-known contemporary criminologist, says "[t]he major criticisms were that his criminal population was not a representative sample of all criminals, that his control group was a fantastic conglomeration of noncriminal civilians, . . . that he emphasized selected characteristics and disregarded others, that he gave no convincing evidence that the criminal's 'inferiority' was inherited, and that he failed to explore other important data that were available."[33] Perhaps even more significant, Hooton failed to recognize that members of his noncriminal control group may, in fact, have been involved in crime but had managed to elude capture and processing by the criminal justice system. In other words, it may have been that the most successful criminals did not appear in Hooton's study group of inmates because they had eluded the law, thereby making their way into his supposedly noncriminal control group. His study may have simply demonstrated that "inferior" criminal specimens are the ones who get caught and end up in prison.

BODY TYPES

Constitutional theories are those which explain criminality by reference to offenders' body types, genetics, and/or external observable physical characteristics. A constitutional or physiological orientation which found its way into the criminological mainstream during the early and mid-twentieth century was that of body types. Also called **somatotyping,** this perspective was primarily associated with the

---

Constitutional theories those which explain criminality by reference to offenders' body types, genetics, and/or external observable physical characteristics.

Somatotyping the classification of human beings into types according to body build and other physical characteristics.

work of **Ernst Kretschmer** and **William H. Sheldon.** Kretschmer, a professor of psychiatry at the German University of Tubingen, proposed a relationship between body build and personality type and created a rather detailed "biopsychological constitutional typology." Kretschmer's somatotypology revolved around three basic mental categories: cycloids (also called cyclothymes), schizoids (or schizothymes), and displastics. The **cycloid** personality, which was associated with a heavyset, soft type of body according to Kretschmer, vacillated between normality and abnormality. Cycloids were said to lack spontaneity and sophistication, and were thought to commit mostly nonviolent property types of offenses. Schizoids, who tended to possess athletic, muscular bodies but, according to Kretschmer, could also be thin and lean, were seen as more likely to be schizophrenic and to commit violent types of offenses. Displastics were said to be a mixed group described as highly emotional and often unable to control themselves. Hence, they were thought to commit mostly sexual offenses and other crimes of passion.

Influenced by Kretschmer, William H. Sheldon utilized measurement techniques to connect body type with personality.[34] Sheldon felt that Kretschmer had erred in including too large an age range in his work. Therefore, he chose to limit

Cycloid a term developed by Ernst Kretschmer to describe a particular relationship between body build and personality type. The cycloid personality, which was associated with a heavyset, soft type of body, was said to vacillate between normality and abnormality.

OLD AMERICAN CRIMINALS

Mosaic of Cranial, Facial, Metric and Morphological Features

MASSACHUSETTS

Narrowest face
Narrowest jaw
Thick beards
Broad, high nasal roots and bridges
Thick nasal tips
Right deflections of nasal septum
Concave profiles ①
External and median eyefolds ②
Small, attached ear lobes ③
Thin integumental lips ④
Membranous lips--upper thin, lower thick
Lip seams absent
Undershot jaw
Facial prognathism ⑤
Right facial asymmetry ⑥
Median chins

FIGURE 5.1   Earnest A. Hooton's "Massachusetts Criminal." Reprinted by permission of the publishers from *Crime and The Man* by Earnest Albert Hooton, Cambridge, Mass: Harvard University Press. Copyright © 1939 by the President and Fellows of Harvard College, renewed 1967 by Mary C. Hooton.

Endomorph a body type originally described as soft and round, or overweight.

Mesomorph a body type originally described as athletic and muscular.

Ectomorph a body type originally described as thin and fragile, with long, slender, poorly muscled extremities, and delicate bones.

his study to 200 boys between the ages of 15 and 21 at the Hayden Goodwill Institute in Boston. Sheldon concluded that four basic body types characterized the entire group. Each type, described partly in Sheldon's words, is as follows:

- The **endomorph,** who is soft and round and whose "digestive viscera are massive and highly developed" (i.e., the person is overweight and has a large stomach).
- The **mesomorph,** who is athletic and muscular and whose "somatic structures . . . are in the ascendancy" (i.e., the person has larger bones and considerable muscle mass).
- The **ectomorph,** who is thin and fragile, and who has "long, slender, poorly muscled extremities, with delicate, pipestem bones."
- The balanced type, which is of average build, being neither overweight, thin, nor exceedingly muscular.

Individuals were ranked along each of the three major dimensions (the balanced type was excluded) using a seven-point scale. A score of 1-1-7, for example, would indicate that a person exhibited few characteristics of endomorphology or mesomorphology, but was predominantly ectomorphic. Sheldon claimed that varying types of temperament and personalities were closely associated with each of the body types he identified. Ectomorphs were said to be cerebrotonic, or restrained, shy, and inhibited. Endomorphs were viscerotonic, or relaxed and sociable. The mesomorphic, or muscular, body type, however, he said was most likely to be associated with delinquency or somatotonia, which he described as "a predominance of muscular activity and . . . vigorous bodily assertiveness." William H. Sheldon's work was supported by constitutional studies of juvenile delinquents conducted by

Endomorphs on the march. A group of would-be actors line up to audition for roles in the movie *Fat Chance.* How might body type relate to criminal activity? *Marty Lederhandler/AP/Wide World Photos.*

Sheldon and Eleanor Glueck, and reported in 1950.[35] The Gluecks compared 500 known delinquents with 500 nondelinquents, and matched both groups on age, general intelligence, ethnical-racial background, and place of residence. Like Sheldon, the Gluecks concluded that mesomorphy was associated with delinquency.

Early biological theorists such as Sheldon, Lombroso, and Gall provide an interesting footnote in the history of criminological thought. Today, however, their work is mostly relegated to dust bins of academic theorizing. Modern biological theories of crime are far more sophisticated than their early predecessors, and it is to these that we now turn.

CHEMICAL AND ENVIRONMENTAL PRECURSORS OF CRIME

Recent research in the area of nutrition has produced some limited evidence that the old maxim "You are what you eat!" may contain more than a grain of truth. Biocriminology has made some significant strides in linking violent or disruptive behavior to eating habits, vitamin deficiencies, genetics, inheritance, and other conditions which impact body tissues. Studies of nutrition, endocrinology, and environmental contaminants have all contributed to advances in understanding such behavior.

One of the first studies to focus on chemical imbalances in the body as a cause of crime was reported in the British medical journal *Lancet* in 1943.[36] Authors of the study linked murder to **hypoglycemia,** or low blood sugar. Low blood sugar, produced by too much insulin in the blood or by near-starvation diets, was said to reduce the mind's capacity to effectively reason or to judge the long-term consequences of behavior. More recent studies have linked excess consumption of refined white sugar to hyperactivity and aggressiveness. Popular books such as *Sugar Blues* provide guides for individuals seeking to free themselves from the negative effects of excess sugar consumption.

To some degree even courts have accepted the notion that excess sugar consumption may be linked to crime. In the early 1980s, for example, Dan White, a former San Francisco police officer, was given a reduced sentence after his lawyers convinced the court that their defendant's consumption of massive amounts of refined white sugar had increased his excitability and lowered his ability to make reasoned decisions. White had been convicted of murdering San Francisco Mayor Moscone and City Councilman Harvey Milk during a dispute in the mayor's office. The night before the killings, White stayed awake drinking Coca-Cola and eating many Twinkies.

More than ten years later, however, a well-conducted 1994 study reported in the *New England Journal of Medicine*[37] seemed to contradict the notion that sugar may lead to hyperactivity. Similarly, neither sugar nor artificial sweeteners were shown to have any link to an increase in learning disabilities. In the study, researchers at Vanderbilt University and the University of Iowa varied the diets of supposedly sugar-sensitive youngsters from ones that were high in sugar, to one that was low in sugar but contained the artificial sweetener aspartame. A third experimental diet contained very little sugar, but had added saccharin. After surveying parents, teachers, and babysitters and testing the study group for changes in memory, concentration,

Hypoglycemia a condition characterized by low blood sugar.

and math skills, the researchers concluded "[w]e couldn't find any difference in terms of their behavior or their learning on any of the three diets."[38] Hence, to date, the evidence concerning sugar's impact on behavior is less than clear.

Allergic reactions to common foods have been reported as the cause of violence and homicide by a number of investigators.[39] Some foods—including milk, citrus fruit, chocolate, corn, wheat, and eggs—are said to produce allergic reactions in sensitive individuals, leading to a swelling of the brain and the brain stem. Involvement of the central nervous system in such allergies, it has been suggested, reduces the amount of learning which occurs during childhood, and may contribute to delinquency as well as to adult criminal behavior. Such swelling is also thought to impede the higher faculties, reducing one's sense of morality and creating conditions that support impulsive behavior.

Some studies have implicated food additives, such as the flavor enhancer monosodium glutamate, dyes, and artificial flavorings in producing criminal violence.[40] Other research[41] has found that coffee and sugar may trigger antisocial behavior. Researchers were led to these conclusions through finding that inmates consumed considerably greater amounts of coffee, sugar, and processed foods than others.[42] It is, however, unclear whether inmates drink more coffee because of boredom, or whether "excitable" personalities feel a need for the kind of stimulation available through coffee consumption. On the other hand, habitual coffee drinkers in nonprison populations have not been linked to crime, and other studies, such as that conducted by Mortimer Gross of the University of Illinois, show no link between the amount of sugar consumed by inmates and hyperactivity.[43] Nonetheless, some prison programs have been designed to limit intake of dietary stimulants through nutritional management and the substitution of artificial sweeteners for refined sugar. Vitamins have also been examined for their impact on delinquency. At least one researcher found that disruptive children consumed far less than optimal levels of vitamins B_3 and B_6 than did nonproblem youths.[44] Some researchers have suggested that the addition of these vitamins to the diets of children who were deficient in them could control unruly behavior and improve school performance.

The role of food and diet in producing criminal behavior, however, has not been well established. The American Dietetic Association and the National Council Against Health Fraud have concluded that no convincing scientific relationship between crime and diet has yet been demonstrated.[45] Both groups are becoming concerned that poor nutrition may result from programs intended to have behavioral impacts, such as those that reduce or modify diets in prisons or elsewhere.

In 1997 British researchers Roger D. Masters, Brian Hone, and Anil Doshi published a study[46] purporting to show that industrial and other forms of environmental pollution cause people to commit violent crimes. The study used statistics from the FBI's Uniform Crime Reporting Program and data from the U.S. Environmental Protection Agency's Toxic Release Inventory. A comparison between the two data sets showed a significant correlation between juvenile crime and high environmental levels of both lead and manganese. Masters and his colleagues suggested an explanation based on a neurotoxicity hypothesis. "According to this approach, toxic pollutants—specifically the toxic metals lead and manganese—cause learning disabilities, an increase in aggressive behavior, and—most importantly—loss of control over impulsive behavior. These traits combine with poverty, social stress, alcohol and drug abuse, individual character, and other social and psychological factors to produce individuals who commit violent crimes."[47]

According to Masters, the presence of excess manganese lowers levels of serotonin and dopamine in the brain—both of which are neurotransmitters associated with impulse control and planning. Masters notes that low blood levels of serotonin are known to cause mood disturbances, poor impulse control, and increases in aggressive behavior. Masters claims that children who are raised from birth on infant formula, and who are not breastfed, will absorb five times as much manganese as breastfed infants. Calcium deficiency is known to increase the absorption of manganese and, says Masters, "a combination of manganese toxicity and calcium deficiency adds up to 'reverse' Prozac."

In support of his thesis Masters cites other studies, the largest of which was an examination of 1,000 black children in Philadelphia that showed that levels of exposure to lead was a reliable predictor of the number of juvenile offenses among the exposed male population, the seriousness of juvenile offenses, and the number of adult offenses.

According to Masters, toxic metals affect individuals in complex ways. Because lead diminishes a person's normal ability to detoxify poisons, he says, it may heighten the effects of alcohol and drugs. Industrial pollution, automobile traffic, lead-based paints, and aging water delivery systems are all possible sources of contamination. In a recent interview, Masters said: "The presence of pollution is as big a factor [in crime causation] as poverty. . . . It's the breakdown of the inhibition mechanism that's the key to violent behavior."[48] When brain chemistry is altered by exposure to heavy metal and other toxins, he said, people lose the natural restraint that holds their violent tendencies in check.

In addition to chemical substances likely to be ingested, other environmental features have also been linked to the likelihood of aggressive behavior. During the early 1980s, for example, Alexander Schauss and his followers[49] were able to show that the use of a specific shade of the color pink could have a calming effect on people experiencing feelings of anger and agitation. Findings indicated that exposure to the color pink produced an endocrine change which caused a tranquilizing effect on the muscles. This involuntary effect, said researchers, was not subject to conscious control. As a result of such studies, jail cells in a number of locales—including Seattle, San Bernardino, San Mateo County (California), Southbridge (Massachusetts), New Orleans, and Charlotte (North Carolina)—were painted pink in hopes that aggressive tendencies among inmates might be reduced. Researchers supported such measures, saying that "the use of pink color in reducing aggression and causing muscular relaxation of inmates is humane and requires no medication or physical force."[50]

HORMONES AND CRIMINALITY

Hormones have also come under scrutiny as potential behavioral determinants. The male sex hormone **testosterone,** for example, has been linked to aggression. Most studies on the subject have consistently shown an apparent relationship between high blood testosterone levels and increased aggressiveness in men. More

Testosterone the primary male sex hormone; produced in the testes, its function is to control secondary sex characteristics and sexual drive.

Davidson County Sheriff Gerald Hedge shows off his newly redecorated jail. The jail sports pink walls, a color that psychologists think may lower the likelihood of aggressive behavior. The blue teddy bears were the sheriff's idea. How do you think offenders will react? *Sonny Hedgecech*

focused studies have unveiled a direct relationship between the amount of the chemical present and the degree of violence used by sex offenders,[51] while other researchers have linked steroid abuse among bodybuilders to destructive urges and psychosis.[52] Contemporary investigations[53] demonstrate a link between testosterone levels and aggression in teenagers, while others[54] show that adolescent problem behavior and teenage violence rise in proportion to the amount of testosterone levels in the blood of young men. In 1987, for example, a Swedish researcher, Dan Olweus,[55] reported that boys aged 15 to 17 showed levels of both verbal and physical aggression which correlated with the level of testosterone present in their blood. Olweus also found that boys with higher levels of testosterone "tended to be habitually more impatient and irritable than boys with lower testosterone levels." He concluded that high levels of the hormone led to increased frustration and habitual impatience and irritability.

In what may be the definitive work to date on the subject, Alan Booth and D. Wayne Osgood[56] conclude that there is a "moderately strong relationship between testosterone and adult deviance,"[57] but suggest that the relationship "is largely mediated by the influence of testosterone on social integration and on prior involvement in juvenile delinquency."[58] In other words, measurably high levels of testosterone in the blood of young men may have some effect on behavior, but those effects are likely to be moderated by the social environment.

A few limited studies have attempted to measure the effects of testosterone on women. Women's bodies manufacture roughly one-tenth the amount of the hormone secreted by men. Even so, subtle changes in testosterone levels in women have

Sex hormones, such as testosterone, have been linked to aggressive behavior. Testosterone also enhances secondary sexual characteristics such as body hair and muscle mass in males. What kinds of crime might be hormonally influenced? *The Kobal Collection.*

been linked to changes in personality and sexual behavior.[59] Few such studies exist, however, and their findings should therefore be regarded as inconclusive.

Fluctuations in the level of female hormones, however, may also bear some relationship to law violation. In 1980 a British court exonerated Christine English of charges that she murdered her live-in lover, after English admittedly ran him over with her car after an argument. English's defense rested on the fact that she was suffering from premenstrual syndrome (PMS) at the time of the homicide. An expert witness, Dr. Katharina Dalton, testified at the trial that PMS had caused Ms. English to be "irritable, aggressive, . . . and confused, with loss of self-control."

Another case[60] involving PMS was decided in 1991 by a Fairfax, Virginia, judge who dismissed drunk driving and other charges against a female orthopedic surgeon named Dr. Geraldine Richter. Richter allegedly kicked and cursed a Virginia state trooper and admitted to having consumed four glasses of wine after being stopped for driving erratically. A Breathalyzer test showed her blood-alcohol level to be nearly 0.13 percent—above the 0.10 percent level Virginia law set for such a violation. Charges against Dr. Richter were dismissed after a gynecologist testified on her behalf, saying that the behavior she exhibited was likely to have been due primarily to PMS.

Although evidence linking PMS to violent and/or criminal behavior is far from clear, some researchers believe that a drop in serotonin levels in the female brain just prior to menstruation might explain the agitation and irritability sometimes associated with premenstrual syndrome. Serotonin has been called a "behavior-regulating chemical" and animal studies have demonstrated a link between low levels of the neurotransmitter present in the brain and aggressive behavior. Monkeys, for example, with low serotonin levels have been found more likely to bite, slap, and chase others of their kind. Low serotonin levels in humans have been linked via studies at the National Institute on Alcohol Abuse and Alcoholism to impulsive crimes. Men convicted of premeditated murder, for example, have been found to have normal serotonin levels, whereas those convicted of crimes of passion have lower levels.[61]

❖❖ GENETICS AND CRIME

CRIMINAL FAMILIES

Some scholars suggest that a penchant for crime may be inherited, and that criminal tendencies are genetically based. Early studies of this type often focused on criminal families, or families that appeared to exhibit criminal tendencies through several generations.

In 1877 **Richard L. Dugdale** (1841–1883) published a study[62] of one such family—the **Juke family.** Dugdale traced the Juke lineage back to a notorious character named Max, a Dutch immigrant who arrived in New York in the early 1700s. Two of Max's sons married into the notorious "Juke family of girls," six sisters, all of whom were said to be illegitimate. Max's male descendants were reputed to be vicious, and one woman named Ada had an especially bad reputation and came to be known as "the mother of criminals." By the time of the study, Dugdale was able to identify approximately 1,200 of Ada's descendants. Included among their numbers were 7 murderers, 60 habitual thieves, 90 or so other criminals, 50 prostitutes, and 280 paupers. Dugdale compared the crime-prone Jukes with another family, the pure-blooded progeny of Jonathan Edwards, a Puritan preacher and one-time president of Princeton University. Descendants of Edwards included American presidents and vice presidents and many successful bankers and businesspeople. None were identified from among the Edwards lineage who had run-ins with the law. In 1915 **Arthur H. Estabrook** published a follow-up to Dugdale's work, in which he identified an additional 715 Juke descendants, including 378 more prostitutes, 170 additional paupers, and 118 other criminals.[63]

Following in the tradition of family tree researchers, **Henry H. Goddard** (1866–1957) published a study[64] of the **Kallikak family** in 1912. Goddard attempted to place the study of deviant families within an acceptable scientific framework via the provision of a kind of control group. For comparison purposes he used two branches of the same family. One branch began as the result of a sexual liaison between Martin Kallikak, a Revolutionary War soldier, and a barmaid whose name is unknown. As a result of this illegitimate union, a son (Martin, Jr.) was born. After the war, Martin, Sr., returned home and married a righteous Quaker girl, and a second line of descent began. Although the second, legitimate branch, produced only a few minor deviants, the illegitimate line resulted in 262 "feebleminded" births and various other epileptic, alcoholic, and criminal descendants. The term *feeble-*

Juke family a well-known "criminal family" studied by Richard L. Dugdale.

Kallikak family a well-known "criminal family" studied by Henry H. Goddard.

minded, which was much in vogue at the time of Goddard's study, was later recast as "mental retardation," whereas people exhibiting similar characteristics today might be referred to as mentally handicapped or mentally challenged. Because feeblemindedness appeared to occur with some predictability in Goddard's study, whereas criminal activity seemed to be only randomly represented among the descendants of either Kallikak line, Goddard concluded that a tendency toward feeblemindedness was inherited, but criminality was not.

Studies such as these, which focused on inherited mental degeneration, led to the **eugenics** movement of the 1920s and early 1930s under which mentally handicapped women were frequently sterilized to prevent their bearing additional offspring. That movement was epitomized in the 1927 U.S. Supreme Court case of ***Buck*** v. ***Bell,***[65] in which Justice Oliver Wendell Holmes, Jr., writing in support of a Virginia statute permitting sterilization, said "[i]t is better for all the world, if instead of waiting to execute degenerate offspring for crime, or to let them starve for their imbecility, society can prevent those persons who are manifestly unfit from continuing their kind."

Eugenics the study of hereditary improvement by genetic control.

THE XYY "SUPERMALE"

Recent developments in the field of human genetics have led to the study of the role of chromosomes, and sex-linked chromosomes in particular, in crime causation. The first well-known study[66] of this type was undertaken by Patricia A. Jacobs, a British researcher who in 1965 examined 197 Scottish prisoners for chromosomal abnormalities through a relatively simple blood test known as *karyotyping.*[67] Twelve members of the group displayed chromosomes which were unusual, and seven were found to have an XYY chromosome. "Normal" male individuals possess an XY chromosome structure, and "normal" female individuals are XX. Some other unusual combinations might be XXX, wherein a woman's genetic makeup contains an extra X chromosome, or XXY, also called Klinefelter's syndrome, in which a man might carry an extra X, or female chromosome. Klinefelter's men often are possessed of male genitalia, but are frequently sterile and evidence breast enlargement and intellectual retardation. The XYY man, however, whose incidence in the prison population was placed at around 3.5 percent by Jacobs, was quickly identified as potentially violent and termed a ***supermale.***

Supermale a male individual displaying the XYY chromosome structure.

Following introduction of the supermale notion into popular consciousness, a number of offenders attempted to offer a chromosome-based defense. In 1969, for example, Lawrence E. Hannell, who was adjudged a supermale, was acquitted of murder in Australia on the grounds of insanity.[68] Such a defense, however, did not work for Richard Speck, another claimed XYY man, convicted of killing eight Chicago nursing students in 1966. It was later learned that Speck did not carry the extra Y chromosome.

To date there have been nearly 200 studies of XYY males. Although not all researchers agree, taken as a group these studies[69] tend to show that supermales

- are taller than the average male, often standing 6′1″ or more;
- suffer from acne or skin disorders;

• are of less than average intelligence;
• are overrepresented in prisons and mental hospitals; and
• come from families with less history of crime or mental illness.

The supermale phenomenon, also called the XYY syndrome, may have been more sensationalism than fact. Little evidence suggests that XYY men actually commit crimes of greater violence than do other men, although they may commit somewhat more crimes overall. A 1976 Danish study[70] of 4,000 men, which found precisely that, may have helped put the issue to rest. The Danish survey, conducted of men born in Copenhagen between 1944 and 1947, also found that the incidence of XYY men was less than 1 percent in the general male population. Other recent researchers have similarly concluded that "studies done thus far are largely in agreement and demonstrate rather conclusively that males of the XYY type are not predictably aggressive."[71]

CHROMOSOMES AND MODERN-DAY CRIMINAL FAMILIES

In 1993 Dutch criminologists caught worldwide attention with their claim that they had uncovered a specific gene with links to criminal behavior. Geneticist Han Brunner, researcher H. Hilger Ropers, and collaborators studied what media sources called "the Netherlands' most dysfunctional family."[72] Although the unnamed family displayed IQs in the near normal range, they seemed unable to control their impulses and often ended up being arrested for violations of the criminal law. Arrests, however, were always of men. Tracing the family back five generations, Brunner found fourteen men whom he classified as genetically given to criminality. None of the women in the family displayed criminal tendencies, although they were often victimized by their crime-prone male siblings. One brother raped a sister and later stabbed a mental hospital staffer in the chest with a pitchfork. Another tried to run over his supervisor with his car. Two brothers repeatedly started fires, and were classified as arsonists. Another brother frequently crept into his sisters' rooms and forced them to undress at knifepoint.

According to Ropers and Brunner, because men have only one X chromosome they are especially vulnerable to any defective gene. Women, with two X chromosomes, have a kind of backup system in which one defective gene may be compensated for by another wholesome and correctly functioning gene carried in the second X chromosome. After a decade of study, which involved the laboratory filtering of a huge quantity of genetic material in a search for the defective gene, Ropers and Brunner announced that they had isolated the specific mutation that caused the family's criminality. The gene, they said, is one that is responsible in the body for production of an enzyme called monoamine oxidase A (MAOA). MAOA is crucially involved in the process by which signals are transmitted within the brain. Specifically, MAOA breaks down the chemicals serotonin and noradrenaline. Both are substances that, when found in excess in the brain, have been linked to aggressive behavior in human beings. Because men with the mutated gene do not produce the enzyme necessary to break down chemical transmitters, researchers surmise, their brains are overwhelmed with stimuli—a situation that results in uncontrollable urges and, ultimately, criminal behavior.

*It is a well known fact that biological weaknesses that make one more susceptible to
cancer and heart attacks can be passed genetically, so why not biological weaknesses
that encourage alcoholism, drug addiction and violent behavior?*

— CLYDE L. CRONKHITE[73]

TWIN STUDIES

Studies of the criminal tendencies of fraternal and identical twins provide a
methodologically sophisticated technique for ferreting out the role of inheritance
in crime causation. Fraternal twins (also called dizygotic or DZ twins) develop from
different fertilized eggs and share only that genetic material common among siblings. Identical twins (also called **monozygotic** or **MZ twins**) develop from the
same egg, and carry virtually the same genetic material.

Monozyotic or MZ twins,
as opposed to dizygotic
(or DZ) twins, develop
from the same egg, and
carry virtually the same
genetic material.

One of the first studies[74] to link MZ twins to criminality was published in the
1920s by the German physician Johannes Lange. Lange examined only seventeen
pairs of fraternal and thirteen pairs of identical twins, but found that in ten of the
thirteen identical pairs both twins were criminal, whereas only two of the seventeen
fraternal pairs exhibited such similarity. Lange's findings drew considerable attention, even though his sample was small and he was unable to adequately separate
environmental influences from genetic ones. The title of his book, *Verbrechen als
Schicksal,* whose English translation is *Crime as Destiny,* indicates Lange's firm conviction that criminality has a strong genetic component.

A much larger twin study[75] was begun in 1968 by the European researchers Karl
Christiansen and Sarnoff Mednick, who analyzed all twins (3,586 pairs) born on a
selected group of Danish islands between 1881 and 1910. Christiansen and
Mednick found significant statistical support for the notion that criminal tendencies are inherited, and concluded that 52 percent of identical twins and 22 percent
of fraternal siblings displayed the same degree of criminality within the twin pair.
Such similarities remained apparent even among twins who had been separated at
birth and who were raised in substantially different environments.

MALE–FEMALE DIFFERENCES IN CRIMINALITY

A number of writers unequivocally recognize that "the male is much more crimi-
nalistic than the female."[76] As Chapter 2 describes, with the exception of crimes
such as prostitution and shoplifting, the number of crimes committed by men routinely far exceeds the number of crimes committed by women in almost any category—and when women commit crimes they are far more likely to assume the role
of followers than leaders.[77] The data on the extent of male–female criminality show
surprising regularity over time. The proportion of homicides committed by men
versus women, for example, has remained more or less constant for decades (see
Table 5.1). In fact, as the table shows and contrary to popular expectations, *male*
perpetrators appear to be involved in an ever larger proportion of murders over the
past thirty-five years. Similarly, the proportion of men murdered by men versus the
proportion of women murdered by women has continuously shown a much larger
propensity for men to murder one another.

⚏

TABLE 5.1

MALE AND FEMALE MURDER PERPETRATORS AS A PERCENTAGE OF ALL ARRESTS FOR HOMICIDE 1960–1996

1960		1975		1980		1996	
Male	*Female*	*Male*	*Female*	*Male*	*Female*	*Male*	*Female*
82.5%	17.5%	84.7%	15.3%	87.2%	12.8%	90.6%	9.4%

Source: Adapted from Federal Bureau of Investigation, *Crime in the United States* (Washington, D.C.: U.S. Department of Justice, 1961, 1976, 1981, and 1997).

If culture exercises the major role in determining criminality, as many social scientists today suggest, then we would expect to see recognizable increases in the degree and nature of female criminality over time, especially as changes in socialization practices, cultural roles, and other ethnographic patterns increase the opportunity for women to commit what had previously been regarded as traditionally male offenses. With the exception of a few crimes, such as embezzlement, drug abuse, and liquor law violations, however, such has not been the case. Although women comprise 51 percent of the population of the United States, they are arrested for only 13 percent of all violent crimes and 26 percent of property crimes[78]—a proportion that has remained surprisingly constant over the years since the FBI began gathering crime data more than half a century ago. Simply put, even with all the cultural changes which have created new possibilities for women in crime, few women have taken advantage of these newfound freedoms. Such apparent differences have existed not only over time, but can be seen in cross-cultural studies as well. Chapter 2 provides additional statistics of this sort.

Such findings are in contrast with the suggestions of authors such as Freda Adler who, in her 1975 book *Sisters in Crime,*[79] proposed that as women entered "nontraditional occupations" and roles, there "would be a movement toward parity with men in the commission of crime in terms of both incidence and type." Darrell Steffensmeir,[80] who studied changes in women's criminality over a twelve-year period following publication of Adler's book, found almost no evidence to support the belief that a new female criminal is emerging, or that female criminality is undergoing the kind of increase Adler might have expected. The lack of contemporary validation for Adler's thesis suggests that something else is occurring; that is, some element other than cultural inhibition or equality of opportunity is preventing women from taking their place alongside men as equals in crime. Biological criminologists suggest that the organic correlates of gender provide the needed explanation.

In evaluating the criminality of women based on statistics alone, however, danger prevails of misidentifying causal factors operative in the behavior itself. Although men consistently commit more murders than women, for example, we should not jump to the conclusion that this bit of evidence shows a genetic predisposition toward interpersonal violence in men which is absent in women. To do so would fail to recognize the role of other causal factors. Observable racial variation in crime rates has provided some writers with a basis for claiming that some racial groups are disproportionately violent—while simultaneously attributing such violence to a genetic basis. A look at the statistics, for example, shows that in the United States blacks are five times as likely as whites to commit murder, three times as likely to commit rape, six times as likely to rob, and twice as likely, on average, to commit any kind of crime.[81] Chapter 2 again provides additional statistics of this sort.

Such statistics can be inherently misleading because—unlike the undeniable and easily observable biological differences that exist between men and women—racial groupings are defined more by convention than by genetics. In fact, some writers suggest that "pure" racial groups no longer exist, and that even historical racial distinctions were based more on political convention than on significant genetic differences.

The criminality of women (or relative lack thereof) is, in all likelihood, culturally determined to a considerable degree. Nonetheless, the consistency of data which routinely show that women are far less likely than men to be involved in most property crimes, and less likely still to commit violent crimes, requires recognition. We have already evaluated the role that testosterone may play in increasing the propensity toward violence and aggression among men. A few authors suggest that testosterone is the agent primarily responsible for male criminality, and that its relative lack in women leads them to commit fewer crimes. Some evidence supports just such a hypothesis. Studies[82] have shown, for example, that female fetuses exposed to elevated testosterone levels during gestation develop masculine characteristics, including a muscular body build and a demonstrably greater tendency toward aggression later in life. Even so, genetically based behavioral differences between men and women are so overshadowed by aspects of the social environment, including socialization, the learning of culturally prescribed roles, the expectations of others, and so on, that definitive conclusions are difficult to reach.

One recently proposed social-psychological explanation[83] for homicidal behavior among women, for example, suggests that men who kill tend to do so out of a need to control a situation, whereas women who kill tend to do so because they have lost control over themselves. The theory says "that women as a group are more 'controlled' than men, particularly with respect to their experience and expression of anger." Such control is said to emanate from the fact that "men are always the subjects and women the objects in [a] male-centric universe."[84] As a consequence of our culture's overemphasis on a woman's looks rather than on her performance, the theory says, women internalize a "self-image on the basis of appearance rather than substance of character," resulting in low self-esteem and low self-confidence. Low self-esteem, the argument goes, necessitates greater self-control and results in lower criminality among women. Such a perspective suggests that women tend to commit homicides only when driven "past the brink" of self-control, thus offering an explanation for why homicides committed by women are generally spontaneous rather than planned, why they usually involve the killing of intimates, and why they generally occur in the home. "Women generally view themselves as part of a collective of relationships around them," say one theorist, "and evaluate their self-worth based on the value and success of these relationships."[85] Hence, when relationships break down, a woman's self-worth may be negated, resulting in a lessening of control—and homicide may ensue.

VIOLENCE LINKED TO GENE DEFECT:

PLEASURE DEFICIT MAY BE THE SPARK

A gene linked to pleasure-seeking behavior and addictions also may play a role in murder and violence, new research suggests. This pleasure gene normally is involved in the flow of dopamine, a powerful brain chemical that provides people with their sense of well-being. When defective, the gene diminishes dopamine function, driving a person to drink, take drugs or engage in other activities that give dopamine a boost.

Studies suggest people who have a variant of the gene, called "DRD2 A1 allele," are prone to becoming smokers, violent alcoholics, gambling addicts and drug addicts.

"We think they're seeking out ways of fixing the lack of pleasure," says Kenneth Blum, University of Texas Health Science Center, San Antonio. "You might be a pleasure seeker for alcohol, drugs, sex or maybe you get it from violence or murder."

In a study presented Wednesday at an American Psychiatric Association meeting, Blum and 17 researchers found the DRD2 A1 allele in:

- Six of 11 children in a residential treatment program for pathological violence but only one of 30 normal children.
- Half of 109 people diagnosed with "schizoid/avoidant" personality. They are introverted, withdrawn, emotionally cold and distant.

Other research by psychoanalyst Anneliese Pontius, Harvard Medical School, has tied schizoid/avoidant disorder to more than a dozen bizarre murders. She is testing her subjects for the DRD2 A1 variant.

If the findings are confirmed, Blum says problem children could be screened for the gene and given drugs, special diets and other treatments known to boost dopamine.

Questions

1. How might genes that are linked to pleasure-seeking behavior lead to crime?
2. Should policies be created to reduce potential criminal activity among persons with the DRD2 A1 allele gene? If so, what might they be?

Source: Tim Friend, "Violence Linked to Gene Defect: Pleasure Deficit May be the Spark," *USA Today,* May 9, 1996, p. 1D. Copyright 1997, *USA Today.* Reprinted with permission.

SOCIOBIOLOGY

In the introduction to his insightful article summarizing sociobiology, Arthur Fisher writes, "[e]very so often, in the long course of scientific progress, a new set of ideas appears, illuminating and redefining what has gone before like a flare bursting over a darkened landscape."[86] To some, **sociobiology**—a theoretical synthesis of biology, behavior, and evolutionary ecology—brought to the scientific community by **Edward O. Wilson** in his seminal 1975 work *Sociobiology: The New Synthesis,*[87] holds the promise of just such a new paradigm. In his book, Wilson defined sociobiology as "the systematic study of the biological basis of all social behavior" and as "a branch of evolutionary biology and particularly of modern population biology." Through his entomological study of social insects, especially ants, Wilson demonstrated that particular forms of behavior could contribute to the long-term survival of the social group. Wilson focused on altruism (selfless, helping behavior) and found that, contrary to the beliefs of some evolutionary biologists, helping behavior facilitates the continuity of the gene pool found among altruistic individuals. Wilson's major focus was to show that the primary determinant of behavior, including human behavior, was the need to ensure the survival and continuity of genetic material from one generation to the next.

Territoriality, another primary tenant of Wilson's writings, was said to explain much of the conflict seen between and among human beings, including homicide, warfare, and other forms of aggression. In Wilson's words, "[p]art of man's problem is that his intergroup responses are still crude and primitive, and inadequate for the extended extraterritorial relationships that civilization has thrust upon him."

> **Sociobiology** the systematic study of the biological basis of all social behavior.

Sociobiologists tell us that certain traits, such as territoriality, are common to both animals and humans. How might territoriality lead to crime? *Paul Lally/Stock Boston.*

The "unhappy result," as Wilson terms it, may be "tribalism," expressed through the contemporary proliferation of street gangs, racial tension, and the hardened encampments of survivalist and separatist groups.

The sad results of territoriality, whatever its cause, can be seen in the deadly adventure of 15-year-old Michael Carter and his companions, who ended up in the proverbial wrong place at the wrong time. On June 18, 1997, Carter, from Highland Township, Michigan, and two of his friends hopped a CSX Transportation train headed for the town of Holly. The three were looking for a free ten-mile ride on their way to see friends. But they missed their jump-off point, sailed past the town of Holly, and ended up in a run-down inner-city ghetto in the middle of Flint, Michigan, around midnight. Soon the three were surrounded by gang members, led into a secluded area, and shot. Carter died at the scene, while friend Dustin Kaiser, also 15, survived a gunshot wound to the head. The 14-year-old girl who had accompanied the boys was raped and shot in the face, but lived.[88]

As sociobiologists tell us, the violence and aggressiveness associated with territoriality is often reserved for strangers. The approach of sociobiology can explain intragroup aggression—or the violence that occurs within groups—and that which occurs between groups. Wilson writes that his theory suggests that, within the group, "a particularly severe form of aggressiveness should be reserved for actual or suspected adultery. In many human societies," he observes, "where sexual bonding is close and personal knowledge of the behavior of others detailed, adulterers are harshly treated. The sin," he adds, "is regarded to be even worse when offspring are produced."[89] Hence, territoriality and acquisitiveness extend, from a sociobiological perspective, to location, possessions, and even other people. Human laws, says Wilson, are designed to protect genetically based relationships which people have with one another, as well as their material possessions and their claimed locations in space. Violations of these intuitive relationships result in crime and in official reactions by the legal system.

Wilson's writing propelled researchers into a flurry of studies intended to test the validity of his assertions. One study,[90] for example, found that Indian adult male Hanuman langurs (a type of monkey) routinely killed the young offspring of female langurs with whom they bonded when those offspring had been sired by other male langurs. A Canadian study[91] of violence in the homes of adoptive children found a human parallel in the langur study, showing that stepchildren run a seventy times greater risk of being killed by their adoptive parent(s) than do children living with their natural parents. Some writers concluded that "murderous behavior, warfare, and even genocide were unavoidable correlates of genetic evolution, controlled by the same genes for territorial behavior that had been selected in primate evolution."[92] Others suggested that biological predispositions developed during earlier stages of human evolution color contemporary criminal activity. Male criminals, for example, tend toward robbery and burglary—crimes in which they can continue to enact their "hunter instincts" developed long ago. The criminality of women, on the other hand, is more typical of "gatherers" when it involves shoplifting, simple theft, and so on.

Human behavioral predilections can be studied in a variety of ways. In the 1989 book *Evolutionary Jurisprudence,*[93] John H. Beckstrom reports upon his examination of over 400 legal documents which, he claimed, showed support for Wilson's contentions that humans tend to act so as to preserve territorial claims, the likelihood of successful reproduction, and the continuation of their own particular genetic material. Beckstrom used legal claims and court decisions in his analysis, spanning over 300 years of judicial activity. Other theorists have gone so far as to imply that, among humans, there may be a gene-based tendency to experience guilt and to develop a conscience. Hence, notions of right and wrong, whether embodied in laws or in social convention, may flow from such a naturalistic origin.

As sociobiology began to receive expanded recognition from American investigators, some social scientists, believing the basic tenants of their profession to be challenged by the movement, began to treat it as "criminology's anti-discipline."[94] John Madison Memory writes, "[b]y the early 1980s sociobiology presented such a significant threat to American criminology that it could no longer be ignored."[95] Criticisms were quick to come. Memory identifies many such critiques, including charges that

- Sociobiology . . . fails to convey the overwhelming significance of culture, social learning, and individual experiences in shaping the behavior of individuals and groups.
- Sociobiology is fundamentally wrong in its depiction of the basic nature of man; there is no credible evidence of genetically based or determined tendencies to act in certain ways.
- Sociobiology is just another empirically unsupported rationale for the authoritative labeling, stigmatization of despised, threatening, powerless minorities.
- Man is so thoroughly different from other animal species, even other primates, that there is no rational basis for the application to man of findings from animal studies.

Many such criticisms were advanced by old guard academicians, some of whom still flourish, in an effort to prevent their own discipline's decline in influence in the face of otherwise convincing sociobiological claims. In the words of one observer, "[m]ost criminologists, like most academicians, were wedded to a **paradigm,** and wedded even to the idea of paradigm, the idea that one great problem solution can permit the explanation of nearly all the unexplained variation in the field."[96] In other words, many criminologists were committed to the idea that one theory (generally their own) could explain all that there was to know about crime and its causes. Fortunately, today many open-minded scholars are beginning to sense the growing need for a new synthesis—for a way in which to integrate the promise of biological theories such as sociobiology with other long-accepted perspectives such as sociology and psychology. As a result, evidence suggests that the field of criminology is now ripe for a new multicausal approach.

Paradigm an example,
model, or theory.

▪▪ CRIME AND HUMAN NATURE: A CONTEMPORARY SYNTHESIS

A decade ago Arnold L. Lieber[97] delivered the invited address at the annual meeting of the American Psychological Association in Denver, Colorado. Lieber used the forum to describe his research, which linked phases of the moon to fluctuations in the incidence of violence among human beings. Nights around full moons, according to Lieber, show a significant rise in crime. Although critics found this type of research nonsensical, police officers, hospital personnel, ambulance drivers, and many late-night service providers who heard of Lieber's talk understood what he was describing. Many such individuals, in their own experience, had apparently seen validation of the "full moon thesis."

Shortly after Lieber's presentation, criminologist **James Q. Wilson** and psychologist **Richard J. Herrnstein** teamed up to write *Crime and Human Nature*,[98] a book-length treatise that reiterates many of the arguments proposed by biological criminologists over the past century. Their purpose, at least in part, was to reopen discussion of biological causes of crime. "We want to show," Herrnstein said, "that the pendulum is beginning to swing away from a totally sociological explanation of crime."[99] Their avowed goal was "not to state a case just for genetic factors, but to state a comprehensive theory of crime that draws together all the different factors that cause criminal behavior."

Constitutional factors that Wilson and Herrnstein cite as contributing to crime include the following.[100]

- *Gender:* "Crime," the authors say, "has been predominantly male behavior."
- *Age:* "In general," they write, "the tendency to break the law declines throughout life."
- *Body Type:* "A disproportionate number of criminals," the authors say, "have a mesomorphic build."
- *Intelligence:* Criminality is said to be clearly and consistently associated with low intelligence.
- *Personality:* Criminals are typically aggressive, impulsive, and cruel.

Although personality, behavioral problems, and intelligence may be related to environment, the authors say "each involve some genetic inheritance." Although Wilson and Herrnstein recognize social factors in the development of personality, they suggest that constitutional factors predispose a person to specific types of behavior, and that societal reactions to such predispositions may determine, to a large degree, the form of continued behavior. Hence, the interplay between heredity, biology, and the social environment may be the key nexus in any consideration of crime causation.

POLICY ISSUES

Biological theories of crime causation present unique challenges to policymakers. According to C. Ray Jeffery, a comprehensive biologically based program of crime prevention and crime control would include

- "Pre- and postnatal care for pregnant women and their infants," to monitor and address potentially detrimental developmental conditions which could lead to heightened aggression and crime later in life.
- Monitoring of children throughout the early stages of their development to identify "early symptoms of behavioral disorder."

- Monitoring of children in their early years to reduce the risk of exposure to violence-inducing experiences such as child abuse and violence committed by other children.
- Neurological examinations, including "CAT, PET, and MRI scans . . . given when the need is evident."
- Biological research, conducted in our nation's prisons and treatment facilities, which might better identify the root causes of aggression and violence. Laws that prevent the experimental use of prison subjects, the analysis of the bodies of executed prisoners, and other similar types of biological investigations must change, says Jeffery.[101]

Jeffery adds that the fundamental orientation of our legal system must change so as to acknowledge contributions of biological criminologists. Such a change would replace or supplement our current "right to punishment" doctrine with a "right to treatment" philosophy. Jeffery concludes his analysis by saying, "[i]f legal and political barriers prevent us from regarding antisocial behavior as a medical problem, and if we do not permit medical research on criminal behavior, how can we ever solve the crime problem?"[102]

The dangers of an overly large dependence on biological approaches to crime, however, raise the specter of a *1984*-type of Orwellian bogey man in charge of every aspect of human social life, from conception to the grave—and include the possible abortion of defective fetuses, capital punishment in lieu of rehabilitation, and enforced sterilization. Precedent for such fears can be found in cases such as *Buck v. Bell*,[103] discussed earlier in this chapter, in which the U.S. Supreme Court, influenced by genetically based perspectives of the times, sanctioned state-enforced sterilization statutes.

Potential links between race and crime, suggested by some researchers, are especially repugnant to many who criticize biological criminology. Ronald Walters, a political scientist at Howard University, observes, "[s]eeking the biological and genetic aspects of violence is dangerous to African-American youth . . . . When you consider the perception that black people have always been the violent people in this society, it is a short step from this stereotype to using this kind of research for social control."[104] According to Gary LaFree and Katheryn K. Russell, "a major reason for moving away from studies of differential crime rates by race, beginning in the 1960s, was to avoid negative associations between race and crime: blacks already were disadvantaged by the economy and the society. Thus, to imply that crime problems were more serious for blacks than for others seemed to be double victimization."[105] Yet, these same authors add, "[n]o group has suffered more than African-Americans by our failure to understand and control street crime."

Although biological theories of crime may have problems, to ignore the potential contributions of biological theorists because of hypothetical policy consequences, or because of the supposed danger of racial prejudice, does a disservice to the science of criminology and denies the opportunity for compassionate and objective researchers to realistically assist in the process of crime reduction. In 1993, for example, the Youth Violence Initiative, begun under President Bush to study problem behavior among American youth, was canceled by the Clinton administration because indications were that it might identify a disproportionate number of racial and ethnic minorities as delinquent. Such head-in-the-sand science does no one any good in the long run, although it may temporarily appease selected political constituencies.

In 1997, in an attempt to bring biological theorizing into the criminological mainstream, Lee Ellis and Anthony Walsh expanded on the theme of genetic predispositions, noting that: "In the case of behavior, nearly all of the effects of genes are quite indirect because they are mediated through complex chains of events occurring in the brain. This means that there are almost certainly no genes for something as complex as criminal behavior. Nevertheless, many genes may affect brain functioning in ways that either increase or reduce the chances of individuals learning various complex behavior patterns, including behavior patterns that happen to be so offensive to others that criminal sanctions have been instituted to minimize their recurrence."[106]

⠿ CRITIQUES OF BIOLOGICAL THEORIES

An excellent contemporary critique of biological perspectives on crime causation is provided by Glenn D. Walters and Thomas W. White, who contend that "genetic research on crime has been poorly designed, ambiguously reported, and exceedingly inadequate in addressing the relevant issues."[107] Walters and White highlight the following specific shortcomings of studies in the area.

- Few biological studies adequately conceptualize of criminality. "Several studies," they say, "have defined criminality on the basis of a single arrest."
- Twin studies, in particular, have sometimes failed to properly establish "whether a pair of twins is monozygotic (MZ) or dizygotic (DZ)." This is because some MZ twins are not identical in appearance, and only a few twin studies have depended on biological testing rather than on a simple evaluation of appearances.
- Problems in estimating the degree of criminality among sample populations are rife in biological (and in many other) studies of criminality. Interview data are open to interpretation and existing statistical data on the past criminality of offenders are not always properly appreciated.
- Methodological problems abound in many studies which attempt to evaluate the role of genetics in crime. Walters and White mention, among other things, the lack of control or comparison groups, small sample sizes, the dropping out of subjects from study groups, biased sampling techniques, and the use of inappropriate forms of statistical analysis.
- Results obtained outside of the United States may not have applicability within this country. Twin studies conducted in Sweden and Denmark provide an example of this potential lack of generalizability.

Walters and White, nonetheless, conclude that "[g]enetic factors are undoubtedly correlated with various measures of criminality," but add that "the large number of methodological flaws and limitations in the research should make one cautious in drawing any causal inferences at this point in time."[108]

SUMMARY

Contemporary criminology has shown considerable reluctance to adapt the contributions of biological theories to an understanding of criminality. An objective understanding of any social phenomenon, however, requires clear consideration of all available evidence. Modern proponents of biological perspectives on crime and crime causation point out that the link between the social environment and human behavior is continuously mediated by the physical brain. Human activity flows from the human mind, and the mind is biologically grounded in the brain. The brain itself is apparently subject to influences from other aspects of the body, such as hormones, neurotransmitters, and the levels of various chemicals in the blood. Such realizations require only a small intellectual leap to the realization that other biological aspects of the human organism may play similar contributory roles in criminal behavior.

Unfortunately, however, for proponents of biological theories that seek to explain crime, the influence of the environment on human behavior appears to be nearly overpowering, and studies purporting to have identified biological determinants of behavior have been thoroughly criticized on methodological and other grounds. For the time being, we must draw the conclusion that while biology provides both a context for, and specific precursors to, human behavior, biological predispositions for behavior in most instances of human interaction are routinely overshadowed by the role of volition, the mechanisms of human thought, and the undeniable influences of socialization and acculturation. Even so, any comprehensive approach to human behavior must give due recognition to the biological precursors of behavior itself.

DISCUSSION QUESTIONS

1. This book emphasizes a social problems versus social responsibility theme. Which perspective would be most supported by biological theories of crime causation? Why?
2. What are the central features of biological theories of crime? How do such theories differ from other perspectives that attempt to explain the same phenomena?
3. Why have biological approaches to crime causation been out of vogue lately? Do you agree or disagree with those who are critical of such perspectives? Why?
4. What does the author of this book mean when he writes, "[o]pen inquiry requires objective consideration of all points of view, and an examination of each for their ability to shed light upon the subject under study"? Do you agree or disagree with that assertion? Why?
5. What are the social policy implications of biological theories of crime? What U.S. Supreme Court case, discussed in this chapter, might presage a type of policy based on such theories?

WEB WATCH

Access the *Criminology Today* home page on the World Wide Web by pointing your browser at www.prenhall.com/cjcentral. Once there, click on *Criminology Today* in order to access the wealth of electronic resources supporting this text.

Onsite resources include (1) "Chapter Links," which provides succinct overviews of critical ideas from the textbook and links selected materials from around the Web to concepts found in the text; (2) "General Reference—Law and Justice Links." Organized by chapter, these links lead to other useful resources on the World Wide Web, such as libraries, electronic discussion lists, and electronic journals; (3) "Criminology Sites on the Web," which lists links to organizations such as the American Society of Criminology and the National Organization for Victims Assistance (NOVA), as well as crime prevention links and statistics on crime and justice. Many other Web-based resources can be accessed via the *Criminology Today* site, including the federal Justice Information Center, the Bureau of Justice Statistics, the FBI, the RAND Corporation, the Vera Institute of Justice, PAVNET (an online "Partnership Against Violence," run by seven different federal agencies), and the National White Collar Crime Center.

Still another feature of the *Criminology Today* Web site is e-mail homework. Homework can be composed onsite and submitted to instructors using the instructor's e-mail address. To use the e-mail homework feature, click on "E-Mail Homework" on the opening page, and then type answers to the questions that appear in the spaces provided. Use your instructor's e-mail address to submit homework answers. The *Criminology Today* Web site also provides links to powerful Web-based search engines that can help you find topics of interest to you as you progress through your course of study. Search engines can be found under the home page heading "Criminology Sites on the Web."

NOTES

[1] Karen J. Winkler, "Criminals Are Born as Well as Made, Authors of Controversial Book Assert," *Chronicle of Higher Education*, January 16, 1986, p. 9.

[2] Anastasia Toufexis, "Seeking the Roots of Violence," *Time*, April 19, 1993, p. 52.

[3] As cited in David Jones, *History of Criminology: A Philosophical Perspective* (Westport, Conn.: Greenwood Press, 1986), p. 1.

[4] For a detailed description of the life of Robert H. Moormann, see John C. C'Anna, "Robert Henry Moormann," *Police*, April 1992, pp. 50–54, 86–88.

[5] C. Ray Jeffery, "Biological Perspectives," *Journal of Criminal Justice Education*, vol. 4, no. 2 (Fall 1993), pp. 292–293.

[6]C. Ray Jeffery, "Genetics, Crime and the Canceled Conference," *The Criminologist,* vol. 18, no. 1 (January/February 1993), pp. 1–8.

[7]Anastasia Toufexis, "Seeking the Roots of Violence," *Time,* April 19, 1993, p. 53.

[8]C. Ray Jeffery, "The Genetics and Crime Conference Revisited," *The Criminologist,* vol. 21, no. 2 (March/April 1996), p. 3.

[9]Lee Ellis and Anthony Walsh, "Gene-Based Evolutionary Theories in Criminology," *Criminology,* vol. 35, no. 2 (1997), pp. 229–276.

[10]Ibid., p. 230.

[11]Jeffery, "Biological Perspectives," p. 298.

[12]Konrad Lorenz, *On Aggression* (New York: Harcourt, Brace & World, 1966).

[13]Ibid., p. 23.

[14]Ibid., p. 38.

[15]Ibid., p. 249.

[16]Ibid., p. 225.

[17]Cesare Lombroso, "Introduction," in Gina Lombroso-Ferrero, *Criminal Man According to the Classification of Cesare Lombroso,* 1911; reprinted Montclair, N.J., 1972 by Patterson Smith, p. xiv.

[18]Charles Darwin, *Descent of Man: And Selection in Relation to Sex,* rev. ed. (London: John Murray, 1874), p. 137.

[19]Lombroso, "Introduction," in Lombroso-Ferrero, *Criminal Man According to the Classification of Cesare Lombroso,* p. xv.

[20]The term *positivism* appears to have its roots in the writings of Auguste Comte (1798–1857), who proposed the use of the scientific method in the study of society in his 1851 work, *A System of Positive Polity.*

[21]As cited in Hermann Mannheim, *Pioneers in Criminology,* 2nd ed. (Montclair, N.J.: Patterson Smith, 1972), p. 29.

[22]*Della Fossetta Cerebellare Mediana in un Criminale,* Institute Lombardo di Scienze e Lettere, 1872, pp. 1058–1065, as cited and translated by Thorsten Sellin, "A New Phase of Criminal Anthropology in Italy," *The Annals of the American Academy of Political and Social Science, Modern Crime,* 525 (May 1926), p. 234.

[23]The English language version appeared in 1895 as Cesare Lombroso, *The Female Offender* (New York: D. Appleton & Co., 1895).

[24]Marvin Wolfgang, "Cesare Lombroso," in Hermann Mannheim, *Pioneers in Criminology,* 2nd ed. (Montclair, N.J.: Patterson Smith, 1972), p. 254.

[25]Charles Goring, *The English Convict: A Statistical Study* (London: His Majesty's Stationary Office, 1913). Reprinted in 1972 by Patterson Smith, Montclair, N.J., p. 15.

[26]Ibid.

[27]Earnest A. Hooton, *Crime and the Man* (Cambridge, Mass.: Harvard University Press, 1939), reprinted by Greenwood Press, Westport, Conn., 1972.

[28]Ibid., pp. 57–58.

[29]Ibid., p. 72.

[30]Ibid., p. 75.

[31]Ibid., p. 388.

[32]Ernest A. Hooton, *The American Criminal: An Anthropological Study* (Cambridge, Mass.: Harvard University Press, 1939).

[33]Stephen Schafer, *Theories in Criminology: Past and Present Philosophies of the Crime Problem* (New York: Random House, 1969), p. 187.

[34]William H. Sheldon, *Varieties of Delinquent Youth* (New York: Harper & Brothers, 1949).

[35]Sheldon and Eleanor Glueck, *Unraveling Juvenile Delinquency* (Cambridge, Mass.: Harvard University Press, 1950).

[36]D. Hill and W. Sargent, "A Case of Matricide," *Lancet,* vol. 244 (1943), pp. 526–527.

[37]Nanci Hellmich, "Sweets May Not Be Culprit in Hyper Kids," *USA Today,* February 3, 1994, p. 1A, reporting on a study reported in the *New England Journal of Medicine.*

[38]Ibid., p. 1A.

[39]See, for example, A. R. Mawson and K. J. Jacobs, "Corn Consumption, Tryptophan, and Cross National Homicide Rates," *Journal of Orthomolecular Psychiatry,* vol. 7 (1978), pp. 227–230; and A. Hoffer, "The Relation of Crime to Nutrition," *Humanist in Canada,* vol. 8 (1975), p. 8.

[40]See, for example, C. Hawley and R. E. Buckley, "Food Dyes and Hyperkinetic Children," *Academy Therapy,* vol. 10 (1974), pp. 27–32; and Alexander Schauss, *Diet, Crime & Delinquency* (Berkeley, Calif.: Parker House, 1980).

[41]"Special Report: Measuring Your Life with Coffee Spoons," *Tufts University Diet & Nutrition Letter,* vol. 2, no. 2 (April 1984), pp. 3–6.

[42]See, for example, "Special Report: Does What You Eat Affect Your Mood and Actions?" *Tufts*

University Diet & Nutrition Letter, vol. 2, no. 12 (February 1985), pp. 4–6.

[43] See *Tufts University Diet & Nutrition Newsletter*, vol. 2, no. 11 (January 1985), p. 2; and "Special Report: Why Sugar Continues to Concern Nutritionists," *Tufts University Diet & Nutrition Letter*, vol. 3, no. 3 (May 1985), pp. 3–6.

[44] A. Hoffer, "Children with Learning and Behavioral Disorders," *Journal of Orthomolecular Psychiatry*, vol. 5 (1976), p. 229.

[45] "Special Report: Does What You Eat Affect Your Mood and Actions?" *Tufts University Diet & Nutrition Letter*, vol. 2, no. 12 (February 1985), p. 4.

[46] Roger D. Masters, Brian Hone, and Anil Doshi, "Environmental Pollution, Neurotoxicity, and Criminal Violence," in J. Rose, ed., *Environmental Toxicology* (London and New York: Gordon and Breach, 1997).

[47] Peter Montague, "Toxics and Violent Crime," *Rachel's Environment & Health Weekly*, no. 551 (June 19, 1997).

[48] Alison Motluck, "Pollution May Lead to a Life of Crime," *New Scientist*, vol. 154, no. 2084 (May 31, 1997), p. 4.

[49] See Alexander G. Schauss, "Tranquilizing Effect of Color Reduces Aggressive Behavior and Potential Violence," *Journal of Orthomolecular Psychiatry*, vol. 8, no. 4 (1979), pp. 218–221; and David Johnston, "Is It Merely a Fad, Or Do Pastel Walls Stop Jail House Brawls?" *Corrections Magazine*, vol. 7, no. 3 (1981), pp. 28–32.

[50] Questions were raised, however, about the long-term effects of confinement in pink cells, and some researchers suggested that extended exposure to the color pink could generate suicidal impulses.

[51] See, for example, R. T. Rada, D. R. Laws, and R. Kellner, "Plasma Testosterone Levels in the Rapist," *Psychomatic Medicine*, vol. 38 (1976), pp. 257–268.

[52] "The Insanity of Steroid Abuse," *Newsweek*, May 23, 1988, p. 75.

[53] Dan Olweus, Mattsson Ake, Daisy Schalling, and Hans Low, "Testosterone, Aggression, Physical and Personality Dimensions in Normal Adolescent Males," *Psychosomatic Medicine*, vol. 42 (1980), pp. 253–269.

[54] Richard Udry, "Biosocial Models of Adolescent Problem Behaviors," *Social Biology*, vol. 37 (1990), pp. 1–10.

[55] Dan Olweus, "Testosterone and Adrenaline: Aggressive Antisocial Behavior in Normal Adolescent Males," in Sarnoff A. Mednick, Terrie E. Moffitt, and Susan A. Stack, eds., *The Causes of Crime: New Biological Approaches* (Cambridge: Cambridge University Press, 1987), pp. 263–282.

[56] Alan Booth and D. Wayne Osgood, "The Influence of Testosterone on Deviance in Adulthood: Assessing and Explaining the Relationship," *Criminology*, vol. 31, no. 1 (1993), pp. 93–117.

[57] Ibid., p. 93.

[58] Ibid.

[59] Richard Udry, Luther Talbert, and Naomi Morris, "Biosocial Foundations for Adolescent Female Sexuality," *Demography*, vol. 23 (1986), pp. 217–227.

[60] "Drunk Driving Charge Dismissed: PMS Cited," *Fayetteville Observer-Times* (North Carolina), June 7, 1991, p. 3A.

[61] Anastasia Toufexis, "Seeking the Roots of Violence," *Time*, April 19, 1993, pp. 52–54.

[62] Richard Louis Dugdale, *The Jukes: A Study in Crime, Pauperism, Disease, and Heredity*, 3rd ed. (New York: G. P. Putnam's Sons, 1895).

[63] Arthur H. Estabrook, *The Jukes in 1915* (Washington, D.C.: Carnegie Institute of Washington, 1916).

[64] Henry Herbert Goddard, *The Kallikak Family: A Study in the Heredity of Feeblemindedness* (New York: Macmillan, 1912).

[65] *Buck* v. *Bell*, 274 U.S. 200, 207 (1927).

[66] P. A. Jacobs, M. Brunton, and M. Melville, "Aggressive Behavior, Mental Subnormality, and the XXY Male," *Nature*, vol. 208 (1965), p. 1351.

[67] Biologists often define *karyotype* as "a photomicrograph of metaphase chromosomes in a standard array." The process of karyotyping typically involves drawing a small sample of blood.

[68] See David A. Jones, *History of Criminology: A Philosophical Perspective* (Westport, Conn.: Greenwood Press, 1986), p. 124.

[69] Many of which have been summarized in J. Katz and W. Chambliss, "Biology and Crime,"

in J. F. Sheley, ed., *Criminology* (Belmont, Calif.: Wadsworth, 1991), pp. 245–272.

[70]As reported by S. A. Mednick and J. Volavka, "Biology and Crime," in N. Morris and M. Tonry, *Crime and Justice: An Annual Review of Research,* vol. 2 (Chicago: University of Chicago Press, 1980), pp. 85–158; and D. A. Andrews and James Bonta, *The Psychology of Criminal Conduct* (Cincinnati: Anderson, 1994), pp. 126–127.

[71]T. Sarbin and J. Miller, "Demonism Revisited: The XYY Chromosomal Anomaly," *Issues in Criminology,* vol. 5 (1970), p. 199.

[72]Geoffrey Cowley and Carol Hallin, "The Genetics of Bad Behavior: A Study Links Violence to Heredity," *Newsweek,* November 1, 1993, p. 57.

[73]Clyde L. Cronkhite, "Biochemistry: An Answer for Curbing Future Criminal Behavior," paper presented at the annual meeting of the Academy of Criminal Justice Sciences, Louisville, KY, March, 1997, p. 4.

[74]Johannes Lange, *Verbrechen als Schicksal* (Leipzig: Georg Thieme, 1929).

[75]Karl O. Christiansen, "A Preliminary Study of Criminality Among Twins," in Sarnoff Mednick and Karl Christiansen, eds., *Biosocial Bases of Criminal Behavior* (New York: Gardner Press, 1977).

[76]C. Ray Jeffery, Biological Perspectives," *Journal of Criminal Justice Education,* vol. 4, no. 2 (Fall 1993), p. 300.

[77]Leanne Fiftal Alarid, James W. Marquart, Velmer S. Burton, Jr., Francis T. Cullen, and Steven J. Cuvelier, "Women's Roles in Serious Offenses: A Study of Adult Felons," *Justice Quarterly,* vol. 13, no. 3 (September 1996), pp. 432–454.

[78]Federal Bureau of Investigation, *Crime in the United States, 1996* (Washington, D.C.: U.S. Department of Justice, 1997).

[79]Freda Adler, *Sisters in Crime: The Rise of the New Female Criminal* (New York: McGraw-Hill, 1975).

[80]Darrell J. Steffensmeir, "Sex Differences in Patterns of Adult Crime, 1965–1977: A Review and Assessment," *Social Forces,* vol. 58 (1980), pp. 1098–1099.

[81]Federal Bureau of Investigation, *Crime in the United States, 1996* (Washington, D.C.: U.S.

Department of Justice, 1997), as computed by the author.

[82]See, for example, D. H. Fishbein, "The Psychobiology of Female Aggression," *Criminal Justice and Behavior,* vol. 19 (1992), pp. 99–126.

[83]Robbin S. Ogle, Daniel Maier-Katin, and Thomas J. Bernard, "A Theory of Homicidal Behavior Among Women," *Criminology,* vol. 33, no. 2 (1995), pp. 173–193.

[84]Ibid., p. 177.

[85]Ibid., p. 179.

[86]Arthur Fisher, "A New Synthesis Comes of Age," *Mosaic,* vol. 22, no. 1 (Spring 1991), pp. 2–9.

[87]Edward O. Wilson, *Sociobiology: The New Synthesis* (Cambridge, Mass.: The Belknap Press of Harvard University Press, 1975).

[88]Janet Zimmerman, "6 Held in Brutal Attack of Mich. Teens," *USA Today,* June 24, 1997, 3A.

[89]Ibid., p. 327.

[90]Sarah Blaffer Hrdy, *The Langurs of Abu: Female and Male Strategies of Reproduction* (Cambridge, Mass.: Harvard University Press, 1977).

[91]Research by Martin Daly and Margo Wilson of McMaster University in Hamilton Canada, as reported in Arthur Fisher, "A New Synthesis II: How Different Are Humans?" *Mosaic,* vol. 22, no. 1 (Spring 1991), p. 14.

[92]Arthur Fisher, "A New Synthesis II: How Different Are Humans?" *Mosaic,* vol. 22, no. 1 (Spring 1991), p. 11.

[93]John H. Beckstrom, *Evolutionary Jurisprudence: Prospects and Limitations on the Youth of Modern Darwinism Throughout the Legal Process* (Urbana, Ill.: University of Illinois Press, 1989).

[94]John Madison Memory, "Sociobiology and the Metamorphoses of Criminology: 1978–2000," unpublished manuscript.

[95]Ibid., p. 11.

[96]Ibid., p. 33.

[97]See, also, Arnold L. Lieber, *The Lunar Effect: Biological Tides and Human Emotions* (Garden City: Anchor Press, 1978).

[98]James Q. Wilson and Richard J. Herrnstein, *Crime and Human Nature* (New York: Simon & Schuster, 1985).

[99]Karen J. Winkler, "Criminals Are Born as Well as Made, Authors of Controversial Book Assert," *The Chronicle of Higher Education,* January 16, 1986, p. 5.

[100]Ibid., p. 8.

[101]Jeffery, "Biological Perspectives," p. 303.

[102]Ibid.

[103]*Buck* v. *Bell*, 274 U.S. 200, 207 (1927).

[104]*Time*, April 19, 1993, p. 53.

[105]Gary LaFree and Katheryn K. Russell, "The Argument for Studying Race and Crime," *Journal of Criminal Justice Education*, vol. 4, no. 2 (Fall 1993), p. 279.

[106]Lee Ellis and Anthony Walsh, "Gene-Based Evolutionary Theories in Criminology," *Criminology*, vol. 35, no. 2 (1997), pp. 229–230.

[107]Glenn D. Walters and Thomas W. White, "Heredity and Crime: Bad Genes or Bad Research?" *Criminology*, vol. 27, no. 3 (1989), pp. 455–485. See, also, P. A. Brennan and S. A. Mednick, "Reply to Walters and White: Heredity and Crime," *Criminology*, vol. 28, no. 4 (November 1990), pp. 657–661.

[108]Ibid., p. 478.

PSYCHOLOGICAL AND

PSYCHIATRIC FOUNDATIONS OF

CRIMINAL BEHAVIOR

Question: "When you put the shotgun up against her left cheek and pulled the trigger, did you love your mother?"

Answer: "Yes."

—LYLE MENENDEZ, TESTIFYING AT HIS TRIAL ON CHARGES THAT HE AND HIS BROTHER KILLED THEIR PARENTS[1]

Society secretly *wants* crime, *needs* crime, and gains definite satisfactions from the present mishandling of it! We condemn crime; we punish offenders for it; but we need it. The crime and punishment ritual is part of our lives!

—KARL MENNINGER[2]

✦ CHAPTER OUTLINE ✦

⟨ IMPORTANT NAMES AND CASES ⟩

Sigmund Freud	Hervey Cleckley	B. F. Skinner
Albert Bandura	Hans Eysenck	*Foucha* v. *Louisiana*

⟨ IMPORTANT TERMS ⟩

correctional psychology	guilty but mentally ill (GBMI)	selective incapacitation
psychopathology	dangerousness	psychopath
alloplastic adaptation	psychological theories	sociopath
psychosis	autoplastic adaptation	neurosis
conditioning	antisocial personality	asocial personality
superego	id	ego
paranoid schizophrenics	psychotherapy	sublimation
psychiatric criminology	schizophrenics	electroencephalogram (EEG)
forensic psychiatry	social learning theory	behavior theory
		Thanatos

CHAPTER 6

229

*Psychological and
Psychiatric
Foundations of
Criminal Behavior*

operant behavior	psychoanalysis	punishments
psychological profiling	rewards	McNaughten rule
irresistible impulse test	insanity	substantial capacity test
	Durham rule	

⊞ INTRODUCTION

On July 22, 1991, a handcuffed man flagged down a police car in suburban Milwaukee.[3] Officers soon learned that the man was Tracy Edwards, a 32-year-old city resident. The lurid story of homosexual abuse and physical attack that Edwards told led investigators to the apartment of a 31-year-old loner named Jeffrey Dahmer. Dahmer was quickly arrested, and a search of his apartment revealed the body parts of at least eleven people. In a confession to police, Dahmer told of how he had repeatedly lured men to his apartment, murdered them, and then dismembered their bodies. Soon police investigations implicated Dahmer in a ten-year killing spree which spanned several states and may have reached as far as Europe. Edwards, whom Dahmer had met in a shopping mall, explained that he went to Dahmer's apartment because "[h]e (Dahmer) seemed so normal."[4] Sadly, one of Dahmer's victims, a 15-year-old boy, had earlier been discovered by police dazed and bleeding—and was returned to Dahmer's apartment after officers concluded that the situation involved nothing but a dispute between homosexual lovers.

Dahmer pleaded insane as a defense to charges of murder, but an expert witness at his trial, psychiatrist Park Dietz, testified that although Dahmer suffered from various psychological disorders, he could have chosen not to kill. Comparing Dahmer's sexual desires with someone who wants money but chooses not to rob, Dietz said, "[t]he choice is exactly the same.... The freedom to make it is exactly the same."[5] In contrasting testimony, another expert witness claimed that Dahmer

Jeffrey Dahmer, perhaps the most infamous serial killer of the twentieth century. What explains the public's seeming fascination with serial killers? *Milwaukee Journal/Sipa Press.*

"had uncontrollable urges to kill and have sex with dead bodies. . . ."[6] Dahmer was sentenced to fifteen consecutive life terms—one each for the murders of fifteen men[7]—but was himself murdered by another inmate in late 1994.

Murder appears to be occurring with increasing frequency throughout the United States. Some years ago, for example, Texan Donald Leroy Evans admitted killing 10-year-old Beatrice Louise Routh.[8] The young girl's homeless mother had given Evans permission to take Beatrice shopping. Soon after his capture, however, Evans—a parolee—confessed to sixty killings and became a suspect in America's worst serial murder case. His arrest came one month before Aileen Wuornos, whom investigators have called the "nation's first true female serial killer," was scheduled to be tried in Florida for killing seven men who had offered her rides; and two months before a gunman smashed a pickup truck through the front window of a Texas cafeteria and shot thirty-one lunchgoers to death. Although Wuornos, an admitted prostitute, claimed self-defense, many suggested that a long-festering hatred of men drove her to kill them.

In 1994, in a case which made headlines around the world, Manassas, Virginia, housewife Lorena Bobbitt was tried on charges of malicious wounding for admittedly severing her allegedly philandering husband's penis with one stroke from a sharp kitchen knife while he slept. Bobbitt drove away with the severed organ still clutched in her fist, and threw it out of her car window onto a grassy field some distance from the couple's apartment. Rescue workers recovered the organ in a predawn search, and it was reattached during hours of microvascular surgery.[9] In defense of her actions she later accused her husband, John, of marital rape. Although he was arrested and charged with raping his wife, a jury voted 12 to 0 to acquit him of all charges.[10]

On the morning immediately following the mutilation, Mrs. Bobbitt had told police that her husband "always [has] an orgasm and he doesn't wait for me. . . . I don't think it's fair, so I pulled back the sheets and I did it." The defense attorney in the case, sounding very much like a pop psychologist, explained Mrs. Bobbitt's actions to the jury in these words: "Why did she cut his penis off? Something happened . . . that drove her over the edge. If this was sheer jealousy, she'd have cut his throat. But what did she attack? . . . The very thing that wounded her."

Finally, in a violent incident which, at the time, helped to further the interests of social responsibility advocates in pending federal crime control legislation, six people were shot to death and another nineteen wounded aboard a Long Island, New York, commuter train near Christmastime in 1993 by Colin Ferguson, a disgruntled Jamaican immigrant. Ferguson, who moved through the train firing as many as forty shots from his semiautomatic handgun, was apparently motivated to commit mass murder by a hatred of white people, whom he blamed for numerous personal failures and other disappointments.[11] Ferguson's actions were explained by Judy Louis, a psychologist at St. John's University in New York City, as the result of a rare delusional disorder. "People who suffer from this [disorder] appear to be rational," said Louis, "except for this delusion they have. The delusion is their focal point." Louis added that people who suffer from the disorder can be difficult to detect. "They can go to the store, they can talk to people and seem perfectly rational."[12] After conducting his own defense, in what some called a mockery of an accused's right to act as his own attorney, Ferguson was convicted of all charges against him.

CHAPTER 6

⟸ 231 ⟹

*Psychological and
Psychiatric
Foundations of
Criminal Behavior*

What motivates people to kill or maim—or even to commit other, less serious offenses? How can many killers "seem so normal" before their crimes—giving no hints of the atrocities they are about to commit? Serial killer, mass murderer, sexual mutilator, even book thief—all must wrestle, before and after the criminal event, with their own personal demons. For answers to questions such as these many people turn to psychological theories. Psychologists are the pundits of the modern age of behaviorism—offering explanations rooted in determinants that lie within *individual actors.* Psychological determinants of deviant or criminal behavior may be couched in terms of exploitive personality characteristics, poor impulse control, emotional arousal, an immature personality, and so on. One contemporary commentator observes that "The major sources of theoretical development in criminology have been—and continue to be—psychological. A theory of criminal conduct is weak indeed if uninformed by a general psychology of human behavior".[13] Other writers go so far as to claim that any criminal behavior is only a symptom of a more fundamental psychiatric disorder.[14]

What is the fundamental distinguishing feature of psychological approaches as opposed to other attempts to explain behavior? Criminologists Cathy Spatz Widom and Hans Toch offer the following insight: ". . . theories are psychological insofar as they focus on the individual as the unit of analysis. Thus any theory that is concerned with the behavior of individual offenders or which refers to forces or dynamics that motivate individuals to commit crimes would be considered to have a psychological component."[15] Another writer, Curt Bartol, defines psychology as "the science of behavior and mental processes."[16] Bartol goes on to say that "[p]sychological criminology . . . is the science of the behavior and mental processes of the criminal. [P]sychological criminology" says Bartol, "focuses on individual criminal behavior—how it is acquired, evoked, maintained, and modified."

⊞ MAJOR PRINCIPLES OF PSYCHOLOGICAL THEORIES

This brief section serves to summarize the central features of **psychological theories** of crime causation.[17] Each of these points can be found elsewhere in this chapter, where they are discussed in more detail. This cursory overview, however, is intended to provide more than a summary—it is meant to be a guide to the rest of this chapter.

Most psychological theories of crime causation make the following fundamental assumptions.

- The individual is the primary unit of analysis.
- Personality is the major motivational element within individuals, because it is the seat of drives and the source of motives.
- Crimes result from abnormal, dysfunctional, or inappropriate mental processes within the personality.
- Criminal behavior, although condemned by the social group, may be purposeful for the individual insofar as it addresses certain felt needs. Behavior can be judged "inappropriate" only when measured against external criteria purporting to establish normality.

Psychological theories those derived from the behavioral sciences and which focus on the individual as the unit of analysis. Psychological theories place the locus of crime causation within the personality of the individual offender.

- Normality is generally defined by social consensus—that is, what the majority of people in any social group agree is "real," appropriate, or typical.
- Defective, or abnormal, mental processes may have a variety of causes, including:
  - a diseased mind
  - inappropriate learning or improper conditioning
  - the emulation of inappropriate role models
  - adjustment to inner conflicts

⊞ EARLY PSYCHOLOGICAL THEORIES

Conditioning a psychological principle which holds that the frequency of any behavior can be increased or decreased through reward, punishment, and/or association with other stimuli.

A twin thread wove through early psychological theories. One strand emphasized behavioral **conditioning,** the other focused mostly on personality disturbances and diseases of the mind. Together, these two foci constituted the early field of psychological criminology. The concept of conditioned behavior was popularized through the work of the Russian physiologist Ivan Pavlov (1849–1936), whose work with dogs won the Nobel Prize in physiology and medicine in 1904. The dogs, who salivated when food was presented to them, were always fed in the presence of a ringing bell. Soon, Pavlov found, the dogs would salivate, as if in preparation for eating, when the bell alone was rung—even when no food was present. Hence, salivation, an automatic response to the presence of food, could be conditioned to occur in response to some other stimulus—demonstrating that animal behavior could be predictably altered via association with external changes arising from the environment surrounding the organism.

Psychopathology the study of pathological mental conditions, that is, mental illness.

The other thread wending its way through early psychological theories was that of mental disease, or **psychopathology.** The concept of psychopathology has been called "one of the most durable, resilient and influential of all criminological ideas."[18] In its original formulation, psychopathology embodied the notion of a diseased mind. It described a particular form of insanity referred to as "moral idiocy," which was thought to have a constitutional, or physiological, basis. The concept is summarized in the words of Nolan Lewis, who wrote during his tenure as director of the New York State Psychiatric Institute and Hospital at Columbia University during World War II that "[t]he criminal, like other people, has lived a life of instinctive drives, of desires, of wishes, of feelings, but one in which his intellect has apparently functioned less effectually as a brake upon certain trends. His constitutional makeup deviates toward the abnormal, leading him into conflicts with the laws of society and its cultural patterns."[19]

THE PSYCHOPATHIC PERSONALITY

Psychopath or **sociopath** a person with a personality disorder, especially one manifested in aggressively antisocial behavior, which is often said to be the result of a poorly developed superego.

The term *psychopathy* comes from the Greek words *psyche* (meaning "soul" or "mind") and *pathos* ("suffering" or "illness"). The word appears to have been coined by the nineteenth-century German psychiatrist, Richard von Krafft-Ebing (1840–1902),[20] and made its way into English psychiatric literature through the writings of Polish-born American psychiatrist Bernard Glueck (1884–1972)[21] and William Healy (1869–1963).[22] The **psychopath,** also called a **sociopath,** was usually viewed as perversely cruel, often without thought or feeling for his victims.[23] By the Second World War, the role of the psychopathic personality in crime causation had become central to psychological theorizing. In 1944, for example, the well-known psychiatrist David Abrahamsen wrote, "[w]hen we seek to explain the riddle of human conduct in general and of antisocial behavior in particular, the solution must be sought in the personality."[24]

The concept of a psychopathic personality, which by its very definition is asocial, was fully developed by **Hervey Cleckley** in his 1964 book *The Mask of Sanity*.[25] Cleckley described the psychopath as a "moral idiot," or as one who does not feel empathy with others, even though that person may be fully cognizant of what is objectively happening around them. The central defining characteristic of a psychopath is *poverty of affect,* or the inability to accurately imagine how others think and feel. Hence, it becomes possible for a psychopath to inflict pain and engage in cruelty without appreciation for the victim's suffering. Charles Manson, for example, whom some have called a psychopath, once told a television reporter, "I could take this book and beat you to death with it, and I wouldn't feel a thing. It'd be just like walking to the drugstore."

In *The Mask of Sanity* Cleckley describes numerous characteristics of the psychopathic personality, some of which are listed here.

- absence of delusions, hallucinations, or other signs of psychosis
- inability to feel guilt or shame
- unreliability
- chronic lying
- superficial charm
- above-average intelligence
- ongoing antisocial behavior
- inability to learn from experience
- self-centeredness

According to Cleckley, psychopathic indicators appear early in life, often in the teenage years. They include lying, fighting, stealing, and vandalism. Even earlier signs may be found, according to some authors, in bedwetting, cruelty to animals, sleepwalking, and fire-setting.[26]

Although the terms *psychopath* and *criminal* are not synonymous, individuals manifesting many of the characteristics of a psychopathic personality are likely, sooner or later, to run afoul of the law. As one writer on the topic says, "[t]he impulsivity and aggression, the selfishness in achieving one's own immediate needs, and the disregard for society's rules and laws bring these people to the attention of the criminal justice system."[27]

The causes of psychopathology are unclear. Somatogenic causes, or those based on physiological features of the human organism, are said to include a malfunctioning of the central nervous system characterized by a low state of arousal that drives the sufferer to seek excitement, and brain abnormalities that may have been present in most psychopaths since birth. Some studies show that an **electroencephalogram (EEG)** taken of a psychopathic patient is frequently abnormal, reflecting "a malfunction of some . . . inhibitory mechanisms" that makes it unlikely the psychopath will "learn to inhibit behavior that is likely to lead to punishment."[28] It is difficult,

Electroencephalogram (EEG) electrical measurements of brain wave activity.

Charles Manson achieved notoriety because he seemed so difficult to understand. What do you think motivated his crimes? *Corbis-Bettmann.*

however, to diagnose psychopathology through physiological measurements because similar EEG patterns also show up in patients with other types of disorders. Psychogenic causes, or those rooted in early interpersonal experiences, are said to include the inability to form attachments to parents or other caregivers early in life, sudden separation from the mother during the first six months of life, and other forms of insecurity during the first few years of life. In short, a lack of love or the sensed inability to unconditionally depend upon one central loving figure (typically the mother in most psychological literature) immediately following birth is often posited as a major psychogenic factor contributing to psychopathic development. Other psychogenic causes have been identified to include deficiencies in childhood role playing, the inability to identify with one's parents during childhood and adolescence, and severe rejection by others.

Most studies of psychopaths have involved male subjects. Researchers have focused little on female psychopaths, and it is believed that only a small proportion of all psychopaths are women.[29] What little research there is suggests that female psychopaths possess many of the same definitive characteristics as do their male counterparts, and that they assume their psychopathic roles at similarly early ages.[30] The lifestyles of female psychopaths, however, appear to emphasize sexual misconduct, including lifestyles involving abnormally high levels of sexual activity. Such research, however, can be misleading because cultural expectations of female sexual behavior inherent in early studies may have not always been in keeping with reality. That is, so little may have been accurately known about female sexual activity to early researchers that the behavior of women judged to be psychopaths may have actually been far closer to the norm than originally believed.

THEORY IN PERSPECTIVE
Types of Psychological and Psychiatric Theories

PSYCHOLOGICAL AND PSYCHIATRIC THEORIES

of criminology are derived from the behavioral sciences and focus on the *individual* as the unit of analysis.

PSYCHIATRIC CRIMINOLOGY, also known as **FORENSIC PSYCHIATRY.** Envisions a complex set of drives and motives operating from recesses deep within the personality to determine behavior.

PERIOD:	1930s–Present
THEORISTS:	Hervey Cleckley, many others
CONCEPTS:	Psychopath, sociopath, antisocial, asocial personality

---

PSYCHOANALYTIC CRIMINOLOGY. A psychiatric approach developed by the Austrian psychiatrist Sigmund Freud which emphasizes the role of personality in human behavior, and which sees deviant behavior as the result of dysfunctional personalities.

PERIOD:	1920s–Present
THEORISTS:	Sigmund Freud and others
CONCEPTS:	Id, ego, superego, sublimation, psychotherapy, Thanatos, neurosis, psychosis, schizophrenia

---

FRUSTRATION-AGGRESSION THEORY. Holds that frustration is a natural consequence of living and a root cause of crime. Criminal behavior can be a form of adaptation when it results in stress reduction.

PERIOD:	1940s–Present
THEORIST:	J. Dollard, Albert Bandura, Richard H. Walters, S.M. Halleck
CONCEPTS:	Frustration, aggression, displacement, catharsis, alloplastic and autoplastic adaptation

---

SOCIAL LEARNING THEORY. A psychological perspective that says people learn how to behave by modeling themselves after others whom they have the opportunity to observe.

PERIOD:	1950s–Present
THEORISTS:	Albert Bandura and others
CONCEPTS:	Interpersonal aggression, modeling, disengagement

BEHAVIOR THEORY. A psychological perspective which posits that individual behavior which is rewarded will increase in frequency, while that which is punished will decrease.

PERIOD:	1940s–Present
THEORISTS:	B. F. Skinner and others
CONCEPTS:	Operant behavior, conditioning, stimulus-response, reward, punishment

Antisocial or asocial
personality refers to
individuals who are
basically unsocialized and
whose behavior pattern
brings them repeatedly
into conflict with society.

The terms *sociopath* and *psychopath* have fallen into professional disfavor in recent years. By 1968 the American Psychiatric Association's *Diagnostic and Statistical Manual of Mental Disorders*[31] had discontinued use of both terms, replacing them with such jargon as antisocial or asocial personality. In that year the APA manual changed to a description of the **antisocial (asocial) personality** type as "individuals who are basically unsocialized and whose behavior pattern brings them repeatedly into conflicts with society. They are incapable of significant loyalty to individuals, groups, or social values. They are grossly selfish, callous, irresponsible, impulsive, and unable to feel guilt or to learn from experience and punishment. Frustration tolerance is low. They tend to blame others or offer plausible rationalization for their behavior."[32] Some recent studies,[33] which attempt to classify criminal offenders by type of mental disorder, have determined that antisocial personalities comprise 46.6 percent of all inmates, while schizophrenics account for 6.3 percent, manic-depressives another 1.6 percent, drug-disordered persons 18.6 percent, depressed individuals 8.1 percent, and alcohol abuse–related suffers another 33.1 percent. A review[34] of twenty such studies found great variation in the degree and type of disorders said to be prevalent among incarcerated offenders. The studies categorized from 0.5 to 26 percent of all inmates as psychotic, 2.4 to 28 percent as mentally subnormal, 5.6 to 70 percent as psychopathic, 2 to 7.9 percent as neurotic, and from 11 to 80 percent of inmates tested as suffering from mental disorders induced by alcoholism or excessive drinking. Generally, however, such studies conclude that few convicted felons are free from mental impairment of one sort or another.

PERSONALITY TYPES AND CRIME

In 1964 **Hans Eysenck,** a British psychiatrist, published *Crime and Personality,*[35] a book-length treatise, in which he explained crime as the result of fundamental personality characteristics linked to individual central nervous system characteristics. Eysenck described three personality dimensions, each with links to criminality. Psychoticism, which Eysenck said "is believed to be correlated with criminality at all stages,"[36] is defined by characteristics such as a lack of empathy, creativeness, tough-mindedness, and antisociability. Psychoticism, said Eysenck, is also frequently characterized by hallucinations and delusions. Extroverts were described as carefree, dominant, and venturesome—operating with high levels of energy. "The typical extravert," Eysenck wrote "is sociable, likes parties, has many friends, needs to have people to talk to, and does not like reading or studying by himself."[37] Neuroticism, the third of the personality characteristics Eysenck described, was said to be typical of people who are irrational, shy, moody, and emotional.

According to Eysenck, psychotics are the most likely to be criminal because they combine high degrees of emotionalism with similarly high levels of extroversion. Individuals with such characteristics, claimed Eysenck, are especially difficult to socialize and to train. Eysenck cited many studies in which children and others who harbored characteristics of psychoticism, extroversion, and neuroticism performed

CHAPTER 6

⟵ 237 ⟶

*Psychological and
Psychiatric
Foundations of
Criminal Behavior*

poorly on conditioning tests designed to measure how quickly they would respond appropriately to external stimuli. Conscience, said Eysenck, is fundamentally a conditioned reflex. Therefore, an individual who does not take well to conditioning will not fully develop a conscience and will continue to exhibit the asocial behavioral traits of a very young child.

Eysenck's approach might be termed *biopsychology,* because he claimed that personality traits were fundamentally dependent upon physiology—specifically upon the individual's autonomic nervous system, which Eysenck described as "underlying the behavioral trait of emotionality or neuroticism."[38] Some individuals were said to possess nervous systems that could not handle a great deal of stimulation. Such individuals, like the introvert, shun excitement and are easily trained. They rarely become criminal offenders. Those who possess nervous systems, however, which need stimulation, said Eysenck, seek excitement and are far more likely to turn to crime. As support for his thesis, Eysenck cited studies of twins showing that identical twins were much more likely than fraternal twins to perform similarly on simple behavioral tests. In particular, Eysenck quoted from the work of J. B. S. Haldane, who was reputed to be a "world-famous geneticist." Haldane, having studied the criminality of thirteen sets of identical twins, concluded, "[a]n analysis of the thirteen cases shows not the faintest evidence of freedom of the will in the ordinary sense of the word. A man of a certain constitution, put in a certain environment, will be a criminal. Taking the record of any criminal, we could predict the behavior of a monozygotic twin placed in the same environment. Crime is destiny."[39] Up to two-thirds of all behavioral variance, claimed Eysenck, could be attributed to "a strong genetic basis."

EARLY PSYCHIATRIC THEORIES

Psychological criminology, with its historically dual emphasis on (1) early forces that shape personality and (2) conditioned behavior, can be distinguished from **psychiatric criminology,** also known as **forensic psychiatry,** which envisions a complex set of drives and motives operating from hidden recesses deep within the personality to determine behavior. David Abrahamsen, a psychiatrist writing in 1944, explains crime this way: "[a]ntisocial behavior is a direct expression of an aggression or may be a direct or indirect manifestation of a distorted erotic drive. Crime," said Abrahamsen, "may . . . be considered a product of a person's tendencies and the situation of the moment interacting with his mental resistance."[40] The key questions to be answered by psychiatric criminology, according to Abrahamsen, are "[w]hat creates the criminal impulse? What stimulates and gives it direction?" A later forensic psychiatrist[41] answered the question this way: "Every criminal is such by reason of unconscious forces within him. . . ." Forensic psychiatry explains crime as caused by biological and psychological urges mediated through consciousness. Little significance is placed upon the role of the environment external to the individual after the first few formative years of life. Psychiatric theories are derived from the medical sciences, including neurology, and, like other psychological theories, focus on the individual as the unit of analysis.

Psychiatric criminology theories derived from the medical sciences, including neurology, and which, like other psychological theories, focus on the individual as the unit of analysis. Psychiatric theories form the basis of psychiatric criminology.

Forensic psychiatry that branch of psychiatry having to do with the study of crime and criminality.

CRIMINAL BEHAVIOR AS MALADAPTION

THE PSYCHOANALYTIC PERSPECTIVE

Psychoanalysis the theory of human psychology founded by Freud on the concepts of the unconscious, resistance, repression, sexuality, and the Oedipus complex.[42]

Psychotherapy a form of psychiatric treatment based on psychoanalytical principles and techniques.

Id the aspect of the personality from which drives, wishes, urges, and desires emanate. More formally, it is the division of the psyche associated with instinctual impulses and demands for immediate satisfaction of primitive needs.[43]

Ego the reality-testing part of the personality; also referred to as the reality principle. More formally, it is the personality component that is conscious, most immediately controls behavior, and is most in touch with external reality.[44]

Superego the moral aspect of the personality; much like the conscience. More formally, it is the division of the psyche that develops by the incorporation of the perceived moral standards of the community, is mainly unconscious, and includes the conscience.[45]

Perhaps the best known psychiatrist of all time is **Sigmund Freud** (1856–1939). Freud coined the term *psychoanalysis* in 1896 and based an entire theory of human behavior on it. From the point of view of psychoanalysis criminal behavior is maladaptive, or the product of inadequacies inherent in the offender's personality. Significant inadequacies may result in full-blown mental illness, which in itself can be a direct cause of crime. The psychoanalytic perspective encompasses diverse notions such as personality, neurosis, psychosis, and more specific concepts such as transference, sublimation, and repression. **Psychotherapy,** referred to in its early days as the "talking cure" because it highlighted patient–therapist communication, is the attempt to relieve patients of their mental disorders through the application of psychoanalytical principles and techniques.

According to Freud, the personality is made up of three components—the id, the ego, and the superego—as shown in Figure 6.1. The **id** is that fundamental aspect of the personality from which drives, wishes, urges, and desires emanate. Freud focused primarily on love, aggression, and sex as fundamental drives in any personality. The id is direct and singular in purpose. It operates according to the pleasure principle, seeking full and immediate gratification of its needs. Individuals, however, were said to rarely be fully aware of the urges that percolate up (occasionally into awareness) from the id, because it is a largely unconscious region of the mind. Nonetheless, from the Freudian perspective each of us carries within our id the prerequisite motivation for criminal behavior. We are, each one of us, potential murderers, sexual aggressors, and thieves—our drives and urges kept in check only by other, controlling aspects of our personalities.

A second component of the personality, the **ego,** is primarily charged with reality testing. Freud's use of the word *ego* should not be confused with popular practice, whereby a person might talk about an "inflated ego" or an "egotistical person." For Freud, the ego was primarily concerned with how objectives might be best accomplished. The ego tends to effect strategies for the individual that maximize pleasure and minimize pain. It lays out the various paths of action that can lead to wish fulfillment. The ego inherently recognizes that it may be necessary to delay gratification to achieve a more fulfilling long-term goal.

The **superego,** the last component of the personality, is much like a moral guide to right and wrong. If properly developed, it assays the ego's plans, dismissing some as morally inappropriate while accepting others as ethically viable. The id of a potential rapist, for example, might be filled with lustful drives, and his ego may develop a variety of alternative plans whereby those drives might be fulfilled, some legal and some illegal. His superego will, however, if the individual's personality is relatively well integrated and the superego is properly developed, turn the individual away from law-violating behavior based on his sensual desires and guide the ego to select a path of action that is in keeping with social convention. When the dictates of the superego are not followed, feelings of guilt may result. The superego is one of the most misunderstood of Freudian concepts. In addition to elements of

CHAPTER 6

239

*Psychological and
Psychiatric
Foundations of
Criminal Behavior*

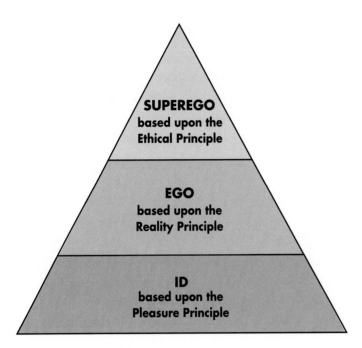

FIGURE 6.1 The Psychoanalytic Structure of Personality.

conscience, the superego also contains what Freud called the *ego-ideal,* which is a symbolic representation of what society values. The ego-ideal differs from the conscience in that it is less forceful in controlling behavior in the absence of the likelihood of discovery.

Although Freud wrote little about crime per se, he did spend much of his time attempting to account for a variety of abnormal behavior, much of which might lead to violations of the criminal law. One way in which a person might be led into crime according to the perspective of psychoanalysis is as the result of a poorly developed superego. In the individual without a fully functional superego, the mind is left to fall back on the ego's reality-testing ability. To put it simply, the ego, operating without a moral guide, may select a path of action which, although expedient at the time, violates the law. Individuals suffering from poor superego development are likely to seek immediate gratification without giving a great deal of thought to the long-term consequences of the choices they may make in the moment.

From the Freudian point of view, inadequate sublimation can be another cause of crime. **Sublimation** is the psychological process whereby one item of consciousness comes to be symbolically substituted for another. Sublimation is often a healthy process. Freud held that the many outstanding accomplishments of the human species have been due to sublimation, through which powerful sexual and aggressive drives are channeled into socially constructive activity. However, crime can result from improper sublimation. According to Freud, for example, a man may hate his mother, his hatred being perhaps the faulty by-product of the striving for adult independence. He may, however, be unable to give voice to that hatred directly. Perhaps the mother is too powerful, or the experience of confronting his mother would be too embarrassing for the man. The man may act out his hatred for his mother, however, by attacking other women whom he symbolically substitutes in

Sublimation the psychological process whereby one aspect of consciousness comes to be symbolically substituted for another.

Sigmund Freud (1856–1939), examining a manuscript in the office of his Vienna home, circa 1930. *Corbis-Bettmann.*

his mind for the mother figure. Hence, from the Freudian perspective, men who beat their wives, become rapists, sexually harass coworkers, or otherwise abuse women may be enacting feelings derived from early life experiences that they would be unable to otherwise express.

Sublimation, like many other psychoanalytical concepts, is a slippery idea. Mother hatred, for example, although a plausible explanation for acts of violence by men against women, is difficult to demonstrate, and the link between such hidden feelings and adult action is impossible to prove. Even so, should an offender be so diagnosed, it would do little good for him to deny the psychoanalytical explanation assigned to him, because doing so would only result in the professional reproach, "yes, but you have hidden knowledge of your true feelings from yourself. You are not aware of why you act the way you do!"

Freud also postulated the existence of a death instinct, which he called **Thanatos.** According to Freud, all living things, which he referred to as "animate matter," have a fundamental desire to relax back into an inanimate state, or death. Living, said Freud, takes energy and cunning. Hence death, at least at some level, is an easier choice because it releases the organism from the need for continued expenditure of energy. Thanatos was seen as contributing to many of the advances made by the human species, and as underlying a large proportion of individual accomplishments. Were it not for a wish to die, operative at some basic instinctual level, said Freud, few people would have the courage to take risks—and without the assumption of risk, precious little progress is possible in any sphere of life. The notion of an innate death wish has been used to explain why some offenders seem to behave in ways that ensure their eventual capture. Serial killers who send taunting

Thanatos a death wish.

messages to the police, terrorists who tell the media of their planned activities or take credit for public attacks, rapists who "accidentally" leave their wallets at the scene, burglars who break into occupied dwellings may all, for the most part unconsciously, be seeking to be stopped, captured, punished, and even killed.

From the Freudian perspective **neurosis,** a minor form of mental illness, may also lead to crime. Neurotic individuals are well in touch with reality, but may find themselves anxious, fearful of certain situations, or unable to help themselves in others. Fear of heights, for example, may be a neurosis, as may be compulsive handwashing or eating disorders. A classic example of the compulsive neurotic can be found in the individual who uses paper towels to open doorknobs, refraining from touching the knob directly for fear of picking up germs. Although such behavior may be unreasonable from the point of view of others, it is reality based (there *are* germs on doorknobs) and, for the individual demonstrating it, probably unavoidable. Most neuroses do not lead to crime. Some, however, can. A few years ago, for example, Stephen Blumberg of Des Moines, Iowa, was sentenced in federal court to nearly six years in prison and fined $200,000 for the theft of more than 21,000 rare books from hundreds of libraries.[46] Blumberg, whose compulsive interest in rare books began at yard sales and with searches in trash dumpsters, may have seen himself as involved in a messianic mission to preserve recorded history. Compulsive shoplifters may also be manifesting another form of neurosis—one in which a powerful need to steal can drive even well-heeled individuals to risk arrest and jail.

Neurosis functional disorders of the mind or of the emotions involving anxiety, phobia, or other abnormal behavior.

THE PSYCHOTIC OFFENDER

For many law-abiding citizens, extreme forms of criminal behavior are often difficult to understand, as the gruesome story of Gary Heidnik illustrates.[47] At his double-murder trial in 1988 Heidnik claimed insanity after he admittedly killed two women and tortured four others. All six women had been held captive in the basement of Heidnik's Philadelphia row house for four months—where they had been shackled with chains. One woman, who was chained to a wall and standing in a puddle of water was electrocuted when Heidnik pushed a live electrical cord against her bare skin. He starved a second woman to death. Heidnik was arrested on March 24, 1987, after one of the captive women escaped and led police to the house. At the scene police found evidence that Heidnik had mixed the ground flesh of at least one victim with dog food and fed it to the other captives.

A jury rejected Heidnik's claim of insanity and convicted him on two charges of first-degree murder. Although he was sentenced to die, Heidnik was still on Pennsylvania's death row as of mid-1997. Assistant District Attorney Charles Gallagher, who prosecuted Heidnik, called the case one of the most complicated he has ever taken to court. "He's an evil man and he did evil things. That's what the death penalty is for," Gallagher said.

Some seemingly inexplicable forms of criminality may be the result of **psychosis.** Whereas neurotic individuals often face only relatively minor problems in living, psychotic people, according to psychiatric definitions, are out of touch with reality in some fundamental way. They may suffer from hallucinations, delusions, or other

Psychosis a form of mental illness in which sufferers are said to be out of touch with reality.

Gary Heidnik. Sentenced to death, Heidnik *wants* to die for his crimes. Should he be executed? *AP/Wide World Photos.*

Schizophrenics mentally ill individuals who are out of touch with reality, and suffer from disjointed thinking.

Paranoid schizophrenics schizophrenic individuals who suffer from delusions and hallucinations.

breaks with reality. The classic psychotic thinks he is Napoleon, or sees spiders covering what others see only as a bare wall. Individuals suffering from a psychosis are said to be psychotic. Psychoses may be either organic, that is, caused by physical damage to, or abnormalities in, the brain, or functional, that is, those with no known physical cause. Gwynn Nettler says "[t]hought disorder is the hallmark of psychosis . . . people are called crazy when, at some extremity, they cannot 'think straight.' "[48] Nettler identifies three characteristics of psychotic individuals: "(1) a grossly distorted conception of reality, (2) moods, and swings of mood, that seem inappropriate to circumstance, and (3) marked inefficiency in getting along with others and caring for oneself."[49] Psychotic persons have also been classified as schizophrenic or paranoid schizophrenic. **Schizophrenics** are said to be characterized by disordered or disjointed thinking, in which the types of logical associations they make are atypical of other people. **Paranoid schizophrenics** suffer from delusions and hallucinations.

Unfortunately, psychiatrists have not been able to agree on definitive schizophrenic criteria that would allow for convenient application of the term. One prominent psychiatrist writes of "how varying . . . schizophrenia may appear, ranging from no striking symptoms at all to conspicuous psychotic features. . . . Thus on the surface," he continues, "the schizophrenic may appear normal and, to some extent, lead a conventional life."[50] The same author later tells us "[s]chizophrenia is not a clearly defined disease. . . . It is characterized rather by a . . . kind of alteration of thinking or feeling. . . ."[51] At the very least, then, we can safely say that schizophrenia is a disorganization of the personality. In its most extreme form, it may manifest itself by way of hallucinations, delusions, and seemingly irrational behavior.

CHAPTER 6

⬤⟫ 243 ⟫⬤

*Psychological and
Psychiatric
Foundations of
Criminal Behavior*

With these caveats in mind, it is fair to say that psychoses may lead to crime in a number of ways. Following the Vietnam War, for example, a number of instances were reported in which former American soldiers suffering from a kind of battle-field psychosis killed friends and family members thinking they were Vietcong soldiers—that is, the enemy. These men, who had been traumatized by battlefield experiences in Southeast Asia, relived their past on American streets. In other crimes committed by psychotics, thought disorders may be less obvious or may only exist temporarily.

THE LINK BETWEEN FRUSTRATION AND AGGRESSION

In his early writings, Freud suggested that aggressive behavior was a response to frustration. Aggression toward others, Freud said, is a natural response to frustrating limitations imposed upon a person. The frustration-aggression thesis was later developed more fully in the writings of J. Dollard,[52] Albert Bandura, Richard H. Walters, and others. Dollard's frustration-aggression theory held that although frustration can lead to various forms of behavior—including regression, sublimation, and aggressive fantasy—direct aggression toward others is its most likely consequence. Because everyone suffers some form of frustration throughout life, beginning with weaning and toilet training, Dollard argued, aggression is a natural consequence of living. Dollard pointed out, however, that aggression could be manifested in socially acceptable ways (perhaps through contact sports, military or law enforcement careers, or simple verbal attacks) and that it could be engaged in vicariously by observing others who are acting violently (as in movies, on television, through popular fiction, and so on). Dollard applied the psychoanalytical term "displacement" to the type of violence which is vented on something or someone not the source of the original frustration and suggested that satisfying one's aggressive urges via observation was a form of "catharsis."

The story of Paul Calden, a former insurance company executive, provides us with an example of the frustration-aggression theory as it applies to real-life crime. In January 1993, the 33-year-old Calden, dressed in a business suit, opened fire with a 9mm semiautomatic handgun on his ex-bosses in the Island Center Cafe, a Tampa, Florida, cafeteria—killing three people and injuring two others. Calden went up to the table where the five were eating, showed them the gun, shouted "[t]his is what you get for firing me!" and pulled the trigger.[53] He had been let go from his position as an underwriter with Fireman's Fund Insurance Company in March 1992. Calden then killed himself. He appears to have been acting out of frustrations born of his experience with having been fired.

Some psychologists have tried to identify what it is that causes some individuals to displace aggression or to experience it vicariously (through catharsis), while others respond violently and directly toward the immediate source of their frustrations. Andrew Henry and James Short,[54] for example, writing in the 1950s, suggested that child-rearing practices are a major determining factor in such a causal nexus. Restrictive parents who both punish and love their children, said Henry and Short, will engender in their children the ability to suppress outward expressions of aggression. When one parent punishes and the other loves, or when both punish but neither show love, children can be expected to show anger directly and perhaps even immediately, because they will not be threatened with the loss of love. Physical punishment, explained Henry and Short, rarely threatens the loss of love, and children so punished cannot be expected to refrain from direct displays of anger.

In 1960 Stewart Palmer[55] studied murderers and their siblings to determine the degree of frustration to which they had been exposed as children. He found that male murderers had experienced much more frustration than their brothers—in fact more than twice as many frustrating experiences, ranging from difficult births to serious illnesses, childhood beatings, severe toilet training, and negative school experiences, were reported by the murderers than by their law-abiding siblings.

▓ CRIME AS ADAPTIVE BEHAVIOR

Some psychiatric perspectives have held that ". . . crime is a compromise, representing for the individual the most satisfactory method of adjustment to inner conflicts which he cannot express otherwise. Thus, his acting out the crime fulfills a certain aim or purpose."[56] One pressing need of many criminals, according to some psychologists, is the need to be punished—that which arises, according to psychiatric theory, from a sense of guilt. Psychiatrists who suggest that the need to be punished is a motivating factor in criminal behavior are quick to point out that such a need may be a closely guarded secret, unknown even to the offender. Hence, from the psychiatric point of view, many drives, motives, and wishes are unconscious or even repressed by people who harbor them. The concept of repression holds that the human mind may choose to keep certain aspects of itself out of consciousness, possibly because of shame, self-loathing, or a simple lack of adequate introspection. The desire for punishment, however, sometimes comes to the fore. In 1993, for example, Westley Dodd was hanged to death by authorities in Washington State for the kidnap, rape, and murder of three little boys four years earlier. Dodd, who said he had molested dozens of children over the course of a decade, sought the death penalty after he was convicted, saying he deserved to die and vowing to sue the American Civil Liberties Union (ACLU) or anyone else who sought to save him.[57]

Crime can be adaptive in other ways as well. Some psychiatrists see it as an adaptation to life's stresses. According to Seymour L. Halleck,[58] turning to crime can provide otherwise disenfranchised individuals with a sense of power and purpose. In Halleck's words, "[d]uring the planning and execution of a criminal act the offender is a free man. . . . The value of this brief taste of freedom cannot be overestimated. Many of the criminal's apparently unreasonable actions are efforts to find a moment of autonomy. . . ."[59] Halleck says that crime can also provide "excellent rationalizations" for perceived inadequacies—especially for those whose lives have been failures when judged against the benchmarks of the wider society. "The criminal is able to say . . ., 'I could have been successful if I had not turned to crime. All my troubles have come to me because I have been bad.'"[60] Hence, crime, according to Halleck, provides "a convenient resource for denying, forgetting or ignoring . . . other inadequacies."

CHAPTER 6

 245

*Psychological and
Psychiatric
Foundations of
Criminal Behavior*

Westley Alan Dodd, hanged in 1993 for murdering young boys whom he molested. "People need to know it's the only thing that will stop me," he said of his execution. Might there have been some other alternative? *Benjamin Benschneider/Seattle Times/Gamma-Liaison, Inc.*

Insofar as the choice of crime reduces stresses which the individual faces by producing changes in the environment (empowerment), it is referred to as an **alloplastic adaptation.** When crime leads to stress reduction as a result of internal changes in beliefs, value systems, and so forth, it is called **autoplastic adaptation.** The offender who is able to deny responsibility for other failures by turning to crime is said to be seeking autoplastic adaptation. Because other forms of behavior may also meet many of the same needs as does crime, Halleck points out that an individual may select crime over various other behavioral alternatives only when no reasonable alternatives are available or when criminal behavior has inherent advantages—as might be the case under instances of economic or social oppression. (That is, individuals who are actively discriminated against may find personal and political significance in violating the laws of the oppressing society.)

In any case, from Halleck's point of view crime "has many advantages even when considered independently of the criminal's conscious or unconscious needs for gratification."[61] In other words, even though crime can be immediately rewarding or intensely pleasureful, says Halleck, such rewards are more "fringe benefits" than anything else. The central significance of criminal behavior for most offenders is that it "is an action which helps one survive with dignity."[62] Halleck tells us that "[w]e cannot understand the criminal unless we appreciate that his actions are much more than an effort to find a specific gratification."[63] In the final analysis, criminal behavior is, from Halleck's point of view, a form of adjustment to stress and oppression.

In another approach to stress as a causative agent in crime commission, Arnold S. Linsky, Ronet Bachman, and Murray A. Straus suggest that stress may lead to aggression toward others and toward oneself (i.e., self-destructive behavior such as

Alloplastic adaptation
that form of adjustment which results from changes in the environment surrounding an individual.

Autoplastic adaptation
that form of adjustment which results from changes within an individual.

suicide, smoking, and abuse of alcohol).[64] Linsky and his colleagues attempt to measure stress at the societal level, arguing that although the relationship between stress and aggression has been studied at the individual level, "the neglect of social stress as an explanation for society-to-society differences in aggression may be partially due to a lack of an objective means of comparing the stressfulness of life in different societies. . . ."[65] Concluding that societal stress levels heighten levels of aggression, the authors suggest that social policies should be created to reduce the impact of stressful events such as having to stop work, foreclosing on a mortgage, and dropping out of school.

Finally, we should recognize that perceptions vary, and although criminal behavior may appear to be a valid choice for some individuals who are seeking viable responses to perceived stresses and oppression, their perceptions may not be wholly accurate. In other words, misperceived stress and oppression may still lead to crime even when far simpler solutions may be found in a more realistic appraisal of one's situation.

⠸ SOCIAL LEARNING THEORY

Social learning theory a psychological perspective that says people learn how to behave by modeling themselves after others whom they have the opportunity to observe.

More recently, **Albert Bandura** has attempted to develop a comprehensive **social learning theory** of aggression. Bandura tells us that "[a] complete theory of aggression must explain how aggressive patterns are developed, what provokes people to behave aggressively, and what sustains such actions after they have been initiated."[66] Although everyone is capable of aggression, he says, "[p]eople are not born with . . . repertories of aggressive behavior. They must learn them." He goes on to say, "the specific forms that aggressive behavior takes, the frequency with which it is expressed, the situation in which it is displayed, and the specific targets selected for attack are largely determined by social learning factors." According to Bandura, people learn by observing others. In some of his early work, Bandura experimented with children who observed adult role models striking inflatable cartoon characters. When the children were observed following their encounter with adult behavior, they too exhibited similarly aggressive behavior toward the models. Bandura also studied violence on television and concluded that "[t]elevision is an effective tutor. Both laboratory and controlled field studies in which young children and adolescents are repeatedly shown either violence or nonviolent fare, disclose that exposure to film violence shapes the form of aggression and typically increases interpersonal aggressiveness in everyday life." A later study,[67] by other researchers, showed that even after ten years the level of violence engaged in by young adults was directly related to the degree of violent television they had been exposed to as children.

Social learning theory also shows how people can model the behavior of others. Bandura explained modeling behavior by reference to the frequent hijacking of domestic airliners to Cuba which occurred in the United States in the late 1960s and early 1970s. Such hijackings, Bandura found, followed immediately on the heels of similar incidents in Eastern European nations under Soviet domination. American hijackings, he said, were simply modeling those in Europe, and hijackers in this country were learning from news accounts of their foreign tutors.

Teenage skinhead brothers Bryan (left) and David Freeman (right) in court with their cousin, Nelson Birdwell III. The brothers pled guilty to charges of killing their parents and 11-year-old brother in 1995. Birdwell was convicted of first-degree murder at trial, and all three were sentenced to life in prison. How might their crimes have been a form of "modeling behavior"? *Reprinted with permission from* The Morning Call, *Allentown, PA.*

Once aggressive patterns of behavior have been acquired, it becomes necessary to show how they can be activated. Aggression can be provoked, Bandura suggests, through physical assaults and verbal threats and insults, as well as by thwarting a person's hopes or obstructing his or her goal-seeking behavior. Deprivation and "adverse reductions in the conditions of life" (a lowered standard of living, the onset of disease, a spouse leaving or caught cheating, etc.) are other potential triggers of aggression. Bandura adds, however, that a human being's ability to foresee the future consequences of present behavior infuses another dimension into the activation of learned patterns of aggression. That is, aggressive behavior can be perceived as holding future benefits for individuals exhibiting it. In short, it can be seen as a means to a desired end.

An example of aggression that resulted from thwarted goal-seeking, and which may have been seen as holding future benefits for the boys involved, occurred on the evening of February 27, 1995. On that evening teenage neo-Nazi "skinhead" brothers, Bryan and David Freeman, bludgeoned their parents and younger brother to death with baseball bats in the family's Allentown, Pennsylvania, home.[68] David was 15 years old at the time of the killings; Bryan was 17. The first to be killed was probably their 48-year-old mother, Brenda, who suffered massive head injuries and stab wounds. Investigators theorize that Brenda confronted the boys after their noisy late-night return home, and was arguing with them when at least one son attacked her, smashing her skull with a club. She fell face down onto the carpeted hallway outside the bedroom her sons shared, trying to protect her head with her hands. One of the boys then jumped on his mother and stabbed her repeatedly in the back. After what may have been a brief conference, the brothers then made their way upstairs to their parents' bedroom, where their 54-year-old father, Dennis, was sleeping. There, they cut their father's throat and clubbed him to death before he could leave the bed. Next, they moved on to the bedroom of their younger brother, Eric, 11, crushing his skull with a hammer as he slept. Viewing the murder scene the next day, Lehigh County Coroner Wayne Snyder called the slayings "the most savage, brutal, cowardly acts of murder I've ever seen."[69]

By all accounts the young Freeman brothers had normal childhoods. Then, about two years prior to the murders, they began to change. The changes were gradual at first, but soon became more pronounced. The boys fell in with a rebellious crowd, took to drinking, and experimented with drugs.[70] Soon they stopped regular school attendance, shaved their heads, began bodybuilding, and paid for a series of garish tattoos to cover their arms and torsos. They began attending white supremacist meetings and collected fascist paraphernalia, including knives. Two weeks before killing their parents, the brothers paid to have their foreheads tattooed: Bryan with "Berserker" and David with "Seig Heil." Run-ins with the police had become routine and, authorities believe, when their parents took away the boys' car and threatened to have them reinstitutionalized, the killings took place.

Bandura also says that individuals sometimes become aggressive because they are rewarded for doing so. The early twentieth-century American concept of a "macho"—virile and masculine—male figure, for example, was often associated with the expectation of substantial reward. The macho male figure was the one who won the most respect from his fellows, inevitably came away with the greatest honors (on the playing field, in school, from the community, etc.), and eventually married the most desirable woman. Whether this perception was accurate, it was nonetheless subscribed to by a significant proportion of American men and, for many decades, served as a guide to daily behavior.

Another form of reward can flow from aggression. Bandura called it the "reduction of aversive treatment." By this he meant that simply standing up for one's self can improve the way one is treated by others. Oftentimes, for example, standing up to a bully is the most effective way of dealing with the harassment one might otherwise face. Similarly, there is an old saying that "the squeaky wheel gets the grease," and it means, quite simply, that people who are the most demanding will be recognized. Aggressive people often get what they go after.

Bandura recognized that all persons have self-regulatory mechanisms that can ameliorate the tendency toward aggression. People reward or punish themselves, Bandura said, according to internal standards they have for judging their own behavior. Hence, aggression may be inhibited in people who, for example, value religious, ethical, or moral standards of conduct such as compassion, thoughtfulness, and courtesy. Nonetheless, Bandura concluded, people who devalue aggression may still engage in it via a process he called "disengagement," whereby rationalizations are constructed which overcome internal inhibitions. Disengagement may result from (1) "attributing blame to one's victims," (2) dehumanization through bureaucratization, automation, urbanization, and high social mobility, (3) vindication of aggressive practices by legitimate authorities, and (4) desensitization resulting from repeated exposure to aggression in any of a variety of forms.

Social learning theory has been criticized for lacking comprehensive explanatory power. How, for example, can striking differences in sibling behavior, when early childhood experiences were likely much the same, be explained? Similarly, why do apparent differences exist between the sexes with regard to degree and type of criminality—irrespective of social background and early learning experiences? More recent versions of social learning theory, sometimes called "cognitive social learning theory,"[71] attempt to account for such differences by hypothesizing that reflection and cognition play a significant role in interpreting what one observes, and in determining responses. Hence, few people are likely to behave precisely as others, because they will have their own ideas about what observed behavior means and about the consequences of emulation.

❖ BEHAVIOR THEORY

Behavior theory has sometimes been called the "stimulus-response approach to human behavior. . . . At the heart of behavior theory is the notion that behavior is determined by environmental consequences which it produces for the individual concerned."[72] When an individual's behavior results in rewards, or in the receipt of feedback which the individual, for whatever reason, regards as rewarding, then it is likely that the behavior will become more frequent. Under such circumstances the behavior in question is said to be reinforced. Conversely, when punishment follows behavior, chances are that the frequency of that type of behavior will decrease. The individual's responses are termed **operant behavior,** because behavioral choices effectively operate upon the surrounding environment to produce consequences for the behaving individual. Similarly, stimuli provided by the environment become behavioral cues, which serve to elicit conditioned responses from individuals. Responses are said to be conditioned according to the individual's past experiences, wherein behavioral consequences effectively defined some forms of behavior as desirable and others as undesirable. Behavior theory is often employed by parents seeking to control children through a series of **rewards** and **punishments.** Young children may be punished, for example, with spanking, the loss of a favored toy (at least for a period of time), a turned-off television, and so forth. Older children are often told what rules they are expected to obey, and the rewards that they can anticipate receiving from adherence to those rules. They also know that punishments will follow if they do not obey the rules.

Rewards and punishments have been further divided into four conceptual categories: (1) positive rewards, which increase the frequency of approved behavior by adding something desirable to the situation—as when a "good" child is given a toy; (2) negative rewards, which increase the frequency of approved behavior by removing something distressful from the situation—as when a "good" child is permitted to skip the morning's chores; (3) positive punishments, which decrease the frequency of unwanted behavior by adding something undesirable to the situation— as when a "bad" child is spanked; and (4) negative punishments, which decrease the frequency of unwanted behavior by removing something desirable from the situation—as when a "bad" child's candy is taken away. According to behavior theory, it is through the application of rewards and punishments that behavior is shaped.

Behavior theory a psychological perspective which posits that individual behavior which is rewarded will increase in frequency, while that which is punished will decrease.

Operant behavior behavior that affects the environment in such a way as to produce responses or further behavioral cues.

Rewards desirable behavioral consequences likely to increase the frequency of occurrence of that behavior.

Punishments undesirable behavioral consequences likely to decrease the frequency of occurrence of that behavior.

Behavior theory differs from other psychological theories in that the major determinants of behavior are envisioned as residing in the environment surrounding the individual rather than actually in the individual. Perhaps the best known proponent of behavior theory is Burrhus Frederic Skinner (1904–1990), popularly referred to as **B. F. Skinner.** Skinner, a former Harvard professor, rejected unobservable psychological constructs, focusing instead on patterns of responses to external rewards and stimuli. Skinner did extensive animal research involving behavioral concepts and created the notion of programmed instruction, which allows students to work at their own pace and provides immediate rewards for learning accomplishments.

Although behavior theory has much to say about the reformation of criminal offenders through the imposition of punishment, the approach is equally significant for its contributions to understanding the genesis of such behavior. As one writer states, "it is the balance of reinforcement and punishment in an individual's learning history which will dictate the presence or absence of criminal behavior."[73] According to the behavioral model, crime results when individuals "receive tangible rewards (positive reinforcement) for engaging in delinquent and criminal behavior, particularly when no other attractive alternative is available."[74]

A few years ago, for example, Sundahkeh "Ron" Bethune, 15, shot and killed a 26-year-old pizza delivery man who gunned his car motor as Bethune attempted to rob him. Ron, who had been dabbling in the drug trade and who could afford high-priced clothing, jewelry, and other accouterments of apparent wealth, was esteemed by many other young people in his Morganton, North Carolina, community. When the delivery man tried to run from Ron in front of a group of his friends, Bethune saw no other choice but to kill him. "I just had to show them I wasn't some little punk,"[75] he said afterward in a prison interview. Ron Bethune did not think of the long-term consequences of his behavior on the night of the killing. All he wanted was to earn the approval of those who were watching him. The crowd's anticipated awestruck response to murder was all the reward Ron needed to pull the trigger that night. He is now serving five years for second-degree murder.

Behavior theory has been criticized for ignoring the role that cognition plays in human behavior. Martyrs, for example, persist in what may be defined by the wider society as undesirable behavior, even in the face of severe punishment—including the loss of their own lives. No degree of punishment is likely to deter a martyr who answers to some higher call. Similarly, criminals who are punished for official law violations may find that their immediate social group interprets criminal punishment as status enhancing. As an acquaintance of the author said, after being released from prison where he had served time for murder, "You woulda thought I had won a Grammy award or somethin'." Members of his community held him in awe. As he walked down the street young people would say, "There goes John! You better not mess with John!" From the point of view of behavior theory, criminal punishments are in danger of losing sway over many forms of human behavior in today's diverse society. Our society's fragmented value system leads to various interpretations of criminal punishments thereby changing the significance of experiences such as arrest, conviction, and imprisonment. In times past, criminal offenders were often shunned and became social outcasts. Today, those who have been adjudicated criminal may find that their new status holds many rewards.

Psychological and Psychiatric Foundations of Criminal Behavior

Insanity (psychological) persistent mental disorder or derangement.[76]

Insanity (law) a legally established inability to understand right from wrong, or to conform one's behavior to the requirements of the law. Also, a defense allowable in criminal courts.

▓ INSANITY AND THE LAW

Insanity is a defense allowable in criminal courts. A criminal defendant may be found not guilty by reason of insanity and avoid punitive sanctions even when it is clear that he or she committed a legally circumscribed act. Legal and psychiatric definitions of insanity, however, rarely coincide. In the words of the U.S. Supreme Court,[77] "It is by now well established that insanity as defined by the criminal law has no direct analog in medicine or science. [T]he divergence between law and psychiatry," the Court has said, "is caused in part by the legal fiction represented by the words 'insanity' or 'insane,' which are a kind of lawyer's catchall and have no clinical meaning." C. Ray Jeffery[78] writes that "[t]hree concepts are confused in the insanity defense": (1) psychiatric, (2) legal, and (3) neurological understandings of mental illness. Even so, psychotic offenders are more likely than most other kinds of criminal wrongdoers to be adjudicated insane or to have their degree of criminal culpability reduced by the courts in recognition of the mental problems they face. The burden of proving a claim of "not guilty by reason of insanity," however, falls upon the defendant.[79] Just as a person is assumed to be innocent at the start of any criminal trial, so too is the person assumed to be sane.

An individual has a right to the opportunity to prove a claim of insanity in court and cannot be forced to take medications during trial that might control the condition. In 1992, for example, the U.S. Supreme Court, in the case of *Riggins* v. *Nevada*,[80] held that the "forced administration of antipsychotic medication" may have impaired the accused's ability to defend himself and violated due process guarantees.

In 1984 the U.S. Congress enacted the Insanity Defense Reform Act (IDRA), part of the 1984 Crime Control and Prevention Act.[81] Congress had been spurred to action by John Hinckley's attempted assassination of then-president Reagan. At trial, Hinckley's lawyers claimed that their client's history of schizophrenia left him

Insanity can be used as a defense against criminal charges. Lorena Bobbitt sobs on the witness stand before acquittal on charges she severed her husband's penis with a kitchen knife. Bobbitt claimed a kind of irresistible impulse. Should she have been acquitted? *Gary Hershorn/Corbis-Bettmann.*

unable to control his behavior, and Hinckley was acquitted of the criminal charges which had been brought against him. Although Hinckley was institutionalized to prevent him from harming others, his release is mandated by federal law which existed at the time of his trial when (and if) he recovers.

Through the IDRA, Congress intended to prohibit the presentation, at trial, of evidence of mental disease or defect, short of legal insanity, to excuse conduct.[82] Insanity under the act is defined as a condition in which the defendant can be shown to have been suffering under a "severe mental disease or defect" and, as a result, "was unable to appreciate the nature and quality or the wrongfulness of his acts."[83] The IDRA also placed the burden of proving insanity squarely on the defendant—a provision that has been unsuccessfully challenged a number of times since the act was passed.

The IDRA created a special verdict of "not guilty by reason of insanity" (NGRI).[84] Through a comprehensive civil commitment procedure, a defendant found NGRI can be held in custody pending a court hearing. The hearing must occur within forty days of the verdict. At the conclusion of the hearing, the court determines whether the defendant should be hospitalized or released. In the words of the U.S. Supreme Court, "[t]he Insanity Defense Reform Act of 1984 ensures that a federal criminal defendant found not guilty by reason of insanity will not be released onto the streets."[85]

The IDRA is especially significant for the fact that it contains a provision which permits mentally ill individuals to be held for trial in the hopes that they will recover sufficiently to permit their trial to proceed. The law allows for an initial hearing to determine the mental status of the defendant. If the defendant is found incompetent to stand trial he will be committed to a hospital "for such a reasonable period of time, not to exceed four months, . . . to determine whether there is a substantial probability that in the foreseeable future he will attain the capacity to permit the trial to proceed; and . . . for an additional reasonable period of time until . . . his mental condition is so improved that trial may proceed. . . ."[86] The law sets no maximum period of confinement, implying only that the defendant will undergo periodic review while institutionalized ". . . if the court finds that there is a substantial probability that within such additional period of time he will attain the capacity to permit the trial to proceed. . . ."

THE MCNAUGHTEN RULE

One of the first instances within the Western legal tradition where insanity was accepted as a defense to criminal liability can be found in the case of Daniel McNaughten (also spelled "M'Naughton" and "M'Naghton"). McNaughten was accused of the 1844 killing of Edward Drummond, the secretary of British Prime Minister Sir Robert Peel. By all accounts McNaughten had intended to kill Peel, but because he was suffering from mental disorganization shot Drummond instead, mistaking him for Peel. At his trial, the defense presented information to show that McNaughten was suffering from delusions, including the belief that Peel's political party was, in some vague way, persecuting him. The court accepted his lawyer's claims and the defense of insanity was established in Western law. Other jurisdictions were quick to adopt

CHAPTER 6

253

*Psychological and
Psychiatric
Foundations of
Criminal Behavior*

⬛

INSANITY AS A DEFENSE UNDER FEDERAL LAW

Federal law permits the defense of insanity, as follows:

Sec. 17. Insanity defense
(a) Affirmative Defense. It is an affirmative defense to a prosecution under any Federal statute that, at the time of the commission of the acts constituting the offense, the defendant, as a result of a severe mental disease or defect, was unable to appreciate the nature and quality or the wrongfulness of his acts. Mental disease or defect does not otherwise constitute a defense.
(b) Burden of Proof. The defendant has the burden of proving the defense of insanity by clear and convincing evidence.

Source: Section 17, Public Law 99-646, Nov. 10, 1986.

the McNaughten rule, as the judge's decision in the case came to be called. The **McNaughten rule** holds that individuals cannot be held criminally responsible for their actions if at the time of the offense either (1) they did not know what they were doing, or (2) they did not know that what they were doing was wrong.

Today the McNaughten rule is still followed by many states when insanity is at issue in criminal cases. Critics of the McNaughten rule say that, although the notion of intent inherent within it appeals well to lawyers, "[i]t is . . . so alien to current concepts of human behavior that it has been vigorously attacked by psychiatrists. An obvious difficulty with the McNaughten rule is that practically everyone, regardless of the degree of his criminal disturbance, knows the nature and quality and rightness or wrongness of what he is doing."[87]

McNaughten rule a standard for judging legal insanity which requires that offenders not know what they were doing, or if they did, that they not know it was wrong.

THE IRRESISTIBLE IMPULSE TEST

The McNaughten ruling opened the floodgates for other types of insanity claims offered as defenses to charges of criminal activity. One interesting claim is that of irresistible impulse. The **irresistible impulse test**—employed by eighteen states, some of which also follow the dictates of McNaughten—holds that a defendant is not guilty of a criminal offense if the person, by virtue of his or her mental state or psychological condition, was not able to resist committing the action in question. Some years ago, for example, a television advertisement claimed that a certain brand of potato chip was so good that, once you opened the container, you couldn't eat just one. Friends of the author would test themselves by purchasing the brand in question, opening the pack, and eating a chip. They would then try and resist the temptation to have another—thereby hoping to prove the commercial wrong. Although this may seem a silly exercise in self-assessment, it did prove a point. The

Irresistible impulse test a standard for judging legal insanity which holds that a defendant is not guilty of a criminal offense if the person, by virtue of his or her mental state or psychological condition, was not able to resist committing the action in question.

commercial, in fact, was right most of the time. Additional chips were almost impossible to avoid for anyone who tried this experiment—especially if they kept the chips around for any length of time!

Of course, eating potato chips is not a crime, even if the chips are irresistible. However, for individuals who suffer from other types of compulsions, some of them criminal, the test may effectively measure their mettle. Even so, it is difficult for anyone to really know whether a given person in a particular situation was able to control his or her behavior. Kleptomania is a disorder in which an individual feels compelled to steal. Kleptomaniacs are often shoplifters, but have also been known to be unable to resist the urge to steal while visiting the homes of friends or relatives.

In 1994, Lorena Bobbitt, whose case was described earlier in this chapter, was found not guilty by virtue of temporary insanity of charges of maliciously wounding her husband by cutting off his penis with a kitchen knife. Her attorneys successfully employed the irresistible impulse defense, convincing the jury that Mrs. Bobbitt acted as a result of irresistible impulse after years of "physical abuse, verbal abuse and sexual abuse" at the hands of her husband. Her attorneys maintained that, while committing the crime, she had a brief psychotic breakdown and could not resist the impulse to maim her husband.

Scientific advances now on the horizon combine with the irresistible impulse test to open a number of intriguing possibilities. One has to do with new colognes and perfumes rumored soon to be marketed. These scents combine the usual toiletries with pheromones—chemical substances that, at least in insect form, have been shown to produce very predictable, and apparently uncontrollable, behavior. Pheromones, which stimulate the olfactory nerves to produce specific chemicals which then target neuroreceptors in the brain, directly alter brain chemistry. Most uses of pheromones to date have been in the area of pest control, where sexual pheromones that attract specific types of male insects, for example, are released into the atmosphere to confuse the insect's mating behavior or to lure pests into a trap. Clearly at issue, if the new products are marketed, will be claims of uncontrollable sexual desire. Will toiletries containing human pheromones lead to instances of sexual attack? If so, will the attackers be held blameless on claims of irresistible impulse, and what will then be the civil liability of the product makers themselves?

THE DURHAM RULE

In 1954 Judge David Bazelon of the U.S. Court of Appeals for the District of Columbia announced a new rule in the case of Monte Durham. In the words of the court: "The rule we now hold is simply that an accused is not criminally responsible if his unlawful act was the product of mental disease or mental defect." Judge Bazelon continued, defining the terms of the court's decision: "We use 'disease' in the sense of a condition which is considered capable of improving or deteriorating. We use 'defect' in the sense of a condition which is not considered capable of either improving or deteriorating and which may be congenital or the result of injury or the residual effect of a physical or mental disease."[88]

CHAPTER 6

⬅️ 255 ➡️

*Psychological and
Psychiatric
Foundations of
Criminal Behavior*

Although this new rule was intended to simplify the adjudication of mentally ill offenders, it has resulted in additional confusion. Many criminal defendants suffer from mental diseases and/or defects. Some show retarded mental development, others are dyslexic, a few are afflicted with Down's syndrome, others have cerebral palsy (which will perhaps meet Judge Bazelon's definition), and a vast number evidence some degree of neurosis or psychosis. The link between any of these conditions and criminal behavior in specific cases, however, is far from clear. Some people struggle with psychological handicaps or mental illnesses all their lives, never engaging in violations of the criminal law. Others, with similar conditions, are frequent law violators. The **Durham rule** provides no way of separating one group from the other.

Finally, some observers have noted the "danger of circularity in the Durham rule." If a person exhibits unusual behavior during the commission of a crime, the criminal behavior itself may be taken as a sign of mental disease—automatically exonerating the offender of criminal culpability.

Durham rule a standard for judging legal insanity which holds that "an accused is not criminally responsible if his unlawful act was the product of mental disease or mental defect."

THE SUBSTANTIAL CAPACITY TEST

In the determination of insanity for purposes of criminal prosecution, nineteen U.S. states adhere to the **substantial capacity test**—a standard embodied in the Model Penal Code of the American Law Institute. The substantial capacity test blends elements of the McNaughten rule with the irresistible impulse standard. Insanity is said to be present when a person lacks "the [substantial] mental capacity needed to understand the wrongfulness of his act, or to conform his behavior to the requirements of the law."[89] A lack of mental capacity does not require total mental incompetence, nor does it mandate that the behavior in question meet the standard of total irresistibility. The problem, however, of determining just what constitutes "substantial mental capacity," or its lack, has plagued this rule from its inception.

Substantial capacity test a standard for judging legal insanity which requires that a person lack "the mental capacity needed to understand the wrongfulness of his act, or to conform his behavior to the requirements of the law."

THE BRAWNER RULE

The Brawner rule, created in 1972 in the case of *U.S. v. Brawner,*[90] is rather unique among standards of its type. This rule, in effect, delegates responsibility to the jury to determine what constitutes insanity. The jury is asked to decide whether the defendant could be *justly* held responsible for the criminal act with which he or she stands charged, in the face of any claims of insanity or mental incapacity. Under the Brawner rule, which has not seen wide applicability, juries are left with few rules to guide them other than their own sense of fairness.

GUILTY BUT INSANE

Frustrated by the seeming inability of criminal courts to effectively adjudicate mentally ill offenders, and by the abuse of insanity claims by offenders seeking to avoid criminal punishments, several states have enacted legislation permitting findings of "guilty but insane" or **"guilty but mentally ill" (GBMI)**. In 1997, for example,

Guilty but mentally ill (GBMI) a finding that offenders are guilty of the criminal offense with which they are charged but, because of their prevailing mental condition, they are generally sent to psychiatric hospitals for treatment rather than to prison. Once they have been declared "cured," however, such offenders can be transferred to correctional facilities to serve out their sentences.

Pennsylvania multimillionaire John E. du Pont was found guilty but mentally ill in the shooting death of former Olympic gold medalist David Schultz during a delusional episode. Although defense attorneys were able to show that du Pont sometimes thought he saw Nazis in his trees, heard the walls talking, and had cut off pieces of his own skin in efforts to remove bugs from outer space, he was held criminally liable for Schultz's death and sentenced to thirteen to thirty years in confinement.

A GBMI verdict means that a person can be held responsible for a specific criminal act, even though a degree of mental incompetence may be present in his or her personality. In most GBMI jurisdictions, a jury must return a finding of "guilty but mentally ill" if (1) every statutory element necessary for a conviction has been proven beyond a reasonable doubt, (2) the defendant is found to have been *mentally ill* at the time the crime was committed, and (3) the defendant was *not* found to have been *legally insane* at the time the crime was committed. The difference between mental illness and legal insanity is crucial, because a defendant can be mentally ill by standards of the medical profession, but sane for purposes of the law.

Upon return of a GBMI verdict, a judge may impose any sentence possible under the law for the crime in question. Offenders adjudicated GBMI are, in effect, found guilty of the criminal offense with which they are charged but, because of their mental condition, are generally sent to psychiatric hospitals for treatment rather than to prison. Once they have been declared "cured," however, such offenders can be transferred to correctional facilities to serve out their sentences.

FEDERAL PROVISIONS FOR THE HOSPITALIZATION OF INDIVIDUALS FOUND "NGRI"

Federal law provides for confinement in a "suitable facility" of criminal defendants found not guilty by reason of insanity.[91] The law mandates a "psychiatric or psychological examination and report" and a hearing to be held within forty days after the not guilty verdict. If the hearing court finds that the person's release would "create a substantial risk of bodily injury to another person or serious damage of property of another due to a present mental disease or defect, the court" in the language of the statute, "shall commit the person. . . ." To be later released, a person committed under the law "has the burden of proving by clear and convincing evidence that his release would not create a substantial risk of bodily injury to another person or serious damage of property of another due to a present mental disease or defect." The person can be discharged "[w]hen the director of the facility in which an acquitted person is hospitalized . . . determines that the person has recovered from his mental disease or defect to such an extent that his release, or his conditional release under a prescribed regimen of medical, psychiatric, or psychological care or treatment, would no longer create a substantial risk of bodily injury to another person or serious damage to property of another. . . ."

The federal statute has been used as a model by many of the states. A few laws, which differ from the federal model, have been held to be unconstitutional, especially when they permit the continued confinement of offenders who have been declared "well," even though they may still be dangerous. In 1992, for example, the U.S. Supreme Court, in the case of **Foucha v. Louisiana,**[92] ordered the release of

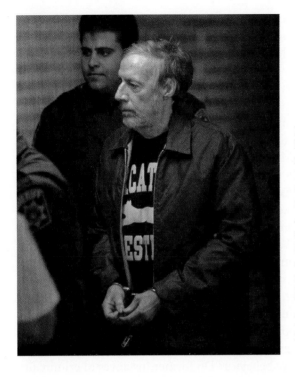

Insanity became an issue at the 1997 Pennsylvania murder trial of multimillionaire John E. du Pont. In 1996 du Pont shot and killed former Olympic wrestling gold medalist David Schultz during a delusional episode. Although defense attorneys were able to show that du Pont sometimes saw Nazis in his trees, heard the walls talking, and cut off pieces of his skin to remove bugs from outer space, he was found guilty but mentally ill, and sentenced to serve 13 to 30 years in confinement. Should he have been absolved of criminal responsibility? *Chris Gardner/AP/Wide World Photos.*

Terry Foucha who had been adjudicated "not guilty by reason of insanity" in the state of Louisiana. Although a psychiatrist later found Foucha to have overcome a drug-induced psychosis which had been present at the time of the crime, a state court ordered Foucha returned to the mental institution in which he had been committed, ruling that he was dangerous on the basis of the same doctor's testimony. The psychiatrist found that although Foucha was "in good shape" mentally, he had "an antisocial personality." Foucha's antisocial personality was described as "a condition that is not a mental disease and is untreatable." The doctor cited the fact that Foucha had been involved in several altercations at the institution, and said that he would not "feel comfortable in certifying that he would not be a danger to himself or to other people." In effect, the Supreme Court struck down a provision of the Louisiana law which made possible continued confinement of recovered persons who had once been deemed not guilty by reason of insanity, when their continued confinement was predicated solely on the basis of the belief that they might represent a continuing danger to the community.

∷ SOCIAL POLICY AND FORENSIC PSYCHOLOGY

Psychological theories continue to evolve. For example, recent research in the field has shown a stability of aggressiveness over time. That is, children who display early disruptive or aggressive behavior have been found, through the use of studies that follow the same individuals over time,[93] likely to continue their involvement in such behavior even as adults. Some researchers have found that aggressiveness appears to stabilize over time.[94] Children who demonstrate aggressive traits early in life

Dangerousness the likelihood that a given individual will later harm society or others; it is often measured in terms of **recidivism,** or as the likelihood of new crime commission or rearrest for a new crime within a five-year period following arrest or release from confinement.

often evidence increasingly frequent episodes of such behavior until, finally, such behavior becomes a major component of the adolescent or adult personality. From such research it is possible to conclude that problem children are likely to become problem adults.

Expanding research of this sort holds considerable significance for those who are attempting to assess **dangerousness,** and to identify personal characteristics which would allow for the prediction of dangerousness in individual cases. The ability to accurately predict future dangerousness is of great concern to today's policymakers. In 1993, for example, Michael Blair, a convicted child molester paroled after serving eighteen months of a ten-year prison sentence, was charged with the kidnap-slaying of young Ashley Estell, who disappeared from a soccer match in Plano, Texas. Ashley was found dead the next day.[95] Similarly, in November of that year, Anthony Cook was executed in Huntsville, Texas, for the slaying of law student Dirck VanTassel, Jr.[96] Cook killed VanTassel only thirteen days after being paroled, robbing him of his wallet, watch, and wedding ring and shooting him four times in the head. Less than a month later, in what was to be a very sad case, Richard Allen Davis, a twice-convicted kidnapper, was arrested for the kidnap-murder of 12-year-old Polly Klaas.[97] Klaas was abducted from a slumber party in her Petaluma, California, home as her mother slept in the next room. Davis had been paroled only a few months earlier after serving an eight-year prison term for a similar offense.

Can past behavior predict future behavior? Do former instances of criminality presage additional ones? Are there other, identifiable, characteristics which violent offenders might manifest that could serve as warning signs to criminal justice decision makers faced with the dilemma of whether to release convicted felons? This, like many other areas, is one in which criminologists are still learning. One recent study[98] found a strong relationship between childhood behavioral difficulties and later problem behavior. According to authors of the study "early antisocial behavior is the best predictor of later antisocial behavior. It appears that this rule holds even when the antisocial behavior is measured as early as the preschool period." Using children as young as 3 years old, researchers were able to predict later delinquency, leading them to conclude that "some antisocial behavioral characteristics may be components of temperament." A second study,[99] which tracked a sample of male offenders for over twenty years, found that stable, but as yet "unmeasured individual differences" account for the positive association which exists between past criminal behavior and the likelihood of future recurrence. A 1996 analysis of recidivism studies[100] by Canadians Paul Gendreau, Tracy Little, and Claire Goggin found that criminal history, a history of preadult antisocial behavior, and "criminogenic needs"—which were defined as measurable antisocial thoughts, values, and behavior—were all predictors of recidivism.

Prediction, however, requires more than generalities. It is one thing to say, for example, that generally speaking 70 percent of children who evidence aggressive behavior will similarly show violent tendencies later in life, and quite another to be able to predict which specific individuals will engage in future violations of the criminal law. **Selective incapacitation** is a policy based on the notion of career criminality.[101] Career criminals, also termed *habitual offenders,* are persons who repeatedly commit violations of the criminal law. Research has shown that only a

Selective incapacitation a social policy which seeks to protect society by incarcerating those individuals deemed to be the most dangerous.

CHAPTER 6

⟺ 259 ⟺

*Psychological and
Psychiatric
Foundations of
Criminal Behavior*

small percentage of all offenders account for most crimes reported to the police. Some studies have found that as few as 8 percent of all offenders commit as many as sixty serious crimes each per year.[102] A recent Wisconsin study found that imprisonment of individuals determined to be career offenders saved the state approximately $14,000 per year per offender when the cost of imprisonment was compared with the estimated cost of new crimes. Researchers in the Wisconsin study concluded that "prison pays" and suggested that the state continue pursuing a policy of aggressive imprisonment of career offenders even in the face of escalating costs and vastly overcrowded prisons. The strategy of selective incapacitation, however, which depends on accurately identifying potentially dangerous offenders out of existing criminal populations, has been criticized by some authors[103] for yielding a rate of "false positives" of over 60 percent. Potentially violent offenders are not easy to identify, even on the basis of past criminal records, and sentencing individuals to long prison terms simply because they are thought likely to commit crimes in the future would no doubt be unconstitutional.

The federal 1984 Comprehensive Crime Control Act,[104] which established the U.S. Sentencing Commission, targeted career offenders. Guidelines created by the commission contain, as a central feature, a "criminal history" dimension which substantially increases the amount of punishment an offender faces based on his or her history of law violations. The sentencing guidelines originally classified a defendant as a career offender if "(1) the defendant was at least 18 years old at the time of the . . . offense, (2) the . . . offense is a crime of violence or trafficking in a controlled substance, and (3) the defendant has at least two prior felony convictions of either a crime of violence or a controlled substance offense."[105] The definition, however, later came under fire for casting individuals with a history of minor drug trafficking into the same category as serial killers and the like.

Definitions of dangerousness are fraught with difficulty because, as some authors have pointed out, "dangerousness is not an objective quality like obesity or brown eyes, rather it is an ascribed quality like trustworthiness." Dangerousness[106] is not necessarily a personality trait which is stable or easily identifiable. Even if it were, recent studies[107] of criminal careers seem to show that involvement in crime decreases with age. Hence, as one author states, if "criminality declines more or less uniformly with age, then many offenders will be 'over the hill' by the time they are old enough to be plausible candidates for preventive incarceration."[108]

No discussion of social policy as it relates to the insights of criminal psychology would be complete without mention of correctional psychology. **Correctional psychology** is concerned with the diagnosis and classification of offenders, the treatment of correctional populations, and the rehabilitation of inmates and other law violators. Perhaps the most commonly used classification instrument in correctional facilities today is the Minnesota Multiphasic Personality Inventory, better known as the MMPI. Based on results of MMPI inventories, offenders may be assigned to various security levels, differing correctional programs, or a variety of treatment programs. Psychological treatment, when employed, typically takes the form of individual or group counseling. Psychotherapy, guided group interaction, cognitive therapy, behavioral modification, and various forms of interpersonal therapy are representative of the range of techniques used.

Correctional psychology that aspect of forensic psychology which is concerned with the diagnosis and classification of offenders, the treatment of correctional populations, and the rehabilitation of inmates and other law violators.

SOCIAL POLICY AND THE PSYCHOLOGY OF CRIMINAL CONDUCT

A practical synthesis of psychological approaches to criminal behavior is offered by D. A. Andrews and James Bonta in their 1994 book *The Psychology of Criminal Conduct*.[109] Andrews and Bonta prefer the term "psychology of criminal conduct," or PCC, to distinguish their point of view from what they call "the weak psychology represented in mainstream sociological criminology and clinical/forensic psychology."[110] Any useful synthesis of contemporary criminal psychology, they claim, should be fundamentally objective and empirical. Clearly they dislike many currently well-accepted perspectives, which they say have "placed higher value on social theory and political ideology than [on] rationality and/or respect for evidence."[111] Specifically, say Andrews and Bonta, "[t]he majority of perspectives on criminal conduct that are most favored in mainstream criminology reduce people to hypothetical fictions whose only interesting characteristics are their location in the social system. Almost without exception . . .," they write, "the causal significance of social location is presumed to reflect inequality in the distribution of social wealth and power." This kind of theorizing, the authors claim, "is a major preoccupation of mainstream textbook criminology, even though such a focus has failed to significantly advance understanding of criminal conduct."[112]

In *The Psychology of Criminal Conduct* Andrews and Bonta do not attempt to develop a new behavioral theory, but rather ask for the objective application of what is now understood about the psychology of crime and criminal behavior. Their book is a call for practical coalescence of what is already known of the psychology of criminal offenders. Such coalescence is possible, they say, through the application of readily available, high-quality psychological findings. The authors claim, for example, that from the nearly 500 published reports on "controlled evaluations of community and correctional interventions," it is possible to conclude that treatment reduces recidivism "to at least a mild degree." Further, a detailed consideration of published studies finds that, among other things, targeting higher-risk cases and using treatments outside of formal correctional settings which extend to an offender's family and peers are all elements of the most effective treatment strategies. Similarly, Andrews and Bonta say, along with objective measures of the success of rehabilitation programs and strategies, effective intervention and treatment services based on the use of psychological assessment instruments which have already demonstrated their validity, empirically established risk factors that can be accurately assessed, and accurately measured community crime rates, are all ready and waiting to make a practical psychology of criminal conduct available to today's policymakers. In the words of Andrews and Bonta, "[t]here exists now an empirically defensible general psychology of criminal conduct (PCC) that is of practical value . . . it should speak to policy advisors, policy-makers and legislators who must come to see that . . . human science is not just [a] relic of a positivistic past."[113] The major remaining issue, say the authors, "on which work is only beginning, is how to make use of what works."[114]

CHAPTER 6

261

*Psychological and
Psychiatric
Foundations of
Criminal Behavior*

PSYCHOLOGICAL PROFILING

During World War II psychologists and psychoanalysts were recruited by the War Department in an attempt to predict future moves enemy forces might make. Psychological and psychoanalytical techniques were applied to the study of Adolph Hitler, the Italian leader Benito Mussolini, the Japanese general and prime minister Tojo Hideki, and other Axis leaders. Such psychological profiling of enemy leaders may have given the allies the edge in battlefield strategy. Hitler, probably because of his heightened sensitivity to symbols, his strong belief in fate, and his German ancestry (Freud was Austrian), became the central figure analyzed by profilers.

Today **psychological profiling** is used to assist criminal investigators seeking to better understand individuals wanted for serious offenses. Profilers develop a list of typical offender characteristics and other useful principles by analyzing crime scene data in conjunction with interviews and other studies of past offenders. In general, the psychological profiling of criminal offenders is based on the belief that almost any form of conscious behavior, including each and every behavior engaged in by the offender during a criminal episode, is symptomatic of an individual's personality. Hence, the way in which a kidnapper approaches his victims, for example, the manner of attack used by a killer, and the specific sexual activities of a rapist, might all help paint a picture of the offender's motivations, personal characteristics, and likely future behavior. Sometimes psychological profiles can provide clues as to what an offender might do following an attack. Some offenders have been arrested, for example, after returning to the crime scene—a behavior typically predicted by specific behavioral clues left behind. Remorseful types can be expected to visit the victim's grave, permitting fruitful stakeouts of cemeteries.

In a well-known study[115] of lust murderers (men who kill and often mutilate victims during or following a forced sexual episode), FBI Special Agents Robert R. Hazelwood and John E. Douglas distinguished between the organized nonsocial and the disorganized asocial types. The organized nonsocial lust murderer was described as exhibiting complete indifference to the interests of society, and as being completely self-centered. He was also said to be "methodical and cunning," as well as "fully cognizant of the criminality of his act and its impact on society." His counterpart, the disorganized asocial lust murderer, was described this way: "The disorganized asocial lust murderer exhibits primary characteristics of societal aversion. This individual prefers his own company to that of others and would be typified as a loner. He experiences difficulty in negotiating interpersonal relationships and consequently feels rejected and lonely. He lacks the cunning of the nonsocial type and commits the crime in a more frenzied and less methodical manner. The crime is likely to be committed in close proximity to his residence or place of employment, where he feels secure and more at ease."[116]

During the 1980s the FBI led the movement to develop psychological profiling techniques through its concentration on violent sex offenders and arsonists. Today, the behavioral sciences unit at the FBI Training Academy in Quantico, Virginia, continues to focus on serial killers, "lust murderers," domestic terrorists, and the like. The unit's activities were popularized a few years ago by the movie *Silence of the*

Psychological profiling the attempt to categorize, understand, and predict the behavior of certain types of offenders based on behavioral clues they provide.

Lambs, starring Jodie Foster and Anthony Hopkins, which portrayed the activities of a serial killer and enforcement activities designed to stop him. Movies, however, may lead the public to put too much stock in behavioral techniques such as psychological profiling. "It's not the magic bullet of investigations," says retired agent Robert Ressler, "[i]t's simply another tool."[117]

SUMMARY

⚡

Psychological and psychiatric theories of criminal behavior emphasize the role of individual propensities and characteristics in the genesis of criminality. Whether the emphasis is on conditioned behavior or on the psychoanalytical foundations of human conduct, such approaches ponder the wellsprings of human motivation, desire, and behavioral choice. Unfortunately, legal strictures have prevented psychology from making the kinds of courtroom contributions of which it appears capable. Even so, some theorists now consider the state of psychological criminology sufficiently advanced to allow for the development of a consistent and dependable social policy in the prediction of dangerousness and the rehabilitation of offenders. Similarly, psychological profiling may soon facilitate informed criminal investigations as well as the prevention of future crime.

DISCUSSION QUESTIONS

⚡

1. This book emphasizes a social problems versus social responsibility theme. Which perspective is best supported by psychological theories of crime causation? Why?
2. How do psychological theories of criminal behavior differ from the other types of theories presented in this book? How do the various psychological and psychiatric approaches presented in this chapter differ from one another?
3. How would the various perspectives discussed in this chapter suggest offenders might be prevented from committing additional offenses? How might they be rehabilitated?
4. How can crime be a form of adaptation to one's environment? Why would an individual choose such a form of adaptation over others that might be available?
5. What is the difference, if any, between the antisocial personality and the psychopath?
6. Which of the various standards for judging legal insanity discussed in this chapter do you find the most useful? Why?

CHAPTER 6

 263

*Psychological and
Psychiatric
Foundations of
Criminal Behavior*

WEB WATCH

Access the *Criminology Today* home page on the World Wide Web by pointing your browser at www.prenhall.com/cjcentral. Once there, click on *Criminology Today* in order to access the wealth of electronic resources supporting this text.

Onsite resources include (1) "Chapter Links," which provides succinct overviews of critical ideas from the textbook and links selected materials from around the Web to concepts found in the text; (2) "General Reference—Law and Justice Links." Organized by chapter, these links lead to other useful resources on the World Wide Web, such as libraries, electronic discussion lists, and electronic journals; (3) "Criminology Sites on the Web," which lists links to organizations such as the American Society of Criminology and the National Organization for Victims Assistance (NOVA), as well as crime prevention links and statistics on crime and justice. Many other Web-based resources can be accessed via the *Criminology Today* site, including the federal Justice Information Center, the Bureau of Justice Statistics, the FBI, the RAND Corporation, the Vera Institute of Justice, PAVNET (an online "Partnership Against Violence," run by seven different federal agencies), and the National White Collar Crime Center.

Still another feature of the *Criminology Today* Web site is e-mail homework. Homework can be composed onsite and submitted to instructors using the instructor's e-mail address. To use the e-mail homework feature, click on "E-Mail Homework" on the opening page, and then type answers to the questions that appear in the spaces provided. Use your instructor's e-mail address to submit homework answers. The *Criminology Today* Web site also provides links to powerful Web-based search engines that can help you find topics of interest to you as you progress through your course of study. Search engines can be found under the home page heading "Criminology Sites on the Web."

NOTES

[1]George J. Church, "Sons and Murderers," *Time*, online edition, October 3, 1993.

[2]Karl Menninger, *The Crime of Punishment* (New York: Viking, 1968).

[3]"Police Fear Killings Span 10 Years," *USA Today*, July 26, 1991, p. 3A.

[4]"Mutilator 'Seemed So Normal,' " *Fayetteville Observer-Times*, July 28, 1991, p. 7A.

[5]"Doctor: Dahmer Wanted to Freeze-Dry a Victim," *Fayetteville Observer-Times*, February 13, 1992, p. 7A.

[6]"Psychiatrist: Dahmer Lacked Will to Stop," *Fayetteville Observer-Times*, February 4, 1992, p. 5A.

[7]"Dahmer: 936 Years for 'Holocaust,' " *USA Today*, February 18, 1992, p. 1A.

[8]"Drifter: I Killed 60 People," *USA Today,* August 15, 1991, p. 1A.

[9]Carlos Sanchez and Marylou Tousignant, "Jury Acquits Bobbitt; Discrepancies, Lack of Evidence Cited," *Washington Post* wire service, November 11, 1993.

[10]Ibid.

[11]"New York Train Gunman a Walking Time Bomb," Reuters wire service, December 12, 1993.

[12]Ibid.

[13]D. A. Andrews and James Bonta, *The Psychology of Criminal Conduct* (Cincinnati: Anderson, 1994), p. 69.

[14]See Adrian Raine, *The Psychopathology of Crime: Criminal Behavior as a Clinical Disorder* (Orlando: Academic Press, 1993).

[15]Cathy Spatz Widom and Hans Toch, "The Contribution of Psychology to Criminal Justice Education," *Journal of Criminal Justice Education,* vol. 4, no. 2 (Fall 1993), p. 253.

[16]Curt R. Bartol, *Criminal Behavior: A Psychosocial Approach,* 3rd ed. (Englewood Cliffs, N.J.: Prentice Hall, 1991), p. 16.

[17]For additional information, see S. Giora Shoham and Mark C. Seis, *A Primer in the Psychology of Crime* (New York: Harrow and Heston, 1993); and Frederic L. Faust, "A Review of *A Primer In The Psychology of Crime,* in *Social Pathology,* vol. 1, no. 1 (January 1995), pp. 48–61.

[18]Nicole Hahn Rafter, "Psychopathy and the Evolution of Criminological Knowledge," *Theoretical Criminology,* vol. 1, no. 2 (May 1997), pp. 235–259.

[19]Nolan D. C. Lewis, "Foreword," in David Abrahamsen, *Crime and the Human Mind* (Montclair, N.J.: Patterson Smith, 1969), p. vii. Originally published in 1944.

[20]As noted by Nicole Hahn Rafter, "Psychopathy and the Evolution of Criminological Knowledge." See Richard von Krafft-Ebing, *Psychopathia Sexualis* (New York: Stein and Day, 1965), reprint of the original 1886 edition; and *Text-Book of Insanity* (Philadelphia: F. A. Davis Company, 1904). First German edition, 1879.

[21]Bernard H. Glueck, *Studies in Forensic Psychiatry* (Boston: Little, Brown, 1916).

[22]William Healy, *The Individual Delinquent* (Boston: Little, Brown, 1915).

[23]Early writings about the psychopath personality focused almost exclusively on men, and most psychiatrists appeared to believe that very few women (if any) possessed such traits.

[24]Ibid., p. 23.

[25]Hervey M. Cleckley, *The Mask of Sanity,* 4th ed. (St. Louis: C. V. Mosby, 1964).

[26]Gwynn Nettler, *Killing One Another* (Cincinnati: Anderson, 1982), p. 179.

[27]Albert I. Rabin, "The Antisocial Personality—Psychopathy and Sociopathy," in Hans Toch, *Psychology of Crime and Criminal Justice* (Prospect Heights, Ill.: Waveland, 1979), p. 330.

[28]R. D. Hare, *Psychopathy: Theory and Research* (New York: John Wiley & Sons, 1970).

[29]L. N. Robins, *Deviant Children Grow Up* (Baltimore: Williams and Wilkins, 1966).

[30]S. B. Guze, *Criminality and Psychiatric Disorders* (New York: Oxford University Press, 1976).

[31]American Psychiatric Association, *Diagnostic and Statistical Manual of Mental Disorders,* 2nd ed. (Washington: APA, 1968).

[32]Ibid., p. 43.

[33]S. Hodgins and G. Cote, "The Prevalence of Mental Disorders Among Penitentiary Inmates in Quebec," *Canada's Mental Health,* vol. 38 (1990), pp. 1–4.

[34]H. Prins, *Offenders, Deviants or Patients? An Introduction to the Study of Socio-Forensic Problems* (London: Tavistock, 1980).

[35]Hans J. Eysenck, *Crime and Personality* (Boston: Houghton Mifflin, 1964).

[36]Hans J. Eysenck, "Personality and Criminality: A Dispositional Analysis," in William S. Laufer and Freda Adler, eds., *Advances in Criminology Theory,* vol. 1 (New Brunswick, N.J.: Transaction, 1989), p. 90.

[37]Eysenck, *Crime and Personality,* pp. 35–36.

[38]Ibid., p. 92.

[39]Ibid., p. 53, citing J. B. S. Haldane, "Foreword," to Johannes Lange, *Crime as Destiny, A Study of Criminal Twins* (London: G. Allen & Unwin, Ltd., 1931), p. 53.

[40]David Abrahamsen, *Crime and the Human Mind* (Montclair, N.J.: Patterson Smith, 1969), p. vii. Originally published in 1944.

[41]P. Q. Roche, *The Criminal Mind: A Study of Communications Between Criminal Law and Psychiatry* (New York: Grove Press, 1958), p. 52.

[42]*The American Heritage Dictionary and Electronic Thesaurus* (Boston: Houghton Mifflin, 1987).

CHAPTER 6

◈ 265 ◈

*Psychological and
Psychiatric
Foundations of
Criminal Behavior*

[43]Ibid.

[44]Ibid.

[45]Ibid.

[46]"Nationline: Book Thief," *USA Today,* August 1, 1991, p. 3A.

[47]Anne Sciater, "Torturer-Killer Wants to Die Today, As Scheduled," *USA Today,* April 15, 1997, p. 2A.

[48]Nettler, *Killing One Another,* p. 159.

[49]Ibid., p. 155.

[50]Abrahamsen, *Crime and the Human Mind,* p. 99.

[51]Ibid., p. 100.

[52]J. Dollard, L. Doob, N. Miller, O. Mowrer, and R. Sears, *Frustration and Aggression* (New Haven, Conn.: Yale University Press, 1939).

[53]Carl Weiser, "This Is What You Get for Firing Me!" *USA Today,* January 28, 1993, p. 3A.

[54]Andrew F. Henry and James F. Short, Jr., *Suicide and Homicide: Economic, Sociological, and Psychological Aspects of Aggression,* (Glencoe, Ill.: Free Press, 1954).

[55]Stewart Palmer, *A Study of Murder* (New York: Crowell, 1960).

[56]Abrahamsen, *Crime and the Human Mind,* p. 26.

[57]Nancy Gibbs, "The Devil's Disciple," *Time,* January 11, 1993, p. 40.

[58]Seymour L. Halleck, *Psychiatry and the Dilemmas of Crime: A Study of Causes, Punishment and Treatment* (Berkeley: University of California Press, 1971).

[59]Ibid., p. 77.

[60]Ibid., p. 78.

[61]Ibid., p. 80.

[62]Ibid.

[63]Ibid.

[64]Arnold S. Linsky, Ronet Bachman, and Murray A. Straus, *Stress, Culture, and Aggression* (New Haven: Yale University Press, 1995).

[65]Ibid., p. 7.

[66]Albert Bandura, "The Social Learning Perspective: Mechanisms of Aggression," in Toch, *Psychology of Crime and Criminal Justice,* pp. 198–236.

[67]M. M. Lefkowitz, L. D. Eron, L. O. Walder, and L. R. Huesmann, "Television Violence and Child Aggression: A Follow-up Study," in G. A. Comstock and E. A. Rubinstein, eds., *Television and Social Behavior,* vol. 3 (Washington, D.C.: U.S. Government Printing Office, 1972), pp. 35–135.

[68]Aminah Franklin, "Brutal, Cowardly Murder: Police Say Threats Preceded Slaying of Salisbury Family," *The Morning Call,* March 1, 1995, p. A1.

[69]Ibid.

[70]David Washburn, "Brothers Cultivated Defiant Attitude," *The Morning Call,* March 1, 1995, p. A4.

[71]Widom and Toch, "The Contribution of Psychology to Criminal Justice Education."

[72]Ibid., p. 253.

[73]C. R. Hollin, *Psychology and Crime: An Introduction to Criminological Psychology* (London: Routledge, 1989), p. 42.

[74]Ibid., p. 254.

[75]"15-Year-Old Killer Feared Being Called a 'Little Punk,'" *Fayetteville Observer-Times,* December 26, 1993, p. 1A.

[76]*The American Heritage Dictionary and Electronic Thesaurus.*

[77]*Foucha* v. *Louisiana,* 504 U.S. 71 (1992).

[78]C. Ray Jeffery, *Criminology: An Interdisciplinary Approach* (Englewood Cliffs N.J.: Prentice Hall, 1990), p. 431.

[79]*Leland* v. *Oregon,* 343 U.S. 790 (1952).

[80]*Riggins* v. *Nevada,* 504 U.S. 127 (1992).

[81]18 U.S.C. Section 17.

[82]See, for example, *U.S.* v. *Pohlot,* 827 F.2d 889, 897 (3d Cir. 1987), cert. denied, 484 U.S. 1011, 108 S.Ct. 710, 98 L.Ed.2d 660 (1988).

[83]18 United States Code §401.

[84]18 U. S. C. Sections 17 and 4242(b).

[85]*Terrance Frank* v. *U.S.,* no. 91-8230. Decided October 13, 1992.

[86]October 12, 1984, P.L. 98-473, title II, Sec. 403(a), 98 Stat. 2057.

[87]Halleck, *Psychiatry and the Dilemmas of Crime,* p. 213.

[88]*Durham* v. *U.S.,* 214 F.2d 862 (D.C. Cir. 1954).

[89]American Law Institute, *Model Penal Code: Official Draft and Explanatory Notes* (Philadelphia: The Institute, 1985).

[90]*U.S.* v. *Brawner,* 471 F.2d 969 (D.C. Cir. 1972).

[91]June 25, 1948, Ch. 645, 62 Stat. 855; Oct. 12, 1984, P.L. 98-473, title II, Sec. 403(a), 98 Stat. 2059; November 18, 1988, P.L. 100-690, title VII, Sec. 7043, 102 Stat. 4400.

[92]*Foucha* v. *Louisiana,* 1992.

[93]See, for example, D. P. Farrington, "Childhood Aggression and Adult Violence: Early Precursors and Later Life Outcomes," in D. J. Pepler

and K. H. Rubin, eds., *The Development and Treatment of Childhood Aggression* (Hillsdale, N.J.: Erlbaum, 1990), pp. 2–29; and R. E. Tremblay, B. Masse, D. Perron, M. LeBlanc, A. E. Schwartzman, and J. E. Ledingham, "Early Disruptive Behavior: Poor School Achievement, Delinquent Behavior and Delinquent Personality: Longitudinal Analyses," *Journal of Consulting and Clinical Psychology,* vol. 60, no. 1 (1992), pp. 64–72.

[94]R. Loeber, "Questions and Advances in the Study of Developmental Pathways," in D. Cicchetti and S. Toth, eds., *Models and Integration: Rochester Symposium on Developmental Psychopathology* (Rochester, N.Y.: University of Rochester Press, 1991), pp. 97–115.

[95]"State Probing Release of Molester Now Charged with Murder," United Press International wire service, Southwestern edition, September 24, 1993.

[96]"Texas Executes Convicted Killer Who Waived Appeals," Reuters wire service, Western edition, November 10, 1993.

[97]Christine Spolar, "California Town Cries as Polly Klaas Is Found; Twice-Convicted Suspect Faces Murder, Kidnapping Charges in Abduction of 12-Year-Old," *Washington Post* wire service, December 6, 1993.

[98]Jennifer L. White, Terrie E. Moffitt, Felton Earls, Lee Robins, and Phil A. Silva, "How Early Can We Tell? Predictors of Childhood Conduct Disorder and Adolescent Delinquency," *Criminology,* vol. 28, no. 4 (1990), pp. 507–528.

[99]Daniel S. Nagin and David P. Farrington, "The Stability of Criminal Potential from Childhood to Adulthood," *Criminology,* vol. 30, no. 2 (1992), pp. 235–260.

[100]Paul Gendreau, Tracy Little, and Claire Goggin, "A Meta-Analysis of the Predictors of Adult Offender Recidivism: What Works!" *Criminology,* vol. 34, no. 4 (November 1996), pp. 575–607.

[101]For one of the first and still definitive works in the area of selective incapacitation, see Peter Greenwood and Allan Abrahamse, *Selective Incapacitation* (Santa Monica, Calif.: Rand Corporation, 1982).

[102]M. A. Peterson, H. B. Braiker, and S. M. Polich, *Who Commits Crimes?* (Cambridge: Oelgeschlager, Gunn and Hain, 1981).

[103]J. Monahan, *Predicting Violent Behavior: An Assessment of Clinical Techniques* (Beverly Hills, Calif.: Sage, 1981).

[104]The 1984 Amendment to Section 200 of Title II (Sec. 200-2304) of P.L. 98-473, is popularly referred to as the "1984 Comprehensive Crime Control Act."

[105]U.S. Sentencing Commission, *Federal Sentencing Guidelines Manual* (Washington, D.C.: U.S. Government Printing Office, 1987), p. 10.

[106]Jill Peay, "Dangerousness—Ascription or Description," in M.P. Feldman, ed., *Developments in the Study of Criminal Behavior,* vol. 2, *Violence* (New York: John Wiley & Sons, 1982), p. 211, citing N. Walker, "Dangerous People," *International Journal of Law and Psychiatry,* vol. 1 (1978), pp. 37–50.

[107]See, for example, Michael Gottfredson and Travis Hirschi, *A General Theory of Crime* (Stanford, Calif.: Stanford University Press, 1990); and Travis Hirschi and Michael Gottfredson, "Age and the Explanation of Crime," *American Journal of Sociology,* vol. 89 (1983), pp. 552–584.

[108]David F. Greenberg, "Modeling Criminal Careers," *Criminology,* vol. 29, no. 1 (1991), p. 39.

[109]D. A. Andrews and James Bonta, *The Psychology of Criminal Conduct* (Cincinnati: Anderson, 1994).

[110]Ibid., p. 1.

[111]Ibid.

[112]Ibid., pp. 20–21.

[113]Ibid., p. 227.

[114]Ibid., p. 236.

[115]Robert R. Hazelwood and John E. Douglas, "The Lust Murderer," *FBI Law Enforcement Bulletin* (Washington: U.S. Department of Justice, April 1980).

[116]Ibid.

[117]Anastasia Toufexis, "Mind Games with Monsters," *Time,* May 6, 1991, pp. 68, 69.

CHAPTER 7

CRIME AND THE ROLE OF THE

SOCIAL ENVIRONMENT

If we would change the amount of crime in the community, we must change the community.

—FRANK TANNENBAUM[1]

Children learn to become delinquents by becoming members of groups in which delinquent conduct is already established. . . .

—ALBERT K. COHEN[2]

I got a 14-shot Beretta and I ain't worried about no police or anybody else.

—BROADWAY GANGSTER CRIP MEMBER "ANTOINE"[3]

Society prepares the crime; the criminal commits it.

—CHINESE PROVERB

❖ CHAPTER OUTLINE ❖

INTRODUCTION
MAJOR PRINCIPLES OF SOCIOLOGICAL THEORIES
SOCIOLOGICAL THEORIES
    The Chicago School
    Culture Conflict
    Subcultural Theory
    Violent Subcultures
    Crime and Social Structure
    Differential Association
    Criminal Careers and Life Course Theory
SOCIAL CONTROL THEORIES
    Containment Theory
    Social Bond Theory
POLICY IMPLICATIONS
CRITIQUE OF SOCIAL-STRUCTURAL THEORIES
SUMMARY

⬅ IMPORTANT NAMES ➡

Ernest Burgess	Richard Machalek	W. I. Thomas
Florian Znaniecki	Robert Park	Henry McKay
Thorsten Sellin	Clifford Shaw	Lloyd Ohlin
Albert Cohen	Richard Cloward	Robert K. Merton
Frederic M. Thrasher	Edwin Sutherland	Walter B. Miller
Gresham Sykes	William Foote Whyte	Franco Ferracuti
Marvin Wolfgang	David Matza	Travis Hirschi
Michael R.	Walter Reckless	Sheldon and Eleanor
Gottfredson	Robert Agnew	Glueck
John Laub	Robert Sampson	Lawrence E. Cohen

⬅ IMPORTANT TERMS ➡

sociological theories	illegitimate opportunity	social-structural theories
social pathology	structure	subcultural theory
social ecology	social structure	containment theory
ecological theory	social disorganization	reaction formation
culture conflict	cohort	differential association
anomie	Chicago school of	learning theory
subculture	criminology	social bond
focal concerns	conduct norms	cohort analysis
social capital	strain theory	evolutionary ecology
social control theory	opportunity structure	defensible space
environmental	criminology of place	broken windows thesis
criminology	life course theories	techniques of
	containment	neutralization

INTRODUCTION

In late July 1993 a tourist traveling home to Mint Hill, North Carolina, from the state's seacoast city of Wilmington, a couple of hundred miles away, was robbed and shot while he napped during a rest period on the shoulder of state Route 74. The murder, like the twenty-two others committed that year in rural Robeson County, North Carolina, would have attracted little attention outside of the local area had it not been for the fact that the dead tourist was 57-year-old James Jordan, father of Chicago Bulls basketball superstar, Michael Jordan. After Jordan was killed, his body was dumped twenty-five miles away in South Carolina's Gum Swamp Creek. The new red Lexus sport coupe that Jordan had been driving showed up later, apparently stripped by teenagers acquainted with the killers.

Two local 18-year-olds, Larry Martin Demery and Daniel Andre Green, were quickly arrested and charged with Jordan's murder. Both had long records of trouble with the law. Demery, a lanky native American with a Guns N' Roses tattoo on his right forearm, was out of work and on parole for check forgery at the time of the murder. In the year preceding the crime, Demery had been charged with four other felonies, ranging from armed robbery to breaking and entering.[4] In one crime attributed to Demery, the robbery of a convenience store, a 61-year-old clerk was struck on the head with a cinder block and seriously injured. When Demery was arrested in the Jordan case, police were already looking for him on four other warrants, all issued for failure to appear for trial on more than a dozen occasions.

Daniel Green's record of law violations was even more serious. In the ninth grade the semiliterate Green was suspended for assaulting the school's principal. He promptly dropped out of school. Shortly afterward, in 1991, Green was convicted of assault with intent to kill after he pled guilty to charges of beating a friend with the blunt side of an axe. The friend, Robert Ellison, 18, was in a coma for months. Demery and Green's life of crime came to an abrupt halt when Demery pled guilty to first-degree murder, turned state's witness in a plea bargain, and helped prosecutors build a case against Green. In 1996 Green was convicted of murdering Jordan and sentenced to life in prison.

A few days after the Jordan killing another murder occurred only a short distance from the spot where Jordan's stolen vehicle was recovered. It happened when U.S. Army Sergeant Kenny French walked into Luigi's Italian Restaurant in Fayetteville, North Carolina, and, without warning, opened fire on the establishment's customers and staff. As he pulled the trigger, French shouted angrily about the Clinton administration's decision to admit avowed homosexuals into military ranks.[5] Killed in the fusillade were the restaurant's owner, his wife, and two customers. Seven other people were shot and injured. Until the time of the mass murder, Sergeant French, who was stationed at Fort Bragg, North Carolina, had been known to friends and former neighbors as a polite young man. French's reasons for killing were variously attributed to individualized factors, including the suicidal death of his abusive father, alcohol abuse, depression, and a discrediting family history of sexual abuse.[6] A jury, however, was unswayed, and French was convicted of murder and sentenced to life in prison.

Although elements of a person's life, as in Kenny French's case, can always be identified as contributing factors in almost any crime, the motivation behind the killing of James Jordan appears to have arisen primarily from social and economic deprivation. Both Green and Demery were born into relative poverty. Both came from families lacking in educational achievement and in the basic skills needed for success in the modern world. Poverty, academic failure, and subcultural values which focused on greed and excitement dictated the direction their lives were to take—and all but ensured their fateful encounter with James Jordan that sultry July afternoon.

❖ MAJOR PRINCIPLES OF SOCIOLOGICAL THEORIES

This brief section serves to summarize the central features of sociological theories of crime causation. Each of these points can be found elsewhere in this chapter, where they are discussed in more detail. This cursory overview, however, is intended to provide more than a summary—it is meant to be a guide to the rest of this chapter.

As this chapter will show, those perspectives on crime causation which have been termed "sociological" are quite diverse; however, most such perspectives build upon the following fundamental assumptions.

- Social groups, social institutions, the arrangements of society, and social roles all provide the proper focus for criminological study.
- Group dynamics, group organization, and subgroup relationships form the causal nexus out of which crime develops.
- The structure of society and its relative degree of organization or disorganization are important factors contributing to the prevalence of criminal behavior.
- Although it may be impossible to predict the specific behavior of a given individual, statistical estimates of group characteristics are possible to achieve. Hence, the probability that a member of a given group will engage in a specific type of crime can be estimated.

Although all sociological perspectives on crime share the foregoing characteristics, particular theories may give greater or lesser weight to the following aspects of social life:

1. the clash of norms and values between variously socialized groups;
2. socialization and the process of association between individuals; and
3. the existence of subcultures and varying types of opportunities.

❖ SOCIOLOGICAL THEORIES

Social structure the pattern of social organization and the interrelationships between institutions characteristic of a society.

Sociological theories place emphasis on the structure of society (or **social structure**), on the relationship between social institutions, and on the types of behavior which tend to characterize *groups* of people. In contrast to more individualized psychological theories, which have what is called a "micro" focus, sociological approaches utilize a "macro" perspective—stressing behavioral tendencies for group members rather than attempting to predict the behavior of specific individuals.

Sociological thought has been dominant in behavioral science literature and has influenced criminological theory construction more significantly than any other perspective during the past half century. This emphasis has probably been due, at least in part, to a widespread American concern with social problems, including civil rights, the women's movement, issues of poverty, and the decline in influence experienced by many traditional social institutions such as the family, government, organized religion, and educational institutions.

This chapter describes various subtypes of sociological theory, including (1) ecological approaches, (2) culture conflict, (3) subcultural approaches, (4) strain theories, (5) differential association, (6) life course theories, and (7) control theories. All share some elements in common, and the classification of a theory into one

THEORY IN PERSPECTIVE

Types of Sociological Theories

SOCIOLOGICAL THEORIES, also known as SOCIAL-STRUCTURAL APPROACHES
Emphasize relationships between social institutions and describe the types of behavior which tend to characterize *groups* of people as opposed to *individuals*.

ECOLOGICAL THEORY OR "CHICAGO SCHOOL." Stresses the demographic and geographic aspects of groups and sees the social disorganization which characterizes delinquency areas as a major cause of criminality and of victimization.

PERIOD:	1920s–1930s
THEORISTS:	Robert Park, Ernest Burgess, W.I. Thomas, Florian Znaniecki, Clifford Shaw, Henry McKay
CONCEPTS:	Demographics, concentric zones, social disorganization, delinquency areas

CULTURE CONFLICT. Suggests that the root cause of crime can be found in a clash of values between variously socialized groups over what is acceptable for proper behavior.

PERIOD:	1930s
THEORISTS:	Thorsten Sellin and others
CONCEPTS:	Conduct norms

DIFFERENTIAL ASSOCIATION. Maintains that criminality, like any other form of behavior, is learned through a process of association with others who communicate criminal values.

PERIOD:	1930s–1960s
THEORISTS:	Edwin Sutherland and others
CONCEPTS:	Differential association; crime as learned; techniques of crime; commission, frequency, duration, priority, and intensity of association

SUBCULTURAL THEORY. Highlights violent and delinquent subcultures, and emphasizes the contribution made by variously socialized cultural groups to the phenomenon of crime.

PERIOD:	1920s–Present
THEORISTS:	Frederic M. Thrasher, William Foote Whyte, Walter B. Miller, Gresham Sykes, David Matza, Franco Ferracuti, Marvin Wolfgang, and many others
CONCEPTS:	Subculture, socialization, focal concerns, delinquency and drift, techniques of neutralization

STRAIN or ANOMIE THEORY. Posits the disjuncture between socially and subculturally sanctioned mean and goals as the cause of criminal behavior.

PERIOD:	1930s–Present
THEORISTS:	Robert K. Merton, Richard Cloward, Lloyd Ohlin, Albert Cohen
CONCEPTS:	Goals, means, opportunity structures, differential opportunity, reaction formation

SOCIAL CONTROL APPROACHES. Ask why people obey rules instead of breaking them.

PERIOD:	1950s–Present
THEORISTS:	Walter C. Reckless, Travis Hirschi, Michael R. Gottfredson, and others
CONCEPTS:	Inner and outer containment, social bond

LIFE COURSE THEORIES. Highlight the development of criminal careers which are seen as the result of various criminogenic influences that impact individuals throughout the course of their lives.

PERIOD:	1930s–Present
THEORISTS:	Sheldon and Eleanor Glueck, Marvin Wolfgang, John Laub and Robert Sampson, Lawrence E. Cohen and Richard Machalek
CONCEPTS:	Career criminality, cohorts, social capital, evolutionary ecology

subcategory or another is often more a matter of which aspects a writer chooses to emphasize rather than the result of any clear-cut definitional elements inherent in the perspectives themselves. Most theories in this chapter can also be termed **social-structural theories,** because they explain crime by reference to various aspects of the social fabric. They name the institutional structure of society and the various formal and informal arrangements between social groups as causes of crime and deviance. Environmental influences, socialization, and traditional and accepted patterns of behavior are all used by social structuralists to portray the criminal as a product of his or her social environment and to depict criminality as a form of acquired behavior.

The term **social pathology** was often associated with early social-structural theories. Social pathology, a concept prevalent in the criminological literature of a few decades ago, was initially defined as "those human actions which run contrary to the ideals of residential stability, property ownership, sobriety, thrift, habituation to work, small business enterprise, sexual discretion, family solidarity, neighborliness, and discipline of will."[7] It referred simply to behavior not in keeping with the prevalent norms and values of the social group. Over time, however, the concept of social pathology changed, and it came to represent the idea that aspects of society may be somehow pathological, or "sick," and may produce deviant behavior among individuals and groups who live under or are exposed to such social conditions. Social pathology has also been associated with the concept of **social disorganization,**[8] a condition said to exist when a group is faced with "social change, uneven development of culture, maladaptiveness, disharmony, conflict, and lack of consensus...."[9]

THE CHICAGO SCHOOL

Some of the earliest sociological theories to receive widespread recognition can be found in the writings of **Robert Park** and **Ernest Burgess.** In the 1920s and 1930s Park and Burgess, through their work at the University of Chicago, developed what became known as **social ecology,** or the ecological school of criminology. Social ecology recognizes that crime always shows an uneven geographical distribution. It attempts to explain such variation by the interrelationship between human beings or human groups and their surroundings. As one writer puts it, social ecology is "the attempt to link the structure and organization of any human community to interactions with its localized environment."[10]

The work of Park and Burgess focused on concentric city zones, which were envisioned much like everexpanding circles on a target (see Figure 7.1), wherein diverse populations and behavioral characteristics predominated. Park and Burgess referred to the central business zone as Zone 1 or the Loop, where retail businesses and light manufacturing were typically located. Zone 2, surrounding the city center, generally contained areas which were in transition from residential areas to business purposes. Zone 3 contained mostly working-class homes, while Zone 4 was occupied by middle-class citizens. Zone 5, consisting largely of suburbs, was called the commuter zone. Early **ecological theories** were formed using 1920s Chicago as a model, hence, the **"Chicago School" of Criminology.** Although their applicability to other cities or to other time periods may be questionable, such

Social-structural theories explain crime by reference to various aspects of the social fabric. They emphasize relationships between social institutions and describe the types of behavior which tend to characterize *groups* of people as opposed to *individuals.*

Social pathology a concept that compares society to a physical organism and sees criminality as an illness.

Social disorganization a condition said to exist when a group is faced with social change, uneven development of culture, maladaptiveness, disharmony, conflict, and lack of consensus.

Social ecology an approach to criminological theorizing that attempts to link the structure and organization of any human community to interactions with its localized environment.

Ecological theory, also called the **Chicago School of Criminology** a type of sociological approach which emphasizes demographics (the characteristics of population groups) and geographics (the mapped location of such groups relative to one another) and sees the social disorganization that characterizes delinquency areas as a major cause of criminality and victimization.

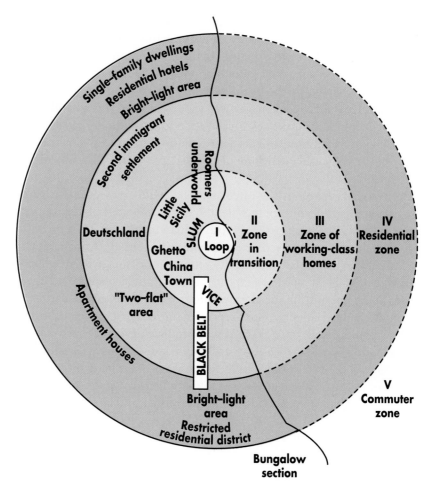

FIGURE 7.1 Chicago's Concentric Zones. *Source:* Robert E. Park, Ernest W. Burgess, and R. D. McKenzie, *The City* (Chicago: University of Chicago Press, 1925), p. 55. Copyright © University of Chicago Press. Reprinted with permission.

theories pointed out the tendency for criminal activity to be associated with transition zones which, because of the turmoil or social disorganization associated with them, were generally characterized by lower property values, marginal individuals, and a general lack of privacy.

Park and Burgess had been strongly influenced by **W. I. Thomas** and **Florian Znaniecki,** who described in their book *The Polish Peasant in Europe and America*[11] the problems Polish immigrants faced in the early 1900s when they left their homeland and moved to the cities of America. Thomas and Znaniecki noted how rates of crime rose among people who had been so displaced, and they hypothesized that the cause was the social disorganization which resulted from the immigrant's inability to successfully transplant guiding norms and values from the home culture into the new one.

Clifford Shaw and **Henry McKay,** other early advocates of the ecological approach, conducted empirical studies of delinquency rates in Chicago. One such study, undertaken in the late 1920s, found that the rate of delinquency among black youths "on the South Side of Chicago decreases regularly by square mile areas from

19.4% in the area adjoining the center of the city to 3.5% in the area five miles from the center of the city."[12]

Even at the height of its popularity, the ecological school recognized that American crime patterns might be different from those found elsewhere in the world, and that crime zones might exist in city areas other than those surrounding the core. Early comparisons of American, European, and Asian data, for instance, found higher crime rates at the so-called city gates (near-suburban areas providing access to downtown) in Europe and Asia.

The greatest contribution the ecological school made to criminological literature can be found in its claim that society, in the form of the community, wields a major influence on human behavior.[13] Similarly, ecological theorists of the Chicago school formalized the use of two sources of information: (1) official crime and population statistics and (2) ethnographic data. Population statistics, also referred to as demographic data, combined with crime information, provided empirical material that gave scientific weight to ecological investigations. Ethnographic information, gathered in the form of life stories, or ethnographies, described the lives of city inhabitants. By comparing one set of data with the other—demographics with ethnographies—ecological investigators were able to show that life experience varied from one location to another, and that personal involvement in crime had a strong tendency to be associated with place of residence.

A Critique of the Ecological School

The ecological school, like many sociological approaches to explaining crime, has been criticized for its tendency to forget the individual. By concentrating on the role social institutions and social disorganization play in crime causation, ecological approaches rarely acknowledge the influence of individual psychology, distinctive biology, or personal choice on criminal activity. This sort of criticism was insightfully advanced by W. S. Robinson in a classic 1950 article.[14] Robinson pointed out the "problematic nature of making individual-level inferences on the basis of aggregate data."[15]

Other authors have suggested that ecological theories give too much credence to the notion that location determines crime and delinquency. The nature of any given location changes over time, and evolutions in land use patterns, such as a movement away from homeownership and toward rental or low-income housing, for example, may seriously affect the nature of a neighborhood and the concomitant quality of social organization found there.

Similarly, rates of neighborhood crime and delinquency may be "an artifact of police decision-making practices,"[16] and bear little objective relationship to the actual degree of law violation in an area. Such police bias, should it exist, may seriously mislead researchers into categorizing certain areas as high in crime when, in fact, they may not be.

Another critique of the ecological school can be found in its seeming inability to differentiate between the condition of social disorganization and the things such a condition is said to cause. What, for example, is the difference between social disorganization and high rates of delinquency? Is not delinquency a form of the very thing said to cause it? As Stephen Pfohl has observed, early ecological writers some-times used the incidence of delinquency as "both an example of disorganization and something caused by disorganization,"[17] making it difficult to gauge the efficacy of their explanatory approach.

Finally, many crimes occur outside of geographic areas said to be characterized by social disorganization. Murder, rape, burglary, incidents of drug use, assault, and so on, all occur in affluent "well-established" neighborhoods as well as in other parts of a community. Likewise, white-collar, computer, environmental, and other types of crime may actually occur with a greater frequency in socially well-established neighborhoods than elsewhere. Hence, the ecological approach is clearly not an adequate explanation for all crime, nor for all types of crime.

EMERGING THEORY

The Criminology of Place

Criminology of place or **environmental criminology** an emerging perspective which emphasizes the importance of geographic location and architectural features as they are associated with the prevalence of criminal victimization.

Ecological approaches to crime causation have found a modern rebirth in what is now called the "criminology of place." The **criminology of place,** also called **environmental criminology,** is an emerging perspective within the contemporary body of criminological theory that emphasizes the importance of geographic location and architectural features as they are associated with the prevalence of victimization. "Hot spots" of crime, including neighborhoods, specific streets, and even individual houses and business establishments, have been identified by recent writers. Lawrence Sherman, for example, tells of a study[1] which revealed that 3 percent of places (addresses and intersections) in Minneapolis produce 50 percent of all calls to the police. Crime, says Sherman, although relatively rare, is geographically concentrated.

Another researcher, Rodney Stark, asks "[h]ow is it that neighborhoods can re-main the site of high crime and deviance rates despite a complete turnover in their populations? ... There must be something about places as such that sustains crime."[2] Stark has developed a theory of deviant neighborhoods. It consists of thirty propositions, including the following:[3]

1. To the extent that neighborhoods are dense and poor, homes will be crowded.
2. Where homes are more crowded there will be a greater tendency to congregate outside the home in places and circumstances that raise levels of temptation and opportunity to deviate.
3. Where homes are more crowded, there will be lower levels of supervision of children.

4. Reduced levels of child supervision will result in poor school achievement, with a consequent reduction in stakes in conformity and an increase in deviant behavior.
5. Poor, dense neighborhoods tend to be mixed-use neighborhoods.
6. Mixed use increases familiarity with and easy access to places offering the opportunity for deviance.

Central to the criminology of place is the **broken windows thesis**[4] which holds that physical deterioration and an increase in unrepaired buildings leads to increased concerns for personal safety among area residents. Heightened concerns, in turn, lead to further decreases in maintenance and repair, and to increased delinquency, vandalism, and crime among local residents—which spawns even further deterioration in both a sense of safety and physical deterioration. Offenders from other neighborhoods are then increasingly attracted by the area's perceived vulnerability.

Even within so-called high-crime neighborhoods, however, crimes tend to be concentrated at specific locations such as street blocks or multiple-family dwellings. This kind of microlevel analysis has also shown, for example, that some units within specific apartment buildings are much more likely to be the site of criminal occurrences than others. Apartments near complex or building entrances appear to be more criminally dangerous, especially if they are not facing other buildings or apartments. Likewise, pedestrian tunnels, unattended parking lots, and convenience stores with clerks stationed in less visible areas are often targeted by criminal offenders.

The criminology of place employs the concept of **defensible space,** a term which evolved out of a conference in 1964 at Washington University in St. Louis, Missouri.[5] Defensible space has been defined as "a surrogate term for the range of mechanisms—real and symbolic barriers, strongly defined areas of influence, and improved opportunities for surveillance—that combine to bring an environment under the control of its residents."[6] The St. Louis conference, which brought criminologists, police officers, and architects face to face, focused on crime problems characteristic of public housing areas. Findings demonstrated that specific architectural changes which enhanced barriers, defined boundaries, and removed criminal opportunity could do much to reduce the risk of crime—even in the midst of high-crime neighborhoods.

The criminology of place holds that location can be as predictive of criminal activity as the lifestyles of victimized individuals or the social features of victimized households. (*Place* has been defined by researchers as "a fixed physical environment that can be seen completely and simultaneously, at least on its surface, by one's naked eyes."[7]) Places can be criminogenic due to the routine activities associated with them. On the other hand, some places host crime because they provide the characteristics that facilitate its commission. In Sherman's study, for example, Minneapolis parks drew "flashers" because they provided "opportunities for concealment" up until the moment when the flasher struck. Changes to the parks, such as moving walkways some distance from trees and shrubbery, can reduce criminal opportunity.

Recognizing the criminology of place, New York City police developed a program a few years ago designed to close businesses with repeated crime problems. Called Operation Padlock, the program appeared to be successful in reducing the incidence

Broken windows thesis a perspective on crime causation which holds that physical deterioration in an area leads to increased concerns for personal safety among area residents, and to higher crime rates in that area. The "broken windows" metaphor says that a broken window, left unattended, invites other windows to be broken, which leads to a sense of disorder that breeds fear and serious crime. Hence, by ignoring minor crimes, we lose opportunities to repair the first signs of disorder and to hold offenders accountable.

Defensible space the range of mechanisms that combine to bring an environment under the control of its residents.

of certain kinds of crime. However, as Sherman points out, "[n]either capital punishment of places (as in arson of crack houses) nor incapacitation of the routine activities of criminal hot spots (as in revocation of liquor licenses) seems likely to eliminate crime. But since the routine activities of places may be regulated far more easily than the routine activities of persons, a criminology of place would seem to offer substantial promise for public policy as well as theory."[8]

[1]Lawrence W. Sherman, Patrick R. Gartin, and Michael E. Buerger, "Hot Spots of Predatory Crime: Routine Activities and the Criminology of Place," *Criminology,* Vol. 27, no. 1 (1989), pp. 27–55.

[2]Rodney Stark, "Deviant Places: A Theory of the Ecology of Crime," *Criminology,* Vol. 25, no. 4 (1987), p. 893.

[3]Ibid., pp. 895–899.

[4]James Q. Wilson and George Kelling, "Broken Windows," *The Atlantic Monthly,* March 1982.

[5]Oscar Newman, *Architectural Design for Crime Prevention* (Washington, D.C.: U.S. Department of Justice, 1973). See also, Oscar Newman, *Defensible Space* (New York: Macmillan, 1972); and Oscar Newman, *Creating Defensible Space* (Washington, D.C.: Office of Housing and Urban Development, 1996).

[6]Oscar Newman, *Defensible Space: Crime Prevention Through Urban Design* (New York: Macmillan, 1972), p. 3. See also Ralph B. Taylor and Adele V. Harrell, "Physical Environment and Crime," National Institute of Justice, May 1996.

[7]"Hot Spots of Predatory Crime," p. 31.

[8]Ibid., p. 49.

CULTURE CONFLICT

Fundamental to ecological criminology was the belief that zones of transition, because they tend to be in flux, harbor groups of people whose values are often at odds with those of the larger, surrounding society. This perspective found its clearest expression in the writings of **Thorsten Sellin** in his 1938 book, *Culture Conflict and Crime.*[18] Sellin maintained that the root cause of crime could be found in different values about what is acceptable or proper behavior. According to Sellin, **conduct norms,** which provide the valuative basis for human behavior, are acquired early in life through childhood socialization. It is the clash of norms between variously socialized groups that results in crime. Because crime is a violation of laws established by legislative decree, the criminal event itself, from this point of view, is nothing other than a disagreement over what should be acceptable behavior. For some social groups, what we tend to call crime is simply part of the landscape—something that can be expected to happen to you unless you take steps to protect yourself. From this point of view, those to whom crime happens are not so much victims as they are simply ill prepared.

Sellin also wrote about culture conflict. **Culture conflict** suggests that the root cause of criminality can be found in a clash of values between variously socialized groups over what is acceptable or proper behavior. In 1997, for example, Danish actress Annette Sorensen was arrested after leaving her toddler in a stroller outside of

Conduct norms the shared expectations of a social group relative to personal conduct.

Culture conflict a sociological perspective on crime which suggests that the root cause of criminality can be found in a clash of values between variously socialized groups over what is acceptable or proper behavior.

a Manhattan restaurant while she sat inside, drinking margaritas with the child's father. Sorensen was charged with endangering the welfare of a child. Her 14-month-old daughter, Liv, was placed in temporary foster care. Sorensen, who was in tears following her arrest, could not understand what had happened. "We do this in Denmark all the time,"[19] the Copenhagen resident told police. Her daughter was soon ordered returned by a city judge, and Sorensen and the child flew home to Denmark, where children are routinely left in strollers outside of restaurants and other public places.[20]

Sellin described two types of culture conflict. The first type, *primary conflict,* arises when a fundamental clash of cultures occurs. Sellin's classic example was that of an immigrant father who kills his daughter's lover following an old-world tradition which demands that a family's honor be kept intact. In Sellin's words, "[a] few years ago, a Sicilian father in New Jersey killed the sixteen-year-old seducer of his daughter, expressing surprise at his arrest since he had merely defended his family honor in a traditional way. In this case . . . [t]he conflict was external and occurred between cultural codes or norms. We may assume that where such conflicts occur . . . norms of one cultural group or area migrate to another and that such conflict will continue so long as the acculturation process has not been completed."[21]

The other type of conflict, called *secondary conflict,* arose, according to Sellin, when smaller cultures within the primary one clashed. So it is that middle-class values, upon which most criminal laws are based, may find fault with inner-city or lower-class norms, resulting in the social phenomenon we call "crime."

In Sellin's day prostitution and gambling provided plentiful examples of secondary conflict. Many lower-class inner-city groups accepted gambling and prostitution as a way of life—if not for individual members of those groups, then at least as forms of behavior which were rarely condemned for those choosing to participate in them. Today, drug use and abuse provide more readily understandable examples. For some segments of contemporary society drug sales have become a source of substantial income, and the conduct norms which typify such groups support at least the relative legitimacy of lives built around the drug trade. In other words, in some parts of America, drug dealing is an acceptable form of business. To those who make the laws, however, it is not. It is from the clash of these two opposing viewpoints that conflict, and crime, emerge.

SUBCULTURAL THEORY

Inherent in the writings of the ecological school is the notion of subculture. Like the larger culture of which it is a part, a **subculture** is a collection of values and preferences which is communicated to subcultural participants through a process of socialization. Subcultures differ from the larger culture in that they claim the allegiance of smaller groups of people. Whereas the wider American culture, for example, may proclaim that hard work and individuality are valuable, a particular subculture may espouse the virtues of deer hunting, male bonding, and recreational alcohol consumption. Although it is fair to say that most subcultures are not at odds with the surrounding culture, some subcultures do not readily conform to the parameters of national culture. Countercultures, which tend to reject and invert the

Subculture a collection of values and preferences which is communicated to subcultural participants through a process of socialization.

Annette Sorensen, right, is comforted by her friend Mette Vajlo after Sorensen—a Danish citizen—was arrested for leaving her baby unattended on a New York street while she and the baby's father ate dinner. Criminologists tell us that conflict is a pervasive part of everyday life—much of it based on a clash of values built on subcultural differences. Was what Sorensen did "wrong"? *Don Halasy/New York Post/Corbis-Bettmann.*

Subcultural theory a sociological perspective that emphasizes the contribution made by variously socialized cultural groups to the phenomenon of crime.

values of the surrounding culture, and criminal subcultures, which may actively espouse deviant activity, represent the other extreme. **Subcultural theory** is a sociological perspective that emphasizes the contribution made by variously socialized cultural groups to the phenomenon of crime.

Some of the earliest writings on subcultures can be found in **Frederic M. Thrasher's** 1927 book, *The Gang.*[22] Thrasher studied 1,313 gangs in Chicago. His work, primarily descriptive in nature, led to a typology in which he described different types of gangs. In 1943, **William Foote Whyte,** drawing on Thrasher, published *Street Corner Society.*[23] Whyte, in describing his three-year study of the Italian slum he called "Cornerville," further developed the subcultural thesis, showing that lower-class residents of a typical slum could achieve success through the opportunities afforded by slum culture—including racketeering and bookmaking.

Focal Concerns

In 1958 **Walter B. Miller** attempted to detail the values that drive members of lower-class subcultures into delinquent pursuits. Miller described *lower-class culture* as "a long established, distinctively patterned tradition with an integrity of its own." In Miller's words, "[a] large body of systematically interrelated attitudes, practices, behaviors, and values characteristic of lower-class culture are designed to support and maintain the basic features of the lower-class way of life. In areas where these differ from features of middle-class culture, action oriented to the achievement and maintenance of the lower-class system may violate norms of the middle class and be perceived as deliberately nonconforming. . . . This does not mean, however, that violation of the middle-class norm is the dominant component of motivation; it is a byproduct of action primarily oriented to the lower-class system."[24]

In the same article, entitled "Lower Class Culture as a Generating Milieu of Gang Delinquency,"[25] Miller outlined what he termed the **focal concerns** or key values of delinquent subcultures. Such concerns included trouble, toughness, smartness, excitement, fate, and autonomy. Miller concluded that subcultural crime and deviance are not the direct consequences of poverty and lack of opportunity, but emanate, rather, from specific values characteristic of such subcultures. Just as middle-class concerns with achievement, hard work, and delayed gratification lead to socially acceptable forms of success, said Miller, so too do lower-class concerns provide a path to subculturally recognized success for lower-class youth.

Miller found that trouble "is a dominant feature of lower class culture." Getting into trouble, staying out of trouble, dealing with trouble when it arises become focal points in the lives of many members of lower-class culture. Miller recognized that getting into trouble was not necessarily valued in and of itself, but seen as an oftentimes necessary means to valued ends. In Miller's words, "[for] men, 'trouble' frequently involves fighting or sexual adventures while drinking; for women, sexual involvement with disadvantageous consequences."[26]

Like many theorists of the time, Miller was primarily concerned with the criminality of men. The lower-class masculine concern with toughness which he identified, Miller admitted, may have been a product of the fact that many men in the groups he examined were raised in female-headed families. Miller's "toughness," then, may reflect an almost obsessive concern with masculinity as a reaction to the perceived threat of overidentification with female role models. In words that sound as applicable today as when they were written, Miller tells us, "[t]he genesis of the intense concern over 'toughness' in lower-class culture is probably related to the fact that a significant proportion of lower-class males are reared in a predominantly female household and lack a consistently present male figure with whom to identify and from whom to learn essential components of a 'male' role. Since women serve as a primary object of identification during the pre-adolescent years, the almost obsessive lower-class concern with 'masculinity' probably resembles a type of compulsive reaction-formation."[27]

Miller described "smartness" as the "capacity to outsmart, outfox, outwit, dupe, take, [or] con another or others and the concomitant capacity to avoid being outwitted, taken or duped oneself. . . . In its essence," said Miller, "smartness involves the capacity to achieve a valued entity—material goods, personal status—through a maximum use of mental agility and a minimum of physical effort."

Excitement was seen as a search for thrills—often necessary to overcome the boredom inherent in lower-class lifestyles. Fights, gambling, picking up women, and making the rounds were all described as derivative aspects of the lower-class concern with excitement. "The quest for excitement," said Miller, "finds . . . its most vivid expression in the . . . recurrent 'night on the town' . . . a patterned set of activities in which alcohol, music, and sexual adventuring are major components."

Focal concerns the key values of any culture, and especially the key values of a delinquent subculture.

Fate is related to the quest for excitement and to the concept of luck or of being lucky. As Miller stated; "[m]any lower-class persons feel that their lives are subject to a set of forces over which they have relatively little control. These are not . . . supernatural forces or . . . organized religion . . . but relate more to a concept of 'destiny' or man as a pawn. . . . This often implicit world view is associated with a conception of the ultimate futility of directed effort toward a goal. . . ."

Autonomy, as a focal concern, manifests itself in statements such as "I can take care of myself" or "No one's going to push me around." Autonomy produces behavioral problems from the perspective of middle-class expectations when it surfaces in work environments, public schools, or other social institutions built on expectations of conformity.

Miller's work derived almost entirely from his study of black inner-city delinquents in the Boston area. As such, it may have less relevance to members of lower-class subcultures at other times, or in other places.

Delinquency and Drift

Members of delinquent subcultures are, to at least some degree, participants in the larger culture that surrounds them. How is it, then, that subcultural participants may choose behavioral alternatives which seemingly negate the norms and values of the larger society? In other words, how can a person give allegiance to two seemingly different sets of values—those of the larger culture and those of a subculture—at the same time?

Gresham Sykes and **David Matza** provided an answer to this question in their 1957 article "Techniques of Neutralization."[28] Sykes and Matza suggested that offenders can overcome feelings of responsibility when involved in crime commission through the use of the following five types of justifications.

1. *Denial of responsibility,* by pointing to one's background of poverty, abuse, lack of opportunity, and so on. Example: "The trouble I get into is not my fault."
2. *Denial of injury,* by explaining how insurance companies, for example, cover losses. Claims that "everyone does it" or that the specific victim could "afford it" fall into this category. Example: "They're so rich, they'll never miss it."
3. *Denial of the victim,* or justifying the harm done by claiming that the victim, for whatever reason, deserved the victimization. Example: "I only beat up drunks."
4. *Condemning the condemners,* by asserting that authorities are corrupt or responsible for their own victimization. Offenders may also claim that society has made them into what they are, and must now suffer the consequences. Example: "They're worse than we are. They're all on the take."
5. *An appeal to higher loyalties,* as in defense of one's family honor, gang, girlfriend, or neighborhood. Example: "We have to protect ourselves."

In the words of Sykes and Matza, "[i]t is our argument that much delinquency is based on what is essentially an unrecognized extension of defenses to crimes, in the form of justifications for deviance that are seen as valid by the delinquent but not by the legal system or society at large."[29]

A few years later Matza went on to suggest that delinquents tended to drift into crime when they found that available **techniques of neutralization** combined with weak or ineffective values espoused by the controlling elements in society. In effect, said Matza, the delinquent "drifts between criminal and conventional action," choosing whichever is the more expedient at the time. By employing techniques of neutralization, delinquents need not be fully alienated from the larger society. When opportunities for crime present themselves, such techniques provide an effective way for overcoming feelings of guilt, and of allowing for ease of action. Matza used the phrase "soft determinism" to describe drift, saying that delinquents were neither forced to make choices because of fateful experiences early in life, nor were they entirely free to make choices unencumbered by the realities of their situation.

More recent studies have found that whereas "only a small percentage of adolescents generally approve of violence or express indifference to violence ... [a] large percentage of adolescents ... accept neutralizations justifying the use of violence in particular situations."[30] The acceptance of such justifications by many young people today is seen as supportive of high levels of adolescent violence. Studies have also found that young people who disapprove of violence but associate with delinquent peers will often use neutralization techniques as justifications for violence in which they personally engage.[31]

> **Techniques of neutralization** culturally available justifications which can provide criminal offenders with the means to disavow responsibility for their behavior.

VIOLENT SUBCULTURES

Some subcultures are decidedly violent, and are built around violent themes and around values supporting violent activities. In 1967 **Franco Ferracuti** and **Marvin Wolfgang** published their seminal work, *The Subculture of Violence: Toward an Integrated Theory of Criminology*,[32] which drew together many of the sociological perspectives previously advanced to explain delinquency and crime. According to some writers,[33] the work of Wolfgang and Ferracuti "was substantively different from the other subculture theories, perhaps because it was developed almost a decade after delinquent-subculture theories and criminology had developed new concerns." Ferracuti and Wolfgang's main thesis was that violence is a learned form of adaptation to certain problematic life circumstances, and that learning to be violent takes place within the context of a subcultural milieu which emphasizes the advantages of violence over other forms of adaptation. Such subcultures are characterized by songs and stories that glorify violence, by gun ownership, and by rituals which tend to stress macho models. They are likely to teach that a quick and decisive response to insults is necessary to preserve one's prestige within the group. Subcultural group members have a proclivity for fighting as a means of settling disputes. Subcultures of violence both expect violence from their members, and legitimize it when it occurs. In Wolfgang's words, "the use of violence ... is not necessarily viewed as illicit conduct, and the users do not have to deal with feelings of guilt about their aggression." In other words, for participants in violent subcultures, violence can be a way of life.

Violent subcultures produce violent acts. Eighteen spent cartridges lay around the body of this New Orleans murder victim. Why are some subcultures "violent," while others are not? *Bryce Lankard.*

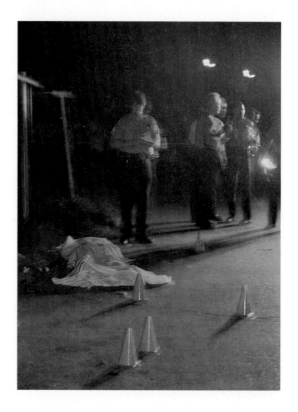

Wolfgang and Ferracuti based their conclusions on an analysis of data which showed substantial differences in the rate of homicides between racial groups in the Philadelphia area. At the time of their study, nonwhite men had a homicide rate of 41.7 per 100,000, versus a homicide rate of only 3.4 for white men. Statistics on nonwhite women showed a homicide rate of 9.3 versus 0.4 for white women. Explaining these findings, Wolfgang and Ferracuti tell us: "[h]omicide is most prevalent, or the highest rates of homicide occur, among a relatively homogeneous subcultural group in any large urban community. . . . The value system of this group, as we are contending, constitutes a subculture of violence. From a psychological viewpoint, we might hypothesize that the greater the degree of integration of the individual into this subculture, the higher the probability that his behavior will be violent in a variety of situations."[34]

Wolfgang and Ferracuti extend their theory of subcultural violence with the following "corollary propositions."[35]

1. No subculture can be totally different from or totally in conflict with the society of which it is a part.
2. To establish the existence of a subculture of violence does not require that the actors sharing in these basic value elements should express violence in all situations.
3. The potential resort or willingness to resort to violence in a variety of situations emphasizes the penetrating and diffusive character of this culture theme.

4. The subcultural ethos of violence may be shared by all ages in a sub-society, but this ethos is most prominent in a limited age group, ranging from late adolescence to middle age.
5. The counter-norm is nonviolence.
6. The development of favorable attitudes toward, and the use of, violence in a subculture usually involves learned behavior and a process of differential learning, association, or identification.
7. The use of violence in a subculture is not necessarily viewed as illicit conduct and the users therefore do not have to deal with feelings of guilt about their aggression.

Other writers have commented on geographical distinctions between violent subcultures in different parts of the United States. A body of criminological literature exists,[36] for example, which claims that certain forms of criminal violence are more acceptable in the southern United States than in northern portions of the country. Some writers have also referred to variability in the degree to which interpersonal violence has been accepted in the South over time, whereas others have suggested that violence in the South might be a traditional tool in the service of social order.[37] Without at least a modicum of expressive violence such as lynchings, dueling, and outright fighting, these authors suggest, southern social solidarity following the Civil War might have been seriously threatened. In short, the notion of a southern violence construct holds that an "infernal trinity of Southerner, violence and weaponry"[38] may make crimes such as homicide and assault more culturally acceptable in the South than in other parts of the country.

In an interesting aside that relates to the chapter-opening story and further illustrates how violent subcultural norms are transmitted from generation to generation, Virginia Demery, 41, the mother of Larry Martin Demery, one of the men arrested and charged with killing Michael Jordan's father, was convicted on September 28, 1993, of using a shotgun in an assault on reporters who came to her mobile home following her son's arrest. Although no one was injured in the incident, reporters who brought criminal charges against her later said that members of the news media should be able to "expect a general amount of civility when they go to interview someone." Ms. Demery gave reporters until the count of five to leave her property but the gun discharged, accidentally she claimed, at the count of two.[39]

The wider culture often recognizes, sometimes begrudgingly and sometimes matter-of-factly, a violent subculture's internal rules. Hence, when one member of such a subculture kills another, the wider society may take the killing less "seriously" than if someone outside the subculture had been killed. As a consequence of this realization, Wolfgang described what he called "wholesale" and "retail" costs for homicide, in which killings that are perceived to occur within a subculture of violence (when both the victim and perpetrator are seen as members of a violent subculture) generally result in a less harsh punishment than do killings which occur outside of the subculture. Punishments, said Wolfgang, relate to the perceived seriousness of the offense, and if members of the subculture within which a crime occurs accept the offense as part of the landscape, so, too, will members of the wider culture which imposes official sanctions on the perpetrator.

Critique of Violent Subcultures Theory

Although subcultural approaches are widely accepted within criminology, the notion of a subculture of violence has been questioned. Canadian criminologist Gwynn Nettler criticizes the subculture of violence thesis by insisting that it is tautological, or circular. That is, saying that people fight because they are violent, or that "they are murderous because they live violently" does little to explain their behavior, according to Nettler. Attributing fighting to "other spheres of violence," he says, may be true, but it is fundamentally "uninformative."

The approach has also been criticized for being racist, because many so-called violent subcultures are said to be populated primarily by minorities. Margaret Anderson says that "[t]he problem with this explanation is that it turns attention away from the relationship of black communities to the larger society and it recreates dominant stereotypes about blacks as violent, aggressive, and fearful. Although it may be true that rates of violence are higher in black communities, this observation does not explain the fact."[40] In sociological jargon, one might say that an observed correlation between race and violence does not necessarily provide a workable explanation for the relationship.

TOT SLAIN IN WRONG TURN ONTO 'AVENUE OF KILLERS'

Is there such a thing as a subculture of violence? Although criminologists disagree, the following article would seem to lend support to the subculture of violence thesis.

Los Angeles—Even if she was old enough to read, 4-year-old Stephanie Kuhen wouldn't have understood the street graffiti that now seems a portent of her death: "Avenue of Killers." That message was scrawled in broken Spanish at the entrance of the alley where Stephanie was shot to death early Sunday.

In the kind of urban nightmare many dread, Stephanie was mortally wounded only blocks from her home when her mother's boyfriend made a wrong turn into a dead-end street used as a hangout by Hispanic hoodlums, police said. A mob of 20 youths barricaded the carload of whites, using trash cans, then opened fire as the driver frantically tried to escape. Stephanie was hit in the head as she lay in her mother's arms in the back seat. Her 2-year-old brother, Joseph, was hit in the foot. He is recovering in a local hospital. Timothy Stone, 25, managed to drive the family home despite a bullet wound in his back. He was treated and released from the hospital Sunday. The other passengers—Stephanie's brother Christopher, 5, mother Robynn Kuhen, 26, and uncle David Dalton, 22—were

Isabel Street—the "Avenue of Killers"—where 4-year-old Stephanie Kuhen was shot to death by gang members. In 1997 three gang members were convicted of her murder. Was Stephanie the victim of a violent subculture? *Bob Riha/Gamma-Liaison, Inc.*

uninjured, although Dalton's baseball cap was creased by a bullet. The family was returning from a barbecue birthday party for a friend.

Stephanie's grandfather said the shooter had to know he was firing on children. "The street was so narrow there was no way they couldn't have seen them in their carseats and everything," David Dalton Sr., 51, said. No arrests have been made in what police are billing an unprovoked ambush slaying.

Although gang violence has been rampant in the working-class neighborhood of Cypress Park for decades, this shooting was different. Hispanic youths generally kill each other in battles over street turf. And they scrupulously avoid injuring young children, police say. "I hope this is not the start

of a new era," said police Detective Robert Lopez.

"She was just a sweet little girl," Dalton said, weeping. "I guess they called it 'Street of Killers' as you drive in, but my kids don't speak Spanish, they didn't know."

In fact, the graffiti at the head of Isabel Street was not a threat but a turf marker, standard in Los Angeles gang neighborhoods, Lopez said. Assassins is the name of a local "set" or subgroup of the Cypress Park area's largest gang, the Avenidas.

The marked block of Isabel Street where Stephanie died long had been known to police as a gang hangout, Lopez said. Neighbors have said that two boarded-up apartment buildings encrusted in graffiti are a favorite spot for late-night teen-age trysts.

Some neighbors complained Monday that police have ignored the drinking, drugs and shootings for too long. "This was an aberration," said Warren Christensen, 52, who lives in the largely white hilltop neighborhood overlooking Cypress Park. "But each year the violence gets farther and farther up the hill."

One Hispanic couple, too fearful to give their names, said drug dealers, not youths, were the real problem. They showed off the elaborate fortifications around their sons' bed: heavy bars and an attack dog. They never call police, they said, because they can't afford a telephone.

"Muy, muy pelligroso, very very dangerous here," the husband said. "I don't fear for myself, but I fear for my children."

Questions

1. What subcultural elements (beliefs, behavior patterns, etc.) may have contributed to Stephanie Kuhen's death?
2. Does the subculture of violence thesis help to explain the behavior of gang members, such as the named Assassins who killed Stephanie? If so, how?
3. What explanations, other than a subculture of violence thesis, might be offered to explain the death of young Stephanie?

Source: Gale Holland, "Tot Slain In Wrong Turn Onto 'Avenue of Killers,'" *USA Today,* September 19, 1995, p. 3A. Copyright 1995, *USA Today.* Reprinted with permission.

CRIME AND SOCIAL STRUCTURE

Strain Theory

In 1938 **Robert K. Merton** offered what is now regarded as a classic statement of the causes of crime in his concept of anomie. *Anomie* is a French word meaning "normlessness," and was popularized by Emile Durkheim in his 1897 book, *Suicide.*[41] Durkheim used the term to explain how a breakdown of predictable social conditions can lead to a feeling of personal loss and dissolution.

Merton's use of the term *anomie* was somewhat different. In Merton's writings[42] **anomie** came to mean a disjunction between socially approved means to success and legitimate goals. This posited strain between goals and means has led to Merton's approach being called **strain theory.** Merton maintained that legitimate goals, involving such things as wealth, status, and personal happiness, were generally defined as desirable for everyone. The widely acceptable means to these goals, however, including education, hard work, financial savings, and so on, were not equally available to all members of society. As a consequence, crime and deviance tended to arise and individuals felt pressed to succeed in approved terms but were not given the tools necessary for such success. In Merton's words, "[i]t's not how you play the game, it's whether you win."[43] Complicating the picture further, Merton maintained, was the fact that not everyone accepted the legitimacy of socially ap-

Anomie a social condition in which norms are uncertain or lacking.

Strain, or **anomie, theory** a sociological approach which posits a disjuncture between socially and subculturally sanctioned means and goals as the cause of criminal behavior.

⧉

FIGURE 7.2

GOALS AND MEANS DISJUNCTURE

	Goals	*Means*
Conformity	+	+
Innovation	+	−
Ritualism	−	+
Retreatism	−	−
Rebellion	±	±

Source: Robert K. Merton, *Social Theory and Social Structure,* 1968 enlarged edition. Copyright 1967, 1968 by Robert K. Merton. Adapted with permission of the Free Press, a division of Macmillan, Inc.

proved goals. Merton diagrammed possible combinations of goals and means as shown in Figure 7.2, referring to each combination as a mode of adaptation.

The initial row in Figure 7.2 signifies acceptance of the goals that society holds as legitimate for everyone, with ready availability of the means approved for achieving those goals. The mode of adaptation associated with this combination of goals and means is called *conformity* and typifies most middle- and upper-class individuals.

Innovation, the second form of adaptation, arises when an emphasis on approved goal achievement combines with a lack of opportunity to participate fully in socially acceptable means to success. This form of adaptation is experienced by many lower-class individuals who have been socialized to desire traditional success symbols such as expensive cars, large homes, and big bank accounts, but who do not have ready access to approved means of acquiring them, such as educational opportunity. Innovative behavioral responses, including crime, can be expected to develop when individuals find themselves so deprived. However, in Merton's words, "[p]overty as such, and consequent limitation of opportunity, are not sufficient to induce a conspicuously high rate of criminal behavior. Even the often mentioned 'poverty in the midst of plenty' will not necessarily lead to this result." It is only insofar as those who find themselves in poverty are pressured to achieve material success and the acquisition of other associated symbols of status that innovation results.

Third, *ritualism* describes the form of behavior that arises when members of society participate in socially desirable means, but show little interest in goal achievement. A ritualist may get a good education, work every day in an acceptable occupation, and outwardly appear to be leading a solid middle-class lifestyle. Yet that person may care little for the symbols of success, choosing to live an otherwise independent lifestyle.

Retreatism describes the behavior of those who reject both the socially approved goals and means. They may become dropouts, drug abusers, or homeless or participate in alternative lifestyles such as communal living. Such individuals are socially and psychologically often quite separate from the larger society around them.

Merton's last category, *rebellion,* signifies a person, or rebel, who wishes to replace socially approved goals and means with some other system. Political radicals, revolutionaries, and antiestablishment agitators may fit into this category. Merton believed that conformity was the most common mode of adaptation prevalent in society, whereas retreatism was least common.

A contemporary version of Merton's anomie theory has been proposed by Steven Messner and Richard Rosenfeld, who suggest that inconsistencies in the American Dream are to be blamed for most criminal activity. Messner and Rosenfeld write: "Our thesis is that the American Dream itself exerts pressures toward crime by encouraging an anomic cultural environment, an environment in which people are encouraged to adopt an 'anything goes' mentality in the pursuit of personal goals."[44]

Differential Opportunity

In the 1960s **Richard Cloward** and **Lloyd Ohlin** published *Delinquency and Opportunity.*[45] Their book, a report on the nature and activities of juvenile gangs, blended the subcultural thesis with ideas derived from strain theory. Cloward and Ohlin saw socially structured opportunities for success as of two types; illegitimate and legitimate. They observed that whereas legitimate opportunities were generally available to individuals born into middle-class culture, participants in lower-class subcultures were often denied access to them. As a consequence, the choice of illegitimate opportunities to success were often seen as quite acceptable by participants in so-called illegitimate subcultures.

Opportunity structure a path to success. Opportunity structures may be of two types: legitimate and illegitimate.

Illegitimate opportunity structure subcultural pathways to success which are disapproved of by the wider society.

Cloward and Ohlin used the term **illegitimate opportunity structure** to describe preexisting subcultural paths to success which are not approved of by the wider culture. Where illegitimate paths to success are not already in place, alienated individuals may undertake a process of ideational evolution through which "a collective delinquent solution" or a "delinquent means of achieving success" may be decided upon by members of a gang. Because the two paths to success, legitimate and illegitimate, differ in their availability to members of society, Cloward and Ohlin's perspective has been termed *differential opportunity.*

According to Cloward and Ohlin, delinquent behavior may result from the ready availability of illegitimate opportunities with the effective replacement of the norms of the wider culture with expedient subcultural rules. Hence, delinquency and criminality may become "all right" or legitimate in the eyes of gang members, and may even form the criteria used by other subcultural participants to judge successful accomplishments. In the words of Cloward and Ohlin, "[a] delinquent subculture is one in which certain forms of delinquent activity are essential requirements for the performance of the dominant roles supported by the subculture."[46] Its "most crucial elements" are the "prescriptions, norms, or rules of conduct that define the activities required of a full-fledged member."[47] "A person attributes legitimacy to a system of rules and corresponding models of behavior," wrote Cloward and Ohlin, "when he accepts them as binding on his conduct."[48] "Delinquents have withdrawn their support from established norms and invested officially forbidden forms of conduct with a claim to legitimacy...."[49]

Cloward and Ohlin noted that a delinquent act can be "defined by two essential elements: it is behavior that violates basic norms of the society, and, when officially known, it evokes a judgment by agents of criminal justice that such norms have been violated."[50] For Cloward and Ohlin, however, crime and deviance were just as normal as any other form of behavior supported by group socialization. In their words, "deviance and conformity generally result from the same kinds of social conditions . . ." and "deviance ordinarily represents a search for solutions to problems of adjustment." In their view, deviance is just as much an effort to conform, albeit to subcultural norms and expectations, as is conformity to the norms of the wider society. They added, however, that "[i]t has been our experience that most persons who participate in delinquent subcultures, if not lone offenders, are fully aware of the difference between right and wrong, between conventional behavior and rule-violating behavior. They may not care about the difference, or they may enjoy flouting the rules of the game, or they may have decided that illegitimate practices get them what they want more efficiently than legitimate practices."[51]

Cloward and Ohlin described three types of delinquent subcultures: (1) criminal subcultures, in which criminal role models are readily available for adoption by those being socialized into the subculture; (2) conflict subcultures, in which participants seek status through violence; and (3) retreatist subcultures, where drug use and withdrawal from the wider society predominate. Each subculture was thought to emerge from a larger, all-encompassing "parent" subculture of delinquent values. According to Cloward and Ohlin, delinquent subcultures had at least three identifiable features: (1) "acts of delinquency that reflect subcultural support are likely to recur with great frequency," (2) "access to a successful adult criminal career sometimes results from participation in a delinquent subculture," and (3) "the delinquent subculture imparts to the conduct of its members a high degree of stability and resistance to control or change."[52]

Cloward and Ohlin divided lower-class youth into four types according to their degree of commitment to middle-class values and/or material achievement. Type I youths were said to desire entry to the middle class via improvement in their economic position. Type II youths were seen as desiring entry to the middle class, but not improvement in their economic position. Type III youth were portrayed as desiring wealth without entry to the middle class. As a consequence, Type III youths were seen as the most crime prone. Type IV youth were described as dropouts who retreated from the cultural mainstream through drug and alcohol use.

Cloward and Ohlin had substantial impact on American social policy through the sponsorship of David Hackett, President John F. Kennedy's head of the newly created Committee on Juvenile Delinquency and Youth Crime. Out of the relationship between the theorists and Hackett, the Mobilization for Youth program, established under the auspices of the 1961 Juvenile Delinquency Prevention and Control Act, was begun with $12.5 million in initial funding in 1962.[53] Mobilization for Youth, a delinquency prevention program based on Cloward and Ohlin's opportunity theory, created employment and educational opportunities for deprived youths.

Reaction Formation

Another criminologist whose work is often associated with both strain theory and the subcultural perspective is **Albert Cohen.** Like Cloward and Ohlin, Cohen's work focused primarily on the gang behavior of delinquent youth. In Cohen's words, "[w]hen we speak of a delinquent subculture, we speak of a way of life that has somehow become traditional among certain groups in American society. These groups are the boys' gangs that flourish most conspicuously in the 'delinquency neighborhoods' of our larger American cities. The members of these gangs grow up, some to become law-abiding citizens and others to graduate to more professional and adult forms of criminality, but the delinquent tradition is kept alive by the age-groups that succeed them."[54]

Cohen argued that youngsters from all backgrounds are generally held accountable to the norms of the wider society through a "middle-class measuring rod" of expectations related to such items as school performance, language proficiency, cleanliness, punctuality, neatness, nonviolent behavior, and allegiance to other similar standards. Like strain theorists, Cohen noted that unfortunately not everyone is prepared, by virtue of the circumstances surrounding their birth and subsequent socialization, for effectively meeting such expectations.

In an examination of vandalism, Cohen[55] found that "nonutilitarian" delinquency, in which things of value are destroyed rather than stolen or otherwise used for financial gain, is the result of middle-class values turned upside down. Delinquent youths, argued Cohen, who are often alienated from middle-class values and lifestyles through deprivation and limited opportunities, can achieve status among their subcultural peers via vandalism and other forms of delinquent behavior.

Children, especially those from deprived backgrounds, turn to delinquency, Cohen claimed, because they experience status-frustration when judged by adults and others according to middle-class standards and goals which they are unable to achieve. Because it is nearly impossible for nonmainstream children to succeed in middle-class terms, they may overcome anxiety through the process of reaction formation, in which hostility toward middle-class values develops. Cohen adapted **reaction formation** from psychiatric perspectives, and used it to mean "the process in which a person openly rejects that which he wants, or aspires to, but cannot obtain or achieve."[56]

Cohen discovered the roots of delinquent subcultures in what he termed the "collective solution to the problem of status." When youths who experience the same kind of alienation from middle-class ideals band together, they achieve a collective and independent solution and create a delinquent subculture. Cohen wrote, "[t]he delinquent subculture, we suggest, is a way of dealing with the problems of adjustment. . . . These problems are chiefly status problems: certain children are denied status in the respectable society because they cannot meet the criteria of the respectable status system. The delinquent subculture deals with these problems by providing criteria of status which these children *can* meet."[57]

Cohen's approach is effectively summarized in a "theoretical scenario" offered by Donald J. Shoemaker,[58] who says that lower-class youths undergo a working-class socialization that combines lower-class values and habits with middle-class success values. Lower-class youth then experience failure in school because they cannot live up to the middle-class norms operative in American educational institutions. They suffer a consequent loss of self-esteem and increased feelings of rejection, leading to dropping out of school and "association with delinquent peers." Hostility and resentment toward middle-class standards grow through reaction formation. Finally, such alienated youths achieve status and a sense of improved self-worth through participation in a gang of like-minded peers. Delinquency and crime are the result.

Reaction formation the process in which a person openly rejects that which he or she wants, or aspires to, but cannot obtain or achieve.

Gangs Today

Gangs have become a major source of concern in contemporary American society. Although the writings of investigators such as Cohen, Thrasher, and Cloward and Ohlin focused on the illicit activities of juvenile gangs in the nation's inner cities, most gang-related crimes of the period involved vandalism, petty theft, and battles over turf. The ethnic distinctions which gave rise to gang culture in the 1920s through the 1950s are today largely forgotten. Italian, Hungarian, Polish, and Jewish immigrants, whose children made up many of the early gangs, have been, for the most part, successfully integrated into the society that is modern America.

Today's gang members are much more likely to be black or Hispanic, and the gangs themselves appear far more violent, drug involved, and intransigent than those studied by the early researchers. A recent NIJ survey[59] found that most gang members (47.8 percent) were African-American youth, while Hispanic youngsters accounted for 42.7 percent of reported gang members. Asian gang membership totaled 5.2 percent of all gang involvement, while whites accounted for only 4.4 percent of gang members nationwide. A 1996 report, also by NIJ, estimated a yearly incidence of 580,331 gang-related crimes—a "12-fold increase over the 46,359 gang crimes estimated to have occurred in 1991."[60] The same report estimated the number of juvenile gangs nationwide at 16,643, with memberships totaling 555,181.

A large-scale project of the National Gang Crime Research Center, known as Project Gangfact, provides a profile of gangs and gang members nationwide. The

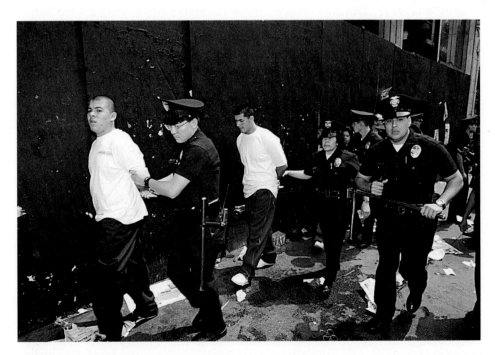

Los Angeles gang members under arrest. Gangs have become a major source of concern in today's society. Why have gangs become such a prominent feature of contemporary society? *Douglas C. Pizac/AP/Wide World Photos.*

1996 Gangfact report,[61] based on data collected by twenty eight researchers in seventeen states, showed that

- the average age for joining a gang, nationally, is 12.8 years of age.
- over half who joined gangs have tried to quit.
- more than two-thirds of gangs have written rules for members to follow.
- over half of all gangs hold regular weekly meetings.
- nearly 30 percent of gangs require their members to pay dues.
- approximately 55 percent of gang members have been recruited by other gang members, while the remainder sought out gang membership.
- most gang members (79 percent) said they would leave the gang if given a "second chance in life."
- four-fifths of gang members reported that their gangs sold crack cocaine.
- most gangs (70 percent) are not racially exclusive, and consist of members drawn from a variety of ethnic groups.
- one-third of gang members report that they have been able to conceal their gang membership from their parents.
- most gangs (83 percent) report having female members, but few allow female members to assume leadership roles.
- many gang members (40 percent) report knowing male members of their gangs who had raped females.

Los Angeles is considered to be the "gang capital"[62] of the United States with more than 143,000 juveniles known to be participating in over 1,142 different gangs as of June 1, 1995.[63] During 1994, Los Angeles County saw 779 gang-related homicides, and over 1,711 injuries were directly caused by gang activity.[64] Drugs form the centerpiece of much Los Angeles gang activity, with large quantities of crack—a highly addictive form of cocaine—being produced and sold by many groups.

The Los Angeles County Sheriff's Department uses a computer system known as GREAT (Gang Reporting, Evaluation, and Tracking) to keep track of gang members, and Los Angeles–area police agencies have resorted to massive arrests to gain some control over the gang problem. The first LAPD sweep focused on city schools, where officers made 127 arrests, half of them for felonies. However, few arrested juveniles remain in custody for long. In California, one report found gang culture flourishing inside of California Youth Authority (CYA) institutions, with members of rival gangs forming branches for protection.[65]

Members of modern youth gangs generally identify with a name (such as the "Crips" and "Bloods," which are well-known Los Angeles–area gangs), a particular style of clothing, symbols, tattoos, jewelry, haircut, and hand symbols. Gangs can be big business. In addition to traditional criminal activities such as burglary, extortion, vandalism, and protection rackets, drug dealing has become a mainstay of many inner-city gangs. Los Angeles police estimate that at least four city gangs earn over $1 million each per week through cocaine sales.[66] The potential for huge drug-based profits appears to have changed the nature of gangs themselves, making them more prone toward violence and cutthroat tactics. Gang killings, including the now infamous drive-by shootings, have become commonplace in our nation's cities.

STUDY EASES FEAR OF TEEN CRIME WAVE

For years criminologists have warned of a coming wave of juvenile crime. Now, new studies, supported by statistics from the U.S. Department of Justice, are beginning to call into question the wisdom of such predictions.

Criminologists and other law enforcement officials now believe a predicted wave of juvenile violence will not occur. Recent declines in juvenile arrests for murder, assault and other violent crimes, they say, is part of a continuing and sustainable downward trend.

On Thursday, Attorney General Janet Reno said a new analysis of FBI crime statistics shows the drop in juvenile arrests for violent crimes in 1995—including murder, assault and rape—was largely driven by a sharp decline in arrests involving children 14 years old and younger. "These numbers offer us . . . a very good lesson," Reno said. "We do not have to face an explosion in youth crime as some have suggested."

The Justice Department analysis goes against the prevailing train of thought among criminologists in recent years. Following sharp increases in juvenile violent crime in the mid-1980s and early 1990s, many criminol-ogists predicted the nation was in line for a crime explosion as the juvenile population rises from 27 million today to 39 million in 2010. But now even Northeastern University professor James Fox, who helped fan national concern about a group he called the "young and the ruthless," has softened his forecast of a juvenile Armageddon. "I get a reputation for being negative, a doomsayer," Fox said in a recent interview. "I never meant there would be a blood bath. Some of it was part of getting people's attention."

Said Jack Levin, director of Northeastern's Program for the Study of Violence and Social Conflict, and an early speculator about a youth apocalypse: "I was wrong."

FBI statistics show drops in every major category of youth violent crime in 1995, down 4% overall. The decline was driven by a 7% decline in arrests involving youngsters 10 to 14.

Questions
1. Is a juvenile crime wave about to burst upon the nation? Why or why not?
2. How has "official" thinking about a coming tidal wave in juvenile crime changed? What has led to such a change in thinking?
3. If criminologists were wrong in their earlier predictions (of rampant juvenile crime on the horizon), how might they have been misled?

Source: Kevin Johnson, "Study Eases Fear of Teen Crime Wave," *USA Today,* December 13, 1996, p. 1A. Copyright 1997, *USA Today.* Reprinted with permission.

Rodney Dailey, a self-avowed former Boston-area drug dealer and gun-wielding gang member, says that in today's gang world, "Shoot before you get shot is the rule."[67] According to Dailey, "[t]hings that normally people would have had fist-fights about can get you shot or stabbed" today. Dailey is founder of Gang Peace, an outreach group which tries to reduce gang-related violence.

Guns have become a way of life for many young gang members. As a young man named Jamaal, hanging around with friends outside Boston's Orchard Park housing project, recently put it, "We don't fight, we shoot." Police in the area describe how values among youth have changed over the past decade or two. Today they "think it's fun to pop someone," they say.

Contemporary researchers, however, are drawing some new distinctions between gangs and violence. A few years ago G. David Curry and Irving A. Spergel, in a study of Chicago communities, distinguished between juvenile delinquency and gang-related homicide.[68] They found that communities characterized by high rates of delinquency do not necessarily experience exceptionally high rates of crime or of gang-related homicides. They concluded that although gang activity may be associated with homicide, "gang homicide rates and delinquency rates are ecologically distinct community problems." Gang-related homicide, they found, seems to be well explained by classical theories of social disorganization and is especially prevalent in areas of the city characterized by in-migration and by the "settlement of new immigrant groups." In their study, high rates of juvenile delinquency seemed to correlate more with poverty, which the researchers defined as "social adaptation to chronic deprivation." According to Curry and Spergel, "[s]ocial disorganization and poverty rather than criminal organization and conspiracy may better explain the recent growth and spread of youth gangs to many parts of the country. Moreover, community organization and social opportunity in conjunction with suppression, rather than simply suppression and incapacitation, may be more effective policies in dealing with the social problem."[69] In proposing a national gang strategy, Finn-Aage Esbensen reminds policymakers that many gang members are delinquent before they become associated with gangs.[70] Esbensen says that "concerns with gang suppression should not supplant efforts to implement effective delinquency intervention and prevention strategies."[71]

General Strain Theory

Strain theory has recently been reformulated by **Robert Agnew**[72] and others into a theory of broader scope, called general strain theory (GST). General strain theory builds on traditional strain theory in several ways. First, it significantly expands the focus of strain theory to include all types of negative relations between an individual and others. Second, GST maintains that strain is likely to have a cumulative effect on delinquency after reaching a certain threshold. Third, general strain theory provides a more comprehensive account of the cognitive, behavioral, and emotional adaptations to strain than traditional strain approaches. Finally, GST more fully describes the wide variety of factors affecting the choice of delinquent adaptations to strain. According to GST, strain occurs when others do the following: (1) prevent or threaten to prevent an individual from achieving positively valued goals; (2) remove or threaten to remove positively valued stimuli that a person possesses; or (3) present or threaten to present someone with noxious or negatively val-ued stimuli. Agnew sees the crime-producing effects of strain as cumulative and concludes that whatever form it takes, "[s]train creates a predisposition for delin-quency in those cases in which it is chronic or repetitive."[73]

In 1994 Raymond Paternoster and Paul Mazerolle[74] tested some of the assump-tions underlying GST through an analysis of data from the National Youth Survey. They found partial support for GST and discovered that negative relations with adults, feelings of dissatisfaction with friends and school life, and the experience of stressful events (e.g., family dissolution) were positively related to delinquency, as was living in an unpleasant neighborhood (one beset by social problems and phys-ical deterioration). When conceived of more broadly as exposure to negative stim-uli, general strain was found to be significantly related to delinquency.

Contrary to Agnew's hypothesis, however, Paternoster and Mazerolle found no evidence that the effects of strain were enhanced when they were experienced for longer periods of time, nor diminished when adolescents classified the dimension of their life in which they experienced strain as "unimportant." Consistent with ear-lier findings,[75] Paternoster and Mazerolle found that feelings of general strain were positively related to later delinquency, regardless of the number of delinquent peers, moral beliefs, self-efficacy, and level of conventional social support. Some support was found for the belief that general strain leads to delinquency by weakening the conventional social bond and by strengthening the unconventional bond with delinquent peers.

A recent analysis by Agnew[76] of other strain theories found that all such theo-ries share at least two central explanatory features. Strain theories, Agnew said, (1) focus "explicitly on negative relationships with others; relationships in which the individual is not treated as he or she wants to be treated," and (2) argue that "adolescents are pressured into delinquency by the negative affective states—most notably anger and related emotions—that often result from negative relation-ships." Agnew also found that strain theories generally describe three different types of negative relationships with others, or forms of "strain": (1) situations in which individuals actively prevent another person from achieving positively valued goals, (2) the intentional removal or threatened removal of something which is positively valued, or (3) the presenting or threatened presenting of negatively val-ued stimuli.

Critique of Strain Theory

Merton's original formulation of strain theory, although it has much of value to say about the consequences of unequal opportunity, is probably less applicable to American society today than it was in the 1930s, because in the last few decades con-siderable effort has been made toward improving success opportunities for all Americans—regardless of ethnic heritage, race, or gender. Hence it is less likely that individuals today will find themselves without the opportunity for choice, as was the case decades ago. Even so, social programs designed to provide equal opportu-nity have had little impact on some apparently well-insulated segments of society where even the semblance of participating in "approved means" may be grounds for derision.

Crime Causation

General strain theories, like those summarized by Agnew, have more contemporary relevance than Merton's original formulation. As Agnew points out, opportunities to legitimate success may be blocked at many junctures in the life course, resulting in strain, frustration, and anger—all of which may produce law-violating behavior in those undergoing such experiences.[77]

Travis Hirschi,[78] however, criticizes strain theory for its inability "to locate people suffering from discrepancy" and notes that human beings are naturally optimistic—a fact, he says, which "overrides . . . aspiration-expectation disjunction." Hirschi concludes that "[e]xpectations appear to affect delinquency, but they do so regardless of aspirations, and strain notions are neither consistent with nor required by the data."

DIFFERENTIAL ASSOCIATION

Learning theory the general notion that crime is an acquired form of behavior, which is learned just as are many other forms of behavior.

Differential association the sociological thesis that criminality, like any other form of behavior, is learned through a process of association with others who communicate criminal values.

One important perspective on criminality is a form of **learning theory** advanced by **Edwin Sutherland** in 1939. Called **differential association,** Sutherland's thesis was that criminality is learned behavior, and that it is learned through a process of association with others who communicate criminal values and who may advocate the commission of crimes. All significant human behavior, according to Sutherland, is learned behavior, and crime, therefore, is not substantively different from any other form of behavior.

Although Sutherland died in 1950, the tenth edition of his famous book, *Criminology,* was published in 1978 under the authorship of Donald R. Cressey, a professor at the University of California at Santa Barbara. The 1978 edition of *Criminology* contained the finalized principles of differential association (which, for all practical purposes, were complete as early as 1947). Nine in number, the principles read as follows:

1. Criminal behavior is learned.
2. Criminal behavior is learned in interaction with other persons in a process of communication.
3. The principal part of the learning of criminal behavior occurs within intimate personal groups.
4. When criminal behavior is learned, the learning includes (a) techniques of committing the crime, which are sometimes very complicated, sometimes very simple, and (b) the specific direction of motives, drives, rationalizations, and attitudes.
5. The specific direction of motives and drives is learned from definitions of the legal codes as favorable or unfavorable.
6. A person becomes delinquent because of an excess of definitions favorable to violation of law over definitions unfavorable to violation of law.
7. Differential associations may vary in frequency, duration, priority, and intensity.
8. The process of learning criminal behavior by association with criminal and anticriminal patterns involves all of the mechanisms that are involved in any other learning.

9. While criminal behavior is an expression of general needs and values, it is not explained by those general needs and values, since noncriminal behavior is an expression of the same needs and values.

Differential association found considerable acceptance among theorists of the mid-twentieth century because it combined then-prevalent psychological and sociological principles into a coherent perspective on criminality. Crime as a form of learned behavior became the catchword of twentieth-century criminology, and biological and other perspectives were essentially abandoned by those involved in the process of theory testing.

Critique of Differential Association

Differential association is not without its critics. Perhaps the most potent criticism is the claim that differential association, because of the way in which Sutherland presented it, is virtually untestable, even though much use has been made of the insights the perspective appears to offer. Other critics also suggest that differential association alone is not a sufficient explanation for crime. If it were, then we might expect correctional officers, for example, to become criminals by virtue of their constant and continued association with prison inmates. Similarly, wrongly imprisoned persons might be expected to turn to crime upon release from confinement. Little evidence suggests that either of these scenarios actually occurs. In effect, differential association does not seem to provide for free choice in individual circumstances, nor for the fact that some individuals, even when surrounded by associates who are committed to lives of crime, are still able to hold onto other, noncriminal, values.

CRIMINAL CAREERS AND LIFE COURSE THEORY

Criminal careers may develop as the result of various criminogenic influences which impact individuals throughout the course of their lives. Career criminality is frequently explained by **life course theories** which provide a kind of summary approach incorporating many other sociological perspectives. Most life course theories recognize that criminogenic influences have their greatest impact during the early stages of life. Hence, such perspectives agree with the widely held belief that children are more impressionable than older people, and that the experiences children have shape them for the rest of their lives.

Life course theories are supported by research dating back more than half a century. During the 1930s, for example, **Sheldon** and **Eleanor Glueck** studied the life cycles of delinquent boys. The Gluecks followed the careers of known delinquents in an effort to identify the causes of delinquency. Data were originally collected through psychiatric interviews with subjects, parent and teacher reports, and via official records obtained from police, court, and correctional files. Surviving subjects were again interviewed between 1949 and 1965. The Gluecks found that family

Life course theories explanations for criminality that recognize that criminogenic influences have their greatest impact during the early stages of life, and hold that experiences which children have shape them for the rest of their lives.

Social capital the degree of positive relationships, with other persons and with social institutions, that individuals build up over the course of their lives.

Cohort analysis a social scientific technique which studies a population that shares common characteristics over time. Cohort analysis usually begins at birth and traces the development of cohort members until they reach a certain age.

Cohort a group of individuals sharing certain significant social characteristics in common, such as gender, time, and place of birth.

Evolutionary ecology an approach to understanding crime that draws attention to the ways people develop over the course of their lives.

dynamics played an especially significant role in the development of criminality, and observed that "the deeper the roots of childhood maladjustment, the smaller the chance of adult adjustment."[79] Delinquent careers, said the Gluecks, tend to carry over into adulthood and frequently lead to criminal careers.

A few years ago, **John Laub** and **Robert Sampson**[80] reanalyzed the data originally gathered by the Gluecks, and found that children who turn to delinquency are frequently those who have trouble at school and at home, and who have friends who are already involved in delinquency. Using a sophisticated computerized analysis of the Gluecks' original data, Laub and Sampson identified "turning points" in a criminal career. Turning points, they found, may occur at any time in such a career, although two especially significant turning points center on the choice of employment and marriage. Employers who are willing to give "troublemakers" a chance and marriage partners who insist on conventional lifestyles can successfully redirect the course of a budding offender's life, according to these authors. Laub and Sampson also developed the concept of **social capital** to refer to the degree of positive relationships with other persons and with social institutions, which individuals build up over the course of their lives. The greater one's social capital, the less the chance of criminal activity.[81]

Life course theory uses a developmental perspective in the study of criminal careers. As a consequence, life course researchers frequently use cohort analysis. **Cohort analysis** usually begins at birth and traces the development of a population whose members share common characteristics, until they reach a certain age. One well-known analysis of a birth **cohort,** undertaken by Marvin Wolfgang during the 1960s, found that a small nucleus of chronic juvenile offenders accounted for a disproportionately large share of all juvenile arrests.[82] Wolfgang studied male individuals born in Philadelphia in 1945 until they reached age 18. He concluded that a relatively small number of violent offenders were responsible for most of the crimes committed by the cohort. Eighteen percent of cohort members accounted for 52 percent of all arrests. A follow-up study found that seriousness of offenses among the cohort increased in adulthood, but that the actual number of offenses decreased as the cohort aged.[83] Wolfgang's analysis, which is also discussed in Chapter 4, has since been criticized for its lack of a second cohort, or control group, against which the experiences of the cohort under study could be compared.[84] More recently, Wolfgang published a cohort analysis of 5,000 individuals born in the Wuchang district of the city of Wuhan in China. The study, from which preliminary results were published in 1996, utilized Chinese-supplied data to compare delinquents with nondelinquents. It found "striking differences in school deportment, achieved level of education, school dropout rate, type of employment, and unemployment rate . . . ."[85] between the two groups.

The ecological perspective on crime control, pioneered by **Lawrence E. Cohen** and **Richard Machalek,**[86] provides a contemporary example of a life course approach. Like other life course theories, **evolutionary ecology** blends elements of previous perspectives—in this case building upon the approach of social ecology— while emphasizing developmental pathways encountered early in life. According to Bryan Vila, "the evolutionary ecological approach . . . draws attention to the ways people develop over the course of their lives. Experiences and environment early in life," says Vila, "especially those that affect child development and the transmission of biological traits and family management practices across generations, seem particular important."[87] According to Vila, evolutionary ecology "attempts to explain how people acquire criminality—a predisposition that disproportionately favors criminal behavior—when and why they express it as crime, how individuals and groups respond to those crimes, and how all these phenomena interact as a dynamic self-reinforcing system that evolves over time."[88]

One of the most comprehensive studies to date which has attempted to detail life pathways leading to criminality began in 1986. The study,[89] a cohort analysis, was sponsored by the U.S. Department of Justice's Office of Juvenile Justice and Delinquency Prevention (OJJDP), and is still producing results.[90] It compiled data on 4,500 youth from three distinct but coordinated projects: the Denver Youth Survey, conducted by the University of Colorado; the Pittsburgh Youth Study, undertaken by University of Pittsburgh researchers; and the Rochester Youth Development Study, fielded by professors at the State University of New York at Albany. The survey sampled youngsters at high risk for serious delinquency and drug use and found that (1) "the more seriously involved in drugs a youth was, the more seriously that juvenile was involved in delinquency," (2) "greater risks exist for violent offending when a child is physically abused or neglected early in life," (3) students who are not highly committed to school have higher rates of delinquency, (4) "poor family life exacerbates delinquency and drug use," and (5) affiliation with street gangs and illegal gun ownership are both predictive of delinquency. The study also found that "peers who were delinquent or used drugs had a great impact on [other] youth." Perhaps the most significant result of the study was the finding that three separate developmental pathways[91] to delinquency exist. The pathways identified by the study are

1. the *authority conflict pathway,* down which subjects appear to begin quite young (as early as 3 or 4 years of age). "The first step," said the study authors, "was stubborn behavior, followed by defiance around age 11, and authority avoidance—truancy, staying out late at night, or running away."
2. the *covert pathway,* which begins with "minor covert acts such as frequent lying and shoplifting, usually around age 10." Delinquents following this path quickly progress "to acts of property damage, such as firestarting or vandalism, around age 11 or 12, followed by moderate and serious forms of delinquency."
3. the *overt pathway,* in which the first step is marked by minor aggression such as "annoying others and bullying—around age 11 or 12." Bullying was found to escalate into "physical fighting and violence as the juvenile progressed along this pathway."

Another recent study that holds the potential to produce substantially significant results began in 1990. The Project on Human Development in Chicago Neighborhoods[92] is jointly sponsored by the National Institute of Justice and the John D. and Catherine T. MacArthur Foundation. Project directors describe their ongoing research as "the major criminologic investigation of this century." The study consists of a longitudinal analysis of how individuals, families, institutions, and communities evolve together, and is now "tracing how criminal behavior develops from birth to age 32." Researchers are planning to follow a total of 11,000 individuals in nine different age groups for eight years. Final project results are scheduled to be reported in 2002. A variety of study methodologies are being utilized, including self-reports, individualized tests and examinations, direct observation, the examination of existing records, and reports by informants. Researchers hope to provide answers to the following questions: (1) "How and why do antisocial and criminal behaviors originate?" (2) "What causes some individuals to continue those behaviors?" and (3) "How and why do some individuals cease law-violating behaviors while others continue?"

Life course theories often point to the need for early intervention through nurturant strategies that build self-control through positive socialization. As Vila points out, "[t]here are two main types of nurturant strategies: those that improve early life experiences to forestall the development of strategic styles based on criminality, and those that channel child and adolescent development in an effort to improve the match between individuals and their environment."[93] Nurturant crime control strategies are discussed in more detail in Chapter 13.

■■ SOCIAL CONTROL THEORIES

CONTAINMENT THEORY

In the 1950s, another student of the Chicago school, **Walter C. Reckless,** wrote *The Crime Problem*.[94] Reckless tackled head-on the realization that most sociological theories, although conceptually enlightening, offered less than perfect predictability. That is, they lacked the ability to predict precisely which individuals, even those exposed to various "causes" of crime, would become criminal. Reckless thought that the sociological perspectives prevalent at the time offered only half of a comprehensive theoretical framework. Crime, Reckless wrote, was the consequence of social pressures to involve one's self in violations of the law, as well as of failure to resist such pressures. Reckless called his approach **containment theory,** and he compared it with a biological immune response, saying that only some people exposed to a disease actually come down with it. Sickness, like crime, Reckless avowed, results from the failure of control mechanisms—some internal to the person, and others external. In the case of sickness, external failures might include unsanitary conditions, the failure of the public health service, the lack of availability of preventative medicine, or the lack of knowledge necessary to make such medicine effective. Still, disease would not result unless the individual's resistance to disease-causing organisms was low, or unless the individual was in some other way weak or susceptible to the disease.

In the case of crime, Reckless wrote, external containment consists of "the holding power of the group." Under most circumstances, Reckless said, "[t]he society, the state, the tribe, the village, the family, and other nuclear groups are able to hold the individual within the bounds of the accepted norms and expectations." In addition to setting limits, Reckless saw society as providing individuals with meaningful roles and activities. Such roles were seen as an important factor of *external containment.*

Containment theory a form of control theory which suggests that a series of both internal and external factors contribute to law-abiding behavior.

Inner containment, said Reckless, "represents the ability of the person to follow the expected norms, to direct himself." Such ability was said to be enhanced by a positive self-image, a focus on socially approved goals, personal aspirations that are in line with reality, a good tolerance for frustration, and a general adherence to the norms and values of society. A person with a positive self-concept can avoid the temptations of crime simply by thinking, "I'm not that kind of person." A focus on approved goals helps keep one on the proverbial straight and narrow path. "Aspirations in line with reality" are simply realistic desires. In other words, if one seriously desires to be the richest person in the world, disappointment will probably result. Even when aspirations are reasonable, however, disappointments will occur—hence the need for a tolerance for frustration. Adherence to the norms and values of the larger society are a basic component of inner containment and a kind of capstone factor.

Reckless's containment theory is diagrammed in Figure 7.3. "Pushes toward crime" represents those factors in an individual's background that might propel him or her into criminal behavior. They include a criminogenic background or upbringing that involves participation in a delinquent subculture, deprivation, biological propensities toward deviant behavior, and psychological maladjustment. "Pulls toward crime" signifies all the perceived rewards crime may offer, including financial gain, sexual satisfaction, and higher status. "**Containment**" is a stabilizing force and, if effective, blocks such pushes and pulls from leading the individual toward crime.

Reckless believed that inner containment was far more effective than external containment in preventing law violations. In his words, "[a]s social relations become more impersonal, as society becomes more diverse and alienated, as people participate more and more for longer periods of time away from a home base, the self becomes more and more important as a controlling agent."

Containment theory was one of the first social control theories to be proposed. Social control approaches argue that social institutions exercise considerable control over individuals, either directly (as in the case of external containment) or indirectly, perhaps through socialization (as in the case of inner containment). **Social control theory** predicts that when social constraints on antisocial behavior are weakened or absent, delinquent behavior will tend to emerge. Rather than stressing causative factors in criminal behavior, however, social control theories tend to ask why people actually obey rules instead of breaking them.[95]

Containment those aspects of the social bond which act to prevent individuals from committing crimes and keep them from engaging in deviance.

Social control theory a perspective which predicts that when social constraints on antisocial behavior are weakened or absent, delinquent behavior emerges. Rather than stressing causative factors in criminal behavior, control theory asks why people actually obey rules instead of breaking them.

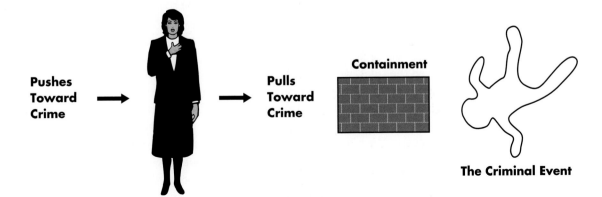

FIGURE 7.3   A diagrammatic representation of containment theory.

SOCIAL BOND THEORY

Social bond the rather intangible link between individuals and the society of which they are a part; created through the process of socialization.

Another form of control theory was popularized by **Travis Hirschi** in his 1969 book *Causes of Delinquency.*[96] Hirschi argued that, through successful socialization, a bond forms between individuals and the social group. When that bond is weakened or broken, deviance and crime may result. Hirschi described four components of the **social bond:** attachment, commitment, involvement, and belief.

In his writings Hirschi cites the psychopath as an example of a person whose attachment to society is nearly nonexistent.[97] Other relatively normal individuals may find their attachment to society loosened through "[t]he process of becoming alienated from others [which] often involves or is based on active interpersonal conflict. Such conflict could easily supply," says Hirschi, "a reservoir of socially derived hostility sufficient to account for the aggressiveness of those whose attachments to others have been weakened."

The second component of the social bond—commitment—reflects a person's investment of time and energies into conforming behavior and the potential loss of rewards that he or she has already gained from that behavior. In Hirschi's words, "[t]he idea, then, is that the person invests time, energy, himself, in a certain line of activity—say, getting an education, building up a business, acquiring a reputation for virtue. Whenever he considers deviant behavior, he must consider the costs of this deviant behavior, the risk he runs of losing the investment he has made in conventional behavior." For such a traditionally successful person, says Hirschi, "a ten-dollar-holdup is stupidity," because the potential for losing what has already been acquired through commitment to social norms far exceeds what stands to be gained. Recognizing that his approach applies primarily to individuals who have been successfully socialized into conventional society, Hirschi adds, "[t]he concept of commitment assumes that the organization of society is such that the interests of most persons would be endangered if they were to engage in criminal acts."

Involvement, for Hirschi, means "engrossment in conventional activities" and is similar to Reckless's concept of meaningful roles. In explaining the importance of involvement in determining conformity, Hirschi cites the colloquial saying that "idle hands are the devil's workshop." Time and energy, he says, are limited, and, if a person is busy at legitimate pursuits, he or she will have little opportunity for crime and deviance.

Belief, the last of Hirschi's four aspects of the social bond, sets his control theory apart from subcultural approaches. Hirschi says that unlike subcultural theory, "control theory assumes the existence of a common value system within the society or group whose norms are being violated . . . . We not only assume the deviant has believed the rules, we assume he believes the rules even as he violates them." How can a person simultaneously believe it is wrong to commit a crime and still commit it? Hirschi's answer is that "[m]any persons do not have an attitude of respect toward the rules of society." That is, although they know the rules exist, they basically do not care. They invest little of their sense of self in moral standards.

In 1990 Hirschi, in collaboration with **Michael R. Gottfredson,** proposed a general theory of crime based on the concepts advanced earlier in control theory.[98] Gottfredson and Hirschi began by asking "What is crime?" Nearly all crimes, they concluded, are mundane, simple, trivial, easy acts aimed at satisfying desires of the moment. Hence, their general theory built on a classical or rational-choice perspective; that is, the belief that crime is a natural consequence of unrestrained human tendencies to seek pleasure and avoid pain. Crime, said Gottfredson and Hirschi, is little more than a subset of general deviant behavior. Hence, they concluded, crime bears little resemblance to the explanations offered in the media, by law enforcement officials, or by most academic thinkers on the subject.

According to Gottfredson and Hirschi, the offender is neither the diabolical genius of fiction nor the ambitious seeker of the American Dream often portrayed by other social scientists. On the contrary, offenders appear to have little control over their own desires. When personal desires conflict with long-term interests, those who lack self-control often opt for the desires of the moment, thus contravening legal restrictions and becoming involved in crime.[99] Central to Gottfredson and Hirschi's thesis is the belief that a well-developed social bond will result in the creation of effective mechanisms of self-control. As others have noted: "For Gottfredson and Hirschi, self-control is the key concept in the explanation of all forms of crime as well as other types of behavior. Indeed, they believe that all current differences in rates of crime between groups and categories may be explained by differences in the management of self-control."[100]

▪▪ POLICY IMPLICATIONS

Theoretical approaches which fault the social environment as the root cause of crime point in the direction of social action as a panacea. In the 1930s, for example, Clifford Shaw, in an effort to put his theories into practice, established the Chicago Area Project. The Chicago Area Project attempted to reduce social disorganization in slum neighborhoods through the creation of community committees. Shaw staffed committees with local residents rather than professional social workers. The project had three broad objectives: (1) improving the physical appearance of poor neighborhoods, (2) providing recreational opportunities for youth, and (3) involving project members directly in the lives of troubled youth through school and courtroom mediation. The program also made use of "curbside counselors," streetwise workers who could serve as positive role models for inner-city youth. Although no effective assessment programs were established to evaluate the Chicago Area Project during the program's tenure, Rand Corporation reviewers in 1984 provided a fifty-year review of the program declaring it "effective in reducing rates of juvenile delinquency."[101]

Similarly, Mobilization for Youth, cited earlier in this chapter as an outgrowth of Cloward and Ohlin's theory of differential opportunity, provides a bold example of the treatment implications of social-structural theories. Mobilization for Youth sought not only to provide new opportunities, but also through direct social action to change the fundamental arrangements of society and thereby address the root causes of crime and deviance. Leaders of Mobilization for Youth decided that "[w]hat was needed to overcome . . . formidable barriers to opportunity . . . was not community organization but community action" that attacked entrenched political interests. Accordingly, MFY promoted "boycotts against schools, protests against welfare policies, rent strikes against 'slum landlords,' lawsuits to ensure poor people's rights, and voter registration."[102] A truly unusual government-sponsored program for its time, Mobilization for Youth was eventually disbanded amid protests that "the mandate of the President's Committee was to reduce delinquency, not to reform urban society or to try out sociological theories on American youths."[103]

A contemporary example of social intervention efforts based on sociological theories can be had in Targeted Outreach,[104] a program now operated by Boys and Girls Clubs of America. The club program had its origins in the 1972 implementation of a youth development strategy based on studies undertaken at the University of Colorado which showed that at-risk youths could be effectively diverted from the juvenile justice system through the provision of positive alternatives. Utilizing a wide referral network made up of local schools, police departments, and various youth service agencies, club officials work to end what they call the "inappropriate detention of juveniles." The program, in its current form, recruits at-risk youngsters—many as young as 7 years old—and diverts them into activities that are intended to promote a sense of belonging, competence, usefulness, and self-control. A sense of belonging is fostered through clubs that provide familiar settings where individuals are accepted. Competence and usefulness are developed through the provision of opportunities for meaningful activities which young people in the club program can successfully undertake. Finally, Targeted Outreach provides its youthful participants with a chance to be heard and, consequently, with the opportunity to influence decisions affecting their future.

To date, Targeted Outreach has served more than 10,000 at-risk youths, although it currently operates through only three local clubs. Plans are for Targeted Outreach to eventually involve more than 1.5 million youngsters between the ages of 7 and 17.

Mobilization for Youth and Targeted Outreach both stand as examples of the kinds of programs that theorists who focus on the social environment typically seek to implement. Social programs of this sort are intended to change the cultural conditions and societal arrangements which are thought to lead people into crime.

KIDS DISOBEY, PARENTS PAY

NEW LAWS DEMAND MORE ACCOUNTABILITY

Huntington, W. Va.—Because her 8-year-old daughter missed 59 days of school, Eva Wilkenson is serving 100 days in jail.

Wilkenson complains that Cabell County Judge L. D. Egnor put her in jail, and her three kids in foster care, to "make an example of me." And the judge doesn't deny he'd like Wilkenson's sentence to scare others.

But what Wilkenson's case may most exemplify is the nation's growing appetite for parental accountability laws.

In a twist on the biblical axiom, these laws visit the sins of the children upon their parents. They make parents

Doing Time: Eva Wilkenson, serving 100 days in a Huntington, W. Va., jail after her daughter missed 59 days of school. Do you agree with the policy of jailing parents for the misdeeds of their children? *Michele Katz/Herald-Dispatch.*

pay—with fines, community service, even jail time—for truancy, vandalism or other misbehavior of children.

Many laws have been on the books for years—100 years, in West Virginia's case. But they're being beefed up, or enforced more vigorously, because other attempts at correcting kids—and parents—don't seem to work.

The crackdown "is very favorably received," says Judge Michael Conese, who since January 1993 has hauled 206 parents of truants into Hamilton, Ohio, municipal court. "People know some parents aren't doing their job, and they have no tolerance."

Nationwide, a range of accountability laws have been passed or proposed:

- In Effingham, Ill., Wednesday, a county judge sentenced Tammy Campe to 12 months probation, 25 hours of community service and $150 in fines for not insisting that her two children go to school.
- In Los Angeles Tuesday night, the city council debated bringing juvenile graffiti "taggers" to court where they'd be spanked with wooden paddles by their parents. The council rejected the notion, "but the fact it was even on the agenda shows people are looking for answers," says Ronald Stephens, an expert on youth issues.
- In the Chicago suburb of Richton Park, Ill., under an ordinance passed in January, parents can be sentenced to as much as $500 in fines and 160 hours of community service—including manual labor—if their children break truancy, curfew, liquor possession and vandalism laws.
- In Honolulu, if a student misses even four hours of school, the police chief may summon parent and child to a special class—and if they don't

attend, the case can go to juvenile court.

- In a dozen states, welfare payments can be docked if kids are truant.

These laws are increasingly popular because "the general public is frustrated with the vandalism, the violence, the lack of social responsibility," says Stephens, who directs Pepperdine University's National School Safety Center. "They're going back to the primary source of control of youngsters . . . the parents."

In Wilkenson's case, school officials cite a 5-year record of truancy problems with her three daughters: the 8-year-old, and 14-year-old twins.

Despite repeated efforts—including getting Wilkenson to sign a contract that her daughters would attend school—officials say the girls frequently were absent, or arrived with head lice.

Early in May, Egnor took one 14-year-old away from Wilkenson after the girl missed 55 school days, and put her in the custody of state social services. On May 11—after 59 absences for the 8-year-old, and 35 for the other 14-year-old—Egnor put those two girls in state custody, and Wilkenson in jail.

Under West Virginia's compulsory attendance law, the parent can be sentenced to up to 20 days in jail for each day of school missed by the child.

"There are some who think we're the scum of the earth for putting this lady in jail, and others who support it," says Bennie Thomas, Cabell County attendance director. "We're not out to get anybody—but we mean for kids to be at school."

When the judge sentenced her, Wilkenson says, "My heart dropped out. And when he said the kids was taken away . . . that's punishing me twice."

Interviewed in jail during her third week there, Wilkenson still seemed stunned: "My lawyer told me I'd never see the inside of a jail."

She acknowledges that her kids sometimes "didn't care whether they went to school." But she insists, "This will not happen ever again. My kids tell me, 'Mommy, we'll go to school every day'" if the judge lets them all go home.

Egnor says he might do that, if Wilkenson uses work-release from jail to clean her house, which her lawyer Keith Newman calls "filthy."

At a hearing June 27, Egnor will review Wilkenson's progress, and consider a request to reduce her sentence and return her kids.

Egnor had received scores of letters and calls, most supporting Wilkenson's jailing: "People are saying, 'It's about time somebody did something serious.'"

Questions

1. Do you believe that parents should be held responsible for the behavior of their underage children? Why or why not?
2. What do you think will be the future of parental accountability laws? Will more jurisdictions pass them? Why or why not?

Source: Patricia Edmonds, "Kids Disobey, Parents Pay," *USA Today,* June 3, 1994, p. 3A. Copyright 1994, *USA Today.* Reprinted with permission.

⠶ CRITIQUE OF SOCIAL-STRUCTURAL THEORIES

Social-structural theories suffer from one general shortcoming that similarly affects most other perspectives on crime causation. In the words of Canadian criminologist Gwynn Nettler, "the conceptual bias of social scientists emphasizes environments—cultures and structures—as the powerful causes of differential conduct. This bias places an intellectual taboo on looking elsewhere for possible causes as, for example, in physiologies. This taboo is . . . strongly applied against the possibility that ethnic groups may have genetically transmitted differential physiologies that have relevance for social behavior."[105]

Nettler is telling us that social scientists downplay the causative role of nonsociological factors. Many believe that such factors are important. But, since sociological theorizing has captured the lion's share of academic attention over the past few decades, the role of other causative factors in the etiology of criminal behavior stand in danger of being shortchanged.

Social-structural approaches also suffer from a seeming inability to explain the behavior of many, even though they may appear applicable to a few. Moreover, some see the inability of social-structural theories to predict which individuals—or at least what proportion of a given population—will turn to crime, as a crucial failure of such perspectives. Although the large majority of persons growing up in inner-city poverty-ridden areas, for example, probably experience an inequitable opportunity structure firsthand, only a relatively small number of those people become criminal. It is true that substantially more people living under such conditions may become criminal than those living in other types of social environments. Nonetheless, a large proportion of persons experiencing strain, as well as a large number of persons raised in deviant subcultures, will still embrace noncriminal lifestyles.

In his book *The Moral Sense,* James Q. Wilson suggests that most people—regardless of socialization experiences and the structural aspects of their social circumstances—may still carry within themselves an inherent sense of fairness and interpersonal morality.[106] If what Wilson suggests is even partially true, then the explanatory power of social-structural theories will inevitably be limited by human nature itself.

SUMMARY

⠶

Sociological theories suggest that the causes of crime lie in the structural arrangements of society and in the way in which social institutions communicate their values to group members. Overall, the concept of subcultures plays an especially important role in sociological theorizing. Even those perspectives that do not speak directly of organized subcultures seem to recognize their significance. Sociological theories also build on the notion that crime is learned in association with others through the process of communication, and that it may result from blocked opportunities for achieving success.

Because sociological theories look to the organization of society for their explanatory power, intervention strategies based on them typically argue for the modification of formal or informal group processes—including the educational process and familial and work arrangements—and to the increased availability of legitimate opportunity structures. Social programs may be created under the exegesis of particular sociological theories, such as the Chicago Area Project or Mobilization for Youth.

WEB WATCH

Access the *Criminology Today* home page on the World Wide Web by pointing your browser at www.prenhall.com/cjcentral. Once there, click on *Criminology Today* in order to access the wealth of electronic resources supporting this text.

Onsite resources include (1) "Chapter Links," which provides succinct overviews of critical ideas from the textbook and links selected materials from around the Web to concepts found in the text; (2) "General Reference—Law and Justice Links." Organized by chapter, these links lead to other useful resources on the World Wide Web, such as libraries, electronic discussion lists, and electronic journals; (3) "Criminology Sites on the Web," which lists links to organizations such as the American Society of Criminology and the National Organization for Victims Assistance (NOVA), as well as crime prevention links and statistics on crime and justice. Many other Web-based resources can be accessed via the *Criminology Today* site, including the federal Justice Information Center, the Bureau of Justice Statistics, the FBI, the RAND Corporation, the Vera Institute of Justice, PAVNET (an online "Partnership Against Violence," run by seven different federal agencies), and the National White Collar Crime Center.

Still another feature of the *Criminology Today* Web site is e-mail homework. Homework can be composed onsite and submitted to instructors using the instructor's e-mail address. To use the e-mail homework feature, click on "E-Mail Homework" on the opening page, and then type answers to the questions that appear in the spaces provided. Use your instructor's e-mail address to submit homework answers. The *Criminology Today* Web site also provides links to powerful Web-based search engines that can help you find topics of interest to you as you progress through your course of study. Search engines can be found under the home page heading "Criminology Sites on the Web."

DISCUSSION QUESTIONS

⬛

1. This book emphasizes a social problems versus social responsibility theme. Which of the theoretical perspectives discussed in this chapter best support the social problems approach? Which support the social responsibility approach? Why?
2. Do you believe ecological theories have a valid place in contemporary criminological thinking? Why or why not?
3. How, if at all, does the notion of a "criminology of place" differ from more traditional ecological theories? Do you see the criminology of place approach as capable of offering anything new over traditional approaches? If so, what?
4. What is a violent subculture? Why do some subcultures stress violence? How might participants in a subculture of violence be turned toward less aggressive ways?
5. Compare and contrast the theories discussed in this chapter, citing differences and similarities between and among them. How, for example, does Reckless's notion of containment differ from Hirschi's idea of a social bond? How is it similar?
6. What policy implications do you think the theories discussed in this chapter hold? What kinds of changes in society and in government policy might be based on the theories discussed here? Would they be likely to bring about a reduction in crime?

NOTES

⬛

[1] Frank Tannenbaum, *Crime and the Community* (Boston: Ginn and Company, 1938), p. 25.

[2] Albert K. Cohen, *Delinquent Boys: The Culture of the Gang* (Glencoe, Ill.: Free Press, 1955).

[3] "L.A.: Waiting on a Razor's Edge," *Newsweek,* March 29, 1993, p. 28.

[4] "Nation, Town 'Shocked' by Slaying," *USA Today,* August 18, 1993, p. 1A.

[5] "Hometown Paints a Portrait of Pain," *Fayetteville Observer-Times,* August 15, 1993, p. 1A.

[6] Ibid., p. 4A.

[7] Edwin M. Lemert, *Social Pathology,* (New York: McGraw-Hill, 1951), p. 3.

[8] For an excellent contemporary review of measuring the extent of social disorganization, see Barbara D. Warner and Glenn L. Pierce, "Reexamining Social Disorganization Theory Using Calls to the Police as a Measure of Crime," *Criminology,* vol. 31, no. 4 (November 1993), pp. 493–513.

[9] Lemert, *Social Pathology* p. 7.

[10] Peter Haggett, "Human Ecology," in Alan Bullock and Oliver Stallybrass, eds., *The Fontana Dictionary of Modern Social Thought* (London: Fontana, 1977), p. 187.

[11] W. I. Thomas and Florian Znaniecki, *The Polish Peasant in Europe and America* (Boston: Gorham, 1920).

[12] Clifford R. Shaw, et al., *Delinquency Areas* (Chicago: University of Chicago Press, 1929).

[13] David Matza, *Becoming Deviant* (Englewood Cliffs, N.J.: Prentice Hall, 1969).

[14] W. S. Robinson, "Ecological Correlation and the Behavior of Individuals," *American Sociological Review,* vol. 15, (1950), pp. 351–357.

[15] Ibid.

[16]Robert J. Bursik, "Social Disorganization and Theories of Crime and Delinquency: Problems and Prospects," *Criminology,* vol. 26, no. 4 (1988), p. 519.

[17]Stephen J. Pfohl, *Images of Deviance and Social Control* (New York: McGraw-Hill, 1985), p. 167.

[18]Thorsten Sellin, *Culture Conflict and Crime* (New York: Social Science Research Council, 1938).

[19]Rick Hampson, "Danish Mom Finds New York Doesn't Kid Around," *USA Today,* May 14, 1997, p. 3A.

[20]Although the practice may seem strange to Americans, the author, while teaching in Iceland, saw firsthand lines of unattended infants bundled into strollers awaiting their parents outside of restaurants and sports centers. The practice seems especially prevalent in Scandinavian countries, where the threat of child abduction is virtually unknown.

[21]Sellin, p. 68.

[22]Frederick M. Thrasher, *The Gang* (Chicago: University of Chicago Press, 1927).

[23]William F. Whyte, *Street Corner Society: The Social Structure of an Italian Slum* (Chicago: University of Chicago Press, 1943).

[24]Walter Miller, "Lower Class Culture as a Generating Milieu of Gang Delinquency," *Journal of Social Issues,* vol. 14, no. 3 (1958), pp. 5–19.

[25]Ibid., p. 19.

[26]Ibid., p. 8.

[27]Ibid., p. 9.

[28]Gresham Sykes and David Matza, "Techniques of Neutralization: A Theory of Delinquency," *American Sociological Review,* vol. 22 (December 1957), pp. 664–670.

[29]Ibid.

[30]Robert Agnew, "The Techniques of Neutralization and Violence," *Criminology,* vol. 32, no. 4 (1994), pp. 555–580.

[31]Ibid.

[32]Franco Ferracuti and Marvin Wolfgang, *The Subculture of Violence: Toward an Integrated Theory of Criminology* (London: Tavistock, 1967).

[33]Frank P. Williams III and Marilyn D. McShane, *Criminological Theory* (Englewood Cliffs, N.J.: Prentice Hall, 1988), p. 79.

[34]Ferracuti and Wolfgang, *The Subculture of Violence,* p. 151.

[35]Ibid.

[36]For an excellent review of the literature, see F. Frederick Hawley, "The Southern Violence Construct: A Skeleton in the Criminological Closet," paper presented at the annual meeting of the American Society of Criminology, 1988.

[37]Bertram Wyatt-Brown, *Southern Honor: Ethics and Behavior in the Old South* (Oxford: Oxford University Press, 1983).

[38]Hawley, "The Southern Violence Construct," p. 27.

[39]"Suspect's Mom Convicted of Shooting at Reporters," *The Fayetteville Observer-Times,* September 29, 1993, p. 1A.

[40]Margaret Anderson, "Review Essay: Rape Theories, Myths, and Social Change," *Contemporary Crises,* vol. 5 (1983), p. 237.

[41]Emile Durkheim, *Suicide: A Study in Sociology* (New York: Free Press, 1897); reprinted and translated in 1951.

[42]Robert K. Merton, "Social Structure and Anomie," *American Sociological Review,* vol. 3 (October 1938), pp. 672–682; and Robert K. Merton, *Social Theory and Social Structure,* rev. ed. (New York: Free Press, 1957).

[43]Robert Merton, *Social Theory and Social Structure* (New York: Glencoe, 1957), p. 190.

[44]Steven F. Messner and Richard Rosenfeld, *Crime and the American Dream* (Belmont, Calif.: Wadsworth, 1994), p. 68.

[45]Richard A. Cloward and Lloyd E. Ohlin, *Delinquency and Opportunity: A Theory of Delinquent Gangs* (Glencoe, Ill.: Free Press, 1960).

[46]Ibid., p. 7.

[47]Ibid., p. 13.

[48]Ibid., p. 16.

[49]Ibid., p. 19.

[50]Ibid., p. 3.

[51]Ibid., p. 37.

[52]Ibid., pp. 12–13.

[53]Stephen J. Pfohl, *Images of Deviance and Social Control,* pp. 224–225.

[54]Cohen, *Delinquent Boys: The Culture of the Gang.*

[55]Ibid., p. 13.

[56]Donald J. Shoemaker, *Theories of Delinquency: An Examination of Explanations of Delinquent Behavior* (New York: Oxford University Press, 1984), p. 102, citing Cohen.

[57]Cohen, *Delinquent Boys,* p. 121.

[58]Shoemaker, *Theories of Delinquency,* p. 105.

[59]G. David Curry, Richard A. Ball, and Robert J. Fox, "Gang Crime and Law Enforcement Recordkeeping," National Institute of Justice, April 1994.

[60]G. David Curry, Richard A. Ball, and Scott H. Decker, "Estimating the National Scope of Gang Crime from Law Enforcement Data," National Institute of Justice, August 1996.

[61]National Gang Crime Research Center, *Achieving Justice and Reversing the Problem of Gang Crime and Gang Violence in America Today: Preliminary Results of the Project Gangfact Study* (Chicago: National Gang Crime Research Center, 1996).

[62]*Criminal Justice Newsletter,* vol. 19, no. 19 (October 3, 1988), p. 2.

[63]Telephone conversation with the Street Crimes Unit, Lost Angeles County Sheriff's Department, June 20, 1995.

[64]Ibid.

[65]Paul Demuro, Anne Demuro, and Steven Lerner, *Reforming the California Youth Authority: How to End Crowding, Diversify Treatments, and Protect the Public—Without Spending More Money* (Bolinas, Calif.: Commonweal Research Institute, 1988).

[66]Carl Rogers, "Children in Gangs," *Criminal Justice 1993–94* (Guilford, Conn.: Dushkin Publishing, 1993), pp. 197–199.

[67]"Youths Match Power, Fear, Guns," *Fayetteville Observer-Times,* September 6, 1993, p. 2A.

[68]G. David Curry and Irving A. Spergel, "Gang Homicide, Delinquency, and Community," *Criminology,* vol. 26, no. 3 (1988), pp. 381–405.

[69]Ibid., p. 401.

[70]Finn-Aage Esbensen, "A National Gang Strategy," in J. Mitchell Miller and Jeffrey P. Rush, eds., *Gangs: A Criminal Justice Approach* (Cincinnati: Anderson, 1996).

[71]See Mary H. Glazier, a review of J. Mitchell Miller and Jeffrey P. Rush, eds., *Gangs: A Criminal Justice Approach* (Cincinnati: Anderson, 1996), in *The Criminologist,* July/April 1996, p. 29.

[72]Robert Agnew, "Foundation for a General Strain Theory of Crime and Delinquency," *Criminology,* vol. 30, no. 1 (1992), pp. 47–87.

[73]Ibid., p. 60.

[74]Raymond Paternoster and Paul Mazerolle, "General Strain Theory and Delinquency: A Replication and Extension," *Journal of Research in Crime and Delinquency,* vol. 31, no. 3 (1994), pp. 235–263.

[75]Robert Agnew and Helene Raskin White, "An Empirical Test of General Strain Theory," *Criminology,* vol. 30, no. 4 (1992), pp. 475–499.

[76]Robert Agnew, "Foundation for a General Strain Theory of Crime and Delinquency," *Criminology,* vol. 30 (February 1992), pp. 47–87.

[77]Ibid.

[78]Travis Hirschi, "Review of Delbert S. Elliott, David Huizinga, and Suzanne S. Ageton, *Explaining Delinquency and Drug Use*" (Beverly Hills, Calif.: Sage, 1985), in *Criminology,* vol. 25, no. 1 (February 1987), p. 195.

[79]Sheldon and Eleanor Glueck, *Delinquents and Nondelinquents in Perspective* (Cambridge, Mass.: Harvard University Press, 1968).

[80]John H. Laub and Robert J. Sampson, "Turning Points in the Life Course: Why Change Matters to the Study of Crime," *Criminology,* vol. 31, no. 3 (1993), pp. 301–325. See also, Robert J. Sampson and John H. Laub, "Crime and Deviance in the Life Course," *Annual Review of Sociology,* vol. 18 (1992), pp. 63–84.

[81]Robert J. Sampson and John H. Laub, *Crime in the Making* (Cambridge, Mass.: Harvard University Press, 1993).

[82]Marvin Wolfgang, Robert Figlio, and Thorsten Sellin, *Delinquency in a Birth Cohort* (Chicago: University of Chicago Press, 1972).

[83]Marvin Wolfgang, Terence Thornberry, and Robert Figlio, *From Boy to Man, From Delinquency to Crime* (Chicago: University of Chicago Press, 1987).

[84]Steven P. Lab, "Analyzing Change in Crime and Delinquency Rates: The Case for Cohort Analysis," *Criminal Justice Research Bulletin,* vol. 3, no. 10 (Huntsville, Texas: Sam Houston State University, 1988), p. 2.

[85]Marvin Wolfgang, "Delinquency in China: Study of a Birth Cohort," National Institute of Justice Research Preview, NIJ, May 1996.

[86]Lawrence E. Cohen and Richard Machalek, "A General Theory of Expropriative Crime: An Evolutionary Ecological Approach," *American Journal of Sociology,* vol. 94, no. 3 (1988), pp. 465–501; and Lawrence E. Cohen and Richard Machalek, "The Normalcy of Crime: From Durkheim to Evolutionary Ecology," *Rationality and Society,* vol. 6 (1994), pp. 286–308.

[87]Bryan Vila, "Human Nature and Crime Control: Improving the Feasibility of Nurturant Strategies," *Politics and the Life Sciences,* March 1997, pp. 3–21.

[88]Ibid.

[89]See Stuart Greenbaum, "Drugs, Delinquency, and Other Data," in *Juvenile Justice,* vol. 2, no. 1 (Spring/Summer 1994), pp. 2–8.

[90]The study, named the "Causes and Correlates of Delinquency," is being conducted by Terence P. Thornberry from the Rochester Youth Development Study at the University of Albany (NY), Rolf Loeber from the Pittsburgh Youth Study at the University of Pittsburgh, and David Huizinga from the Denver Youth Survey at the University of Colorado.

[91]For another interesting analysis, see Robert J. Sampson and John H. Laub, *Crime in the Making* (Cambridge, Mass.: Harvard University Press, 1993).

[92]See Felton J. Earls and Albert J. Reiss, *Breaking the Cycle: Predicting and Preventing Crime* (Washington, D.C.: National Institute of Justice, 1994).

[93]Vila, p. 10.

[94]Walter C. Reckless, *The Crime Problem,* 4th ed. (New York: Appleton-Century-Crofts, 1967).

[95]For a good overview of social control approaches, see George S. Bridges and Martha Myers, eds., *Inequality, Crime, and Social Control* (Boulder, Col.: Westview Press, 1994).

[96]Travis Hirschi, *Causes of Delinquency* (Berkeley: University of California Press, 1969).

[97]Ibid.

[98]Michael Gottfredson and Travis Hirschi, *A General Theory of Crime* (Stanford, Calif.: Stanford University Press, 1990).

[99]See also Michael R. Gottfredson and Travis Hirschi, "Criminality and Low Self-Control," in John E. Conklin, ed., *New Perspectives in Criminology* (Boston: Allyn and Bacon, 1996).

[100]Werner Einstadter and Stuart Henry, *Criminological Theory: An Analysis of Its Underlying Assumptions* (Fort Worth: Harcourt Brace, 1995), p. 189.

[101]Steven Schlossman et al., *Delinquency Prevention in South Chicago: A Fifty-Year Assessment of the Chicago Area Project* (Santa Monica, Calif.: Rand Corporation, 1984).

[102]J. Robert Lilly, Francis T. Cullen, and Richard A. Ball, *Criminological Theory: Context and Consequences* (Newbury Park, Calif.: Sage, 1989), p. 80.

[103]Lamar T. Empey, *American Delinquency: Its Meaning and Construction* (Homewood, Ill.: Dorsey, 1982), p. 243.

[104]Robert W. Sweet, Jr., "Preserving Families to Prevent Delinquency," *Office of Juvenile Justice and Delinquency Prevention Model Programs 1990* (Washington, D.C.: U.S. Department of Justice, April 1992).

[105]Gwynn Nettler, *Killing One Another* (Cincinnati: Anderson, 1982), p. 54.

[106]James Q. Wilson, *The Moral Sense* (New York: The Free Press, 1993).

CHAPTER 8

THE MEANING OF CRIME—

SOCIAL PROCESS PERSPECTIVES

It's like it ain't so much what a fellow does, but it's the way the majority of folks is looking at him when he does it.

—WILLIAM FAULKNER[1]

Plainly, it is of crucial importance that we distinguish between the meaning of the act to the actor . . . and its meaning to us as scientists.

—ABRAHAM KAPLAN[2]

Deviation is criminal only if effectively reacted to and symbolized as such.

—EDWIN M. LEMERT[3]

The stigmatized and the normal are part of each other; if one can prove vulnerable, it must be expected that the other can too.

—ERVING GOFFMAN[4]

⊞ CHAPTER OUTLINE ⊞

INTRODUCTION
MAJOR PRINCIPLES OF SOCIAL PROCESS PERSPECTIVES
SOCIAL PROCESS PERSPECTIVES
    The Group Perspective: Labeling
    Reintegrative Shaming
    Dramaturgy
    Phenomenology
    Victimology: The Study of the Victim
    Policy Implications
SUMMARY

⇐ IMPORTANT NAMES ⇒

Frank Tannenbaum	Edwin M. Lemert	Howard Becker
John Braithwaite	Erving Goffman	Stanton Samenow
Samuel Yochelson	Hans von Hentig	Benjamin Mendelsohn
Richard Quinney	Margaret Fry	Stephen Schafer
Henry Ellenberger	Marvin E. Wolfgang	Stuart Henry
Dragan Milovanovic		

⇐ IMPORTANT TERMS ⇒

tagging	primary deviance	secondary deviance
labeling	moral enterprise	stigmatic shaming
reintegrative shaming	dramaturgical perspective	constitutive criminology
impression management	discrediting information	victimology
phenomenology	social process theories	victimogenesis
victim-proneness	penal couple	total institutions
postcrime victimization	VOCA	victim impact
restitution	OJJDP	statement
victim–witness	victim-precipitated	phenomenological
assistance programs	criminal homicide	criminology
interactionist perspectives		

⊞ INTRODUCTION

In late 1993 James Hamm found himself at the center of a vicious controversy. Hamm, a convicted murderer, had served eighteen years in prison for shooting a man in the head over a drug deal gone bad and was about to enter the Arizona State University school of law. Hamm had been paroled in June 1992 after Arizona's parole board judged him "rehabilitated." While in prison Hamm, a former divinity student, earned a bachelor's degree in sociology and had been active in Middle

Ground, a prisoner rights group. While the 45-year-old Hamm worked on getting an education, students at the university were challenging his access to law school, saying that a convicted murderer did not deserve to be admitted. Mark Killian, the Arizona Republican house speaker, claimed, "There are a lot of hard-working young people out there who could not get into law school because he did."[5] Members of the Arizona Board of Regents, which runs the state's public universities, called for a review of policies on admitting ex-convicts to the schools. Nonetheless, Hamm, who scored in the top 5 percent of all applicants taking the law school admissions test nationwide, seemed to hold excellent promise as a student. In Hamm's words, the controversy surrounding him "touches on feelings about crime, criminals, recidivism, the failure of the criminal justice system. . . .[6] I'm a lightning rod for those feelings," he said.

The case of James Hamm provides an example of how society's continued reaction to what it defines as criminal behavior can change the course of an offender's life—often for the worse—even after he has paid his "dues." As a certain professor liked to say, while there are plenty of ex-cons, there is no such thing as an "ex-ex-con." Or "once a con, always a con." Society, it seems, never forgets.

▟ MAJOR PRINCIPLES OF SOCIAL PROCESS PERSPECTIVES

This brief section serves to summarize the central features of social process theories of crime causation. Each of these points can be found elsewhere in this chapter, where they are discussed in more detail. This cursory overview, however, is intended to provide more than a summary—it is meant to be a guide to the rest of this chapter.

Most social process theories of crime causation make the following fundamental assumptions.

- The nature of social reality is in flux; what we think of as social reality is a construction—specifically, an artifact of socialization and social interaction. In short, human beings are seen as coproducers of their social worlds.
- The meaning of events and experiences is conferred upon them by the participants in any interaction. Social actors define the situations in which they are involved.
- Meaning is derived from previous learned experiences and is conferred upon experiences in typical and recurring ways.
- Behavior is criminal insofar as others define it as such and agree to its meaning.
- Criminal behavior is variously interpreted by the offender, the victim, agents of social control, and society.
- Deviant individuals and criminal offenders achieve their status by virtue of social definition, rather than because of inborn traits.
- Continued criminal activity may be a consequence of limited opportunities for acceptable behavior which follow from the negative responses of society to those defined as criminal.

• Career offenders participate in a worldview that differs from the worldview of the conformist and that grants legitimacy to nonconformist activity.

▦ SOCIAL PROCESS PERSPECTIVES

Social process theories also known as inter-actionist perspectives emphasize the give-and-take which occurs between offender, victim, and society—and specifically between the offender and agents of formal social control such as the police, courts, and correctional organizations.

The theories discussed in this chapter are typically called **social process theories,** or **interactionist perspectives,** because they depend on the action (or reaction) of society to the offender (or to the victim) for their explanatory power—that is, upon the *process* of social interaction occurring between society, the victim, and the offender. Social process theories emphasize the give-and-take which occurs between offender, victim, and society—and specifically between the offender and agents of formal social control such as the police, courts, and correctional organizations. Another term frequently applied to the perspectives outlined in this chapter is *interactionist,* because the notion of give-and-take implies some activity to which a response is made. A shortcoming of at least some of the theories discussed in this chapter, however, is that they make only a casual attempt to explain the genesis of criminal behavior, focusing instead on the consequences of such behavior for those undertaking it, for the victims of law-breaking behavior, and for society.

THE GROUP PERSPECTIVE: LABELING

Tagging like labeling, the process whereby an individual is negatively defined by agencies of justice.

An early description of lasting societal reaction to deviance can be found in the work of **Frank Tannenbaum.** Tannenbaum's book, *Crime and the Community,* was published in 1938 and popularized the term ***tagging*** to explain what happens to offenders following arrest, conviction, and sentencing. Tannenbaum told his readers that crime was essentially the result of "two opposing definitions of the situation," between the delinquent and the community at large. "This conflict over the situation," he said, "is one that arises out of a divergence of values. As the problem develops, the situation gradually becomes redefined. The attitude of the community hardens definitely into a demand for suppression. There is a gradual shift from the definition of the specific acts as evil to a definition of the individual as evil, so that all his acts come to be looked upon with suspicion.... From the community's point of view, the individual who used to do bad and mischievous things has now become a bad and unredeemable human being.... The young delinquent becomes bad because he is defined as bad and because he is not believed if he is good. There is a persistent demand for consistency in character. The community cannot deal with people whom it cannot define."[7]

Tannenbaum used the phrase "dramatization of evil" to explain the process whereby an offender comes to be seen as ultimately and irrevocably "bad." After the process has been completed, Tannenbaum said, the offender "now lives in a different world. He has been tagged.... The process of making the criminal, therefore, is a process of tagging...." Once a person has been defined as bad, few legitimate opportunities remain open to him or to her. As a consequence, the offender finds that only other people who have been similarly defined by society as bad are avail-

THEORY IN PERSPECTIVE
Types of Social Process Theories

SOCIAL PROCESS THEORIES also known as **INTERACTIONIST PERSPECTIVES**

Emphasize the give-and-take which occurs between offender, victim, and society—and specifically between the offender and agents of formal social control such as the police, courts, and correctional organizations.

LABELING. An interactionist perspective which sees continued crime as a consequence of limited opportunities for acceptable behavior which follow from the negative responses of society to those defined as offenders.

PERIOD: 1938–1940 and 1960s–1980s, 1990s revival
THEORISTS: Frank Tannenbaum, Edwin M. Lemert, Howard Becker, John Braithwaite, and others
CONCEPTS: Tagging, labeling, outsiders, moral enterprise, primary and secondary deviance, reintegrative shaming

DRAMATURGY. An interactionist perspective which depicts human behavior as centered around the purposeful management of impressions, and which seeks to gain explanatory power from the analysis of social performances.

PERIOD: 1960s–Present
THEORISTS: Erving Goffman and others
CONCEPTS: Total institutions, impression management, back and front regions, performances, discrediting information, stigma, spoiled identity

PHENOMENOLOGICAL CRIMINOLOGY. Details the existence of criminal reality via exploration of the worldview or mind-set characteristic of committed career offenders. (Phenomenology, as a philosophical perspective, means the study of the contents of human consciousness without regard to external convention or prior assumptions.)

PERIOD: 1970s–Present
THEORISTS: Stanton Samenow, Samuel Yochelson, Stuart Henry, Dragan Milovanovic
CONCEPTS: Phenomenological method, constitutive criminology, social construction of reality, criminal worldview

VICTIMOLOGY. The study of victims and their contributory role, if any, in crime causation.

PERIOD: 1930s–Present
THEORISTS: Hans von Hentig, Benjamin Mendelsohn, Henry Ellenberger, Marvin E. Wolfgang, Margaret Fry, Stephen Schafer
CONCEPTS: Victim proneness, penal couple, victim-precipitated homicide, victimogenesis, restitution, victim impact statements, VOCA

Primary deviance initial deviance often undertaken to deal with transient problems in living.

Secondary deviance that which results from official labeling and from association with others who have been so labeled.

Labeling an interactionist perspective which sees continued crime as a consequence of limited opportunities for acceptable behavior which follow from the negative responses of society to those defined as offenders.

Moral enterprise a term which encompasses all the efforts a particular interest group makes to have its sense of propriety enacted into law.

able to associate with him or with her. This continued association with negatively defined others leads to continued crime.

Using terminology developed by **Edwin M. Lemert,** it became fashionable to call an offender's initial acts of deviance primary deviance and continued acts of deviance, especially those resulting from forced association with other offenders, secondary deviance. **Primary deviance,** Lemert pointed out, may be undertaken to solve some immediate problem or to meet the expectations of one's subcultural group. Hence, the robbery of a convenience store by a college student temporarily desperate for tuition money, although not a wise undertaking, may be the first serious criminal offense ever committed by the student. The student may well intend for it to be the last, but if arrest ensues and the student is "tagged" with the status of a criminal, then secondary deviance may occur as a means of adjustment to the negative status. In Lemert's words, "[w]hen a person begins to employ his deviant behavior or a role based upon it as a means of defense, attack, or adjustment to the overt and covert problems created by the consequent societal reaction to him, his deviation is secondary."[8]

Secondary deviance becomes especially important because of the forceful role it plays in causing tagged individuals to internalize the negative labels which have been applied to them. Through such a process, labeled individuals assume the role of the deviant. According to Lemert, "[o]bjective evidences of this change will be found in the symbolic appurtenances of the new role, in clothes, speech, posture, and mannerisms, which in some cases heighten social visibility, and which in some cases serve as symbolic cues to professionalization."[9]

The name most often associated with labeling theory is that of **Howard Becker.** In 1963 Becker published *Outsiders: Studies in the Sociology of Deviance,*[10] a work in which the **labeling** perspective found its fullest development. In *Outsiders,* Becker, among other things, described the deviant subculture of jazz musicians and the process by which an individual becomes a marijuana user. His primary focus, however, was to explain how a person becomes labeled an outsider, as "a special kind of person, one who cannot be trusted to live by the rules agreed on by the group."[11] The central fact about deviance, says Becker, is that it is a social product, that "it is created by society." Society creates both deviance and the deviant person by responding to circumscribed behaviors. The person who engages in sanctioned behavior is, as part of the process, labeled a deviant. In Becker's words, "social groups create deviance by making the rules whose infraction constitutes deviance, and by applying those rules to particular people and labeling them as outsiders. From this point of view, deviance is not a quality of the act the person commits, but rather a consequence of the application by others of rules and sanctions. . . . The deviant is one to whom that label has been successfully applied."[12]

In developing labeling theory, Becker attempted to explain how some rules come to carry the force of law, while others have less weight or apply only within the context of marginal subcultures. His explanation centered on the concept of **moral enterprise,** a term which he used to encompass all the efforts a particular interest group makes to have its sense of propriety embodied in law. "Rules are the products of someone's initiative," said Becker, "and we can think of the people who exhibit such enterprise as moral entrepreneurs."[13]

An early example of moral enterprise can be found in the Women's Christian Temperance Union (WCTU), a group devoted to the idea of prohibition. The WCTU was highly visible in its nationwide fight against alcohol—holding marches and demonstrations, closing drinking establishments, and lobbying legislators. Press coverage of the WCTU's activities swayed many politicians into believing that lawful prohibition of alcoholic beverages was inevitable, and an amendment to the U.S. Constitution soon followed—ushering in the age of prohibition. Moral enterprise is similarly used, Becker claimed, by other groups seeking to support their own interests with the weight of law. Often the group that is successful at moral enterprise does not represent a popular point of view. The group is simply more effective than others at maneuvering through the formal bureaucracy that attends the creation of legislation.

Becker was especially interested in describing deviant careers—the processes by which individuals become members of deviant subcultures and take on the attributes associated with the deviant role. Becker argued that most deviance, when it first occurs, is likely to be transitory. That is, it is unlikely to occur again. However, transitory deviance can be effectively stabilized in a person's behavioral repertoire through the labeling process. Once a person is labeled "deviant," opportunities for conforming behavior are seriously reduced. Behavioral opportunities that remain open are primarily deviant ones. Hence, throughout the person's career, the budding deviant increasingly exhibits deviant behavior, not so much out of choice, but rather because his or her choices are restricted by society. Additionally, successful deviants must acquire the techniques and resources necessary to undertake the deviant act (be it drug use or bank robbery), and develop the mind-set characteristic of others like them. Near the completion of a deviant career, the person who has been labeled a deviant internalizes society's negative label, assumes a deviant self-concept, and is likely to become a member of a deviant subgroup. Becker says, "[a] drug addict once told me that the moment she felt she was really 'hooked' was when she realized she no longer had any friends who were not drug addicts."[14] In this way, says Becker, deviance finally becomes a "self-fulfilling prophecy." Labeling, then, is a cause of crime insofar as the actions of society in defining the rule breaker as deviant push the person further in the direction of continued deviance.

Labeling theory contributed a number of unique ideas to the criminological literature. They include the notions that

1. Deviance is the result of social processes involving the imposition of definitions, rather than the consequence of any quality inherent in human activity itself.
2. Deviant individuals achieve their status by virtue of social definition, rather than because of inborn traits.
3. The reaction of society to deviant behavior and to actors who engage in such behavior is the major element in determining the criminality of the person and of the behavior in question.
4. Negative self-images follow from processing by the formal mechanisms of criminal justice, rather than precede delinquency.

5. Labeling by society and handling by the justice system tend to perpetuate crime and delinquency rather than reduce it.

Becker's typology of delinquents helped explain the labeling approach. It consisted of those whom he called (1) the pure deviant, (2) the falsely accused deviant, and (3) the secret deviant. The pure deviant is one who commits norm-breaking behavior and whose behavior is accurately appraised as such by society. An example might be the burglar who is caught in the act of burglary, then tried and convicted. Such a person, we might say, has gotten what he deserves. The falsely accused individual is one who, in fact, is not guilty, but is labeled deviant nonetheless. The falsely accused category in Becker's typology demonstrates the power of social definition. Innocent people sometimes end up in prison, and one can imagine that the impact of conviction and of the experiences which attend prison life can leave the falsely accused with a negative self-concept and with group associations practically indistinguishable from those of the true deviant. In effect, the life of the falsely accused is changed just as thoroughly as is the life of the pure deviant by the process of labeling. Finally, the secret deviant violates social norms, but his or her behavior is not noticed, and negative societal reactions do not follow. The secret deviant again demonstrates the power of societal reaction—in this case by the very lack of consequences.

Recently, Mike S. Adams proposed a general social learning theory of crime and deviance incorporating components of labeling theory and differential association.[15] Adams contends that "labeling effects are mediated by associations with delinquent peers." He concludes that labeling is not a direct cause of delinquency and crime, but "appears to cause delinquency indirectly via the effects of associations with delinquent peer groups." In other words, "the causal chain linking primary to secondary deviance must incorporate links that account for the effects of associations with delinquent [peers]."[16]

Critique of Labeling

The labeling approach, although it successfully points to the labeling process as a reason for continued deviance and as a cause of stabilization in deviant identities, does little to explain the origin of crime and deviance. Likewise, few, if any, studies seem to support the basic tenants of the theory. Critics of labeling have pointed to its "lack of firm empirical support for the notion of secondary deviance," and "many studies have not found that delinquents or criminals have a delinquent or criminal self-image."[17]

Also, there is a lack of unequivocal empirical support for the claim that contact with the justice system is fundamentally detrimental to the personal lives of criminal perpetrators. Even if that supposition were true, however, one must ask, would it ultimately be better that offenders not be caught and forced to undergo the rigors of processing by the justice system? Although labeling theory hints that official processing makes a significant contribution to continued criminality, it seems unreasonable to expect that offenders untouched by the system would forego the rewards of future criminality.

PAYING FOR CRIME WITH SHAME:

JUDGES SAY 'SCARLET LETTER' ANGLE WORKS

Labeling theory says that people who commit deviant acts may continue down aberrant pathways because of the labels society applies to them. Others, however, argue that the application of labels can contribute to the reformation of offenders. The following story, about the use of public shaming to stop crime, seems to support the latter view.

If prison time or heavy fines are not enough to stop crime, some judges believe public humiliation will. Shaming criminals, a practice as ancient as the Old Testament, is making a comeback. Courts across the USA are handing down sentences that include a good dose of public branding, from allowing a woman assaulted by her ex-husband to spit in his face to forcing child molesters to post signs in front of their homes describing their crimes.

The Boston District Attorney's office added a new twist this month to the crime of sex solicitation. Convicted "johns" are given brooms and shovels, and spend four hours sweeping the streets of Chinatown, an area rife with prostitution. The public is invited to watch the men cleaning up streets and alleys littered with used condoms.

The rise in shame as punishment is being dubbed a return to "scarlet letter" days, when sentences were meant to not only punish but deter wrongdoers through public humiliation. Judges, facing the problems of prison overcrowding and the high cost of incarceration, already have been relying on alternative sentences such as community service. But some legal experts believe judges are adding humiliation to the mix to soothe a public hungry for retribution.

The trend is disturbing to some, especially when there are no statistics that prove shame works. "It's an embarrassment to the criminal justice system and all done in the guise of law and order to appease the victims," says Knoxville lawyer Jim A. H. Bell, who serves on the board of the National Association of Criminal Defense Lawyers. He is skeptical that debasing criminals will rehabilitate them or deter others. "It's all done for shock value."

Texas District Judge Ted Poe of Houston, famous for some very unusual sentences, is used to such criticism. He's sentenced convicted wife batterers to apologize to their wives in front of women's groups. He has some criminals spend hundreds of hours cleaning horse manure in the Houston Police Department's stables. He barred a 66-year-old music teacher who molested two of his students from playing the piano until the end of his 20-year probation, made him give up his $16,000 piano and post a sign on his front door warning anyone under 18 to stay away.

He made a teen-ager who had vandalized 13 schools go back to every one of the schools, apologize to the students and answer questions. "It was wonderful. They wanted to know why he was a mean person," says Poe, who believes the sentence taught the vandal and the students a lesson. "The greatest deterrent to criminal conduct is public humiliation," he says.

Poe admits that he reserves most of his shame sentences for defendants with "an attitude" or contempt for the system. The teen-ager, for example, told the court that he went on his vandalism spree because he got bored after his cable TV went out.

Poe designed a special sentence for Steven Dodd, convicted of interfering with child custody after he took his two children out of state for five years.

Dodd received 180 days in jail and 20 hours a month cleaning the Houston Police Department's stables during the entire stretch of a 10-year probation. "That's a lot of horse manure," says Dodd, 47, whose sentence was eventually suspended after six years and 1,572 hours in the horse barns. "It's definitely a deterrent. I don't want to go back and do something like that again." Dodd drove 91 miles each way three to four times a month to get from his home in Onalaska, Texas, to the Houston police stables. It gave him plenty of time to "look at what I'd done."

Questions

1. Can shame, in your opinion, serve as an effective deterrent? Why or why not?
2. If you think shame might be an effective deterrent, with what kinds of crimes might it be most effective?
3. What do you think of Knoxville lawyer Jim A. H. Bell's comment that shame as a punishment is "an embarrassment to the criminal justice system . . .?"

Source: Haya El Nasser, "Paying for Crime With Shame: Judges Say 'Scarlet Letter' Angle Works," *USA Today,* June 26, 1996, p. 1A. Copyright 1996, *USA Today.* Reprinted with permission.

REINTEGRATIVE SHAMING

In what some see as a contemporary offshoot of labeling theory, **John Braithwaite** and colleagues at the Australian National University (ANU) reported initial results of their studies on reintegrative shaming in 1997.[18] Braithwaite, with Lawrence Sherman of the University of Maryland and Heather Strang at ANU, compared the effectiveness of traditional court processing of criminal offenders with a restorative justice approach operating in Canberra, Australia, known as "diversionary conferencing." The diversionary conferencing approach "consists of an emotionally intense meeting, led by a police officer, between admitted offenders and their supporters, usually family and friends, and the victim of the offense, together with their supporters. In the absence of a direct victim, a representative of the community in which the offence occurred expresses the victim perspective on the events. The group discusses the consequences of the offense for all the parties and then determines what restitution the offenders must comply with to repair the harm for which they are responsible and so avoid going to court."[19]

Called RISE, for Reintegrative Shaming Experiments, the ongoing project is assessing the efficacy of each approach using criteria such as: (1) prevalence and frequency of repeat offending, (2) victim satisfaction with the process, (3) estimated cost savings within the justice process, (4) changes in drinking or drug use behavior among offenders, and (5) perceptions of procedural justice, fairness, and protection of rights.

At the core of the study is Braithwaite's belief that two different kinds of shame exist. One he calls "stigmatic shaming." **Stigmatic shaming** is thought to destroy the moral bond between the offender and the community. The other type of shame, **reintegrative shaming,** is thought to strengthen the moral bond between the offender and the community. According to Braithwaite, "stigmatic shaming is what American judges employ when they make an offender post a sign on his property saying 'a violent felon lives here,' or a bumper sticker on his car saying 'I am a drunk driver.' Stigmatic shaming sets the offender apart as an outcast—often for the rest of the offender's life. By labeling him or her as someone who cannot be trusted to obey the law, stigmatic shaming says the offender is expected to commit more crimes."

Braithwaite's alternative to stigmatic humiliation is "to condemn the crime, not the criminal." Through carefully monitored diversionary conferences Braithwaite hopes to give offenders the opportunity to rejoin the community as law-abiding citizens. To earn the right to a fresh start, says Braithwaite, offenders must express remorse for their past conduct, apologize to any victims, and repair the harm caused by the crime.

Preliminary results from the RISE study support the claimed value of reintegrative shaming. To date, however, most such results are being measured through interviews with offenders following diversionary conferences. Findings show that offenders are far more likely to feel ashamed of their crimes if handled through conferences rather than through formal court processing. Final results of the RISE project will be available around the year 2000.

DRAMATURGY

Another interactionist approach to the study of criminology can be found in the work of **Erving Goffman.** Goffman's 1959 book, *The Presentation of Self in Everyday Life,*[20] introduced students of criminology to the concept of dramaturgy. The **dramaturgical perspective** says that individuals play a variety of nearly simultaneous social roles, such as mother, teacher, daughter, wife, and part-time real estate agent—and that such roles must be sustained in interaction with others. Shakespeare's famous claim that "[a]ll the world's a stage, and all the men and women merely players: They have their exits and their entrances; and one man in his time plays many parts"[21] provides a good summation of Goffman's dramaturgical approach.

Goffman argued that social actors present themselves more or less effectively when acting out a particular role, and that role performances basically consist of managed impressions. Through communications, both verbal and nonverbal, social actors define the situations in which they are involved. A medical doctor, for

Stigmatic shaming that form of shaming, imposed as a sanction by the criminal justice system, that is thought to destroy the moral bond between the offender and the community.

Reintegrative shaming that form of shaming, imposed as a sanction by the criminal justice system, that is thought to strengthen the moral bond between the offender and the community.

Dramaturgical perspective, also **dramaturgy** a theoretical point of view which depicts human behavior as centered around the purposeful management of interpersonal impressions.

Impression management
the intentional enactment
of practiced behavior
which is intended to
convey to others one's
desirable personal
characteristics and social
qualities.

example, may wear a lab coat and a name tag with her title emblazoned on it, carry a stethoscope and other medical accouterments, and introduce herself as "*Dr. Smith.*" Each choice the doctor makes, in what she wears, says, or how she acts, is intended to convey, according to Goffman, medical authority—and to thereby establish certain rules of interpersonal interaction, that is, to demand a certain appropriate kind of subservience from specified others, including patients, nurses, laboratory technicians, and so on. Medical doctors may, by way of their esoteric knowledge and the awe they inspire in patients and family members of patients, mystify their audiences and thereby gain compliance with their wishes, which makes their jobs easier. Criminals, through a similar process of managed impressions, and by way of the fear they engender in their victims, may likewise achieve cooperation.

Impression management, according to Goffman, is a complex process involving a never-ending give-and-take of information. Back regions (such as dressing rooms) in which actors prepare for their roles, front regions (such as offices where furniture, degrees, and plaques are carefully placed), and personal displays of status or role occupancy all play a role in the management of impressions. When impression management has been successful, says Goffman, dramatic realization has occurred. "Together," he says, "the participants contribute to a single overall definition of the situation which involves not so much a real agreement as to what exists but rather a real agreement as to whose claims concerning what issues will be temporarily honored."[22]

Goffman also claims that a performer can "be completely taken in by his own act," or, on the other hand, "the performer may not be taken in at all by his own routine"[23] and may not be the person he represents himself as being. When the performer is not duped, but others are, then the performance is a sham or a fraud. In such cases of misrepresentation, he says, "we may take a harsh view of performers such as confidence men who knowingly misrepresent every fact about their lives, [but] we may have some sympathy for those who have but one fatal flaw and who attempt to conceal the fact that they are, for example, ex-convicts."[24]

Deviant behavior finds its place in the dramaturgical perspective through the concept of "discreditable disclosure." Some actors, says Goffman, may find themselves discredited by the introduction of new information, especially by information they have sought to hide. When such **discrediting information** is revealed, the flow of interaction is disrupted, and the nature of the performance may be altered substantially. In an example from real life, which was made into a play and the 1993 movie *M. Butterfly,*[25] a French diplomat in China spent twenty years living with a Beijing opera singer, never knowing that "she" was really a "he." Such an interpersonal relationship must have required nothing less than heroic impression management, with the potential for discrediting information always close at hand.

Discrediting information
information that is
inconsistent with the
managed impressions
being communicated in a
given situation.

Goffman would say that "[t]o be a given kind of person" requires the dramatic realization of one's claimed status. What one *is* depends on how successful one is at acquiring the abilities necessary to convince others of one's claims. In his words, "[a] status, a position, a social place is not a material thing . . . it is a pattern of appropriate conduct, coherent, embellished, and well articulated . . . it is . . . something that must be enacted and portrayed, something that must be realized."[26]

Goffman's work takes on considerable relevance for criminology in his later writings, especially his book *Stigma: Notes on the Management of Spoiled Identity.*[27] In

The Taming of the Shrew, performed in Tucson, Arizona. Some criminologists suggest that people, like actors on a stage, intentionally present themselves to others in ways calculated to produce predictable social responses. How might criminals manipulate impressions? *First Image/The Image Works.*

Stigma, Goffman advances the notion that discredited, or stigmatized, individuals differ significantly from "normals" in the way that society responds to them. "By definition . . .," he says, "we believe that a person with a stigma is not quite human. On this assumption we exercise varieties of discrimination, through which we effectively, if often unthinkingly, reduce his life chances. We construct a stigma-theory, an ideology to explain his inferiority and account for the danger he represents. . . . We tend to impute a wide range of imperfections on the basis of the original one. . . ."[28] Stigmata (the plural of stigma) may be physical (such as birthmarks), behavioral (such as theft), or ideational (such as a low rank in the proverbial pecking order).

In *Stigma,* Goffman is primarily concerned with how "normals" and stigmatized individuals interact. At times, says Goffman, discredited individuals are known to others before they come into contact with them. When that happens, normal people approach the stigmatized with expectations of encountering further stigmatizing behavior. When discrediting information does not precede interpersonal encounters, the stigmatized individual may attempt to "pass" as normal using various techniques of concealment including aliases and misrepresentation.

According to Goffman, societal reactions, although they may forcibly create social identities, are also instrumental in the formation of group identities. When similarly discredited individuals come together in like-minded groups, they may align themselves against the larger society. In so reacting, they may justify their own deviant or criminal behavior. At the conclusion of *Stigma,* Goffman reminds us, "[t]he normal and the stigmatized are not persons, but rather perspectives. These are generated in social situations during mixed contacts by virtue of the unrealized norms that are likely to play upon the encounter."[29]

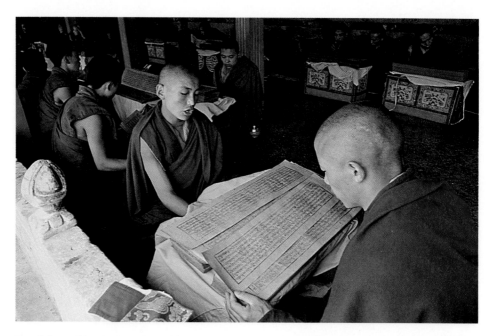

People in total institutions share all aspects of their lives—such as these monks in a Buddhist monastery. How is a prison like a monastery? *Eastcott/Momatiuk/Woodfin Camp & Associates.*

Total institutions facilities from which individuals can rarely come and go, and in which communal life is intense and circumscribed. Individuals in total institutions tend to eat, sleep, play, learn, and worship (if at all) together.

In another book, *Asylums,*[30] Goffman describes **total institutions**—facilities from which individuals can rarely come and go, and in which communal life is intense and circumscribed. Individuals in total institutions tend to eat, sleep, play, learn, and worship (if at all) together. Military camps, seminaries, convents, prisons, rest homes, and mental hospitals are all types of asylums according to Goffman. Goffman believed that residents of total institutions bring "presenting cultures" with them to their respective facilities. In the case of prisons, for example, some inmates carry street culture into correctional facilities, whereas others, from different walks of life, bring a variety of other cultural baggage. However, residents, says Goffman, undergo a period of "disculturation," during which they drop aspects of the presenting culture that are not consistent with existing institutional culture—a culture they must acquire.

A criminology of relevance . . . should not only be empirical, but rooted in minute understandings of the varied groundings of experience.

—PETER K. MANNING[31]

Critique of Dramaturgy

Goffman's work has been criticized as providing a set of "linked concepts"[32] rather than a consistent theoretical framework. Other critics have faulted Goffman for failing to offer suggestions for institutional change or for not proposing treatment modalities based on his assumptions. Goffman's greatest failing may be in taking the analogy of the theater too far and convincing readers that real life is but a form of playacting. According to George Psathas, one of Goffman's critics, "[p]erforming and being are not identical."

Erving Goffman was a sociologist and one-time president of the American Sociological Association. Unfortunately for the field of criminology, Goffman said very little directly about crime and criminality. Although he made a number of analytical references to prisons in *Asylums,* Goffman's work has been given wider applicability to criminology by his followers.

PHENOMENOLOGY

The phenomenological tradition within social science holds that social reality is a perceptual construct, that is, a generally agreed upon consensus as to what people, things, places, and so on *mean.* Reality is effectively defined for each person through socialization into a preexisting culture of agreed upon understandings. Your understanding of these words, for example, is predicated upon your learning of the English language along with a host of words that carry specific meanings for you. Because you and I give words pretty much the same meanings, you can understand what is written on this page, along with what it is that I wish to convey.

Along with words, the process of socialization establishes certain things as agreed upon facts. Most individuals who are successfully socialized into Western culture, for example, accept the "scientific way" of doing things, and reject explanations which are overly mystical. They believe, say, that the earth's moon congealed into orbit around the planet out of space "dust" and that its orbit is sustained by its speed, trajectory, and the mutual attraction between the earth and the moon. They tend to reject the belief, say, that the moon harbors an independent consciousness which interacts with, and influences, events on earth on a grand scale (although some people, in fact, do believe this).

Once society provides us with a language and a set of beliefs about the nature of reality, or agreed upon facts, it has prepared us for encountering new experiences and interpreting them in patterned, fairly predictable ways. We interpret things we encounter in light of previous knowledge and experiences. Hence, the next uniformed individual I encounter who wears a badge, I will probably "grasp" (in my mind) as a police officer. My interpretation of the experience could be wrong. He or she might be an actor or actress dressed in a police uniform, a private security officer, a Halloween partygoer, or a con artist attempting to mislead me. However, my responses toward this individual are likely to depend on my socially predicated understanding of whom it is I am dealing with. Hence, although it is generally safe to assume that uniformed individuals with badges are actually police personnel, a number of unscrupulous characters have used the full assemblage of police identifiers—including uniforms, marked cars with sirens and lights, and other accouterments—to perpetrate crimes. In a number of instances, women have been attacked and raped by such impostors after stopping their cars for what they thought were police vehicles.

For most people, the process of socialization builds the foundation necessary for successful interaction with others. It allows for understanding and provides a life rich in meaning. Without the socially derived concepts with which we interpret the world, our lives would indeed lack meaning in the phenomenological sense.

Phenomenology the study of the contents of human consciousness without regard to external conventions or prior assumptions.

Samuel Yochelson and Stanton Samenow, however, in detailed discussions with forensic, or criminal, psychiatric patients discovered that such individuals possessed a criminal mind which painted a picture of reality quite different from that generally accepted by normal people.[33] A criminal way of life and a concomitant criminal way of thinking emerged. It was as though, in effect, the committed career offender lived in a different world than the one commonly populated by others. As other writers have observed, "[t]he criminal world attracts its members from among habitual offenders by providing a ready-made system of meaning. Criminal reality—criminals' perception of the world—is the mechanism through which life becomes comprehensible for offenders. It tells criminals who they are, who others are, which actions are significant and what they mean. In short, it endows criminal life with purpose."[34]

Although phenomenological understandings can be extended to individual cases of criminality, they seem to make the most sense when used to explain the concept of crime itself. In 1970, for example, **Richard Quinney** published *The Social Reality of Crime,* which outlined a number of propositions detailing how crime is constituted out of societal interaction. Crime, according to Quinney, is "a definition of human conduct that is created by authorized agents in a politically organized society."[35] Quinney went on to say that "criminal definitions describe behaviors that conflict with the interests of segments of society that have the power to shape public policy." He also asserted that "criminal definitions are applied by the segments of society that have the power to shape the enforcement and administration of criminal law. . . ." In his analysis Quinney recognized that class identification is crucial in determining which individuals are likely to violate the law. "Persons in the segments of society whose behavior patterns are not represented in formulating and applying criminal definitions," he wrote, "are more likely to act in ways that will be defined as criminal than those in the segments that formulate and apply criminal definitions." Quinney summarized his understanding of crime in these words: "The social reality of crime is constructed by the formulation and application of criminal definitions, the development of behavior patterns related to criminal definitions, and the construction of criminal conceptions."

Stuart Henry and **Dragan Milovanovic,** two contemporary proponents of **phenomenological criminology,** use the term **constitutive criminology** to refer to the process by which human beings create "an ideology of crime that sustains it as a concrete reality."[36] "We are concerned," they write, "with the ways in which human agents actively coproduce that which they take to be crime." For Henry and Milovanovic, the idea of crime itself is a social construction, and researchers, they say, should recognize that criminals and victims are also "emergent realities." Concepts such as *crime, criminal, victim,* and so forth are codetermined by individual actors in the crime and justice drama, and by society itself which confers meaning upon human interaction through ready-made and preexisting concepts. In fact, say these writers, crime and crime control are not "object-like entities," but social constructions. To treat them as anything else is to limit one's self to the perception of distinctions which, for all their social and cognitive power, are merely arbitrary. In short, write Henry and Milovanovic, "crime is both *in* and *of* society." Note, however, that constitutive criminology, which focuses on the social process by which crime and criminology become cultural realities, is not to be confused with constitutional criminology, a biological approach which holds that one's physical constitution plays a role in crime causation.[37]

Phenomenological criminology the study of crime as a social phenomenon that is created through a process of social interaction.

Constitutive criminology the study of the process by which human beings create an ideology of crime that sustains it (the notion of crime) as a concrete reality.

Unfortunately, for those unschooled in the phenomenological tradition, much of the terminology used by modern-day constitutive criminologists partially obfuscates the subject matter with which they are dealing. Their writings can be instructive, nonetheless. Henry and Milovanovic, for example, write ". . . human agents transform events that they see or experience as micro events into summary representations, or mind patterns, by relying on routine practices through which they convince themselves of having achieved the appropriate representation of these events; these are then objictified in coherent narrative constructions. . . . [N]o clearer example exists than the very categorization of the diversity of human conflicts and transgressions into crime, or of the multitude of variously motivated acts of personal injury into violent crime or types of violent crime. . . ."[38] In other words, some of the things that people do are called crimes by virtue of a kind of mental shorthand or stereotyping that others impose upon them. Likewise, notions that law and order are desirable and that crime and incivility are displeasing are created and maintained through social agreement. Or, in the words of Henry and Milovanovic, "[f]rom the perspective of constitutive criminology, then, control institutions are the relations among human agents acting to police the conceptual distinctions among discursively constructed social structures."[39]

Although their work may be more tangential than central to the phenomenological movement in criminology, some criminologists classify the writings of **Stanton Samenow,** a clinical research psychologist, and **Samuel Yochelson,** a psychiatrist, as phenomenological criminology because these researchers employed a technique they called "phenomenologic reporting." According to Yochelson and Samenow, phenomenologic reporting is "an intense probe of a criminal's stream of thinking throughout the day."[40] Although Samenow and Yochelson could just as easily be characterized as psychological or psychiatric criminologists, we include their work here because of their insistence that career offenders participate in a criminal worldview quite different from the worldview of conformists, and because of their assertion that criminality is an attitude toward life that begins in early childhood and is unlikely to ever abate.

Samenow and Yochelson worked with the criminally insane (those found not guilty by reason of insanity, or NGBRI) at St. Elizabeth's Hospital in Washington, D.C., during the 1960s and early 1970s. Career offenders, according to Yochelson and Samenow, demonstrate fifty-two "errors in thinking," including[41]

1. a lack of interest in schooling
2. the belief that work is for "suckers"
3. a propensity toward chronic lying—even when there seems to be no point in it
4. early sexual activity and a "great deal of sexual thinking," accompanied by sexual immaturity and an inability to form meaningful romantic relationships
5. the ability to postpone criminal activity if threatened with negative consequences
6. a disdain for rules except when their application may benefit the criminal
7. deriving enjoyment from reckless and law-violating behavior, such as vandalism
8. dropping out of normal society early in life

9. untrustworthiness, irresponsibility, and a focus on the "here and now" at the expense of the future
10. boredom with routine activity and concomitant restlessness
11. a know-it-all attitude in many situations
12. expensive tastes, but no "responsible" understanding of the value of money
13. the tendency to steal "almost anything that is not tied down or too heavy to move"
14. a sporadic commitment to formalized religion, along with a "compartmentalization" of religion from the rest of life
15. extreme fear of pain and of physical injury, accompanied by many other fears
16. chronic anger, often toward the world in general and most everything it holds
17. hesitancy to apply the term *criminal* to themselves

According to Yochelson and Samenow, "[e]ach participant in the study had committed literally thousands of crimes, but had been apprehended very few times. From early in life, the patterns grew and grew...." Most criminals, they tell us, were already well on their way to lives of crime as children. "The criminal child," they write, "sets himself apart. He does not confide in his family, and he conceals ideas and emotional reactions. Because he lies so often and engages in forbidden activity, he is ever distrustful and suspicious of other family members."[42]

Finally, Yochelson and Samenow conclude, "the criminal is not a victim of circumstances. He makes choices early in life, regardless of his socioeconomic status, race, or parents' child-rearing practices."[43] The significance of environmental factors in the development of criminality, or in its treatment, is rejected by these theorists. "Changing the environment," say Yochelson and Samenow, "does not change the man." Hence, providing new opportunities for legitimate success will not reorient the criminal, but rather will be interpreted by the career offender as providing new opportunities for the commission of additional crimes. From the point of view of Yochelson and Samenow, teaching a committed offender how to weld, as many prison reeducation programs do, provides the criminal not so much with a tool for employment on the outside, as it does with a device for continued criminality—to be used for safecracking, breaking and entering, vehicle theft, and so on.

Similarly, other phenomenological writers have pointed out, "[i]f poverty and unemployment are principal sources of crime, as many sociologists suggest, then all we have to do is provide jobs and decent incomes. And yet most hardened criminals spurn conventional employment and mock those who work for a living."[44]

To change career criminals, Yochelson and Samenow argued, a total conversion of the offender's personality is required. In their own notes, dictated as their studies progressed, they observed, "I am convinced there is no helping these people unless there is a 'metamorphosis.' 'Change' is not a sufficiently descriptive term for the degree of overhauling that is necessary." After all, if crime is the result of an internally consistent worldview which characterizes career offenders to the same extent as a normal worldview typifies the rest of us, then it would seem no less easy a task to convert the criminal into a conformist than to move conformists toward criminality.

Critique of Phenomenology

Some critics have called phenomenological criminology nihilistic, by which they mean that, in their opinion, it offers few practical solutions to the problem of crime. In effect, they say, phenomenological approaches may challenge well-accepted concepts such as crime and justice (by portraying them as arbitrary social constructions), but offer nothing in their place. Although social policies based on phenomenological concepts in the field of criminology may be hard to locate, this kind of criticism is not entirely deserved. It will be answered, in part, in the last chapter, when phenomenological criminology is discussed further under the rubric of "peacemaking criminology."

Other criticisms may be more valid. Concepts in phenomenological criminology are difficult to test and to verify. How, for example, can sociological experiments be constructed that explore the suggested process of cultural creation which is said to give rise to stereotypical concepts such as crime and justice? The fact that phenomenological writers have couched their own ideas in terminology that is itself not easy to grasp has made theory testing all the more difficult.

When criminologists attempt to apply phenomenological principles to specific situations, critiques can be even more telling. In the case of Yochelson and Samenow's "phenomenologic reporting," for example, the population under study consisted of hospitalized offenders diagnosed as mentally ill. Generalizability becomes a problem when attempting to extend theoretical findings developed from observations based on such a population. Whether traits demonstrated by offenders diagnosed as mentally ill can be expected to characterize other criminal offenders—even career ones—is highly debatable. Another shortcoming of Yochelson and Samenow's work pertains to the relatively small number of offenders they interviewed. Additionally, because these people were all institutionalized in a Washington, D.C.–area hospital, it becomes difficult to extend findings to offenders in other parts of the country.

VICTIMOLOGY: THE STUDY OF THE VICTIM

Some people are labeled "criminals" by the justice system and take on a deviant identity. Others, as a consequence of forced entanglements, come to be defined as "victims" and assume the social characteristics appropriate for that role. The process by which one comes to be victimized, the interaction between criminal and victim through which victimization occurs, and the meaning given to victimization after it has occurred all suggest that victimization can be subsumed under a social process perspective on criminality.

Just as criminals have been studied to determine what kinds of social and personal experiences they have, so, too, have criminologists advocated close scrutiny of victims. As a field of study **victimology,** or the study of victims, has closely paralleled the development of criminology. As was characteristic of the wider body of criminological theory, early victimologists stressed constitutional factors which propelled the victim toward the victimization. The adjudged degree of an individual's potential for victimization was termed **victim-proneness.**

Victimology the study of victims and their contributory role, if any, in crime causation.

Victim-proneness the degree of an individual's likelihood of victimization.

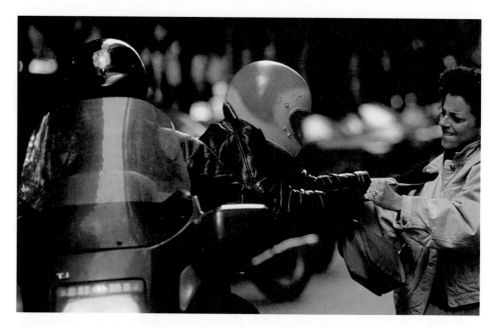

Purse snatchers in action. Why do victimologists suggest that some people contribute to their own victimization? *Buu-Turpin/Gamma-Liaison, Inc.*

One of the earliest writers in the field, **Hans von Hentig,**[45] depicted crime poetically—as a duet played by two. Hans von Hentig appears to have been heavily influenced by a popular German language novel of the time, entitled *The Murdered One Is Guilty.*[46] "In a sense," says von Hentig, "the victim shapes and moulds the criminal."[47] Comparing the victim and criminal to carnivore and prey, he writes, "In a certain sense, the animals which devour and those that are devoured complement each other.... To know one we must be acquainted with the complementary partner."[48]

Von Hentig created a typology, or classificatory scheme, of victims based on what he saw as biological or situational weaknesses. Weaknesses could be physically, socially, psychologically, or environmentally based. Anything that puts the potential victim at a disadvantage relative to the criminal predator, constituting "easy prey" so to speak, found a place in his typology. His scheme consisted of the following categories.

General Classes of Victims

The young—weak by virtue of age and immaturity

The female—often less physically powerful than the male

The old—incapable of physical defense, and the object of confidence schemes

The mentally defective—unable to think clearly

Immigrants—unsure of the rules of conduct in the surrounding society

Minorities—racial prejudice may lead to victimization or unequal treatment by the agencies of justice

Dull normals—the "born victims of swindlers"

Psychological Types of Victims

The depressed—submissive by virtue of emotional condition

The acquisitive or greedy—the act of always wanting more propels such individuals into victimization

The wanton or overly sensual—ruled by passion and thoughtlessly seeking pleasure

The lonesome—similar to the acquisitive type of victim, by virtue of wanting companionship or affection

The heartbroken—like the lonesome, if only temporarily

The tormentor—a victim who asks for it, often from his or her own family and friends

Other types include the blocked, exempted, and fighting victims. Blocked victims were those on whom the tables were turned, as in cases when the swindler becomes swindled or the attacker ends up injured. In like fashion, blackmailers often end up dead. Von Hentig also wrote of "victim areas," or parts of the country to which tourists and others with money are drawn. Similarly attracted are the criminals who prey upon them. Recent incidents involving foreign tourists in Florida were presaged by this kind of thinking. Likewise, inner-city areas rich in crime were seen as creating a special relationship between victim and criminal. Criminals in such areas were described as "deleterious mosquitoes. . . . [B]ut," wrote von Hentig, "they could not exist if there were no social swamps."[49]

On occasion, said von Hentig, the law creates a victim where there is none at all. The man who visits a prostitute—a willing participant in the offense of prostitution—can, from some perspectives, be classified as a victim. Likewise, the prostitute herself can fall into the category of victim, although as von Hentig says, as in cases of statutory rape, "even the gratified female is supposed to be victimized if the law does not give her consent legal strength."[50]

Finally, according to von Hentig, in some cases victim and criminal are the same. Arson, burglary, auto theft, and other property crimes in which insurance coverage is sought and false police reports filed are forms of criminal activity that typify such criminals and victims.

Von Hentig used colloquial information, preexisting statistical data, documented individual experiences, and personal observations to support his concepts. Although he did not undertake any empirical research of his own, von Hentig's ideas helped propel the importance of the victim into the forefront of criminological thinking during the 1950s and 1960s.

Some criminologists trace the development of the field of victimology to even earlier writings, including those of **Benjamin Mendelsohn.** In 1937 Mendelsohn, a European defense attorney, published a paper[51] advocating the study of victims. Three years later Mendelsohn published *Rape in Criminology*,[52] claiming that women possess formidable natural defenses against the crime of rape (including the biologically sheltered position of sex organs, the strength of leg muscles relative to the rest of the body, and so on). He intended to provide ammunition to criminal lawyers defending clients accused of rape by pointing out certain personal characteristics (including temperament, modesty, and credibility) which made some women easier targets of rape than others.

Like von Hentig, Mendelsohn created his own classification of victim types. Mendelsohn's typology was based on the degree of guilt that the victim brought to the criminal event. It included the following six categories.

1. The completely innocent victim. Such a person, said Mendelsohn, is an "ideal victim" in popular perception. In this category he placed persons victimized while they were unconscious, and child victims.
2. Victims with only minor guilt, and those victimized due to ignorance. Mendelsohn used the example of a woman who attempts a self-administered abortion and pays with her life.
3. The victim who is just as guilty as the offender, and the voluntary victim. Suicide committed by a couple, solicited euthanasia, and other forms of suicide were included in this category.
4. The victim more guilty than the offender. This category was described as containing persons who provoked the criminal or actively induced their own victimization.
5. The most guilty victim, or the victim "who is guilty alone." Attackers killed by would-be victims in the act of defending themselves were placed into this subgroup.
6. The imaginary victim. Here Mendelsohn allowed for the fact that some individuals file false police reports, or believe themselves to have been victimized when in fact they have not been. Senile people, mentally ill individuals, children, and others could fall into this category, he said.

Penal couple a term that describes the relationship between victim and criminal. Also, the two individuals most involved in the criminal act—the offender and the victim.

Mendelsohn is generally credited with creating the term *victimology,* as well as the concept of the **penal couple** which describes the relationship between victim and criminal. He also coined the term *victimal* to describe the victim counterpart of the criminal, and the word *victimity* which signified the opposite of criminality. In his writings Mendelsohn called for the development of victimology as a field of study independent from criminology. He foresaw the creation of an international institute for victimological research as part of the United Nations and called for the creation of an international society of victimology which would support its own journal (which he called the *International Review of Victimology*).

Victimogenesis the contributory background of a victim as a result of which he or she becomes prone to victimization.

In 1954 **Henry Ellenberger,** an American psychiatrist, introduced the concept of **victimogenesis**[53] to explain how persons can undergo life experiences that eventually place them in circumstances which contribute to their future victimization. Just as a criminal experiences events in life which lead to criminality, Ellenberger said, so too, many victims undergo a process of socialization that results in less caution, a proclivity to associate with possible offenders, an increased likelihood of frequenting places associated with criminal activity, and a generally higher risk of criminal victimization.

Victim-precipitated homicide killing in which the "victim" was the first to commence the interaction or was the first to resort to physical violence.

In 1957 **Marvin E. Wolfgang** popularized the term **victim-precipitated criminal homicide,** in his study[54] of murders in Philadelphia between 1948 and 1952. "[V]ictim-precipitated cases," said Wolfgang, "are those in which the victim was the first to show and use a deadly weapon, to strike a blow in an altercation—in short, the first to commence the interplay or resort to physical violence."[55] Wolfgang found that victims who brought about their own homicide were more likely than other murder victims to be black men with previous police records, especially involving assault, who were killed by stabbing in a situation where alcohol was present. Significantly, he found, many victim-precipitated homicides were committed by women, often wives. Hence, mate-killing, where threatened wives turn the tables on their abusive husbands, seemed to typify the victim-precipitated criminal homicides that Wolfgang studied.

Some years later Wolfgang, writing in consort with Thorsten Sellin,[56] introduced a typology of victims based on victim-offender relationships. They described:

1. Primary victimization—in which an individual falls victim to crime
2. Secondary victimization—in which an impersonal agency such as a business is victimized
3. Tertiary victimization—in which the government or public order is offended, perhaps through regulatory violations
4. Mutual victimization—in which the participants in an offense willingly involve themselves, such as drug sales, gambling, and fornication
5. No victimization—a category reserved for juvenile status offenses that could not be committed by an adult, such as the buying of cigarettes by an underage person

The Dynamics of Victimization

Some authors[57] have identified a number of procedural models which can be applied to a study of the victimization process, that is, for the purpose of understanding the experience the victim undergoes during and following victimization. The "victims of crime model," developed by Bard and Sangrey,[58] says that three stages are involved in any victimization: (1) the stage of impact and disorganization, during and immediately following the criminal event; (2) recoil, during which the victim formulates psychological defenses and deals with conflicting emotions of guilt, anger, acceptance, and desire for revenge (the state of recoil is said to last from three to eight months); and (3) the reorganizational stage, during which the victim puts his or her life back together and gets on with daily living in a more or less normal fashion. Some victims do not successfully adapt to the victimization experience, and a maladaptive reorganizational stage may last for many years.

Another model with applicability to the victimization experience is the "disaster victim's model," originally developed to explain the coping behavior of victims of natural disasters. This model outlines four stages in the victimization process: (1) preimpact, which describes the state of the victim prior to being victimized; (2) impact, or the stage at which victimization occurs; (3) postimpact, which entails the degree and duration of personal and social disorganization that follows victimization; and (4) behavioral outcome, which describes the victim's adjustment, or lack thereof, to the victimization experience.

Finally, the model developed by Elizabeth Kubler-Ross to describe the stages that dying persons go through has some applicability to the victimization process. Kubler-Ross described a five-part transitional process of denial, anger, bargaining, depression, and acceptance.[59] Victims often either deny the likelihood of their own victimization or believe that "this can't be happening to me." After the victimizing event many victims feel anger, and some express rage toward their victimizers. Bargaining occurs when victims negotiate with themselves as well as with family members, representatives of the criminal justice community, and social service providers over how the victimization experience should be personally interpreted and about how it should be officially handled. Acceptance occurs when the victim finally acknowledges that victimization has occurred, and the victim makes the adjustments necessary to go on with life. Of course, as in the case of other models, the Kubler-Ross model allows for maladjustment in the final phase as some victims never successfully integrate the victimization experience into their psyches in a way that avoids reduction in the quality of their lives.

The problem of crime always gets reduced to, "What can be done about criminals?" Nobody asks, "what can be done about victims?"

— R O B E R T   R E I F F [60]

The Victim as a Social Construct

Richard Quinney, whose contribution to the field of criminology is discussed elsewhere in this volume, argues that the victim is a social construction. That is, the wording of laws, the theoretical explorations of criminologists, and the cultural and institutional arrangements of society, all contribute to defining certain social actors as criminals and others as victims. The only real difference between the two, says Quinney, is convention and, one might add, happenstance.

In a 1972 article entitled "Who Is the Victim," Quinney wrote, ". . . criminologists have tended to share a singular conception of reality. . . . Breaking out of the theory of reality that had dominated criminological thought, we would begin to conceive of the victims of police force, the victims of war, the victims of the 'correctional' system, the victims of state violence, the victims of oppression of any sort. Because criminologists have tended to rely on a particular theory of reality, they have excluded these victims."[61] Fundamentally, says Quinney, the concept of victimization relates to one's notion of morality and corresponding understanding of social reality. "To argue," he writes, "that abortion is victimless is to exclude the living fetus as a victim. To regard the person who loses property as a victim is to value the sanctity of private property."

From some points of view, the victim, or at least the degree of victimization, is a cultural artifact. For example, potential murder victims who do not die because they receive prompt medical assistance thwart application of the term *homicide*. In a recent study of the availability of medical resources (especially quality hospital emergency services), William G. Doerner[62] found that serious assaults may "become" homicides where such resources are lacking, but that homicides can be prevented via the effective utilization of capable medical technology. Hence, societal decisions on the distribution and placement of advanced medical support equipment and personnel can lower homicide rates in selected geographic areas. In Doerner's words, "the causes of homicide transcend the mere social world of the combatants."[63] This kind of perspective bears more than a passing relationship to the criminology of place, discussed in a box in the previous chapter.

Critique of Victimology

Victimologists move much of the onus for criminality from the offender to the victim, claiming that the victim's behavior, appearance, physical or psychological makeup, or circumstances of birth and upbringing contribute significantly to victimization and are, at least to some degree, the cause of the criminal act itself. Although some of these claims may have a certain objective reality, the current political reality of crime—that is, the perception by the majority of Americans that the nation is swamped with far too much crime and the commonly expressed feeling that offenders should be held thoroughly accountable for their actions—seems to dictate a general lack of acceptance for such victimological perspectives.

However, in an article entitled "The Art of Savage Discovery: How to Blame the Victim," William Ryan explains that most victims of commonplace property and violent crimes are members of the lower class.[64] As a consequence, blaming the victim has become something of a popular undertaking for certain groups in society, in particular the middle and upper classes. According to Ryan, most members of the middle and upper classes sympathize with victims, but they are not about to do anything to change the all too prevalent conditions in society (poverty, unemployment, discrimination, and the like) which generate crime and lead to victimization. "The victim blamer," says Ryan, "is a middle-class person who is doing reasonably well in a material way; he has a good job, a good income, a good house, a good car. Basically, he likes the social system pretty much the way it is. . . ." Such people, Ryan says, employ a two-pronged approach to the problem of crime. First, they see victims as fated to be poor, uneducated, and victimized. Second, and somewhat contradictorily, they "want to make the victims less vulnerable, send them back into battle with better weapons, thicker armor, a higher level of morale. . . . What weapons," he asks, ". . . might they have lacked when they went into battle? Job skills? Education? What armor was lacking that might have warded off their wounds? Better values? Habits of thrift and foresight? And what might have ravaged their morale? Apathy? Ignorance? Deviant lower-class culture patterns?" Because the typical middle-class victim-blamer values precisely those attributes that so many lower-class victims lack, says Ryan, he or she is apt to blame the victim for choosing to be ill equipped to deal with the challenges of crime and of criminal victimization itself.

A History of the Victim

In early times, victims took the law into their own hands. If they were able to apprehend their victimizers, they enacted their own form of revenge and imposed some form of personal retaliation. The Code of Hammurabi (circa 1750 B.C.), one of the earliest known legal codes, required that many offenders make restitution. If the offender could not be found, however, the victim's family was duty bound to care for the needs of the victim. This early period in history has been called the

Golden Age of the Victim, because victims were not only well cared for, but also had considerable say in imposing punishments upon apprehended offenders.

Eventually, however, crimes came to be understood as offenses against society, and the victim was forgotten. By the late Middle Ages the concept of "King's Peace" had emerged, wherein all offenses were seen as violations of imperial law. It became the duty of local governments to apprehend, try, and punish offenders, effectively removing the victim from any direct involvement in judicial decision making. Victims were expected only to provide evidence of a crime and to testify against those who had offended them. Society's moral responsibility toward making victims "whole again" was forgotten, and victims as a class were moved to the periphery of the justice process. Justice for the victim was forgotten, translated instead into the notion of justice for the state.

The situation remained pretty much the same until the 1960s, when renewed interest in the plight of victims led to a resurgence of positive sentiments around the world. Such sentiments were soon translated into a flurry of laws intended to provide compensation to victims of violent crimes.

Compensation for criminal injury is not unknown throughout history. More than a hundred years ago Jeremy Bentham advocated "mandatory restitution, to be paid by a state compensation system, in cases of property crime."[65] Long before that, the Code of Hammurabi specified that

> If a man has committed robbery ... that man shall be put to death. If the robber is not caught, the man who has been robbed shall formally declare what he has lost ... and the city ... shall replace whatever he has lost for him. If it is the life of the owner that is lost, the city or the mayor shall pay one maneth of silver to his kinfolk.

The first modern victim compensation statute was adopted by New Zealand in 1963. Known as the Criminal Injuries Compensation Act, it provided an avenue for claims to be filed by victims of certain specified violent crimes. A three-member board was empowered to make awards to victims. A year later, partially in response to a movement led by the social reformer **Margaret Fry,** Great Britain established a similar board. In 1965 the state of California passed the first piece of American legislation intended to assist victims of crime. Simultaneously the New York City Council passed a "Good Samaritan" statute designed to pay up to $4,000 to persons suffering physical injuries while going to the aid of others being victimized by crime. Other states soon joined the bandwagon, and today all fifty states and the District of Columbia have passed legislation providing for monetary payments to crime victims, although legislatures have rarely funded programs at the level of received requests.

All states require applicants to meet certain eligibility requirements, and most set award maximums. A number of states set minimum loss limits (similar to deductible provisions in insurance policies) and have established a "needs test," whereby only needy crime victims are eligible for compensation. Likewise, some states deny awards to family members of the offender, as in the case when a son assaults a father. In all states, payments for medical assistance, lost wages, and living expenses are commonly made. Victims who are responsible in some significant way for their own victimization are generally not reimbursed for losses under existing laws.

The concept of victim compensation rests upon at least seven philosophical underpinnings:[66]

1. Strict liability theory, which claims that compensation is due victims because the social contract between victim and society (specifically, the government) has been broken by the experience of victimization. The duty of the government, says liability theory, is to safeguard its citizens, and when safeguards fail, the injured citizen is due compensation.

2. Government negligence theory, a very selective approach, which holds that the negligent actions of government representatives, including law enforcement officers, jailers, correctional personnel, and the like should result in appropriate forms of compensation.

3. Equal protection theory, which says that compensation should serve to ameliorate imbalances in society, including the huge variation in crime risk that citizens living in different parts of the nation face.

4. Humanitarian theory, which advocates compensation because of the suffering victims undergo.

5. Social welfare theory, similar to humanitarian theory, which says that victims should be compensated if they are in need. Social welfare approaches might exclude compensatory payments to well-heeled victims, but make them available on an as-needed basis to less fortunate members of society who undergo the victimization process.

6. Crime prevention theory, which holds that compensation programs will encourage more citizens to report crime, thereby resulting in more effective law enforcement programs.

7. Political motives theory, which says that victim compensation is in vogue with the voting public and that any politician desiring continued election will support the concept.

Although many tout the benefits of victim compensation programs, a recent study of the effectiveness of government-sponsored compensation programs in New York and New Jersey[67] found that most victims had generally negative attitudes toward the programs which were supposed to help them. According to the study, "[r]espondents were dissatisfied with delays, inconveniences, poor information, inability to participate, and the restrictive eligibility requirements. These sentiments, coupled with the large number of award applications that were denied, produced strongly negative attitudes among victims toward victim compensation."[68]

Current Directions in Victimology

Victims experience many hardships extending beyond their original victimization, including the trauma of testifying, uncertainty about their role in the justice process, lost time at work, trial delays, fear of retaliation by the defendant, and a

Postcrime victimization or secondary victimization refers to problems in living which tend to follow from initial victimization.

Victim–witness assistance programs counsel victims, orient them to the justice process and provide a variety of other services such as transportation to court, child care during court appearances, and referrals to social service agencies.

Victims of Crime Act (VOCA) passed by the U.S. Congress in 1984, it helps support local and state victim assistance programs.

general lack of knowledge of what is expected of them as the wheels of justice grind forward. Problems which follow from initial victimization are referred to as **postcrime victimization,** or **secondary victimization.** Police, employer, and spouse insensitivity can all exacerbate the difficulties crime victims face. Even hospitals that charge high fees for medical records, and social service agencies that swamp applicants in a plethora of forms, can contribute to the victim's sense of continuing victimization.[69]

In recent years a number of victims' assistance programs, designed to provide comfort and assistance to victims of crime, have developed across the nation.[70] The earliest of these programs began as grassroots movements designed to counsel victims of rape. In 1975 a national survey identified only twenty-three victims' assistance programs in the United States.[71] By 1986 the number had grown to over six hundred, and estimates today place the number of such programs at nearly one thousand. Some authors have drawn a distinction between victim service programs, which emphasize therapeutic counseling, and victim–witness assistance programs, which provide a wide array of services.

Most **victim–witness assistance programs,** although small and often staffed by local volunteers, typically counsel victims, orient them to the justice process, and provide a variety of other services such as transportation to court, child care during court appearances, and referrals to social service agencies when additional assistance is needed. A recent survey[72] found that most organizations explain the court process to victims (71.2 percent of all organizations surveyed), make referrals to other agencies (68.4 percent), provide court escorts (65.2 percent), help victims fill out victim compensation forms (64.1 percent), attempt to educate the public as to the needs of victims (60.9 percent), advocate with employers on behalf of victims (60.3 percent), and provide transportation to court (59.2 percent).[73]

Two large public groups, the National Organization for Victims Assistance (NOVA) and the National Victims Center, both located in the Washington, D.C., area, provide leadership in victims' education, lobby the federal Congress, and hold conferences and workshops designed to assist local victim–witness assistance programs.

In 1982 the President's Task Force on Victims of Crime recommended sixty-eight strategies that could be used by federal, state, and local governments to improve the plight of crime victims. Legislation based on task force recommendations resulted in the **Victims of Crime Act (VOCA),** passed by Congress in 1984. VOCA established the federal Crime Victims Fund which uses monies from fines and forfeitures collected from federal offenders to supplement state support of local victims' assistance programs and state victim compensation programs.

Victims' advocates argue that a victims' rights amendment to the U.S. Constitution is needed to provide the same kind of fairness to victims that is routinely afforded defendants in criminal proceedings. In 1996 a victims' rights amendment to the U.S. Constitution was proposed by three senators. Although the proposal failed to pass Congress due to difficulties in wording, proponents of the legislation remain active as this book goes to press. A modified version of the proposal is soon likely to come before Congress again. The wording of the original 1996 proposal is reproduced in a box in this section.

THEORY VERSUS REALITY

A Proposed Victims' Rights Amendment to the U.S. Constitution

Senate Joint Resolution 65, introduced on September 30, 1996, by Senators Jon Kyl and Dianne Feinstein, proposed a victims' rights amendment to the U.S. Constitution. Although the proposal failed to garner the votes needed to pass Congress, proponents of the legislation anticipate that efforts toward a victims' rights amendment will continue. The text of the Kyl–Feinstein resolution is reproduced here.

Proposing an amendment to the Constitution of the United States to protect the rights of crime victims. (Introduced in the Senate)

IN THE SENATE OF THE UNITED STATES
September 30, 1996

Mr. KYL (for himself, Mrs. FEINSTEIN, and Mr. EXON) introduced the following joint resolution; which was read twice and referred to the Committee on the Judiciary

JOINT RESOLUTION

Proposing an amendment to the Constitution of the United States to protect the rights of crime victims.

Resolved by the Senate and House of Representatives of the United States of America in Congress assembled (two-thirds of each House concurring therein), That the following article is proposed as an amendment to the Constitution of the United States, which shall be valid for all intents and purposes as part of the Constitution when ratified by the legislatures of three-fourths of the several States within seven years from the date of its submission by the Congress:

Article

SECTION 1. Victims of crimes of violence and other crimes that Congress and the States may define by law pursuant to section 3, shall have the rights to notice of and not to be excluded from all public proceedings relating to the crime; to be heard if present and to submit a statement at a public pre-trial or trial proceeding to determine a release from custody, an acceptance of a negotiated plea, or a sentence; to these rights at a parole proceeding to the extent they are afforded to the convicted offender; to notice of a release pursuant to a public or parole proceeding or an escape; to a final disposition free from unreasonable delay; to an order of restitution from the convicted offender; to have the safety of the victim considered in determining a release from custody; and to notice of the rights established by this article.

SECTION 2. The victim shall have standing to assert the rights established by this article; however, nothing in this article shall provide grounds for the victim to challenge a charging decision or a conviction, obtain a stay of trial, or compel a new trial; nor shall anything in this article give rise to a claim for damages against the United States, a State, a political subdivision, or a public official; nor shall anything in this article provide grounds for the accused or convicted offender to obtain any form of relief.

SECTION 3. The Congress and the States shall have the power to enforce this article within their respective Federal and State jurisdictions by appropriate legislation, including the power to enact exceptions when required for compelling reasons of public safety.

SECTION 4. The rights established by this article shall be applicable to all proceedings occurring after ratification of this article.

SECTION 5. The rights established by this article shall apply in all Federal, State, military, and juvenile justice proceedings, and shall also apply to victims in the District of Columbia, and any commonwealth, territory, or possession of the United States.

Victim Impact Statements

Victim impact statement a written document which describes the losses, suffering, and trauma experienced by the crime victim or by the victim's survivors. In jurisdictions where victim impact statements are used, judges are expected to consider them in arriving at an appropriate sentence for the offender.

One consequence of the burgeoning national victim–witness rights movement has been a call for the use of victim impact statements prior to the sentencing of convicted criminal defendants. A **victim impact statement** is typically a written document which describes the losses, suffering, and trauma experienced by the crime victim or by the victim's survivors. In jurisdictions where victim impact statements are used, judges are expected to consider them in arriving at an appropriate sanction for the offender.

Although the drive to mandate inclusion of victim impact statements in sentencing decisions has gathered much momentum, their final role has yet to be decided. The Victim Task Force, commissioned by then-president Reagan shortly after he took office, recommended adoption of a change to the Sixth Amendment of the U.S. Constitution. The task force specifically recommended adding the words "Likewise, the victim, in every criminal prosecution shall have the right to be present and to be heard at all critical stages of judicial proceedings."[74] Although such an amendment may be long in coming, significant federal legislation has already occurred. The 1982 Victim and Witness Protection Act[75] requires victim impact statements to be considered at federal sentencing hearings, and places responsibility for their creation on federal probation officers.

Some states have gone the federal government one better. In 1984 the state of California, for example, passed legislation[76] to allow victims a right to attend and participate in sentencing and parole hearings. Approximately twenty states now have laws mandating citizen involvement in sentencing. When written victim impact statements are not available, courts may invite the victim to testify directly at sentencing.

The legality of victim impact statements, although in doubt for some time, appears to have been decisively upheld by the U.S. Supreme Court in the 1991 case of

Payne v. *Tennessee.*[77] The *Payne* case began with a 1987 double murder, in which a 28-year-old mother and her 2-year-old daughter were stabbed to death in Millington, Tennessee.[78] A second child, 3-year-old Nicholas Christopher, himself severely wounded in the incident, witnessed the deaths of his mother and young sister. In a trial following the killings, the prosecution claimed that Pervis Tyrone Payne, a 20-year-old retarded man, had killed the mother and child after the woman resisted his sexual advances. Payne was convicted of both murders. At the sentencing phase of the trial, Mary Zvolanek, Nicholas's grandmother, testified that the boy continued to cry out daily for his dead sister.

In contrast to some earlier decisions which had cast doubt on the admissibility of victim impact statements, the Court in the *Payne* case held that such statements may be appropriately used at sentencing hearings because "[v]ictim impact evidence is simply another form or method of informing the sentencing authority about the specific harm caused by the crime in question. . . ."

Victim Restitution

The victims' movement has also spawned a rebirth of the concept of restitution. **Restitution** is punishment through imposed responsibility—in particular, the payment of compensation to the victim. Restitution encompasses the notion that criminal offenders should shoulder at least a portion of the financial obligations required to make the victim whole again. Not only does restitution help make the victim whole again, it places responsibility for the process back upon the offender who caused the loss of wholeness initially. Advocates of restitution, which works through court-imposed fines and garnishments, claim that, as a sentence, it benefits society by leading to an increased sense of social and individual responsibility on the part of convicted offenders.

> **Restitution** a criminal sanction, in particular the payment of compensation by the offender to the victim.

Stephen Schafer, who wrote the book *The Victim and His Criminal*[79] in 1968, is commonly credited with repopularizing the concept of restitution. Schafer discussed three forms of restitution: (1) compensatory fines, which are imposed in addition to other court-ordered punishments and which compensate the victim for the actual amount of loss; (2) double or treble damages, in which offenders are required, as punishment, to pay the victim back more than the amount of the original injury; and (3) restitution in lieu of other punishment, where the offender discharges any criminal responsibility by compensating the victim. In the last form of restitution, no other criminal penalties are imposed if the offender meets the restitution obligations.

The 1982 President's Task Force on Victims of Crime recognized the inequitable financial consequences that often follow criminal victimization with these words: "It is simply unfair that victims should have to liquidate their assets, mortgage their homes, or sacrifice their health or education or that of their children while the offender escapes responsibility for the financial hardship he has imposed. It is unjust that a victim should have to sell his car to pay bills while the offender drives to his probation appointments. The victim may be placed in a financial crisis that will last a lifetime. If one of the two must go into debt, the offender should do so."[80] The report went so far as to recommend that legislation be passed requiring restitution in all criminal cases and that mandates be established requiring judges to order restitution in cases where victims have suffered financially, unless compelling reasons to the contrary could be demonstrated.

A year later, in 1983, the American Bar Association, in its *Guidelines for Fair Treatment of Crime Victims and Witnesses,* recommended that "victims of a crime involving economic loss, loss of earnings, or earning capacity should be able to expect the sentencing body to give priority consideration to restitution as a condition of probation."[81]

According to Susan Hillenbrand,[82] the change in perspective which the American system of justice underwent in the 1970s and 1980s meant that restitution was no longer seen "solely as a punitive or rehabilitative measure," but came to be understood "as a matter of justice to crime victims. . . ." Even today, however, Hillenbrand says, efforts to evaluate restitution programs "have largely assessed outcomes in terms of correctional objectives rather than in terms of benefits to victims."[83] Nonetheless, Hillenbrand offers, "restitution need not be viewed as an all or nothing proposition for either victims or defendants in order to benefit both. The fact that the criminal justice system has goals other than restoration of crime victims should not be of concern to victims as long as their own needs are included among the goals of the system."[84]

Today restitution is widely operative in sentencing practice. The state of Texas is one of a growing number of states that utilize restitution as a major component of its statewide alternatives to prison. The Texas Residential Restitution Program operates numerous community-based centers, housing selected nonviolent felony offenders who work at regular jobs in the community, pay for their support and for the support of their families, and make restitution to their victims. On the national level, the **Office of Juvenile Justice and Delinquency Prevention (OJJDP)** has developed a monetary and direct victim service program for juvenile courts called RESTTA (Restitution, Education, Specialized Training, and Technical Assistance Program). RESTTA provides local juvenile courts with the information needed to make restitution a meaningful part of the disposition process for juvenile offenders.

Contemporary restitution programs, although typically well intended, are often mired in a number of problems. Chief among them are the difficulties associated with actually collecting restitution. Offenders are typically poor, lower class, and ill motivated to participate meaningfully in restitution programs. Overworked courts often order restitution and then do little to remedy the situation when offenders do not make their payments. In the words of Thomas C. Castellano, who conducted a 1992 survey of restitution studies, "the extant studies indicate room for concern and very little suggestion that adult restitution, particularly the mere imposition of a restitution order, achieves its desired effect on offender behavior."[85]

Office of Juvenile Justice and Delinquency Prevention (OJJDP) a national program that develops monetary and direct victim service programs for juvenile courts.

POLICY IMPLICATIONS

As we have been remarking throughout this chapter, both offenders and victims are stigmatized through social processes involving the formal and informal imposition of labels. Removal of the stigmata would, at least theoretically, restore both to their precrime state.

Labeling theory, in particular, would seem to predict that reverse labeling could occur, and might offer an attractive treatment technique to counteract the effects of the labeling process. Based on this proposition some programs have attempted to change convicts by having them participate in esteem-building workshops, developing strategies whereby correctional staff might officially accord them positive labels, and by providing them with the experience of self-enhancing public rituals such as graduation ceremonies. No such efforts have resulted in positive reports of realistic and lasting behavioral changes, nor of lowered recidivism rates. Similarly, existing evidence suggests that even equipping offenders with new identities and relocating them to new areas (as in witness protection programs) does little to change their fundamental approach to life. In like manner, phenomenological perspectives seem to hold little hope for a successful change in the worldview of career offenders. As a consequence, no individualized treatment strategies seem to be offered by either of these perspectives which might result in a realistic hope for offender rehabilitation. Imprisonment, with dangerous offenders held indefinitely, appears to be the best possible social policy that could be predicated on the theories offered here.

Studies of victims' compensation programs discussed earlier in this chapter seem to express a common caution: such programs can be effective provided they are intelligently managed and do not further expose victims to additional secondary victimization through less than effective bureaucracy. Moreover, money may not be as important to most victims as are practical assistance and fair representation within the justice system. Hence, legislation enhancing the rights of victims and local victims' assistance programs may be the best ways of channeling energies currently existing within the burgeoning victims' movement.

SUMMARY

▚

This chapter discussed a wide variety of perspectives, from labeling, through dramaturgy and phenomenology, to the rebirth of the victims' rights movement. Similarly, we have used both the terms *social process approach* and *interactionist perspective* to classify the theories found here. More fundamental to each of this chapter's perspectives, however, is the concept of social meaning, and this chapter might be appropriately titled "the search for social meaning."

When individual offenders are labeled criminal or deviant, the meaning which their presence holds for the group of which they are a part, as well as the personal significance of their own lives, have been inexorably changed. They will rarely be seen the same (in the predeviant state) again. In like fashion, when offenders internalize an acquired or imposed deviant self-conception, the meaning of their own lives changes and any future decisions they will make take on a new significance in light of the new self-image. Some people, as Erving Goffman points out, work diligently to create impressions that convey particular sorts of meaning to others around them.

Finally, victims often find their lives dramatically modified by the victimization experience. Things previously taken for granted, such as evening strolls in the neighborhood, may never seem the same again (especially if the person was the victim of a mugging or of a random act of violence). Hence, each perspective covered in this chapter examines the interaction that occurs between individuals, and looks closely at the interaction between criminals and their victims. This chapter teaches us that social interaction is a process which is open to analysis, and that the ultimate outcome of any significant interaction is always a new experience or the reinterpretation of previous experiences—that is, the creation of new meanings.

WEB WATCH

Access the *Criminology Today* home page on the World Wide Web by pointing your browser at www.prenhall.com/cjcentral. Once there, click on *Criminology Today* in order to access the wealth of electronic resources supporting this text.

Onsite resources include (1) "Chapter Links," which provides succinct overviews of critical ideas from the textbook and links selected materials from around the Web to concepts found in the text; (2) "General Reference—Law and Justice Links." Organized by chapter, these links lead to other useful resources on the World Wide Web such as libraries, electronic discussion lists, and electronic journals; (3) "Criminology Sites on the Web," which lists links to organizations such as the American Society of Criminology and the National Organization for Victims Assistance (NOVA), as well as crime prevention links and statistics on crime and justice. Many other Web-based resources can be accessed via the *Criminology Today* site, including the federal Justice Information Center, the Bureau of Justice Statistics, the FBI, the RAND Corporation, the Vera Institute of Justice, PAVNET (an online "Partnership Against Violence," run by seven different federal agencies), and the National White Collar Crime Center.

Still another feature of the *Criminology Today* Web site is e-mail homework. Homework can be composed onsite and submitted to instructors using the instructor's e-mail address. To use the e-mail homework feature, click on "E-Mail Homework" on the opening page and then type answers to the questions that appear in the spaces provided. Use your instructor's e-mail address to submit homework answers. The *Criminology Today* Web site also provides links to powerful Web-based search engines that can help you find topics of interest to you as you progress through your course of study. Search engines can be found under the home page heading "Criminology Sites on the Web."

DISCUSSION QUESTIONS

1. This book emphasizes a social problems versus social responsibility theme. Which of the theoretical perspectives discussed in this chapter (if any) best support the social problems approach? Which (if any) support the social responsibility approach? Why?
2. This chapter begins with a discussion of the labeling process. Give a few examples of the everyday imposition of positive, rather than negative, labels. Why is it so difficult to successfully impose positive labels on individuals previously labeled negatively?
3. Do you believe that Erving Goffman's dramaturgical approach, which sees the world as a stage and individuals as actors upon that stage, provides any valuable insights into human affairs? If so, what are they? Do you believe that Goffman takes his analogy too far? If so, how?
4. Explain the concept of phenomenology in your own words. How might it be applied to the study of a subject matter other than crime and criminality? Do you agree with critics that phenomenological criminology is nihilistic? Why or why not?
5. Review the proposed victims' rights constitutional amendment presented in a theory box in this chapter. Do you favor or oppose amending the U.S. Constitution to recognize the rights of crime victims? Defend your position.

NOTES

[1] William Faulkner, *As I Lay Dying* (New York: Random House, 1964).

[2] Abraham Kaplan, *The Conduct of Inquiry: Methodology for Behavioral Science* (San Francisco: Chandler, 1964), p. 32.

[3] Edwin M. Lemert, *Social Pathology: A Systematic Approach to the Theory of Sociopathic Behavior* (New York: McGraw-Hill, 1951), p. 284.

[4] Erving Goffman, *The Presentation of Self in Everyday Life* (Garden City, N.Y.: Doubleday, 1959), p. 135.

[5] "Killer's Admission to Law School Criticized," *Fayetteville Observer-Times,* September 12, 1993, p. 14A.

[6] Ibid.

[7] Frank Tannenbaum, *Crime and the Community* (New York: Atheneum Press, 1938), pp. 17–18.

[8] *Social Pathology,* p. 76.

[9] Ibid.

[10] Howard Becker, *Outsiders: Studies in the Sociology of Deviance* (New York: Free Press, 1963).

[11] Ibid., p. 1.

[12] Ibid., p. 9.

[13] Ibid., p. 147.

[14] Ibid., pp. 37–38.

[15] Mike S. Adams, "Labeling and Differential Association: Towards A General Social Learning Theory of Crime and Deviance," *American Journal of Criminal Justice,* vol. 20, no. 2 (1996), pp. 147–164.

[16] Ibid., p. 160.

[17] Randy Martin, Robert J. Mutchnick, and W. Timothy Austin, *Criminological Thought: Pioneers Past and Present* (New York: Macmillan, 1990), p. 368.

[18] Four papers have been released in the RISE series to date. They are: Lawrence W. Sherman and Heather Strang, *The Right Kind of Shame for Crime Prevention* (Canberra, Australia: Australian National University, 1997); Heather Strang and Lawrence W. Sherman, *The Victim's Perspective* (Canberra, Australia: Australian

National University, 1997); Lawrence W. Sherman and Geoffrey C. Barnes, *Restorative Justice and Offenders' Respect for the Law* (Canberra, Australia: Australian National University, 1997); and Lawrence W. Sherman and Heather Strang, *Restorative Justice and Deterring Crime* (Canberra, Australia: Australian National University, 1997).

[19] *RISE Working Papers: Introduction* (Canberra, Australia: Australian National University, 1997).

[20] *The Presentation of Self in Everyday Life.*

[21] William Shakespeare, *As You Like It* [1598–1600], Act II, Scene 7, line 139.

[22] *The Presentation of Self in Everyday Life,* pp. 9–10.

[23] Ibid., p. 17.

[24] Ibid., p. 60.

[25] "People," *USA Today,* September 13, 1993, p. 2D.

[26] Ibid., p. 75.

[27] Erving Goffman, *Stigma: Notes on the Management of Spoiled Identity* (Englewood Cliffs, N.J.: Prentice Hall, 1963).

[28] Ibid., p. 5.

[29] Ibid., p. 138.

[30] Erving Goffman, *Asylums: Essays on the Social Situation of Mental Patients and Other Inmates* (Garden City, N.Y.: Anchor Books, 1961).

[31] Peter K. Manning, "On the Phenomenology of Violence," *The Criminologist,* vol. 14, no. 4 (July/August 1989), pp. 1, 4–6, 22.

[32] Laurie Taylor, "Erving Goffman," *New Society,* December 1968, p. 836.

[33] Samuel Yochelson and Stanton E. Samenow, *The Criminal Personality: A Profile for Change* (New York: Jason Aronson, 1976); *The Criminal Personality: The Change Process* (New York: Jason Aronson, 1977); and *The Criminal Personality: The Drug User* (Northvale, N.J.: Jason Aronson, 1986).

[34] Frank Schmalleger, "World of the Career Criminal," *Human Nature,* March 1979.

[35] Richard Quinney, *The Social Reality of Crime* (Boston: Little Brown, 1970), p. 15.

[36] Stuart Henry and Dragan Milovanovic, "Constitutive Criminology: The Maturation of Critical Theory," *Criminology,* vol. 29, no. 2 (May 1991), p. 293.

[37] See also Stuart Henry and Dragan Milovanovic, *Constitutive Criminology: Beyond Postmodernism* (London: Sage, 1996); and Dragan Milo-

vanovic, *Postmodern Criminology* (Hamden, Conn.: Garland, 1997).

[38] Ibid., p. 302.

[39] Ibid.

[40] Samuel Yochelson and Stanton E. Samenow, *The Criminal Personality: A Profile for Change* (New York: Jason Aronson, 1976), p. 41.

[41] Yochelson and Samenow, *The Criminal Personality: A Profile for Change.*

[42] Ibid., Volume 1, p. 129.

[43] Ibid., Volume 1, p. 249.

[44] "World of the Career Criminal."

[45] Hans von Hentig, *The Criminal and His Victim: Studies in the Sociobiology of Crime* (Archon Books, 1967), reprinted from the 1948 Yale University Press edition.

[46] As noted by Stephen Schafer, *The Victim and His Criminal: A Study in Functional Responsibility* (New York: Random House, 1968).

[47] Ibid., p. 384.

[48] Ibid., p. 385.

[49] Ibid., p. 399.

[50] Ibid., p. 402.

[51] Benjamin Mendelsohn, "Method to Be Used by Counsel for the Defence in the Researches Made into the Personality of the Criminal," *Revue de Droit Pénal et de Criminologie* (Brussels), Fall 1937, p. 877.

[52] Benjamin Mendelsohn, *Rape in Criminology* (Rome: Giustizia Penale, 1940).

[53] See Henry Ellenberger, "Relations Psychologiques entre le Criminel et sa Victime," *Revue Internationale de Criminologie et de Police Technique* (Geneva), no. 2, 1954.

[54] Marvin E. Wolfgang, "Victim-Precipitated Criminal Homicide," *Journal of Criminal Law, Criminology and Police Science,* vol. 48, no. 1 (1957), pp. 1–11.

[55] Ibid.

[56] Thorsten Sellin and Marvin E. Wolfgang, *The Measurement of Delinquency* (New York: John Wiley & Sons, 1964).

[57] Rosa Casarez-Levison, "An Empirical Investigation of the Coping Strategies Used by Victims of Crime: Victimization Redefined," in Emilio Viano, ed., *Critical Issues in Victimology: International Perspectives* (New York: Spring, 1992).

[58] M. Bard and D. Sangrey, *The Crime Victim's Book,* 2nd ed. (New York: Brunner/Mazel, 1986).

[59]Elizabeth Kubler-Ross, *On Death and Dying* (New York: Macmillan, 1969).

[60]Robert Reiff, *The Invisible Victim: The Criminal Justice System's Forgotten Responsibility* (New York: Basic Books, 1979), p. xi.

[61]Richard Quinney, "Who Is the Victim," *Criminology,* vol. 10, no. 2 (1972), pp. 314–323.

[62]William G. Doerner, "The Impact of Medical Resources on Criminally Induced Lethality: A Further Examination," *Criminology,* vol. 26, no. 1 (February 1988), pp. 171–177.

[63]Ibid., p. 177.

[64]William Ryan, "The Art of Savage Discovery," in Adalberto Aguirre, Jr. and David V. Baker, eds., *Sources: Notable Selections in Race and Ethnicity* (Guilford, Conn.: Dushkin/McGraw-Hill, 1995).

[65]Steven Rathgeb Smith and Susan Freinkel, *Adjusting the Balance: Federal Policy and Victim Services* (Westport, Conn.: Greenwood Press, 1988), p. 13.

[66]Robert Elias, *Victims of the System: Crime Victims and Compensation in American Politics and Criminal Justice* (New Brunswick, N.J.: Transaction, 1983), pp. 24–26.

[67]Ibid.

[68]Ibid., p. 245.

[69]For a good review of the issues in the area, see Robert C. Davis, Arthur J. Lurigio, and Wesley G. Skogan, *Victims of Crime,* 2nd ed. (Thousand Oaks, Calif.: Sage, 1997).

[70]For a good review of the issues involved, see Robert C. Davis, Arthur J. Lurigio, and Wesley G. Skogan, *Victims of Crime,* 2nd ed. (Thousand Oaks, Calif.: Sage, 1997); and Leslie Sebba, *Third Parties: Victims and the Criminal Justice System* (Columbus, Ohio: Ohio State University Press, 1996).

[71]Albert R. Roberts, *Helping Crime Victims* (Newbury Park, Calif.: Sage, 1990).

[72]Ibid., p. 31.

[73]See also "Victim Assistance Programs: Whom They Service, What They Offer," A National Institute of Justice, *Update* (May 1995).

[74]President's Task Force on Victims of Crime, *Final Report* (Washington, D.C.: U.S. Government Printing Office, 1982).

[75]P.L. 97-291.

[76]Proposition 8, *California's Victims' Bill of Rights.*

[77]*Payne* v. *Tennessee,* 501 U.S. 808 (1991).

[78]"What Say Should Victims Have?" *Time,* May 27, 1991, p. 61.

[79]Stephen Schafer, *The Victim and His Criminal: A Study in Functional Responsibility* (New York: Random House, 1968).

[80]The President's Task Force on Victims of Crime, *Final Report* (Washington, D.C.: U.S. Government Printing Office, 1982).

[81]American Bar Association, *Guidelines for Fair Treatment of Crime Victims and Witnesses* (Chicago: ABA, 1983), p. 22.

[82]Susan Hillenbrand, "Restitution and Victim Rights in the 1980s," in Arthur J. Lurigio, Wesley G. Skogan, and Robert C. Davis, eds., *Victims of Crime: Problems, Policies, and Programs* (Newbury Park, Calif.: Sage, 1990), p. 192.

[83]Ibid., p. 196.

[84]Ibid.

[85]Thomas C. Castellano, "Assessing Restitution's Impact on Recidivism: A Review of the Evaluative Literature" in Viano, *Critical Issues in Victimology: International Perspectives,* p. 240.

PART THREE

CRIME IN THE MODERN WORLD

Our country will not truly be safe again until all Americans take personal responsibility for themselves, their families, and their communities...."

—President Clinton, commenting at the signing of the $30 billion Violent Crime Control and Law Enforcement Act of 1994.

POLITICAL REALITIES

AND CRIME

Social stratification breeds envy. And that leads to crime . . . .

—NATALYA LEMESHEVA, RUSSIAN SCHOOL TEACHER[1]

To move beyond criminal justice is to move beyond capitalism.

—RICHARD QUINNEY[2]

[I] attribute the social and psychological problems of modern society to the fact that society requires people to live under conditions radically different from those under which the human race evolved.

—THE UNABOMBER

There's a little bit of the Unabomber in most of us.

—ROBERT WRIGHT[3]

❖ CHAPTER OUTLINE ❖

INTRODUCTION: POLITICS AND CRIME
LAW AND SOCIAL ORDER PERSPECTIVES
    The Consensus Perspective
    The Pluralistic Perspective
    The Conflict Perspective
RADICAL-CRITICAL CRIMINOLOGY
    Radical Criminology Today
    Critical Criminology
    Radical-Critical Criminology and Policy Issues
    Critiques of Radical-Critical Criminology
TERRORISM
    Countering the Terrorist Threat
STATE-ORGANIZED CRIME
SUMMARY

⬅ IMPORTANT NAMES ➡

Roscoe Pound	Karl Marx	George Vold
Richard Quinney	William Chambliss	Austin Turk
Raymond J. Michalowski		

⬅ IMPORTANT TERMS ➡

consensus model	pluralistic perspective	conflict perspective
radical criminology	proletariat	social class
Marxist criminology	critical criminology	terrorism
state-organized crime	bourgeoisie	

❖ INTRODUCTION: POLITICS AND CRIME

At approximately 3 A.M. on a snowy January morning in 1994, "Big Oleg" Korotaev, 44, a former champion Russian boxer, was shot in the head and died on New York City's Brighton Beach Avenue. The shot that killed Korotaev, who was among the highest ranking of Russia's emerging organized crime figures, could be heard all the way to Moscow's Spassky Street. That's where Russian police General Gennady F. Chebotarev runs an office charged with tracking the growing worldwide threat represented by Russia's crime bosses and the organizations they run.

    Russian criminal organizations rapidly gained in power and influence during the tumultuous period of social upheaval which surrounded the demise of the former Soviet government. They now have roots that reach around the globe. In this country Russian organized crime groups have been reported operating in Boston,

Philadelphia, San Francisco, and Los Angeles, as well as in New York. These groups—using skills first developed to dodge the bureaucracy of the old Soviet system—have become expert at forgery, medical insurance fraud, credit card scams, narcotics distribution, and contract killings.

One favorite area of activity perfected by Russian criminal organizations is that of gasoline tax fraud. FBI Director Louis Freeh estimates that "Russian émigrés involved in tax-evasion schemes in this country now control the sale of more than 50 million gallons of gasoline a month, on which $7 million in federal excise taxes is evaded."[4] The Russians set up fake fuel companies, selling gasoline at "tax-included" prices—but never paying the fuel tax to local or federal revenue offices. One such scam, which resulted in the indictment of fourteen persons in Pennsylvania and New Jersey, produced an estimated $14.8 million in illegal gains for the Russian masterminds behind the plan, who quickly fled to their native country to launder the ill-gotten gains.

Money laundering is a relatively simple undertaking in Russia. There American money is more valuable than gold, and official regulations do not require the reporting of cash transactions in any amount. New to capitalism, Russia has yet to implement U.S.-style money-laundering laws that mandate the reporting of large cash bank transactions. Although lax Russian laws are a help, Russian gangsters are undeniably thorough. Commenting on "Big Oleg's" murder, one New York detective remarked, "One thing we know is that you don't solve Russian homicides."[5]

▓ LAW AND SOCIAL ORDER PERSPECTIVES

The rapid growth of Russian organized crime highlights the close link between crime and politics which exists not only in Russia, but also throughout the world. In the old Soviet Union, for example, communism precluded the existence of certain forms of crime. People were cared for by the state, and—at least theoretically—most types of private property simply did not exist. Hence, those crimes of theft or destruction of property that took place were generally regarded as crimes against the state, the entity to which most property formally belonged. Soviet understandings of crime which characterized the period were couched in terms of communist ideology and seen as the direct result of the immoral tendency toward capitalism.

As Russian laws changed following the downfall of the Soviet system, so too did the characteristic nature of crime and criminal activity within Russian society. Not only were new *opportunities* for criminal activity created by the changing social structure, but new *categories* of criminal activity were called into being by changed laws. An understanding of the interplay between formalized law and social order is critical to any study of criminology. Following are three analytical perspectives that shed some light on this subject.

- the consensus perspective
- the pluralist perspective
- the conflict perspective

Consensus model an
analytical perspective on
social organization which
holds that most members
of society agree as to what
is right and what is wrong,
and that the various
elements of society work
together in unison toward
a common and shared
vision of the greater good.

THE CONSENSUS PERSPECTIVE

The **consensus model** of social organization is built around the notion that most members of society agree on what is right and wrong, and that the various elements of society—including institutions such as churches, schools, government agencies, and businesses—work together toward a common and shared vision of the greater good. According to **Raymond J. Michalowski,** whose excellent analytical work is used to describe each of the three major approaches discussed in this section, the consensus perspective is characterized by four principles:[6]

- A belief in the existence of core values. The consensus perspective holds that commonly shared notions of right and wrong characterize the majority of society's members.
- The notion that laws reflect the collective will of the people. Law is seen as the result of a consensus, achieved through legislative action, and represents a kind of social conscience.
- The assumption that the law serves all people equally. From the consensus point of view, the law not only embodies a shared view of justice, but is itself perceived to be just in its application.
- The idea that those who violate the law represent a unique subgroup with some distinguishing features. The consensus approach holds that law violators must somehow be improperly socialized, psychologically defective, or suffer from some other lapse which leaves them unable to participate in what is otherwise widespread agreement on values and behavior.

The consensus perspective was operative in American politics and characterized social scientific thought in this country throughout much of the early 1900s. It found its greatest champion in **Roscoe Pound,** former dean of the Harvard School of Law and one of the greatest legal scholars of modern times. Pound developed the notion that the law is a tool for engineering society. The law, Pound said, meets the needs of men and women living together in society, and can be used to fashion society's characteristics and major features. Pound distilled his ideas into a set of jural postulates. Such postulates, Pound claimed, explain the existence and form of all laws insofar as laws reflect shared needs. Pound's postulates read as follows:[7]

- In civilized society men and women[8] must be able to assume that others will commit no intentional aggressions upon them.
- In civilized society men and women must be able to assume that they may control for beneficial purposes what they have discovered and appropriated to their own use, what they have created by their own labor, and what they have acquired under the existing social and economic order.
- In civilized society men and women must be able to assume that those with whom they deal in the general intercourse of society will act in good faith and hence
  1. Will make good reasonable expectations that their promises or other conduct will reasonably create.

2. Will carry out their undertakings according to the expectations which the moral sentiment of the community attaches thereto.

3. Will restore specifically or by equivalent what comes to them by mistake or unanticipated or (via a) not fully intended situation whereby they receive at another's expense what they could not reasonably have expected to receive under the circumstances.

- In civilized society men and women must be able to assume that those who are engaged in some course of conduct will act with due care not to cause an unreasonable risk of injury upon others.

- In civilized society men and women must be able to assume that those who maintain things likely to get out of hand or to escape and do damage will restrain them or keep them within their proper bounds.

THE PLURALISTIC PERSPECTIVE

Contrary to the assumptions made by consensus thinkers, however, it has become quite plain to most observers of the contemporary social scene that not everyone agrees on what the law should say. Society today is rife with examples of conflicting values and ideals. Consensus is hard to find. Modern debates center on issues such as abortion, euthanasia, the death penalty, the purpose of criminal justice agencies in a diverse society, social justice, the rights and responsibilities of minorities

Paul Hill, sentenced to die for the murders of a Florida abortion clinic doctor and the doctor's security escort. Hill's self-righteous attitude reflects the plurality of values characteristic of society today. Why did some people see Hill as a martyr? *Steve Mawyer/Corbis-Bettmann.*

and other underrepresented groups, women's issues, the proper role of education, economic policy, social welfare, the function of the military in a changing world, environmental concerns, and appropriate uses of high technology. As many contemporary public forums would indicate, there exists within America today a great diversity of social groups, each with its own point of view regarding what is right and what is wrong, and each with its own agenda. Add to that the plethora of self-proclaimed individual experts busily touting their own points of view, and anything but a consensus of values seems characteristic of society today.

Such a situation is described by some writers as pluralistic. A **pluralistic perspective** mirrors the thought that a multiplicity of values and beliefs exists in any complex society, and that different social groups will each have their own set of beliefs, interests, and values. A crucial element of this perspective, however, is the assumption that although different viewpoints exist, most individuals agree on the usefulness of law as a formal means of dispute resolution. Hence, from a pluralistic perspective the law, rather than reflecting common values, exists as a peace-keeping tool that allows officials and agencies within the government to settle disputes effectively between individuals and among groups. It also assumes that whatever settlement is reached will be acceptable to all parties because of their agreement on the fundamental role of law in dispute settlement. The basic principles of the pluralist perspective include the following notions.[9]

Pluralistic perspective an analytical approach to social organization which holds that a multiplicity of values and beliefs exist in any complex society, but that most social actors agree on the usefulness of law as a formal means of dispute resolution.

- Society consists of many and diverse social groups. Differences in age, gender, sexual preference, ethnicity, and the like often provide the basis for much naturally occurring diversity.
- Each group has its own characteristic set of values, beliefs, and interests. Variety in gender, sexual orientation, economic status, ethnicity, and other forms of diversity produce interests which may unite like-minded individuals, but which may also place them in natural opposition to other social groups.
- A general agreement exists on the usefulness of formalized laws as a mechanism for dispute resolution. People and groups accept the role of law in the settlement of disputes and accord decisions reached within the legal framework at least a modicum of respect.
- The legal system is value neutral. That is, the legal system is itself thought to be free of petty disputes or above the level of general contentiousness which may characterize relationships between groups.
- The legal system is concerned with the best interests of society. Legislators, judges, prosecutors, attorneys, police officers, and correctional officials are assumed to perform idealized functions that are beyond the reach of the everyday interests of self-serving groups. Hence, such official functionaries can be trusted to act in accordance with the greater good, to remain unbiased, and to maintain a value-free system for the enforcement of laws.

According to the pluralistic perspective, conflict is essentially resolved through the peace-keeping activities of unbiased government officials exercising objective legal authority.

THE CONFLICT PERSPECTIVE

A third point of view, the **conflict perspective,** maintains that conflict is a fundamental aspect of social life itself that can never be fully resolved. At best, according to this perspective, formal agencies of social control merely coerce the unempowered or the disenfranchised to comply with the rules established by those in power. From the conflict point of view, laws become a tool of the powerful, useful in keeping others from wresting control over important social institutions. Social order, rather than being the result of any consensus or process of dispute resolution, rests upon the exercise of power through law. Those in power must work ceaselessly to remain there, although the structure which they impose on society—including patterns of wealth-building that they define as acceptable and circumstances under which they authorize the exercise of legal power and military might—gives them all the advantages they are likely to need. The conflict perspective can be described in terms of six key elements.[10]

> **Conflict perspective** an analytical perspective on social organization which holds that conflict is a fundamental aspect of social life itself and can never be fully resolved.

THEORY IN PERSPECTIVE

Law and Social Order Approaches

CONSENSUS MODEL

Holds that most members of society agree as to what is right and what is wrong, and that the various elements of society work together in unison toward a common and shared vision of the greater good.

PLURALISTIC PERSPECTIVE.   Holds that a multiplicity of values and beliefs exist in any complex society, but that most social actors agree on the usefulness of law as a formal means of dispute resolution.

CONFLICT PERSPECTIVE.   Holds that conflict is a fundamental aspect of social life itself and can never be fully resolved.

RADICAL CRIMINOLOGY.   Holds that the causes of crime are rooted in social conditions which empower the wealthy and the politically well organized, but disenfranchise those less fortunate.
PERIOD: 1960s–Present
THEORISTS: Karl Marx, Richard Quinney, William Chambliss, Raymond Michalowski
CONCEPTS: Social class, bourgeoisie, proletariat

- Society is made up of diverse social groups. As in the pluralist perspective, diversity is thought to be based on distinctions which people hold to be significant, such as gender, sexual orientation, social class, and the like.
- Each group holds to differing definitions of right and wrong. Moralistic conceptions and behavioral standards vary from group to group.
- Conflict between groups is unavoidable. Conflict is based on differences held to be socially significant (such as ethnicity, gender, and social class) and is unavoidable because groups defined on the basis of these characteristics compete for power, wealth, and other forms of recognition.
- The fundamental nature of group conflict centers on the exercise of political power. Political power is the key to the accumulation of wealth and to other forms of power.
- Law is a tool of power and furthers the interests of those powerful enough to make it. Laws allow those in control to gain what they define (through the law) as legitimate access to scarce resources and to deny (through the law) such access to the politically disenfranchised.
- Those in power are inevitably interested in maintaining their power against those who would usurp it. The powerful strive to keep their power.

The conflict perspective was brought to criminology early in the twentieth century, but popularized by **George Vold** in 1958. Vold described social conflict as "a universal form of interaction" and said that groups are naturally in conflict as their interests and purposes "overlap, encroach on one another and (tend to) be competitive."[11] Vold also addressed the issue of social cohesion, noting that as intergroup conflict intensified, loyalty of individual members to their groups increased. "It has long been realized that conflict between groups tends to develop and intensify the loyalty of group members to their respective groups,"[12] Vold wrote. But Vold's most succinct observation of the role conflict plays in contributing to crime was expressed in these words: "The whole political process of law making, law breaking, and law enforcement becomes a direct reflection of deep-seated and fundamental conflicts between interest groups. . . . Those who produce legislative majorities win control over the power," said Vold, "and dominate the policies that decide who is likely to be involved in violation of the law."[13]

In other words, from Vold's point of view, powerful groups make laws, and those laws express and protect their interests. Hence, the body of laws that characterize any society is a political statement, and crime is a political definition imposed largely upon those whose interests lie outside of that which the powerful, through the law, define as acceptable. In his writings about conflict Vold went so far as to compare the criminal with a soldier, fighting, through crime commission, for the very survival of the group whose values he or she represents. In Vold's words: "[t]he individual criminal is then viewed as essentially a soldier under conditions of warfare: his behavior may not be 'normal' or 'happy' or 'adjusted'—it is the behavior of the soldier doing what is to be done in wartime."[14] Vold's analogy, probably influenced by the proximity in time of his writing to World War II, was meant to express the idea that crime was a manifestation of denied needs and values, that is, the cultural heritage of disenfranchised groups who were powerless to enact their interests in legitimate fashion. Hence, theft becomes necessary for many poor people, especially those left unemployed or unemployable by the socially acceptable forms of wealth distribution defined by law.

Another early conflict theorist, **Austin Turk,** said that in the search for an explanation of criminality, "one is led to investigate the tendency of laws to penalize persons whose behavior is more characteristic of the less powerful than of the more powerful and the extent to which some persons and groups can and do use legal processes and agencies to maintain and enhance their power position vis-à-vis other persons and groups."[15] In his 1969 seminal work, *Criminality and Legal Order,*[16] Turk wrote that in any attempt to explain criminality, "it is more useful to view the social order as mainly a pattern of conflict" rather than to offer explanations for crime based on behavioral or psychological approaches. Turk, like most other conflict criminologists, saw the law as a powerful tool in the service of prominent social groups seeking continued control over others. Crime was the natural consequence of such intergroup struggle because it resulted from the definitions imposed by the laws of the powerful upon the disapproved strivings of the unempowered.

"MARTYR" OR MURDERER?

ABORTION PROTESTER'S DEATH SENTENCE

The conflict perspective seems better suited to an understanding of many contemporary social issues, among them the heated battle between pro-lifers and pro-choice advocates over abortion, as the article in this box shows.

When Paul Hill used a 12-gauge shotgun to kill an abortion clinic's doctor, abortion rights supporters—and many foes—called him a monster.

Tuesday, Hill may have graduated from monster to martyr when he was sentenced to die in Florida's electric chair for the July murders of John Bayard Britton and his escort, James Barrett, in Pensacola.

"He'll be a good poster boy for murder in the future," said David Gunn, Jr., the son of a doctor killed in 1993 by another protester.

The National Right to Life Committee denounced violence. "The murders committed by Paul Hill were deplorable and reprehensible," says President Wanda Franz.

But radical abortion rights foes hailed Hill.

"He's a hero and a martyr in my book," says Christian Action Group's Roy McMillan of Jackson, Miss. "I believe in killing people in just wars . . . and there's a war in the womb."

Now, "we are going to execute someone who simply did for a stranger something every father in America would do to protect his children."

Almost from the time he joined demonstrations outside Pensacola's abortion clinics, activists watched as the articulate, soft-spoken former minister and father of three grew more fervent in his protests.

First, his fetus posters became more graphic, his shouting more intense.

"Mommy, don't let them kill me!" he cried out to women at The Ladies Center clinic.

Then, in March 1993, when another protester shot and killed abortion doctor David Gunn in Pensacola, Hill stunned the Bible Belt community by proclaiming he was part of a group that believes in "justifiable homicide" to stop abortion.

The Gunn slaying, Hill said last week on *Eye to Eye With Connie Chung,* "literally changed my life."

The double murder occurred 17 months later. Britton's wife was wounded, too.

On *Eye to Eye,* Hill said he has no regrets: "I have done something that I think the Lord is pleased with. I know . . . I'm going to heaven when I die."

Michael Bray, who served four years in prison in connection with the bombings of seven Washington, D.C.–area clinics, calls Hill an inspiration.

"If a martyr is one who dies for a just cause, yes," Bray said. "If he dies for doing what is good and right, yes. Therefore, I say yes."

Abortion rights activists say they're terrified such talk will provoke more violence.

"We are on red alert," says Eleanor Smeal of the Feminist Majority Foundation.

Smeal and others are urging the federal government to step up enforcement of a new law that makes it a crime to block access to clinics or threaten or harm workers. Hill also was convicted under that law.

Already, members of the new Republican-controlled Congress are considering ways to limit its scope.

"Those who commit violence ought to have federal penalties," says Rep. Chris Smith (R., N.J.). But the law goes too far, so "we're going to take a (new) look at it."

Barrett's son Bruce said Hill's sentence should send a powerful message. "It's real important that the state showed that this kind of violence is not going to be condoned, and the only way to do that is to give the maximum penalty," he said. Hill "shot my father in the face with a shotgun. He shot Dr. Britton in the head . . . and he had planned to do it for a long time."

Questions

1. How is it that some people view Paul Hill as a common criminal, while others see him as a hero—even a martyr? How can otherwise law-abiding citizens condone the killing of abortion clinic workers?
2. What does the debate over abortion have to tell us about the role of law in society, and about how laws are made and enforced?
3. What other issues can you identify which are officially law violations, but which have numerous proponents?

Source: Mimi Hall, "'Martyr' or Murderer? Abortion Protester's Death Sentence Ignites Debate," *USA Today,* December 7, 1994, p. 3A. Copyright 1994, *USA Today.* Reprinted with permission.

RADICAL-CRITICAL CRIMINOLOGY

The conflict perspective is thoroughly entrenched in **radical criminology,** which is also diversely known as, or related to, schools of thought referred to as new, critical, or Marxist criminology. Radical criminology, which appeared on the American scene in the 1970s, has its roots in the writings of nineteenth-century social utopian thinkers. Primary among them is **Karl Marx,** whose writings on the conflicts inherent in capitalism led to the formulation of communist ideals and, many would say, to the rise of communist societies the world over.

According to Marx two fundamental social classes exist within any capitalistic society: the haves and the have nots. Marx termed these two groups the proletariat and the bourgeoisie. The **proletariat** encompasses the large mass of people, those who are relatively uneducated and who are without power. In short, the proletariat are the workers, whereas the **bourgeoisie** are the capitalists—the wealthy owners of the means of production (i.e., the factories, businesses, and other elements of a society's organizational infrastructure). Although Marx was German, the terms *proletariat* and *bourgeoisie* were taken from Marx's knowledge of the French language, and are in turn derived from Latin. In ancient Rome, for example, that city's lowest class was propertyless and were individually referred to as *proletarius.*

According to Marx, the proletariat, since they possessed neither capital nor the means of production such as factories, land, or natural resources, must earn their living by continuously selling their labor. The bourgeoisie, on the other hand, are the capitalist class who, by nature of their very position within society, stand opposed to the proletariat in ongoing class struggle. Marx saw such struggle between classes as inevitable to the evolution of any capitalistic society, and believed that the natural outcome of such struggle would be the overthrow of capitalistic social order and the birth of a truly classless, or communistic, society.

RADICAL CRIMINOLOGY TODAY

Contemporary radical criminology is the intellectual child of three important historical circumstances: (1) the ruminations of nineteenth-century social utopian thinkers referred to earlier, including Friedrich Engels, Georg Wilhelm, Friedrich Hegel, Karl Marx, George Simmel, and Max Weber; (2) the rise of conflict theory in the social sciences; and (3) the dramatic radicalization of American academia in the 1960s and 1970s.

Radical criminologists of today are considerably more sophisticated than their Marxist forebearers. Contemporary radical criminology holds that the causes of crime are rooted in social conditions which empower the wealthy and the politically well organized, but disenfranchise those less fortunate. William Chambliss, a well-known spokesperson for radical thinkers, succinctly summarizes the modern perspective in these words: "what makes the behavior of some criminal is the coercive power of the state to enforce the will of the ruling class."[17]

Central to the perspective of radical criminology is the notion of social class. Some authors maintain that "class is nothing but an abbreviation to describe a way of living, thinking, and feeling." For most sociologists, however, the concept of

Radical criminology a perspective which holds that the causes of crime are rooted in social conditions which empower the wealthy and the politically well organized, but disenfranchise those less fortunate. Radical criminology is sometimes called **Marxist criminology.**

Proletariat in Marxian theory, the working class.

Bourgeoisie in Marxian theory, the class of people which owns the means of production.

The tomb of Karl Marx, in Highgate Cemetery, London, England. Marxist thought underpins the writings of many radical criminologists. How did Marxism influence criminology? *Rex Features USA Ltd.*

Social class distinctions made between individuals on the basis of important defining social characteristics.

social class entails distinctions made between individuals on the basis of significant defining characteristics such as race, religion, education, profession, income, wealth, family background, housing, artistic tastes, aspirations, cultural pursuits, child-rearing habits, speech, accent, and so forth. Individuals are assigned to classes by others and by themselves on the basis of characteristics which are both ascribed and achieved. Ascribed attributes are those with which a person is born, such as race or gender, while achieved characteristics are acquired through personal effort or chance over the course of one's life and include such things as level of education, income, place of residence, and profession.

Although Marx concerned himself with only two social classes, most social scientists today talk in terms of at least three groups: upper, middle, and lower class. Some, such as Vance Packard,[18] have distinguished between five hierarchically arranged classes (the real upper, semiupper, limited-success, working, and real lower) while further subdividing classes 'horizontally' according to ascribed characteristics such as race and religion.

Conflict theorists of the early and mid-1900s saw in the concept of social class the rudimentary ingredients of other important concepts such as authority, power, and conflict. Ralf Dahrendorf, for example, wrote that "classes are social conflict groups the determinant of which can be found in the participation in or exclusion from the exercise of authority."[19] For Dahrendorf, conflict was ubiquitous, a fundamental part of and coextensive with any society. "Not the presence but the absence of conflict is surprising and abnormal," he wrote, "and we have good reason to be suspicious if we find a society or social organization that displays no evidence of conflict. To be sure, we do not have to assume that conflict is always violent and uncontrolled . . . [and] we must never lose sight of the underlying assumption that conflict can be temporarily suppressed, regulated, channeled, and controlled but that neither a philosopher-king nor a modern dictator can abolish it once and for all."[20]

From Dahrendorf's perspective, it was power and authority which were most at issue between groups, and over which class conflicts arose. Dahrendorf also recognized that situations characterized by conflict are rarely static, and it is out of conflict that change arises. For Dahrendorf, change could be either destructive or constructive. Destructive change brings about a lessening of social order, whereas constructive change increases cohesiveness within society.

Two highly visible proponents of radical criminology today are **Richard Quinney** and **William Chambliss.** In 1971 Chambliss, along with Robert T. Seidman, published an intellectually renowned volume entitled *Law, Order, and Power.* Their work represented something of a bridge between earlier conflict theorists and the more radical approach of Marxists. Through its emphasis on social class, class interests, and class conflict, *Law, Order, and Power* presented a Marxist perspective stripped of any overt references to capitalism as the root cause of crime. "The more economically stratified a society becomes," Chambliss and Seidman wrote, "the more it becomes necessary for the dominant groups in the society to enforce through coercion the norms of conduct which guarantee their supremacy."[21] Chambliss and Seidman outlined their position in four propositions, as follows:[22]

- The conditions of one's life affect one's values and norms. Complex societies are composed of groups with widely different life conditions.
- Complex societies are therefore composed of highly disparate and conflicting sets of norms.
- The probability of a given group's having its particular normative system embodied in law is not distributed equally but is closely related to the political and economic position of that group.
- The higher a group's political or economic position, the greater the probability that its views will be reflected in laws.

Chambliss also believed that middle- and upper-class criminals are more apt to escape apprehension and punishment by the criminal justice system, not because they are any smarter or more capable of hiding their crimes than are lower class offenders, but because of a "very rational choice on the part of the legal system to pursue those violators that the community will reward them for pursuing and to ignore those violators who have the capability for causing trouble for the agencies."[23]

By the 1970s, however, as American academia became increasingly radicalized, Chambliss's writings assumed a much more Marxian flavor. In an article published in 1975, Chambliss once again recognized the huge power gap separating the "haves" from the "have nots."[24] Crime, he said, is created by actions of the ruling class which define as criminal such things as undertakings and activities that contravene the interests of the rulers. At the same time, he said, members of the ruling class will inevitably be able to continue to violate the criminal law with impunity, because it is their own creation.

By 1975, the Marxian flavor of Chambliss's writing had become undeniable. He began using Marxist terminology. "[A]s capitalist societies industrialize and the gap between the bourgeoisie and the proletariat widens," he wrote, "penal law will expand in an effort to coerce the proletariat into submission."[25] For Chambliss, the economic consequences of crime within a capitalistic society were partially what perpetuated it. "[C]rime reduces surplus labor," he wrote, "by creating employment not only for the criminals but for law enforcers, welfare workers, professors of criminology, and a horde of people who live off the fact that crime exists...."[26] Socialist societies, claimed Chambliss, should reflect much lower crime rates than capitalist societies because a "less intense class struggle should reduce the forces leading to and the functions of crime."

Although Chambliss provides much of the intellectual bedrock of contemporary radical criminology, that school of thought found its most eloquent expression in the writings of Richard Quinney. In 1974 Quinney, in an attempt to challenge and change American social life for the better, set forth his six Marxist propositions for an understanding of crime, as follows:[27]

- American society is based on an advanced capitalist economy.
- The state is organized to serve the interests of the dominant economic class, the capitalist ruling class.
- Criminal law is an instrument of the state and ruling class to maintain and perpetuate the existing social and economic order.
- Crime control in capitalist society is accomplished through a variety of institutions and agencies established and administered by a governmental elite, representing ruling class interests, for the purpose of establishing domestic order.
- The contradictions of advanced capitalism—the disjunction between existence and essence—require that the subordinate classes remain oppressed by whatever means necessary, especially through the coercion and violence of the legal system.
- Only with the collapse of capitalist society and the creation of a new society, based on socialist principles, will there be a solution to the crime problem.

A few years later, Quinney published *Class, State, and Crime*, in which he argued that almost all crimes committed by members of the lower classes are necessary for the survival of individual members of those classes. Crimes, said Quinney—in fashion reminiscent of Vold's notion of the criminal as a soldier—are actually an attempt by the socially disenfranchised "to exist in a society where *survival* is not assured by other, collective means."[28] "Crime is inevitable under capitalist conditions," concludes Quinney, because crime is "a response to the material conditions of life. Permanent unemployment—and the acceptance of that condition," wrote Quinney, "can result in a form of life where criminality is an appropriate and consistent response."[29] The solution offered by Quinney to the problem of crime is the development of a socialist society. "The *ultimate meaning* of crime in the development of capitalism," he writes, "is the need for a socialist society."[30]

Contemporary radical criminology attributes much of the existing propensity toward criminality to differences in social class, and in particular to those arrangements within society which maintain class differences. As Quinney puts it, "classes are an expression of the underlying forces of the capitalist mode of production. . . ."[31] "Within the class structure of advanced capitalism," he writes, "is the dialectic that increases class struggle and the movement for socialist revolution." Table 9.1 depicts the class structure of the United States as Quinney portrayed it.

TABLE 9.1

CLASS STRUCTURE OF THE UNITED STATES
WITH ESTIMATED PERCENTAGES OF THE ADULT POPULATION

Capitalist Class 1.5%	Owns and controls production; wields state power
Petty Bourgeoisie 18.5%	Professionals, middle management, bureaucrats

Working Class
 	
80%
	Technical and skilled working class, 25%
	
	Technical, 10%
	   teachers
	   nurses
	   medical technicians
	
	Skilled, 15%
	   craftsmen
	   clerical
	   sales
	   operatives
	   transport
	   industrial
	
	Unskilled working class, 55%
	
	Unskilled, 30%
	   industrial labor
	   service
	   office
	   sales
	   clerical
	
	Reserve army, 15%
	   unemployed
	
	Pauperized poor, 10%

Source: Richard Quinney, *Class, State, and Crime: On the Theory and Practice of Criminal Justice* (New York: David McKay, 1977), p. 77. Reprinted with permission.

Critical criminology a
perspective focused on
challenging traditional
understandings and on
uncovering false beliefs
about crime and criminal
justice.

CRITICAL CRIMINOLOGY

Some writers distinguish between critical criminology and radical criminology, claiming that the former is simply a way of critiquing social relationships that lead to crime, while the latter constitutes a proactive call for a radical change in the social conditions which lead to crime.

Gresham Sykes explains **critical criminology** this way: "it forces an inquiry into precisely how the normative content of the criminal law is internalized in different segments of society, and how norm-holding is actually related to behavior."[32] As David A. Jones states in his insightful *History of Criminology*, however, "Sometimes, it may be difficult to distinguish 'critical' from a truly Marxist criminology. One basis, advanced by Marvin Wolfgang, is that 'critical' criminology is 'more reactive than proactive,' meaning that 'critical' criminology does not aim to overthrow the 'ruling class' so much as it may criticize the way it believes such a group dominates society."[33]

A cogent example of the critical perspective in contemporary criminology can be had in the work of Elliott Currie.[34] Currie claims "that 'market societies'—those in which the pursuit of private gain becomes the dominant organizing principle of social and economic life—are especially likely to breed high levels of violent crime." Market societies, says Currie, are characterized by more than free enterprise and a free market economy. They are societies in which the striving after personal economic gain runs rampant and becomes the hallmark of social life. The conditions endemic to market societies lead to high crime rates because they undercut and overwhelm more traditional principles that "have historically sustained individuals, families and communities." The United States is the world's premier market society, says Currie, and its culture provides "a particularly fertile breeding ground for serious violent crime." Similarly, the recent and dramatic rise in crime rates in former communist countries throughout Europe can be explained by the burgeoning development of new market societies in those nations. According to Currie, seven "profoundly criminogenic and closely intertwined mechanisms" operate in a market society to produce crime. They are:

- "The progressive destruction of livelihood," which results from the long-term absence of opportunities for stable and rewarding work—a consequence of the fact that market societies view labor "simply as a cost to be reduced" rather than as an asset with intrinsic value.
- "The growth of extremes of economic inequality and material deprivation," which causes many children to spend their developmental years in poverty.
- "The withdrawal of public services and supports, especially for families and children," resulting from the fact that "it is a basic operating principle of market society to keep the public sector small . . .".
- "The erosion of informal and communal networks of mutual support, supervision, and care," brought about by the high mobility of the work force characteristic of market societies.
- "The spread of a materialistic, neglectful, and 'hard' culture," which exalts brutal forms of individualized competition.

- "The unregulated marketing of the technology of violence," including the ready availability of guns, an emphasis on advancing technologies of destruction (such as the military), and mass-marketed violence on television and in the media.
- "The weakening of social and political alternatives," leaving people unable to cope effectively with the forces of the market society which undermine their communities and destroy valuable interpersonal relationships.

Currie suggests that as more nations emulate the 'market society' culture of the United States, crime rates throughout the world will rise. An increasing emphasis on punishment, and the growth of huge prisons systems, says Currie, will consequently characterize most of the world's nations in the twenty-first century.

RADICAL-CRITICAL CRIMINOLOGY AND POLICY ISSUES

Some contemporary writers on radical criminology tell us that "Marxist criminology was once dismissed as a utopian perspective with no relevant policy implication except revolution. At best, revolution was considered an impractical approach to the problems at hand. Recently, however, many radicals have attempted to address the issues of what can be done under our current system."[35]

Most radical-critical criminologists of the current genre recognize that a sudden and total reversal of existing political arrangements within the United States is highly unlikely. They have begun to focus, instead, on promoting a gradual transition to socialism and to socialized forms of government activity. These middle-range policy alternatives include "equal justice in the bail system, the abolition of mandatory sentences, prosecution of corporate crimes, increased employment opportunities, and promoting community alternatives to imprisonment."[36] Likewise, programs to reduce prison overcrowding, efforts to highlight injustices within the current system, the elimination of racism and other forms of inequality in the handling of both victims and offenders, growing equality in criminal justice system employment, and the like are all frequently mentioned as midrange strategies for bringing about a justice system that is more fair and closer to the radical ideal.

Raymond Michalowski well summarizes the policy directions envisioned by today's radical-critical criminologists when he says, "[w]e cannot be free from the crimes of the poor until there are no more poor; we cannot be free from domination of the powerful until we reduce the inequalities that make domination possible; and we cannot live in harmony with others until we begin to limit the competition for material advantage over others that alienates us from one another."[37]

Even so, few radical-critical criminologists seem to expect to see dramatic changes in the near future. As Michael J. Lynch and W. Byron Groves explain, "[i]n the end, the criminal justice system has failed as an agent of social change because its efforts are directed at an individual as opposed to social remedies. . . . For these reasons, radicals suggest that we put our efforts into the creation of economic equality or employment opportunities to combat crime."[38]

CRITIQUES OF RADICAL-CRITICAL CRIMINOLOGY

Radical-critical criminology has been criticized for its nearly exclusive emphasis on methods of social change at the expense of well-developed theory. As *William* v. *Pelfrey* explains, "[i]t is in the Radical School of Criminology that theory is almost totally disregarded, except as something to criticize, and radical *methods* are seen as optimum."[39]

Radical-critical criminology can also be criticized for failing to recognize what appears to be at least a fair degree of public consensus about the nature of crime, that is, that crime is undesirable and that criminal activity is to be controlled. Were criminal activity in fact a true expression of the sentiments of the politically and economically disenfranchised, as some radical criminologists claim, then public opinion might be expected to offer support for at least certain forms of crime. Even the sale and consumption of illicit drugs, however—a type of crime which may provide an alternative path to riches for the otherwise disenfranchised—is frequently condemned by residents of working-class communities.[40]

An effective criticism of Marxist criminology, in particular, centers on the fact that Marxist thinkers appear to confuse issues of personal politics with what could otherwise be social reality. As a consequence of allowing personal values and political leanings to enter the criminological arena, Marxist criminologists have frequently appeared to sacrifice their objectivity. Jackson Toby, for example, claims that Marxist and radical thinkers are simply building upon an "old tradition of sentimentality toward those who break social rules."[41] Such sentimentality can be easily discounted, he says, when we realize that "[c]olor television sets and automobiles are stolen more often than food and blankets."[42]

Marxist criminology has also been refuted by contemporary thinkers who find that it falls short in appreciating the multiplicity of problems that contribute to the problem of crime. Some years ago, for example, the astute criminologist Hermann Mannheim critiqued Marxian assumptions by showing how "subsequent developments" have shown that "Marx was wrong in thinking: (a) that there could be only two classes in a capitalist society . . .; (b) that . . . class struggle was entirely concerned with the question of private property in the means of production; (c) that the only way in which fundamental social changes could be effected was by violent social revolution; [and] (d) that all conflicts were class conflicts and all social change could be explained in terms of class conflicts. . . ."

Mannheim went on to point out that the development of a semiskilled work force along with the advent of highly skilled and well-educated workers has led to the creation of a multiplicity of classes within contemporary capitalistic societies. The growth of such classes, said Mannheim, effectively spreads the available wealth in those societies where such workers are employed and reduces the likelihood of revolution.

Marxist criminology has also suffered a considerable loss of prestige among many would-be followers in the wake of the collapse of the former Soviet Union and its client states in Eastern Europe and other parts of the world. With the death of Marxist political organizations and their agendas, Marxist criminology seems to have lost some of its impetus. Many would argue that, in fact, the work of writers such as Quinney and Chambliss presaged the decline of Soviet influence and had already moved Marxist and radical criminology into new areas—effectively shedding the reigns of world communism and ending any association with its institutional embodiment in specific parts of the world. The work of Elliott Currie (discussed earlier in this chapter), and others, is now leading in a post-Marxist direction, while retaining a critical emphasis on the principles out of which radical criminology was fashioned.

▓ TERRORISM

From the perspective of radical criminology, crime can be a political statement. Quinney, for example, says that "criminality is the beginning of a conscious rebellion against capitalist conditions."[43] When crime becomes a conscious and intentionally chosen response to conditions of societal oppression, then it becomes a revolutionary tool. Hence, as alluded to earlier, some thinkers not only explain crime as the result of political oppression and the inequitable distribution of wealth and power in society, but view it as a form of terrorism that is more or less consciously waged against the state by the disenfranchised.

Unfortunately for such thinkers, however, the fact is that most crimes committed today appear to victimize precisely those who are already the most victimized by existing arrangements of wealth and power, that is, the working class poor and the unemployed. Quinney recognizes this when he says, "to the extent that crime is directed against members of the working class, crime remains counterrevolutionary. Much, if not most crime continues to victimize those who are already oppressed by capitalism. . . ."[44] Even so, it is true that those who see themselves as actively excluded from effective participation in political decision making may turn to other means to have their voices heard. When awareness translates into alienation, conscious calls for terrorist activity may erupt.

The FBI defines **terrorism** as "a violent act or an act dangerous to human life in violation of the criminal laws of the United States or of any state to intimidate or coerce a government, the civilian population, or any segment thereof, in furtherance of political or social objectives."[45] From the radical point of view discussed earlier in this chapter, terrorism is simply another example of the control by state monopolies over definitions of crime. Hence, a contrasting definition of terrorism is "behaviors which menace the social, economic, and political order."[46]

Regardless of definitional distinctions, both conservative and radical approaches seem to agree that "the primary distinction between violent criminal acts and terrorist acts has to do with the political motivation or ideology of the offender."[47] Hence, bombings, hostage taking, and other similar terroristlike acts which are undertaken for mere individual or pecuniary gain, when no political or social objectives are sought by the perpetrators, would not qualify as "terrorism" under either approach. However, as both definitions reveal, terrorists probably do not think of themselves as "criminal," preferring instead the "revolutionary" label.

Today the United States is faced with two types of terrorism: international and domestic. Although the number of terrorist attacks on U.S. interests around the world has shown an overall decline in recent years, it would be a mistake to assume that international terrorism is no longer a serious threat. As one observer on the

Terrorism a violent act or an act dangerous to human life in violation of the criminal laws of the United States or of any state to intimidate or coerce a government, the civilian population, or any segment thereof, in furtherance of political or social objectives.

subject states, "[w]hile the number of terrorist attacks generally is declining, the audacity of terrorists and their choice of targets . . . are in some ways more alarming than ever. As long as the United States remains actively engaged in the world, as it clearly must, there will be governments and groups committed to the use of violence to attack U.S. interests and further their own political goals."[48]

In 1996, the horrific truck bombing of U.S. military barracks in Dhahran, Saudi Arabia, validated that observation. Nineteen U.S. Air Force personnel were killed, and more than 250 others injured, in the blast that destroyed the Khobar Towers housing complex. A forty-person Pentagon task force headed by retired U.S. Army General Wayne Downing later concluded that the Pentagon had failed to take terrorist threats seriously.

Truck bombs pale in comparison with the destructive power of nuclear weapons, the availability of which appears to be rapidly increasing in today's black market. In 1997, for example, two Lithuanian nationals, Alexander Porgrebeshski, 28, and Alexander Darichev, 36, were arrested in Miami and charged with trying to sell Soviet-era nuclear weapons to federal agents posing as arms brokers for drug dealers. The two were caught on videotape negotiating the sale of Bulgarian-made tactical nuclear weapons. Dennis Fagan, chief agent at the U.S. Customs Service Miami office, said that the incident "shows there are people out there who have the ability to move weapons—strategic weapons—around the world."[49] Today's loose control over nuclear weapons and weapons-grade fissionable materials is the direct result of the collapse of the Soviet Union at the close of 1980s. That country's dissolution seriously lessened the ability of Russian and former East-block authorities to retain control over cold war stockpiles of nuclear weapons.

In a 1997 press briefing,[50] Ambassador Philip C. Wilcox, Jr.,[51] who has primary responsibility within the U.S. government for developing, coordinating, and implementing American counterterrorism policy, said "terrorists appear to be using much more lethal explosives against mass noncombatant targets." Ambassador Wilcox noted that "American businesses have been singled out for scores of terrorists attacks overseas," and added that: "Terrorism is also a more lethal threat than it has ever been in the past because of growing access of terrorists to technology." He provided an interesting analogy, saying: "In the year 1605, a would-be terrorist named Guy Fawkes tried to blow up the British House of Commons. He used 29 barrels of gunpowder. Fortunately, the plot was foiled. Today, that job could have been done with a small plastic charge concealed in a briefcase. Now, conventional explosives are readily available and the technology to make them and, worse yet, terrorists have increasing access to materials of mass destruction—nuclear, chemical, and biological." Ambassador Wilcox also noted that: "In today's volatile mix of religious fanaticism, pathological terrorists, and other dangerous and perverse forces and their access to modern technology increases the danger of terrorism tremendously. Terrorists not only have access to these materials of technological resources, another form of technology—the expansion of international media and communications—gives them a much, much broader stage upon which to perform, to intimidate, and to terrorize."

According to the U.S. State Department,[52] the number of international terrorist acts in 1996 fell to a twenty-five-year low. There were 296 such acts in 1996, compared with 665 in 1987 (the peak year since official record keeping began). Of the

296 acts of international terrorism in 1996, 251 were attacks against property in which there were no human casualties. There is, however, an opposite trend developing in the number of persons killed. In 1996, 311 persons died as the result of terrorist activity, whereas *only* 177 died during the previous year.

A more accurate measure of terrorism may be that produced by Pinkerton Risk Assessment Services, which uses a much broader definition of terrorism (one that counts politically motivated violence committed inside a country by its own citizens) than does the State Department. Pinkerton says that terrorist attacks worldwide have increased to record levels, and claims that the number of people killed yearly in worldwide terrorist attacks recently rose above 10,000 for the first time since the company began keeping records.[53]

The possibility of terrorism within U.S. borders was highlighted by the 1993 bombing of the World Trade Center in New York City and the ensuing fire and smoke which caused six deaths and nearly one thousand injuries while leaving a five-story crater under the building, was the only externally directed terrorist incident in 1993 that claimed American lives. One year and six days after the explosion, Nidal Ayyad, Ahmad Ajaj, Mohammad Salameh, and Mahmud Abouhalima—all Islamic fundamentalists who had entered the United States from the Middle East— were convicted of all charges that the U.S. government had brought against them, including conspiracy to bomb buildings, explosive destruction of property, and assault on a federal officer. After the bombing it was discovered, however, that plotters had targeted other vital city areas, including the United Nations and the Holland and Lincoln Tunnels. Had those plots been successfully implemented, many more lives would have been lost and an untold amount of social disruption would have occurred within the northeastern United States. In 1995 Sheik Oma Abdel-Rahman, the mastermind behind the Trade Center bombing, and eight other Muslim fundamentalists were convicted in a federal court on charges related to the bombing. Evidence showed that they plotted to start a holy war, and conspired to commit assassinations within the United States, and to bomb the United Nations.[54] The Sheik was sentenced to life in prison.

Observers say that the bombing of the World Trade Center may be just the beginning of a new and especially violent campaign of terrorism directed at American citizens both at home and abroad. As one terrorism expert recently put it, "The U.S. and its Arab allies are losing steadily to Islamic forces energized by several new trends in the Middle East. . . . It is tempting to dismiss the fundamentalists accused of bombing the World Trade Center and planning a host of other violent actions in New York as deranged fanatics, and amateurish ones at that. Yet, to do so is to ignore the fact that radical Islamists, in the U.S. and the Middle East, are pursuing an ambitious political agenda. It also is tempting to characterize the fundamentalists as a fringe group on the periphery of Middle Eastern politics, when, actually, their destabilizing activities are at the center of the region's troubles. Without illusions, Washington must recognize that the slow triumph of militant Islam in the Middle East not only will pose a major threat to the U.S.'s position in the region, but also will bring terrorism to American shores."[55]

Another expert explains it this way: "The U.S. has long been a major terrorist target, but most of the assaults on Americans and their organizations have taken place overseas. Terrorist attacks inside the U.S. have been extremely rare. There are

Devastation in downtown Oklahoma City—the result of a massive terrorist truck bomb detonated in front of the Alfred P. Murrah federal building in 1995. In 1997 Timothy McVeigh was convicted in federal court of 11 charges in the bombing—ranging from conspiracy to first-degree murder—and sentenced to death. Why is domestic terrorism increasing? *David Longstreath/AP/Wide World Photos.*

many reasons, though, to think that may change. As the only remaining super-power, the U.S. already is the Great Satan to Islamic fundamentalists—the protector of Israel, supporter of the perceived infidel Mubarak, prime enemy of theocratic Iran. But there could well be many other groups with grievances: Bosnian Muslims who think the U.S. has abandoned them to slaughter; Kurds who think Washington has left them to the cruelties of Saddam Hussein, the Turkish government or both. Indeed, the U.S. could be a target for just about any group that feels itself aggrieved and believes the one (remaining) superpower has caused its troubles or could stop them but won't bestir itself."[56]

The 1995 terrorist bombing of the Alfred P. Murrah federal building in downtown Oklahoma City, Oklahoma, in which 168 people died and hundreds more were wounded, demonstrated just how vulnerable the United States is to terrorist attack. The nine-story building, which included offices of the Social Security Administration, Drug Enforcement Administration, the Secret Service, the Bureau of Alcohol, Tobacco, and Firearms, and a daycare center called America's Kids, was devastated by the homemade bomb. The fertilizer and diesel fuel device used in the attack was estimated to have weighed approximately 1,200 pounds. It was left in a parked rental truck on the 5th Street side of the building. The blast left a crater thirty feet wide and eight feet deep, and spread debris over a ten-block area.

In June 1997 a federal jury found 29-year-old Timothy McVeigh guilty of eleven counts ranging from conspiracy to first-degree murder in the bombing. Jurors concluded that McVeigh had conspired with Terry Nichols, a friend he had met while both were in the army, and with unknown others, to use a truck bomb to destroy the Murrah Building. Prosecutors argued that the attack was intended to revenge the 1993 assault on David Koresh's Branch Davidian complex in Waco, Texas, which left seventy-eight cult members dead. The Waco incident happened two years to the day before the Oklahoma City attack. Following the guilty verdicts, McVeigh was sentenced to death.[57] If executed, he will be the first person under federal jurisdiciton to be put to death since 1963. McVeigh's co-conspirator, Terry Nichols, was convicted of eight counts of involuntary manslaughter, but escaped the death penalty.

The very freedoms which allow America to serve as a model of democracy to the rest of the world have made it possible for terrorist or terrorist-affiliated groups to operate within the United States relatively unencumbered. For example, the Islamic Committee for Palestine, which some have described as a quasi-radical group with possible terrorist links, operates from a base in Tampa, Florida, from which it sponsors conferences, meetings, and speakers. Recent occasions have featured representatives of the fanatic Palestinian Islamic Jihad organization, and Sheik Abd al-Aziz Odeh, the group's spiritual leader, has addressed groups there. Similarly in attendance has been Rachid al-Ghanouchi, the leader of Tunisia's outlawed al-Nahda.

Many U.S.-based terrorists may have direct links with those who control them from abroad. Others, however, may simply be motivated by a spiritual kinship with foreign ideas. Vincent Cannistraro, former head of the CIA's counterterrorism center, has spoken to the issue. "What they're providing," says Cannistraro of the radical Muslim countries and their governments, "is a world vision, a means of direct participation in God's plan. That can be very appealing."[58]

Many terrorist organizations exist within other nations, however. Included among them are the Japanese Red Army, the Lebanese Hezballah, the Provisional Irish Republican Army in the United Kingdom, the Abu Nidal Organization, the ETA in Spain, Peruvian Shinning Path (*Sendero Luminoso*) guerrillas, the Palestinian Hamas, Islamic Jihad, and the Popular Front for the Liberation of Palestine-General Command. Some such organizations enjoy state sponsorship, whereas others do not. "Some terrorist groups that do not enjoy state sponsorship," says Timothy E. Wirth, U.S. undersecretary of state for global affairs, "have tried to develop independent means of support. Some groups have resorted to crimes such as bank robbery or extortion, while others, particularly in the Andean region, have developed close working relationships with drug dealers."

COUNTERING THE TERRORIST THREAT

Secretary Wirth recently testified before Congress on the growing threat of international terrorism. "Working in close consultation with the Congress," Wirth said, "successive Administrations have developed a set of principles that continue to

THEORY VERSUS REALITY

The Unabomber and Domestic Terrorism

In April 1996, Harvard-educated Theodore Kaczynski, 52, a Lincoln, Montana, recluse, was arrested and charged with the infamous Unabomber terrorist bombings. Kaczynski admitted the bombings in early 1998, and was sentenced to life in prison without parole

The Unabomber's 18-year-long mail bomb campaign had targeted universities, airlines, and researchers. The attacks killed three people, and injured twenty-three others in sixteen separate bombing incidents. Prior to Kaczynski's arrest, a fifty-six-page, 35,000-word "manifesto" had been mailed to offices of the *New York Times, Washington Post,* and *Penthouse* magazine. Titled "Industrial Society and Its Future," the Unabomber manifesto was a rambling thesis condemning American social institutions and high technology—and calling for a new social order based on a return to simpler times. It blamed many of the world's existing problems on the industrial revolution and forecasted an Orwellian future, in which helpless humans are controlled by computers. Excerpts from the manifesto were widely published and helped lead to Kaczynski's capture. The manifesto's introductory paragraphs (which use the word *we* in referring to the bomber) are printed here.

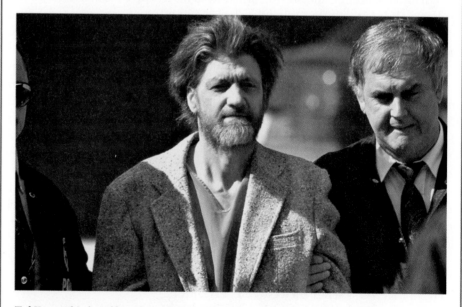

Ted Kaczynski, the self-confessed "Unabomber." Kaczynski is said to be responsible for 16 bombings over an 18-year period. The bombings resulted in 3 deaths and 23 injuries. What motivates criminals like the Unabomber? *S. O'Sullivan/Sygma.*

The Industrial Revolution and its consequences have been a disaster for the human race. They have greatly increased the life-expectancy of those of us who live in "advanced" countries, but they have destabilized society, have made life unfulfilling, have subjected human beings to indignities, have led to widespread psychological suffering (in the Third World to physical suffering as well) and have inflicted severe damage on the natural world. The continued development of technology will worsen the situation. It will certainly subject human beings to greater indignities and inflict greater damage on the natural world, it will probably lead to greater social disruption and psychological suffering, and it may lead to increased physical suffering even in "advanced" countries.

The industrial-technological system may survive or it may break down. If it survives, it MAY eventually achieve a low level of physical and psychological suffering, but only after passing through a long and very painful period of adjustment and only at the cost of permanently reducing human beings and many other living organisms to engineered products and mere cogs in the social machine. Furthermore, if the system survives, the consequences will be inevitable: There is no way of reforming or modifying the system so as to prevent it from depriving people of dignity and autonomy.

If the system breaks down the consequences will still be very painful. But the bigger the system grows the more disastrous the results of its breakdown will be, so if it is to break down it had best break down sooner rather than later.

We therefore advocate a revolution against the industrial system. This revolution may or may not make use of violence; it may be sudden or it may be a relatively gradual process spanning a few decades. We can't predict any of that. But we do outline in a very general way the measures that those who hate the industrial system should take in order to prepare the way for a revolution against that form of society. This is not to be a POLITICAL revolution. Its object will be to overthrow not governments but the economic and technological basis of the present society . . .

DISCUSSION QUESTIONS

1. What motivated the Unabomber? Why did he advocate a "revolution against the industrial system"?
2. Do you think that the Unabomber really believed his bombings would create a better world? If so, how did he think they would bring about such change?

guide us as we counter the threat posed by terrorists."[59] According to Wirth these principles dictate that the U.S. government must

Make no concessions to terrorists.

Continue to apply increasing pressure to state sponsors of terrorism.

Forcefully apply the rule of law to international terrorists.

Help other governments improve their capabilities to counter the threats posed by international terrorists.

Terrorist bombings can be costly. Here an Israeli soldier examines the aftermath of a terrorist bombing of a Tel Aviv bus. Is the United States adequately prepared to deal with the threat of international terrorism? *Shaul Golan/Yedioth Aharonoth/Sygma.*

"Our counter-terrorism strategy," testified Wirth, "has three key elements—to implement our policy of 'no concessions,' to keep pressure on state sponsors, and to apply the rule of law. These basic policies," Wirth added, "have served us well in the past, and will do so in the future . . ." and, said Wirth, apply "equally well to groups such as the Abu Nidal Organization, or a small and unnamed group that may come together to undertake only a single attack."

▓ STATE-ORGANIZED CRIME

In his 1988 presidential remarks to the American Society of Criminology, William J. Chambliss addressed the issue of what he called "state-organized crime."[60] Chambliss characterized **state-organized crime** as "acts defined by law as criminal and committed by state officials in the pursuit of their job as representatives of the state."[61] Examples, said Chambliss, include a nation's "complicity in piracy, smuggling, assassinations, criminal conspiracies, acting as an accessory before or after the fact, and violating laws that limit their activities." Limits on activities would encompass such restrictions as legal regulations against spying on citizens, campaign contribution rules, the legislative earmarking of funds not to be diverted for other purposes, prohibitions against the selling of arms to belligerent nations, and statutes contravening official support for terrorism.

State-organized crime, Chambliss advised those in attendance, "does not include criminal acts that benefit only individual officeholders," including such things

State-organized crime
acts defined by law as criminal and committed by state officials in the pursuit of their job as representatives of the state.

as the acceptance of bribes or the "illegal use of violence by the police against individuals, unless such acts . . . violate existing criminal law and are official policy." In his speech Chambliss gave examples of the kinds of things that *do* constitute state-organized crime. Among the activities mentioned were occurrences as diverse as (1) the state-supported pirates who worked for France, England, and Holland against Spanish and Italian interests centuries ago; (2) America's enlistment of pirates during the War of 1812 to fend off attacks by British naval vessels; (3) French colonial profits derived from the opium trade in Indochina, which helped finance colonial governments there; (4) the use of the CIA-sponsored airline, Air America, during the Vietnam War to transport illegal opium to market in order to finance anti-Communist mountain tribes in their militant activities against the North Vietnamese army; (5) money laundering activities of U.S.-sponsored banks in Australia during the war in Southeast Asia; and (6) the plan by members of the National Security Council, the Department of Defense, and the CIA, later uncovered in Senate hearings in 1986, to sell arms to Iran and to use money from those sales to support the activities of Contra rebels in Nicaragua.

This last example is perhaps best known to contemporary Americans, who will recall the indictment and prosecution of Lt. Colonel Oliver North and the investigations of Theodore Shackley, Thomas Clines, and Major General Richard Secord which followed from Senate suspicions that the 1985 Borland Amendment had been violated. The Borland Amendment forbade any U.S. official from assisting the Nicaraguan Contra rebels—either directly or indirectly.

Chambliss also categorizes as state-organized crime American-sponsored coups in Guatemala, Nicaragua, the Dominican Republic, and Vietnam. "[I]nvolvement in these coups," he says, "was never legally authorized." To bring his point home, Chambliss adds, "the murders, assassinations, and terrorist acts that accompany coups are criminal acts by law, both in the United States and in the country in which they take place." The DEA, the CIA, and the FBI have all been involved in such illegal clandestine activities, according to Chambliss, although they sometimes hide their involvement by establishing puppet or client organizations—such as the feared Chilean secret service (DINA) formed during the CIA-sponsored overthrow of Chilean president Salvador Allende in 1970.

Internal crimes committed by governments include such things as medical experimentation on unwilling subjects, as might have occurred following World War II when American soldiers were exposed to nuclear blasts and the dangerous fallout that followed; experiments by the CIA involving hefty doses of LSD and other drugs on unsuspecting subjects provide yet another example of crimes committed by our own government within American borders. Finally, Chambliss cites the example of a 30-year-old FBI-run operation called CONTELPRO, which was intended to "disrupt, harass, and discredit groups that the FBI decided were in some way 'un-American.'" Targeted were the American Civil Liberties Union, representatives of the 1970s antiwar movement, militant black groups, and even organizations such as the NAACP. Chambliss calls CONTELPRO "the most flagrant violation of civil rights by federal agencies" in the nation's history, although some would argue that the internment of American civilians of Japanese descent at concentrationlike camps during World War II exceeded even the FBI's harassment program in its flagrant violation of the rights of American citizens.

Many examples of state-organized crime committed by nations around the world could be given. Government-sponsored drug trade remains a major area of state-organized criminal activity. Chambliss says that "[t]oday, we see nations such as Turkey, Bolivia, Colombia, Peru, Panama, and the Bahamas encouraging the export of illegal drugs while condemning them publicly."

Although it is imperative that state-organized crime be studied, such study is fraught with difficulties including the need[62]

- To acquire reliable information on modern-day state-organized crime, which is difficult as sources of such information are themselves inherently unreliable.
- For comparisons between styles of government and "political, economic, and social systems" across different historical time frames to learn why some "forms of social organization are more likely to create state-organized crime than others."
- To explore and identify parallels between state-organized criminality and the criminality of police and of other agencies of enforcement.

SUMMARY

❖

Politics and crime are inextricably intertwined. Sometimes the actions undertaken by government officials are themselves criminal, while on other occasions governments may act to shield law violators or even assist citizens in the violation of official dictums. More significantly, however, the very action of legislative bodies in defining crime through the making of statutory law reveals the crucial nexus between social organization and the use of law as a tool of the powerful. The form of social organization endemic to a society produces a set of intergroup relationships that ultimately define which individuals and which groups are empowered to make law. Those who find themselves excluded from such important decision-making processes will either find alternative paths to success or turn to other means to empower themselves.

DISCUSSION QUESTIONS

❖

1. This book emphasizes a social problems versus social responsibility theme. Which of the theoretical perspectives discussed in this chapter (if any) best support the social problems approach? Which (if any) support the social responsibility approach? Why?
2. Explain the difference between the consensus, pluralistic, and conflict perspectives. Which comes closest to your way of understanding society? Why?
3. What is Marxist criminology? How, if at all, does it differ from radical criminology? From critical criminology?

4. Does the Marxist perspective hold any significance for contemporary American society? Why or why not?
5. Define *terrorism.* Do you think that society will experience more or less terrorism in the future? How will forms of terrorism change in the future?
6. What is state-organized crime? Give examples of such crime. How can it be controlled?
7. What lessons can be learned from the 1995 terrorist bombing of the Alfred P. Murrah federal building in downtown Oklahoma City, Oklahoma? How likely do you believe such attacks may be in the future? How can we, as a nation, guard against them?

WEB WATCH

Access the *Criminology Today* home page on the World Wide Web by pointing your browser at www.prenhall.com/cjcentral. Once there, click on *Criminology Today* in order to access the wealth of electronic resources supporting this text.

Onsite resources include (1) "Chapter Links," which provides succinct overviews of critical ideas from the textbook and links selected materials from around the Web to concepts found in the text; (2) "General Reference—Law and Justice Links." Organized by chapter, these links lead to other useful resources on the World Wide Web, such as libraries, electronic discussion lists, and electronic journals; (3) "Criminology Sites on the Web," which lists links to organizations such as the American Society of Criminology, and the National Organization for Victims Assistance (NOVA), as well as crime prevention links and statistics on crime and justice. Many other Web-based resources can be accessed via the *Criminology Today* site, including the federal Justice Information Center, the Bureau of Justice Statistics, the FBI, the RAND Corporation, the Vera Institute of Justice, PAVNET (an online "Partnership Against Violence," run by seven different federal agencies), and the National White Collar Crime Center.

Still another feature of the *Criminology Today* Web site is e-mail homework. Homework can be composed onsite and submitted to instructors using the instructor's e-mail address. To use the e-mail homework feature, click on "E-Mail Homework" on the opening page and then type answers to the questions that appear in the spaces provided. Use your instructor's e-mail address to submit homework answers. The *Criminology Today* Web site also provides links to powerful Web-based search engines that can help you find topics of interest to you as you progress through your course of study. Search engines can be found under the home page heading "Criminology Sites on the Web."

NOTES

⬧⬧

[1]Natasha Alova, "Russia-Juvenile Crime," Associated Press wire service, Northern edition, February 9, 1994.

[2]Richard Quinney, *Class, State, and Crime: On the Theory and Practice of Criminal Justice* (New York: David McKay, 1977), p. 145.

[3]Robert Wright, "The Evolution of Despair," Time, August 28, 1995.

[4]Michael J. Sniffen, "Russian Crime," Associated Press wire service, May 24, 1994.

[5]Ibid.

[6]Raymond J. Michalowski, "Perspectives and Paradigm: Structuring Criminological Thought," in Robert F. Meier, ed., *Theory in Criminology* (Beverly Hills, Calif.: Sage, 1977), pp. 17–39.

[7]Roscoe Pound, *Social Control Through the Law: The Powell Lectures* (Hamden, Conn.: Archon, 1968), pp. 113–114.

[8]Although Pound's postulates originally made reference only to "men" we have here used the now-conventional phrase "men and women" throughout the postulates to indicate that Pound was speaking of all persons within the social group. No other changes to the original postulates have been made.

[9]Adapted from Michalowski, "Perspectives and Paradigm: Structuring Criminological Thought."

[10]Ibid.

[11]George B. Vold, *Theoretical Criminology* (New York: Oxford University Press, 1958), p. 205.

[12]Ibid., p. 206.

[13]Ibid., pp. 208–209.

[14]Ibid., p. 309.

[15]Austin Turk, *Criminality and Legal Order* (Chicago: Rand McNally, 1969), p. vii.

[16]Ibid.

[17]William J. Chambliss, "Toward a Political Economy of Crime," in C. Reasons and R. Rich, *The Sociology of Law* (Toronto: Butterworth, 1978), p. 193.

[18]Vance Packard, *The Status Seekers* (London: Harmondsworth, 1961).

[19]Ralf Dahrendorf, *Class and Class Conflict in An Industrial Society* (Stanford, Calif.: Stanford University Press, 1959).

[20]Ralf Dahrendorf, "Out of Utopia: Toward a Reorientation of Sociological Analysis," *American Journal of Sociology,* vol. 64 (1958), pp. 115–127.

[21]William Chambliss and Robert T. Seidman, *Law, Order, and Power* (Reading, Mass.: Addison-Wesley, 1971), p. 33.

[22]Adapted from ibid., pp. 473–474.

[23]William J. Chambliss, *Crime and the Legal Process* (New York: McGraw-Hill, 1969), p. 88.

[24]William J. Chambliss, "Toward a Political Economy of Crime," *Theory and Society,* vol. 2 (1975), pp. 152–153.

[25]Ibid.

[26]Ibid., p. 152.

[27]Richard Quinney, *Critique of the Legal Order: Crime Control in Capitalist Society* (Boston: Little, Brown, 1974), p. 16.

[28]Richard Quinney, *Class, State, and Crime: On the Theory and Practice of Criminal Justice* (New York: David McKay, 1977), p. 58.

[29]Ibid., p. 58.

[30]Ibid., p. 61.

[31]Ibid., p. 65.

[32]Gresham M. Sykes, "Critical Criminology," *Journal of Criminal Law and Criminology,* vol. 65 (1974), pp. 206–213.

[33]David A. Jones, *History of Criminology: A Philosophical Perspective* (Westport, Conn.: Greenwood, 1986), p. 200.

[34]Elliott Currie, "Market, Crime, and Community," *Theoretical Criminology,* vol. 1, no. 2 (May 1997), pp. 147–172.

[35]Michael J. Lynch and W. Byron Groves, *A Primer in Radical Criminology,* 2nd ed. (Albany, N.Y.: Harrow and Heston, 1989), p. 126.

[36]Ibid., p. 128.

[37]Raymond J. Michalowski, *Order, Law, and Crime: An Introduction to Criminology* (New York: Random House, 1985), p. 410.

[38]Lynch and Groves, *A Primer in Radical Criminology,* p. 130.

[39]Pelfrey, *The Evolution of Criminology,* p. 86.

[40]For a good overview of critiques of radical criminology, see J. F. Galliher, "Life and Death

of Liberal Criminology," *Contemporary Crisis,* vol. 2, no. 3 (July 1978), pp. 245–263.

[41] Jackson Toby, "The New Criminology Is the Old Sentimentality," *Criminology,* vol. 16 (1979), pp. 516–526.

[42] Ibid.

[43] Richard Quinney, *Class, State and Crime: On the Theory and Practice of Criminal Justice* (N.Y.: David McKay, 1977), p. 99.

[44] Ibid., p. 103.

[45] Federal Bureau of Investigation, Counterterrorism Section, *Terrorism in the United States, 1987* (Washington, D.C.: FBI, December 1987).

[46] Lynch and Groves, *A Primer in Radical Criminology,* p. 39.

[47] Ibid., p. 39.

[48] Peter Flory, "Terrorism Must Continue to Be a Top Priority," *Insight on the News,* vol. 10, no. 21 (May 23, 1994), pp. 37–38.

[49] Catherine Wilson, "Two Accused in Nuke Sale Sting," Associate Press wire service, June 30, 1997.

[50] Available on the World Wide Web at http://www.state.gov/www/global/terrorism/ 1996report/970430.html, as of July 2, 1997.

[51] Ambassador Wilcox is the State Department's coordinator for counterterrorism.

[52] U.S. Department of State, *Patterns of Global Terrorism, 1996* (Washington, D.C.: U.S. Government Printing Office, 1997).

[53] As cited in George J. Church and Sophfronia Scott Gregory, "The Terror Within," *Time,* July 5, 1993, p. 22.

[54] Bruce Frankel, "Sheik Guilty in Terror Plot," *USA Today,* October 2, 1995, p. 1A. Sheik Abdel-Rahman and codefendant El Sayyid Nosair were both sentenced to life in prison. Other defendants received sentences of be-tween 25 and 57 years in prison. See Sascha Brodsky, "Terror Verdicts Denounced," United Press International wire service, January 17, 1996.

[55] Bradford R. McGuinn, "Should We Fear Islamic Fundamentalists?" *USA Today* (magazine), vol. 122, no. 2582 (November 1993), pp. 34–35.

[56] George J. Church and Sophfronia Scott Gregory, "The Terror Within," *Time,* July 5, 1993, pp. 22–28.

[57] The death penalty was imposed for the first-degree murders of eight federal law enforcement agents who were at work in the Murrah Building at the time of the bombing. While the killings violated Oklahoma law, only the killings of the federal agents fell under federal law, which makes such murders capital offenses.

[58] Ibid.

[59] Timothy E. Wirth, *Meeting the Challenge of International Terrorism,* U.S. Department of State Dispatch, vol. 4, no. 29 (July 19, 1993), pp. 516–520.

[60] The material in this section is taken from William J. Chambliss, "State-Organized Crime— The American Society of Criminology, 1988 Presidential Address," *Criminology,* vol. 27, no. 2 (1989), pp. 183–208.

[61] Another useful definition of state criminality is offered by Gregg Barak as "the harm illegally or legally organized and inflicted upon people by their own governments or the governments of others. . . ." See Gregg Barak, "Crime, Criminology, and Human Rights: Toward an Understanding of State Criminality," in Gregg Barak, ed., *Varieties of Criminology: Readings from a Dynamic Discipline* (Westport, Conn.: Praeger, 1994), pp. 253–267.

[62] Chambliss "State-Organized Crime," pp. 203–204.

CHAPTER 10

WHITE-COLLAR AND

ORGANIZED CRIME

More money has been stolen at the point of a fountain pen than at the point of a gun.

—WOODY GUTHRIE

No longer is the criminologist a middle-class observer studying lower-class behavior. He now looks upward at the most powerful and prestigeful strata, and his ingenuity in research and theory will be tested, indeed.

—DONALD J. NEWMAN[1]

"Do you know what the Mafia is?"
"The what?"
"The Mafia? M-a-f-i-a?"
"I'm sorry. I don't know what you're talking about."

—CRIME BOSS SALVATORE MORETTI RESPONDING TO QUESTIONS DURING THE KEFAUVER INVESTIGATION OF ORGANIZED CRIME.

❖ CHAPTER OUTLINE ❖

═══ IMPORTANT NAMES ═══

Edwin Sutherland	Herbert Edelhertz	Gilbert Geis
Gary S. Green	Travis Hirschi	Michael Gottfredson
John Braithwaite	James W. Coleman	

═══ IMPORTANT TERMS ═══

white-collar crime	environmental crime	corporate crime
occupational crime	Mafia	*Cosa Nostra*
Kefauver Committee	*omerta*	organized crime
ethnic succession	RICO	money laundering
organized crime	asset forfeiture	

❖ INTRODUCTION

A few years ago retiree George Salmon read an advertisement in a local newspaper calling for investors to support a new concept in wireless cable television transmissions. Wireless cable systems send television programs to homes using microwaves, and serve around 500,000 subscribers nationwide.[2] Salmon called the company's representative and was told he could make as much as a 300 percent return on his investment in a short time. Attracted by the promise of quick riches, Salmon sent

$10,000 to Broadcast Holdings in Costa Mesa, California. Broadcast Holdings promised to develop wireless cable systems in Missouri, Tennessee, and Oregon. Two years later, however, Broadcast Holdings closed after state regulators, charging that the company was trading unregistered securities, raided its offices. In all likelihood Salmon will never see any part of his investment again.

According to a recent issue of *Worth* magazine,[3] wireless cable is the fraud *du jour*—or the scam of the day. Since 1992, says the magazine, "unscrupulous promoters have raised over $300 million in questionable deals to set up wireless systems. . . ." Such promotions, touting other products, have been common for decades. In the 1960s and 1970s many rushed to invest in shares of fake goldmining and energy companies, spurred in part by the Arab oil embargo of 1973 which caused long "gas lines" to form in America's cities and towns. During the 1980s and early 1990s fraudulent securities dealers hawked international, telecommunications, and biomedical stocks and other sometimes worthless equities almost with impunity, advertising in some of the country's most widely read financial journals and newspapers.

Financial scandals have a long and ubiquitous history in the United States, sometimes involving government regulators themselves. In 1929, for example, the Teapot Dome scandal embroiled the administration of President Warren Harding. The scandal began in 1921, when Secretary of the Interior Albert B. Fall secretly leased naval oil reserves at Teapot Dome, Wyoming, and Elk Hills, California, to developers without asking for competitive bids. A Senate investigation later revealed that large sums of federal money had been loaned to developers without interest. Fall was eventually fined and sent to prison, and a 1927 U.S. Supreme Court decision ordered the fields restored to the U.S. government.

WHITE-COLLAR CRIME

In 1939 famed criminologist **Edwin Sutherland** defined white-collar crime during his presidential address to the American Sociological Society. **White-collar crime,** said Sutherland, consists of violations of the criminal law "committed by a person of respectability and high social status in the course of his occupation." (Today we say ". . . in the course of *his* or *her* occupation.") Many criminologists do not properly understand crime, Sutherland claimed, because they fail to recognize that the secretive violations of public and corporate trust by those in positions of authority are, in fact, just as criminal as predatory acts committed by persons of lower social standing.

As Sutherland told those gathered for the address: My thesis is that the traditional "conception(s) and explanations of crime [are] misleading and incorrect; that crime is in fact not closely correlated with poverty or with the psychopathic and sociopathic conditions associated with poverty, and that an adequate explanation of criminal behavior must proceed along quite different lines. The conventional explanations are invalid principally because they are derived from biased samples. The samples are biased in that they have not included vast areas of criminal behavior of persons not in the lower class. . . ."[4]

White-collar crime violations of the criminal law committed by a person of respectability and high social status in the course of his or her occupation.

The criminality of upper-class persons "has been demonstrated again and again in the investigations of land offices, railways, insurance, munitions, banking, public utilities, stock exchanges, the oil industry, real estate, reorganization committees, receiverships, bankruptcies and politics," said Sutherland.[5] For still other examples, Sutherland pointed to those he called "the robber barons" of the nineteenth century, citing Cornelius Vanderbilt's famous response to inquiries about his sometimes flagrantly illegal activities. "You don't suppose you can run a railroad in accordance with the statutes, do you?" the wealthy Vanderbilt reportedly quipped.

In a later study that is still widely cited by criminologists, Sutherland reported on the frequency with which the nation's seventy largest corporations violated the law.[6] He found that each of the corporations he studied had been sanctioned by courts or by administrative commissions, and that the typical corporation had an average of fourteen decisions against it. Ninety-eight percent of corporations are recidivists, or commit crime after crime, Sutherland said, while 90 percent could be called habitual criminals under the habitual offender statutes which existed at the time of his study. "Sixty of the corporations (had) decisions against them for restraint of trade, fifty-four for infringements (generally, of patents), forty-four for unfair labor practices, twenty-seven for misrepresentation in advertising, twenty-six for (illegal) rebates, and forty-three for miscellaneous offenses,"[7] wrote Sutherland. He also found that of the seventy largest corporations studied, "thirty were either illegal in their origin or began illegal activities immediately after their origin. . . ." Such businesses may have been built upon price-fixing, unregulated commodities offerings, or via unlawful and clandestine negotiations with government regulators.

The only real difference between modern-day white-collar criminals and those of the past is that they are more sophisticated, Sutherland claimed. Although no hard and fast figures were available to Sutherland, he estimated that the "financial cost of white-collar crime is probably several times as great as the financial cost of all the crimes which are customarily regarded as the 'crime problem.'"[8]

Sutherland also noted that white-collar criminals are far less likely to be investigated, arrested, or prosecuted than are other types of offenders. When they are—on rare occasions—convicted, white-collar criminals are far less likely to receive active prison terms than are "common criminals." If they are sent to prison, the amount of time they are ordered to serve is far less than one would expect given the amount of damage their crimes inflict on society. The deference shown white-collar criminals, according to Sutherland, is due primarily to their social standing. Many white-collar criminals are well respected in their communities, and many take part in national affairs. Few are perceived as mean spirited or even ill intentioned. Private citizens who do not fully understand business affairs sometimes assume that those charged with white-collar crimes were unwittingly caught up in obscure government regulations or that government agencies chose to make examples of a few unfortunate, but typical, businessmen or women.

Given these kinds of sentiments, criminologists felt compelled for years to address the question, "Is white-collar crime, crime?" As recently as 1987 writers on the subject were still asking, "Do persons of high standing commit crimes?"[9] Although most criminologists today would answer the question with a resounding "yes," members of the public have been far slower to accept the notion that violations of the criminal law by businesspeople share conceptual similarities with street crime.

Attitudes, however, are changing as more headline-making charges are being filed against corporations and their representatives for illegal activities.

Examples of contemporary white-collar crime abound. The insider trading scam of stock market tycoon Ivan Boesky and the securities fraud conviction of junk bond king Michael Milken a few years ago show how fortunes can be amassed through white-collar law violations. Boesky was estimated to have netted a profit of $250 million for himself and a few close friends, while Milken paid a $600 million fine—far less than the amount he is estimated to have reaped from illegal trading.

The nationwide savings and loan (S&L) disaster of the 1980s, which some have called the "biggest white-collar crime in history," serves as another modern-day example of white-collar crime. The savings and loan fiasco was the result of years of intentional mismanagement and personal appropriation of funds by institutional executives. Although the actual amount of money lost or stolen during the scandal may never be known, it is estimated to run into the hundreds of billions of dollars. The collapse of just one such institution, Charles Keating's California-based Lincoln Savings and Loan Association, cost taxpayers—who were left to redeem the insolvent institutions—approximately $2.5 billion, while the collapse of Neil Bush's Silverado Banking S&L in Denver cost nearly $1 billion. Some experts say that the final "bail-out" of S&Ls nationwide will cost American taxpayers $500 billion[10]— much more than has ever been stolen in all bank robberies throughout the history of our country.

Another type of white-collar crime sprang from the low interest rates characteristic of the early and mid-1990s. Sham banking operations, often with high-sounding names and seemingly prestigious addresses, flourished—offering high interest rates and double-digit rates of return on investments held by the bank.

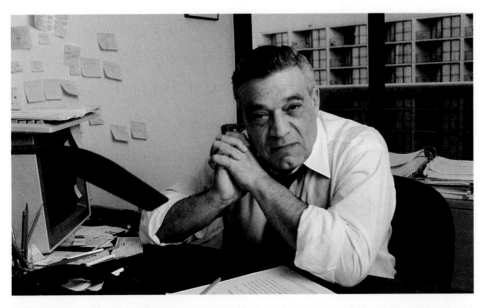

Miami businessman David Paul shown here after his conviction on sixty-eight counts of bank fraud. Paul was chairman of south Florida's CenTrust Bank, one of the nation's largest savings and loans. Should white-collar criminals be punished the same as other offenders? *Miami Herald Publishing Co.*

Unfortunately such "phantom banks," as they were dubbed by the federal comptroller of the currency, evaporated as quickly as they were formed, leaving investors stunned and sometimes penniless. Some of the schemes involved the sale of certificates of deposit in offshore banks such as those in the Caribbean; others bilked investors into buying millions of dollars of what was supposed to be newly privatized Russian stock; while still more offered the seemingly irresistible chance to earn exorbitant returns through sophisticated overseas investments. Recently, the Federal Deposit Insurance Corporation (FDIC) issued a list of sixty unregulated business entities illegally conducting banking businesses within the United States. Canadian officials added another two hundred suspects to the list. As one expert on illegal banking operations explained, "[i]t's difficult to prosecute the criminals who run phantom banks because many times the victims are unwilling to press charges or the schemes take months to unravel. . . ."[11]

An even more recent white-collar crime appears to have been involved in the 1997 bankruptcy of Canadian gold prospector Bre-X Minerals Ltd. In the mid-1990s Bre-X officials claimed that assayed ore from the company's Busang mine in Indonesia proved that it owned what was likely to be the world's largest gold reserve. In what some have called "the greatest stock fraud of the century," shares of the company's stock soared from pennies to a value of $206 each. After a number of debacles, including the suspicious death of the company's chief geologist who fell from a helicopter over the Indonesian jungle, the company admitted the truth of an independent report which showed that the company's claims were based on falsified data.[12] Bre-X shareholders were left with worthless stock certificates, while the company's vice president of exploration filed for residency status in the Cayman Islands where he owned approximately $6 million worth of beachfront homes.

Also in 1997, shares of Mercury Finance Company tumbled on the New York Stock Exchange when the company revealed that it would have to lower its reported earnings over the previous four years by about $90 million, due to accounting irregularities. After the announcement, Mercury Finance defaulted on millions of dollars in debt and was served with a search warrant by FBI agents seeking the business's financial records. The company lost more than $2 billion in market capitalization in one day when the stock plunged following the announcement that it would slash reported earnings. Investigations into the actions of officers of Bre-X and Mercury Finance are ongoing at the time of this writing.

CORPORATE CRIME

Corporate malfeasance, another form of white-collar crime, has been dubbed "corporate crime." **Corporate crime** may be defined as "a violation of a criminal statute either by a corporate entity or by its executives, employees, or agents acting on behalf of and for the benefit of the corporation, partnership, or other form of business entity."[13] Corporate crimes come in many forms—ranging from prior knowledge about exploding gas tanks on Pinto automobiles and GM pickup trucks to price-fixing and insider securities trading. Culpability, which often results in civil suits against a corporation along with possible criminal prosecutions, is greatest where company officials can be shown to have had advance knowledge about product defects, dangerous conditions, or illegal behavior on the part of employees.

Corporate crime a violation of a criminal statute either by a corporate entity or by its executives, employees, or agents acting on behalf of and for the benefit of the corporation, partnership, or other form of business entity.

Two of the most massive corporate liability issues in U.S. history were settled in September 1994. In one case, U.S. District Court Judge Sam Pointer gave final approval to a class action suit against makers and sellers of silicon gel breast implants.[14] The decision had taken years to reach and cleared the way for implant recipients to be paid $4.25 billion over thirty years. Of the 2 million American women who have had breast implants, approximately 90,000 filed claims under the action. Women whose claims are approved could each receive between $105,000 and $1.4 million, depending on age, health, and medical condition. Claimants had argued that many of the parties involved in the manufacture and surgical implantation of the implants were aware of the dangers represented by their products but had opted to market them anyway.

In an interesting aside, which many claimed was a continuing effort to cover up critical issues in the case, Mayo Clinic researchers reported in the prestigious *New England Journal of Medicine* at the time of the implant settlement that no link could be found between implants and autoimmune and other disorders reportedly suffered by women claiming to be negatively affected by the implants. It was later revealed that financial support for the study had come from precisely those groups with the most to lose in the financial settlement. Among the contributors were the American Society of Plastic and Reconstructive Surgeons ($500,000), Plastic Surgery Education Foundation ($300,000), American Society of Aesthetic Plastic Surgeons ($210,000), Dow Corning ($500,000), and Bristol-Myers Squibb ($100,000).[15]

The second corporate liability case settled in 1994 involved Union Carbide Corporation which agreed to sell its entire remaining holdings in Union Carbide India Limited to the Indian company McLeod Russel India.[16] McLeod Russel was the highest bidder in a closed-door auction ordered by India's Supreme Court as part of the American company's punishment for a chemical leak at its storage facilities in Bhopal, India, on December 3, 1984. The Bhopal tragedy, which many claim was due to criminal negligence, caused more than 3,000 deaths and disabled thousands of townspersons. Union Carbide had originally been ordered by Indian state courts to pay $81 million to the government as compensation for disaster victims. The country's Supreme Court later ordered the company to pay $470 million as final compensation. Another court then required the seizure of Union Carbide's remaining Indian assets and ordered that they be sold to the highest bidder. Union Carbide officials, who were threatened with murder charges, left the country.

On June 20, 1997, the largest product liability settlement in history was reached between state attorneys general and representatives of the tobacco industry.[17] According to the terms of the agreement, tobacco companies agreed to pay $368.5 billion over twenty-five years, in compensation for the harmful effects of tobacco, and to reimburse the states and the federal government for monies spent on medical problems associated with tobacco use. Companies are to continue to pay an additional $15 billion per year after the first twenty-five years. Part of the money is to be used to fund a major antismoking campaign. In return, the industry is to receive some protection from legal liability in cases filed by individuals and government agencies. Under the terms of the agreement, individual smokers could still sue companies within the tobacco industry, but punitive damages would be disallowed (i.e., only *actual* damages would be permitted). As of this writing, the pact still has to be approved by Congress and the president.

Crimes against the environment have recently become an area of special concern to criminologists. Why have such offenses only recently been recognized as crimes? *J. Muir Hamilton/Stock Boston.*

Environmental crimes
violations of the criminal law which, although typically committed by businesses or by business officials, may also be committed by other persons or organizational entities, and which damage some protected or otherwise significant aspect of the natural environment.

Product liability cases, such as that involving the tobacco companies, are not necessarily based on violations of the criminal law. A relatively new area of corporate and white-collar criminality, which is defined solely in terms of violations of the criminal law, however, is that of crimes against the environment.[18] **Environmental crimes** are violations of the criminal law which, although typically committed by businesses or by business officials, may also be committed by other persons or organizational entities, and which damage some protected or otherwise significant aspect of the natural environment.

Whaling in violation of international conventions, for example, constitutes a form of environmental crime. So, too, does intentional pollution, especially when state or federal law contravenes the practice. Sometimes negligence may contribute to environmental criminality, as in the case of the 1,000-foot *Valdez* supertanker owned by Exxon Corporation that ran aground off the coast of Alaska in 1989, spilling 11 million gallons of crude oil over 1,700 miles of pristine coastline. In September 1994 an Alaskan jury ordered Exxon to pay $5 billion in punitive damages to 14,000 people affected by the 1989 spill, and another $287 million in actual damages to commercial fishermen in the region.

Other acts against the environment violate more conventional statutes, although their environmental impact may be obvious. The devastating fires set in oil fields throughout Kuwait by retreating Iraqi Army troops during the Gulf War provide an example of arson which resulted in global pollution while it negatively impacted fossil fuel reserves throughout much of the Middle East. These intentional fires, while properly classified as environmental criminality, also serve as an example of ecological terrorism because they were set for purposes of political intimidation.

DEFINITIONAL EVOLUTION OF WHITE-COLLAR CRIME

One early writer on white-collar crime explained, "[t]he chief criterion for a crime to be 'white-collar' is that it occurs as a part of, or a deviation from, the violator's occupational role."[19] This focus on the violator, rather than on the offense, in deciding whether to classify a crime as "white collar" was well accepted by the 1967 Presidential Commission on Law Enforcement and Administration of Justice. In its now classic report, *The Challenge of Crime in a Free Society,*[20] members of the commission wrote, "[t]he 'white-collar' criminal is the broker who distributes fraudulent securities, the builder who deliberately uses defective material, the corporation executive who conspires to fix prices, the legislator who peddles his influence and vote for private gain, or the banker who misappropriates funds in his keeping."

WHITE-COLLAR CRIME

The Initial Statement

At least one eminent criminologist has called the concept of white-collar crime "the most significant . . . development in criminology, especially since World War II . . ."[21] The roots of the concept go back to 1939 when Edwin Sutherland first coined the term *white-collar crime* in his presidential address to the American Sociological Society. Details of that address are discussed elsewhere in this chapter. His speech, however, concluded with the following five points:

1. White-collar criminality is real criminality, being in all cases in violation of the criminal law.
2. White-collar criminality differs from lower-class criminality principally in an implementation of the criminal law, which segregates white-collar criminals administratively from other criminals.
3. The theories of the criminologists that crime is due to poverty or to psychopathic and sociopathic conditions statistically associated with poverty are invalid because, first, they are derived from samples which are grossly biased with respect to socioeconomic status; second, they do not apply to the white-collar criminals; and third, they do not even explain the criminality of the lower class, since the factors are not related to a general process characteristic of all criminality.
4. A theory of criminal behavior which will explain both white-collar criminality and lower-class criminality is needed.
5. A hypothesis of this nature is suggested in terms of differential association and social disorganization.

Source: Edwin Sutherland, "White-Collar Criminality," *American Sociological Review,* vol. 5 (February 1940), pp. 1–12.

Over the past few decades, however, the concept of white-collar crime has undergone considerable refinement.[22] The reason, according to the U.S. Department of Justice, is that "the focus [in cases of white-collar crime] . . . has shifted to the nature of the crime instead of the persons or occupations involved." The methods used to commit white-collar crime, such as the use of a computer, and the special skills and knowledge necessary for attempted law violation, have resulted in a contemporary understanding of white-collar crime that emphasizes the type of offense being committed, rather than the social standing or occupational role of the person committing it. Some reasons for this shift are due to changes in the work environment and in the business world itself. Others are pragmatic. In the words of the Justice Department: "[t]he categorization of 'white-collar crime' as crime having a particular *modus operandi* [committed in a manner that utilizes deception and special knowledge of business practices and committed in a particular kind of economic environment] is of use in coordinating the resources of the appropriate agencies for purposes of investigation and prosecution."

Between the early definitions of white-collar crime and those which came later, many other investigators refined the conceptual boundaries surrounding the term. **Herbert Edelhertz,** for example, defined white-collar crime as any "illegal act or series of illegal acts committed by nonphysical means and by concealment or guile, to obtain money or property, to avoid the payment or loss of money or property, or to obtain business or personal advantages."[23] **Gilbert Geis,** another early writer on the subject, grappled with the notion of "upperworld crime," which he called "a label designed to call attention to the violation of a variety of criminal statutes by persons who at the moment are generally not considered, in connection with such violations, to be the 'usual' kind of underworld and/or psychologically aberrant offenders."[24] Many writers, however, were quick to realize that upperworld or white-collar crime might have its counterpart in certain forms of blue-collar crime committed by members of less prestigious occupational groups. Hence, the term *blue-collar crime* emerged as a way of classifying the law-violating behavior of persons involved in the appliance and automobile repair business, yard maintenance activities, house cleaning, and general installation services.

Finally, in an effort to bring closure to the concept of work-related crime, the term *occupational crime* emerged as a kind of catchall category. **Occupational crime** can be defined as "any act punishable by law that is committed through opportunity created in the course of an occupation which is legal."[25] Occupational crimes include the job-related law violations of both white- and blue-collar workers. One of the best typologies of occupational crime to emerge in recent years is that offered by **Gary S. Green** in his book *Occupational Crime.*[26] Green identifies the four categories of occupational crime as follows:

- *Organizational Occupational Crime:* crimes committed for the benefit of an employing organization. In such instances only the organization or the employer benefits, not individual employees.
- *State Authority Occupational Crime:* crimes by officials through the exercise of their state-based authority. Such crime is occupation specific, and can only be committed by persons in public office or by those working for such persons.

Occupational crime any act punishable by law which is committed through opportunity created in the course of an occupation that is legal.

- *Professional Occupational Crime:* crimes by professionals in their capacity as professionals. The crimes of physicians, attorneys, psychologists, and the like are included here.
- *Individual Occupational Crime:* crimes by individuals as individuals. This is a kind of catchall category and includes personal income tax evasion, the theft of goods and services by employees, the filing of false expense reports, and the like.

CAUSES OF WHITE-COLLAR CRIME

When Sutherland first coined the term *white-collar crime* he wrote, "a hypothesis is needed that will explain both white-collar criminality and lower-class criminality...." The answer Sutherland gave to this own challenge was that "white-collar criminality, just as other systematic criminality, is learned...." He went on to apply elements of his now famous theory of differential association theory (discussed in Chapter 7) to white-collar crime, saying that "it is learned in direct or indirect association with those who already practice the behavior...."

Other authors have since offered similar integrative perspectives. **Travis Hirschi** and **Michael Gottfredson,** for example, in a recent issue of the journal *Criminology,* published half a century after Sutherland's initial work, wrote, "[i]n this paper we outline a general theory of crime capable of organizing the facts about white-collar crime at the same time it is capable of organizing the facts about all forms of crime."[27] Their analysis of white-collar crime focuses squarely on the development of the concept itself. Hirschi and Gottfredson suggest that if we were not aware of the fact that the concept of white-collar crime arose "as a reaction to the idea that crime is concentrated in the lower class, there would be nothing to distinguish it from other" forms of crime.[28] "It may be, then," they write, "that the discovery of white-collar criminals is important only in a context in which their existence is denied by theory or policy." In other words, nothing is unusual about the idea of white-collar crime other than the fact that many people are loath to admit that high-status individuals commit crimes just as do those of lower status.

In fact, say Hirschi and Gottfredson, white-collar criminals are motivated by the same forces that drive other criminals: self-interest, the pursuit of pleasure, and the avoidance of pain. White-collar crimes certainly have special characteristics. They are not as dangerous as other "common" forms of crime; they provide relatively large rewards; the rewards they produce may follow quickly from their commission; sanctions associated with them may be vague or only rarely imposed; and they may require only minimal effort from those with the requisite skills to engage in them.

Hirschi and Gottfredson conclude, however, that criminologists err in assuming that white-collar criminality is common, or that it is as common as the forms of criminality found among the lower classes. They reason that the personal characteristics of most white-collar workers are precisely those which we would expect to produce conformity in behavior. High educational levels, a commitment to the status quo, personal motivation to succeed, deference to others, attention to conventional appearance, and other inherent aspects of social conformity—all of which tend to characterize those who operate at the white-collar level—are not the kinds of personal characteristics associated with crime commission. "In other words," say Hirschi and Gottfredson, "selection processes inherent to the high end of the occupational structure tend to recruit people with relatively low propensity to crime."[29]

One other reason most criminologists are mistaken about the assumed high rate of white-collar criminality, Hirschi and Gottfredson tell us, is because "white-collar researchers often take organizations as the unit of analysis" and confuse the crimes committed by organizational entities with those of individuals within those organizations. Similarly, rates of white-collar offending tend to lump together the crimes of corporations with crimes committed by individual representatives of those organizations when making comparisons with the rate of criminal activity among blue-collar and other groups.

A complementary perspective by Australian criminologist **John Braithwaite** says that white-collar criminals are frequently motivated by a disparity between corporate goals and the limited opportunities available to businesspeople through conventional business practices.[30] When pressured to achieve goals which may be unattainable within the existing framework of laws and regulations surrounding their business's area of endeavor, innovative corporate officers may turn to crime to meet organizational demands.[31]

Braithwaite believes that a general theory covering both white-collar and other forms of crime can be developed by focusing on inequality as the central explanatory variable in all criminal activity.[32] Although alienation from legitimate paths to success may lead lower-class offenders to criminal activity in an effort to acquire the material possessions necessary for survival, greed can similarly motivate relatively successful individuals to violate the law in order to acquire even more power and more possessions.[33] New types of criminal opportunities and new paths to immunity from accountability are constituted by concentrations of wealth and power. Inequality thus worsens both crimes of poverty motivated by the need to survive, and crimes of wealth motivated by greed.

Braithwaite also suggests that corporate culture socializes budding executives into clandestine and frequently illegal behavioral modalities—making it easier for them to violate the law when pressures to perform mount. The hostile relationship that frequently exists between businesses and the government agencies that regulate them may further spur corporate officers to evade the law. Braithwaite emphasizes his belief that the potential for shame associated with discovery—whether by enforcement agencies, the public, or internal corporate regulators—can have a powerful deterrent effect on most corporate executives because they are fundamentally conservative individuals who are otherwise seeking success through legitimate means.[34]

Braithwaite also recommends implementation of an "accountability model," which would hold all those responsible for corporate crimes accountable.[35] Rather than merely punishing corporations through fines, personal punishment meted out to corporate lawbreakers, says Braithwaite, should have the potential to substantially reduce white-collar offending.[36]

In sum, Braithwaite contends that an integrated theory of organizational crime would include insights garnered from: (1) strain theories, as to the distribution of legitimate and illegitimate opportunities; (2) subcultural theory, as applied to business subcultures; (3) labeling theory, on the way stigmatization can foster criminal subculture formation, and (4) control theory, as to how potential white-collar offenders can be made accountable.[37]

DEALING WITH WHITE-COLLAR CRIME

Certain forms of occupational crime may be easier to address than others. Individual occupational crimes may especially be subject to reduction by concerted enforcement and protective efforts, including enhanced IRS auditing programs, theft deterrent systems, and good internal financial procedures. Consumer information services can help eliminate fraudulent business practices, and increases in both victim awareness and reporting can help target both businesses and individuals responsible for various forms of white-collar or occupational crime.

However, as Donald J. Newman has observed, "[i]f white-collar crime is intrinsic to and normative within the value structure of our society, then no punishment or treatment program will effectively eradicate it."[38] Similarly, Gary S. Green points out that "[p]rofessional occupational criminals will probably continue to enjoy immunity from prosecution. Hence, they are unlikely to be deterred by sanction or threat and are unlikely to be formally disqualified by their professional organizations. They will therefore feel free and be free to continue or begin their criminal activities."[39]

In his insightful book *The Criminal Elite: The Sociology of White-Collar Crime*,[40] **James W. Coleman** suggests four areas of reform through which white-collar crime might be effectively addressed:

- *Ethical:* Ethical reforms include such things as working to establish stronger and more persuasive codes of business ethics. Courses on ethical business might be offered in universities, and corporations could school their employees in right livelihood.
- *Enforcement:* Enforcement reforms center on the belief that white-collar criminals must be more severely punished, but also include such things as better funding for enforcement agencies dealing with white-collar crime, larger research budgets for regulatory investigators, and the insulation of enforcement personnel from undue political influence.
- *Structural:* Structural reforms "involve basic changes in corporate structure" to make white-collar crime more difficult to commit. Coleman suggests adding members of the public to corporate boards of directors; changing the process whereby corporations are chartered to include control over white-collar crime; enhancing the flow of information between businesses, the public, and administrative bodies; and the "selective nationalization of firms that have long records of criminal violations."
- *Political:* Political reforms, according to Coleman, center on eliminating campaign contributions from corporations and businesses, but also include increasing the level of fairness in determining government grants, government purchases, and government contracts. The government, says Coleman, must

also police itself. Although this includes enforcement of laws now on the books which are intended to regulate the activities of elected officials and administrative personnel, Coleman concludes that ". . . there is some question about how effectively the government can ever police itself."

ORGANIZED CRIME

Organized crime the unlawful activities of the members of a highly organized, disciplined association engaged in supplying illegal goods and services, including but not limited to gambling, prostitution, loan-sharking, narcotics, labor racketeering, and other unlawful activities of members of such organizations.

Organized criminal groups have always existed. An early written account[41] of **organized crime** describes the activities of Jonathan Wild, a notorious brigand of the early 1700s. Wild was born in Wolverhampton, Staffordshire, England, in 1682 to "persons of decent character and station." Wild received a formal education, which was unusual for the times, and at age 15 was apprenticed to a buckle maker. Married at 22, Wild left his wife and new son a year later for the excitement of nearby London. Not long after his arrival in the city, Wild was arrested for nonpayment of debts and thrown into Wood-street Compter, a prison which held debtors and other prisoners—both male and female. During the four years he spent in prison Wild became intimate with a female inmate by the name of Mary Milliner, who was described as "one of the most abandoned prostitutes and pickpockets on the town. . . ." Wild later said that he also used his time in prison to "learn the secrets of the criminals there under confinement." Upon release he shared a home with Milliner, calling her his wife.

Milliner ran a bar on what was then known as Cock Alley in Cripplegate, one of the most notorious parts of London. Soon the bar became a hangout for thieves and other criminals. Wild capitalized on the situation and began purchasing all types of stolen goods and fencing them to merchants and the general public. As one writer of the times observed, "[h]e was at first at little trouble to dispose of the articles brought to him by thieves at something less than their real value, no law existing for the punishment of the receivers of stolen goods. . . ." However, the authorities, hearing of Wild's organized criminal activity, soon passed a law forbidding the receipt and sale of stolen items. As a consequence, the value of stolen goods plummeted. Soon, however, Wild discovered a way around the new law. One commentator described his solution this way: Wild called a meeting of thieves in the city and proposed "that when they made prize of anything, they should deliver it to him . . . saying that he would restore the goods to the owners by which means greater sums might be raised, while the thieves would remain perfectly secure from detection." Soon Wild was running the largest criminal organization in England and evading the law by returning stolen goods to their rightful owners in exchange for handsome rewards.

As he rose in both power and wealth, Wild displayed ruthless organizational skills. If a thief or burglar in Wild's gang demanded too much money or threatened to unmask the operation, Wild would have him apprehended and hanged—collecting whatever official reward had been offered for the felon's capture. As Wild's organization grew, he hired ships to transport excess inventory to France, the Netherlands, and Belgium. Soon he was trading internationally in stolen goods and living in grand style. Because of his ability to gather intelligence throughout the criminal underworld as well as in the ghettos of London, Wild gained the confidence of advisors to King George I—a relationship that kept him out of harm's way for many years. With the death of George I, however, and increasing British hostility to criminal activity, Wild was finally arrested and charged with running a criminal organization. Sentenced to hang, Wild was executed at Tyburn Prison on May 24, 1725.

HISTORY OF ORGANIZED CRIME IN THE UNITED STATES

Much of what most Americans traditionally think of today as organized crime— the **Mafia** or *Cosa Nostra*—has roots which predate the establishment of the United States as a sovereign power. For hundreds of years secret societies, the products of extreme poverty, feudalism, a traditional disregard for the law, and (some would say) national temperament, have flourished in Italy.[42] During the nineteenth century the Italian Camorra, based in Naples, became infamous for extortion and murder. The Camorrian code demanded total silence, and the organization issued printed licenses to its members to kill.

Italian criminal organizations that migrated to the United States with the wave of European immigrants during the late nineteenth and early twentieth centuries included the Mafia and the Black Hand. The Black Hand (in Italian, *La Mano Negro*) "specialized in the intimidation of Italian immigrants,"[43] typically extorting protection monies and other valuables. The Black Hand became especially powerful in Detroit, St. Louis, Kansas City, and New Orleans.

The Mafia, with roots in Sicily, worked to become a quasi-police organization in the Italian ghetto areas of the burgeoning American cities of the industrial era— often enforcing its own set of laws or codes when official intervention was lacking. One of the first well-documented conflicts between the Mafia and American law enforcement came on March 13, 1909, when New York City police officials learned that NYPD Lieutenant Joseph Petrosino had been assassinated upon his arrival in Palermo, Italy. Petrosino had gone to Palermo to investigate allegations that Mafia bosses in New York City were importing Black Hand assassins from the "old country" to do their dirty work. He was killed as he visited the Palermo Court of Justice by a single bullet allegedly fired by Mafia boss Vito Cascio Ferro. Although Ferro was arrested and charged with the crime, local deputies provided him with an alibi, and he was never convicted.

Secret societies in Italy were all but expunged during the 1930s and early 1940s under the fascist dictator Benito Mussolini. Surviving Mafia members became vehemently antifascist, sentiments that endeared them to American and allied intelligence services during World War II. Following the war, mafioso leaders resumed their traditional positions of power within Italian society, and links grew between American criminal organizations and those in Italy.

In his comprehensive book *Organized Crime,*[44] Howard Abadinsky reports that the first mention of the Mafia in New York can be found in a *New York Times* article dated October 21, 1888. The article quotes police inspector Thomas Byrnes as saying that a murder victim named Antonio Flaccomio was "an Italian fruit dealer and a member of a secret society. . . ." The society, said Byrnes, was called the Mafia; its members were fugitives from Sicily, an island in the south of Italy.

Cosa Nostra (literally, "our thing")or **Mafia** a term signifying organized crime, and one of a variety of names for the Outfit, the Mob, the Syndicate, or the Organization.

Ethnic succession the
continuing process
whereby one immigrant
or ethnic group succeeds
another through
assumption of a particular
position in society.

A ROSE BY ANY OTHER NAME—*THE COSA NOSTRA*

Other organized criminal groups, including Jewish and Irish gangs, flourished in
New York City prior to the arrival of large numbers of Italian immigrants in the late
1800s. Ethnic succession has been as much a reality in organized crime as in most
other aspects of American life. **Ethnic succession** refers to the continuing process
whereby one immigrant or ethnic group succeeds another through assumption of
a particular position in society.

Throughout the late nineteenth and early twentieth centuries, for example,
Jewish gangsters such as Meyer Lansky, Benjamin "Bugsy" Siegel, "Dutch" Schultz,
and Lepke Buchalter ran many of the "rackets" in New York City, only to have their
places taken by Italian immigrants arriving a few years later. Almost forgotten today is Arnold Rothstein, a famous Jewish gangster who was able to translate many
ill-gotten gains into real estate holdings and other legitimate commercial ventures.
Among those who remember, Rothstein has been called the "most important orga-
nizer and innovator"[45] among Jewish criminal operatives in turn-of-the-century
New York, and the "Godfather" of organized crime in the city. Italian-American organized criminals are themselves not immune to ethnic succession, which has continued into the present day, with gangs of African-Americans, Hispanic-Americans,
and Asian-Americans now running significant aspects of the drug trade and controlling other illicit activities in many parts of the country.

Even so, organized criminal activity in the United States throughout the last half
century has largely been the domain of Italian-American immigrants and their
descendants—especially those of Sicilian descent. As one observer notes, "to beat rival organizations, criminals of Sicilian descent reproduced the kind of illegal

Much of what the public believes about
organized crime comes from images
such as this one of Humphrey Bogart,
starring in the 1951 movie *The Enforcer*.
Has the government won the war
against organized crime? *Archive Photos.*

groups they had belonged to in the old country and employed the same rules to make them invincible."[46] Hence, it was not long before American Mafia leaders had taken over from their criminal predecessors, many of whom were either killed or forced to turn to more legitimate forms of enterprise.

As a consequence of historical events that are well documented, it is both realistic and useful to discuss American organized crime primarily in terms of Sicilian–American involvement. A few caveats must be recognized, however. For one thing, although many Sicilians who emigrated to this country either had ties to, or experience with, Mafia organizations in the old country, most did not. Many Sicilian-Americans, in fact, emigrated to America to escape Mafia despotism at home, and most became productive members of their adopted society. Relatively few involved themselves in organized crime. Those who did created an organization known variously as the Mafia, the Outfit, the Mob, *La Cosa Nostra* (our thing), the syndicate, or simply, the organization. Other terms applied to Sicilian-American organized crime include crime cartel and the confederation.

Joseph Valachi is generally credited with popularizing the term *Cosa Nostra.* In 1963, Valachi, a member of the Genovese crime family, used the term while testifying before the McClellan Committee which was holding hearings into organized crime. Following the hearings, the name *Cosa Nostra* became increasingly popular both with the American press and public, and has at least partially replaced the term *Mafia* as the *nom de jour* of Italian-American criminal organizations.

The term *Mafia,* however, is still in widespread use. Hence, in the paragraphs that follow, Sicilian-American organized criminal groups are referred to as both Mafia and *Cosa Nostra*—terms which have been used interchangeably by police investigators, the press, the public, and government commissions over the years.

Mob informant Joseph Valachi testifying before Senate investigators in 1963. How has organized crime changed since Valachi's time? *Locs Mags (UPI)/Corbis-Bettmann.*

PROHIBITION AND OFFICIAL CORRUPTION

By the 1920s Mafia influence extended to most American cities. But it was the advent of Prohibition that gave organized crime its vital financial wherewithal. In 1919 the U.S. Congress passed the 18th Amendment to the U.S. Constitution, ushering in an age of prohibition on the manufacture, transportation, and sale of alcoholic beverages. The 18th Amendment reads as follows:

> Section 1. After one year from the ratification of this article the manufacture, sale, or transportation of intoxicating liquors within, the importation thereof into, or the exportation thereof from the United States and all territory subject to the jurisdiction thereof for beverage purposes is hereby prohibited.
>
> —*U.S. Constitution*
> *Amendment XVIII [1919]*

In many ways the advent of Prohibition was a godsend for Mafia leaders. Prior to Prohibition, Mafia operations in American cities were "small time," concerned mostly with gambling, protection rackets, and loansharking. Many mafiosi, however, also belonged to a fraternal brotherhood called *Unione Siciliana* whose members were well versed in the manufacture of low-cost high-proof untaxed alcohol,[47] an expertise which had been brought from their native country. In addition, the existing infrastructure of organized crime permitted easy and efficient entry into the running and sale of contraband liquor. As one writer explained, "[b]y its nature, bootlegging required national (even international) organization. The liquor came from Canada or Europe, necessitating an extranational arrangement. It rode at anchor outside the territorial limits in bottoms belonging to the underworld. It had to be picked up by small craft to be smuggled ashore. The contraband had to get by the Coast Guard, Customs, and cops. The cargo had to be loaded on trucks, carried across bridges and highways, protected against hijackers, delivered to warehouses, [and] redistributed to retailers. And somewhere, somehow, there had to be collectors, bookkeepers, accountants, enforcers, personnel men, and masterminds to make the rum-running pay."[48]

Prohibition provided existing Mafia families the opportunity for accumulation of unheralded wealth. As Abadinsky puts it, "Prohibition enabled men who had been street thugs to become crime overlords."[49] Others describe it this way: "Prohibition proved to be the catalyst that established the wealth and power of modern organized crime syndicates."

The huge profits to be had from bootlegging led to the wholesale bribery of government officials and to the quick corruption of many law enforcement officers throughout the country. Nowhere was corruption more complete than in Chicago, where runners working for organized crime distributed illegal alcohol under police protection,[50] and corrupt city government officials received regular payoffs from criminal cartels.

In 1929 President Herbert Hoover appointed the National Commission on Law Observance and Enforcement, better known as the Wickersham Commission—

after its chairman, George Wickersham. The commission produced a series of four-teen reports. Three of them, *Observance and Enforcement of Prohibition, Lawlessness in Law Enforcement,* and *The Police,* either mentioned or decried the corrupting influence Prohibition was having on professional law enforcement in America. Fourteen years after it had been passed, the 18th Amendment was repealed, and with it Prohibition ended.

Section 1. The eighteenth article of amendment to the Constitution of the United States is hereby repealed.

—*U.S. Constitution*
Amendment XXI [1933]

Unfortunately, the heritage of Prohibition-associated corruption is still with us. Official corruption has become an institutionalized part of American life in some parts of the country. As one writer explains, "American cities have a long history of corrupt relations between some illegal enterprises and local police or politicians. For criminal entrepreneurs, payments to politicians or police can be viewed either as normal business expenses in return for services to the enterprise or as extortionate demands that eat into the profits of the enterprise. For police and politicians, levying regular assessments on illegal entrepreneurs has provided a source of extra income as well as a way to oversee neighborhood enterprises that could not be legally controlled. Historically, oversight by local political organizations (or the police) has been the most important source of coordination for illegal enterprises in American cities."[51]

In 1967 the Task Force on Organized Crime, part of President Johnson's Commission on Law Enforcement and Administration of Justice, concluded that "[a]ll available data indicate that organized crime flourishes only where it has corrupted local officials."[52] Sometimes the roots of corruption reach far deeper. As one writer notes, "the line between organized crime and corrupt officials is often unclear, at times nonexistent. . . . In both Chicago and New York those who ran organized criminal activities, gambling and prostitution, were political figures and often elected officials."[53]

CENTRALIZATION OF ORGANIZED CRIME

The Prohibition era was a tumultuous time for American organized crime. While its leaders grappled for the huge profits to be reaped from the sale of illegal alcohol, they simultaneously worked to consolidate power. Gang warfare—not unlike the drive-by shootings and execution-style slayings which now characterize inner-city youth gangs—was the order of the day.

One of the most infamous gangland wars of all time erupted in Chicago in the mid-1920s when Alphonse "Al" Capone, an up-and-coming thug, decided to make a citywide grab for power. Following a number of spectacular killings (dubbed "massacres" by the press), Capone was successful in forging a crime syndicate under which he declared himself the leader of all of Chicago's organized crime families. For a time his claim remained disputed, primarily by George 'Bugs' Moran who had inherited the leadership of a local gang. In a bid to end competition, Capone lured Moran's men to a garage on Chicago's east side on the ruse that a truckload of boot-legged liquor was soon to arrive. Once inside the garage, Moran's men were surprised by five of Capone's executioners. Three were dressed as police officers, while the other two wore plain clothes. The uniformed men ordered the Moran gang against the garage wall, where the plain clothes killers machine-gunned them to death. The killings became known as the St. Valentine's Day massacre and established Capone as undisputed ruler of organized crime in Chicago.

Similar efforts at consolidation were being made nationwide. On April 15, 1931, influential New York City crime figure "Joe the Boss" Giuseppe Masseria was gunned down in a restaurant in the Coney Island section of Brooklyn. His killing, part of what has been called the Castellammarese War, appears to have been ordered by another of the city's bosses, Salvatore Maranzano. Following Masseria's death, Maranzano declared himself the "boss of bosses" over all of New York's crime families. Maranzano, however, soon lost favor with more "Americanized" Mafia figures, and was himself killed in September 1931 by armed men who entered his office disguised as immigration officials.

During the next two days, thirty Mafia leaders died in similar gang-ordered executions across the country. By the close of 1931, when the smoke settled and the killings stopped, the Mafia had become an integrated, coordinated criminal organization able to settle most disputes internally and capable of shielding its activities from the prying eyes of investigators. A 1939 expose written by J. Richard Davis, former attorney for one of New York's crime families, credited the centralization of control to the rise of "Charlie Lucky," also known as "Lucky Luciano" (born Charles Luciano), who "became leader of the *Unione Siciliani* in 1931. . . . The 'greasers' in the *Unione*," wrote Davis, "were killed off, and the organization was no longer a loose, fraternal order of Sicilian blackhanders and alcohol cookers, but rather the framework for a system of alliances which were to govern the underworld."[54] Another author described it this way: "in 1931 organized crime units across the United States formed into monopolistic corporations, and those corporations, in turn, linked themselves together in a monopolistic cartel."[55]

Following 1931, Mafia activity went underground. The Mafia's success at hiding its operations was so great that one expert was able to write, "there is a considerable body of police opinion in the United States which holds that the Mafia in America died in September 1931, on 'Purge Day.'"[56]

As the 1967 President's Commission on Law Enforcement and Administration of Justice observed, Mafia activity remained nearly invisible and investigations of Mafia operations lay dormant until the 1950s. In the words of the commission: "[a]fter World War II there was little national interest in the problem (of organized crime) until 1950, when the U.S. Attorney General convened a national conference on organized crime."[57]

Organized crime reemerged into the national spotlight in 1951 when the federal Special Committee to Investigate Organized Crime in Interstate Commerce[58] (better known as the **Kefauver Committee,** after its chairman Estes Kefauver) reported that "a nationwide crime syndicate known as the Mafia operate(s) in many

Kefauver Committee
formed in 1951, was the better known name for the Federal Special Committee to Investigate Organized Crime in Interstate Commerce.

large (American) cities, and the leaders of the Mafia usually control the most lucrative rackets in their cities."[59] Although the Kefauver Committee, which interviewed hundreds of witnesses, noted that it had "found it difficult to obtain reliable
data concerning the extent of Mafia operation, the nature of Mafia organization,
and the way it presently operates," it was able to reach the following conclusions.

- A nationwide crime syndicate exists, known as the Mafia, whose tentacles are
  found in many large cities.
- The American Mafia has international linkages that appear most clearly in
  connection with narcotics traffic.
- Mafia leaders are usually found in control of the most lucrative rackets in their
  cities.
- Indications suggest centralized direction and control in these rackets, but
  leadership appears to be in a group rather than in a single individual.

Public interest in organized crime was again roused when authorities learned of
a national meeting of at least seventy-five leaders of criminal cartels scheduled for
November 1957. The purpose of the meeting, held at the home of Joseph Barbara
in the small New York town of Apalachin, was never uncovered. Some speculate that
syndicate leaders may have met to split up the empire of the recently murdered
Albert Anastasia—who was himself reputed to have been a ruthless killer. Barbara,
born in Castellammarese del Golfo, Italy, was boss of a northeastern Pennsylvania
crime family and died two years after the meeting.

The 1957 meeting resulted in raids on Barbara's house and the arrest of many
well-known organized crime figures. In 1959 Joseph Bonanno and twenty-six others were convicted of obstruction of justice for their refusal to reveal the meeting's
purpose. Their convictions, however, were overturned in 1960 by the U.S. Supreme
Court which, in *U.S. v. Bufalino*,[60] reasoned that the suspects had been arrested
without probable cause.

The picture that eventually emerged from years of federal investigations into
Italian-American organized criminal groups was of twenty-four crime families operating in the United States under the direction of a "commission," whose membership consisted of the bosses of the nation's most powerful families. The following, taken directly from the 1967 President's Commission report, summarizes what
was believed to be true of organized crime at the time of the report: "Today the core
of organized crime in the United States consists of 24 groups operating as criminal
cartels in large cities across the nation. Their membership is exclusively Italian, they
are in frequent communication with each other, and their smooth functioning is in-
sured by a national body of overseers.... The wealthiest and most influential core
groups," the report concluded, "operate in States including New York, New Jersey,
Illinois, Florida, Louisiana, Nevada, Michigan, and Rhode Island." The report
placed membership in organized crime at 5,000 nationwide, and said that "[e]ach
of the 24 groups is known as a 'family' with membership varying from as many as
700 men to as few as 20."

Family organization was said to consist of (1) a boss, whose primary functions
were described as "maintaining order and maximizing profits," (2) an underboss,
who was said to collect information for the boss and to relay messages to and from

him, (3) the counselor, or consigliere, who serves as an advisor, (4) numerous lieutenants, or *caporegime,* some of whom "serve as chiefs of operating units," and (5) soldiers or *soldati,* representing the lowest level of family membership, and who "operate a particular illicit enterprise" such as a loansharking operation, a lottery, a smuggling operation, etcetera. "Beneath the soldiers," the commission found, "are large numbers of employees and . . . agents who are not members of the family and not necessarily of Italian descent. These are people who do most of the actual work in the various enterprises." Unlike the family members who give them orders, "they have no buffers or other insulation from law enforcement." The structure of a typical Sicilian-American organized crime family is shown in Figure 10.1.

The President's Commission also found that organized crime members swear allegiance to a code of conduct which "stipulates that underlings should not interfere with the leaders' interests and should not seek protection from the police. They should be 'standup guys' who go to prison in order that the bosses may amass fortunes. The code gives leaders exploitative authoritarian power over everyone in the organization. Loyalty, honor, respect, absolute obedience—these are inculcated in family members through ritualistic initiation and customs within the organization, through material rewards, and through violence."[61]

COSA NOSTRA TODAY

Some writers maintain that at least twenty-four organized crime families of Sicilian-American heritage continue to operate throughout the United States today. Of these, the largest number (five) operate out of New York. They are the[62]

Luciano/Genovese Family (300–400 members)
Mineo/Gambino Family (400–500 members)
Reina/Lucchese Family (125 members)
Profaci/Colombo Family (100 members)
Bonanno Family (75 members)

Chicago is home to other influential *Cosa Nostra* families, including the Carlisi family (sometimes called the "Outfit"), while the Scarfo (run by Nicodemo "Little Nicky" Scarfo) and Stanfa organizations still operate in Philadelphia. New Orleans serves as headquarters for the Marcello gang (headed by Carlos Marcello), and organized crime in New England is controlled by Ray Patriarca, Jr., and his henchmen, while the Civella mob runs racketeering activities in Kansas City, Missouri.

ACTIVITIES OF ORGANIZED CRIME

The 1976 federal Task Force on Organized Crime identified five types of activity which may qualify as organized crime: racketeering, vice operations, theft/fence rings, gangs, and terrorism.

Whatever its source, however, money is the centerpiece of, and primary motivation for, all organized criminal activity. Near the start of the Great Depression, the

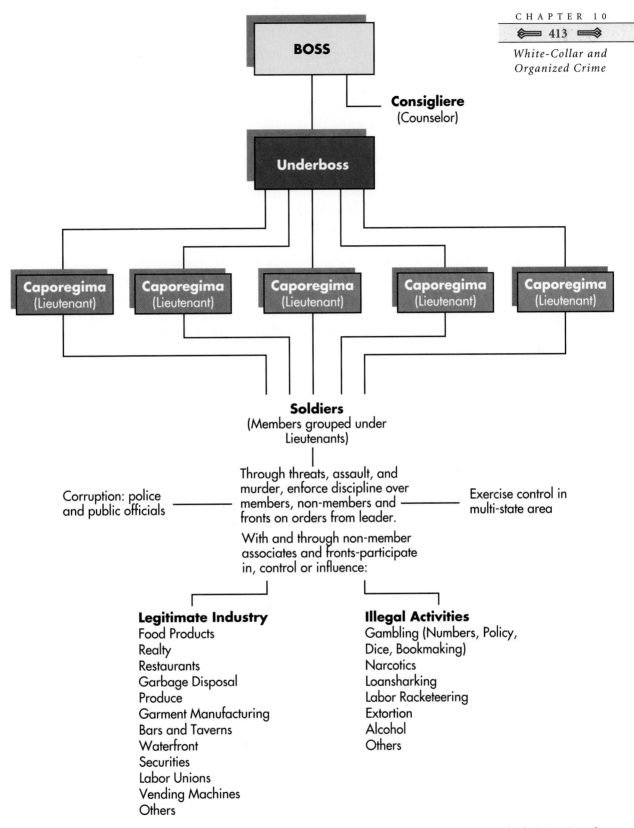

FIGURE 10.1   A Typical Organized Crime Family. *Source:* President's Commission on Law Enforcement and Administration of Justice, *The Challenge of Crime in a Free Society* (Washington, D.C.: U.S. Government Printing Office, 1967), p. 47.

notorious Chicago gangster Al Capone achieved the distinction of being listed in the *Guiness Book of World Records* as having the highest income of any individual in a single year—more than $105 million in 1927.[63]

Things haven't changed much since Capone's day. As one expert on organized crime explains, "it is cash that dominates every aspect of the mob machines.... The mobsters' working days are spent worrying about and scheming over money, and finally, quarreling and killing for money, almost all of it derived illegitimately."[64] The same expert gives the example of Philadelphia crime boss Nicky Scarfo, who "even considered killing his own wife, Domenica, over money when he learned that 'little by little, she had robbed him of around four hundred thousand' for her gambling sprees at Trump Plaza in Atlantic City." No amount of money seems too small for concern, and—as in much of the wider society—money often becomes a way of keeping score as to who has been the most successful at what they have done.

Throughout the past half-century Sicilian-American criminal cartels have continued to be involved in (1) the establishment and control of both legalized and illicit forms of gambling, including lotteries, bookmaking, horse-race wagering, and bets on athletic contests; (2) loansharking, which involves the lending of money at rates far higher than legally prescribed limits; (3) large-scale drug trafficking; (4) the fencing of stolen goods, including securities; (5) infiltration of legitimate businesses, including labor unions and corporations that can be used as quasi-legitimate fronts for money laundering, and so on; and (6) labor union racketeering via which legitimate businesses are intimidated through threats of strikes, walk-outs, and sabotage.

In some states, where lotteries are now government run, the organized crime's "take" from illegal gambling has been reduced. Not to be outdone, however, Sicilian-American operatives have moved into legitimate gambling, reportedly buying stakes in casinos in Nevada, New Jersey, and elsewhere. The Flamingo Hotel, the first elaborate hotel-casino in Las Vegas, was said to have been built by crime boss "Bugsy" Siegel and funded by organized crime leaders throughout the country.[65] Cleveland syndicate leader Moe Dalitz is reputed to have financed the Stardust Hotel, and federal officials claim that at least $14 million was illegally skimmed from the hotel's operations between 1973 and 1983.[66] Although New Jersey has made herculean efforts to keep organized crime from influencing casino operation in Atlantic City, some writers point out that "Local 54 of the Hotel Employees and Restaurant Employees Union . . . which represents 22,000 casino hotel employees, has long been dominated by the Bruno family of Philadelphia."[67]

Organized crime is involved in many other kinds of rackets besides gambling. Some evidence suggests, for example, that organized crime today is becoming increasingly active in the illegal copying and distribution of copyrighted software, music, and other forms of recorded media including videotapes, compact discs, and cassette tapes. The provision of elaborately staged videotaped pornographic productions, including "snuff movies" (in which a sex "star" is actually killed on screen), and elements of child pornography can also be traced to organized criminal activity.

Some sense of the profit derived from the activities of organized crime can be gained from official estimates of the money being collected by Nicodemo "Little Nicky" Scarfo's gang at the time of Scarfo's indictment in 1986 on charges of first-

Anthony Accetturo (center), an alleged leader of the Lucchese crime family, celebrates after his acquittal on federal racketeering charges. The trial lasted nearly two years. How does the "code" of organized crime protect its members? *Peter Cannata/AP/Wide World Photos.*

degree murder. Scarfo operated illegitimate businesses throughout Philadelphia and southern New Jersey. When he was arrested his gang was estimated to be taking in "$25,000,000 to $30,000,000 annually from illegal gambling (numbers, video poker, sports betting), and millions more from loansharking, shakedowns of drug dealers and labor union racketeering. Even bigger deals were in the making: Scarfo was preparing to control more than $200,000,000 in Philadelphia waterfront-development projects, as well as to infiltrate the union benefits plans of Atlantic City's bartenders and waitresses."[68]

CODE OF CONDUCT

A strict code of conduct governs behavior among members of organized Sicilian-American criminal groups. This code, sometimes called *omerta* (or "manliness"), is unwritten. Members are formally introduced to the code through an initiation ritual which has changed little since it was brought to American shores by Sicilian immigrants well over a hundred years ago. The code of **omerta** functions to concentrate power in the hands of crime bosses while ensuring their protection. As officials with one federal task force stated, "[t]hose aspects of the code which prohibit appealing to outside authorities for justice while at the same time advocating great loyalty, respect and honor are probably most essential to the concentration of power in the hands of a few, and hence to exploitation of lower-status men by their leaders."[69]

A few years ago the FBI electronically eavesdropped on a house in Medford, Massachusetts, in which Joseph Russo, a New England *Cosa Nostra* consigliere, conducted an initiation ritual for four new family members. Twenty-one men

Omerta the informal, unwritten code of organized crime which demands silence and loyalty, among other things, of family members.

attended the candlelit ceremony. This was the first time authorities had ever captured a *Cosa Nostra* induction on tape. As each young man swore to uphold *omerta* and took a vow of silence never to betray the organization or tell its secrets, he held a burning picture of a Catholic saint and prayed: "*Come si brucia questa santa, cosi si brucera la mia anima*" (as burns this saint, so will burn my soul), a reference to the death awaiting anyone who violates the code.[70]

Another initiate described his induction into Philadelphia's Scarfo gang this way:[71] "I was driven to this million-dollar house in Philadelphia, with a big swimming pool and a big table laid out with food—shrimp, steaks, meatballs, peppers, olives, spaghetti—and about forty chairs. I was on cloud nine. Scarfo is at the head of this long table and says, 'Nick, do you know why you're here?' I said, 'No.' You're supposed to say no. . . . So next, he says, 'We want you to be one of us. Now, look around this table and tell me if there is anyone you have bad feelings with.' I look around and say 'no'. . . . So he makes a speech about how much I've done for the family and then says that I have the freedom to leave now and that I'll always be their friend. There would be no hard feelings if I didn't want to join. I said, 'No, I want to be one of you'. . . . Scarfo points to a gun and a knife on a table and asks if I'd use these for any of these friends around the table. Then he lights a small piece of tissue paper in my hand while I say, 'May I burn like the saints in hell if I ever betray any of my friends.' He also pricks my trigger finger. Then you go around the table and kiss everyone. Then we have a feast and then you're told the rules. In the days that follow, you go around and meet the guys who weren't at the ceremony. Then word just seems to spread everywhere you go. And everywhere you go, the respect that you receive from nonmembers is enormous."

The rules of the Scarfo family, said this inductee, included the following: "the family doesn't fool with kidnapping, counterfeit money or bonds. You can shake down or rob drug dealers, but you can't protect them, lend them money or deal drugs yourself. No fooling with a member's wife. You can't even look at another guy's wife. That's automatic death. Even hitting another member is automatic death. He can ask for your life. You're supposed to report once a week to your *capo*, unless there's a good excuse. You can't go out of town without telling him. You always have to touch base. You're also told that silence is the code and this thing comes first. It comes before your mother, your father, your sister, your brother."[72]

Federal investigators and others studying organized crime have identified seven general features characteristic of the code sworn to by family members everywhere.

- Do not be an informer. Do not "rat" on others and do not sell out.
- Be a member of the team. Be loyal to members of the organization.
- Do not interfere with the interests of others. Do not rock the boat.
- Be rational. Do not engage in battle if you cannot win.
- Be a man of honor. Have class. Be independent.
- Respect women and your elders.
- Be a "stand-up" guy ("stand-up guys" take the "rap," shielding others). Keep your eyes and ears open and your mouth shut.

Like any informal unwritten code, *omerta* has many other implicit rules and is fraught with nuances fully understood only to those raised within its traditions. The code, however, imposes two clear and indisputable requirements on all family members: (1) obey your superiors, and (2) keep silent. Failure to adhere closely to either rule means death. The 1967 President's Commission report stated it this way: "The basic principle of justice in the Sicilian Mafia, as in American organized crime, is deterrence from deviation by means of the threat of certain, swift, uniform and severe punishment."

An example is provided by the recent FBI investigation focusing on New York City crime boss John Gotti (then head of the Gambino family), which yielded a wealth of secretly recorded conversations between Gotti and other organized crime figures. This is what Gotti told his underboss, Frank "Frankie Loc" Locascio, about why a subordinate had to die: "Anytime you got a partner who don't agree with us, we kill him," Gotti explained. "He didn't rob nothin'. Know why he's dying?" Gotti continued. "He's gonna die because he refused to come in when I called. He didn't do nothing else wrong."

The code of *omerta* is similar to the values found among career criminals everywhere. As one federal report stated, "there is a striking similarity between both the code of conduct and the enforcement machinery used in the confederation of organized criminals and the code of conduct and enforcement machinery which governs the behavior of prisoners."[73]

OTHER ORGANIZED CRIMINAL GROUPS

According to Howard Abadinsky, a hallmark of true criminal organizations is that they function independently of any of their members, including their leaders, and have a continuity over time as personnel within them change.[74] The example given by Abadinsky is of the James Gang, which dissolved with the death of its leader, Jesse James. In contrast, says Abadinsky, "[w]hen Al Capone was imprisoned fifty years later, the 'Capone Organization' continued, and in its more modern form (the 'Outfit') it continues to operate in Chicago."[75]

Although, until now, we have restricted our discussion of organized crime to Sicilian-American criminal enterprise, it is both useful and realistic to mention the existence of other organized criminal groups in the United States—each characterized by some degree of organizational continuity which is independent of its membership. Among such criminal associations are groups which have been diversely referred to as the Black Mafia, the Cuban Mafia, the Haitian Mafia, Colombian Cartels, the Russian Mafia, Asian criminals (Chinese Tongs and street gangs, Japanese Yakuza, and Vietnamese gangs), and others. Included here, as well, might be inner-city gangs (the most well known of which are probably the Los Angeles Crips and Bloods, and the Chicago Vice Lords), international drug rings, outlaw motorcycle gangs (such as the Hell's Angels and the Pagans), and other looser associations of small-time thugs, prison gangs, and drug dealers.

Noteworthy among these groups are the Latino organized bands, including Dominican, Colombian, Mexican, and Cuban importers of cocaine and other drugs. Although it is not known precisely how much cocaine has entered this country illegally, much of it has been handled by the Medellin and Cali Cartels headquartered in Colombia, South America. The Medellin and Cali Cartels consist of approximately thirty-five organized groups that often cooperate with one another and who have financed their own small armies for protection of both their operations and their personnel. Although recent arrests and some deaths have cut into the cartels' influence, it is believed that they are still responsible for the majority of cocaine entering the United States illegally.

Although it is difficult to categorize such a diversity of groups with any consistency, it is impossible to discuss each of them in a volume of this size. Whether, however, the principle of ethnic succession (discussed earlier) will ever fully apply to organized criminal activity is open to debate—although in some American cities *Cosa Nostra* operatives have already begun to be replaced by Puerto Rican, African-American, and even Russian gangs. In part, such replacement is due to federal and state law enforcement efforts which have seriously impacted activities of the mob in some areas of the United States.

Where Sicilian-American organized criminal activity continues to flourish, however, connections with the "old country" sometime still remain. In late 1994, for example, New York City police, in conjunction with federal authorities, announced the arrest of seventy-nine suspects in New York and Italy, all charged with drug conspiracy. Drug-running activities were said to have centered on New York City's Famous Original Ray's Pizza Restaurant on Third Avenue near Forty-third Street. Authorities alleged that the pizza parlor was used as a halfway point in an international drug ring whose ultimate aim was to provide cocaine to "three long-standing organized crime groups in Italy, where cocaine sells for three times what it costs in New York."[76] Among those arrested were Aniello, Francesco, and Roberto Ambrosio—brothers of Italian-American descent who ran the pizzeria.

ORGANIZED CRIME AND THE LAW

For many years American law enforcement agencies had few special weapons in the fight against organized crime. Instead, they prosecuted organized criminal operatives under statutes directed at solitary offenders, using laws such as those against theft, robbery, assault, gambling, prostitution, drug abuse, and murder. Innovative prosecutors have at times drawn upon other statutory resources in the drive to indict leaders of organized crime. On October 17, 1931, for example, Al Capone was convicted on various charges of income tax evasion after federal investigators were able to show that he had paid no taxes on an income in excess of $1 million. Laws regulating the sale of alcohol and drugs, and statutes circumscribing acts of prostitution have also been used against organized criminals, although with varying degrees of success.

The first federal legislation aimed specifically at curtailing the activities of organized crime is known as the Hobbs Act, although the term actually denotes a series of statutes that were passed beginning in 1946. In essence, the Hobbs Act made it a violation of federal law to engage in any form of criminal behavior that interferes with interstate commerce. It also criminalized interstate or foreign travel in furtherance of criminal activity, and made it a crime to use the highways, telephone, or mail in support of activities such as gambling, drug trafficking, loansharking, and other forms of racketeering.

RICO an acronym for the
Racketeer Influenced and
Corrupt Organization
statute, which was part of
the federal Organized
Crime Control Act of 1970.

The single most important piece of federal legislation ever passed which specifically targets the activities of organized crime is RICO. **RICO** is an acronym for the Racketeer Influenced and Corrupt Organization statute, which was part of the federal Organized Crime Control Act of 1970. The Organized Crime Control Act defines organized crime as "the unlawful activities of the members of a highly organized, disciplined association engaged in supplying illegal goods and services, including but not limited to gambling, prostitution, loansharking, narcotics, labor racketeering, and other unlawful activities of members of such organizations." The RICO portion of the act sweepingly brought together under one single piece of legislation the many and diverse activities of American organized crime and made each punishable in a variety of new ways. RICO did not make racketeering itself illegal, but rather focused on the ill-gotten gains derived from such activity—specifying that it shall be unlawful for anyone involved in a *pattern* of racketeering to derive any income or proceeds from that activity. Given the continuing significance of the RICO statute, it is worthwhile to reproduce here that statute's definition of racketeering activity, which includes

(A) any act or threat involving murder, kidnapping, gambling, arson, robbery, bribery, extortion, dealing in obscene matter, or dealing in narcotic or other dangerous drugs, which is chargeable under State law and punishable by imprisonment for more than one year;

(B) any act that is indictable under any of the following provisions of title 18, United States Code: section 201 (relating to bribery), section 224 (relating to sports bribery), sections 471, 472, and 473 (relating to counterfeiting), section 659 (relating to theft from interstate shipment) . . . section 664 (relating to embezzlement from pension and welfare funds), sections 891–894 (relating to extortionate credit transactions), section 1029 (relating to fraud and related activity in connection with access devices), section 1084 (relating to the transmission of gambling information), section 1341 (relating to mail fraud), section 1343 (relating to wire fraud), section 1344 (relating to financial institution fraud), sections 1461–1465 (relating to obscene matter), section 1503 (relating to obstruction of justice), section 1510 (relating to obstruction of criminal investigations), section 1511 (relating to the obstruction of State or local law enforcement), section 1512 (relating to tampering with a witness, victim, or an informant), section 1513 (relating to retaliating against a witness, victim, or an informant), section 1951 (relating to interference with commerce, robbery, or extortion), section 1952 (relating to racketeering), section 1953 (relating to interstate transportation of wagering paraphernalia), section 1954 (relating to unlawful welfare fund payments), section 1955 (relating to the prohibition of illegal gambling businesses), section 1956 (relating to the laundering of monetary instruments), section 1957 (relating to engaging in monetary transactions in property derived from specified unlawful activity), section 1958 (relating to use of interstate commerce facilities in the commission of murder-for-hire), sections 2251–2252 (relating to sexual exploitation of children), sections 2312 and 2313 (relating to interstate transportation of stolen motor vehicles), sections 2314 and 2315 (relating to interstate transportation of stolen property), section 2321 (relating to trafficking in certain motor vehicles or motor vehicle parts), sections 2341–2346 (relating to trafficking in contraband cigarettes), sections 2421–2424 (relating to white slave traffic),

(C) any act that is indictable under title 29, United States Code, section 186 (dealing with restrictions on payments and loans to labor organizations) or section 501(c) (relating to embezzlement from union funds),

(D) any offense involving fraud connected with a case under title 11, fraud in the sale of securities, or the felonious manufacture, importation, receiving, concealment, buying, selling, or otherwise dealing in narcotics or other dangerous drugs, punishable under any law of the United States, or

(E) any act that is indictable under the Currency and Foreign Transactions Reporting Act.

Asset forfeiture the authorized seizure of money, negotiable instruments, securities, or other things of value.

Punishments provided for under RICO include **asset forfeiture,** which makes it possible for federal officials to seize the proceeds of those involved in racketeering. In the words of the statute: "Whoever violates any provision of . . . this chapter shall be fined . . . or imprisoned not more than 20 years (or for life if the violation is based on a racketeering activity for which the maximum penalty includes life imprisonment), or both, and shall forfeit to the United States, irrespective of any provision of State law . . . any property . . . derived from any proceeds that the person

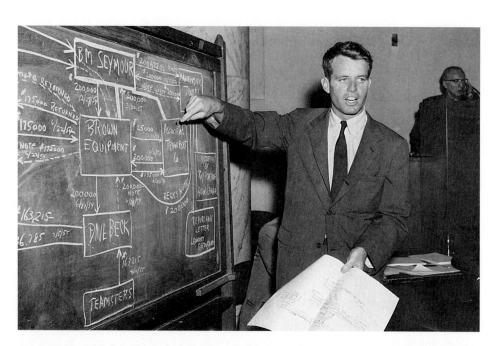

Attorney General Robert Kennedy describing a link between the Teamsters and organized crime. How influential is organized crime in American society today? *UPI/Corbis-Bettmann.*

obtained, directly or indirectly, from racketeering activity or unlawful debt collection. . . ." Hence, as a result of RICO, federal agents are empowered to seize the financial and other tangible fruits of organized criminal activity including businesses, real estate, money, equities, gold and other commodities, vehicles including airplanes and boats, and just about anything else that can be shown to have been acquired through a pattern of racketeering activity.

Money Laundering

Money laundering refers to the process by which illegal gains are disguised as legal income. A more formal definition is offered by the National Institute of Justice, which says that money laundering is "the process of converting illegally earned assets, originating as cash, to one or more alternative forms to conceal such incriminating factors as illegal origin and true ownership."[77]

Title 18, Section 1956 of the U.S. Criminal Code specifically prohibits what it calls the "laundering of monetary instruments" and defines money laundering as efforts "to conceal or disguise the nature, the location, the source, the ownership, or the control of the proceeds of specified unlawful activity. . . ." To assist in the identification of money launderers, a provision of the 1986 federal Money Laundering Control Act requires that banks report to the government all currency transactions in excess of $10,000. This requirement is, of course, well known to high-end money launderers who routinely evade it by dealing in commodities such as gold, using foreign banks, or by making a series of smaller deposits and transfers.

Reliable official estimates of the amount of money laundered in the United States are hard to establish. A decade ago, however, the President's Commission on Organized Crime estimated that approximately $15 billion of illicit U.S. drug proceeds moved illegally every year into international financial channels.[78] Of that amount, $5 billion was thought to be taken out of the country as currency.

A few years ago, the most notorious of foreign banks set up to serve the needs of money launderers, drug dealers, terrorists, and other assorted ne'er-do-wells, was closed when banking regulators in the United States, England, and several other countries seized branch assets and arrested many of the bank's officers. The Bank of Credit and Commerce (BCCI), International, was chartered in Luxembourg and opened branches throughout the world, including at least one in the Bahamas—islands already known for their role in the provision of infamous "off-shore" banking services which, while trading in currencies internationally, offer customers considerable secrecy and very limited reporting requirements.

BCCI soon grew into one of the largest banks in the world, and opened offices in seventy-two countries. Its friends in America included Jimmy Carter, Washington lawyer Clifford Clark, and the powerful senator Orrin Hatch.[79] Although evidence suggests that BCCI may have provided assistance to U.S. CIA operatives, it also "served to smuggle arms to Syria, Iran, and Libya, and to launder money for the Medellin cartel and Golden Triangle drug warlord Khun Sa."[80] After repeated indictments of top officials, BCCI closed its doors in 1991. During the decade or so

Money laundering the process of converting illegally earned assets, originating as cash, to one or more alternative forms to conceal such incriminating factors as illegal origin and true ownership.

that it was in existence, however, it is estimated that many billions of dollars flowed through its numerous branch offices—the majority of it from drug cartels and terrorist organizations seeking to hide the source of their revenues.

In December 1993 the bipartisan President's Commission on Model State Drug Laws released its report which included a comprehensive package of forty-four model state laws designed to crack down on drug and alcohol abuse throughout the country. "Money and property are the economic lifeblood of the illegal drug industry,"[81] the report concluded, and suggested that asset forfeiture, including expedited property seizure, evictions, and strict controls on money laundering, was the best means available for fighting the problem.

If anything, however, the money laundering problem appears to be getting worse. A 1994 report by the Senate Permanent Subcommittee on Investigations found, for example, that "billions of dollars are now leaving our country every year to be put into the flow of commerce and returned to this country as laundered capital. . . ."[82]

In that same year, however, in what many experts saw as contrary to the trend in enforcement activities needed to curb organized crime and drug trafficking, the U.S. Supreme Court made money laundering convictions harder to obtain. The case involved Waldemar and Loretta Ratzlaf, high-stakes gamblers from Oregon with lines of credit at fifteen casinos in New Jersey and Nevada.[83] In 1988, in an apparent attempt to hide $160,000 in gambling losses from the IRS, the Ratzlafs went to several banks in Nevada and California and bought cashier's checks of less than $10,000 each to pay the debt. Their check purchases came under IRS scrutiny as a result of an investigation into the couple's 1986 tax return. In that year, casino records showed that the couple had engaged in large cash transactions with a number of casinos, but had reported no gambling income.

Authorities accused the Ratzlafs of "organizing financial transactions" to evade the currency-reporting requirement of the 1986 federal Money Laundering Control Act. Both Ratzlafs were convicted in federal court in Nevada on charges of conspiracy and interstate travel in aid of racketeering. Mr. Ratzlaf was sentenced to fifteen years in prison and fined $26,300, while Ms. Ratzlaf was sentenced to ten months of home detention and fined $7,900.

The couple's lawyers appealed through the Ninth U.S. Circuit Court of Appeals, and finally to the U.S. Supreme Court. The Court, in a 5 to 4 decision, found in favor of the Ratzlafs, saying that federal authorities had failed to prove that the couple knew they were violating the law. The words of Justice Ruth Bader Ginsburg summarize the opinion of the majority: "Not all currency structuring serves an illegal goal. . . . Under the government's construction an individual would commit a felony against the United States by making cash deposits in small doses, fearful that the bank's reports would increase the likelihood of burglary, or in an endeavor to keep a former spouse unaware of his wealth."

In a separate dissenting opinion, however, Justice Harry A. Blackmun criticized the Court's majority, writing, "Waldemar Ratzlaf—to use an old phrase—will be laughing all the way to the bank." Ratzlaf, said Blackmun, "was anything but uncomprehending as he traveled from bank to bank converting his bag of cash to cashier's checks in $9,500 bundles" to pay the debt.

⠿ POLICY ISSUES: THE CONTROL OF ORGANIZED CRIME

In a cogent analysis of organized crime Gary W. Potter tells us that "[t]he question of what we (should) do about organized crime is largely predicated on how we conceptualize (of) organized crime."[84] Potter criticizes current policies for focusing "almost exclusively on *criminal* aspects of organized crime." It is, says Potter, "the *organized* aspects of organized crime which offer the most useful data for formulating future policy."

To understand organized crime, and to deal effectively with it, according to Potter, we must study the social context within which it occurs. Such study reveals "that organized crime is simply an integral part of the social, political, and economic system," says Potter. Any effective attack on organized crime, therefore, would involve meeting the demands of the consumers of organized crime's products and services. Potter suggests this can be accomplished either by punishing the consumer more effectively or by educating such individuals as to the perils of their own behavior.

Fighting corruption in politics and among law enforcement personnel and administrators is another track Potter suggests in the battle against organized crime. If organized crime has been successful at least partially because it has been able to corrupt local politicians and enforcement agents, then, Potter asks, why not work to reduce corruption at the local level?

Howard Abadinsky recommends four approaches to the control of organized crime, each involving changes at the policymaking level.[85]

1. Increasing the risk of involvement in organized crime by increasing the resources available to law enforcement agencies that are useful in fighting organized crime. A greater proportion of tax revenues, for example, might be moved into the fight against organized crime. The 1994 Violent Crime Control and Enforcement Act, which puts more law enforcement officers on the streets, should be helpful in freeing up others to investigate organized crime.
2. Increasing law enforcement authority so as to increase the risks of involvement in organized crime. Money laundering statutes that expand the scope of law enforcement authority, racketeering laws, and forfeiture statutes all may be helpful in this regard. Abadinsky also suggests providing a special "good faith" exception "to the exclusionary rule in prosecutions involving RICO violations."[86]
3. Reducing the economic lure of involvement in organized crime by making legitimate opportunities more readily available. Educational programs, scholarships, job training initiatives, and so on might all play a role in such a strategy.
4. Decreasing organized criminal opportunity through decriminalization or legalization. This last strategy is perhaps the most controversial. It would decriminalize or legalize many of the activities from which organized crime now draws income. State-run gambling and the ready availability of narcotics and other substances, now subject to widespread abuse through state-controlled facilities, provide examples of the kinds of policy changes necessary to achieve this goal.

Salvatore "Sammy the Bull" Gravano, who admitted to nineteen murders, entered the federal witness protection program in 1995. He has been called the "most significant witness in the history of organized crime." Will the government be able to protect Gravano? *J. Markowitz/Sygma.*

Strict enforcement of existing laws is another option. It is a strategy that has recently been used with considerable success by a number of federal and state law enforcement operations which have targeted organized crime. In 1987, for example, Nicholas "The Crow" Caramandi agreed to testify in eleven criminal trials against organized crime figures, resulting in more than fifty-two convictions mostly in the Pennsylvania and New Jersey areas. Caramandi had bargained for lessened sentences in his own convictions on murder, racketeering, and extortion charges. A few years ago, Caramandi was released from prison and now lives far from Philadelphia, under the federal witness relocation program with a new identity and a mob-ordered sentence of death hanging over him.

One of the most spectacular mob trials in recent years was that of John Gotti, who until recently headed New York's Gambino family. Over the years Gotti had been arrested on many occasions and prosecuted at least five times for various offenses. His ability to escape conviction earned him the title "the Teflon don." That changed on April 2, 1992, when Gotti was convicted on thirteen federal charges, including murder and racketeering. Following trial, Gotti was sentenced to life in prison without possibility of parole. Gotti's major mistake appears to have been to personally participate in several executions, including that of Paul Castellano, his predecessor. Gotti and his underboss, Locascio, are now both in federal prison, while Gotti's son, John, Jr., is thought to be running the family.

Gotti's downfall came at the hands of Salvatore "Sammy the Bull" Gravano, a former underboss in the Gambino crime family. Gravano, who admitted to nineteen murders, shared family secrets with federal investigators in return for leniency and succor through the federal witness protection program. Gravano also spent days on the witness stand testifying against his former boss. Federal prosecutor Zachary Carter later called Gravano "the most significant witness in the history of organized crime."[87] In 1997 Gravano again assumed center stage when he testified in federal district court in Brooklyn as the star prosecution witness in the murder and racketeering trial of Vincent Gigante, reputed head of the powerful Genovese crime family. Gravano was assailed by defense lawyers for admittedly being a notorious liar and for leading "a life of lies," facts he largely admitted in his best-selling book, *Underboss.*[88]

Some say that, in the face of increased law enforcement activity, the *Cosa Nostra* is doomed. According to the FBI, most major crime families have now been decimated by enhanced investigation efforts, often supplemented by wiretaps and informant testimony. The FBI claims that a total of 1,173 *Cosa Nostra* bosses, soldiers, and associates throughout the country have been convicted during the last six years alone. Imprisoned bosses now include not only New York's John Gotti, but Los Angeles' Peter Milano, and the leaders of Kansas City's Civella family. Also, a few years ago thirteen members of New England's Patriarca family were convicted of murdering Billy Grasso, one of their underbosses, and sent to prison.

Can the *Cosa Nostra* survive such pressure? Nicholas Caramandi says "yes." "It's such a bureaucracy . . . this thing of ours," says Caramandi. "You can't kill it. . . . It's the second government. . . . We serve needs. People come to us when they can't get justice, or to borrow money that they can't get from the bank. . . . It never dies. It's as powerful today as it ever was. It's just more glorified and more out in the open."[89] The Mob, says Caramandi, reaches all the way to the highest levels of political power. Survival is assured through well-placed friends in America's highest elected offices.

One expert believes that "[t]he Mafia, *Cosa Nostra,* will not be recognizable by the end of the century." John Gotti thinks otherwise. "This is gonna be *Cosa Nostra* till I die," he told his underbosses just before his arrest. "Be it an hour from now or be it tonight or a hundred years from now, it's gonna be *Cosa Nostra.*"

SUMMARY

This chapter discusses white-collar and organized crime. Unfortunately, observations made about both forms of crime, as valid and useful as they may be, rarely rise above the level of organized conjecture. Hence, it is impossible at this point to describe a theory of white-collar crime, or a theory of organized crime, except insofar as those concepts can be contained within other theoretical perspectives—as was the case with Sutherland's attempt to explain white-collar crime in terms of differential association. John Braithwaite's attempt to integrate a variety of theoretical approaches into a general theory which explains all forms of crime, including white-collar crime, may be the most comprehensive theory of organizational crime to date.

Although both white-collar and organized crime appear prevalent in the United States today, and organized and white-collar criminals often share similar goals such as acquiring wealth and social position, there appears to be considerable variation in commitment between the two types of offenders. Many organized criminals evidence a long tradition of criminal involvement, often in the form of racketeering, which is largely unknown to most white-collar offenders. Similarly, organized crime wraps its members in a kind of deviant subculture with a detailed code of conduct which affects its members throughout their lives. White-collar criminals, on the other hand, have typically achieved positions of power and social respectability through conformity and approved forms of achievement. They often come from cultural backgrounds that are supportive of adherence to the law. Hence, most white-collar offenders are probably drawn to criminal activity for the immediate financial rewards it offers, whereas organized criminals are more apt to see crime as a way of life and to condemn the conformist activity of others.

If such differences are true, then white-collar crime may be effectively prevented by strict enforcement efforts which, by their very example, serve as a strong general deterrent to other would-be offenders. Organized criminal groups, on the other hand, given their long-standing commitment to criminal activities, are unlikely to be impacted by such threats.

WEB WATCH

Access the *Criminology Today* home page on the World Wide Web by pointing your browser at www.prenhall.com/cjcentral. Once there, click on "Criminology Today" to access the wealth of electronic resources supporting this text.

Onsite resources include (1) "Chapter Links," which provides succinct overviews of critical ideas from the textbook and links selected materials from around the Web to concepts found in the text; (2) "General Reference—Law and Justice Links." Organized by chapter, these links lead to other useful resources on the World Wide Web such as libraries, electronic discussion lists, and electronic journals; (3) "Criminology Sites on the Web," which lists links to organizations such as the American Society of Criminology, and the National Organization for Victims Assistance (NOVA), as well as crime prevention links, and statistics on crime and justice. Many other Web-based resources can be accessed via the *Criminology Today* site, including the federal Justice Information Center, the Bureau of Justice Statistics, the FBI, the RAND Corporation, the Vera Institute of Justice, PAVNET (an online "Partnership Against Violence," run by seven different federal agencies), and the National White Collar Crime Center.

Still another feature of the *Criminology Today* Web site is e-mail homework. Homework can be composed onsite and submitted to instructors using the instructor's e-mail address. To use the e-mail homework feature, click on "E-Mail Homework" on the opening page, and then type answers to the questions that appear in the spaces provided. Use your instructor's e-mail address to submit homework answers. The *Criminology Today* Web site also provides links to powerful Web-based search engines that can help you find topics of interest to you as you progress through your course of study. Search engines can be found under the home page heading "Criminology Sites on the Web."

DISCUSSION QUESTIONS

1. What is the difference between organized crime and white-collar crime? What linkages, if any, might exist between the two?
2. What types of white-collar crime has this chapter identified? Is corporate crime a form of white-collar crime? Is occupational crime a form of white-collar crime?
3. Describe a typical organized crime family, as outlined in this chapter. Why does a crime family contain so many different "levels"?
4. What is *money laundering?* How might money laundering be reduced or prevented? Can you think of any strategies this chapter does not discuss for the reduction of money laundering activities in the United States? If so, what are they?
5. What strategies for combating the activities of organized crime are discussed in this chapter? Which seem best to you? Why? Can you think of any other strategies that might be effective? If so, what might they be?

NOTES

[1] Donald J. Newman, "White-Collar Crime: An Overview and Analysis," *Law and Contemporary Problems,* vol. 23, no. 4 (Autumn 1958).

[2] Kathleen Murray, "The Fraud du Jour Is Wireless Cable," *Worth,* October 1994, p. 118.

[3] Ibid., pp. 118–120.

[4] Edwin H. Sutherland, "White-Collar Criminality," *American Sociological Review,* vol. 5, no. 1 (February 1940), pp. 2–10.

[5] Ibid.

[6] Edwin H. Sutherland, "Crime of Corporations," in Albert Cohen, Alfred Lindesmith, and Karl Schuessler, eds., *The Sutherland Papers* (Bloomington: Indiana University Press, 1956), pp. 78–96.

[7] Ibid.

[8] Edwin H. Sutherland, "White-Collar Criminality."

[9] Travis Hirschi and Michael Gottfredson, "Causes of White-Collar Crime," *Criminology,* vol. 25, no. 4 (1987), p. 952.

[10] *USA Today,* April 2, 1991, pp. B1–2.

[11] Karen Gullo, " 'Phantom' Banks Across the Country Bilking Investors," Associated Press, September 11, 1994.

[12] James Cox, "Gold Dust or Bust," *USA Today,* April 17, 1997, p. 1B.

[13] Michael L. Benson, Francis T. Cullen, and William J. Maakestad, *Local Prosecutors and Corporate Crime* (Washington, D.C.: National Institute of Justice, 1993).

[14] Michael Clements, "Breast Implant Pact OK'd: $4.25 Billion Is Available to Claimants," *USA Today,* September 2, 1994, p. 1A.

[15] "Plastic Surgeons, Manufacturers Helped Finance Breast-Implant Study," *USA Today,* September 2, 1994, p. 10A.

[16] Rahul Sharma, "Union Carbide Quits India a Decade After Bhopal," Reuters wire service, September 9, 1994.

[17] Details of the described agreement come from: CNN Interactive, "Koop, Kessler Have Doubts About Tobacco Deal." Web posted June 22, 1997.

[18] Of course, environmental damage inflicted by corporations can result in civil liability as well as violate criminal statutes.

[19] Donald J. Newman, "White-Collar Crime: An Overview and Analysis," *Law and Contemporary Problems,* vol. 23, no. 4 (Autumn 1958).

[20] President's Commission on Law Enforcement and Administration of Justice, *The Challenge of Crime in a Free Society* (Washington, D.C.: U.S. Government Printing Office, 1967), p. 47.

[21] Donald J. Newman, "White-Collar Crime: An Overview and Analysis."

[22] For excellent reviews of the evolution of the concept of white-collar crime, see K. Schlegel and

D. Weisburd, "White-Collar Crime: The Parallax View," in Kip Schlegel and David Weisburd, eds., *White-Collar Crime Reconsidered* (Boston: Northeastern University Press, 1992), pp. 3–27; and K. Schlegel and D. Weisburd, "Returning to the Mainstream: Reflections on Past and Future White-Collar Crime Study," in Schlegel and Weisburd, eds., *White-Collar Crime Reconsidered,* pp. 352–365.

[23]Herbert Edelhertz, *The Nature, Impact and Prosecution of White-Collar Crime* (Washington, D.C.: National Institute of Law Enforcement and Criminal Justice, 1970).

[24]Gilbert Geis, "Upperworld Crime," in Abraham S. Blumberg, ed., *Current Perspectives on Criminal Behavior: Original Essays on Criminology* (New York: Alfred A. Knopf, 1974).

[25]Gary S. Green, *Occupational Crime* (Chicago: Nelson-Hall, 1990), p. 12.

[26]Ibid., p. 16.

[27]Hirschi and Gottfredson, "Causes of White-Collar Crime," p. 949.

[28]Ibid., p. 951.

[29]Ibid., p. 960.

[30]Braithwaite began many of his studies of white-collar crime with investigations into the criminal activities of pharmaceutical company executives. See, for example, John Braithwaite, *Corporate Crime in the Pharmaceutical Industry* (London: Routledge & Kegan Paul, 1984).

[31]For a test of this thesis, see Anne Jenkins and John Braithwaite, "Profits, Pressure and Corporate Lawbreaking," *Crime, Law, and Social Change,* vol. 20, no. 3 (1993), pp. 221–232.

[32]John Braithwaite, "Poverty, Power, White-Collar Crime and the Paradoxes of Criminological Theory," *Australian and New Zealand Journal of Criminology,* vol. 24, no. 1 (1991), pp. 40–48.

[33]Toni Makkai and John Braithwaite, "Criminological Theories and Regulatory Compliance," *Criminology,* vol. 29, no.2 (1991), pp. 191–217.

[34]John Braithwaite and Gilbert Geis, "On Theory and Action for Corporate Crime Control," *Crime and Delinquency,* vol. 28, no. 2 (1982), pp. 292–314. See also Brent Fisse and John Braithwaite, *The Impact of Publicity on Corporate Offenders* (Albany, N.Y.: State University of New York Press, 1983).

[35]Brent Fisse and John Braithwaite, "Accountability and the Control of Corporate Crime: Making the Buck Stop," in Mark Findlay and Russell Hogg, eds., *Understanding Crime and Criminal Justice* (North Ryde, Australia: Law Book Company, 1988), pp. 93–127.

[36]Brent Fisse and John Braithwaite, *Corporations, Crime and Accountability* (New York: Cambridge University Press, 1994).

[37]John Braithwaite, "Criminological Theory and Organizational Crime," *Justice Quarterly,* vol. 6, no. 3 (1989), pp. 333–358.

[38]Newman, "White-Collar Crime: An Overview and Analysis."

[39]Green, *Occupational Crime,* p. 256.

[40]James William Coleman, *The Criminal Elite: The Sociology of White-Collar Crime* (New York: St. Martins, 1989).

[41]The details of this account are taken from Camden Pelham, *The Chronicles of Crime: The Newgate Calendar—A Series of Memoirs and Anecdotes of Notorious Characters* (London: T. Miles, 1887), pp. 57–65.

[42]Much of the information in this section comes from Julian Symons, *A Pictorial History of Crime* (New York: Bonanza Books, 1966).

[43]Ibid.

[44]Howard Abadinsky, *Organized Crime,* 4th ed. (Chicago: Nelson-Hall, 1994).

[45]Ibid., p. 112.

[46]Luigi Barzini, *The Italians* (New York: Atheneum, 1965).

[47]Howard Abadinsky, *Organized Crime,* 4th ed., p. 132.

[48]Gus Tyler, "The Crime Corporation," in Abraham S. Blumberg, ed., *Current Perspectives on Criminal Behavior: Original Essays on Criminology* (New York: Alfred A. Knopf, 1974), p. 197, citing Hank Messick, *The Silent Syndicate* (New York: Macmillan, 1966), pp. vii–xii.

[49]Abandinsky, *Organized Crime,* p. 173.

[50]John Kilber, *Capone: The Life and World of Al Capone* (Greenwich, Conn.: Fawcett, 1971).

[51]Mark H. Haller, "Illegal Enterprise: A Theoretical and Historical Interpretation," *Criminology,* vol. 28, no. 2 (May 1990), p. 209.

[52]President's Commission on Law Enforcement and Administration of Justice, *Task Force*

Report: Organized Crime (Washington, D.C.: United States Government Printing Office, 1967), Appendix A.

[53] Anthony E. Simpson, *The Literature of Police Corruption* (New York: The John Jay Press, 1977).

[54] J. Richard Davis, "Things I Couldn't Tell Till Now," *Collier's*, August 19, 1939, p. 35.

[55] Robert W. Ferguson, *The Nature of Vice Control in the Administration of Justice* (St. Paul: West, 1974), p. 379.

[56] Symons, *A Pictorial History of Crime*, p. 226.

[57] President's Commission on Law Enforcement and Administration of Justice, *The Challenge of Crime in a Free Society*, p. 196.

[58] Special Committee to Investigate Organized Crime in Interstate Commerce, U.S. Senate, 82nd Congress, 1951.

[59] President's Commission on Law Enforcement and Administration of Justice, *The Challenge of Crime in a Free Society*, p. 192, citing the Kefauver Committee report.

[60] *U.S. v. Bufalino*, 285 G.2d. 408 (1960).

[61] President's Commission on Law Enforcement and Administration of Justice, *The Challenge of Crime in a Free Society*, p. 195.

[62] As identified by Abadinsky in *Organized Crime*.

[63] As cited by Abadinsky in ibid., pp. 186–187.

[64] William Sherman, "Kingpins of the Underworld," *Cosmopolitan*, vol. 212, no. 3 (March 1992), pp. 158–162.

[65] Abadinsky, *Organized Crime*, pp. 311–312.

[66] Ibid., p. 313.

[67] Ibid., p. 313.

[68] Richard Behar, "In the Grip of Treachery," *Playboy*, vol. 38, no. 11 (November 1991), p. 92.

[69] President's Commission on Law Enforcement and Administration of Justice, *Task Force Report: Organized Crime*.

[70] "Kingpins of the Underworld."

[71] Behar, "In the Grip of Treachery."

[72] Ibid.

[73] President's Commission on Law Enforcement and Administration of Justice, *Task Force Report: Organized Crime*, p. 41.

[74] Howard Abadinsky, *Organized Crime*.

[75] Abadinsky, *Organized Crime*, p. 5.

[76] Joseph B. Treaster, "In Pizza Connection II, 79 Seized in Raids in New York and Italy," *New York Times*, September 16, 1994, p. 1A.

[77] Clifford Karchmer and Douglas Ruch, "State and Local Money Laundering Control Strategies," *NIJ Research in Brief* (Washington, D.C.: NIJ, 1992), p. 1.

[78] President's Commission on Organized Crime, *The Cash Connection: Organized Crime, Financial Institutions, and Money Laundering* (Washington, D.C.: U.S. Government Printing Office, 1984).

[79] According to Abadinsky, *Organized Crime*, p. 427.

[80] Ibid.

[81] United Press wire service, Northern edition, "Presidential Commission Presents Recommendation on Drug Control," December 13, 1993.

[82] Carolyn Skorneck, "Money Laundering," Associated Press wire service, Northern edition, April 7, 1994.

[83] Laurie Asseo, "Scotus-Money Reporting," Associated Press wire service, Northern edition, January 11, 1994.

[84] Gary W. Potter, *Criminal Organizations: Vice, Racketeering, and Politics in an American City* (Prospects Heights, Ill.: Waveland, 1994), p. 183.

[85] Abadinsky, *Organized Crime*, p. 507.

[86] Ibid., p. 508.

[87] "5-Year Prison Term for Mafia Turncoat," *USA Today*, September 27, 1994, p. 3A.

[88] Peter Maas, *Underboss: Sammy the Bull Gravano's Story of Life in the Mafia* (New York: HarperCollins, 1997). According to Ronald Kuby, an attorney suing Gravano to reclaim book royalties under New York's "Son of Sam" law, a roundabout method had been used to pay Gravano in order to avoid the provisions of the law. Kuby claimed that documents would show that author Peter Mass, Gravano, HarperCollins, and International Creative Management, the agent for the book, had conspired to hide payments made to Gravano.

[89] Behar, "In the Grip of Treachery."

DRUG ABUSE AND CRIME

I believe that the struggle between East and West has been replaced by the world's struggle against drugs.

—INTERPOL SECRETARY-GENERAL RAYMOND KENDALL[1]

Drug dealers no longer count their money. They weigh it.

—HOUSTON, TEXAS, POLICE LIEUTENANT[2]

I don't feel that was a crime.

—FORMER U.S. SURGEON GENERAL JOYCELYN ELDERS, WHEN ASKED WHETHER HER SON, CONVICTED OF SELLING COCAINE TO AN UNDERCOVER OFFICER, MIGHT COMMIT OTHER CRIMES WHILE FREE ON BAIL.[3] ELDERS LOST HER JOB.

✳ CHAPTER OUTLINE ✳

⇐ IMPORTANT TERMS ⇒

drug-defined crimes	drug-related crimes	dangerous drugs
pharmaceutical	heroin signature	drug trafficking
diversion	program (HSP)	asset forfeiture
designer drugs	interdiction	psychoactive
legalization	decriminalization	substances

✳ INTRODUCTION

In early July 1997, the childhood home of Mexico's top drug lord, Amado Carrillo Fuentes, was prepared for his funeral.[4] Dirty blankets lay over an open crypt, candles burned in the home's small chapel, which was adorned with figures of Jesus, the Virgin of Guadalupe, and Jesus Malverde—claimed by drug dealers as their patron saint. Five-foot rose wreaths lined the pathway to the house, where hundreds of wooden chairs stood stacked against walls.

  Although mourners gathered to pay respects to Carrillo's mother and sisters, there could be no funeral. Carrillo's body was in the possession of Mexican authorities, who were busy studying and cataloging the corpse. Carrillo, the authorities said, had died two days earlier in a botched attempt by plastic surgeons to change his appearance.

Before his death Carrillo, the 42-year-old son of Mexican peasants, had replaced the Medellin cartel's Pablo Escobar as the biggest shipper of cocaine to U.S. cities—earning an estimated $100 million a month in the illicit drug trade. Much of the money was used to pay off thousands of local, state, and federal officials (both in Mexico and in the United States). Carrillo earned the nickname "Lord of the Skies" after arranging to ferry Colombian cocaine into the United States. At one time he was said to have brought jumbo jet loads of cocaine from Columbia to Mexico, smuggling it across the Mexican–Texas border. At the time of his death, Carrillo's organization had nearly displaced Colombian drug merchants in New York and other American cities, and Carrillo's net worth was estimated to have reached an astounding $25 billion![5]

Carrillo had been very open in his drug dealing until the arrest in February 1997 of General Jesus Gutierrez Rebollo, former head of Mexico's federal antidrug agency. It was reputed that Carrillo would even stroll around the plazas in Juarez, Mexico, to show that he was above the law. On the run from the Mexican national police (the *Federales*) since the general's arrest, Carrillo died in a desperate attempt to escape a closing dragnet of law enforcement officials. U.S. drug agents were told that Carrillo succumbed to heart failure at a Mexico City hospital following ten hours of extensive plastic surgery. Doctors who had performed the operation—for which Carrillo had rented an entire floor of the hospital, cordoning it off with heavily armed guards—fled after his death. Prior to surgery, Carrillo had just returned from Russia, where he had been trying to arrange a safe haven for his family and his money. In an interesting footnote to this story, rumors started circulating throughout Mexico following Carrillo's death that he had been secretly assassinated by DEA agents who slipped lethal drugs into the medications used during the drug lord's plastic surgery. Many Mexicans believed the rumors because Carrillo died on the Fourth of July—American Independence Day. His death on that date, said the rumor mill, was a silent message to other drug runners, putting them on notice that they might be next.[6]

HISTORY OF DRUG ABUSE IN THE UNITED STATES

Carrillo's death illustrates the desperation that today often characterizes the lives of those involved with illegal drugs—from the highest level "dealers," to the saddest and most addicted of users. The widespread use of illegal drugs affects all segments of society. Sadder still is the fact that almost all forms of illicit drug use in America are associated with other forms of criminality. Drugs, and their relationship to crime, provide one of the most significant policy issues of our time. Famed *Washington Monthly* columnist Paul Savoy recently reported polls showing that Americans "are so fearful about the drug-driven crime epidemic that more than half of those polled . . . expressed an opinion [which] favored cutting back the constitutional rights of criminal defendants and overruling Supreme Court decisions that limit police conduct in gathering evidence."[7]

Psychoactive substances
those substances that
affect the mind, mental
processes, or emotions.

The rampant and widespread use and abuse of mind- and mood-altering drugs, so commonplace in the United States today, is of relatively recent origin. Throughout the 1800s and early 1900s, the use of illegal drugs in America was mostly associated with artistic individuals and fringe groups. One hundred years ago drug abuse, as we understand it today, was almost exclusively confined to a subsegment of musicians, painters, poets, and other highly imaginative individuals seeking to enhance their creativity. Although it is true that medicinal elixirs of the period contained a variety of potent substances, including cocaine, alcohol, and opium, the lives of relatively few Americans were seriously affected at the time by any drug other than alcohol. One significant exception existed in the form of "opium dens" that flourished in West Coast cities and eventually made their way across the country as a result of increased Asian immigration. Some Chinese immigrants brought opium products with them and introduced other segments of the American population to opium smoking.

Psychoactive substances gained widespread acceptance during the hippie movement, a period of newfound freedoms embraced by a large number of American youth during the late 1960s and early 1970s. The movement, which was characterized by slogans such as "if it feels good, do it" and "tune in, turn on, drop out," promoted free love, personal freedom, experimentation with subjective states of consciousness, and "mind expansion." Cheech and Chong movies, "flower power," paisley clothes, bell-bottom jeans, long hair on men, and Eastern religions all flourished within the context of a drug-fed countercultural movement.

One influential figure in the drug-inspired movement of the times was the Harvard professor Dr. Timothy Leary. Leary formed the League of Spiritual Discovery in the mid-1960s, describing it as "an orthodox, psychedelic religion that permits the use of LSD and marijuana as sacraments by League members." With the advent of the hippie era, marijuana, LSD, hashish, psyliocybin, and peyote burst upon the

Smoker in an opium den in Chinatown, San Francisco, circa 1925. Why did American attitudes toward drugs change? *UPI/Corbis-Bettmann.*

national scene as an ever growing number of individuals began to view drugs as recreational substances and more and more young people identified with the tenor of the period.

It was during this time, apparently, that President Bill Clinton's experiments with marijuana took place. Clinton revealed during the 1992 presidential campaign that he had smoked marijuana as a youth, claiming that he never inhaled.

EXTENT OF ABUSE

Current data on drug abuse in the United States are available through a variety of publications such as the *National Household Survey on Drug Abuse (NHSDA),* conducted annually by the Substance Abuse and Mental Health Services Administration (SAMHSA); the National Narcotics Intelligence Consumers Committee's *NNICC Report,* published in conjunction with the Drug Enforcement Administration (DEA); the National Institute of Justice's (NIJ) annual *Drug Use Forecasting* (DUF) report; the Office of National Drug Control Policy's (ONDCP) *Pulse Check: National Trends in Drug Abuse,* which reports at least once a year on drug use trends; and annual reports published by the federal Drug Abuse Warning Network (DAWN).

According to the most recent data,[8] "current" illegal drug use in the United States—as measured by the number of people who report having used an illicit drug in the previous month—declined steadily over the thirteen years from 1979 to 1992, with a leveling off of the decline beginning in 1992. In 1979, the highest year on record, 24.3 million people reported recent illegal drug use, while by 1992 the number had dropped to a low of 11.4 million.[9] It rose to 11.7 million in 1993, and 12.8 million in 1995, although increases in the nation's population mean that the larger numbers may not be statistically significant.

NHSDA estimates that approximately 9.8 million persons currently use marijuana or hashish, and approximately 7 million of them use only marijuana, the rest in combination with other drugs. Marijuana users represent 4.7 percent of the nation's population aged 12 and older. Marijuana is by far the most prevalent drug used, because approximately three-quarters (77 percent) of current illicit drug users used either marijuana or hashish in 1995. Notably, the annual number of new users of marijuana has risen every year since 1991. An estimated 1.5 million Americans are current cocaine users, representing less than 1 percent of the nation's population aged 12 and older.

If *NHSDA* survey results are accurate, they would seem to indicate that drug abuse is now substantially less of a problem than it was two decades ago. The largest ever annual estimate of marijuana use put routine users at 22.5 million in 1979, while the largest cocaine use estimate was 5.3 million in 1985—figures far greater than those of today. Growth of the American population in the meantime gives the estimated decline even greater weight. "Compared with 1979, when 24.3 million current users represented 13.7 percent of the population age 12 and older, the 12.8 million users currently reported compose 6.1 percent of the U.S. population 12-years of age or older."[10] The survey found that rates of drug use show substantial variation by age. Among youth aged 12 to 13, 4.5 percent are current illicit drug users. The highest rates were found among young people ages 16 to 17 (15.6 percent) and ages 18 to 20

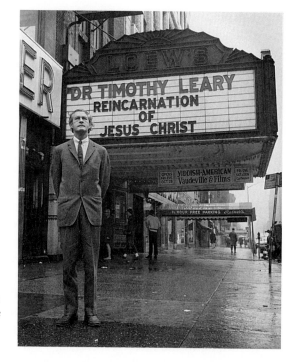

Dr. Timothy Leary, guru of the 1960s
new consciousness movement, shown
here in New York in 1966. Leary died in
1996, and his ashes were shot into space
a year later. What was Leary's message?
UPI/Corbis-Bettmann.

(18.0 percent). Rates of use were lower in each successive age group, with approximately 1 percent of persons age 50 and older reporting current illicit use.

According to the most recent edition of *NHSDA,* nearly half of young adults ages 21 to 25 have tried illicit drugs at least once in their lifetime, and 12 percent are current users. More than half of adults ages 26 to 44 have tried illicit drugs, but rates of current use are only 8.3 percent for those aged 26 to 34, and 5.6 percent for those aged 35 to 44.

The survey found some significant differences in drug use related to race and sex, and noted that: "The rate of current illicit drug use for blacks (7.9 percent) remained somewhat higher than for whites (6.0 percent) and Hispanics (5.1 percent)...." The survey also concluded that men continued to have a higher rate of illicit drug use than women (7.8 versus 4.5 percent). Specifically, in most categories for which data were gathered (including marijuana, cocaine, crack, inhalants, hallucinogens, stimulants, sedatives, tranquilizers, analgesics, and alcohol), men reported rates of abuse higher than that of women, while blacks reported only slightly higher rates of abuse than whites. Individual drug categories, however, exhibited notable differences. Black respondents, for example, were nearly three times as likely as whites, and twice as likely as Hispanics, to report the use of crack cocaine. Whites exceeded both blacks and Hispanics in reported use of inhalants, and twice as many whites as blacks reported having ever used hallucinogens. Similarly, reported illegal use of psychotherapeutic drugs (especially stimulants) was substantially greater among whites than among blacks or Hispanics, with white males showing the highest rate of such abuse. Finally, more whites (87 percent) than any other category (blacks, 79 percent; Hispanics, 77 percent) reported ever having used alcohol, and more whites reported having used alcohol within the past month than any other racial group.

The survey noted other significant differences as well. Black males, for example, reported a rate of cocaine, crack, and marijuana use that was twice that of black females. Whites reported somewhat greater use of anabolic steroids than did other groups, and blacks reported the highest frequency of heroin abuse—with the use of needles by black males for the purpose of drug injection exceeding the frequency of reported needle use for any other category. The use of needles, which is known to spread AIDS, was highest (when rates were computed) among black males aged 26 to 34.

As in previous surveys, illicit drug use rates remain highly correlated with educational status. Among young adults 18 to 34 years old, those who have not completed high school have the highest rate of use (15.4 percent), whereas college graduates have the lowest rate of use (5.9 percent). This finding is despite the fact that young adults at different educational levels are equally as likely to have tried illicit drugs in their lifetime (50 percent of those not completing high school and 52 percent of college graduates). Hence, the more education a person receives, the more likely that person is to discontinue using drugs with age.

Current employment status was found to be highly correlated with rates of illicit drug use. *NHSDA* found that 14.3 percent of unemployed adults (age 18 and older) were illicit drug users, compared with 5.5 percent of full-time employed adults. Of all current illicit drug users age 18 and older (7.4 million adults), 71 percent were employed, including 5.4 million full-time workers and 1.9 million part-time workers.

NHSDA also provides a perspective on the future of drug abuse in the United States. In the words of survey authors:

Newly developed estimates of trends in drug use incidence (i.e., initiation) provide a different measure of the drug use situation. They can provide an early indication of emerging patterns of use. The estimated annual number of new marijuana users increased from 1.4 million in 1991 to 2.3 million in 1994, indicating no signs of any reversal of the upward trends in prevalence. The recent upturn in illicit drug use among youths has important implications for substance abuse prevention and treatment efforts. In terms of prevention, there is an obvious need to focus immediate attention on children and adolescents. In the long run, the increasing proportion of young people using illicit drugs will probably result in continuing pressure on the substance abuse treatment system in future years, as many new drug users progress to addiction and require intervention. Reports of increasing heroin and methamphetamine use have [also] been prominent over the past few years, based on data from medical examiners, emergency departments, and drug treatment facilities . . . .

The NHSDA continues to show the aging of the drug using population. Cohorts who were teenagers and young adults in the 1960s and 1970s are now older, and although most no longer use illicit drugs, many still do. This aging cohort, composed primarily of the baby boom, is adding increasingly to the '35 and older' age group shown in NHSDA reports. Thus, the proportion of drug users that are age 35 and older continues to increase (from 10 percent of users in 1979 to 27 percent of users in 1995). Data from the Drug Abuse Warning Network (DAWN) on drug-related hospital emergency department episodes also show the impact of the aging cohort of drug users. In 1979, 12 percent of patients with cocaine episodes were age 35 and older. By 1985 the proportion was 19, and by 1995 it was 43.

Many of the drug users in this aging cohort have used drugs for many years and have developed severe drug problems. This may partly explain the continuing rise in hospital emergency department episodes, which are more likely to involve these heavy users than occasional users or those who use only marijuana. Cocaine-related emergency room visits have increased from 5,000 in 1981 to 29,000 in 1985 (the peak year for past month cocaine prevalence in the NHSDA) to 142,000 in 1995. Heroin-related emergency room visits have increased from 12,000 in 1979 to 76,000 in 1995.

As *NHSDA* authors realize, it is important to recognize the limitations of government surveys, including *NHSDA* for measuring the prevalence of *heavy* drug use. They write: "Sample size, coverage, and validity problems are likely to be more pronounced for NHSDA estimates of heavy users than for other measures generated by the survey. Therefore, estimates of heavy use are considered conservative, and changes over time are generally not statistically significant. For example, the NHSDA has produced estimates of about 600,000 frequent cocaine users with no significant changes in the size of this population since 1985. By using various other data sources and making a number of assumptions (many of which are of uncertain validity), researchers have estimated that there are over 2 million frequent cocaine users in the U.S. . . . Clearly there is considerable uncertainty about the size of the heavy drug-using population."

Whereas the use of illicit drugs provides one measure of the drug problem facing our country, the ready availability of such drugs provides another. Data from the National Crime Victimization Survey[11] show that two of three students ages 12 to 19 report ready availability of illegal drugs at their school. Students in public schools report a wider availability of drugs than do those in private schools, and students in higher grades (ninth through twelfth) report more drugs available to them than do those in the lower grades. Similar rates of availability were reported by white students (69 percent of whom said drugs were available to them at school) and black students (67 percent), and by students living in cities (66 percent), suburban areas (67 percent), and those in rural areas (71 percent).

COSTS OF ABUSE

The true costs of drug abuse are difficult to measure. Included among them would be measurable expenditures such as those for law enforcement activities intended to prevent drug growing, importation, and use; criminal justice case processing; drug treatment programs; money laundering; and time lost from work as a result of drug involvement. More difficult to quantify, but equally real, are other costs related to drug abuse such as sickness resulting from exposure to controlled substances, drug-related crime, the fragmentation of families and other relationships caused by illegal drug use, changes in attitudes and worldview induced among substantial segments of the American population by drug-crime fear, lost human potential, and the image of the United States on the world stage.

DRUG WAR CLAIMING "ENTIRE GENERATION" OF YOUNG BLACKS

Ex-Newark, N.J., police director Hubert Williams, who helped lead a government probe into last year's deadly Los Angeles riots, doesn't frighten easily.

But his voice grows grim when Williams looks at the results of a *USA Today* study that shows blacks are four times as likely as whites to be arrested for drugs.

"You'd almost have to be blind not to see the time bomb we're creating," says Williams, president of the Police Foundation, a research organization.

Williams and others say the racial disparity in drug arrests is the result of the drug war's decade-long focus on arrest and imprisonment instead of prevention and treatment.

Critics say the disparity has created a self-fulfilling cycle of police suspicion and arrest for black people.

And in communities nationwide, it has worsened festering racial tensions and fostered resentment on all sides.

"It's almost legal genocide," charges A. J. Kramer, who has a front-line view of the drug war as chief of the federal public defender office in Washington,

Webster: Black lawyers' leader says, "It's almost like they're arresting nobody but African Americans." Why are a seemingly disproportionate number of black people arrested in the battle against drugs? *Bob Riha/Gamma-Liaison, Inc.*

D.C. "We're locking up an entire generation of young black Americans."

Echoes Allen Webster, president of the National Bar Association, a black lawyers' group: "It's almost like they're arresting nobody but African Americans."

Critics say part of the solution is to provide job opportunities for idle young people, especially in the inner-city; more antidrug programs; and diversion programs that get small-time users treatment, not jail.

Even some die-hard drug warriors want a change.

Detroit Judge Leonard Townsend, 57, watches with dismay as a parade of defendants, most of them black, passes through Courtroom 702. "Oh, God. Hundreds, hundreds—it's just unbelievable."

Townsend agrees the law has to "put a boot to their posteriors" when big-time dealers ask for leniency during sentencing. But almost half the cases in Detroit's criminal court involve small-time users—"victims"—Townsend calls them.

"We end up with all the little fish in the net . . . bogged down with cases that shouldn't be here."

Ed Dennis, former criminal division chief in the Bush Justice Department, acknowledges "some pretty deep-rooted" social problems in the inner city.

But Dennis, who is black, says the violent drug trade demanded "firm ac-

tion" by police. Go ahead and spend more money on social programs, he says, "but you don't have to give up on law enforcement."

John Laux, police chief in Minneapolis, doesn't want to give up. But he concedes: "We're all trapped into this language of a 'war on drugs.' "

"There's a mindset of what war means—it means guns, it means violence, it means oppression. I was certainly guilty of using that same term . . . and I think that sends the wrong message."

Next door in St. Paul, Police Chief William Finney says he has to scrounge for private donations for half of the money that goes to police-sponsored drug prevention programs in his city.

"For the last 12 years we suffered from people who said . . . 'Let them eat cake,' " he says. "So we're eating cake and selling dope on the street corner."

In Berkeley, Calif., officials have already begun community policing and are working on treatment and prevention programs. But assistant city manager Weldon Rucker says little can be done without a major federal effort to produce jobs and expand antidrug services.

Harriet Walden of Seattle, founder of Mothers Against Police Harassment, says it doesn't get much simpler than this: "We're filling up our jails with people who need treatment or jobs or better education."

Questions

1. In this article, A. J. Kramer, chief of the federal public defender office in Washington, D.C., says, "We're locking up an entire generation of young black Americans . . ." because of drugs. What do you think are the root causes of such high arrest rates among young blacks today?

2. Do you believe that young black Americans are, in fact, more involved in illegal drug-related activities than other groups? On what do you base your belief?

3. Allen Webster, president of the National Bar Association, says "It's almost like they're arresting nobody but African Americans." What do you see as alternatives, if any, to the current situation? If you do see alternatives, how might they be implemented?

Source: Sam Vincent, "Drug War Claiming 'Entire Generation' of Young Blacks," *USA Today,* July 27, 1993, p. 7A. Copyright 1993, *USA Today.* Reprinted with permission.

Acquired immunodeficiency syndrome (AIDS), for example, many cases of which can be traced to intravenous drug use, has proven to be a costly disease in social terms. Researchers at the Centers for Disease Control say that AIDS "is already the leading cause of death of black and Hispanic men aged 25 to 44. Preliminary data," says the CDC, "indicate AIDS has become the second leading cause of death among black women aged 25 to 44."[12] Homicide is the second leading cause of death for black and Hispanic men in that age group. The CDC finds seventy-three AIDS cases for every 100,000 black women, but only five per 100,000 white women. Of AIDS cases among minority women, 47 percent are traceable to intravenous drug use while 37 percent appear due to heterosexual intercourse.

Tables 11.1 and 11.2 show the estimated financial and social costs of illegal drug use in the United States per year. Table 11.1 includes dollar amounts spent on systemwide efforts at drug control, and Table 11.2 lists types of costs that are much more difficult to quantify.

▚ TYPES OF ILLEGAL DRUGS

By convention, controlled substances are generally grouped according to both pharmacological and legal criteria into the following seven categories: stimulants, depressants, cannabis, narcotics, hallucinogens, anabolic steroids, and inhalants. A separate eighth category, that of dangerous drugs, provides a kind of legal and definitional catchall. The Drug Enforcement Administration (DEA) uses the term *dangerous drugs* to refer to "broad categories or classes of controlled substances other than cocaine, opiates, and cannabis products."[13] Each category, and some of the drugs it contains, is described in the following paragraphs.[14] Table 11.3 summarizes the differences between drug categories.

Dangerous drugs a term used by the Drug Enforcement Administration (DEA) to refer to "broad categories or classes of controlled substances other than cocaine, opiates, and cannabis products."

⋮⋮

TABLE 11.1

DIRECT COSTS OF ILLEGAL DRUG USE

Type of Cost	Millions
Federal drug expenditures (FY 1998 request)	$15,976
All law enforcement	7,157
Interdiction	2,028
Investigations	1,288
International	640
Prosecution	584
Corrections	1,265
Intelligence	104
State and local assistance	1,016
Regulatory compliance	31
Other law enforcement	201
Drug prevention	1,483
Drug treatment	1,752
All research and development	450
State and local drug crime expenditures	5,240
Enforcement of drug laws	2,007
Adjudication of drug law violators	123
Correction of drug law violators	3,072
State prisons	1,158
Local jails	890
Juveniles	224
Probation, pardon, and parole	677
Other corrections	122
Other criminal justice	38
Health care costs for illegal drug users	2,272
Short-stay hospitals	1,242
Specialty institutions	570
Office-based physicians	52
Support services	201
Other professional services	17
Medical care for drug-related AIDS cases	126
Support services for drug-related AIDS cases	64
Total	$23,488

Note: Figures are author estimates from a variety of sources, including Office of National Drug Control Policy, *The National Drug Control Strategy, 1997: FY 1998 Budget Summary* (Washington, D.C.: ONDCP, 1997); and Bureau of Justice Statistics, *Drugs, Crime and the Justice System: A National Report* (Washington, D.C.: U.S. Government Printing Office, 1993).

TABLE 11.2

INDIRECT COSTS OF ILLEGAL DRUG USE

Criminal justice expenditures on drug-related crime
- Investigating robberies, burglaries, and thefts for drug money and adjudicating and punishing the offenders
- Investigating assaults and homicides in the drug business (or by a drug user who has lost control) and adjudicating and punishing the offenders

Health care costs
- Injuries resulting from drug-related child abuse or neglect
- Injuries from drug-related accidents
- Injuries from drug-related crime
- Other medical care for illegal drug users, including volunteer services and outpatient services, such as emergency room visits
- Resources used in nonhospital settings

Lost productivity costs
- Of drug-related accident victims
- Of drug-related crime victims
- Time away from work and homemaking to care for drug users and their dependents
- Drug-related educational problems and school dropouts
- Offenders incarcerated for drug-related or drug-defined crimes

Other costs to society
- Loss of property values due to drug-related neighborhood crime
- Property damaged or destroyed in fires, and in workplace and vehicular accidents
- Agricultural resources devoted to illegal drug cultivation or production
- Toxins introduced into public air and water supplies by drug production
- Workplace prevention programs such as drug testing and employee assistance programs
- Averting behavior by potential victims of drug-related crime
- Pain and suffering costs to illegal drug users and their families and friends

Source: Bureau of Justice Statistics, *Drugs, Crime and the Justice System: A National Report from the Bureau of Justice Statistics* (Washington, D.C.: U.S. Government Printing Office, December 1992).

TEENS AND DRUGS

Drug use among American teenagers showed a significant decline during the 1980s. Now, however, use is on the rise once again—and all kinds of drugs are involved. As this story shows, experts disagree as to the cause.

The U.S.A. could lose a decade of progress against drug abuse unless the recent rapid increase in use among teen-agers can be halted.

A federal survey out Tuesday shows nearly 11 percent of the 22 million U.S. teen-agers are using drugs—mostly marijuana but also cocaine and LSD and other hallucinogens.

Donna Shalala, secretary of Health and Human Services, said illicit drug use among 12- to 17-year-olds has more than doubled since 1992, after years of decline. Teen drug use began its decline in the 1980s and did not begin to rise again until 1991–92.

Now the National Household Survey on Drug Abuse, which included 17,747 people older than 12, shows drugs have become so widespread among teens that in a classroom of 25, three are drug users. If the current rate of increase continues, within four years drug use among U.S. teens will reach the peak level of 1979, which is nearly twice that of today, experts say.

"I have a 20-year-old daughter. When she was in middle school she was never offered drugs in the 8th grade," says James Copple of the Community Anti-Drug Coalitions of America, Alexandria, Va. "My 14-year-old was offered drugs six times in the 8th grade, so I get a very real sense that the drug issue and peer pressure around drug abuse is far more intense today."

The question parents, politicians, anti-drug advocates and law enforcement officials want answered is why is drug use among teens climbing again? Republicans point the finger at President Clinton and criticize his drug-fighting efforts. But Copple and others say many factors are to blame.

Charts released by the White House National Office of Drug Control Policy show increased marijuana use followed a relaxing of attitudes about the dangers of the drug after 1991. "Twelfth-graders' disapproval of marijuana peaked in 1990, and their perception of its harmfulness peaked in 1991," says retired Army general Barry McCaffrey, director of the office.

Lee Brown, former drug policy director and now professor of sociology at Houston's Rice University, blames several factors for the increase in teen drug use: Baby boomers who used drugs now have children using them, and the boomer parents are finding it hard to argue with their children about behavior that they themselves engaged in. There is a "reglamorization" of drug use going on in the entertainment and communication industries. The mainstream media aren't paying as much attention to the problem as they used to.

"It was on the radar screen up until the (Persian Gulf) war," Brown says. "When we went to the gulf war, it never surfaced as an issue again." As a result, funding from corporations that had been working to combat drug use dropped 30 percent, he says. "There was a belief that we'd won the war on drugs, which was far, far from the truth." Copple credits the decline in drug use in the 1980s to programs such as Safe and Drug Free Schools and the Community Partnership Coalition, which raised teen awareness of drugs' dangers.

And instead of seeing marijuana smoking in popular teen movies such as *Clueless,* the public saw frequent images of fried eggs depicting the brain on drugs—a TV campaign that got $350 million of free air time for public service announcements, Copple says.

Anti-drug advocate Jessica Hulsey, 19, who was taken away from her

Photo illustration of a high school student snorting cocaine. In a typical American classroom, three of twenty-five students use drugs. What accounts for the recent rise in teen drug use? *Matt Mendelsohn Photography.*

drug-addicted parents as a child, agrees that perceptions of the dangers of drugs have changed in recent years. "Drug use among teen-agers is increasing at an alarming rate while the perceived risk is decreasing," says Hulsey, a Princeton University junior. "That's one thing we need to change. They just don't see (drug use) as a big deal. Like, pot? 'It won't hurt me.' Heroin? 'We can handle it.' "

Her mother began smoking marijuana at 13, says Hulsey, who has seen the worst of its effects. "My mother started when she was 13 with pot and alcohol, then she went on to LSD and cocaine, and when my younger sister was born it was heroin," Hulsey says. "She lost 15 years to drug abuse and doesn't remember much of those years, and she's been in recovery for 10 years." Her father is now addicted to crack cocaine, she says. "Crack does incredible things to human beings. It deteriorates the body and takes away part of the soul."

McCaffrey says federal studies show a person who begins smoking marijuana at age 13 is 79 times more likely to become a drug addict as an adult.

But members of *USA Today's* Teen Panel say the use of marijuana is now so widespread that teens don't really even consider it a drug:

"I think marijuana as a drug is being promoted a lot more in movies, music and music videos," says Kyle Haden, 17, of Bethel Park, Pa. "You see it so much that you don't think it is illegal. I listen to a lot of rappers brag about it."

"As far as general teen use, marijuana is definitely on the rise," says Tighe Herren, 16, of Louisville, Ky. "It is so popular, so well known, it is around everywhere. Nobody is afraid of the consequences of selling it or buying it."

"Marijuana is a big, big thing," says Jennifer Tyus, 17, Decatur, Ill. "I mean, like, there are people who smoke a joint in a car outside school, and when they come in, you can just smell it on them. There are a lot of people doing it."

"I see it at parties," says Renee Benavidez, 18, Stockton, Calif. "It is so kind of regular it isn't considered a drug anymore. It is so normal, everybody does it."

Hulsey says kids decide to smoke marijuana for many reasons: broken families, trouble with parents and peer pressure. And she says the teen-age years are simply a difficult and vulnerable time when self-confidence is often lacking.

But there's also plain curiosity. And in the absence of a strong and powerful message on the danger, children will try it.

"They want to know what it is all about," Benavidez says. "And really, they do it just so they can be cool." Says Herren: "It is really easy to get. You don't have to go find a dealer anymore. It is everywhere."

If the trend is to be stopped, grassroots education and prevention efforts directed at teens must become a primary focus of federal efforts, says Copple. Currently, only $500,000 of the nation's $15 million dollar anti-drug budget goes to community programs, he says.

Parents, too, must be sure their children have good information and sound decision-making skills. "You can't tell youth what choices they have to make," Hulsey says, "but you can give the information and the skills they need to make positive choices for themselves."

And these efforts must begin early. "Parents have no influence at all once their kid hits 14 or 15," Herren says. "You've lost them. They will make up their own minds."

Questions

1. According to this story, "the question parents, politicians, anti-drug advocates and law enforcement officials want answered is why is drug use among teens climbing again?" What do you think?
2. This article speaks of the "reglamorization" of drug use. What is *reglamorization?* How might the effects of reglamorization be reduced?
3. This article says that many teenagers today do not even consider marijuana a "drug." What accounts for this shift in perception?

Source: Tim Friend, "Teens and Drugs: Today's Youth Just Don't See the Dangers," *USA Today*, August 21, 1996, 1A. Copyright 1996, *USA Today*. Reprinted with permission.

STIMULANTS

Stimulants include amphetamines such as Dexedrine and Benzedrine and other drugs such as cocaine, crack, and ice (methamphetamine). Stimulants act as their name implies—they stimulate the central nervous system and result in higher heart rate, elevated blood pressure, and increased mental activity. Legitimate uses of

⬛

TABLE 11.3

DIFFERENCES IN DRUG CATEGORIES AND CHARACTERISTIC CONTROLLED SUBSTANCES

Drugs	*Federal Schedule*	*Names*	*Physical Dependency*	*Psychological Dependency*
Stimulants				
Cocaine	II	coke, flake, snow	Possible	High
Amphetamines	II, III	Benzedrine, Dexedrine, Ice	Possible	High
Methylphenidate	II	Ritalin	Possible	High
Depressants				
Cloral hydrate	IV	Noctec, Somnos	Moderate	Moderate
Barbiturates	II, III, IV	Amobarbital, Phenobarbital, Secobarbital	High-Mod.	High-Mod.
Methaqualone	II	Optimil, Parest, Quaalude, Sopor	High	High
Benzodiazepines	IV	Ativan, Azene, Clonopin, Dalmane, Diazepam, Librium, Valium	Low	Low
Cannabis				
Marijuana	I	pot, Acapulco gold, grass, reefer, weed	Unknown	Moderate
Hashish	I	hash, hash oil	Unknown	Moderate
Narcotics				
Opium	II, III, V	Dover's Powder, Paregoric	High	High
Morphine	II, III	Morphine, Pectoral syrup	High	High
Codeine	II, III, V	Codeine, Robitussin A-C	Moderate	Moderate
Heroin	I	Diacetylmorphine, horse, smack	High	High
Methadone	II	Dolophine, Methadone, Methadose	High	High
Hallucinogens				
LSD	I	acid, microdot	None	Unknown
Mescaline, peyote	I	Mesc, buttons, cactus	None	Unknown
Amphetamine variants	I	2, 5-DMA, PMA, STP MDA, MMDA, TMA	Unknown	Unknown
Phencyclidine	II	PCP, angel dust, hog	Unknown	High
Steroids				
Anabolic steroids	III	Anabolin, Androlone, Durabolin, Kabolin	Low	High
Inhalants				
Various common substances		Laughing gas, nitrous oxide, gasoline, freon toluene, amyl nitrite, butyl nitrite, acetate	Low	High

stimulants include increased alertness, reduced fatigue, weight control, and topical analgesic (pain-killing) action. Such drugs are used illegally, however, by those seeking to produce states of excitability and feelings of competence and power.

Cocaine, the use of which has spread rapidly through American population centers, is available in powdered form or as small "rocks" of crack. Crack cocaine, which is much less expensive than powdered cocaine, is made by mixing cocaine powder with water and baking soda or ammonia. It is usually smoked in a "crack pipe" and is named for the fact that it gives off crackling sounds when burned.

Powdered cocaine is inhaled or snorted, but it may also be mixed with volatile chemicals and "freebased" or smoked and injected. Cocaine produces effects similar to other stimulants—euphoria, a sense of intense stimulation, psychic and physical well-being, and what may seem like boundless energy—although cocaine "highs" are generally both more intense and immediate than are those produced by other drugs. Prolonged cocaine use can cause delusions, hallucinations, weight loss, and overall physical deterioration.

Cocaine sells in Colombia, South America, for between $1,350 and $3,900 per pound and $6,600 and $11,350 (80 percent pure) per pound in the United States at the wholesale level. Once cut and diluted (cocaine is often mixed with sugar and other substances), the American retail price of powdered cocaine skyrockets to between $36,300 and $136,000 per pound. Crack cocaine sells for between $3 and $40 per vial, each of which contains several small "rocks." The Office of National Drug Control Policy (ONDCP) estimates that the total annual amount spent on illegal cocaine in the United States is approximately $18 billion.

Other stimulants include amphetamines with street names such as "bennies," "speed," and "uppers." Amphetamines act to produce mental alertness and increase the ability to concentrate. They are used medically to treat narcolepsy, obesity, and some forms of brain dysfunction. They also cause talkativeness, reduce fatigue, and result in wakefulness. Abuse produces irritability, overexhaustion, and—in cases of prolonged abuse—psychosis and death from cardiac arrest.

One drug now catching the attention of many is methamphetamine, which is a stimulant chemically related to other amphetamines, but with stronger effects on the central nervous system. Street names for the drug include "speed," "meth," and "crank." Methamphetamine is used in pill form, or in powdered form by snorting or injecting.[15] Crystallized methamphetamine known as "ice," "crystal," or "glass" is a smokable and still more powerful form of the drug. Effects of methamphetamine use include increased heart rate and blood pressure, increased wakefulness, insomnia, increased physical activity, decreased appetite, and anxiety, paranoia, or violent behavior. The drug is easily made in simple home "laboratories" from readily available chemicals, and recipes describing how to produce the substance circulate on the Internet. Methamphetamine appeals to the abuser because it increases the body's metabolism and produces euphoria and alertness, and gives the user a sense of increased energy. Methamphetamine, an increasingly popular drug at raves (all-night dancing parties), is not physically addictive but can be psychologically addictive. High doses or chronic use of the drug increases nervousness, irritability, and paranoia.

In 1996, growing popularity of methamphetamine led to passage of the federal Comprehensive Methamphetamine Control Act. The act is discussed in more detail later in this chapter.

DEPRESSANTS

The depressant family includes barbiturates, sedatives, and tranquilizers with names such as Nembutal®, Seconal®, Phenobarbital®, Quaalude, Sopor, Valium®, Librium®, Thorazine®, and Equanil®. Depressants are used legitimately to obtain release from anxiety, for the treatment of psychological problems, and as mood elevators. Illegitimate users employ such substances to produce intoxication and to counter the effects of other drugs or in the self-treatment of drug withdrawal.

Depressants are often prescribed by physicians seeking to control patients' stress-related symptoms and to induce relaxed states and even sleep. Individuals who have experienced recent traumatic events, for example, may find that the temporary use of prescribed depressants helps to alleviate the psychic distress that they would otherwise feel. If abused, however, depressants may lead to psychological dependence and to addiction.

CANNABIS

The cannabis category includes marijuana, hashish, cannabis plants, sinsemilla, and hashish oil—all of which are collectively referred to as "marijuana." Marijuana is a relatively mild, nonaddictive drug with limited hallucinogenic properties. The primary active chemical in marijuana is tetrahydrocannabinol. Although legitimate uses for cannabis have not been fully recognized, some research suggests that the substance can be used in the treatment of pain and glaucoma, and as a supplement to cancer chemotherapy—in which cannabis appears to have the ability to control the nausea associated with chemotherapy. Marijuana is used illegitimately to induce states of euphoria, gaiety, detachment, relaxation, intoxication, and focused awareness. Time distortion, increased sex drive, enhanced appetite, uncontrollable giddiness, and short-term memory loss tend to accompany its use.

Street names for marijuana include pot, grass, and weed. Most marijuana is smoked in the form of dried leaves, stems, and flowers of the marijuana plant (or, more accurately, the Indian hemp plant), although processed marijuana "oil" and the cake form of hashish are also widely available. Hashish is made from resins found on the surface of the female marijuana plant and is considerably more potent than other forms of cannabis.

Most of the marijuana consumed in the United States is either grown within the country or comes from Mexico. Although one marijuana plant produces between one and two pounds of dried leaves and stems, marijuana is generally sold to consumers in one-ounce bags. A pound of dried marijuana costs dealers between $450 and $2,700, while users pay between $25 and $1,000 per one-ounce bag depending on the reputed potency of the particular variety they are purchasing. Single marijuana cigarettes, sometimes called "joints" or "reefers," sell for $1 to $5. Overall, the Office of National Drug Control Policy estimates that the total amount spent on illegal marijuana in the United States is approximately $9 billion annually.

NARCOTICS

Narcotics, including such drugs as opium, morphine, heroin, methadone, codeine, and dilaudid, have a number of legitimate uses including pain relief, antidiarrheal action, and cough suppression. Street use of these drugs is intended to induce pleasure, euphoria, a lack of concern, and general feelings of well-being. The use of narcotics produces drowsiness and relaxation, accompanied by a dreamlike state of reverie. Narcotics are thought to mimic or enhance the activity of endorphins, which are proteins produced by the brain and which control pain and influence other subjective experiences.

Heroin and morphine, which are generally sold as white powdered substances, are derived from opium and usually injected into the body, although they may also be smoked or eaten. Sometimes users inject these drugs under the skin, a practice called "skin-popping," but most addicts prefer direct intravenous injections for the strong and immediate effects produced.

One pound of 70 to 90 percent pure heroin sells in Southeast Asia for between $2,700 and $5,000. At the wholesale level in the United States the same substance brings between $40,000 and $110,000 per pound, while midlevel dealers pay up to $270,000 for that amount. Dealers, however, "cut" the drug, effectively diluting it with a variety of other substances. One writer describes it this way: "Once in the United States, heroin may be stepped on (diluted) as many as seven to ten times. What started out in some remote Asian laboratory as 99 percent pure heroin is cut with lactose (milk sugar, a by-product of milk processing), quinine, cornstarch, or almost any other powdery substance that will dissolve when heated . . . [u]ltimately, the heroin sold on the street is less than 10 percent pure and sometimes as little as 1 percent to 4 percent pure."[16] Street-level dealers sell diluted heroin in 0.1 gram single-dose bags for as much as $46 each, which translates into an effective retail price of more than $2 million per pound for imported heroin. The ONDCP estimates that the total amount spent on heroin in the United States is approximately $12 billion annually.

Although narcotics, including heroin, tend to be highly toxic when taken in large doses, frequent users build up tolerances and require ever larger doses for the desired effects to be induced. Physical addiction may result in drug dependence, and symptoms of withdrawal may appear if the drug is not available. Withdrawal symptoms include nervousness, restlessness, severe abdominal cramps, watery eyes, nasal discharge, and—in later stages—vomiting, diarrhea, weight loss, and pain in the large muscles of the body, especially the back and legs.

HALLUCINOGENS

Hallucinogens, which include drugs such as LSD (lysergic acid diethylamide), PCP, peyote, mescaline, psilocybin, MDA, MDMA, belladonna, and mandrake, have no official legitimate use. Street use of these drugs is intended to produce "mind expansion," hallucinations, creative mental states, and perceptual distortions—all of which have been popularly called "psychedelic experiences" or "trips."

The exact process by which hallucinogens act upon the mind is not known, and the effects of such drugs may be unpredictable. LSD "trips," for example, may produce pleasurable hallucinations and sensations, or may result in frightening experiences for the user. During such episodes uncontrollable nightmarish phantasms may appear to the user who is no longer able to distinguish external reality from his or her own subjective states.

ANABOLIC STEROIDS

Anabolic steroids include the substances nandrolene, oxandrolene, oxymetholone, and stanozolol. Steroids are used legitimately for purposes of weight gain; the treatment of arthritis, anemia, and connective tissue disorder; and in the battle against certain forms of cancer. Some body builders, professional athletes, and others, however, seeking to build body bulk and to increase strength have created a secondary market in steroids that has resulted in their ready availability through illegal channels of distribution.

INHALANTS

Inhalants include a wide variety of psychotropic substances such as nitrous oxide, carbon tetrachloride, amyl nitrite, butyl nitrite, chloroform, freon, acetate, and toluene. They are highly volatile substances which generally act as central nervous system depressants. Inhalants are found in fast-drying glues, nail polish remover, room and car deodorizers, lighter fluid, paint thinner, kerosene, cleaning fluids, households sealants, and gasoline. Although some of these substances, such as ether, nitrous oxide, amyl nitrate, and chloroform, have legitimate medical uses, others are employed only to produce a sense of lightheadedness often described in colloquial terms as a "rush." The use of inhalants "can disturb vision, impair judgment, and reduce muscle and reflex control."[17]

Inhalants have been called "gateway drugs," or substances that initiate young people into illicit drug usage. Easy access to these chemicals is assured by the fact that few inhalants are subject to legislative control beyond simple administrative regulations. In fact, most inhalants are easily available, being found on household shelves, in hardware stores, and on the shelves of general merchandisers.

According to self-reports from members of surveyed households who are 12 years or older, 11.9 million Americans have used inhalants at some point in their lives, and 2.4 million report the use of such drugs within the past month.[18] Among high school seniors, only marijuana use is more widespread than the use of inhalants.[19] Sixteen percent of high school seniors report having experimented with some form of inhalant prior to graduation.

Pharmaceutical diversion
the process by which
legitimately manufactured
controlled substances are
diverted for illicit use.

PHARMACEUTICAL DIVERSION AND DANGEROUS DRUGS

The pharmaceutical diversion and subsequent abuse of legitimately manufactured controlled substances is a major source of drug-related addictions or dependencies, medical emergencies, and deaths. **Pharmaceutical diversion** occurs through illegal prescribing by physicians and illegal dispensing by pharmacists and their assistants. "Doctor shopping," the process of finding a physician who is overly liberal in the type and amount of drug prescribed, and visitations to numerous physicians for the purpose of collecting large quantities of prescribed medicines are practices which exacerbate the problem. Depressants, including sedatives, tranquilizers, and antianxiety drugs (especially Xanax® and Valium®), along with stimulants and anabolic steroids constitute the types of drugs most often diverted.

A number of drugs, especially those which fall into the "designer" category, are manufactured in clandestine drug facilities, which are sometimes called "basement laboratories" because they are operated by individuals out of personal homes and apartments. As the National Institute of Justice notes, "[c]landestine laboratories range from small crude operations in sheds, bathtubs, mobile homes, boats, and motel rooms to highly sophisticated operations with professional quality laboratory glassware and equipment."[20] **Designer drugs** are so named because "they are new substances designed by slightly altering the chemical makeup of other illegal or tightly controlled drugs."[21] Designer drugs such as Nexus, a new reputed aphrodisiac, usually fall under the rubric "synthetic narcotic," or "synthetic hallucinogen."

Designer drugs new
substances designed by
slightly altering the
chemical makeup of other
illegal or tightly controlled
drugs.

Reflecting the high social cost of drugs, fans in Seattle mourn the death of Kurt Cobain, after *Nirvana's* lead singer committed suicide. Drugs were once called "the love of Cobain's brief life."[23] How could drugs be so attractive? *Grant M. Haller/Sygma.*

Designer drugs require the use of a number of specifically identifiable chemicals in their production. Similarly, opium, cocaine, and other naturally occurring psychoactive substances necessitate the use of chemicals in step-by-step processes that leave them ready for street-level distribution and consumption. The Chemical Diversion and Trafficking Act (CDTA) of 1988 placed the distribution of eight essential chemicals used in the production of illicit drugs, as well as twelve "precursor chemicals" (from which drugs could be made), under federal control. The CDTA also regulates the distribution of machines which can produce pharmaceutical capsules and tablets. In 1994 the Domestic Chemical Diversion Control Act[22] added thirty-two other chemicals to the list, bringing the total number of drug-related chemical substances under federal control to fifty-two.

DRUG TRAFFICKING

In everyday usage the phrase "drug trafficking" can have a variety of meanings. On the one hand, it can refer to smuggling, that is, the illegal shipment of controlled substances across state and national boundaries. On the other, it can mean the sale of controlled substances. Hence, in colloquial usage, a person who "traffics" in drugs may simply sell them. Technically speaking, **drug trafficking** "includes manufacturing, distributing, dispensing, importing, and exporting (or possession with intent to do the same) a controlled substance or a counterfeit substance."[24] Federal law enforcement agencies, in their effort to reduce trafficking, focus largely on the prevention of smuggling and on the apprehension of smugglers.

> Drug trafficking includes manufacturing, distributing, dispensing, importing, and exporting (or possession with intent to do the same) a controlled substance or a counterfeit substance.

Drugs such as cocaine, heroin, and LSD are especially easy to smuggle, because relatively small quantities of the drugs can be adulterated with other substances to provide large amounts of illicit commodities at street level. Figure 11.1 provides a map of major cocaine trafficking routes (sometimes called *pipelines*) into the United States. Most cocaine that enters the United States originates in the Western Hemisphere, especially in the South American nations of Colombia, Ecuador, Peru, and Bolivia. Transportation routes into the United States include (1) shipment overland from South America through Central America, (2) direct shipments to U.S. ports concealed in containers or packed with legitimate products, (3) flights into the United States via commercial airplanes or in private aircraft, and (4) airdrops to vessels waiting offshore for smuggling into the United States.

Most cocaine entering the United States is smuggled aboard maritime vessels. Fishing vessels with hidden compartments, cargo ships plying international waters, and even private submersibles have all been used in smuggling operations. In 1993, for example, Colombian authorities seized a 22-foot-long semisubmersible vessel engaged in smuggling cocaine into Puerto Rico, where it was scheduled for repackaging and shipment to the continental United States. Recent large seizures of cocaine include 2.7 metric tons discovered hidden in canvas bags amidst a shipment of coffee beans imported into Miami; and 7 metric tons discovered aboard the fishing vessel *Don Celso*, and seized by Ecuadorian authorities at the Port of Esmeraldes.[25]

Some trafficking methods are highly creative. As one DEA reports, "[u]nusual methods of concealment [found] cocaine concealed in a shipment of beach towels,

FIGURE 11.1   Cocaine Trafficking: Major
Countries of Origin and Routes of Transportation
into the United States. *Source:* Bureau of Justice
Statistics, *Drugs, Crime and the Justice System: A
National Report* (Washington, D.C.: U.S.
Government Printing Office, 1993), p. 47.

inside spools of industrial thread, inside cans of lard, sealed within quartz crystals,
in drums of fruit pulp, in fish meal, and in avocado paste. In addition, U.S. Customs
Service and U.S. Fish and Wildlife officers seized several kilograms of cocaine from
within a shipment of boa constrictors. The cocaine, wrapped in condoms, had been
inserted into the snakes' intestines."[26]

The DEA follows heroin trafficking through its **heroin signature program (HSP),** which identifies the geographic source area of a heroin sample through the laboratory detection of specific chemical characteristics in the sample which are peculiar to a source area. The signature program employs special chemical analyses to identify and measure chemical constituents of a sample of seized heroin. Results of the HSP show that 17 percent of heroin in the United States originates in Southeast Asia, 62 percent in South America, 16 percent in Southwest Asia, and 5 percent in Mexico. According to the DEA, most heroin originating in Southeast Asia is produced in the Golden Triangle area which encompasses Burma, Laos, and Thailand. Shipments are "controlled by ethnic Chinese criminal groups . . . while U.S.-based ethnic Chinese traffickers with links to these international criminal groups (are) the most prolific importers and distributors of Southeast Asian heroin"[27] within the United States. HSP data were based on examination of over 800 random samples, including some obtained through undercover purchases, domestic seizures, and seizures made at U.S. ports of entry.

Heroin signature program (HSP) a DEA program that identifies the geographic source area of a heroin sample through the detection of specific chemical characteristics in the sample peculiar to the source area.

▚ DRUGS AND CRIME

While the manufacture, sale, transportation, and use of controlled substances is itself criminal, drugs and crime are also linked in other ways. Persons so habituated to the use of illegal drugs that they steal to support their "habit," the drug importer who kills a rival dealer, and the offender who commits a criminal act due to the stimulation provided by drugs, all provide examples of how drug abuse may be linked to other forms of criminal activity.

Recognizing these differences, the Bureau of Justice Statistics distinguishes between drug-defined and drug-related crimes. **Drug-defined crimes** are "violations of laws prohibiting or regulating the possession, use, or distribution of illegal drugs."[28] The costs of all drug-defined crime, says the BJS, is directly attributable to illegal drug use. **Drug-related crimes,** on the other hand, "are not violations of drug laws but are crimes in which drugs contribute to the offense." Illegal drug use, says BJS, "is related to offenses against people and property in three major ways: (1) pharmacologically drugs can induce violent behavior, (2) the cost of drugs induces some users to commit crimes to support their drug habits, [and] (3) violence often characterizes relations among participants in the drug distribution system."[29]

According to the U.S. Department of Justice, "there is extensive evidence of the strong relationship between drug use and crime." This relationship can be summarized in the following three points, each of which, the department says, is supported "by a review of the evidence."[30]

Drug-defined crimes violations of laws prohibiting or regulating the possession, use, or distribution of illegal drugs.

Drug-related crimes crimes in which drugs contribute to the offense (excluding violations of drug laws).

- Drug users report greater involvement in crime and are more likely than nonusers to have criminal records.
- Persons with criminal records are much more likely than ones without criminal records to report being drug users.
- Crimes rise in number as drug use increases.

One initiative that attempts to measure the degree to which criminal offenders use controlled substances is the Drug Use Forecasting (DUF) program of the

National Institute of Justice. Begun in 1987, DUF measures drug use among persons coming into contact with the criminal justice system by tracking drug use among booked arrestees in twenty four cities across the nation. DUF data are collected in booking facilities using trained local staff members who obtain voluntary and anonymous urine specimens and interviews from samples of booked arrestees. DUF methodologists report that volunteerism runs high, with "more than 90 percent of the arrestees approached agreeing to be interviewed. Approximately 80 percent of those interviewed provide urine specimens."[31]

Collected urine specimens are sent to a central laboratory for analysis. All specimens are analyzed for the presence of ten drugs: cocaine, opiates, marijuana, PCP, methadone, benzodiazepines (for example, Valium), methaqualone, propoxyphene (i.e., Darvonlike substances), barbiturates, and amphetamines. Tests can detect the use of most drugs within the past two to three days, and marijuana and PCP use can be detected as long as three weeks after ingestion.

Recent DUF data from twenty-three cities show that male arrestees throughout the country are likely to test positive for the presence of one or more drugs. DUF city-by-city data for 1996 show that in twenty of the twenty-three sites where measurements were taken, more than 60 percent of adult male arrestees tested positive for at least one illicit drug (other than alcohol).[32] In only one site (San Jose) did less than 50 percent of arrestees test positive for at least one drug. The rate of illegal drug use ranged from a high of 83 percent of sampled female arrestees in Manhattan (a statistic that exceeds even the rate of illicit drug use by male arrestees for that area), to a low of 35 percent of arrested women in New Orleans.[33] Cocaine was the most widely abused drug among arrestees in most cities, although evidence suggests that its use may be declining. Propoxyphene, barbiturates, and methaqualone were found in relatively few (less than 3 percent) arrestees.

According to the NIJ "drug use among arrestees remains at high levels, especially for cocaine. In many sites," says the report, "cocaine use has shown an increase."[34] The DUF report concludes that "examination of drug use trends among arrestees across the United States clearly shows that drug use continues to be a serious problem. Although some success has been noted in decreasing drug use among the general population, DUF data indicate that these successes have not reached those persons who are coming into contact with the criminal justice system."[35]

Other information on drug use by offenders at the time of the offense comes from the NCVS, which gathers data from victims of violent crimes who are asked to report their impressions about offenders. In a recent year, for example, 33 percent of all victims of violent crime included in the survey reported that they believed their assailants were under the influence of drugs or alcohol at the time the crime occurred. Another 46 percent of victims stated that they did not know whether the offender was under the influence of drugs.

Offender self-reports gathered by Bureau of Justice Statistics researchers show that among jail inmates[36]

- 44 percent used illegal drugs in the month before the offense for which they were arrested;
- 30 percent used illegal drugs daily in the month before the offense;
- 27 percent used illegal drugs at the time of the offense; and

• cocaine and crack cocaine were the drugs most commonly abused by jail inmates.

Surveys of state prison inmates reveal much the same pattern. Of inmates in state prisons, 61 percent say that they or their victims were under the influence of drugs or alcohol at the time of the offense, 50 percent report having been under the influence of alcohol or drugs, and 30 percent say their victims were under the influence of alcohol or drugs.[37] Nearly 40 percent of youths incarcerated in long-term state-operated facilities report having been under the influence of illegal drugs at the time of their offense.[38] When self-reports of jail and state prison inmates are evaluated to determine the proportion reporting having ever used drugs, nearly 80 percent of adult inmates report such use, while 83 percent of incarcerated juveniles say they have used drugs at some point in their lives.[39]

Surveys of drug-related crime have also been conducted in recent years. Interviews with adult prison inmates, for example, determined that 24 percent of female and 16 percent of male inmates committed their offenses to get money to buy drugs. The same surveys show that approximately 30 percent of all robberies, burglaries, and thefts are committed to obtain drug money, while 5 percent of murders result from such criminal activities.[40]

ILLEGAL DRUGS AND OFFICIAL CORRUPTION

Sometimes the corrupting influence of drugs and drug money extends beyond street crime and street criminals. Lucrative drug profits have the potential to corrupt official agents of control as the recent Mollen Commission study of police corruption in New York City found. The Mollen Commission, headed by former Judge Milton Mollen, made its report on July 6, 1994, and found that the severity of police corruption in New York City has worsened drastically since previous investigations into the subject. According to the report, "police have crossed the line into actively engaging in criminal activity including robbery, drug dealing and even a killing."[41] It called today's corrupt police, "criminals in blue uniforms," contrasting the severity of their illegal activity with prior forms of corruption that simply involved turning a "blind eye" to crime.

Much illegal police activity was found to be drug related, with drug monies providing powerful incentives toward corruption. The report found that police officers in certain precincts banded together and regularly robbed drug dealers, sold drugs, and conducted illegal raids to confiscate additional drugs for personal gain. The commission found that "some precincts were much more prone to corruption, particularly in minority communities because of high levels of drug activity within their borders. . . . Unlike 20 years ago, when an officer took bribes it was to turn his head away from crime. This time these (bad) cops are the criminals," Judge Mollen said, commenting on the commission's report.[42]

It is not only police officers who face the threat of corruption from the lucrative monetary rewards to be reaped from dealing drugs. A few years ago,[43] for example, twenty District of Columbia corrections officers and employees were given stiff prison sentences after being convicted of drug smuggling activities. Even with those

Vast amounts of money associated with the illegal drug trade have the potential to corrupt public officials and agents of control. How can that potential be reduced? *Steve Starr/Saba Press Photos, Inc.*

convictions, however, few believed that corruption in the District's prisons had been ended. U.S. District Judge Royce Lamberth, who sentenced the former officers, observed that "even as the latest prison guard drug ring was being shut down . . . corruption continues today as I sit in this courtroom."[44]

■ SOCIAL POLICY AND DRUG ABUSE

The history of drug control policy in the United States is as interesting as it is diverse. According to some authors, "[a]lcohol prohibition marked the first legal recognition of problems emanating from substance abuse."[45] In reality, however, the 18th Amendment, which was ratified in 1919 and prohibited the manufacture, sale, and transportation of alcoholic beverages, was preceded by the Harrison Act, the first major piece of federal antidrug legislation. The Harrison Act, passed by Congress in 1914, required anyone dealing in opium, morphine, heroin, and cocaine or their derivatives to register with the federal government and to pay a $1.00 per year tax. The act, however, only authorized the registration of physicians, pharmacists, and other medical professionals, effectively outlawing "street" use of these drugs. However, by 1920 court rulings severely curtailed the use of heroin for medical purposes, saying its prescribed use only prolonged addiction. Hence, the beginning of complete federal prohibition over at least one major drug can be traced to that time.

In 1937 passage of the Marijuana Tax Act effectively outlawed marijuana, a federal stance that was reinforced by the Boggs Act of 1951. The Boggs Act also man-

Houston police remove 600 pounds of marijuana found in false tops of trucks brought from Mexico. Are our borders adequately patrolled? *Gregg Smith/Saba Press Photos, Inc.*

dated deletion of heroin from the list of medically useful substances and required its complete removal from all medicines. The 1956 Narcotic Control Act increased penalties for drug traffickers and made the sale of heroin to anyone under age 18 a capital offense.

The most comprehensive federal legislation to address controlled substances to date is the 1970 Comprehensive Drug Abuse Prevention and Control Act. Title 2 of that act is referred to as the Controlled Substances Act (CSA). It established five schedules that classify psychoactive drugs according to their medical use, degree of psychoactivity, and adjudged potential for abuse. Table 11.4 outlines the various drug schedules under federal law. Penalties under federal law are generally more severe for possession of higher category substances (Schedule I being the highest), but vary by amount possessed, the purpose of possession (for sale or personal use, etc.), and the offender's criminal history.

Another federal initiative, the 1988 Anti-Drug Abuse Act, proclaimed the goal of a "Drug-Free America by 1995." Although many of the act's provisions, such as the preamble that contained the "drug-free" phrase, were more rhetoric than substance, the act substantially increased penalties for recreational drug users and made weapons purchases by suspected drug dealers more difficult. The law also denied federal benefits—ranging from loans (such as federal student loans) to contracts and licenses—to federal drug convicts.

In 1991 steroids were added to the list of Schedule III controlled substances by congressional action, and in 1996 the Drug-Induced Rape Prevention Act[46] increased penalties for trafficking in the drug Rohypnol®, which is known as the "date rape drug" because of its growing use by "young men [who] put doses of the drug in women's drinks without their consent in order to lower their inhibitions."[47] Rohypnol® (whose generic name is flunitrazepam) is a powerful sedative manufactured by Hoffmann-LaRoche Pharmaceuticals. A member of the benzodiazepine family of depressants, it is legally prescribed in sixty-four countries for insomnia and as a preoperative anesthetic. Seven to ten times more powerful than Valium®, Rohypnol® is easily available on the black market. It dissolves easily in drinks and can leave anyone who unknowingly consumes it unconscious for hours—making them vulnerable to sexual assault. The drug is variously known as "roples," "roche," "ruffles," "roofies," and "rophies" on the street.

RECENT LEGISLATION AND CURRENT POLICY

Recent drug control legislation of note includes the Comprehensive Methamphetamine Control Act of 1996 (CMCA), and relevant portions of the Violent Crime Control and Law Enforcement Act of 1994. The CMCA: (1) contains provisions for the forfeiture and seizure of chemicals used in the manufacture of methamphetamine, (2) added iodine to the list of chemicals controlled under the Chemical Diversion and Trafficking Act of 1988 and the Domestic Chemical Diversion Control Act of 1993, (3) created new reporting requirements for distributors of combination products containing ephedrine, pseudoephedrine, and phenylpropanolamine, and (4) increased penalties for the manufacture and possession of equipment used to make controlled substances.

TABLE 11.4

SCHEDULED DRUGS UNDER FEDERAL LAW

Schedule	Abuse Potential	Examples of Drugs Covered	Some Effects	Medical Use
I	Highest	heroin, LSD, hashish, marijuana, designer drugs, methaqualone	Unpredictable effects, severe psychological or physical dependence, or death	No accepted use; some are legal for limited research use only
II	High	morphine, PCP, codeine, cocaine, methadone, Demerol, benzedrine, dexedrine	May lead to severe psychological or physical dependence	Accepted use with restrictions
III	Medium	codeine with aspirin or Tylenol, some amphetamines, anabolic steroids	May lead to moderate or low physical dependence or high psychological dependence	Accepted use
IV	Low	Darvon, Talwin, phenobarbital, Equanil miltown, Librium, diazepam	May lead to limited physical or psychological dependence	Accepted use
V	Lowest	Over-the-counter or prescription compounds with codeine, Lomatil, Robitussin A–C	May lead to limited physical or psychological dependence	Accepted use

Source: Adapted from DEA, *Drugs of Abuse,* 1996 edition (Web posted at http://www.usdoj.gov/dea/pubs/abuse/contents.htm).

The far-reaching Violent Crime Control and Law Enforcement Act of 1994 included a number of drug-related provisions. Specifically the act:

- Authorized $1 billion in Edward Byrne Memorial Formula Grant Program monies to reduce or prevent juvenile drug- and gang-related activity in federally assisted, low-income housing areas.
- Authorized $1.6 billion for direct funding to localities around the country for anticrime efforts, such as drug treatment, education, and jobs, through a legislative subsection known as the Local Partnership Act.
- Allocated other drug treatment monies for the creation of state and federal programs to treat drug-addicted prisoners. The act also created a treatment schedule for all drug-addicted federal prisoners and requires drug testing of federal prisoners upon release.
- Provided $1 billion for drug court programs for nonviolent offenders with substance abuse problems. Participants will be intensively supervised, given drug treatment, and subjected to graduated sanctions—ultimately including prison terms—for failing random drug tests.
- Provided stiff new penalties for drug crimes committed by gang members and tripled penalties for using children to deal drugs near schools and playgrounds.
- Established "Drug Free Zones" by increasing penalties for drug dealing in areas near playgrounds, schoolyards, video arcades, and youth centers.
- Increased penalties for drug dealing near public housing projects.
- Expanded the federal death penalty to include large-scale drug trafficking and mandated life imprisonment for criminals convicted of three drug-related felonies.
- Created special penalties for drug use and drug trafficking in prison.

Throughout the years, major policy initiatives in the battle against illicit drugs have included (1) antidrug legislation and strict enforcement, (2) interdiction, (3) forfeiture, (4) crop control, and (5) antidrug education and treatment.[48]

Current policy is much in keeping with calls for the strict enforcement of antidrug abuse laws, although much enforcement emphasis in recent years has shifted from targeting users to the arrest, prosecution, and incarceration of the distributors of controlled substances. Similar shifts have occurred among employers, some of whom no longer wait for drug-influenced behavioral problems to arise, but instead require routine drug testing as a condition of employment and retention.

In 1996 nearly 1.5 million persons were arrested for drug law violations throughout the United States.[49] One-third of all arrests, however, were for the sale and/or manufacture of controlled substances. Although the percentage of arrests for drug distribution increased by more than 130 percent between 1983 and 1996, the number of arrests for drug possession increased by only about 40 percent during the same period. Enforcement activities within the United States also include the seizure and destruction of illegal drugs and clandestine drug laboratories. In 1996 domestic seizures of marijuana and cannabis-related substances totaled 142.9 metric tons, while 270 clandestine laboratories were seized and destroyed throughout the country. Of the total number of laboratories seized, 218 were involved in the manufacture of the stimulant methamphetamine.

Interdiction an international drug control policy that aims to stop drugs from entering the country illegally.

Interdiction is an international drug control policy that aims to stop drugs from entering the country illegally. In the first half of 1996, for example, U.S. agents seized 11 metric tons of cocaine from commercial maritime vessels entering the United States.[50] Most arrests occurred at the Port of Miami. In 1994 the Federal-wide Drug Seizure System (FDSS) reported that domestic cocaine seizures totaled 111 metric tons. Foreign seizures of cocaine, most of which occurred in source countries and along trafficking routes, were reported to exceed 155 metric tons of the drug. Heroin seizures in 1996 amounted to 1.5 metric tons domestically and another 23 metric tons internationally. Such amounts, however, represent mere drops in the proverbial bucket. DEA estimates of worldwide opium production, for example, exceeded 4,200 metric tons in 1996, while cocaine production in South American source countries was estimated at around 760 metric tons—most of which eventually found its way into the United States.[51]

A third strategy, crop control, has both international and domestic aspects. During 1996, for example, 3 million cultivated marijuana plants were seized throughout the United States, while the Colombian National Police and Colombian armed forces combined efforts to destroy cocaine fields and cocaine processing laboratories. Similarly, Mexican officials reported the eradication of 7,900 hectares of opium poppies in 1996, while Pakistan reported the destruction of 867 hectares.

Asset forfeiture the authorized seizure of money, negotiable instruments, securities, or other things of value. In federal antidrug laws: the authorization of judicial representatives to seize all monies, negotiable instruments, securities, or other things of value furnished or intended to be furnished by any person in exchange for a controlled substance, and all proceeds traceable to such an exchange.

Forfeiture, or **asset forfeiture,** is another strategy in the battle against illegal drugs. Forfeiture is a legal procedure that authorizes judicial representatives to seize "all moneys, negotiable instruments, securities, or other things of value furnished or intended to be furnished by any person in exchange for a controlled substance . . . [and] all proceeds traceable to such an exchange."[52] Unfortunately, asset forfeiture laws have at times been abused by enforcement agencies. As one writer explains, "There have, in the past, been cases where innocent parties have had property seized and had to spend a considerable amount on lawyers' fees to get it back. Parents have had homes confiscated because children sold drugs there. Farms have been taken even though the owners were acquitted of growing marijuana on an isolated part of the property."[53] Recent U.S. Supreme Court decisions, however, now require that property owners be given notice of any pending seizures, and the opportunity to respond to government charges.[54] The Court has also acted to restrain seizures of property far more valuable than the proceeds of the underlying crime with which the property owner has been charged.[55]

Antidrug education and drug treatment, the final strategies to be discussed in this section, have gained significant popularity over the past decade. Those favoring educational attacks on the problem of drug abuse are quick to claim that other measures have not been effective in reducing the incidence of abuse. Antidrug education programs often reach targeted individuals through schools, corporations, and media campaigns. A short TV commercial of a few years ago, for example, recited the lines, "This is your brain. This is your brain on drugs," while showing a picture of an egg, followed by an egg sizzling in a frying pan. School-based programs are numerous, with many being built on the principles developed by Project D.A.R.E., which stands for Drug Abuse Resistance Education, began as a joint effort of the Los Angeles Police Department and the Los Angeles Unified School District in 1983. D.A.R.E. uses uniformed police officers and other "experts" to explain issues of drug abuse to school-aged children and attempts to build resistance to what might otherwise be portrayed by youthful peers as attractive drug-related activities. D.A.R.E. focuses on developing competent decision-making skills, combating negative forms of peer pressure, and meaningful alternatives to drug usage. Unfortunately for advocates of such programs, however, a number of recent studies have questioned the effectiveness of D.A.R.E-type interventions, finding—after repeated evaluations—that its "effects on drug use, except for tobacco use, are nonsignificant."[56]

Recent policy initiatives at the federal level have begun to once again emphasize treatment and the prevention of drug abuse through education. In 1994, for example, President Bill Clinton announced "a new national attack on drug addiction."[57] The program was aimed largely at hard-core drug users, although it also involved a three-pronged approach including (1) working with countries that produce drugs to go after kingpins, (2) destroying drug cartels, and (3) using better technology and "smarter efforts" in interdiction. In the president's words, "this strategy does more than ever before to help hard-core drug users into treatment programs where they belong."[58] The new program represented at least a partial shift away from interdiction and a movement toward greater prevention, education, and treatment. Monies budgeted for interdiction efforts under the new program were reduced by $94 million below year-ago levels.[59]

Other proposals by the Clinton administration include a welfare reform plan that "would require substance abuse treatment as a condition for receiving welfare benefits."[60] Under the plan, recipients of Aid to Families with Dependent Children (AFDC) would be required to take jobs limiting their benefits to two years, and "recipients with disabilities, including severe addiction, would be temporarily deferred from work, but would be required to develop 'employability plans' that lead to work."[61]

POLICY CONSEQUENCES

There can be little doubt that the "war on drugs" has been a costly one. In fiscal year 1998 alone, the federal government's drug control budget exceeded $15.9 billion.[62] Domestic law enforcement activities (i.e., federal law enforcement programs within the nation's borders) accounted for the lion's share of federal antidrug expenditures (52.8 percent), while demand reduction (i.e., educational activities) programs absorbed 34 percent of the antidrug budget. Interdiction at the nation's borders, a separate expenditure category, accounted for another $1.6 billion (or 10 percent of the total budget).[63] When state monies spent on the control of illegal drugs and the enforcement of drug laws are added to funds spent on antidrug abuse education, and the personal and social costs of drug abuse identified earlier, the total cost of the war on drugs has been enormous.

The drug war has been costly in other ways as well. James Inciardi describes the current situation this way: "As an outgrowth of the U.S. 'war on drugs' during the 1980s and early 1990s, all phases of the criminal justice process have become 'drug driven.' "[64] The same could be said of the nation's system of civil justice. "Although at first blush it may seem unrelated," says writer J. Michael McWilliams, "the 'war on drugs' has had a major impact on the civil justice system at both the state and federal levels. Our courts, like all of government and commerce, are institutions of limited resources. To the extent that court resources must be diverted to deal with the enormous influx of drug prosecutions, these resources are not available to resolve civil matters.... In some jurisdictions, drug cases account for as much as two-thirds of the criminal case filings. America's major cities have been especially affected."[65] In Los Angeles, for example, three-quarters of all criminal prosecutions are for drug charges or drug-related crimes.[66]

Strict enforcement has combined with a lock-em-up philosophy to produce astonishingly high rates of imprisonment for drug offenders. The proportion of federal prisoners who are drug offenders rose from 38 percent in 1986 to 58 percent in 1991 and, according to the Bureau of Prisons, is nearly 60 percent today.[67] Part of the increase is due to congressional action that, beginning in 1986, required high mandatory minimum sentences in drug cases so that even first offenders were sentenced to long prison terms instead of probation. Today, approximately 70 percent of all first offenders in federal prisons are serving drug sentences. This is also true of 85 percent of illegal immigrants who are federal prisoners and 66 percent of female federal prisoners.[68]

ALTERNATIVE DRUG POLICIES

A number of alternative drug control policies have been tried on both state and local levels. Primary among them have been legalization and decriminalization. Both strategies are "based on the assumption that drug abuse will never be eliminated."[69] Whereas **decriminalization** typically reduces criminal penalties associated with the personal possession of a controlled substance, **legalization** eliminates "the laws and associated criminal penalties that prohibit its production, sale, distribution, and possession."[70] Decriminalization enhances personal freedoms in the face of state control, whereas legalization "is aimed," in part, "at reducing the control that criminals have over the drug trade."[71] Other arguments in favor of legalization include the following notions.

Decriminalization (of drugs) reduces criminal penalties associated with the personal possession of a controlled substance.

Legalization (of drugs) eliminates the laws and associated criminal penalties that prohibit the production, sale, distribution, and possession of a controlled substance.

- In a free society people should be permitted to do what they want, as long as they don't harm others. Drug use is considered by many to be a "victimless crime," which harms no one other than the user. Existing drug laws, say advocates of legalization, make criminals out of otherwise law-abiding individuals.
- Keeping drugs illegal means that they will continue to be high priced. Legalizing them could greatly lower the price. The expense of illicit drugs, kept artificially high by their illegal status, encourages the commission of many drug-related crimes, such as robbery and burglary, by users seeking to feed their habits. Legalize drugs, some argue, and many other forms of crime will decline.
- Legalizing drugs would also reduce other forms of "vice," such as prostitution, pornography, and gambling, because many such offenses are also committed in an effort to obtain money to purchase high-priced drugs.
- Legalizing drugs would reduce the influence of criminal cartels now closely involved in the production, transportation, and sale of controlled substances.

- The illegal status and associated high cost of drugs indirectly victimizes others, such as the family members of drug abusers, property owners in drug-infested areas, and taxpayers who must foot the enforcement bill. Legalization would end these forms of victimization.
- Drug legalization would dramatically reduce the opportunity for official corruption, which is now frequently associated with the illicit drug trade. Enforcement agents, politicians, correctional officers, and representatives of the judiciary would cease to be subject to corrupting influences dependent upon the vast financial resources available to drug trafficking cartels.
- The legalization of drugs would result in increased tax revenues, because drugs could be taxed just as alcohol and cigarettes are today.
- The legalization of drugs would allow for better control over public health issues related to drug use. The spread of AIDS, for example, caused in large part by the use of dirty needles in heroin injection, could be better controlled if sterilized needles were made legally available. Similarly, drug quality and potency could be monitored and ensured, resulting in fewer overdoses and emergency room visits by drug users now uncertain of the chemical composition of the substances they consume.

Were controlled substances to be legalized, they might still be dispensed under controlled conditions (as in liquor stores), and penalties might still accrue to those who used them injudiciously (as while driving a car).

In 1996 California and Arizona voters passed resolutions in their respective states legalizing the medical use of marijuana under certain circumstances. The thrust of California's Proposition 215, which the voters approved, is contained in the following language taken from the proposition: (A) To ensure that seriously ill Californians have the right to obtain and use marijuana for medical purposes where that medical use is deemed appropriate and has been recommended by a physician who has determined that the person's health would benefit from the use of marijuana in the treatment of cancer, anorexia, AIDS, chronic pain, spasticity, glaucoma, arthritis, migraine, or any other illness for which marijuana provides relief. (B) To ensure that patients and their primary caregivers who obtain and use marijuana for medical purposes upon the recommendation of a physician are not subject to criminal prosecution or sanction.

Although the California law permits possession of marijuana for valid medicinal purposes, buying and selling the drug remain illegal—meaning that legitimate users may have to grow their own supply, or buy it on the black market. Arizona law requires prescribing physicians to write a scientific opinion explaining why the drug is appropriate for a specific patient, and a supportive second opinion is required before the drug can be legally used.

Opponents of legalization argue that reducing official control over psychoactive substances is immoral and socially irresponsible, and would result in heightened costs to society from drug abuse. Lost time from work, drug-induced criminality (especially violence), the loss of personal self-control, and the severing of important social relationships would all accompany legalization such thinkers argue—suggesting that drug legalization would simply increase the types of problems now associated with alcohol abuse. Opponents of legalization also hold that drug laws are enforceable, and that we are winning the war against drugs. Having laws not entirely enforceable is no reason to eliminate them, they say. Laws against murder and rape, for example, have not entirely eliminated such crimes, and there is no conclusive evidence that laws seriously reduce the numbers of crimes committed in any category in which intense needs or emotions are involved as motivating factors.

SUMMARY

Drug abuse has a long and varied history in American society. Policy responses to abuse have been equally diverse. Although recent statistics on drug use show some decline, a hard-core population of illicit drug users remains. Strategies to reduce the flow of illegal drugs into this country, while meeting with some success, are being increasingly supplemented with programs of education and treatment intended to reduce the demand for controlled substances. In the meantime, the potential for official corruption in the face of a lucrative drug trade remains high. Drug traffickers are now in control of vast amounts of money, leading some to suggest that only legalization can solve the secondary problems of drug-related crime, official corruption, and drug-related public health concerns.

DISCUSSION QUESTIONS

1. This book emphasizes a social problems versus social responsibility theme. Which of the social policy approaches to controlling drug abuse discussed in this chapter (if any) appears to be predicated upon a social problems approach? Which (if any) is predicated upon a social responsibility approach? Explain the nature of the relationship.
2. What are some of the costs of illicit drug use in the United States today? Which costs can be more easily reduced than others? How would you reduce the cost of illegal drug use?
3. What is the difference between decriminalization and legalization? Should drug use remain illegal? What do you think of the arguments in favor of legalization? Those against?
4. What is the difference between drug-defined and drug-related crime? Which form of crime is more difficult to address? Why?
5. What is *asset forfeiture?* How has asset forfeiture been used in the fight against controlled substances? How have recent U.S. Supreme Court decisions limited federal asset seizures? Do you agree that such limitations were necessary? Why or why not?

WEB WATCH

Access the *Criminology Today* home page on the World Wide Web by pointing your browser at www.prenhall.com/cjcentral. Once there, click on "Criminology Today" to access the wealth of electronic resources supporting this text.

Onsite resources include (1) "Chapter Links," which provides succinct overviews of critical ideas from the textbook and links selected materials from around the Web to concepts found in the text; (2) "General Reference—Law and Justice Links." Organized by chapter, these links lead to other useful resources on the World Wide Web such as libraries, electronic discussion lists, and electronic journals; (3) "Criminology Sites on the Web," which lists links to organizations such as the American Society of Criminology, and the National Organization for Victims Assistance (NOVA), as well as crime prevention links and statistics on crime and justice. Many other Web-based resources can be accessed via the *Criminology Today* site, including the federal Justice Information Center, the Bureau of Justice Statistics, the FBI, the RAND Corporation, the Vera Institute of Justice, PAVNET (an online "Partnership Against Violence," run by seven different federal agencies), and the National White Collar Crime Center.

Still another feature of the *Criminology Today* Web site is e-mail homework. Homework can be composed onsite and submitted to instructors using the instructor's e-mail address. To use the e-mail homework feature, click on "E-Mail Homework" on the opening page, and then type answers to the questions that appear in the spaces provided. Use your instructor's e-mail address to submit homework answers. The *Criminology Today* Web site also provides links to powerful Web-based search engines that can help you find topics of interest to you as you progress through your course of study. Search engines can be found under the home page heading "Criminology Sites on the Web."

NOTES

[1]Melanie Goodfellow, "Interpol Head Says Drugs a Threat to Democracy," Reuters wire service, October 4, 1994.

[2]"Presidential Commission Presents Recommendation on Drug Control," United Press International wire service, Northern edition, December 13, 1993.

[3]"Perspectives," *Newsweek,* September 12, 1994, p. 19.

[4]The information in this section comes from Niko Price, "Drug Lord's Body Hangs In Limbo," Associated Press wire service, July 6, 1997; and Michael J. Sniffen, "DEA Eyes Drug Death Aftermath," Associated Press wire service, July 7, 1997.

[5]"Did U.S. Anti-Narcotics Agents Kill the Lord of the Skies?" *The Independent,* London. Via Simon & Schuster NewsLink, July 12, 1997.

[6]Reported in: "Did U.S. Anti-Narcotics Agents Kill the Lord of the Skies?" *The Independent,* London. Via Simon & Schuster NewsLink, July 12, 1997.

[7]Paul Savoy, "When Criminal Rights Go Wrong: Forget Liberal. Forget Conservative. Think Common Sense," *Washington Monthly,* vol. 21, no. 11 (December 1989), p. 36.

[8]Data in this section are derived from: Substance Abuse and Mental Health Services Administration, *National Household Survey on Drug Abuse 1995* (Washington, D.C.: U.S. Government Printing Office, 1996).

[9]U.S. Department of Health and Human Services, *National Household Survey on Drug Abuse* (Washington, D.C.: U.S. Government Printing Office, 1994).

[10]Carolyn Skorneck, "Drug Use," Associated Press wire service, July 20, 1994.

[11]Bureau of Justice Statistics, *Drugs and Crime Facts, 1993* (Washington, D.C.: U.S. Department of Justice, August 1994), p. 25.

[12]Mike Cooper, "CDC Charts Impact of AIDS Among Blacks, Hispanics," Reuters wire service, September 8, 1994.

[13]National Narcotics Intelligence Consumers Committee, *The NNICC Report 1996: The Supply of Illicit Drugs to the United States* (Arlington, VA: The Drug Enforcement Administration, 1997), p. 69.

[14]Most of the information in the paragraphs that follow is taken from ibid. and Office of National Drug Control Policy, *Pulse Check: National Trends in Drug Abuse* (Washington, D.C.: ONDCP, 1997).

[15]Much of the information in this section comes from the National Institute on Drug Abuse's world wide web site at http://www.nida.nih. gov (November 1, 1997); and from Office of National Drug Control Policy, *Pulse Check: Special Report; Methamphetamine Trends in Five Western States and Hawaii* (Washington, D.C.: ONDCP, 1997).

[16]James A. Inciardi, *The War on Drugs II* (Mountain View, Calif.: Mayfield, 1992), p. 69.

[17]Michael D. Lyman and Gary W. Potter, *Drugs in Society: Causes, Concepts and Control* (Cincinnati: Anderson, 1991), p. 45.

[18]National Inhalant Prevention Coalition, world wide web site: www.inhalants.org, October 25, 1997.

[19]Ibid.

[20]Sherry Green, "Preventing Illegal Diversion of Chemicals: A Model Statute" (Washington, D.C.: National Institute of Justice, November 1993), p. 2.

[21]Ibid., p. 79.

[22]Called the "Domestic Chemical Diversion Control Act of 1993," the provisions of this legislation became effective April 16, 1994.

[23]Malcom Jones et al., "The Fallout of the Burnout," *Newsweek,* April 25, 1994, p. 68.

[24]As defined by federal law and precedent.

[25]National Narcotics Intelligence Consumers Committee, *The NNICC Report 1996* (Arlington, VA: The Drug Enforcement Administration, 1997).

[26]NNICC, *The NNICC Report 1993.*

[27]Ibid., p. 35.

[28]Bureau of Justice Statistics, *Drugs, Crime and the Justice System,* (Washington, D.C.: U.S. Government Printing Office, 1992), p. 2.

[29]Ibid., p. 126.

[30]Ibid., p. 2.

[31]National Institute of Justice, *Drug Use Forecasting 1992 Annual Report: Drugs and Crime in America's Cities* (Washington, D.C.: National Institute of Justice, 1993), p. 2.

[32]National Institute of Justice, *Drug Use Forecasting 1996: Annual Report on Adult and Juvenile Arrestees* (Washington, D.C.: NIJ, December 1997).

[33]Ibid.

[34]National Institute of Justice, *Drug Use Forecasting 1992 Annual Report,* p. 4.

[35]Ibid.

[36]Bureau of Justice Statistics, *Drug and Crime Facts, 1993,* pp. 4–5.

[37]Ibid., p. 6.

[38]Ibid.

[39]Ibid., p. 7.

[40]Ibid., p. 8.

[41]United Press International wire service, Northeastern edition, "Study: Bad NYC Cops 'Criminals in Blue,'" July 7, 1994.

[42]Ibid.

[43]In July, 1994.

[44]"Judgment on Corrections," *Washington Post* wire service, July 5, 1994.

[45]Lyman and Potter, *Drugs in Society,* p. 256.

[46]Public Law 104–305.

[47]" 'Rophies' Reported Spreading Quickly Throughout the South," *Drug Enforcement Report,* June 23, 1995, pp. 1–5.

[48]For an excellent overview of policy initiatives in the area of drug control, see Doris Layton MacKenzie and Craig D. Uchida, *Drugs and Crime: Evaluating Public Policy Initiatives* (Thousand Oaks, Calif.: Sage, 1994).

[49]Federal Bureau of Investigation, *Crime in the United States, 1996* (Washington, D.C.: U.S. Government Printing Office, 1997).

[50]National Narcotics Intelligence Consumers Committee, *The NNICC Report 1996: The Supply of Illicit Drugs to the United States* (Arlington, VA: The Drug Enforcement Administration, 1997).

[51]Ibid., pp. 16 and 34.

[52]21 U.S.C., section 881 (a) (6).

[53]"Notice, Hearing and Seizure," *Washington Post* on-line, December 16, 1994.

[54]*United States* v. *James Daniel Good Real Property,* 114 S. Ct. 492, 126 L. Ed. 2d 490 (1993).

[55]*Austin* v. *U.S.,* 113 S. Ct. 2801, 15 L. Ed. 2d 448 (1993).

[56]Fox Butterfield, no headline, *New York Times* news service online, 7:06 EST, April 16, 1997, citing Office of Justice Programs, *Preventing Crime: What Works, What Doesn't, What's Promising* (Washington, D.C.: U.S. Department of Justice, 1997).

[57]Juliana Gruenwald, "Clinton Unveils Anti-Drug Strategy with More Money," United Press International wire service, Northeastern edition, February 9, 1994.

[58]Ibid.

[59]Associated Press wire service, "Drug Strategy-Box," February 9, 1994.

[60]"Required Treatment Option Included in Welfare Proposal," *Substance Abuse Letter,* July 19, 1994, p. 1.

[61]Ibid.

[62]Office of National Drug Control Policy, *The National Drug Control Strategy, 1997: FY 1998 Budget Summary* (Washington, D.C.: ONDCP, 1997). Web posted at http://ncjrs.org/htm/tables.htm#table1.

[63]Ibid.

[64]James A. Inciardi, *Criminal Justice* (Orlando: Harcourt Brace Jovanovich, 1993), p. v.

[65]J. Michael McWilliams, "Setting the Record Straight: Facts About Litigation Costs and Delay," *Business Economics,* vol. 27, no. 4 (October 1992), p. 19.

[66]Ibid.

[67]Bureau of Justice Statistics, *Prisoners in 1996* (Washington, D.C.: U.S. Department of Justice, June 1997).

[68]"Who Is in Federal Prison?" *Washington Post,* October 3, 1994.

[69]Lyman and Potter, *Drugs in Society,* p. 316.

[70]Inciardi, *The War on Drugs II,* p. 239 (note *d*).

[71]Lyman and Potter, *Drugs in Society,* p. 316.

THE HIGH-TECH OFFENDER

Crime is not static. Existing patterns get displaced by new ones.

—GEORGETTE BENNETT[1]

As surely as the future will bring new forms of technology, it will bring new forms of crime . . .

—CYNTHIA MANSON AND CHARLES ARDAI[2]

The rise of a new kind of economy, never before known, threatening to many, demanding rapid changes in work, life style, and habits, hurls large populations—terrified of the future—into spasms of diehard reaction. It opens cleavages that fanatics rush to fill. It arms all those dangerous minorities who live for crisis in the hopes of catapulting themselves onto the national or global stage and transporting us all into a new Dark Age.

—ALVIN TOFFLER[3]

⚙ CHAPTER OUTLINE ⚙

⟸ IMPORTANT TERMS ⟹

computer crime	cybercrime	threat analysis
computer abuse	computer-related crime	federal interest
computer virus	bulletin board system (BBS)	computers
audit trail	hacker	phone phreak
TEMPEST	cyberspace	expert systems
Internet	DNA fingerprinting	data encryption
Daubert standard	or profiling	software piracy

⟸ IMPORTANT CASES AND LAWS ⟹

Frye v. *United States*	*Daubert* v. *Merrell Dow Pharmaceuticals, Inc.*
Reno v. *ACLU*	Communications Decency Act (1996)

⚙ INTRODUCTION

Sometimes science is stranger than fiction. Not long after she was raped, an Indiana woman thought she spotted her attacker walking down a city street. A quick call to police resulted in the man's arrest. His name was Robert Flowers. Flowers vehemently denied committing the crime, but a sample of his blood was sent to a crime laboratory for DNA analysis.[4] Although test results confirmed that his DNA did not precisely match DNA in the rapist's semen, it came surprisingly close. Following further investigation police arrested Flowers' look-alike brother and charged him with the crime. The brother's DNA proved a perfect match and he was convicted of the rape.

❖ CRIME AND TECHNOLOGY

Technology and criminology have always been closely linked. Early forms of technology, including the telegraph, the telephone, and the automobile, were embraced by agents of law enforcement as soon as they became available. Evidence derived from fingerprint and ballistics analysis is routinely employed by prosecutors, and emerging technologies promise to keep criminologists and law enforcement agents in step with high-tech offenders.

Technology, of course, can be employed by both crime fighters and by those who break the law. The con artist using telephones in a financial scam, the robber who uses a firearm and drives a getaway car, even the murderer who wields a knife—all employ at least rudimentary forms of technology in the crimes they commit.

Technology, which is taken for granted today, was at one time almost unthinkable. Telephones, for example, were invented scarcely a century ago, and mass-produced automobiles are newer still. Even firearms are of relatively recent origin if one considers the entire history of humankind, and the manufacture of contemporary cutting instruments would be impossible were it not for an accumulation of technological expertise beginning with the progress in metallurgy during the Iron Age.

As technology advances, it facilitates new forms of behavior. Just as we can be sure that everyday life in the future will be substantially different from life today, so too can we be certain that tomorrow's crimes will differ from those of today. In the future, personal crimes of violence and traditional property crimes will undoubtedly continue to occur, but advancing technology will create new and as yet unimaginable opportunities for criminals positioned to take advantage of it and of the power such technology will afford.

A frightening preview of such possibilities can be had in events surrounding the collapse of the Soviet Union a decade ago.[5] The resulting social disorganization in that part of the world made the acquisition of fissionable materials, stolen from former Soviet stockpiles, simple for even relatively small outlaw organizations. In what has since become a nightmare for authorities throughout the world, Middle Eastern terrorist groups are known to be making forceful efforts to acquire former Soviet nuclear weapons and the raw materials necessary to manufacture their own bombs. Some evidence also suggests that nuclear weapons parts may have already been sold to wealthy international drug cartels and organized criminal groups who may now be hoarding them to use as bargaining chips against possible government prosecution. Speaking before the House of Representatives Foreign Affairs Committee, CIA Director James Woolsey warned recently of the possibility "that Russian organized crime groups will be able to obtain and sell nuclear weapons or weapons-grade materials as a target of opportunity. We should not rule out the prospect," Woolsey said, "that organized crime could be used as an avenue for terrorists to acquire weapons of mass destruction."[6] In 1997 Russian Defense Minister Igor Rodionov issued a similar warning.[7] Rodionov said his country's cash-starved armed forces are in such a perilous state that, possibly, nuclear missiles and weapons systems may not be controllable in the future.

NUCLEAR SMUGGLING
A BOMB WAITING TO GO OFF

Reports of nuclear material being smuggled out of Russia are alarming U.S. officials and scientists, who say Iraq, Libya, and Iran could build atomic bombs if they laid their hands on it.

"There could be enough in circulation for big trouble," says David Albright, president of the Institute for Science and International Security Studies. "But we don't know if we're seeing the tip of the iceberg or the whole thing."

"This is a matter that is serious and ought to be treated with a great deal of urgency by all governments," says State Department Spokesman Mike McCurry. U.S. officials in Moscow officially conveyed the concern on Tuesday, he said.

Germany reports more than half a pound of 87% pure plutonium 239 arrived on a flight from Moscow last week. It was confiscated by police posing as buyers willing to pay $250 million. It was the fourth, and largest, seizure of nuclear material in Germany in the past four months—all of it attributed to Russian sources by German officials.

William Potter, of the Monterey, California, Institute of International Studies, says far more material may have been smuggled than has been caught.

This latest seizure and one back in May of "superpure" material are particularly troubling, he says, because they suggest high-level complicity.

Last week's shipment was in a sophisticated package, and on the same flight as a top Russian energy official, perhaps because smugglers thought they wouldn't be carefully checked traveling with him.

Just the fact they knew his schedule "may be an indication of involvement of senior parties in the nuclear industry," said Potter, who has testified before Congress on nuclear smuggling.

"This isn't a bunch of amateurs," agrees Albright.

Russia has tons of leftover plutonium, enough for 40,000 to 50,000 nuclear bombs, and an accounting system U.S officials say is so loose tons go unaccounted for. The other former Soviet states of Belarus, Ukraine, and Khazakstan also have stockpiles.

Because only a few pounds of plutonium are needed for a bomb, U.S. officials are pressing the Russians, who publicly deny any problem, to redouble security. To a rogue nation seeking atomic weapons, creating the nuclear core is the toughest part. Usually, it takes tens of thousands of people years of work to manufacture the highly radioactive ingredients.

But John Pike of the Federation of American Scientists says a few hundred of the right people, scientists, machinists, and engineers, could quickly construct a bomb if they had the raw materials.

"It ain't going to be six guys in a garage who are going to slap this together in the back of a van," he says.

But a nation like Iraq could do it he says.

The publicity surrounding the seizures may be an attempt to show smugglers that they are more likely to be caught in a "sting" than to get rich.

But with thousands of people who worked in Russia's nuclear program facing the lure of easy wealth, the task of perfectly protecting the stockpiles is formidable. And it must be near perfect.

"Even if we have a system that is 99.9% pure ... we're still talking about a few Hiroshimas between friends," Pike says.

Questions

1. Why has nuclear smuggling become a problem for international law enforcement agencies? What are the potential consequences of such smuggling?
2. What kind of policies might the United States implement which could reduce the threats represented by smuggled nuclear materials?

Source: Steve Komarow, "Nuclear Smuggling: A Bomb Waiting to Go Off," *USA Today,* August 17, 1994, p. 6A. Copyright 1994, *USA Today.* Reprinted with permission.

HIGH TECHNOLOGY AND CRIMINAL OPPORTUNITY

The twenty-first century has been described by some as representing the epitome of the postindustrial information age. Information, as many now recognize, is vital to the success of any endeavor, and certain forms of information hold nearly incalculable value. Patents on new products, the chemical composition of innovative and effective drugs, corporate marketing strategies, and the financial resources of competing corporations are all forms of information whose illegitimate access might bestow unfair advantages upon unscrupulous competitors. Imagine, for example, the financial wealth and market share which would accrue to the first pharmaceutical company to patent an effective AIDS cure. Imagine, as well, the potential profitability inherent in the information describing the chemical composition of that drug—especially to a competitor who might beat the legitimate originator of the substance to the patent desk, or who might use stolen information in a later bid to challenge patents already issued.

Such a scenario is not far fetched. In 1995, for example, the huge pharmaceutical manufacturer Merck[8] filed a request with the federal government and the regulatory agencies of twenty-seven other countries for permission to market its new medicine, Fosamax. Fosamax, a drug intended to reverse the effects of osteoporosis in postmenopausal women, was described as a corporate centerpiece in the plan to ensure Merck's leadership position among pharmaceutical manufacturers worldwide. The introduction of Fosamax to the pharmaceutical marketplace, along with ongoing clinical trials, was announced only after years of guarded negotiations and developmental research. The carefully crafted introduction was intended to ensure Merck's clear claim to ownership of the chemical compound in Fosamax, which should prove highly profitable for the company. Merck officials estimated the osteoporosis health care market in the United States alone at $10 billion annually.

High-tech criminals seeking illegitimate access to computerized information, and to the databases that contain it, have taken a number of routes. One is the path of direct access, by which office workers or corporate spies, planted as seemingly innocuous employees, violate positions of trust and use otherwise legitimate work-related entry to a company's computer resources to acquire wanted information. Such interlopers typically steal data during business hours under the guise of normal work routines.

Another path of illegal access is sometimes called "computer trespass" and involves remote access to targeted machines. Anyone equipped with a home computer and a modicum of knowledge about computer modems, telecommunications, and log-on procedures has easy access to numerous computer systems across the country. Many such systems have few, if any, security procedures in place to thwart would-be invaders. In one recent case, for example, a Silicon Valley software company learned that a fired software developer had been using her telephone to enter its computers.[9] By the time she was caught, the woman had copied several million dollars' worth of the company's programs. It was later learned that the stolen software had been slated for illicit transmission to collaborators in Taiwan. Had the scheme succeeded, many thousands of "pirated" copies of the software would have been distributed at great financial loss to the legitimate copyright owners. In a similar scenario, a Florida television news editor was recently arrested after moving to a new job with a different station for allegedly entering the computer of his former employer via telephone and copying researched stories.[10]

More exotic techniques used to steal data stored in computers extend to reading the electromagnetic radiation produced by such machines. Electromagnetic field (EMF) decoders, originally developed for military purposes, are capable of scanning radio frequency emanations generated by all types of computers. Key stroke activity, internal chip-processed computations, disk reads, and the like can all be detected and interpreted at a distance by such sophisticated devices under favorable conditions. Computers secured against such passively invasive practices are rarely found in the commercial marketplace. Those available to commercial organizations generally conform to a security standard developed by the U.S. military called **TEMPEST.**

Some criminal perpetrators intend simply to destroy or alter data without otherwise accessing or copying the information. Disgruntled employees, mischievous computer **hackers,** business competitors, and others may all have varied degrees of interest in destroying the records or computer capabilities of a company.

TEMPEST a standard developed by the U.S. government that requires that electromagnetic emanations from computers designated as "secure" be below levels that would allow radio receiving equipment to "read" the data being computed.

Hacker a person who views and uses computers as objects for exploration and exploitation.

Coincidence or espionage? Before the dissolution of the Soviet Union, Eastern bloc scientists succeeded in building a copy of the American space shuttle, pictured here. Experts suspected that the Soviet model would not have been possible without information stolen from United States research archives. Why is technology difficult to protect? *(left) Phil Sandlin-Canapress Photo Service/AP/Wide World Photos; (right) Terry Renna-Canapress Photo Service/AP/Wide World Photos.*

In what proved to be the first criminal prosecution of a person accused of creating a **computer virus,** Texas programmer Donald Gene Burleson was arrested in 1988 for allegedly infecting a former employer's computer with a program designed to destroy the information it contained. Since Burleson's arrest, many other would-be imitators have taken similar paths of revenge. According to Richard Baker, author of the respected *Computer Security Handbook,* "the greatest threat to your computers and data comes from inside your company, not outside. The person most likely to invade your computer," says Baker, "is not a gawky youngster in some other part of the country but an employee who is currently on your payroll."

Technically speaking, **computer crime,** which involves a wide variety of potential activities, is any violation of a federal or state computer crime statute. A recent estimate by the prestigious accounting firm Ernst & Young puts the cost of computer crime in the United States at between $3 billion and $5 billion a year.[12] Global estimates of lost revenues due to software piracy dwarf even that estimate. **Software piracy,** or the unauthorized and illegal copying of software programs, appears rampant. According to the Software Publishing Association (SPA), global losses from software piracy totaled $11.2 billion in 1996.[13] The study estimates that, of the 523 million new business software applications used globally during 1996, 225 million units—nearly one in every two—were pirated. According to SPA, 46 percent of all software in use in the world has been copied illegally. Some countries have especially

Virus (computer) a set of computer instructions that propagates copies or versions of itself into computer programs or data when it is executed.[11]

Computer crime any violation of a federal or state computer crime statute.

Software piracy the unauthorized and illegal copying of software programs.

high rates of illegal use. Of all the computer software in use in Vietnam, for example, it is estimated that 99 percent has been illegally copied. On a dollar basis most piracy occurs in Asia and Pacific-rim countries ($4 billion), while Europe and North America each account for approximately $3.5 billion worth of revenue losses to software manufacturers.

According to some experts, "that may be just the beginning." As one technological visionary observes, "Our society is about to feel the impact of the first generation of children who have grown up using computers. The increasing sophistication of hackers suggests that computer crime will soon soar, as members of this new generation are tempted to commit more serious offenses."[14] Table 12.1 lists five major categories of computer crime, with examples of each.

TABLE 12.1
CATEGORIES OF COMPUTER CRIME

Internal computer crimes
Trojan horses
Logic bombs
Trap doors
Viruses

Telecommunications crimes
Phone phreaking
Hacking
Illegal Web sites
Misuse of telephone systems

Computer manipulation crimes
Embezzlements
Frauds

Support of criminal enterprises
Databases to support drug distributions
Databases to support loan sharking
Databases to support illegal gambling
Databases to keep records of illegal client transactions
Money laundering

Hardware/software thefts
Software piracy
Thefts of computers
Thefts of microprocessor chips
Thefts of trade secrets

Source: Adapted from Catherine H. Conly and J. Thomas McEwen, "Computer Crime," *NIJ Reports,* January/February, 1990, p. 3.

Thou shalt not steal thy neighbor's data.
—*INTERLOCK® SECURITY DEVICES ADVERTISEMENT*

While the theft or damage of information represents one area of illegitimate criminal activity, the use of technology in direct furtherance of criminal enterprise constitutes another. Illegal activity based on advanced technologies is as varied as are the technologies themselves. Nuclear blackmail may represent the extreme technologically based criminal threat, whereas telephone fraud and phone "phreaking" are examples of low-end crimes that depend on modern technology for their commission. Some authors prefer the term *cybercrime* to distinguish crimes that involve the use of computers or the manipulation of digital data from other technologically sophisticated crimes.

Phone phreaks are a category of cybercriminals who use special dial-up access codes and other restricted technical information to avoid long-distance charges. Some are able to place calls from pay phones, while others fool telephone equipment into billing other callers. As a top telecommunications security expert explains it, "many organizations discover they have been victims of telephone fraud only after their telephone bill arrives in a carton instead of an envelope."[15]

As some companies have been surprised to learn, the responsibility for payment of stolen telephone time may rest with them. A year ago, for example, a U.S. district court ordered Jiffy Lube International, Inc., to pay AT&T $55,727 for long-distance calls made by computer hackers who had stolen the company's access codes. Judge Frank Kaufman said the law "squarely places responsibility upon a customer, such as Jiffy Lube, for all calls whether or not authorized. . . ."[16] In effect, Judge Kaufman sent a message to corporations nationwide that they can be held responsible for ensuring the security of their own telephone services.

A new form of phone phreaking emerged only a year or two ago. It involves the electronic theft of cellular telephone numbers and access codes. Thieves armed with simple mail-order scanners and low-end computers can "literally grab a caller's phone number and identification number out of the air."[17] Say experts, "Those numbers are [then] used to program computer chips, which are placed inside other cellular phones—or 'clones'—so the long-distance calls appear on the victim's bill."[18] Such high-profile figures as New York Mayor Rudolph Giuliani and his police commissioner have been among recent victims of cellular phone piracy.

Other types of crime may be perpetrated using the telephone. The federal Violent Crime Control and Law Enforcement Act of 1994, for example, made it illegal to use interstate telephone lines in furtherance of telemarketing fraud, and also expanded federal jurisdiction to cover cases of insurance fraud and frauds committed against the elderly even when such crimes do not involve use of the mail or telephone.

TECHNOLOGY AND CRIMINAL MISCHIEF

Not all computer crime is committed for financial gain. Some types of computer crime, including the creation and transmission of destructive computer viruses, "worms," and other malicious forms of programming code, might better be classified as criminal mischief. Perhaps not surprisingly, these types of activities are

Cybercrime crime committed with the use of computers, or via the manipulation of digital forms of data. Another term for computer crime.

Phone phreak a person who uses switched, dialed-access telephone services as objects for exploration and exploitation.

typically associated with young technologically sophisticated male miscreants, seeking a kind of clandestine recognition from their computer-literate peers. Computer crimes committed by youthful and idealistic offenders may represent a new form of juvenile delinquency—one aimed at expressing dissatisfaction with the status quo. As one security expert said, "kids in the '90s will be like kids in the '60s—they are going to care about social issues, and that caring is going to rub off onto the computer business. A lot of establishment computers are going to get trashed, as kids find a cause and express their concern with non-violent electronic protest."[19]

Viruses have already shown signs of becoming effective terroristlike tools in the hands of young, disaffected technonerds intent on attacking or destroying existing social institutions. As previously defined, a computer virus is simply a computer program that is designed to secretly invade computer systems and to modify either the way in which they operate or alter the information they store. Other types of destructive programs are logic bombs, worms, and Trojan horse routines. Distinctions between such programs are based largely either on the way in which they infect targeted machines or on the way in which they behave once they have managed to find their way into a computer. Table 12.2 lists a few of the better-known computer viruses.

Viruses may spread from one machine to another via modem (when files are downloaded), through networks or direct links (such as that provided by popular programs such as LapLink Pro or the Windows™ "Direct Connection" option), and through the exchange of floppy disks, CD-ROM discs, or magnetic backup media. Most viruses hide inside of executable computer software, or in the so-called boot

TABLE 12.2

COMPUTER VIRUSES

Hundreds of computer viruses have been identified. Viruses come in many varieties, and are often given interesting names. Following were the most frequently occurring viruses affecting personal computers in mid-1997.

Monkey	Anticoms	Wazzu
Concept	NYB	Form
Antiexe	Anticmos	Stealth-C
MDMA	Junkie	One-Half
SAT-BUG	Ripper	

Other common viruses include:

Anthrax	Disk Killer	Jerusalem
Armageddon	Enigma	Kamikaze
Bandit	Fu Manchu	Friday 13th
Lucifer	Michaelangelo	Black Monday
Brain	Gotcha	Stealth
Chaos	Stoned	Holocaust
Ping Pong-B	Dark Avenger	Invader

Source: Steve Alexander, "Viruses," *Computerworld,* June 2, 1997, p. 88.

sectors of floppy or hard disks. Recently, however, rogue codes known as Macro viruses have been secreted into text documents. The most famous of these, the Concept virus, affects users of Microsoft's Word software. Similarly, HTML (hypertext markup language) files, which form the backbone of the World Wide Web, may be infected with viruses lurking inside of Java script or Macromedia Shockwave generated code. Some users also worry that "cookies," or small programs sent to users' machines by servers on the Web, may spread viruses.

Perhaps the most insidious forms of destructive programming making the rounds of the computer world today are polymorphic viruses. A polymorphic virus is one that uses advanced encryption techniques to assemble varied (yet entirely operational) clones of itself. Hence, polymorphic viruses have the ability to alter themselves once they have infected a computer. This strategy is effective in circumventing most security devices that depend on scanning techniques to recognize viral signatures. Simply put, when viruses change they can no longer be recognized. In typical leapfrog fashion, when crime-fighting techniques are overtaken and surpassed by new technologies favoring law breakers and then later regain ascendancy, polymorphic viruses have—over the last few years—largely rendered signature-based antivirus scanning technologies obsolete. Unfortunately, although many hardware devices and software products now on the market offer some degree of virus protection to individual and commercial users, new viruses are constantly being created which may soon have the ability to circumvent all security procedures now in place. The only fully effective technique for avoiding viral contamination is the complete and total isolation of computer equipment—a strategy as unlikely to be maintained as it is to be implemented.

COMPUTER CRIME AND THE LAW

In the early years of computer-based information systems, states often tried to prosecute unauthorized computer access under preexisting property crime statutes, including burglary and larceny laws. Unfortunately, because the actual carrying off of a computer is quite different from simply making a copy of some of the information it contains or altering such information, juries frequently could not understand the applicability of such laws to high-tech crimes, and offenders were often exonerated. As a result, all states and the federal government developed computer crime statutes specifically applicable to invasive activities aimed at illegally accessing stored information. Federal statutes of relevance to crimes committed with or against computer equipment and software include (1) the Communications Decency Act (CDA), which is Title 5 of the Telecommunications Act of 1996,[20] (2) the Computer Fraud and Abuse Act of 1984 and its amendments—especially Section 290001 of Title 29 of the Violent Crime Control and Law Enforcement Act of 1994 that is known as the Computer Abuse Amendments Act of 1994, (3) the Electronic Communications Privacy Act of 1986, (4) the National Stolen Property Act, (5) the Federally Protected Property Act, and (6) the Federal Wiretap Act of 1968.

Federal laws protect mostly equipment defined as **federal interest computers,** which includes machines owned by the federal government or a financial institution, or those that are accessed across state lines without prior authorization. The

Federal interest computers those that are the property of the federal government, that belong to financial institutions, or are accessed across state lines without authorization.

U.S. Criminal Code, Title 18, Section 1030(a), defines as criminal the intentional unauthorized access to a computer used exclusively by the federal government or any other computer used by the government when such conduct affects the government's use. The same statute also defines as criminal the intentional and unauthorized access to two or more computers in different states and conduct that alters or destroys information and causes loss to one or more parties in excess of $1,000.[21] Punishment specified under federal law is a maximum sentence of five years, and a fine of up to $250,000 upon conviction. The Computer Abuse Amendments Act of 1994, however, adds the provision that "[a]ny person who suffers damage or loss by reason of a violation of [this] section . . . may maintain a civil action against the violator to obtain compensatory damages and injunctive relief or other equitable relief." The 1994 provision is intended to support civil actions in federal court against computer criminals by those suffering monetary losses as a result of computer crimes.

In 1996 President Clinton signed the **Communications Decency Act** (CDA) into law. The CDA, which is Title 5 of the Telecommunications Act of 1996,[22] sought to protect minors from harmful material on the Internet. A portion of the CDA criminalized the knowing transmission of obscene or indecent messages to any recipient under 18 years of age. Another section prohibited the knowing, sending, or displaying to a person under 18 any message "that, in context, depicts or describes, in terms patently offensive as measured by contemporary community standards, sexual or excretory activities or organs." The law provided acceptable defenses for those who took "good faith . . . effective . . . actions" to restrict access by minors to prohibited communications, and to those who restricted such access by requiring certain designated forms of age proof, such as a verified credit card or an adult identification number.

Shortly after the law was passed, however, the ACLU and a number of other plaintiffs filed suit against the federal government, challenging the constitutionality of the law's two provisions relating to the transmission of obscene materials to minors. In 1996 a three-judge federal district court entered a preliminary injunction against enforcement of both challenged provisions, ruling that they contravened First Amendment guarantees of free speech. The government then appealed to U.S. Supreme Court. The Court's 1997 decision, *Reno* v. *ACLU*,[23] upheld the lower court's ruling, and found that the CDA's "indecent transmission" and "patently offensive display" provisions abridge "the freedom of speech" protected by the First Amendment. Justice John Paul Stevens wrote for the majority: "It is true that we have repeatedly recognized the governmental interest in protecting children from harmful materials. But that interest does not justify an unnecessarily broad suppression of speech addressed to adults."

CDA supporters have worked to draft a new version of the law that can pass constitutional muster. Many doubt, however, that they can succeed, acknowledging that the Court has placed the Internet in the same category as newspapers and other print media, where almost no regulation is permitted.

The computer crime laws of individual states are not modeled after federal legislation. As a result they contain great variation. Texas law, for example, distinguishes between only two areas of illegal use of a computer: "harmful access" and "breach of computer security." A *breach of security* occurs when an individual simply uses a computer or gains unauthorized "access to data stored or maintained by a computer without the effective consent of the owner or licensee of the data [when] the actor knows that there exists a computer security system intended to prevent him from gaining access" to the computer or the data it contains. *Harmful access* is defined under Texas law as unauthorized computer use (without the consent of the owner) when "the actor knows that there exists a computer security system intended to prevent him from making that use of the computer." Harmful access only occurs, however, when, in the words of the Texas statute, the offender

1. damages, alters, or destroys a computer, computer program or software, computer system, data, or computer network.
2. causes a computer to interrupt or impair a government operation, public communication, public transportation, or public service providing water or gas.
3. uses a computer to tamper with government, medical, or educational records, or receive or use records that were not intended for public dissemination, or gain an advantage over business competitors.
4. obtains information from or introduces false information into a computer system to damage or enhance the data or credit records of a person.
5. causes a computer to remove, alter, erase, or copy a negotiable instrument; inserts or introduces a computer virus into a computer program.

Under Texas law, the lack of a well-publicized security system becomes an open invitation for anyone seeking to invade the computer systems of others—for whatever purpose. If a theft of data takes place, no crime has occurred unless a security system was in place and efforts to secure the system were visible to the perpetrator. According to state law in Texas, however, "a person commits an offense if the person intentionally or knowingly gives a password, identifying code, personal identification number, debit card number, bank account number, or other confidential information about a computer security system to another person without the effective consent of the person employing the computer security system to restrict the use of a computer or to restrict access to data stored or maintained by a computer."

In contrast to Texas, the state of Virginia specifically defines computer crime according to the following categories: "theft of computer services, computer invasion of privacy, computer trespass, computer fraud, [and] personal trespass by computer" (via which physical injury accrues to someone by virtue of unauthorized access to a computer, as may happen in the case of disruption of utility services). The laws of two other states, Colorado and Wisconsin, are shown in separate boxes in this chapter. The Colorado statute, as can be easily seen, is quite succinct, whereas Wisconsin's is quite detailed.

Ambiguities in existing computer-crime laws, complicated by rapid changes in technology, can make it difficult even to tell when a crime has occurred. In 1995, for example, University of Michigan student Jacob Alkhabaz (A.K.A. Jake A. Baker), 20, became the first person ever indicted for writing something on the Internet when he was arrested by the FBI and charged with five counts of interstate transmission of threats.[24] Alkhabaz had posted a series of stories on the Internet about his fantasy of torturing, raping, and murdering a female classmate. One of his messages contained the phrase, "Just thinking about it anymore doesn't do the trick. I need to do it." Another note read: "Torture is foreplay, rape is romance, snuff (killing) is climax."[25]

Computer-related crime
any illegal act for which
knowledge of computer
technology is involved for
its investigation,
perpetration, or
prosecution.

Computer abuse any
incident without color of
right associated with
computer technology in
which a victim suffered or
could have suffered loss,
and/or a perpetrator by
intention made or could
have made gain.

Although he might have been punished by a sentence of up to five years in prison, Detroit U.S. District Judge Avern Cohn threw out the charges after Alkhabaz spent twenty-nine days in jail.[26] Cohn ruled that Alkhabaz's violent-sounding Internet writings were protected under the free speech clause of the U.S. Constitution. Notably, Alkhabaz had been charged with "communicating threats" rather than "computer crime" because his activities were not specifically covered under federal computer crime laws. Had they been, a different verdict might have resulted.

Such cases as that of "Jake Baker" illustrate how certain, as of yet unimaginable, future illegitimate activities employing computer equipment may not be adequately covered by existing law. On the other hand, some crimes committed with the use of a computer may be more appropriately prosecuted under "traditional" laws. For that reason some experts distinguish among computer crime (defined earlier), computer-related crime, and computer abuse. **Computer-related crime** is "any illegal act for which knowledge of computer technology is involved for its investigation, perpetration, or prosecution," whereas **computer abuse** is said to be "any incident without color of right associated with computer technology in which a victim suffered or could have suffered loss and/or a perpetrator by intention made or could have made gain."[27]

WHAT IS A COMPUTER CRIME?

The Wisconsin Computer Crime Law
A considerable difference exists between the physical theft of computer equipment and the theft through copying of information stored in computers. The Wisconsin state computer crime statute, which makes a good attempt at distinguishing between these two types of offenses, is excerpted here. The statute is also notable for the fact that it recognizes a wide range of activities as possible forms of computer crime.

State of Wisconsin
Criminal Statutes
Chapter 293, Laws of 1981
943.70 Computer crimes:

(2) Offenses Against Computer Data and Programs.

(a) Whoever willfully, knowingly and without authorization does any of the following may be penalized as provided in paragraph (b):

1. Modifies data, computer programs or supporting documentation.
2. Destroys data, computer programs or supporting documentation.
3. Accesses data, computer programs or supporting documentation.
4. Takes possession of data, computer programs or supporting documentation.

  5. Copies data, computer programs or supporting documentation.
  6. Discloses restricted access codes or other restricted access information to unauthorized person.

(b) Whoever violates this subsection is guilty of:

  1. A Class A misdemeanor unless subd. 2, 3 or 4 applies.
  2. A Class E felony if the offense is committed to defraud or to obtain property.
  3. A Class D felony if the damage is greater than $2,500 or if it causes an interruption or impairment of governmental operations or public communication, of transportation or of a supply of water, gas or other public service.
  4. A Class C felony if the offense creates a situation of unreasonable risk and high probability of death or great bodily harm to another.

(3) Offenses Against Computers, Computer Equipment or Supplies.

(a) Whoever willingly, knowingly and without authorization does any of the following may be penalized as provided in paragraph (b):

  1. Modifies computer equipment or supplies that are used or intended to be used in a computer, computer system or computer network.
  2. Destroys, uses, takes or damages a computer, computer system, computer, network or equipment or supplies used or intended to be used in a computer, computer system, or computer network.

(b) Whoever violates this subsection is guilty of:

  1. A Class A misdemeanor unless sub. 2, 3 or 4 applies.
  2. A Class E felony if the offense is committed to defraud or obtain property.
  3. A Class D felony if the damage to the computer, computer system, computer network, equipment or supplies is greater than $2,500.
  4. A Class C felony if the offense creates a situation of unreasonable risk and high probability of death or great bodily harm to another.

Penalties for Infractions

939.50(3) Penalties for felonies are as follows:

  (a) For a Class A felony, life imprisonment.
  (b) For a Class B felony, imprisonment not to exceed 20 years.
  (c) For a Class C felony, a fine not to exceed $10,000 or imprisonment not to exceed 10 years, or both.
  (d) For a Class D felony, a fine not to exceed $10,000 or imprisonment not to exceed 5 years, or both.
  (e) For a Class E felony, a fine not to exceed $10,000 or imprisonment not to exceed 2 years, or both.

939.51(3) Penalties for misdemeanors are as follows:

  (a) For a Class A misdemeanor, a fine not to exceed $10,000 or imprisonment not to exceed 9 months, or both.

(b) For a Class B misdemeanor, a fine not to exceed $1,000 or imprisonment not to exceed 90 days, or both.

(c) For a Class C misdemeanor, a fine not to exceed $500 or imprisonment not to exceed 30 days, or both.

COLORADO REVISED STATUTES

TITLE 18. Criminal Code
ARTICLE 5.5. Computer Crime
C.R.S. 18-5.5-102 (1990)
18-5.5-102. Computer crime

(1) Any person who knowingly uses any computer, computer system, computer network, or any part thereof for the purpose of devising or executing any scheme or artifice to defraud; obtaining money, property, or services by means of false or fraudulent pretenses, representations, or promises; using the property or services of another without authorization; or committing theft commits computer crime.

(2) Any person who knowingly and without authorization uses, alters, damages, or destroys any computer, computer system, or computer network described in section 18-5.5-101 or any computer software, program, documentation, or data contained in such computer, computer system, or computer network commits computer crime.

❖ A PROFILE OF COMPUTER CRIMINALS

In 1997 FBI agents arrested Adam Quinn Pletcher, 21, and charged him with trying to extort $5.25 million from Microsoft founder and chairman Bill Gates. Pletcher,[28] a loner from Illinois who spent hours in front of his computer, allegedly sent several letters to Gates demanding the money and threatening to kill him or his wife, Melinda, if Gates did not respond to an America Online service known as "NetGirl." The service, an online dating forum, was to serve as a secure medium for the exchange of messages between Gates and the extortionist. FBI agents nabbed Pletcher after he sent a disk to Gates which held erased files containing the names of Pletcher's parents. Some months earlier Pletcher had made headlines in Chicago when he was accused of running scams on his Internet Web page, including the sale of fake driver's licenses, telling people he could get them cars at bargain prices then pocketing their money, running an illegal raffle that solicited $10 chances to win an expensive automobile, and offering "free" pagers that cost more than $50 in service charges. By all accounts Pletcher was a hacker—a technologically sophisticated loner.

Robert T. Morris, Jr., inventor of the infamous "internet worm," leaving a New York federal court.
How do computer crimes impact society? *Michael J. Okoniawski/AP/Wide World Photos.*

It is from hacker subculture that computer criminals tend to come. Hackers and
hacker identities are a product of **cyberspace,** that quasi-etheric realm where computer technology and human psychology meet. Cyberspace exists only within electronic networks, and is the place where computers and human beings interact with
one another. For many hackers, cyberspace provides the opportunity for impersonal interpersonal contact, technological challenges, and game playing. Fantasy
role-playing games are well developed within cyberspace and may engross many
"wave riders," who appear to prefer what in technological parlance is called "virtual
reality" to the external physical and social worlds that surround them. As one writer
states, "cyberspace is hacker heaven."[29]

Literature that glorifies cyberspace and the people who inhabit it is called cyberpunk. An understanding of cyberpunk literature is crucial for those wanting to
gain an appreciation for how hackers think. According to Paul Saffo of the Institute
for the Future in Menlo Park, California, "anyone trying to make sense of computing in the 1990s should add some cyberpunk books to their reading lists."[30] "Cyberpunk," says Saffo, "may become the counterculture movement" of the future. He
adds that "the cyberpunk trend is likely to be matched by an increase in the number of cyber-outlaws penetrating networks for criminal ends." Young, idealistic, and
immature, hackers of this genre typically take on pseudonyms by which they can be
identified by other hackers, but which also provide at least the illusion of
anonymity. Names such as Phiber Optik, Acid Phreak, Knight Lightning, Time
Lord, Nightcrawler, and Dark Angel are only a few of the many pseudonyms that
are either now in use or that have been used by hackers in recent years. A psychological and social profile of today's hackers is provided in a box in this chapter.

Some of the most infamous computer hackers of recent years, those comprising
the Atlanta-based "Legion of Doom," fit the hacker profile well. A few years ago,
three Legion members were sentenced to prison terms of fourteen to twenty-one

months and ordered to pay $233,000 each in restitution to BellSouth Corporation for breaking into its computer systems and stealing confidential data. Following expiration of their jail time, some Legion members found themselves sought after by high-tech employers seeking to exploit their skills in the development of proprietary computer security systems. Other "legionnaires" formed a company called Comsec Data Security to help provide private business with the expertise necessary to fend off electronic intrusions.

THEORY VERSUS REALITY
The Computer Hacker

A PSYCHOLOGICAL AND SOCIAL PROFILE

Computer hackers generally share the following social and personal characteristics.

1. Young: often 14 to 19 years of age.
2. Intelligent: IQ probably over 120, with the ability to articulate well.
3. "Nerdy": socializes poorly with peers, but may have close friends among like-minded fellows.
4. "WASP"-like: likely to be white, Protestant, and from a middle- or upper-middle-class background.
5. Fond of gadgets, especially computer-related hardware.
6. Academic performer: likely to perform well on individual academic assignments, such as tests and term papers. Unlikely to perform well on group assignments.
7. Self-perceived hero:

   Sees self as empowering humankind via an abstract victory over the "machine."

   Sees self as assisting humanity via participation in the fight against dehumanizing organizations (i.e., may seek to "liberate" information in the belief that information should be freely shared by all).

8. Counter-culture participant: has likely read, or is familiar with, the following books:

   William Gibson's *Neuromancer*
   John Brunner's *Shockwave Rider*
   William Gibson's *Count Zero*
   William Gibson's *Mona Lisa Overdrive*
   Clifford Stoll's *The Cuckoo's Egg*
   Melissa Scott's *Trouble and Her Friends*

9. Self-descriptions include feelings of boredom and apathy.
10. Favorite activities include computer games and/or other games emphasizing a fantasy world (i.e., Dungeons and Dragons).
11. Membership in a thrill-seeking subcultural group of computer hackers, usually taking on the name of a fantasy world character. Communicates to various other members of subculture via a computer bulletin board or via direct computer linkages.
12. Feelings experienced when accessing a secure computer system are often referred to in terms of drug-taking and sexual activity ("getting high," "orgasmic," "the big thrill," etc.).

Source: Adapted with permission from Robert W. Taylor, "Computer Crime," in C. R. Swanson, N. C. Chamelin, and L. Territo, *Criminal Investigation* (New York: Random House, 1991).

THE HISTORY AND NATURE OF HACKING

Some authors[31] have suggested that computer hacking began with creation of the interstate phone system and direct distance dialing (DDD) implemented by AT&T in the late 1950s. Early switching devices used audible tones that were easily duplicated by electronics hobbyists, and "blue boxes" capable of emulating such tones quickly entered the illicit marketplace.

Although phone phreaking has been practiced for more than forty years, a form of illegal telephone access that has recently come to the fore is voice-mail hacking. Private voice-mailboxes used for storing verbal messages have become the targets of corporate raiders and young vandals alike. In a recent case, two teenaged New York City brothers caused an estimated $2.4 million in lost business by gaining illegal access to the New Hampshire–based International Data Group's voice-mail system. The brothers were angry at not having received a poster promised with their magazine subscription. Security experts at the company first thought that the mailboxes were malfunctioning, but were alerted to the intentional disruptions by obscene outgoing messages planted by the brothers that greeted unsuspecting callers.[32]

Voice-mail fraud, another form of telephone crime, involves schemes in which mailbox access codes are shared in such a way that callers to 800 numbers can leave messages for one another in voice-mailboxes, thereby avoiding personal long-distance charges.[33] Companies that provide access to voice-mail systems through 800 numbers often learn of the need for access code security only after they find themselves the victims of such schemes.

Although the hacker lifestyle may have begun with phone phreaking, phone phreaks represent only one type of hacker. Hackers can be distinguished both on the basis of purpose and on their method of operation. Such categorization, however, is merely descriptive. Other more useful distinctions can be made on the basis of personality and lifestyle. Some experts[34] have suggested that hackers can be classified according to psychological characteristics into the following groups.

Mark Abene (left), known in hacker circles as Phiber Optik. Abene was sent to federal prison in 1994 for "computer intrusion" involving machines owned by Southwestern Bell Telephone Company. Computer hacker Kevin Mitnick (right), arrested in 1995 following the alleged theft of thousands of credit card numbers from NETCOM, an Internet service provider. According to some, "Mitnick represents our worst fears about what hackers can do." Just what *do* we fear from "hackers"? *(left) Robert Maass/SIPA Press; (right) Bob Jordan/AP/Wide World Photos.*

- *Pioneers:* individuals who are fascinated by the evolving technology of telecommunications and explore it without knowing exactly what they were going to find. Few hard-core criminals are found among this group.
- *Scamps:* hackers with a sense of fun. They intend no overt harm.
- *Explorers:* hackers who are motivated by their delight in the discoveries associated with breaking into new computer systems. The farther away such systems are geographically from the hacker's physical location, or the more secure such systems are, the more excitement associated with breaking into them.
- *Game players:* those who enjoy defeating software or system copy protection and who seek systems with games to play. Hacking itself becomes a game for this sort of hacker.
- *Vandals:* malicious hackers who deliberately cause damage with no apparent gain for themselves. The 414 Gang in Milwaukee, for example, which broke into the Sloan-Kettering Cancer Institute's computers and wiped out patients' records, provides an example of this type of hacker.
- *Addicts:* classic computer "nerds" who are literally addicted to hacking and to computer technology. They may also be addicted to illicit drugs, as some hacker bulletin board systems post information on drugs as well as on modems, passwords, and vulnerable systems.

Psychologist Percy Black contends the existence of an underlying theme in all cases of hacking. It is, he says, "the search for a feeling of power, possibly stemming from a deep-seated sense of powerlessness."[35] Hence, hacking may serve as com-

TECHNOLOGICAL ATTRACTION

The attraction computer hacking holds is well captured in this passage by
Melissa Scott in her cyberpunk adventure novel, *Trouble and Her Friends:*

> Trouble's on the net tonight, riding the high data like a cowboy, the plains of light stark
> around her. The data flows and writhes like grass in the virtual wind. IC(E)—Intru-
> sion Countermeasures (Electronic)—rises to either side, prohibiting the nodes, and
> the old urge returns . . . She can almost taste what lies behind that barrier, files and
> codes turned to candy-color shapes good enough to eat, and remembers the sweet-
> sour tang, the glorious greed of gorging on the good bits, sorting them in an eye-blink
> by taste and smell, faster and more sure than anyone else in the business . . ."

Source: Melissa Scott, *Trouble and Her Friends* (Garden City, N.J.: Science Fiction Book Club, 1994).

pensation for feelings of personal inferiority. By challenging the machine, and by
winning against machine culture, hackers go through a kind of rite of passage into
adulthood whereby they prove themselves capable of success.

Because most hackers are young adolescent males, however (see Figure 12.1), it
may be important to realize, as one expert on hackers says, "Their other favorite
risky business is the time-honored adolescent sport of trespassing. They insist on
going where they don't belong. But then teen-age boys have been proceeding uninvited since the dawn of human puberty. It seems hard-wired. The only innovation
is in the new form of the forbidden zone and the means of getting in it. . . ."[36]

*The ease with which electronic impulses can be manipulated, modified and erased is
hostile to a deliberate legal system.*

—ANNE W. BRANSCOMB[37]

Unfortunately, however, not all computer hackers are simply kids trying their
hand at beating technological challenges. As Garry M. Jenkins, assistant director of
the U.S. Secret Service, put it around the time of Operation Sun Devil (a joint two-
year undercover operation of Secret Service and local and state law enforcement
personnel, along with the private security operatives of AT&T, PacBell, BellSouth,
MCI, U.S. Sprint, NYNEX, and others), "Recently, we have witnessed an alarming
number of young people who, for a variety of sociological and psychological reasons, have become attached to their computers and are exploiting their potential in
a criminal manner. Often, a progression of criminal activity occurs that involves
telecommunications fraud (free long-distance phone calls), unauthorized access to
other computers (whether for profit, fascination, ego, or the intellectual challenge),
credit card fraud (cash advances and unauthorized purchases of goods), and then
moves on to other destructive activities like computer viruses. . . . Our experience

shows that many computer hacker suspects are no longer misguided teenagers mischievously playing games with their computers in their bedrooms. Some are now high-tech computer operators using computers to engage in unlawful conduct."[38]

Not all high-tech crimes are committed using computer technology. Many technologically sophisticated professional criminals operate today, some of whom use the diverse fruits of high technology in the furtherance of serious criminal activity. The theft of money is a major area of such activity. A couple of years ago, for example, technologically sophisticated thieves in New York City rolled a fake automatic teller machine (ATM) into the local Buckland Hills shopping mall. Although the machine did not dispense money, it did record the information contained on the magnetic strips of legitimate banking cards inserted by would-be customers. Personal information numbers (PINs) which the customers entered were also recorded. Armed with the necessary codes for legitimate accounts, the thieves then fabricated their own cards and used them to withdraw thousands of cash dollars from ATM machines across the city.

Although most people probably think of money as dollar bills, money today is really only information—information stored in a computer network, possibly located within the physical confines of a bank, but more likely existing as bits and bytes of data on service providers' machines. Typical financial customers give little thought to the fact that very little "real" money is held by their bank, brokerage house, mutual fund, or commodities dealer. Nor do they often consider the threats

FIGURE 12.1   Ages of computer-crime defendants at time of arrest. *Source:* National Council on Crime and Delinquency, as reported in Larry Coutourie, "The Computer Criminal: An Investigative Assessment," *The FBI Law Enforcement Bulletin,* September 1989, p. 21.

to their financial well-being by activities such as electronic theft or the sabotage of existing accounts. Unfortunately, however, the threat is very real. Computer criminals equipped with enough information, or able to ferret out the data they need, can quickly and easily send vast amounts of money anywhere in the world.

Although billions of dollars' worth of electronic transactions occur every day, no reliable estimates exist as to the losses suffered in such transactions due to the activities of technologically aware criminal perpetrators. Accurate estimates are lacking largely because sophisticated high-tech thieves are so effective at eluding apprehension, and even detection, that reliable loss figures are impossible to ascertain.

World Wide Web sites and a computer **bulletin board system (BBS)** can also facilitate criminal activity. In 1993, for example, U.S. Customs Service agents involved in Operation Longarm, carried out raids in eighteen different states on child pornographers and suspected pedophiles using names taken from a pedophile board. According to the Customs Service, the computerized transmission of illegal pornography among pedophiles is rapidly becoming more popular than smutty magazines.[39] Similarly, in 1994, Robert and Carleen Thomas were convicted of violating antiobscenity laws, on the grounds that their California online service (Amateur Action) was used to transmit obscene materials across state lines to Tennessee. On January 29, 1996, the U.S. Court of Appeals for the Sixth Circuit upheld the Thomas's conviction.

Other Web sites and bulletin boards may serve as illicit drug information exchange centers, and even a few may be run by organized criminal groups. As one expert explains, "some BBS's are being infiltrated by organized crime syndicates because of the potential for selling stolen computer components, blackmail, and narcotics distribution. Pirate [illegal boards, or those that make copyrighted software freely available] BBS operators have been known to threaten the lives of undercover investigators who have infiltrated their systems."[40]

> **Bulletin board system (BBS)** a computer accessible by telephone used like a bulletin board to leave messages and files for other users.

COMPUTER CRIME AS A FORM OF WHITE-COLLAR CRIME

White-collar crime is discussed in detail in Chapter 10. It is important here, however, to recognize that a number of contemporary analysts believe that computer crime may be nothing other than a new form of white-collar crime. Some suggest that it is white-collar crime *par excellence*—that is, the ultimate expression of white-collar crime.

In what may be the definitive work to date on high-tech professional crime, Donn B. Parker, author of the National Institute of Justice's *Computer Crime: Criminal Justice Research Manual*,[41] compares white-collar criminals with computer criminals. Both share what Parker calls "common criminal behavior-related issues," such as the following:

- Both types of acts are often committed through nonviolent means, although certain industrial, consumer, and environment-related crimes have life-threatening consequences.
- Access to computers or computer storage media, through employment-related knowledge or technical skills, is often needed.

- These acts generally involve information manipulations that either directly or indirectly create profits or losses.
- These crimes can be committed by an individual, several individuals working in collusion, and/or organizations, with the victims in the latter case ranging from individual clients, customers, or employees or other organizations.

According to Parker, computer crime and white-collar crime also share the following similarities.

- These crimes are often difficult to detect, with discovery quite often started by accident or by customer complaint rather than as the result of direct investigation.
- The general public views many of these acts as less serious than crimes involving physical violence.
- These crimes cost individuals, organizations, and society large amounts of resources.
- Prevention of these crimes requires a combination of legal, technical, managerial, security, and audit-monitoring controls.

▓ THE INFORMATION SUPERHIGHWAY AND DATA SECURITY

There is much talk today about an "information superhighway" that is about to be constructed with federal tax dollars, and which will soon put information of all kinds at the fingertips of anyone with a computer, a modem, and a little technical knowledge. Although funding details and the exact structure of the information superhighway remain a bit uncertain, the notion of such a data thoroughfare is closely intertwined with future expectations for our society and for the world as a whole. The historical development of the United States, which has long been a world leader in technology, was greatly facilitated by the development of railroads, river traffic, roads, and interstate highways. In short, transportation and the ability to move goods and people did much to build America and to ensure its place of prominence in the world.

As we enter the twenty-first century, America has begun to leave behind its industrial roots and is moving toward becoming a service-oriented information-rich society. John Naisbitt, author of *Megatrends*, explains it this way: "the transition from an industrial to an information society does not mean manufacturing will cease to exist or become unimportant. Did farming end with the industrial era? Ninety percent of us produced 100 percent of the food in the agricultural era; now 3 percent of us produce 100 percent. . . . In the information age, the focus of manufacturing will shift from the physical to more intellectual functions on which the physical depends."[42]

Although goods and materials will always need to be created, transported, and distributed, it is information that will form the lifeblood of the coming world order. Information, many pundits believe, will be the most valuable resource of the new age, comparable to—and even exceeding—the value which natural resources such as oil, gas, coal, and gold held over the past few centuries. As Naisbitt states, "information is an economic entity because it costs something to produce and because people are willing to pay for it."[43] Nations that are able to effectively manage valuable information, and can make it accessible to their citizens, will find enhanced productivity and greater wealth as a reward.

One vocal proponent of the information superhighway is Vice President Al Gore. Following his election to the U.S. Senate in 1984, Gore worked tirelessly to ensure that a high-speed fiber-optic computer network would be built throughout the nation, providing the backbone for future information development. Before becoming vice president, Gore was chairman of the Senate's Subcommittee on Science, Technology, and Space. Almost single-handedly he conceived of and authored the High Performance Computing Act of 1990, which laid the groundwork for federal government support of the data superhighway. During his fight to win the legislation's passage, Gore drew an effective contrast between modern telecommunications and the invention of the printing press centuries ago. "Gutenberg's invention," he said, "which so empowered Jefferson and his colleagues in their fight for democracy, seems to pale before the rise of electronic communications and innovations, from the telegraph to television, to the microprocessor and the emergence of a new computerized world—an information age."[44]

The highly touted information superhighway is a visionary way of moving data quickly, and a way of making information accessible to masses of citizens who can use it productively. Some suggest that the information superhighway already exists in the form of the Internet. The **Internet,** which is the world's largest computer network, had its beginnings a couple of decades ago with the linkage of military and scientific computer facilities already existing on the Arpnet and Milnet. Today the Internet consists of a vast resource of tens of thousands of computers around the world that are all linked together.

The Internet currently provides for electronic mail, mailing lists, news groups, and file transfer capability, and provides the backbone of the World Wide Web. Although Internet access had originally been restricted to commercial users, researchers, and university personnel, access to the Internet is routine for many people today. Commercial service providers such as America Online, CompuServe, and Prodigy offer Internet gateways, and a large number of direct Internet access providers furnish Internet access to anyone able to pay small monthly fees. Web browsers make it easy to search the tremendous amount of information on the Web and to interact with other Internet users.

Unfortunately, as the Internet has grown, it has been targeted by hackers and computer criminals, some of whom have introduced rogue computer programs into the network's machines. In 1988, for example, the infamous Internet "worm" written by Cornell University graduate student Robert T. Morris, Jr., circulated through computers connected to the Internet, effectively disabling many of them. Morris was later arrested and sentenced in 1990 to 400 hours of community service and three years probation. He was also fined $10,000. Since Morris's day, many other hackers have found loopholes in the software and hardware supporting the Internet.

In 1996, in response to the growing threat to the nation's information systems, President Clinton created the Commission on Critical Infrastructure Protection.[45] The commission was charged with assessing threats to the nation's computer

Internet the world's largest computer network.

networks, and to recommend policies to protect them. Security issues related to information systems which control the nation's telecommunications, electric power, oil and gas, banking and finance, transportation, water supply, emergency services, and government operations were studied by the commission, which issued its report in October of 1997. Among its recommendations, the commission proposed: (1) establishing an Information Analysis and Warning Center to collect information on computer security breaches in industry and government, (2) creating legislation to permit private companies to conduct special background checks when hiring computer experts for sensitive positions, (3) creating a White House office to coordinate the information security roles of government, including the departments of Commerce, Defense, Energy, Justice, Treasury, and Transportation, and (4) quadrupling research on cyberspace security to $1 billion by the year 2004.[46]

It's just a matter of time before we have a cyber Pearl Harbor.

—JAMIE GORELICK, DEPUTY U.S. ATTORNEY GENERAL[47]

▓ TECHNOLOGY IN THE FIGHT AGAINST CRIME

Technology is a double-edged sword. On the one hand, it arms evildoers with potent new weapons of crime commission, while on the other it provides police agencies and criminal justice personnel with powerful tools useful in the battle against crime. Law enforcement capabilities and criminally useful or evasive technologies commonly leapfrog one another. Consider, for example, the relatively simple case of traffic radar, which has gone through an elaborate technological evolution from early "always-on" units through trigger-operated radar devices to today's sophisticated laser speed-measuring apparatus. Each change was an attempt by enforcement agencies to keep a step ahead of increasingly sophisticated radar detection devices marketed to drivers everywhere. Although cutting-edge laser speed units are invisible to most radar detectors, laser radar detectors *do* exist. Their usefulness, however, is open to debate because they generally alert the speeding driver too late to respond. On the other hand, radar jamming devices are now increasingly used by people apparently intent on breaking speed limit laws, and laser jammers may soon be sold. Not to be outdone, suppliers to enforcement agencies have created radar-detector detectors which are used by authorities in states where radar detectors have been outlawed.[48]

Other than traffic radar, some of the most potent technology in law enforcement service today includes computer databases of known offenders, machine-based expert systems, cellular communications, electronic eavesdropping, DNA analysis, and less-than-lethal weapons. Recent advances, for example, in transponder-based automated vehicle location (AVL) systems now use patrol car–based transmitters in tandem with orbiting satellites to pinpoint police vehicle locations to within fifty feet. Dispatchers making use of such information can better allocate resources available on a given shift and are able to substantially reduce police response times in crisis situations. Similarly, chip-based transponders are now being installed in private vehicles to deter thieves and to help trace stolen automobiles.

Computer-aided dispatch (CAD) systems, representing yet another area of advanced crime-fighting technology, are becoming increasingly sophisticated. In ju-

Less-than-lethal weapons are undergoing review by law enforcement agencies nationwide. Here a test dummy is encased in incapacitating polyester slime. When might such weapons be used? *Sandia National Laboratories.*

risdictions where CAD systems function, police dispatchers are prompted by computers for important information which allows them to distinguish one place from another (such as the location of a particular McDonald's restaurant) within a city. CAD computers can also quickly provide information about how often officers have been called to a given site and tell responding officers what they might expect to find based on past calls from that location. As one writer[49] enticingly states, "Imagine this response from a 911 call-taker: 'Yes, Ms. Smith, we are aware that beer-drinking youths at the corner of Hollywood and Vine have been a problem over the past six weeks, and in fact, we've responded seven times to requests to disperse them. As soon as one of our patrol cars frees up on a robbery call, I'll be sure that it goes over to disperse the group. And by the way, we are unaware of any serious crimes that can be attributed to these youths. But please feel free to call us immediately if you observe any criminal activities.'" The same software that facilitates such a response will routinely inform responding officers about police experience with the suspects, provide background checks as a matter of course, tell whether they are likely to find registered guns at the address, and relay information about outstanding warrants on anyone who lives there. It can also inform dispatchers when responding officers do not call back after a statistically determined period of time for that type of call—alerting them to potential threats to officer safety.

Other even more innovative crime-fighting technologies are on the horizon. The "Spiderman snare," for example, now being tested for its usefulness in incapacitating fleeing suspects, is a fine net sixteen feet in diameter. Compressed into a small shotgun-like shell, the net has small weights at its circumference and is designed to wrap itself around a target when fired. The snare's impact is harmless, and test subjects report being able to watch with open eyes as the net wraps around them. Similarly, a disco-like strobe light which quickly disorients human targets is on drawing boards. The special frequency light emitted by the strobe rapidly causes intense dizziness, leaving subjects unable to resist cuffing and arrest. Operators wear special glasses designed to counter the influence of the light. Finally, a form of electronic warfare is on the verge of being launched against speeders driving today's high-tech computer-equipped cars. Because high-speed chases pose a substantial danger to the public, scientists have developed an aimed electromagnetic pulsing device that can be used to temporarily disable a vehicle's electrical system, causing the engine to stall. The prototype is said to be safe enough to use on vehicles driven by pacemaker-equipped drivers.

As new technologies are developed, their potential usefulness in law enforcement activities is evaluated by the FBI, the National Institute of Justice (NIJ), and other agencies. NIJ's Technology Assessment Program (TAP) focuses on four areas of advancing technology: protective equipment, such as "bulletproof" vests and other body armor; forensic sciences, including the applicability of advances in DNA technology; transportation and weapons, such as electronic "stun guns" and other new less-than-lethal weapons; and communications and electronics, including computer security, electronic eavesdropping, and so on. Other groups, such as the National Computer Security Association (NCSA), the American Cryptography Association (ACA), and the American Society for Industrial Security (ASIS), bring more specialized high-tech expertise to the private security and public law enforcement professions.

DNA FINGERPRINTING

DNA fingerprinting or profiling the use of biological residue found at the scene of a crime for genetic comparisons in aiding the identification of criminal suspects.

DNA profiling or, as it is commonly called, **DNA fingerprinting,** received much attention during the widely publicized criminal and civil trials of former media superstar and gridiron great O. J. Simpson—whose trials occupied a large portion of the American media spotlight from 1995 until 1997. In those cases, DNA evidence appeared to show that Simpson, who was accused of the double murder of Nicole Brown Simpson and Ronald Goldman, was present at the crime scene at the time of the killings. In Simpson's criminal trial, defense attorneys chose to not attack the credibility of DNA testing technology, claiming instead that the blood evidence was planted by "crooked cops" out to frame Simpson.

Although DNA evidence failed to provide a conviction in the Simpson criminal case, it apparently was more persuasive in his civil trial a year later. Experts point to the fact, however, that after years of debate over population variability, the genetic patterns of isolated ethnic groups and other arcane issues, lawyers and scientists finally agree that DNA testing has the power to definitively match blood, semen, or other biological residue recovered at a crime scene to a given individual.[50] As a consequence, Simpson's defense attorneys in both trials did not waste time arguing that the blood in question belonged to someone other than Simpson. They were forced to focus instead on the possibility of mishandling, laboratory contamination, or the planting of evidence.

Former football superstar O.J. Simpson. DNA evidence played a central role in Simpson's double-murder trial. What can DNA evidence tell investigators? *LAPD.*

A person's genetic code is contained in his or her DNA (deoxyribonucleic acid), whose composition is unique to each individual except in the case of identical twins. DNA samples can be taken from blood, hair, semen, saliva, or even small flakes of skin left at the scene of a crime. In cases of rape, for example, semen or pubic hairs left behind by the perpetrator and removed from the victim or gathered at the scene can provide the DNA evidence necessary for identifying a suspect. In cases of murder, victims sometimes fight with their attackers, retaining small bits of the killer's skin under their fingernails—thereby providing a tissue sample useful in DNA analysis.

After processing, DNA profiles appear like bar codes on X-ray images. A small difference in such codes can exonerate a suspect in the eyes of expert analysts—or provide nearly irrefutable evidence of guilt.

DNA evidence is long lasting, with even fossilized DNA now being used to reconstruct genetic maps of long-extinct plant and animal species. Although DNA analysis is theoretically possible using only a single cell, most reputable DNA laboratories require a considerably greater quantity of material to conduct an effective analysis. That, however, may soon change. Using a technique called polymerase chain-reaction technology, a Nobel Prize–winning technique, minute strands of DNA can be effectively amplified so that even the identity of a person taking a single puff from a cigarette can be accurately established. Although the cost and complexity of such enhancement are still prohibitive, technological advances are expected to bring the technique within the range of forensic analysts within a decade.

The National Research Council calls DNA profiling "a highly reliable forensic tool,"[51] while admitting that it is not infallible. Although obvious differences in scrutinized DNA samples can easily eliminate a suspect, testing provides less certainty with positive identification. Human error in conducting the tests is perhaps the greatest threat to reliable results. As of this writing, at least twenty states and the federal government generally accept DNA evidence in criminal trials. Other jurisdictions, including California, are less clear in their recognition of DNA test-ing, and trial judges in those states may off-handedly exclude the use of such evi-dence when experts disagree as to its validity.

In 1993 the U.S. Supreme Court, in the civil case of ***Daubert*** v. ***Merrell Dow Pharmaceuticals, Inc.,***[52] revised the criteria for the admissibility of scientific evi-dence by rejecting a previous admissibility standard established in the 1923 case of ***Frye*** v. ***United States.***[53] The *Daubert* Court ruled that the older *Frye* standard re-quiring "general acceptance" of a test or procedure by the relevant scientific com-munity "is not a necessary precondition to the admissibility of scientific evidence…" The baseline rule for the admissibility of scientific evidence, said the Court, is es-tablished by Rule 402 of the *Federal Rules of Evidence,* which was published after *Frye* and supersedes it. Rule 402 says that, in a trial, "[a]ll relevant evidence is admissi-ble, except as otherwise provided by the Constitution of the United States, by Act of Congress, by these Rules, or by other rules prescribed by the Supreme Court pur-suant to statutory authority." The Court went on to say that although "the *Frye* test was displaced by the Rules of Evidence [that] does not mean … that the Rules them-selves place no limits on the admissibility of purportedly scientific evidence. Nor is the trial judge disabled from screening such evidence. To the contrary, under the Rules the trial judge must ensure that any and all scientific testimony or evidence admitted is not only relevant, but reliable." The real test for the admissibility of sci-entific expert testimony, said the Court, is for the trial judge to decide "at the out-set . . . whether the expert is proposing to testify to (1) scientific knowledge that (2) will assist the trier of fact to understand or determine a fact in issue." The Court concluded that the task of the trial judge is one of "ensuring that an expert's testi-mony both rests on a reliable foundation and is relevant to the task at hand. Perti-nent evidence based on scientifically valid principles," said the Court, "will satisfy those demands."

The plaintiffs in *Daubert* did not argue the merits of DNA testing, but claimed, instead, that the drug Bendectin caused birth defects. Nonetheless, the **Daubert standard** eased the criteria for the introduction of scientific evidence at both civil and criminal trials—and effectively cleared the way for the use of DNA evidence in the courtroom.[54] Specifically, the *Daubert* Court found that the following factors may be used to determine whether any form of scientific evidence is reliable.

- whether it has been subject to testing
- whether it has been subject to peer review
- known or potential rates of error
- the existence of standards controlling application of the techniques involved

One observer, discussing the general quality of DNA identification methods, notes: "the challenges today are no longer technical; instead they lie in taking the technology and building a meaningful legal infrastructure around it."[55] In other words, it appears to be only a matter of time until DNA evidence will be accepted throughout jurisdictions nationwide (and, probably, worldwide). Once that occurs, it is likely that DNA databases, similar in purpose to now widely used fingerprint archives, will be established in individual states and at the national level. Today a number of states and the federal government (through the FBI laboratory) have begun building digitized forensic DNA databases. FBI crime laboratory director John W. Hicks notes, "We're doing about 2,500 profiles a year right now.... In a few years, it should be in the tens of thousands."[56] Although at this point there has been no coordination between the federally funded multibillion-dollar Human Genome Initiative and forensic DNA programs, future collaboration between the two could lead to truly explosive growth in the use of human DNA in criminal case processing.

In 1995 British police, operating under the aegis of a new nationwide crime bill, became the first national police force in the world to begin routine collection of DNA samples from anyone involved in a "recordable" offense (a serious crime).[57] As scientific techniques continue to be refined it appears likely that genetic profiling will become one of the most significant crime-fighting technologies of the twenty-first century. In the words of one forensics expert, "genetic profiling—the use of biotechnology to identify the unique characteristics of an individual's DNA—is about to become as prevalent as the Breathalyzer and more important than the fingerprint."[58]

In 1996 the National Institute of Justice released the most comprehensive report to date on the applicability of DNA testing to criminal case processing. The report, entitled *Convicted by Juries, Exonerated by Science*,[59] called DNA testing "the most important technological breakthrough of twentieth-century forensic science," and provided a detailed review of twenty-eight cases in which postconviction DNA evidence exonerated defendants who had been sentenced to lengthy prison terms. The twenty-eight cases were selected on the basis of a detailed examination of records which indicated that the convicted defendants might have actually been innocent. The men in the study had served, on average, seven years in prison, and most had been tried and sentenced prior to the widespread availability of reliable DNA testing.

The report concluded that "momentum is growing, spurred in part by the public's education from the Simpson trial, for DNA testing in criminal cases. Juries may begin to question cases where the prosecutor does not offer 'conclusive' DNA test results if the evidence is available for testing. More defense attorneys in court-appointed cases may file motions for DNA testing and request the State to pay for the tests ..."

COMPUTERS AS CRIME-FIGHTING TOOLS

The widespread use of computers and computer applications in a diversity of professions has been one of the most far-reaching social phenomena of recent years. Computers are now used to keep records of every imaginable sort, from point-of-sale contacts to inventory maintenance and production schedules. Even organized criminal groups have been known to use computers to record criminal transactions. Computers assist in the design of new technologies and aid in the assignment of resources to problem areas. Police departments, prisons, and courts now commonly employ computer software to schedule facilities and personnel; to keep track of defendants, witnesses, and cases; and to keep account of budgetary matters.

Computers also connect people. The world's largest computer network, the Internet, now contains a number of law–and law enforcement–oriented news groups and also provides access to United Nations and worldwide crime data through its link to the United Nations Criminal Justice Information Network. Other computer services, such as CompuServe and America Online, provide access to security information and to software useful in law enforcement administration. Specialized World Wide Web sites such as the Society of Police Futurists International's home page, the International Association of Chiefs of Police site, and the SEARCH Group's file server all link law enforcement professionals and criminologists throughout the country.

Other innovative computer technologies facilitate the work of enforcement agents. Among them are automated fingerprint identification systems or AFIS (often with interstate and even international links), computerized crime scene simulations and reenactments, expert systems, and online clearinghouses containing data on criminal activity and on offenders. AFIS, a technology developed some years ago by Hewlett-Packard and Cogent Systems, allows investigators to complete in a matter of minutes what would otherwise consume weeks or months of work manually matching a suspect's fingerprints against stored records. AFIS computers are able to compare and eliminate from consideration 1,200 fingerprints per second, leading to the identification of a suspect in a short time. New "Live-Scan" technology, developed jointly by IBM and Identix, allows for the easy inkless digitizing of fingerprints from live suspects. In like manner, the Bureau of Alcohol, Tobacco, and Firearms' (ATF) new Bulletproof software takes a 360-degree picture of a bullet's ballistic characteristics and then compares it with others stored in a database to isolate a small universe of potential matches.

Once crime-related information or profiles of criminal offenders have been generated they are typically stored in a database and often made accessible to law enforcement agencies at other sites. Some of today's most widely used online criminal information services are the FBI's National Crime Information Center (NCIC), the Violent Criminal Apprehension Program (VICAP), and METAPOL—an information-sharing network run by the Police Executive Research Forum (PERF). Other specialized database programs now track inner-city gang activity and gang membership, contain information on known sexual predators, and describe missing children.

One leader in the development of law enforcement services is the Criminal Justice Information Services Division (CJISD) of the FBI. CJISD was created in 1993 to provide state-of-the-art information services to the justice community and to assist in the future development of such services. One contemporary law enforcement–oriented software program, called COPS (for Criminal Offender Profiling System), allows for the desktop integration of digitized mug shots, videotaped images, computerized fingerprint data, and text-based information such as criminal records—all in one automated file folder.

PC radios provide another high-tech weapon in the war on crime. These devices—which are essentially combinations of laptop computers and police radios—were initially tested by the Baltimore, Maryland, police department. Mobile data terminals placed in police cars are proving useful in the apprehension of both traffic violators and other more serious offenders. Officers use PC radios to (1) obtain motor vehicle information, (2) get detailed information when answering a call, and (3) report incidents either by saving data on disk or by transmitting it to other locations, such as police headquarters. PC radios have also helped befuddle drug dealers who themselves routinely use police scanners to keep abreast of enforcement activities. The digitized transmissions of such devices consist of machine code that cannot be easily read by drug dealers or other criminals trying to outguess the police.

Forensic expert systems, representing yet another computerized law enforcement technology, deploy machine-based artificial intelligence to draw conclusions and make recommendations to investigators and others interested in solving problems related to crime and its commission. **Expert systems,** developed by professional "knowledge engineers" who work with "knowledge bases" and computer software called "inference engines," attempt to duplicate the decision-making processes used by skilled investigators in the analysis of evidence and in the recognition of patterns which such evidence might represent. One such system is currently being perfected by the FBI's National Center for the Analysis of Violent Crime (NCAVC). The NCAVC expert system attempts to profile serial killers by matching clues left at a crime scene with individual personality characteristics. While the NCAVC system is becoming increasingly sophisticated, it has not yet replaced human investigators. As one FBI developer puts it, "there is certainly no possibility that the system we are devising will ever replace skilled human profilers. Rather, the system will function as a profiler's assistant or consultant."[60]

Finally, a number of specialized computer software programs such as ImAger, which is produced by Face Software, Inc., and Compusketch, a product of Visatex Corporation, assist police artists in rendering composite images of suspects and missing victims.

> **Expert systems** computer hardware and software that attempt to duplicate the decision-making processes used by skilled investigators in the analysis of evidence and in the recognition of patterns which such evidence might represent.

◆ COMBATING COMPUTER CRIME

In 1982, sales of information security products to private companies and government agencies totaled $51 million. By 1992 expenditures exceeded $220 million, and in 1997 $425 million was spent to protect critical information.[61]

Gadgets, however, are not enough. Any effective program intended to secure a company or business operation against the threat of high-tech crime must be built on a realistic threat analysis. **Threat analysis,** sometimes called risk analysis, involves a complete and thorough assessment of the kinds of perils facing an organization. Some risks such as floods, tornadoes, hurricanes, and earthquakes arise from natural events and are often unpredictable. Others, including fire, electrical outages, and disruptions in public services, may be of human origin—but equally difficult to presage. Theft, employee sabotage, and terrorist attacks constitute yet another category of risk—those brought about by intentional human intervention. Responses to unpredictable threats can, nonetheless, be planned and strategies for dealing with almost any kind of risk can be implemented. Unless and until an organization adequately assesses the threats to its continuing operation, however, it will be unable to formulate a plan to effectively deal with such risks. Hence, threat analysis is a must for businesses and other organizations preparing to meet the many diverse challenges of today's world.

Once specific threats are identified, strategies tailored to dealing with them can be introduced. For example, one powerful tool useful in identifying instances of computer crime when they occur is the audit trail. Properly defined, an **audit trail**

> **Threat analysis** (or **risk analysis**) involves a complete and thorough assessment of the kinds of perils facing an organization.

> **Audit trail** a sequential record of computer system activities that enables auditors to reconstruct, review, and examine the sequence of states and activities surrounding each event in one or more related transactions from inception to output of final results back to inception.

is "a sequential record of system activities that enables auditors to reconstruct, review, and examine the sequence of states and activities surrounding each event in one or more related transactions from inception to output of final results back to inception."[62] In other words, audit trails, which (once implemented) are recorded in some form of computer memory, trace and record the activities of computer operators and facilitate the apprehension of computer criminals.

Unfortunately, although most large companies and financial institutions have fairly extensive computer security programs, few small business, schools, hospitals, and individuals have any real understanding of the need for security in the use of their computers. "What is surprising about computer crime," says computer security expert Kenneth Rosenblatt, "is how little is being done to deter it: industry will not beef up security, the police are not equipped to catch electronic thieves, and judges do not hand down the kind of sentences that will impress would-be computer criminals. New strategies are urgently needed."[63]

POLICE INVESTIGATION OF COMPUTER CRIME

Unfortunately, even with new laws for backup, few police departments are prepared with either the time or qualified personnel to effectively investigate crimes committed by computer criminals. When it comes to computer crime investigations, one technology expert concludes, "[p]olice departments are simply unsuited to the task."[64] Although specialized computer-crime units have been created in some jurisdictions, they are often poorly funded and seriously understaffed. The cities of Los Angeles, Philadelphia, and Baltimore now have field units, as do the Illinois State Police, the Tarrant County, Texas, District Attorney's Office, the Arizona State Attorney General's Office, and the Santa Clara County (California) District Attorney's Office.

Most state and local police departments, however, have no specialized computer crime units. Nor do they have personnel skilled in the investigation of such crimes. Most officers know little about tracing the activities of computer criminals, and some police investigators find it difficult to understand how a crime can actually have occurred when nothing at the scene appears to be missing or damaged. Horror stories of botched police investigations are plentiful and include tales of officers standing by while high-tech offenders perform seemingly innocuous activities that destroy evidence, of seized floppy disks allowed to bake in the sun on the dashboards of police vehicles, and of the loss of evidence stored on magnetic media due to exposure to police clipboards and evidence lockers containing magnets.

Police departments also sometimes intentionally avoid computer crime investigations because they may be complex and demanding. The amount of time and money spent on computer crime investigations, it is often felt, could better be spent elsewhere. It is not unusual for computer crime investigations to cross state lines and to involve a number of telecommunications companies and other services. Additionally, investigators who spend a lot of time on crimes involving computers tend to not be promoted as readily as their more glamorous counterparts in homicide and property crime divisions, and personnel who are truly skilled in computer applications are apt to take jobs with private industries where pay scales are far higher than in police work. As a consequence of these considerations and others, many police departments and the investigators who staff them frequently accord computer crime a low priority, focusing instead on highly visible offenses such as murder and rape, and seeing computer crime victims as too wealthy to be seriously impacted by the crimes they experience.

One expert summed up the situation this way: "Because computer crime is too much for traditional law enforcement to handle, the bulk of computer offenses go unpunished. Probably fewer than 250 cases have been prosecuted in the United States during the past decade. At this rate, prosecutions are too rare to deter computer crime. If an offender is convicted, the usual penalties are also not much of a deterrent."[65]

The situation is changing, however, thanks to federal intervention. A few years ago the FBI formed its National Computer Crime Squad (NCCS)[66] to investigate violations of the federal Computer Fraud and Abuse Act of 1984 (CFAA),[67] and other federal computer crime laws. The NCCS is charged with investigating computer crimes in the areas of (1) intrusions of public switched networks (telephone company networks), (2) major computer network intrusions, (3) network integrity violations, (4) privacy violations, (5) industrial espionage, (6) pirated computer software, and (7) other crimes when the computer is centrally involved in committing a criminal offense. The NCCS operates out of the FBI's Washington, D.C., metropolitan field office, and has national jurisdiction. It coordinates many of its activities with investigative agencies in foreign countries when U.S. interests are involved. The FBI is now in the process of creating individual computer crime investigation teams in each of its fifty-six field offices within the United States.

One of the first large-scale NCCS operations took place in 1997, when FBI agents raided the homes and offices of about a dozen computer bulletin board system (BBS) operators and webmasters suspected of pirating software in eight cities. The operation, code-named "Cyber Strike," resulted from NCCS monitoring of Internet Relay Chat (IRC) channels and file transfers over the Internet. Software vendors praised the FBI's action. "We're tremendously impacted by software piracy," said Kathy Tom, spokeswoman for Autodesk, Inc., makers of AutoCAD software— a computer-aided design tool used by engineers and architects. "For every one copy of AutoCAD that is sold, seven or eight are stolen," she said.[68]

DEALING WITH COMPUTER CRIMINALS

While any effective policy for dealing with computer and high-tech crime must recognize the issues associated with personal freedoms and individual rights in the information age, a second aspect of effective policy necessarily relates to crime control. How can high-tech criminals be deterred? If they succeed in committing criminal acts, how can they be reformed? Kenneth Rosenblatt,[69] who focused on computer crimes during his work as a California district attorney, suggests three sanctions that he feels would be especially effective in deterring high-tech offenders.

1. confiscating equipment used to commit a computer crime
2. limiting the offender's use of computers
3. restricting the offender's freedom to accept jobs involving computers

Such penalties, says Rosenblatt, could be supplemented by a few days or weeks in a county jail—with longer periods of incarceration applicable in serious cases. "In my experience," Rosenblatt adds, "one of the best ways to hurt computer offenders, especially young hackers, is to take away their toys."

▓ POLICY ISSUES

PERSONAL FREEDOMS IN THE INFORMATION AGE

The continued development of telecommunications resources has led not only to concerns about security and data integrity, but also to an expanding interest in privacy, free speech, and personal freedoms. While the Constitution guarantees each of us in its First and Fourth Amendments freedom of speech and security in our "persons, houses, papers, and effects, against unreasonable searches and seizures," it is understandably silent on the subject of electronic documents and on advanced forms of communication facilitated by technologies which did not exist at the time of the Constitutional Convention.

Within the context of contemporary society we are left to ask, "What is paper? What is speech?" Do electronic communications qualify for protection under the First Amendment, as does the spoken word? In an era when most houses are wired for telephone usage, and many support data links that extend well beyond voice capabilities, it becomes necessary to ask what constitutes one's "home" or one's "speech." What, exactly, is *speech*? Does electronic mail qualify as speech? Where does the concept of a "home" begin and end for purposes of constitutional guarantees? Do activities within the home that can be accessed from without (as when a computer BBS is run out of a home) fall under the same constitutional guarantees as a private conversation held within the physical confines of a house?

These and questions like them will be debated for years to come. In 1990, however, concerned individuals banded together to form the Electronic Frontier Foundation (EFF), a citizens' group funded by private contributions that set for itself the task of actively assisting in refining notions of privacy and legality as they relate to telecommunications and other computer-based media. In the foundation's own words: "The Electronic Frontier Foundation (EFF) was founded in July of 1990 to ensure that the principles embodied in the Constitution and the Bill of Rights are protected as new communications technologies emerge. From the beginning, EFF has worked to shape our nation's communications infrastructure and the policies that govern it in order to maintain and enhance First Amendment, privacy and other democratic values. We believe that our overriding public goal must be the creation of Electronic Democracy. . . ."[70] As Mitch Kapor, EFF cofounder and president of Lotus Development Corporation, explained, "It is becoming increasingly obvious that the rate of technology advancement in communications is far outpacing the establishment of appropriate cultural, legal and political frameworks to handle the issues that are arising. . . ."

The EFF, which also supports litigation in the public interest, has been an active supporter of the Palo Alto, California–based public advocacy group Computer Pro-

PRESS RELEASE ANNOUNCING THE FORMATION OF THE ELECTRONIC FRONTIER FOUNDATION

In 1990 the Electronic Frontier Foundation (EFF) came into being. What follows are excerpts from the original press release announcing formation of the EFF.

For Immediate Release

NEW FOUNDATION ESTABLISHED TO ENCOURAGE COMPUTER-BASED COMMUNICATIONS POLICIES

Washington, D.C., July 10, 1990—Mitchell D. Kapor, founder of Lotus Development Corporation and ON Technology, today announced that he, along with colleague John Perry Barlow, has established a foundation to address social and legal issues arising from the impact on society of the increasingly pervasive use of computers as a means of communication and information distribution. The Electronic Frontier Foundation (EFF) will support and engage in public education on current and future developments in computer-based and telecommunications media. In addition, it will support litigation in the public interest to preserve, protect and extend First Amendment rights within the realm of computing and telecommunications technology.

Initial funding for the Foundation comes from private contributions by Kapor and Steve Wozniak, co-founder of Apple Computer, Inc. The Foundation expects to actively raise contributions from a wide constituency.

Source: The Electronic Frontier Foundation.

---

fessionals for Social Responsibility (CPSR). CPSR maintains a "Computing and Civil Liberties Project" much in keeping with EFF's purpose. Initial EFF litigation focused on a request for full federal government disclosure of information regarding the seizure of Jackson Games computer equipment. Jackson Games, an Austin, Texas–based game manufacturer, was a target in the U.S. Secret Service's Operation Sun Devil. In a second action, the foundation sought amicus curiae (friend of the court) status in a federal case against Craig Neidorf, a 20-year-old University of Missouri student who had been editor of the electronic newsletter *Phrack World News*. EFF also supported challenges to the Communications Decency Act that resulted in the 1997 Supreme Court ruling in *Reno* v. *ACLU* (which found key provisions of the act unconstitutional).

⬥ WHAT THE FUTURE HOLDS

Data encryption the
process by which informa-
tion is encoded, making it
unreadable to all but its
intended recipients.

Exactly what the future holds no one knows. Of one thing we can be sure, however.
New technologies will continue to give rise to new forms of crime, and novel forms
of criminality will engender innovative enforcement efforts. Although it is impossible to discuss every possible answer to crimes which take advantage of high technology for their commission, data encryption can serve as an example of the types
of techniques which may find widespread use in the twenty-first century and beyond. **Data encryption** is the process by which information is encoded, making it
unreadable to all but its intended recipients.

Vice President Al Gore has described the potential held by data encryption
technologies in these words: "Encryption is a law and order issue since it can be used
by criminals to thwart wiretaps and avoid detection and prosecution. It also has
huge strategic value. Encryption technology and cryptoanalysis turned the tide in
the Pacific and elsewhere during World War II."[71]

Many forms of encryption are now in use. Most can be "broken" through the
use of supercomputers tasked with uncovering the codes upon which they are built.
A few years ago, an encryption technology consisting of a hardware-software combination known as the "clipper chip" was proposed by the federal government. The
clipper chip was the product of the desire to maintain a balance between the American public's right to privacy and the need for law enforcement agencies to gather
information on criminal activities. Clipper (also called key escrow encryption) is a
powerful encryption technology that scrambles communications, making them
unintelligible to anyone without the required decryption code. To date, clipper encryption has never been compromised, and even the most powerful supercomputers have been unable to decode clipper-encrypted documents.

As of this writing, the Clinton administration supports continued development
and implementation of clipper technology and is promoting it for use by private
citizens and businesses with a legitimate need for private communications. The
government fears, however, that criminals could also use the technology to render
their communications unintelligible to investigators. Original plans called for government agencies, and the government alone, to hold the electronic "key" needed
to decode clipper messages. Under that proposal, the key would have been separated
into two pieces so that unauthorized snooping by government agents could have
been avoided. The "pieces" necessary for decryption of a particular message would
have been joined when enforcement agents obtained search warrants, and then
would have been used to decode communications of a suspected criminal nature.[72]

Because clipper technology is so powerful, however, and because the proposed
plan only allowed government agencies to hold needed decryption keys, critics
charged that abuses of the technology could easily occur. Government officials, they
said, might conduct unauthorized and secretive decryptions. Moreover, important
information could be kept from the public by government officials bent on secrecy—so thoroughly encrypted that its very existence might be unknown. Under
such circumstances, critics argued, the Freedom of Information Act would lose its
power, and government agencies could enter an electronic underground inaccessi-
ble to the public and without the need for public accounting.

In 1996, in an effort to sidestep critics, Attorney General Janet Reno withdrew the suggestion that decoding technology should be held by the federal government. Instead, Reno proposed that decryption codes be kept by third parties, independent of the government.[73] Such organizations, called "escrow companies," would turn over only the information needed to decrypt specific messages, and then only when decryption was legally authorized through a court-supervised investigation. By 1998, however, industry officials and citizens groups appeared to have been successful in their demands that high-tech companies be allowed to hold their own decryption keys—making them available to the government only when subpoenaed to do so. In any event, the battle over encryption technologies may soon become moot, because well-financed criminal organizations may one day develop their own encryption technologies rivaling any of those now available.

*We live in the Space Age, but we've left our cops in the Iron Age. . . . Our kids play
with more sophisticated electronic toys than the crude implements we give most of
our police officers. . . . I don't see why we can give our military brilliant, 20th century
technology to fight wars overseas but can't do the same thing for our police, who are
fighting a war at home—the war against violence on our streets.[74]*

—*REP. CHARLES E. SCHUMER (D., N.Y.)*
CHAIRMAN OF THE HOUSE JUDICIARY
SUBCOMMITTEE ON CRIME

SUMMARY

⚍

High-tech crimes hold the potential to vastly change our understanding of crime. Illegal wire transfers of huge asset stores, nuclear subterfuge, and computer crime are emerging as novel forms of criminal enterprise. Some forms of high-tech crime hold dangers never before imagined. One incident of nuclear terrorism, for example, holds the potential to destroy more property and to claim more human lives than decades of traditional criminal activity.

The very nature of contemporary society dictates that crimes exploiting high technology will always be with us. It can only be hoped that enforcement technologies continue to keep abreast of technologies that serve criminal purposes. Unfortunately, however, no one is able to realistically assess even the current extent of high-tech crime, let alone accurately imagine the form future high-tech crimes will take.

Efforts to control high-tech crime open a Pandora's box of issues related to individual rights in the face of criminal investigation and prosecution. Such issues extend from free speech considerations to guarantees of technological privacy in the midst of digital interconnectedness. As we begin the twenty-first century, it is incumbent upon us to strike an acceptable balance between constitutional guarantees of continued freedom of access to legitimate activities based on high technology, and enforcement initiatives which can deal effectively with the massive threat high-tech crimes represent.

WEB WATCH

Access the *Criminology Today* home page on the World Wide Web by pointing your browser at www.prenhall.com/jcentral. Once there, click on "Criminology Today" to access the wealth of electronic resources supporting this text.

Onsite resources include (1) "Chapter Links," which provides succinct overviews of critical ideas from the textbook and links selected materials from around the Web to concepts found in the text; (2) "General Reference—Law and Justice Links." Organized by chapter, these links lead to other useful resources on the World Wide Web such as libraries, electronic discussion lists, and electronic journals; (3) "Criminology Sites on the Web," which lists links to organizations such as the American Society of Criminology and the National Organization for Victims Assistance (NOVA), as well as crime prevention links and statistics on crime and justice. Many other Web-based resources can be accessed via the *Criminology Today* site, including the federal Justice Information Center, the Bureau of Justice Statistics, the FBI, the RAND Corporation, the Vera Institute of Justice, PAVNET (an online "Partnership Against Violence," run by seven different federal agencies), and the National White Collar Crime Center.

Still another feature of the *Criminology Today* Web site is e-mail homework. Homework can be composed onsite and submitted to instructors using the instructor's e-mail address. To use the e-mail homework feature, click on "E-Mail Homework" on the opening page and then type answers to the questions that appear in the spaces provided. Use your instructor's e-mail address to submit homework answers. The *Criminology Today* Web site also provides links to powerful Web-based search engines that can help you find topics of interest to you as you progress through your course of study. Search engines can be found under the home page heading "Criminology Sites on the Web."

DISCUSSION QUESTIONS

1. This book emphasizes a social problems versus social responsibility theme. Which perspective best explains the involvement of capable individuals in criminal activity necessitating skills in the area of high technology? What is the best way to deal with such criminals?
2. What is the difference between high-tech crime and traditional forms of criminal activity? Will the high-tech crimes of today continue to be the high-tech crimes of tomorrow? Why or why not?
3. What forms of high-tech crime can you imagine which this chapter has not discussed? Describe each briefly.
4. Do you believe that high-tech crimes will eventually surpass the abilities of enforcement agents to prevent or solve them? Why or why not?

5. What different kinds of high-tech offenders can you imagine? What is the best way to deal with each such offender? Give reasons for your answers.

NOTES

⚏

[1]Georgette Bennett, *Crimewarps: The Future of Crime in America* (New York: Anchor, 1987), p. xiii.

[2]Cynthia Manson and Charles Ardai, *Future Crime: An Anthology of the Shape of Crime to Come* (New York: Donald I. Fine, 1992), p. ix.

[3]Alvin Toffler, *Powershift: Knowledge, Wealth, and Violence at the Edge of the 21st Century* (New York: Bantam, 1990), p. 255.

[4]See Matt Crenson, "DNA in Court," Associated Press wire service, January 26, 1997.

[5]The U.S.S.R. was officially dissolved on December 31, 1991.

[6]Robert Green, "CIA Warns of Nuclear Threat from Russian Gangs," Reuters wire service, June 27, 1994.

[7]"Fears Grow Over Russia's Nuclear Arsenal," Reuters NewMedia, February 7, 1997, 10:53 AM EST.

[8]Merck and Co., Inc., *Interim Report for the Period Ended June 30, 1994*, p. 4.

[9]Kenneth Rosenblatt, "Deterring Computer Crime," *Technology Review*, vol. 93, no. 2 (February/March 1990), pp. 34–41.

[10]Ibid.

[11]This and most other definitions related to computer crime in this chapter are taken from Donn B. Parker, *Computer Crime: Criminal Justice Resource Manual* (Washington, D.C.: National Institute of Justice, 1989).

[12]Rosenblatt, "Deterring Computer Crime."

[13]Software Publishing Association, "Global Study Shows Increase In Software Units Pirated: Nearly One In Every Two Business Applications Is Pirate Copy," May 7, 1997. Web posted at: http://www.spa.org/piracy/releases/96pir.htm. See also Software Publishing Association, "More Than $13 Billion Lost Worldwide To Software Piracy Joint BSA/SPA Survey Reveals." Web posted at: http://www.spa.org/piracy/releases/spa_bsa.htm.

[14]Gary H. Anthes, "Software Pirates' Booty Topped $13B, Study Finds," *Computerworld*, January 6, 1997, p. 24.

[15]Stephen R. Purdy, "Protecting Your Telephone Systems Against Dial-Tone Thieves," *Infosecurity News*, July/August 1993, p. 43.

[16]"Out Slicked," *Infosecurity News*, July/August 1993, p. 11.

[17]Paul Keegan, "High Tech Pirates Collecting Phone Calls," *USA Today*, September 23, 1994, p. 4A.

[18]Ibid.

[19]Paul Saffo, "Desperately Seeking Cyberspace," *Personal Computing*, May 1989, p. 248.

[20]Public Law 104-104, 110 Stat. 56.

[21]As described in M. Gemignani, "Viruses and Computer Law," *Communications of the ACM*, vol. 32 (June 1989), p. 669.

[22]Public Law 104-104, 110 Stat. 56.

[23]*Reno* v. *ACLU* (1997), No. 96-511. Decided June 26, 1997.

[24]Brian S. Akre, "Internet-Torture," Associated Press wire service, February 10, 1995.

[25]Ibid.

[26]Jim Schaefer and Maryanne George, "Internet User's Charges Dismissed U.S. Criticized for Pursuing U-M Case," *Detroit Free Press* online, June 22, 1995.

[27]Parker, *Computer Crime: Criminal Justice Resource Manual*.

[28]Steve Miletich, no title, *Seattle Post-Intelligencer*, via Simon & Schuster NewsLink online, May 21, 1997.

[29]Saffo, "Desperately Seeking Cyberspace," p. 247.

[30]Ibid.

[31]J. Bloombecker, "A Security Manager's Guide to Hacking," *DATAPRO Reports on Information Security*, Report #IS35-450-101, 1986.

[32]Marc Robins, "Case of the Ticked-Off Teens," *Infosecurity News*, July/August 1993, p. 48.

[33]For more information, see Ronald R. Thrasher, "Voice-Mail Fraud," *FBI Law Enforcement Bulletin*, July 1994, pp. 1–4.

[34]J. Maxfield, "Computer Bulletin Boards and the Hacker Problem," *EDPACS, the Electric Data Processing Audit, Control and Security*

Newsletter (Arlington, Va.: Automation Training Center, October 1985).

[35]Percy Black, personal communication, 1991. As cited in M. E. Kabay, "Computer Crime: Hackers" (undated electronic manuscript).

[36]John Perry Barlow, "Crime and Puzzlement: in Advance of the Law on the Electronic Frontier," *Whole Earth Review,* Fall 1990, p. 44.

[37]Anne W. Branscomb, "Common Law for the Electronic Frontier," *Scientific American,* September 1991.

[38]As cited in Barlow, "Crime and Puzzlement."

[39]"Computer Porn," *Time,* March 15, 1993, p. 22.

[40]Maxfield, "Computer Bulletin Boards and the Hacker Problem."

[41]Parker, *Computer Crime: Criminal Justice Resource Manual.*

[42]John Naisbitt, *Megatrends: Ten New Directions Transforming Our Lives* (New York: Warner Books, 1982), p. 36.

[43]Ibid.

[44]Al Gore, "Infrastructure for the Global Village," *Scientific American,* September 1991, p. 150.

[45]Gary H. Anthes, "White House Launches Cybershield," *Computerworld,* July 22, 1996, p. 29.

[46]M. J. Zuckerman, "Clinton to Get Cyberterror Plan," *USA Today,* October 9, 1997, p. 1A.

[47]As quoted in Gary H. Anthes, "White House Launches Cybershield," *Computerworld,* July 22, 1996, p. 29.

[48]For insight into how security techniques often lag behind the abilities of criminal perpetrators in the high-technology arena, see James A. Fagin, "Computer Crime: A Technology Gap," *International Journal of Comparative and Applied Criminal Justice,* vol. 15, nos. 1 and 2 (Spring/Fall 1991), pp. 285–297.

[49]Richard Larson, "The New Crime Stoppers: State-of-the-Art Computer Technology Promises a Return to Neighborhood-Oriented Policing," *Technology Review,* vol. 92, no. 8 (November/December 1989), p. 26.

[50]See Matt Crenson, "DNA in Court," Associated Press wire service, January 26, 1997.

[51]Michael Schrage, "Today, It Takes a Scientist to Catch a Thief," *Washington Post* on-line, March 18, 1994.

[52]*Daubert* v. *Merrell Dow Pharmaceuticals, Inc.,* 113 S. Ct. 2786 (1993).

[53]*Frye* v. *United States,* 54 App. D.C. 46, 47, 293 F. 1013, 1014 (1923).

[54]For the application of *Daubert* to DNA technology, see Barry Sheck, "DNA and *Daubert,*" *Cardozo Law Review,* vol. 15 (1994), p. 1959.

[55]Schrage, "Today, It Takes a Scientist to Catch a Thief."

[56]Ibid.

[57]"British Police to Use DNA to Catch Burglars," Reuters wire service, June 16, 1994.

[58]Schrage, "Today, It Takes a Scientist to Catch a Thief."

[59]Edward Connors, Thomas Lundregan, Neal Miller, and Tom McEwen, *Convicted by Juries, Exonerated by Science: Case Studies in the Use of DNA Evidence to Establish Innocence After Trial* (Washington, D.C.: National Institute of Justice, 1996).

[60]Roland Reboussin, "An Expert System Designed to Profile Murderers," in Frank Schmalleger, ed., *Computers in Criminal Justice: Issues and Applications* (Bristol, Ind.: Wyndham Hall Press, 1990), p. 239.

[61]"Increased Spending for Security," *Infosecurity News,* July/August 1993, p. 11; 1997 figure is a projection.

[62]Don B. Parker, *Computer Crime,* p. xiii.

[63]Kenneth Rosenblatt, "Deterring Computer Crime," *Technology Review,* vol. 93, no. 2 (February/March 1990), pp. 34–41.

[64]Ibid.

[65]Ibid.

[66]The NCCS can be found on the World Wide Web at http://www.fbi.gov/programs/nccs/comcrim.htm.

[67]As modified in 1986, 1988, and later years.

[68]Wylie Wong, "FBI Targets BBS Operators, Seizes Hardware in Software Piracy Sting," *Computerworld,* February 3, 1997, p. 24.

[69]Ibid.

[70]EFF statement of purpose, from the EFF forum on CompuServe, as of August 22, 1994.

[71]The White House, Office of the Vice President, "Statement of the Vice President," February 4, 1994.

[72]Department of Justice press release, "Attorney General Makes Key Escrow Encryption Announcements," February 4, 1994.

[73]Richard Cole, "Reno-Computer Security," Associated Press wire service, June 14, 1996.

[74]Taken from Marcy Gordon, "Hi-Tech for Cops," Associated Press wire service, Northern edition, July 22, 1994.

PART FOUR

RESPONDING TO CRIMINAL BEHAVIOR

We cannot predict with any confidence that in the more benign post-scarcity environment of future societies humans will become more like angels and less like beasts.

—*Bernard Gendron*[1]

Crime is . . . an ever-present condition, even as sickness, disease, and death. It is perennial as spring and as recurrent as winter.

—*Frank Tannenbaum*[2]

CHAPTER 13
Criminology and Social Policy

CHAPTER 14
Future Directions in Criminology

CRIMINOLOGY

AND SOCIAL POLICY

Criminology should be concerned with real-world applications of its research.

—JOAN PETERSILIA, PAST-PRESIDENT, THE AMERICAN SOCIETY OF CRIMINOLOGY[3]

A mortal battle for the national conscience is being waged as I write and you read. The jousting . . . will determine what we, in the future, will label as "crime" and how we react to it.

—GEORGETTE BENNETT[4]

Fundamentally, our capacity to extinguish criminality and lawlessness lies in the moral training and moral stature of our people.

—PRESIDENT HERBERT HOOVER[5]

❖ CHAPTER OUTLINE ❖

❖ IMPORTANT TERMS ❖

public policy
deterrence strategy
Kriminalpolitik
three strikes
nurturant strategy

Law Enforcement
    Assistance Admini-
    stration (LEAA)
habitual offender
    statutes

social epidemiology
protection/avoidance
    strategy

❖ IMPORTANT LAWS AND GROUPS ❖

Wickersham Commission
Omnibus Crime Control and Safe Streets Act of 1967
National Advisory Commission on Criminal Justice Standards and Goals
Comprehensive Crime Control Act of 1984
Anti-Drug Abuse Act of 1988
Brady Handgun Violence Prevention Act of 1993
Violent Crime Control and Law Enforcement Act of 1994

❖ INTRODUCTION

In the study of crime, as in many other areas, life often imitates art. On September 7, 1996, rapper Tupak Shakur, well known for his starring role in the movie *Poetic Justice,* was gunned down after leaving a Mike Tyson fight in Las Vegas. Shakur had been born in the Bronx in 1971 and was raised by a Black Panther mother. He died at a local hospital a week after being attacked. Shakur's violent past included a shooting that injured two off-duty Atlanta police officers, a conviction on sodomy charges in New York City,[6] and a previous mugging during which the rapper was shot four times. The mugging occurred in 1994 as Shakur was awaiting sentencing after being convicted of assault and battery in an attack on his former film director, Allen Hughes.[7] During his brief rise to stardom, Shakur's brand of "gangsta rap" was condemned by former Vice President Dan Quayle, who charged that Shakur's violent lyrics had led a youth to kill a Texas state trooper.

Six months after Shakur died, the Notorious B.I.G., or Biggie Smalls—another of gangsta rap's best known entertainers—was killed in a hail of gunfire. The 24-year-old B.I.G., whose given name was Christopher Wallace, was shot shortly after midnight on March 9, 1997, as he sat in the passenger seat of a GMC Suburban at a red light in downtown Los Angeles. He died a short time later at Cedars-Sinai Medical Center. B.I.G., a former drug dealer and street hustler from the rough Bedford-Stuyvesant section of Brooklyn, New York, had burst on the gangsta rap scene in 1994 with his million-selling album *Ready to Die.*

About the time B.I.G. died, another infamous rapper, Snoop Doggy Dogg, and his bodyguard McKinley Lee, were acquitted of murder charges in the 1993 slaying of Phillip Woldermariam. Woldermariam, a member of the Venice Shoreline Crips, had been shot twice in the back after meeting with Snoop. Snoop, whose birth name is Calvin Broadus, was born in Long Beach, California, in 1971. Others like Snoop have profited mightily by selling images of urban violence to mainstream youth. As a result of highly lucrative album sales, Snoop had no problem posting a $2 million bond following his arrest.[8] A $25 million wrongful death suit filed by Woldermariam's family was settled out of court in late 1996 for an undisclosed sum.

The car in which gangsta rapper Biggie Smalls, known as the Notorious B.I.G., was shot and killed in 1997. Some claim that violent themes in "ghetto rap" lead to crime. What do you think? *Mike Meadows/AP/Wide World Photos.*

The violent exploits of gangsta rappers is replete with other examples. A few years before Shakur died, Flavor Flav (William Drayton), a singer with the group Public Enemy, was arrested for firing a .38-caliber pistol at a neighbor. By the time of Flav's arrest, Ice-T's song *Cop Killer* had been blamed in the 1992 shooting deaths of two Las Vegas police officers who were ambushed and killed by four juveniles. The juveniles continued to sing *Cop Killer* lyrics following their arrest.[9] *Body Count*, the Time-Warner album on which *Cop Killer* appears, was shipped to stores in a miniature body bag.

A year later, rapper Dr. Dre (A.K.A. Andre Young) directed an eighteen-minute video of a Snoop performance called *Murder Was the Case*. Dre said he wanted to package the video with Oliver Stone's *Natural Born Killers*.[10] *Murder* and *Killers* were both quickly criticized by law enforcement organizations, parents' groups, and black leaders decrying the lyrics of gangsta music.[11] The Reverend Arthur L. Cribbs, Jr., a black minister writing in a national editorial, called gangsta rap "nothing but modern-day violence and vulgarity wrapped and packaged in blackface."[12] Cribbs claimed the music "would not be widespread if white megarecord companies did not put filth on sale for big dollars." Soon, radio stations began banning violent rap music. WBLS-FM in New York and KACE-FM in Los Angeles announced that they would no longer play rap songs that encouraged violence, KPWR-FM in Los Angeles masked offensive words, and WCKZ-FM in Charlotte limited gangsta rap to late-night hours.

Gangsta rap and "hip hop" music have been condemned by many who claim that their lyrics promote antisocial and violent behavior. But whether gangsta rap is indeed a cause of crime, or merely a quasi-poetic rendering of the social conditions characteristic of many inner-city American communities today, is less than clear. The real problems, some claim, are outside rap music, not within it. Gangsta rap supporters suggest that rap may be the wake-up call needed to end black-on-black violence, which now seems out of control, and that by raising public awareness it may do more to reduce violence than any government-sponsored program.

❖ FEDERAL ANTICRIME INITIATIVES

A number of public interest groups and influential politicians—among them, the National Political Congress of Black Women, U.S. Attorney General Janet Reno, and Senator Carol Moseley-Braun (D-Ill.)—are calling for congressional investigations into the possible behavioral consequences of rap music, hoping that lawmakers will enact some sort of legislative control over the airing of offensive lyrics.[13] Should Congress undertake to control the potentially crime-inspiring effects of rap music, its action will be just one of the latest in a long series of federal government initiatives in the war against crime.

Some understanding of how public policy—especially crime control policy—is created is essential in the study of criminology. Before we trace the development of public policies in the crime control area, however, a definition of the term *public policy* is in order. **Public policy,** also called social policy, is "a course of action that government takes in an effort to solve a problem or to achieve an end."[14] Analysts of public policy have observed that policies undergo five stages in their development.[15]

Public policy a course of action that government takes in an effort to solve a problem or to achieve an end.

- identification of the problem
- agenda setting or the prioritization of problems
- policy formation
- program implementation
- program evaluation and reassessment

As Jeff Ferrell notes, however, "As all criminologists know, criminality is decided as much by legal and political authorities, and by their strategies of criminalization, enforcement, and control, as by criminals themselves."[16] One could easily add that crime-fighting policies are probably more the result of politics than they are the direct outcome of social science research and data. As Nancy E. Marion, a leading figure in the public policy arena, observes: "Presidential and congressional initiatives have been largely symbolic gestures rather than coherent attempts to deal effectively with crime."[17] The Massachusetts Institute for a New Commonwealth, which is especially interested in issues of crime control, puts it equally succinctly. The institute asserts: "Opportunities to reduce crime are systematically neglected, as policy making is dominated by the need to appease the public's justifiable fear and anger and by a wide variety of organizational and professional interests and ideological postures. The simple question, 'What policies would minimize crime?' is rarely raised, and even more rarely debated on its merits. There is little careful analysis of which actions by police, courts, prosecutors, and corrections authorities would most reduce crime, and even less serious attention to the contributions of non-criminal justice agencies and policies to crime control."[18]

THE HOOVER ADMINISTRATION

Although the development of policies to combat crime and the conditions that cause it have traditionally been the responsibility of state and local governments, crime control became a part of the federal approach to social problems in the United States more than half a century ago. In the foreword to James D. Calder's *The Origins and Development of Federal Crime Control Policy*,[19] George H. Nash writes: "While all complicated social policies and institutional arrangements have many roots . . . the decisive movement in the development of comprehensive federal crime control was the period between 1929 and 1933, the presidency of Herbert Hoover." Calder puts it even more succinctly. "The administration of Herbert Clark Hoover, thirty-first president of the United States," he writes, "marks the origins of federal crime-control policy."[20] Calder argues that a trilogy of factors combined to usher in an era of federal crime-control policies: "the proliferating stress on the judicial system" associated mostly with Prohibition; "the emergence of new perspectives in law, sociology, and criminology, and the rise of academically-trained social scientists eager to apply their knowledge to reform of the legal system," and "the election in 1928 of a president committed to reform and receptive to the approaches of the activist social scientists."[21] Other events of the era, including the sensational kidnapping of young Charles Augustus Lindbergh, Jr., better known as "the Lindbergh baby"; the rapid rise in influence of organized crime; the visibility of gang warfare; media coverage of notorious criminals; and the effects of the Great Depression on crime rates everywhere, all necessitated serious and decisive anticrime action by the Hoover administration.

In 1929 Max Lowenthal, a Hoover administration insider, called crime and its control, "the dominant issue before the American people."[22] The opening words of Hoover's inaugural address focused the first order of business for the new administration upon "the failure of our system of criminal justice." Hoover observed that "crime had increased . . . and confidence in the system of criminal justice had decreased."[23] When Hoover assumed office, Calder observes, "[t]he popular belief was that crime had increased and governments at all levels had become less able to control its growth."[24] During his campaign for the presidency, Hoover promised if elected to initiate a scientific study of crime and law enforcement. The promise was fulfilled with the 1929 appointment of George Woodard Wickersham to chair Hoover's Commission on Law Observance and Enforcement. Wickersham, a lawyer with an outstanding professional reputation, had been U.S. attorney general during the Taft administration. Wickersham's views coincided with Hoover's in many policy areas, and the two men were in constant communication during the **Wickersham Commission** hearings.

The Hoover administration developed policy initiatives in the areas of police, courts, and corrections. Interest centered on[25]

- developing "objectives to improve justice system practices and to reinstate law's role in civilized governance" (which was the mandate of the Wickersham Commission).
- exploring the extent to which "Prohibition was the basis for general disrespect of the law."
- investigating the extent to which deadly force was a necessary or reasonable law enforcement tool (an issue which arose after a number of innocent citizens were killed by federal and state enforcement agents determined to stop fleeing Prohibition law violators).
- controlling the illegal manufacture, sale, and importation of heroin, morphine, and opium.
- development of a system of reliable information gathering, including crime statistics, which could be used in the further development of crime-fighting policies.
- codification of federal law enforcement activities, including the elimination of overlapping law enforcement activities by different agencies.
- increasing professionalism among the federal judiciary, especially through the removal and replacement of incompetent or corrupt government prosecutors.
- streamlining the federal court system, improving court procedures, and ending the massive congestion then found in federal courtrooms across the country.
- combating organized crime and reducing its influence throughout America.
- reforming the system of federal prisons so that it might not only punish, but reform and provide a visible sense of deterrence to others contemplating criminal activity.
- elimination of abusive and unprofessional prison management.
- reducing prison overcrowding and decreasing idleness among prisoners.

Development of federal criminal justice policy during the Hoover administration era made use of "the services of the best experts in the country"—men and women such as August Vollmer, former chief of police in Berkeley, California; Roscoe Pound, dean of the Harvard Law School; Henry W. Anderson, president of the Virginia Bar Association; Ada L. Comstock, president of Radcliffe College; Mabel Willebrandt, a highly visible Prohibition supporter; Sanford Bates, director of the Federal Bureau of Prisons; Frank J. Loesch, a judge and Chicago antigang leader; and many other policy leaders and critical thinkers of the times.

Unfortunately, however, policymaking groups, most notably the Wickersham Commission, did not include broad representation of blacks or other racial and ethnic minorities. Although some citizens expressed concerns that "blacks had endured more than a century of police abuse, rigged court rooms, and harsh prison treatment and that they were overrepresented in crime statistics for reasons that demanded inquiry,"[26] Hoover decided that the appointment of ethnic minorities to policymaking groups solely for the purpose of including them "would violate his principle of having no special interests represented"[27] and might produce less than objective results.

Nonetheless, the Hoover era set the tone for federal criminal justice policies that were to follow—a tone already identified in the October 1929 preliminary report of the Wickersham Commission which said: "We found that with huge investments in plant and personnel and with great operating costs, the country has been proceeding largely in a haphazard manner, without any inventory of the available facts, without commensurate research for checking a great social evil, without the application of the principles that have been so successful in some of the professions, in many businesses and in the social sciences."[28]

Many Hoover-era reforms eventually proved themselves effective. As James D. Calder observes, "Hoover's administration was the first to give formal policy attention to federal prisons and prisoners. Under his leadership, prison administration, historically ignored, was transformed from an antiquated and rawly inadequate collection of penitentiaries into a model system."[29] Other reforms were also well received. Prison expansion got underway, activities of the federal parole board were streamlined and centralized, and new federal district court standards were introduced reducing the high cost of repeated and redundant appeals which had been clogging the nation's courts.

FEDERAL POLICY FOLLOWING WORLD WAR II

By the end of World War II the nation basked in the glow of economic expansion as industrial production, greatly enhanced by the demands of war, turned to peaceful purposes. Unfortunately, however, domestic tranquillity was about to be disrupted by the baby-boom generation, who were themselves an offshoot of the enthusiasm which accompanied the end of the war. Baby boomers, born in the decade following 1945, contributed significantly to rising crime rates around 1960 as they began to reach their early teen years. Rising rates made crime and its control an important political issue during the presidency of John F. Kennedy (1961–1963). The Kennedy administration expanded federal crime-control policies to address

Law Enforcement Assistance Administration (LEAA) a federal program established under Title 1 of the Omnibus Crime Control and Safe Streets Act of 1967, designed to provide assistance to police agencies.

juvenile crime and the rights of indigent defendants to be afforded counsel. Under the direction of Robert Kennedy, U.S. attorney general during his brother's administration, federal anticrime efforts also focused on combating organized crime—which was seen as a crime-control issue that transcended state boundaries.

After Kennedy was assassinated in 1963, Lyndon Baines Johnson was sworn in as the thirty-sixth president of the United States—serving until 1969. Although Barry Goldwater had highlighted issues of crime and violence during the 1964 presidential campaign, Johnson capitalized on them, playing to rising crime fears identified by pollsters at the time. Johnson established the President's Commission on Law Enforcement and Administration of Justice and it formed part of his drive toward building what he called "The Great Society." Johnson's charge to the commission consisted partially of these words: "The problem of crime brings us together. Even as we join in common action, we know there can be no instant victory. Ancient evils do not yield to easy conquest. We cannot limit our efforts to enemies we can see. We must, with equal resolve, seek out new knowledge, new techniques, and new understanding."[30]

The commission's report, *The Challenge of Crime in a Free Society,* which was published in February 1967, laid the groundwork for many anticrime initiatives which were to follow. True to its Democratic roots, the commission saw crime as the inevitable result of poverty, unemployment, low educational levels, and other social and economic disadvantages. It proposed legislation, passed in the form of the **Omnibus Crime Control and Safe Streets Act of 1967,** to "eliminate the social conditions that bring about crime." Title 1 of the Safe Streets Act established the **Law Enforcement Assistance Administration (LEAA),** with the mandate of providing technical and financial assistance to the states for the purpose of improving and strengthening law enforcement activities at the local level. The LEAA spent hundreds of millions of dollars before it was disbanded.

At the time of the commission's 1967 report, crime was far less a reality than it is today. Although fear of crime was widespread in the late 1960s, the crime rate was less than a third of what it is now. Carjackings, crack cocaine, drive-by shootings, metal detectors in schools, mass murder, drug cartels, and gang warfare with automatic weapons were unfamiliar. Even so, as the crime rate rose, personal security became a major concern of the American public. It was during this period that the nation's "war on crime" took on its modern tenor.

Although the true cause of rising crime rates that characterized the period from 1960 to 1975 may never be known, many possibilities have been suggested, ranging from maturing baby boomers (discussed earlier) to the dissolution of institutions of social control such as the family, churches, and schools. Whatever the reason, it soon became clear that federal crime-control policies were no match for the underlying social forces fueling the rapid rise in crime.

When Richard Milhous Nixon became president of the United States in 1969, federal efforts at crime control took on a decidedly Republican cast. Nixon "sought all out war on crime, frequently with little concern for the accused. In his efforts to get criminals out of circulation, Nixon advocated mandatory minimum sentences, fewer pretrial releases for multiple offenders, generally heavier penalties, and selection of judges who were strict on crime."[31] As the nation's law enforcers, courts, and correctional systems became hopelessly overworked, high rates of recidivism were cited as the basis for an emerging new "lock-em-up" policy which emphasized retribution and deterrence by example. The war on crime turned increasingly conservative and calls for swift and certain penalties, accompanied by increased punishments including the reduction or abolition of parole and early release, were made into law. Nixon also commissioned the **National Advisory Commission on Criminal Justice Standards and Goals in 1971.** In its reports, the commission called for improved police–community relations and enhanced communications between criminal justice agencies.

As some writers have observed, the first phase of the federal war on crime was based on a social philosophy that attempted to address underlying cultural and social conditions which fed crime. Unfortunately, however, even as massive federal funding infused social welfare programs, crime continued to rise. Social programs themselves faced growing criticism that they tended to perpetuate the very problems they were intended to address.

THE REAGAN–BUSH YEARS

The first phase in the war on crime ended approximately in 1981 with the election of President Ronald Reagan. During the Reagan administration (1981–1988) two new fronts in the war on crime emerged. One, which some writers have called a "war on criminals," meant that less attention would be paid to the root causes of crime, and more attention would be devoted to holding individual offenders responsible for their crimes. In support of this first front, Congress passed the **Comprehensive Crime Control Act of 1984,** a far-reaching law that mandated new sentencing guidelines, eliminated parole at the federal level, limited the use of the insanity defense, and increased penalties associated with drug dealing. Typical of Republican approaches to the problem of crime, Reagan insisted that, "[c]hoosing a career in crime is not the result of poverty or of an unhappy childhood or of a misunderstood adolescence; it's the result of a conscious, willful, selfish choice made by some who consider themselves above the law, who seek to exploit the hard work and, sometimes, the very lives of their fellow citizens."[32]

The second front in the Reagan administration's war on crime focused on drugs and their relationship to criminal activity. Some analysts claim that drug control provided the single most important issue on Reagan's crime-control agenda. Reagan believed that drugs contributed, both directly and indirectly, to much of the nation's crime problem. He was strongly opposed to the legalization or decriminalization of controlled substances, and in 1985 persuaded Congress to pass legislation criminalizing the manufacture, distribution, and possession of designer drugs. Under Reagan's leadership, Congress passed the **Omnibus Anti-Drug Abuse Act of 1988** which substantially increased penalties for recreational drug users and created a new cabinet-level position to coordinate the drug-fighting efforts of the federal government. The position, dubbed by the press as the "Drug Czar," was initially filled by William Bennett (a Bush appointee) who brought federal antidrug efforts to national attention when he declared Washington, D.C., a "drug zone" in 1989. "Drug zone" designation made the city, and others like it, eligible for federal drug-fighting assistance.

The war on drugs was well supported throughout the early 1990s by federal and state tax dollars. In 1991 alone government agencies nationwide spent nearly $24 billion[33] to fight the drug war, with most of the money going to criminal justice efforts—and very little to rehabilitation or counseling initiatives outside the system. Of all monies spent to combat drugs, 79 percent went to criminal justice agencies, and only 21 percent reached agencies focused on rehabilitation and educational activities. State and local governments spent a total of $15.9 billion on criminal justice activities such as incarcerating prisoners and paying for police, according to a report by the Office of National Drug Control Policy. States paid $6.8 billion in 1991 to support their prisons and local jails, with an additional $4.2 billion in state monies going to fund police services. Judicial and legal services cost states $1.5 billion. Per capita spending on antidrug efforts varied greatly, ranging from only $13 per citizen per year in South Dakota to over $154 per person per year in Alaska. Average per capita spending by state and local governments was $63.08. Even with the aid of such massive expenditures, the war on drugs had little immediate result other than grossly overworked criminal justice agencies and intolerably overcrowded jails and prisons.

❖ CRIME-CONTROL PHILOSOPHIES TODAY

The contemporary situation is the cumulative result of the aforementioned historical initiatives.[34] Today's policy approach to crime control is twin pronged. One prong, that of crime control, defines crime as an issue of individual responsibility. The other, which is being cast in the guise of a public health agenda, sees criminals as victims of a kind of rampant social pathology that has turned them into offenders. Previously in Chapter 1, the first prong was termed the "social responsibility perspective," and the second approach the "social problems perspective."

Those who portray crime as the result of poor social conditions stress the need for improvements in the American infrastructure and continue to battle for an expansion of educational and employment opportunities for the disenfranchised. One new aspect of the social problems approach is its recasting in terms of social epidemiology. In terminology akin to the old social pathology approach of the Chicago school, some contemporary politicians and criminologists now view crime and the conditions that create it in terms of a disease model.[35] The word *epidemiology* refers to the study of epidemics and diseases, and the phrase **social epidemiology** has come to mean the study of social epidemics and diseases of the social order. Hence, the social epidemiologic approach holds that crime arises from festering conditions which promote social ills, and that individuals caught in an environment within which crime may be communicated display symptoms of this disease and suffer from its maladies. Crime becomes an illness, a social malady, but one which can be cured if the necessary resources could be dedicated to its treatment and eradication. Recognizing that crime and violence have reached epidemic proportions, such thinkers advance solutions based on what is, in effect, a public health model. Crime as a disease becomes a new kind of social problem—one which shifts responsibility for law violations away from individuals "afflicted" with criminality and toward the society that is ultimately responsible for their control.

Social epidemiology the study of social epidemics and diseases of the social order.

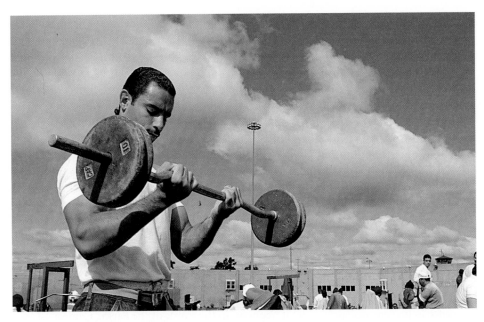

Prison weight-lifting bans, popular in some states, reflect a growing frustration with unsuccessful crime-control policies. Should recreational opportunities in prison be reduced? *Steve Lehman/SABA Press Photos, Inc.*

As a consequence of continued frustration at being unable to end the ongoing avalanche of American crime, however, and due to a lack of proven programs for ensuring the rehabilitation of criminal offenders, the social responsibility perspective is now in ascendancy. Policies at both the state and federal level are more focused on strict enforcement of existing laws and on strict punishments.[36] Prisons are being built apace, while tough legislation which will fill even more prisons is being passed at a feverish pitch. Americans, fed up with both crime and with the fear it engenders, are pushing their political representatives for creation of conservative policy tools to deal with it.

Reflecting such get-tough-on-crime attitudes, lawmakers have recently targeted what they see as "soft" prisons—institutions where inmates spend their days lifting weights, watching television, reading newspapers, going to the dining hall, and living in air-conditioned relaxation. In some states, legislators—citing the 1993 Lucasville, Ohio, prison riot in which inmates threatened guards with barbells—have introduced legislation designed to limit the leisure activities of inmates. Others argue that prisoners should not have the opportunity to build strength while in prison only to victimize innocent people once released. Prisoners, on the other hand, are opposed to the lawmakers' newfound conservative fervor. Harvey Garlotte, a convicted murderer serving a life sentence in the South Mississippi Correctional Facility, recently watched guards as they began to confiscate previously permitted private TV sets. "If they're going to take the TVs and all," Garlotte said, "things are going to blow apart."[37]

T H E O R Y   V E R S U S   R E A L I T Y

Crime as Disease: A Social Epidemiological Approach

The social epidemiological approach to "crime as disease" has a growing number of adherents. Among them is the San Francisco–based Pacific Center for Violence Prevention, which serves as the policy center for a unique, statewide effort in California, known as the youth Violence Prevention Initiative. Adapting methods originally designed to prevent nonviolent causes of injury, the Pacific Center follows a public health approach in attempting to develop workable interventions to prevent youth violence. In so doing, the Pacific Center focuses on policies which address causes of youth violence to prevent violence before it happens. In the words of the Pacific Center:

Violence is a public health issue, and violence prevention is a public health mandate. Violence results in premature death, serious injury and disability in populations. These are the concern of public health agencies and advocates. The public health model suggests that efforts to prevent violence, like those to prevent injury and infectious diseases, should consider the interaction between host, agent and environment. The host for violent injury is the person who is at risk of harming or being harmed by himself or herself or another person. The agent for violent injury is the weapon, be it a gun, knife, fist, foot, broken bottle or baseball bat. The environment for violent injury has three components: physical, economic, and social. Examples of the physical environment of violent injury are dark streets, abandoned buildings, bedrooms, bar rooms and work sites. The economic environment of violent injury includes limited social, recreational and educational activities, high levels of poverty and unemployment, particularly among young males. The social environment of violent injury includes fear, hopelessness, sexism and racism. Comprehensive programs to prevent violence cannot ignore the interaction among host, agent and environment. Within the public health approach, efforts to prevent violence necessitate identifying and addressing the root causes of violence . . .

Not everyone agrees with such an approach, however. Edgar A. Suter, M.D., head of Doctors for Integrity in Policy Research, Incorporated, says:

Treating crime as a disease—the essence of the 'public health' approach to gun violence—is as illogical and ineffectual as the converse, treating disease as a crime. We would mock any criminologist who advocated criminalizing disease by measures such as fines for obesity or jail time for tobacco-related emphysema. We would condemn the police if they invaded bedrooms to ensure the use of condoms in the crusade against AIDS. The silliness of such proposals are readily apparent, yet are no more illogical and insupportable than the proposals by advocates of the 'public health' model of gun violence, banning or severely restricting good citizens' access to guns simply because a tiny fraction of guns are misused by predatory aberrants. It is a distorted concept, indeed, that the rights of good people, the most virtuous and productive citizens, should be defined—more precisely, restrained—by the criminal actions of predators in our society.

DISCUSSION QUESTIONS

1. Do you believe that crime and violence can be effectively portrayed in terms of a disease model? Why or why not?
2. What are the advantages and disadvantages of a disease model of crime and violence?
3. With which perspective do you most closely agree—that of the Pacific Center for Violence Prevention, or Dr. Suter? Why?

Sources: The Pacific Center for Violence Prevention web site, http://www.traumafdn.org/pcvp2.html; and E.A. Suter, W.C. Waters, G.B. Murray, et al. "Violence in America: Effective Solutions," *Journal of the Medical Association of Georgia*, vol. 85 (1995), pp. 253–263.

Suppose I told you that it is time to start thinking of communicable disease as a criminal and legal issue, rather than a public health issue, and . . . to recognize that "Disease is a crime."

—DAVID B. KOPEL[38]

TYPES OF CRIME-CONTROL STRATEGIES

The dichotomous values which underlie modern-day policymaking reflect fundamental differences in philosophical and political orientations.[39] Even so, the range of effective crime-control alternatives available to reformers of any political bent is essentially limited to three types of strategies. These three strategies—identified by Bryan Vila,[40] one of the most seminal contemporary analysts of contemporary public policy—differ in terms of "strategic focus." That is, they are distinguishable from one another "by whether they attempt to block opportunities for crime, alter the outcome of conscious or unconscious decision-making that precedes a criminal act, or alter the broad strategic style with which people approach many aspects of their lives."[41] The three strategies are

- Protection/avoidance strategies
- Deterrence strategies
- Nurturant strategies

Protection/avoidance strategies "attempt to reduce criminal opportunities by changing people's routine activities, increasing guardianship, or incapacitating

Protection/avoidance strategy a crime-control strategy that attempts to reduce criminal opportunities by changing people's routine activities, increasing guardianship, or by incapacitating convicted offenders.

Which crime-control policies work are the subject of considerable debate. Here, meditators affiliated with Maharishi International University work to lower crime in Washington, D.C. Later research showed a statistically significant reduction in D.C.-area crime rates during the meditative session. Do you think the observed effect was "real"? *Courtesy Maharishi International University.*

Deterrence strategy a crime-control strategy that attempts to diminish motivation for crime by increasing the perceived certainty, severity, or celerity of penalties.

Nurturant strategy a crime-control strategy that attempts to forestall development of criminality by improving early life experiences and channeling child and adolescent development into desirable directions.

convicted offenders."[42] Incapacitating convicted offenders via incarceration or through the use of electronic monitoring devices provide examples of protection/ avoidance strategies. Target hardening through the use of architectural design, crime prevention programs such as neighborhood watch, and increased policing also fit this category.

Deterrence strategies "attempt to diminish motivation for crime by increasing the perceived certainty, severity, or celerity of penalties."[43] New and tougher laws, quicker trial court processing, harsher punishments, and faster imposition of sentences are all deterrence strategies.

Nurturant strategies "attempt to forestall development of criminality by improving early life experiences and channeling child and adolescent development" into desirable directions. They "focus on prevention of criminality rather than its remediation or control."[44] Nurturant strategies include increased infant and maternal health care, child care for the working poor, training in parenting skills, enhanced public education, and better programs to reduce the number of unwanted pregnancies.

A comprehensive crime-control strategy, say many criminologists, would be "a balanced mix of protection/avoidance, deterrence, and nurturant strategies."[45] Achieving the most effective balance in a politically sensitive world, however, is a difficult undertaking. Many large and influential political constituencies continue to press for crime-control measures which emphasize protection/avoidance and deterrence strategies while virtually ignoring those in the nurturant category.

EXPANSION OF DEATH PENALTY TO NONMURDERS FACES CHALLENGES

Deterrence strategies of crime control "attempt to diminish motivation for crime by increasing the perceived certainty, severity, or celerity of penalties."[1] Deterrence strategies include tough laws, quick trial court processing, and fast sentence imposition. The death penalty is the toughest deterrent strategy of all. As the following story shows, a nationwide movement to expand the application of capital punishment is now taking place.

Judy Benitez works days, nights and weekends counseling rape victims, including children she describes as "terribly wronged, tragically robbed." So why is the New Orleans woman working hard to overturn a Louisiana law that gives the death penalty to people who rape children?

"We're not pro-perpetrator, it's just that this law accomplishes nothing," says Benitez, who runs the Louisiana Foundation Against Sexual Assault. "At best, it's a feel-good gesture. At worst, it's counterproductive."

State and national legislators and some local prosecutors seemingly do not agree. While the death penalty once was reserved for the most heinous premeditated murders, it has been expanded to apply to a growing variety of crimes. The list now includes some crimes, like child rape, in which the victim is not killed.

In 1994, Congress reacted to a spate of high profile public crimes by increasing the number of federal offenses that could lead to the death penalty from 13 to about 60. Murders related to immigrant smuggling, torture, terrorism, marine sabotage, drive-by shootings and sexual exploitation of children now qualify for death sentences under federal law. Congress broke ground by applying the death penalty to "drug kingpins," key members of groups that traffic in large amounts of narcotics. It was the first time, other than in cases of spying or treason, that the federal death penalty had been applied to cases in which no one is killed. Some states were quick to follow.

Twelve men are being prosecuted under Louisiana's 1995 rape law, which allows prosecutors to pursue the death penalty for the rape of a child under age 12. No one has yet been convicted under the law, which the U.S. Supreme Court is considering for review.

The Supreme Court, which in 1977 barred use of the death penalty in adult rape cases, is expected to decide whether to take the case later this year. Meanwhile, other prosecutors are testing the limits of the death penalty.

Last week, in Winston-Salem, N.C., Assistant District Attorney Vincent Rabil asked a jury to order the execution of Thomas Jones. A motorist with two previous drunken driving convictions, Jones was impaired by drugs and alcohol when he caused the deaths of two college students. Instead, the jury sentenced Jones to life without parole.

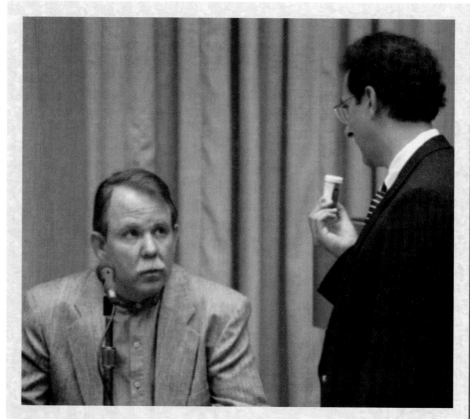

Prosecutor Vincent Rabil shows defendant Thomas Jones his pills with instructions to not drink or drive. Jones was on trial for his life after consuming the pills along with alcohol, and causing a traffic accident in which two people died. Do you think that drunk drivers who kill should be put to death? *AP/Wide World Photos.*

Rabil has been consulted by about 18 other prosecutors and a state attorney general contemplating similar prosecutions. This summer, he plans to seek the death penalty in a second vehicular homicide case.

"The death penalty is appropriate (in these cases) as a question of justice," Rabil says. "These perfectly innocent young women didn't have to die. They died because someone did something he had been warned not to do by his mother, his wife, the police, his doctor, which is get in a car and drive (impaired). That's a far more intentionally reckless act than many other crimes (eligible for the death penalty.)"

But there are signs that the expansion of the death penalty is provoking a backlash. Last year, moves to expand the death penalty were blocked in Illinois, California and Washington state. Supporters of the death penalty have opposed its expansion on grounds that too broad a penalty may be vulnerable to attack.

"We have a death penalty that is effective today because it is consistently applied only to the worst of our murders," says Michael Rushford, president of the Criminal Justice Legal Foundation. The Sacramento group opposes attempts to abolish capital punishment. "The best way to weaken it is to extend it so far that it becomes ridiculous. Then, it's open to a (legal challenge), and anything could happen."

The legal fight is now in Louisiana. Death penalty foes challenged the state's child rape law last year, after a prosecutor in Monroe sought the execution of a father accused of raping his daughter and two stepdaughters, ages 5, 8 and 9, in one afternoon. The man had AIDS. The opponents won in a lower court by arguing that the law, which applies when the victim is under 12, is too broad and that the penalty is too severe. Benitez of the Louisiana Foundation Against Sexual Assault, added a practical consideration: Making rape punishable by death takes away the incentive to let the victim live. But the Louisiana Supreme Court reversed the ruling and upheld the law, saying child rape is "like no other crime."

New Orleans lawyer John Holdridge has asked the U.S. Supreme Court to overturn that decision. He says the Louisiana law allowing the death penalty in child rape is fatally flawed. "It's just an easy sound bite for politicians," he says.

If the Supreme Court takes the case, Holdridge expects it to apply the same reasoning used in 1977, when it struck down the death penalty in adult rape cases on the grounds that the penalty was disproportionate to the crime.

Jerry Jones, the Monroe district attorney prosecuting the child rape case, disagrees. "These children have had their future, however much they have, greatly damaged," Jones says. "There are some situations where the death penalty is just plain deserved. This is one of them."

Questions

1. As a crime deterrent strategy, how effective do you think the death penalty really is? How might the deterrent impact of capital punishment vary from case to case?
2. Do you agree with Jerry Jones that "there are some situations where the death penalty is just plain deserved"? Why or why not?
3. Will the expansion of the death penalty to new types of crimes lead to lower crime rates? Why or why not?

Source: Richard Willing, "Expansion of Death Penalty to Nonmurders Faces Challenges," *USA Today*, May 14, 1997, p. 6A.
[1]Bryan Vila, "A General Paradigm for Understanding Criminal Behavior: Extending Evolutionary Ecological Theory," *Criminology*, vol. 32, no. 3 (August 1994), pp. 311–359.

RECENT FEDERAL POLICY INITIATIVES

THE BRADY LAW

One result of the growing conservative push which characterized the late 1980s and early 1990s was the **Brady Handgun Violence Prevention Act of 1993.** The Brady law, which is primarily a protection/avoidance strategy, was the last act passed by Congress in 1993. It was signed into law by President Clinton on November 30 of that year. The law was named after former President Ronald Reagan's White House press secretary, Jim Brady, who was shot in the head during John Hinckley's 1981 attempted assassination of Reagan. Brady, although seriously injured and impaired for life, survived.

The purpose of the Brady law is to "provide for a waiting period before the purchase of a handgun and for the establishment of a national instant criminal background check system, to be contacted by firearms dealers before the transfer of any firearm."[46] Under the law, firearms dealers must register with the federal government and are required to notify law enforcement officials of all handgun purchase applications. Federal officials will then check a potential buyer's background.[47] Purchases of handguns may be disapproved for (1) individuals under indictment for, or convicted in any court of, a crime punishable by imprisonment for a term exceeding one year; (2) fugitives from justice; (3) unlawful users of or those addicted to any controlled substance; (4) those adjudicated as mentally defective, or persons who have been committed to a mental institution; (5) illegal aliens, or those who are in the United States unlawfully; (6) persons who have not been discharged from the armed forces under honorable conditions; and (7) "a person who, having been a citizen of the United States, has renounced such citizenship." Gun dealers not abiding by the provisions of the law may have their licenses suspended or revoked and may be fined up to $5,000 per illegal transaction. Twenty-seven states and territories must comply with the law, but the District of Columbia and twenty-three states are exempt from the law's provisions because they have more stringent laws already in effect.

As of this writing, the national background checking system, called Instacheck, is not yet fully in place. The five-day waiting period for handgun purchases is to be phased out after the national system is fully operational.

Handgun victim James Brady sits to the right of President Clinton as the Brady Bill is signed into law. Much recent anticrime policy in the United States has focused on gun control. Do you think that the government has the right to restrict gun ownership? *Gary Hershorn/Reuter/Corbis-Bettmann.*

In an effort to reduce firearm theft, especially during the interstate shipment of weapons, the Brady law also requires that "[n]o common or contract carrier shall require or cause any label, tag, or other written notice to be placed on the outside of any package, luggage, or other container that such package, luggage, or other container contains a firearm."

Proponents of the Brady law believed that the widespread and ready availability of guns throughout the United States was a significant factor contributing to the crime problem. Statistics seem to support that view. Recent reports[48] by the Bureau of Justice Statistics, for example, found that approximately 1.3 million crimes are committed annually in the United States with handguns. Handguns are used in an ever-growing percentage of violent crimes, and overall handgun use is up—at the same time that the crime rate is dropping. According to the BJS, 92 percent of crimes committed with handguns are nonfatal. Handguns are used, however, in 55.6 percent of the nation's murders, and offenders armed with handguns commit one in every eight nonfatal violent crimes, including rape, robbery, and assault. The BJS also found that young black males comprise the group most victimized by handgun crime. Annually, approximately forty handgun victimizations occur for every 1,000 black males age 16 to 19 in the U.S. population—four times the rate for young white males. Other findings showed that offenders fired their weapons in 17 percent of all nonfatal handgun crimes, missing the victim four of five times, and that approximately 21,000 victims are wounded by handguns each year. The BJS also reports that, on average, 340,000 firearms are stolen yearly.

Opponents of the Brady law, however, are not convinced it will reduce crime. As Rep. Harold Volkmer (D-Mo.) said at the time the bill was being debated in the Senate: "A waiting period imposes a burden on those who obey the law. Getting criminals off the street is the only way to solve the crime problem. It is ludicrous to think that tougher gun laws will stop criminals." The strongest and most vocal opposition to handgun control, however, comes from the National Rifle Association (NRA), which claims the Brady law and other measures like it are unconstitutional.

In January 1994, Philip Toth, 25, became the first person formally accused of violating the Brady law.[49] Toth was charged in U.S. District Court in Cedar Rapids, Iowa, with stealing guns from a licensed firearms dealer, now a federal offense under the law. In April of that same year John Arnold, a Fort Walton Beach, Florida, gun dealer, became the first person convicted under the law.[50] He had been charged with stealing five guns from the Gulf Breeze, Florida, Pistol Parlor in January 1994.

Other gun law changes may be in the works. Following passage of the Brady law, President Clinton said that he was intrigued by an idea raised by New York City Mayor Rudolph Giuliani, "calling for either the federal government or the states to establish gun licensing and training systems for potential gun owners, similar to current licensing requirements for motorists."

THE VIOLENT CRIME CONTROL
AND LAW ENFORCEMENT ACT OF 1994

Another direct result of get-tough crime-control attitudes is the **Violent Crime Control and Law Enforcement Act of 1994.** At first blush, the act, which was passed by Congress in response to increasingly hard-nosed voter sentiment about crime, appears primarily representative of a deterrence strategy, although it also contains elements of the protection/avoidance approach. Conservative critics of the law, however, which was passed by a Democratic-controlled Congress under the leadership of a Democratic president, claim that it is really a liberal agenda in disguise and that its funding of social programs in the fight against crime moves it in the direction of nurturant strategies. In fact, the law tries to be all things, and attempts to address the needs of a wide diversity of political constituencies. As a result, it embodies aspects of each of the three types of crime-control strategies identified earlier.

The 1994 law, one of the most sweeping pieces of federal anticrime legislation of all time, provided massive funding for increased law enforcement and correctional resources, including $30.2 billion over six years for crime reduction efforts through the Violent Crime Reduction Trust Fund. Savings from the president's reductions in the federal work force, as calculated by the Congressional Budget Office—and locked in by reductions in federal budget caps—are expected to fund the more than $30 billion in crime bill initiatives.

Under the act—through whose auspices funding continues to flow—state and local law enforcement agencies were slated to receive $10.8 billion, including (1) $8.8 billion to put 100,000 police officers on the streets in community policing programs; (2) $245 million for rural anticrime and antidrug efforts; (3) $130 million for technical automation grants for law enforcement agencies; and (4) $200 million for college scholarships for students who agree to serve as police officers and for scholarships for in-service officers.

Another $2.6 billion was slated to go to enhance the activities of federal enforcement agencies, including $250 million to the FBI, $150 million to the DEA, $1.2 billion to the Immigration and Naturalization Service and Border Patrol, $50 million to United States Attorneys, $550 million to the Treasury Department, $200 million to the Justice Department, and $200 million to federal courts.

Prisons across the nation are receiving $9.7 billion, including (1) $7.9 billion in grants to the states to build and operate prisons and incarceration alternatives such as boot camps to ensure that additional prison cells will be available to put—and keep—violent offenders behind bars; and (2) $1.8 billion to states for costs of incarcerating criminal illegal aliens.

Another $6.1 billion was earmarked for crime prevention efforts, including (1) $90 million to create an interagency Ounce of Prevention Council to coordinate new and existing crime prevention programs; (2) $567 million for after-school, weekend, and summer "safe haven" programs to provide children with positive activities and alternatives; (3) $243 million to provide in-school assistance to at-risk children, including education, mentoring, and other programs; (4) $1.6 billion to fight violence against women; (5) $1.6 billion for direct funding to localities around the country for anticrime efforts, such as drug treatment, education, and jobs under a portion of the bill called the Local Partnership Act; (6) $626 million for model crime prevention programs targeted at high-crime neighborhoods; (7) $270 million for lines of credit to community development corporations to stimulate business and employment opportunities for low-income, unemployed, and underemployed individuals; and (8) $383 million for drug treatment programs for state ($270 million) and federal ($113 million) prisoners.

Another $377 million was earmarked for a new Local Crime Prevention Block Grant program to be distributed to local governments to be used as local needs dictate for, among other things, (1) antigang programs, (2) midnight sports leagues to give at-risk youth nightly alternatives to the streets, (3) the establishment of boys and girls clubs in low-income housing communities and the encouraging of police officers to live in those communities, (4) partnerships between senior citizen groups and law enforcement to combat crimes against elderly Americans, (5) partnerships between law enforcement and social service agencies to fight crimes against children, and (6) supervised centers for divorced or separated parents to visit their children in "safe havens" when a history of risk of physical or sexual abuse is indicated.

Drug courts that target nonviolent offenders with substance abuse problems were funded to the tune of $1 billion. Participants in such programs will be intensively supervised, given drug treatment, and subjected to graduated sanctions—ultimately including prison terms—for failing random drug tests.

The act also increased control over firearms including (1) a ban on the manufacture of nineteen military-style assault weapons; (2) prohibiting the sale or transfer of a gun to a juvenile and possession of a gun by a juvenile; (3) prohibiting gun sales to, and possession by, persons subject to family violence restraining orders; and (4) strengthening federal licensing standards for firearms dealers.

Likewise, the act targeted gangs and youth violence by (1) providing new, stiff penalties for violent and drug crimes committed by gangs; (2) tripling penalties for using children to deal drugs near schools and playgrounds; and (3) enhancing penalties for all crimes using children and for recruiting and encouraging children to commit a crime.

The law also (1) created drug-free zones by increasing penalties for drug dealing near playgrounds, schoolyards, public housing projects, video arcades, and youth centers; (2) authorized adult treatment of 13-year-olds charged with the most violent of crimes (murder, attempted murder, aggravated assault, armed robbery, and rape); (3) enhanced federal penalties for acts of terrorism; (4) expanded the federal death penalty to cover about sixty offenses, including terrorism, murdering a law enforcement officer, large-scale drug trafficking, drive-by shootings, and carjacking in which death occurs; (5) mandated life imprisonment for criminals convicted of three violent felonies or drug offenses (the famous "three strikes and you're out" provision); and (6) increased or created new penalties for over seventy criminal offenses, primarily covering violent crimes, drug trafficking, and gun crimes such as drive-by shootings, the use of semiautomatic weapons, drug use and drug trafficking in prison, the possession of guns and explosives by convicts, sex offenses and assaults against children, crimes against the elderly, interstate gun trafficking, aggravated sexual abuse, gun smuggling, arson, hate crimes, and drunk driving.

In response to the complaints of state governments that the federal government was not taking seriously its responsibility to oversee the nation's borders and stem the flow of illegal immigrants, the law designated $1.2 billion for immigration enforcement, including (1) a summary procedure to speed deportation of aliens who have been convicted of crimes; (2) increased penalties for smuggling aliens and for document fraud; and (3) monies to hire new border patrol agents, asylum reform, and other immigration enforcement activities.

In the area of victims rights, the bill (1) allowed victims of violent and sex crimes to speak at the sentencing of their assailants, (2) required sex offenders and child molesters to pay restitution to their victims, and (3) prohibited diversion of victims' funds to other federal programs.

Finally, the 1994 legislation increased federal criminal penalties for various types of fraud, including (1) telemarketing fraud targeted at senior citizens and multiple victims, (2) computer crime offenses, (3) a new federal offense of major fraud by insurance companies against their policyholders, and (4) credit card offenses.

For all its complexity, there are those who suspect that the Violent Crime Control and Law Enforcement Act of 1994 was primarily a political product, intended to appease a variety of constituencies. As Alfred Blumstein explains: "The legislative amalgam . . . contained an astonishing array of programs and provisions costing 30 billion dollars. Some were intended to satisfy doves (e.g., prevention programs, drug courts), many more were directed at satisfying the hawks (e.g., major subsidies for prisons, three-strikes law, capital punishment), but very few were directed at satisfying the owls, those who would like to substitute more rationality for the ideology that dominates crime-control policy."[51]

⬥⬥

CRIME FIGHTING: WHAT WORKS

Eugene H. Methvin

If you were America's anti-crime czar, with full powers to invest $30 billion to make our cities safe again, where would you put it? This year, Congress chose to divide the money three ways. It spent $13.5 billion to hire more cops, $9.8 billion to build more prisons, boot camps and "alternate facilities," and $6.9 billion for "prevention" programs ranging from "self-esteem" classes to "gang resistance education" and a "Junior Officers in Training" program for high schoolers.

If America's bureaucracies knew how to target "prevention" dollars, crime would not be a national issue. We have spent literally trillions on programs like those Congress prescribed.

How about investing in cops? In 1992, the U.S. had 534,000. They made fewer than 4 million felony arrests, and only 381,500 convicted felons landed in prison. Thus, the average cop is lucky to get a single serious felon locked away each year. The cops waste enormous time and money chasing the same criminals, collaring them, processing them and sitting in court—only to see them go free for one reason or another.

It costs an estimated $75,000 to put a single cop on the streets in high-crime districts, but only about $17,000 a year to keep a convicted criminal behind bars. Thus we can keep four career criminals locked up for the price of one cop on the street, and prevent far more crime.

Studying locales as diverse as London, Copenhagen, Philadelphia, Dayton, Racine, Phoenix and Utah, criminologists have demonstrated that each year's crop of young males contains a tiny and stable minority of serious habitual offenders who commit well over half of the violent and serious crime.

A pioneering study of all 31,436 men born in Copenhagen in the years between 1944 and 1947 found that just 0.6% of offenders committed 43.4% of the violent crime.

In our own country, the National Youth Survey followed 1,725 juveniles of both sexes aged 11 to 17, carefully selected to represent all U.S. youngsters, for 15 years. Just 32 became high-rate offenders and multiple drug users. This tiny fraction, about 4% of the males, accounted for half of all the serious crimes committed by the entire group. They committed 30 to 40 violent crimes and hundreds of lesser crimes, year after year, on into adulthood.

Violence has escalated in recent years not because the number of criminals has grown but chiefly because this tiny fraction of high-rate offenders has increased both the frequency and intensity of their violence.

Consider a recent study, reported in the Fall 1994 edition of the journal *Criminology*, that followed 6,310 California prisoners released in 1962 and 1963. They were selected to represent all 25,000 California inmates at the time. These were bad hombres: 56% had been in prison before, and 44% were in for violent offenses, burglary or robbery.

Over the next 26 years, these convicts were arrested 30,464 times. Moreover, since criminologists know criminal repeaters get away with a dozen or more crimes per arrest, these 6,310 convicts undoubtedly contributed over a quarter-million crimes to California's crime rate.

For the 4,897 who were rearrested, 54.4% of the charges involved nuisance offenses, such as parole violations, drunk driving, disorderly conduct, gambling and drug possession or use. But the group also scored arrests for 10,000 serious crimes.

What if, instead of sending these career criminals on repeated trips through the revolving door, we had simply "locked 'em up and thrown away the key" in 1962?

To have kept all 6,310 in prison for 26 years would have cost California something like $1.3 billion. As it was, they cost the state a good chunk of that amount anyway—on investigation, prosecution and incarceration for their subsequent crimes.

A rough guess for California's taxpayers' net out-of-pocket costs for that "extra" law enforcement activity would be half the $1.3 billion. So the added cost to prevent almost 10,000 serious crimes—including 184 homicides, 2,084 assaults, 126 kidnappings, 144 rapes, 2,756 burglaries, 655 auto thefts, and 1,193 robberies would be well under a billion—a real bargain.

So where would you invest to cut crime in America: "prevention," cops, or prisons?

Eugene H. Methvin, a *Reader's Digest* senior editor in the Washington editorial office, has covered the criminal justice system for more than forty years.

Source: Reprinted with permission of *Investor's Business Daily.* Guest Editorial. Eugene H. Methvin, "Crime Fighting: What Works?" November 2, 1994, p. A2.

Three-strikes a provision
of some criminal statutes
which mandates life
imprisonment for
criminals convicted of
three violent felonies or
serious drug offenses.

"THREE-STRIKES" LEGISLATION

One interesting and controversial aspect of the Violent Crime Control and Law Enforcement Act of 1994 is its "three-strikes" provision. The **three-strikes** provision, a deterrence strategy, reads as follows:

Mandatory life imprisonment:

Notwithstanding any other provision of law, a person who is convicted in a court of the United States of a serious violent felony shall be sentenced to life imprisonment if—

(A) the person has been convicted (and those convictions have become final) on separate prior occasions in a court of the United States or of a State of—

(i) 2 or more serious violent felonies; or

(ii) one or more serious violent felonies and one or more serious drug offenses; and

(B) each serious violent felony or serious drug offense used as a basis for sentencing under this subsection, other than the first, was committed after the defendant's conviction of the preceding serious violent felony or serious drug offense.

On August 14, 1995, Thomas Lee Farmer, 43, of Des Moines, Iowa, became the first person sentenced under the federal "three-strikes" law.[52] Farmer, who had three previous convictions for murder, robbery, and conspiracy to commit murder dating back to 1971, was convicted of trying to rob a Waterloo, Iowa, grocery store at gunpoint. Farmer received a mandatory life prison term.

Three-strikes laws are part of a relatively new nationwide initiative intended to keep repeat offenders behind bars.[53] Nationally, many states are in the process of adopting three-strikes laws, which are a kind of **habitual offender statute.** Such laws generally require that offenders who are convicted of three or more serious crimes be sentenced to a lengthy prison term (often life behind bars) following their third conviction. Although three-strikes laws may be new, habitual offender statutes are not, and thirty-five states already have some form of habitual offender statute on the books. One of the first states to pass an habitual offender statute was Illinois. The Illinois law, which was enacted in 1978, covers only violent offenses. It sounds, however, like a three-strikes law because it mandates a life sentence without parole for people convicted of their third so-called class X felony. Fewer than a hundred offenders are currently serving sentences under the Illinois habitual offender statute.

Other states have recently joined the "get tough on crime" bandwagon. In the spring of 1994, for example, California legislators passed the state's now famous "three strikes and you're out" bill. Amid much fanfare, Governor Pete Wilson signed the three-strikes measure into law, calling it "the toughest and most sweeping crime bill in California history." California's law, which is retroactive (in that it counts offenses committed before the date the legislation was signed), requires a 25-year-to-life sentence for three-time felons with convictions for two or more serious or violent prior offenses. Criminal offenders facing a "second strike" can receive up to double the normal sentence for their most recent offense. Under the law, parole consideration is not available until at least 80 percent of an offender's sentence has

**Habitual offender
statutes** laws intended to
keep repeat criminal
offenders behind bars.
Lately these laws have
gained new attention
under the rubric of "three
strikes and you're out."

been served. In 1996, however, the California Supreme Court, in the case of *People
v. Superior Court of San Diego—Romero*,[54] cast the future of the three-strikes law in
California into doubt. The court ruled that—regardless of the law—California
judges retain the discretion to reduce three-strike sentences, and to avoid counting
previous convictions at sentencing, "in furtherance of justice." Efforts to modify
California's three-strikes law ensued. As of this writing, however, they have been unsuccessful. By mid-1997, twenty-two states had passed three-strikes legislation—
and other states were considering the same. Some states enacted even tougher laws.
Georgia, for example, passed a two-strikes law. Georgia's law, one of the stiffest in
the nation, requires that murderers and persons convicted of a second violent
felony be sentenced to life in prison without parole.

Unfortunately, get-tough policies may not provide the solution those who advocate them seek. In an excellent analysis of crime-control policy,[55] Bryan Vila
presents research findings which tend to show that nurturant strategies—those
that attempt to get at the root causes of crime and that address child welfare
needs—are more effective than others in the long run. "We know full well that the
most serious and intractable types of crime have their roots in the very child welfare problems that are neglected as we trash through one ineffective war on crime
after another," says Vila. "[P]olitical support for nurturant programs might be ob-
tainable," he says, "if we could reverse the vicious cycle of media sensationalism,
short-sighted policy, and public impatience that encourages ineffective 'quick
fixes' for crime."[56]

▓ INTERNATIONAL POLICIES

The United States is not the only country fighting crime with strict legal mandates.
Indeed, a growing conservatism in many other countries, coupled with new concerns about crime, have led a number of nations to recently enact legislation designed to curb crime through strategies of deterrence. In 1994, for example, the
British parliament passed the Criminal Justice and Police Bill, marking the return
to a get-tough English crime policy. British Home Secretary Michael Howard called
the legislation "the most comprehensive attempt to tackle crime [in England] in
more than three decades."[57]

The degree to which British social policy shifted with passage of the bill can be
easily seen in one feature of the legislation, which removed a suspect's right to silence. According to Howard, "the right of silence, [is] an age-old feature of Britain's
justice system that has been copied in many countries, [but which] was a charter for
terrorists and professional criminals." Prior to the bill's passage suspects were told
that they had a right to remain silent under police questioning, and that anything
they might say could be taken down and be used as evidence against them. The bill
mandates that suspects now be told only that failure to mention relevant information during questioning at the police station may damage their case. Another feature of the 1994 statute gives courts wide powers to sentence persistent offenders
aged 12 to 14 and doubles the maximum permissible sentence in institutions for
youthful offenders.

Kriminalpolitik the
political handling of
crime, or a criminology-
based social policy.

CAN WE SOLVE THE PROBLEM OF CRIME?

In 1956 the European writer H. Bianchi[58] emphasized what he saw as the difference between criminology and what he termed *Kriminalpolitik.* Criminology, said Bianchi, should be considered a "metascience" or "a science of wider scope (than that of criminal law, jurisprudence, criminal justice, or corrections) whose terminology can be used to clarify the conceptions of its subdisciplines. Far from being a mere auxiliary to the criminal law," said Bianchi, "it is therefore superior to it."[59]

For Bianchi, and other writers of the time, the concept of **Kriminalpolitik** referred to the political handling of crime, or—as we might say today—a criminology-based social policy. Bianchi believed that if criminology were to remain pure, it could not afford to sully its hands, so to speak, with political concerns. Today, however, the image esteemed by criminologists and the expectations they hold for their discipline are quite different than they were in Bianchi's time. Many criminologists expect to work hand-in-hand with politicians and policymakers, forging crime-control agendas based on scientific knowledge and criminological theorizing. Some would say that this change in attitude represents a maturation of the discipline of criminology.

Whether effective crime-control policies can ever be implemented, however, is another question. A number of critics argue that only drastic policy-level changes

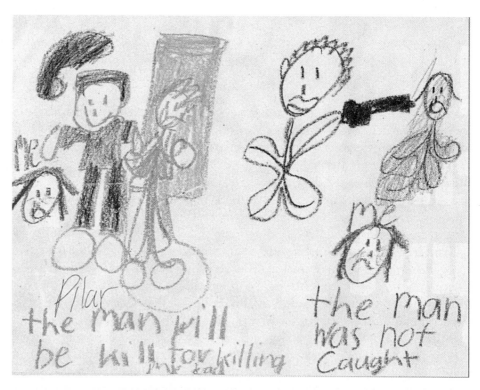

The American voting public is "fed up" with crime, a fact symbolized by this drawing. A child's grief expressed through art—"The man will be kill for killing my dad. . . . The man was not caught," the young artist writes. How might the experience of criminal victimization influence a child's development? *Illustration by Pilar Martin.*

can address the real issues that underlie high rates of crime and criminal activity. Drug legalization, the elimination of guns throughout America, nightly curfews, and close control of media violence, say such reformers, may be necessary before crime can be curbed. "Reforms that substantially will lower the crime rate are unlikely because of cultural taboos," says Lawrence Friedman, a Stanford University law professor and author of the book *Crime and Punishment in American History.* According to Friedman, "[i]f you add up all the taboos we have—against legalization of drugs, real gun control, paying taxes for social programs we might at least try—it's hard not to come to the conclusion that there isn't much we can do about crime."[60] Many existing taboos, say such thinkers, are rooted in citizens' demands for individual freedoms. "At one time in South Korea," says Friedman, "they had an absolute curfew between midnight and 5 A.M. The police kept everyone off the streets. It was as hard on burglars as other citizens and very effective at squelching crime. But most Americans would consider that an unacceptable inroad on their personal lives."

Complicating the picture further is the fact that numerous interest groups, each with its own agenda, are clamoring to be heard by policymakers. As Robert D. Pursley states, "[o]ur nation's efforts to deal with crime remind us that crime, among other things, is a highly political issue that has been transformed into a racially volatile subject. This issue provides an excellent window into political policymaking. Opposing ideological lines have divided our efforts to develop comprehensive anticrime programs. Deep fissures in our social fabric have contributed to conflicting attitudes about crime and its control."[61]

Racial divisiveness has created one of those fissures. Pursley writes: "Our anticrime programs and studies of traditional street crimes, especially those involving violence, show that such crimes are disproportionately the acts of young African-American males. So long as black men commit violent crimes at a rate that is six to eight times higher than that found among whites and three to four times higher than that among Latino males, race and crime will be threads of the same cloth. These facts have become unpopular and certainly not politically correct to discuss in certain circles, but they remain facts. No attempt to silence those who raise such issues by denouncing them as 'racists' can conceal these statistics."[62]

Pursley is telling us, in effect, that for some groups in some locales, violations of the criminal law are simply part of the landscape. Among certain segments of the American population, crime may be an accepted way of doing business and criminal activity, even when discovered, might not necessarily be stigmatizing. Moreover, those who commit crimes may hold positions of prestige or highly visible public offices when their constituencies fail to condemn illicit behavior. Ultimately they may even serve as role models to youngsters—albeit dubious ones. Although such a perspective is undoubtedly a minority point of view, it seriously impacts the ability of policymakers to establish consistent policies in the battle against crime.

A symbol of the divisiveness that today characterizes public attitudes toward crime was the November 1994 election of Marion Barry, a convicted drug felon and former federal inmate, to head the government of Washington, D.C. In 1990 Barry, who had been D.C. mayor for twelve years, was videotaped smoking crack cocaine during an FBI sting operation, convicted of illegal drug use, and sent to prison. A mere five years later, following release from federal prison, he was once

Washington, D.C., mayor, Marion Barry with his wife, Cora. Barry, a convicted drug felon, was reelected to office in 1994—symbolizing the diversity of attitudes Americans hold toward criminal activity. How could Barry be reelected mayor? *Tim Dillon/USA Today.*

again heading the government of our nation's capitol—reelected at a time when the federal government and many of the states were moving toward ultraconservative crime-control and antidrug policies. During the election, Barry vowed that he would not submit to random drug tests if elected. In May 1996, Barry suddenly left Washington and checked into a thirty-two-acre religious retreat outside St. Louis. Many said that Barry was trying to kick a continuing drug habit. At the time, law enforcement sources told a CNN reporter that they "have recently been receiving more numerous and credible reports that Barry has been using drugs. Sources even say that the reports include first-hand accounts of alleged drug sales. But authorities have not substantiated them."[63]

In 1997 Congress stripped Barry of most of his power, and appointed a control board to run the city. Nonetheless, Barry says he would run for reelection in 1998.

SYMBOLISM AND PUBLIC POLICY

When all the political crime-fighting rhetoric has ended, and all the dollars have been spent, some expect that crime will still be with us. Many analysts of the contemporary scene see all crime-control policies, especially those at the federal level, as largely symbolic. As Nancy E. Marion explained (a few years ago), "No one could effectively argue that the federal government under any modern president has successfully reduced the amount of criminal activity in the United States. The FBI reports yearly that crime has not gone down, but only continues to increase [Marion was writing in 1993]. Further, the number of people using drugs has not gone down. Therefore, it can be said that the federal government is not making any progress in their fight against crime."[64]

Why is this so? Marion states because, "many of the policies supported by the federal government may in actuality be symbolic gestures to appease the public rather than attempts to reduce crime. One reason for the presence of symbolic policies . . . is simply that the federal government cannot reduce crime—it is not within the government's capacity to do so."[65] Marion says that congressional power is fragmented through the influence of special interest groups, and as a result, the potential of crime-control initiatives is effectively dispersed by the time any legislation is enacted. In addition, says Marion, the American political system is decidedly shortsighted, focusing only on issues that are likely to win elections. Similarly, due to changes in incumbents (often every two to four years), it is impossible to establish consistent crime-control policies. Whereas a Democratic president may hold office for four years, for example, it is likely that a Republican president will take office with the next elections—and in the meantime a nearly continuous shuffling of cabinet members, senators, representatives, U.S. Supreme Court justices, agency heads, federal judges, and so on is occurring. Similar changes at the state level ensure constant modification of laws, enforcement practices, and criminal sanctions. Without a consistent, long-term, national, and interstate approach to crime fighting, Marion suggests, crime can never be effectively reduced.

Even consistent policies may be inaccurately targeted. As one author explains, "[o]ne reason we cannot stop crime in the United States is because many elements of the crime problem we believe to be true simply are not. Because of the way crime is presented in the media, crime events 'become distorted and are given unprecedented social consideration.' These myths help to sustain our views of crime, criminals, and the system as a whole."[66] Part of the mythology of crime, some claim, is belief in criminological theories of limited usefulness. Another problem flows from our inability to effectively conceptualize of crime itself. Laws may merely reflect moral conceptions of the political majority. Both morality and law are subject to change, making it difficult to accurately define crime. A final difficulty is one of accurately measuring the extent of crime. Although exhaustive efforts have been made toward achieving accuracy in measurement, experts are still unable to ascertain the true rate of crime in the United States. Hence, as critics of contemporary crime-fighting policies indicate, if we do not fully understand what crime is, or what causes it, how can we create an effective policy for controlling it?

Some people, such as Alfred Blumstein, say the answer is possibly found in increased expenditures on criminological research. According to Blumstein: "That we are in this confused state is not surprising when we recognize that the nation spends less than $25 million per year for research at the National Institute of Justice on the problem that seems to be the nation's greatest concern. Contrast this with $11 billion for health research at the National Institutes of Health, $600 million on mental health, and $165 million for dental research. With so small a research effort, it is not surprising that we reach out for programs with little ability to assess the impact that they might have on the intended objective, and that we operate in a pre-Galilean mode when we debate crime policy."[67]

⠶

THE NATIONAL CRIMINAL JUSTICE
COMMISSION RECOMMENDATIONS

In 1996 the National Criminal Justice Commission, a project of the National Center on Institutions and Alternatives, in Alexandria, Virginia, released its report on American criminal justice. The report, entitled *The Real War on Crime,* was the result of a two-year undertaking by a nonpartisan group of citizens and experts intended to assess the state of America's criminal justice system. The goals of the commission were to provide a comprehensive assessment of the American criminal justice system, to offer solutions to reduce violence, to recommend policies to make American communities safer, and to determine if America's war on crime has been a worthwhile undertaking.

The commission made "10 recommendations to shift the fundamental direction of U.S. crime policy." Those recommendations, which are reproduced here in the original wording provided by the commission, were:

- Decrease the reliance on prisons as the primary response to criminal behavior. Impose a three-year moratorium on new prison construction until a systematic assessment of prison needs can be completed. Replace many prison sanctions with alternative programs that are less expensive and often more effective at reducing crime.
- Replace the war on drugs with a policy of harm reduction where the police work with public health professional to stem illegal drug use. Drug addiction should be treated as a public health challenge rather than a criminal justice problem.
- Balance criminal justice spending with resources spent on other civic activities. Stop doing what doesn't work, and invest resources in proven prevention programs and other crime fighting alternatives.
- Restore the internal balance of the criminal justice system so judges have more discretion at sentencing and victims of crime receive better treatment by the court system.
- Commission an independent clearinghouse to gather and report objective criminal justice information to the public. The clearinghouse should be separate from the Department of Justice.
- At all levels of government create crime councils to develop a coordinated anti-crime strategy. This council should be created at the city, county, state, and national level. They should include representatives of law enforcement, prosecutors, social service professionals, public health specialists, child welfare officials, crime victims, and representatives of other government agencies concerned with crime prevention.
- Reduce violence by using innovative approaches developed in the field of public health; and reduce the harmful effects of violence by passing gun control legislation at the federal level.

- Commit ourselves to reducing poverty in order to reduce street crime. Funds should be provided so each child can enter an early childhood development program.
- Eliminate racial bias and reduce racial disparity with the criminal justice system.
- Shift ourselves from an agenda of "war" to an agenda of "peace." Wars against American citizens are wars that nobody can win.

Source: The National Center on Institutions and Alternatives world wide web site, January 2, 1997.

COSTS OF CRIME AND PUNISHMENT:

MORE PRISONS SAVE MONEY, BUT ONLY UP TO A POINT

Charles Oliver

The good news is that serious crime is down in America. The bad news is that it's still unacceptably high.

The Justice Department estimates that Americans face some 49 million attempted crimes each year. This high level of crime imposes an enormous burden on its victims: lost property, lost wages, medical bills, pain and suffering. It adds up to hundreds of billions of dollars.

Seen in this light, many criminologists say, the cost of keeping a crook in prison is pretty small. Many studies show that prison does cut crime and America's vast prison-building of the last two decades made sense.

But other data show that jailing more people longer may reach a point of diminishing returns. In other words, the likely costs of releasing certain offenders who could commit new crimes are less than the cost of keeping them in jail.

There's no doubt that crime itself costs Americans big money. A recent report from the U.S. government's National Institute for Justice found that crime costs Americans $105 billion each year in lost earnings and medical costs. Throw in pain and suffering and reduced quality of life, and the total cost soars to $451 billion each year. That's roughly $1,800 for each man, woman and child in the U.S.

Violent crime, including drunken driving, child abuse and arson, makes up the biggest part of that total—$426 billion. Property crime, like burglary and auto theft, costs $25 billion. The total includes $45 billion paid each year by insurance firms to crime victims. But it doesn't include costs of the criminal justice system. Nor does it count private actions to cut crime such as hiring security guards or buying alarm systems. The NIJ didn't try to put a cost on so-called victimless crimes, such as drug use or prostitution.

Although property crime is more common, violent crime costs more. This is due to the effects of injuries to victims: lost wages, medical costs and reduced quality of life. For instance, 3% of all U.S. medical spending results from violent crime, and 14% of injury-related medical costs come from violent crime. Violent crime causes wage losses that equal 1% of all earnings.

A breakdown of these costs by crime type shows that the typical arson costs $54,000 per victim and assault $31,000 per victim. Compare that with the cost of keeping an inmate in prison: $20,000 to $30,000 a year. The U.S. has some 1.1 million people behind bars. That costs about $22 billion to $30 billion a year.

What does that money buy? Criminologists still disagree over the exact effect jail has on crime. But a growing body of research suggests that jailing crooks can cut crime, and it seems that money for prisons is generally well-spent.

On average, rape costs $110,000 per victim, for instance. If jailing a rapist for two years prevents even one rape, the trade-off makes economic sense. And jailing career criminals can often stop them from committing many crimes. In the late '70s, the Rand think tank conducted a survey of prisoners in Texas, Michigan and California. "We found the median number of non-drug crimes committed in the year before incarceration was 15" by each prisoner, said Allan Abrahams, a researcher in Rand's criminal justice program.

In 1990, researchers John J. DiIulio and Anne Morrison Piehl did a similar survey of Wisconsin prisoners. In 1993, DiIulio and Piehl questioned prisoners in New Jersey. In each state, the median number of crimes committed in the year before incarceration was 12 per prisoner.

Crime Costs

DiIulio and Piehl estimate that the median social cost of that crime was $70,098. In other words, half the prisoners cost society more than $70,098 and half less in the year before getting jailed.

They divided that sum by $25,000. That's a rough figure for the cost of keeping one person in prison for a year. This gave them a cost-benefit ratio of 2.80. For every dollar society spends to keep someone locked up, it saves $2.80 from averted crimes.

In the past, putting more people behind bars has had substantial results. Patrick A. Langan is a researcher at the Bureau of Justice Statistics. He looked at the tripling of the U.S. prison population from 1975 to 1989. He says it kept violent crime 10% to 15% below what it would have been. "That translates into 390,000 murders, rapes, robberies and aggravated assaults in 1989 alone," Langan said.

That's a hefty cut. But notice that to get that 15% reduction, the U.S. had to triple its prison population. If the U.S. tripled its prison population again, it likely would see a smaller reduction in crimes.

A 1993 report by the National Research Council looked at the crime-cutting effects of jailing crooks. It found that incarceration is subject to the law of diminishing returns. In other words, each increase in prison population has a smaller impact on crime.

The effects of incarceration seem to drop as prison populations increase for two reasons. First, a large amount of crime is committed by a relatively small number of offenders. Because of their high rates of activity, they are the most likely to be caught and incarcerated, and because of their prior criminal records, they are likely to draw longer sentences. Thus, these criminals already spend a good part of their criminal careers behind bars. Increases in the prison population bring in successively less serious offenders, and the number of crimes prevented per inmate drops.

Second, most criminals' careers are fairly short, generally peaking in activity in a crook's early 20s. Imprisoning someone at an early age can take a real bite out of crime. Keeping that person in jail well into his 40s or 50s typically doesn't.

Increasing the length of time served gives increasing prison space to older felons. These are persons who would likely stop committing crimes even if they were released into the community.

Even DiIulio and Piehl say that prison doesn't always pay. "The public and its purse could benefit if 10% to 25% of prisoners were under some other form of correctional supervision or released from custody altogether," they wrote.

The cost of imprisoning these criminals is greater than the costs of crimes they would commit if free. Such crooks are basically property offenders, petty thieves and burglars. This isn't to say that these criminals should be left on the street. A lower-cost punishment, such as supervised probation or home confinement, may make sense.

DiIulio and Piehl are critical of parole. They note that half of all parolees will commit another crime within three years of their release. DiIulio also claims that one in three violent crimes are committed by those on parole, probation or pretrial release.

That said, DiIulio and Piehl still criticize moves to abolish parole completely or almost completely. Half of all parolees DON'T commit another crime, they note. "No doubt a large fraction of the parole population should be imprisoned. But a no-parole policy lowers rather than increases the chances that the system will sort offenders more cost-effectively," they write.

This raises the question of whether our prison resources are being used well. About 20% of state prison inmates are serving time on drug charges. That's up from 8.6% in 1986. Nearly two-thirds of federal inmates are doing time for drug crimes. That's up from one-third in 1986.

DiIulio and Piehl don't back legalizing drugs, but they argue that no drug sales are prevented by locking up drug criminals. That view has been backed by other analysts who can't be accused of being soft on crime. Leading criminologist James Q. Wilson is one of these.

It seems that imprisoning a drug dealer simply opens up a job opportunity for another dealer. The same is not true of locking up a rapist, for example.

A Morals Issue?

Of course, one can, and some people do, argue for locking up drug criminals on purely moral grounds. They say long prison terms are what such crimes demand. And, to be sure, many drug criminals also commit other crimes, so locking up these people may help cut crime.

But some drug criminals are simply drug criminals, and on purely practical grounds some wonder whether it makes sense to put them in prison.

Nobel-winning economist Milton Friedman, for instance, has said drugs should be made legal. Others say it may be better to give nonviolent drug criminals some cheaper form of punishment, such as home confinement, fines or mandatory drug treatment.

It's tough to tell how many prisoners have committed only drug crimes. But DiIulio and Piehl found some interest-

ing facts about New Jersey inmates. One-fourth did no crimes other than sell drugs in the four months before entering jail. And 3% committed no crimes other than drug possession.

Letting such persons out of prison would free cells that could house violent criminals. Legalizing drugs or just giving drug criminals alternative sentences could save taxpayers money, too. But many worry about what sort of message it would send.

Source: Reprinted with permission of *Investors Business Daily.* Charles Oliver, "Costs Of Crime And Punishment: More Prisons Save Money, But Only Up To A Point", May 20, 1996.

Despite the claims of quantitative criminologists, the failures of criminal justice [policy] in any society cannot truly be measured in quantitative terms because such failures qualitatively erode the core of social civility; people lose trust in each other, in their social obligations, in their systems of social control, and finally in themselves.

—SAM S. SOURYAL[68]

SUMMARY

Although crime has always been a part of American society, comprehensive efforts at crime control, at least at the federal level, originated during the Depression years of the twentieth century. Efforts to reduce crime, however, although well intentioned, are fraught with political uncertainties resting largely upon fundamental disagreements within American society itself as to the sources of crime and the most appropriate means for combating it. Bryan Vila, whose work is cited throughout this chapter, summarizes the contemporary situation this way: "Lack of a unified criminological framework has fostered shortsighted, inconsistent, and ineffective crime-control policies. Theoretical ambiguity made it easier for policymakers to base their decisions on politics rather than science. Lacking a reasonable complete and coherent explanation of the causes of crime, they have been free to shift the focus of crime-control efforts back and forth from individual-level to macro-level causes as the political pendulum swung from right to left. This erratic approach hindered crime-control efforts and fed the desperate belief that the problem of crime is intractable."[69]

Although answers to the crime problem appear to face formidable obstacles, all may not be lost. Fundamental social changes including the development of high moral values through education, the elimination (or significant reduction) of poverty, increased opportunities for success at all levels, and decriminalization of certain offenses may all be combined some day into a workable strategy for the management of criminal activity within the United States. In any event, major inroads into the crime problem cannot be made until American society, and especially those parts of it which are now accepting of criminal activity and the conditions that produce it, undergo a fundamental change in orientation.

WEB WATCH

Access the *Criminology Today* home page on the World Wide Web by pointing your browser at www.prenhall.com/cjcentral. Once there, click on "Criminology Today" to access the wealth of electronic resources supporting this text.

Onsite resources include (1) "Chapter Links," which provides succinct overviews of critical ideas from the textbook and links selected materials from around the Web to concepts found in the text; (2) "General Reference—Law and Justice Links." Organized by chapter, these links lead to other useful resources on the World Wide Web such as libraries, electronic discussion lists, and electronic journals; (3) "Criminology Sites on the Web," which lists links to organizations such as the American Society of Criminology and the National Organization for Victims Assistance (NOVA), as well as crime prevention links and statistics on crime and justice. Many other Web-based resources can be accessed via the *Criminology Today* site, including the federal Justice Information Center, the Bureau of Justice Statistics, the FBI, the RAND Corporation, the Vera Institute of Justice, PAVNET (an online "Partnership Against Violence," run by seven different federal agencies), and the National White Collar Crime Center.

Still another feature of the *Criminology Today* Web site is e-mail homework. Homework can be composed onsite and submitted to instructors using the instructor's e-mail address. To use the e-mail homework feature, click on "E-Mail Homework" on the opening page, and then type answers to the questions that appear in the spaces provided. Use your instructor's e-mail address to submit homework answers. The *Criminology Today* Web site also provides links to powerful Web-based search engines that can help you find topics of interest to you as you progress through your course of study. Search engines can be found under the heading "Criminology Sites on the Web."

DISCUSSION QUESTIONS

1. This book emphasizes a social problems versus social responsibility theme. What types of anticrime social policies might be based on the social responsibility perspective? The social problems approach? Why?
2. What are the two major policy approaches discussed in this chapter? What are the major differences between the two? With which do you most closely identify? Why?
3. What are the three types of crime-control strategies this chapter describes? Which comes closest to your own philosophy? Why?
4. Explain the social epidemiologic approach to reducing crime. In your opinion is the approach worthwhile? Why or why not?
5. If you were in charge of government crime reduction efforts, what steps would you take to control crime in the United States? Why would you choose those particular approaches?

NOTES

[1] Bernard Gendron, *Technology and the Human Condition* (New York: St. Martins, 1977), p. 255.

[2] Frank Tannenbaum, "Foreword," in Henry Elmer Barnes and Negley K. Teeters, *New Horizons in Criminology* (Englewood Cliffs, N.J.: Prentice Hall, 1943), p. v.

[3] Joan Petersilia, "Policy Relevance and the Future of Criminology—The American Society of Criminology, 1990 Presidential Address," *Criminology,* vol. 29, no. 1 (1991), pp. 1–15.

[4] Georgette Bennett, *Crimewarps: The Future of Crime in America* (Garden City, N.Y.: Anchor/Doubleday, 1987), p. xix

[5] James D. Calder, *The Origins and Development of Federal Crime Control Policy* (Westport, Conn.: Praeger, 1993), p. 211.

[6] Although charged with sodomy, Shakur was convicted on three lesser counts of sexual abuse. See Samuel Maull, "Shakur Trial," Associated Press wire service, December 2, 1994.

[7] James T. Jones IV, "Real-Life Woes Beset Actor/Rapper," *USA Today,* February 11, 1994, p. 2A.

[8] $1 million for himself and another $1 million for his bodyguard. See "Prosecutors Mull Second Trial for Rapper," Reuter wire service, February 23, 1996.

[9] Dennis R. Martin, "The Music of Murder," *ACJS Today,* November/December 1993, pp. 1, 3, 20.

[10] Kendall Hamilton and Allison Samuels, "Dr. Dre's New 'Hood: Hollywood," *Newsweek,* August 22, 1994, p. 45.

[11] See, for example, Elizabeth Snead, "Dogg's 'Murder' Video has Plenty of Bite," *USA Today,* October 13, 1994.

[12] Arthur L. Cribbs, Jr., "Gangsta Rappers Sing White Racists' Tune," *USA Today,* December 27, 1993, p. 9A.

[13] Some authors also hold that the nature and frequency with which crime stories appear in other popular media, such as newspapers, may influence the rate of criminal activity in society. For a thorough analysis of newspaper crime data, see H. L. Marsh, "Comparative Analysis of Crime Coverage in Newspapers in the United States and Other Countries from 1960–1989: A Review of the Literature," *Journal of Criminal Justice,* vol. 19, no. 1 (1991), pp. 67–79.

[14] James E. Anderson, *Public Policymaking: An Introduction* (Boston: Houghton Mifflin, 1990).

[15] Nancy E. Marion, *A History of Federal Crime Control Initiatives, 1960–1993* (Westport: Praeger, 1994), p. 3. For a more detailed analysis of the process by which crime control policies are created, see Paul Rock, "The Opening Stages of Criminal Justice Policy Making,"

British Journal of Criminology, vol. 35, no. 1 (Winter 1995).

[16]Jeff Ferrell, "Criminological *Verstehen:* Inside the Immediacy of Crime," *Justice Quarterly,* vol. 14, no. 1 (1997), p. 16.

[17]Nancy E. Marion, *A History of Federal Crime Control Initiatives, 1960–1993* (Westport: Praeger, 1994), abstract.

[18]The Massachusetts Institute for a New Commonwealth, "Criminal Justice in Massachusetts: Executive Summary," July 7, 1997; http://www.massinc.org/reports/cjim/exec.html

[19]Calder, *The Origins and Development of Federal Crime Control Policy.*

[20]Ibid., p. 1.

[21]Ibid., pp. ix–x.

[22]Ibid., p. 85.

[23]Ibid., p. 5.

[24]Ibid., p. 6.

[25]Ibid., various pages.

[26]Ibid., p. 83.

[27]Ibid.

[28]Ibid., citing the Commission, p. 102.

[29]Ibid., p. 157.

[30]The President's Commission on Law Enforcement and Administration of Justice, *The Challenge of Crime in a Free Society* (Washington, D.C.: U.S. Government Printing Office, 1967), p. xii.

[31]Steven A. Shull, *Domestic Policy Formation: Presidential-Congressional Partnership?* (Westport, Conn.: Greenwood Press, 1983), p. 41.

[32]"Remarks at the Annual Conference of the National Sheriff's Association in Hartford, Connecticut," *Public Papers of the President* (June 20, 1984), pp. 884–888.

[33]Carolyn Skorneck, "Anti-Drug Spending," Associated Press wire service, December 2, 1993.

[34]For an excellent overview of historical initiatives as well as contemporary suggestions for crime-control strategies, see James Q. Wilson and Joan Petersilia, *Crime: Twenty-Eight Leading Experts Look at the Most Pressing Problem of Our Time* (San Francisco: Institute for Contemporary Studies Press, 1995).

[35]See Arthur L. Kellermann, "Understanding and Prevention Violence: A Public Health Perspective," National Institute of Justice, June 1996.

[36]For an excellent discussion of the policies associated with law, punishment, and social control, see Thomas G. Blomberg and Stanley Co-

hen, eds., *Punishment and Social Control: Essays in Honor of Sheldon L. Messinger* (Hawthorne, N.Y.: Aldine de Gruyter, 1995).

[37]Richard Stratton, "Even Prisoners Must Have Hope," *Newsweek,* October 17, 1994, p. 90.

[38]David B. Kopel, "Guns, Germs, and Science," *Journal of the Medical Association of Georgia,* vol. 84 (June 1995), p. 269.

[39]For an excellent up-to-date review of policy issues in the crime-control area, see James Houston and William W. Parsons, *Criminal Justice and the Policy Process* (Chicago: Nelson-Hall, 1997).

[40]Bryan Vila, "A General Paradigm for Understanding Criminal Behavior: Extending Evolutionary Ecological Theory," *Criminology,* vol. 32, no. 3 (August 1994), pp. 311–359.

[41]Bryan Vila, "Could We Break the Crime Control Paradox?" paper presented at the annual meeting of the American Society of Criminology, Miami, November 1994.

[42]Bryan Vila, "Human Nature and Crime Control: Improving the Feasibility of Nurturant Strategies," *Politics and the Life Sciences,* March 1997, pp. 3–21.

[43]Vila, "A General Paradigm for Understanding Criminal Behavior."

[44]Vila, "Human Nature and Crime Control," p. 10.

[45]Ibid., p. 11.

[46]103rd Congress, H.R. 1025 ("The Brady Bill"), January 5, 1993, p. 1.

[47]A portion of the Brady Handgun Violence Prevention Act requiring the "chief law enforcement officer" of each local jurisdiction to conduct background checks and perform related tasks on an interim basis until a national checking system became operative, was struck down by the U.S. Supreme Court as unconstitutional in 1997. The Court, in *Printz* v. *U.S.* (1997) and *Mack* v. *U.S.* (1997), held that the constitutional principle of "dual sovereignty" prohibited direct federal control over state officers.

[48]Marianne W. Zawitz, *Guns Used in Crime: Firearms, Crime, and Criminal Justice* (Annapolis Junction, Md: Bureau of Justice Statistics, July 1995); and Michael R. Rand, *Guns and Crime: Handgun Victimization, Firearm Self-Defense, and Firearm Theft* (Annapolis Junction, Md: Bureau of Justice Statistics, April 1994).

[49]"Iowa Man Believed First to Be Charged Under Brady Bill," United Press International wire service, Northern edition, January 11, 1994.

[50]"Brady-First Conviction," Associated Press wire service, Northern edition, April 14, 1994.

[51]Alfred Blumstein, "Seeking the Connection between Crime and Punishment," *Jobs & Capital* (Santa Monica: Milken Institute for Job & Capital Formation), Winter 1995, vol. 4.

[52]National Association of Criminal Defense Lawyers, "Three Strikes Laws: Absurd and Unnecessary," NACDL Web posted at *www.criminaljustice.org/media/pr000005*.htm, November 1, 1997.

[53]For an excellent overview of the issues in the area, see David Shichor and Dale K. Sechrest, *Three Strikes and You're Out* (Thousand Oaks, Calif.: Sage, 1996).

[54]*People* v. *Superior Court of San Diego—Romero,* 917 P.2d 628 (California Supreme Court, 1996).

[55]Vila, "Could We Break the Crime Control Paradox?"

[56]Ibid., abstract.

[57]"Right of Silence to Go in New British Crime Bill," Reuters wire service, December 17, 1993.

[58]H. Bianchi, *Position and Subject-Matter of Criminology* (Amsterdam, 1956).

[59]Hermann Mannheim, *Comparative Criminology* (New York: Houghton Mifflin, 1965), p. 18.

[60]"Can Anything Really Be Done?" *USA Today* (magazine), vol. 122, no. 2587 (April 1994), p. 6.

[61]Robert D. Pursley, *Introduction to Criminal Justice,* 6th ed. (New York: Macmillan, 1991), p. 677.

[62]Ibid.

[63]Mark Feldstein, "Barry's absence stirs talk of drug relapse," CNN online, May 4, 1996, *http://cnn.com/US/9605/04/marion.barry/index*.html

[64]Marion, *A History of Federal Crime Control Initiatives, 1960–1993,* p. 250.

[65]Ibid., p. 244.

[66]Ibid., p. 249.

[67]Alfred Blumstein, "Seeking the Connection between Crime and Punishment," *Jobs & Capital* (Santa Monica: Milken Institute for Job & Capital Formation), Winter 1995, vol. 4.

[68]Sam S. Souryal, "What Does the United Nations Have to Do With Justice," *Journal of Criminal Justice Education,* vol. 7, no. 2 (Fall 1996), p. 338.

[69]Vila, "Could We Break the Crime Control Paradox?" p. 3.

CHAPTER 14

FUTURE DIRECTIONS

IN CRIMINOLOGY

I seriously doubt that this country has the will to address . . . its crime problems . . . We could in theory make justice swifter and more certain, but we will not. We could vastly improve the way in which our streets are policed, but some of us won't pay for it and the rest of us won't tolerate it . . . We could alter the way in which at-risk children experience the first few years of life, but the opponents of this . . . are numerous and the bureaucratic problems enormous. Meanwhile, just beyond the horizon, there lurks a cloud that the winds will soon bring over us. By the end of this decade there will be a million more people between the ages of fourteen and seventeen . . . This extra million will be half male. Six percent of them will become high rate, repeat offenders—thirty thousand more young muggers, killers and thieves than we have now. Get ready.

—JAMES Q. WILSON[1]

As we go forth into the future a world of crime as yet unknown awaits us.

—CYNTHIA MANSON AND CHARLES ARDAI[2]

❖ CHAPTER OUTLINE ❖

INTRODUCTION TO THE FUTURE
FUTURE CRIMES
THE NEW CRIMINOLOGIES
    Postmodern Criminology
    Rational Choice Theory
    Feminist Theory
    Peacemaking Criminology
    Realist Criminology
    Theory Integration
POLICIES OF THE FUTURE
SUMMARY

≈ IMPORTANT NAMES ≈

William Tafoya	Richter H. Moore, Jr.	Georgette Bennett
Stuart Henry	Dragan Milovanovic	Gene Stephens
Lawrence Cohen	Marcus Felson	Ronald Clarke
Derek Cornish	Freda Adler	Rita J. Simon
Kathleen Daly	Meda Chesney-Lind	John Hagan
Harold E. Pepinsky	Richard Quinney	Walter DeKeseredy
Jock Young		

≈ IMPORTANT TERMS ≈

futurist	future criminology	participatory justice
environmental scanning	scenario writing	futures research
lifestyle theory	routine activities theory	strategic assessment
rational choice theory	situational crime prevention	situational choice theory
target hardening	power-control theory	displacement
peacemaking criminology	realist criminology	feminist criminology
deconstructionist theories	postmodern criminology	restorative justice
peace model		

❖ INTRODUCTION TO THE FUTURE

Futurist one who studies the future.

Future criminology the study of likely futures as they impinge on crime and its control.

Emile Durkheim once observed that crime and deviance are a natural part of any social world. Although the form of criminal activity varies with the nature of society, it is unlikely that any human future will be free of crime. People who study the future are called **futurists;** futurist criminologists try to imagine how crime will appear in both the near and distant future. **Future criminology** is the study of likely futures as they relate to crime and its control.

From our present point of view, multiple futures exist, each of which is more or less probable and each of which may or may not come to pass. In other words, the future contains an almost limitless number of possibilities, any of which might unfold but only a few of which actually will. The task of the futurist is to effectively distinguish between these impending possibilities, assessing the likelihood of each, and making more or less realistic forecasts based on such assessments.

Some assumptions about the future, such as estimates of future world populations, can be based on existing and highly credible public or private statistics and mathematical analyses of trends. Others, however, are more intuitive and result from the integration of a wide range of diverse materials derived from many different sources. As one futurist explains, "Before we can plan the future, we must make some assumptions about what that future will be like. . . . Assumptions about the future are not like assumptions in a geometry exercise. They are not abstract statements from which consequences can be derived with mathematical precision. But we need to make some assumptions about the future in order to plan it, prepare for it, and prevent undesired events from happening."[3]

Best known among groups that study the future is the World Future Society, which publishes *The Futurist,* a journal of well-considered essays about probable futures. Individual futurists who have become well known to the general public include Alvin Toffler, author of the trilogy of futurist titles *Future Shock,*[4] *Powershift,*[5] and *The Third Wave;*[6] John Naisbitt, author of *Megatrends: Ten New Directions Transforming Our Lives;*[7] and Peter F. Drucker—who has written many books with futuristic themes, among them *Managing for the Future* and *Post-Capitalist Society.* Within criminology the Society of Police Futurists International (PFI) represents the cutting edge of research into future crime-control policy. PFI evolved from a conference of approximately 250 educators and practitioners representing most states and twenty different nations that was held at the FBI National Academy in Quantico, Virginia, in 1991. PFI members apply the principles of futures research to gain an understanding of the world as it is likely to be in the future.[8]

Futures research has been described as "a multidisciplinary branch of operations research" whose principal aim "is to facilitate long-range planning based on (1) forecasting from the past supported by mathematical models, (2) cross-disciplinary treatment of its subject matter, (3) systematic use of expert judgment, and (4) a systems-analytical approach to its problems."[9] In the words of PFI founder **William Tafoya,** "[f]utures research offers both the philosophy and the methodological tools to analyze, forecast, and plan in ways rarely seen" in crime-control planning. "Guided by insight, imagination, and innovation, a new perspective awaits criminal justice professionals willing to attempt creative new approaches to dealing with crime and criminals."[10]

Central to futures research are the techniques of environmental scanning, scenario writing, and strategic assessment.[11] **Environmental scanning** "is a systematic effort to identify in an elemental way future developments (trends or events) that could plausibly occur over the time horizon of interest"[12] and that might impact one's area of concern. In other words, it is impossible to predict the future without having some sense of what is happening now, especially where important trends are concerned. **Scenario writing** builds upon environmental scanning by attempting to

Futures research a multidisciplinary branch of operations research whose principal aim is to facilitate long-range planning based on (1) forecasting from the past supported by mathematical models, (2) cross-disciplinary treatment of its subject matter, (3) systematic use of expert judgment, and (4) a systems-analytical approach to its problems.

Environmental scanning a systematic effort to identify in an elemental way future developments (trends or events) that could plausibly occur over the time horizon of interest, and that might impact one's area of concern.

Scenario writing a technique intended to predict future outcomes, and builds upon environmental scanning by attempting to assess the likelihood of a variety of possible outcomes once important trends have been identified.

Strategic assessment a
technique that assesses the
risks and opportunities
facing those who plan for
the future.

assess the likelihood of a variety of possible outcomes once important trends have been identified. Scenario writing develops a list of possible futures and assigns each a degree of probability or likelihood. **Strategic assessment** provides an appreciation of the risks and opportunities facing those who plan for the future.

A comprehensive futures research approach, for example, might identify an important trend that shows affluent middle- and upper-class citizens fleeing cities and suburbs for the safety of enclosed residential enclaves surrounded by secure perimeters and patrolled by paid private security personnel. Many likely scenarios could then be envisioned, including a further decline in America's cities as the moneyed classes abandon them, continued growth of street and property crimes in metropolitan areas, and rampant victimization of the urban working poor. Although crime-control strategies might be developed to counter the imagined threat to cities, many risks must be considered in any planning. A serious decline in the value of the dollar, for example, as recently experienced, may cause gated communities to unravel and may create a shortfall of tax dollars that would be needed to pay for enhanced policing in cities. The influx of new and large immigrant populations, likely to add to the burgeoning number of inner-city dwellers, could add another new dimension to overall crime-control planning.

Such issues have been the concern of a number of outstanding thinkers in the field of criminology. Futurists who have made their mark on criminology include Georgette Bennett, Gene Stephens, William "Bill" Tafoya, and Richter H. Moore, Jr. Their work and other emerging theoretical explanations for crime and new suggestions for crime-control policy are discussed in this chapter.

⚏ FUTURE CRIMES

Murder, rape, robbery, and other types of "everyday" crime which have become mainstays of contemporary criminological analysis will continue to occur in the future, to be sure, but other new and emergent forms of criminality will grow in frequency and number. Recently, for example, Joseph F. Coates, president of the future-oriented "think tank" of Coates & Jarratt, predicted that by the year 2025, "Socially significant crime—that is, the crimes that have the widest negative effects—in the advanced nations will be increasingly economic and computer based. Examples include disruption of business, theft, introduction of maliciously false information, and tampering with medical records, air traffic control, or national-security systems."[13] Another futurist predicts that "[t]he top guns of twenty-first-century criminal organizations will be educated, highly sophisticated, computer-literate individuals who can wield state-of-the-art information technology to the best advantage—for themselves and for their organizations."[14]

In a wide-ranging overview of future crimes, **Richter H. Moore, Jr.,** paints a picture of future criminality that includes many dimensions. Already present are elements of what Moore predicts: "computer hackers are changing bank records, credit accounts and reports, criminal-history files, and educational, medical, and even military records."[15] Identity manipulation, says Moore, will be a nexus of future criminality. "By the twenty-first century," he writes, "genetic-based records will in-

A female officer calls her base. Community policing, a strategy by which law enforcement officials stay in close touch with citizens, holds great hope for the future. What is new in community policing? *Sidney/The Image Works.*

clude a birth-to-death dossier of a person and will be the method of criminal identification." As the human genome project proceeds apace, the complete mapping of human DNA comes closer to reality. Already the U.S. military is using genetic testing to provide unique identification codes to each of its soldiers. In the event of war, such codes will allow for the identification of human remains from as little as a single cell. DNA coding, unique to each of us, may soon form the basis for nearly foolproof identification technologies which will take the science of personal identification far beyond fingerprinting, blood-type matching, or photography. The science of bioengineering, however, which is now undergoing clinical trials in the treatment of various forms of disease, may soon be clandestinely employed for the illegal modification of human DNA, with the goal of effectively altering a person's identity. It is but one more step by which the theft of computer-based genetic identification records could make it possible for one person to effectively imitate another in our future society.

Moore describes many other crimes of the future. "By the next century," he says, "criminal organizations will be able to afford their own satellites." Drug trafficking and money-laundering operations could be coordinated via satellite communications, couriers and shipments could be tracked, and satellite surveillance could provide alerts of enforcement activity. Likewise, says Moore, "[p]rostitution rings will use modern technology to coordinate global activities," and children and fetuses may "become subject to unlawful trafficking." The illegal disposal of toxic materials, an activity which organized crime has already explored, may become even more profitable for criminal entrepreneurs as many more hazardous substances are produced in the face of ever-tighter controls. The supply of nuclear materials and military-quality armaments to "private armies ... terrorists, hate groups, questionable regimes, independent crime groups, and individual criminals" will be a fact of life in the next century, as will the infiltration of governments and financial institutions by sophisticated criminals whose activities are supported by large, illegally acquired fortunes.

Another writer, **Georgette Bennett,** whose seminal book *Crimewarps*[16] was published in 1987 and helped establish the study of criminal futures as a purposeful endeavor, says that American society is about to experience major changes in both what society considers criminal and in who future offenders will be. Some areas of coming change that Bennett predicts are

- the decline of street crime, such as robbery and assault;
- an increase in white-collar crimes, especially high-technology crimes;
- increasing female involvement in crime;
- increased crime commission among the elderly;
- a shift in high crime rates from the "Frost Belt" to the "Sun Belt;" and
- safer cities, with increasing criminal activity in small towns and rural areas.

❖ THE NEW CRIMINOLOGIES

Along with futures research, new and emerging criminological theories provide a picture of what criminology will be like in the years and decades to come. In an intriguing article entitled "Explaining Crime in the Year 2010,"[17] L. Edward Wells suggests that "[w]hen it comes to explaining crime, we seem to have an embarrassment

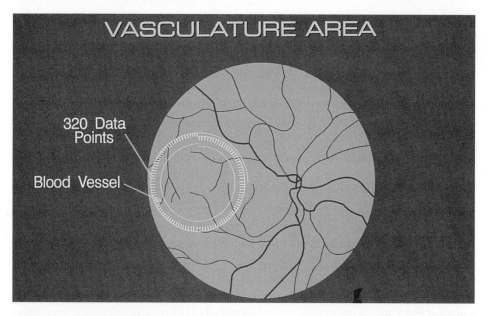

Diagram of a retinal image used for identification purposes. The security of sensitive sites and the accurate identification of personnel are being increasingly served by advanced technologies such as retinal imaging. Are such technologies foolproof? *Courtesy Eye Dentify, Inc.*

of riches but a poverty of results." In other words, although many explanations for criminal behavior have come and gone, "none has proven noticeably more effective in explaining, predicting, or controlling crime." That may be about to change, says Wells. Contemporary criminological theorizing is interdisciplinary and conservative in its approach to crime causation, and major changes in the premises upon which criminological theories are built are unlikely without significant ideological shifts or changes in basic components of the social structure such as the economy, the political system, or the family. Significant social change, however, can bring about the need for new theoretical formulations, says Wells. "Legal events in the 1960s and 1970s," for example, "changed abortion from a criminal act to a routine medical procedure. . . ."[18] Similarly, an aversion to even minor forms of physical force may now be leading to a redefinition of crimes such as child abuse, spousal abuse, elder abuse, and sexual aggression. Hence, our basic understanding of criminal violence may be undergoing a fundamental modification that will require a concomitant change in our attempts to theorize about its causes.

Wells sees similar possibilities for theoretical change about to be introduced by advances in scientific knowledge. Should the human genome project, for example, yield definitive evidence that some forms of aggression and violence are biologically grounded, it will provide the basis for an entirely new and emergent group of biological explanations for at least certain forms of criminal activity.

Wells makes a number of specific predictions about the future of criminological theorizing. Among them, he predicts that future explanations of crime will be[19]

1. more eclectic than past theories, and less tied to a single theoretical tradition or discipline;
2. more comparative and less confined to a single society or single dominant group within society;
3. predominantly *individualistic* rather than collective, and *voluntaristic* rather than deterministic;
4. more applied and pragmatic in orientation;
5. more oriented toward explaining white-collar crime; and
6. reflective of a renewed appreciation for the biological foundations of human behavior and will assign more theoretical substance to biological and medical factors.

Unfortunately, from approximately 1960 until 1985 criminology suffered through a few "black decades" in which theory building fell by the wayside as a generation of criminologists trained in quantitative analysis repeatedly tested existing ideas at the expense of developing new ones. In the mid-1980s, however, a new and dynamic era of theory building was unleashed. Frank P. Williams and Marilyn D. McShane explain: "[a]s if the restraints on theory building had created a pent-up demand, criminologists began exploring new theoretical constructs during the 1980s. Slowly at first, and then with great rapidity, theoretical efforts began to emerge."[20] Although space does not permit a detailed discussion of the various fast-growing new approaches, a few of the most significant ones will be discussed in the pages that follow.

Postmodern criminology
a brand of criminology
that developed following
World War II, and that
builds on the tenets
inherent in postmodern
social thought.

POSTMODERN CRIMINOLOGY

Some significant, yet new theoretical approaches now emerging within criminology are largely the result of postmodernist thought. Most such theories can be lumped together under the rubric postmodern criminology. **Postmodern criminology** applies understandings of social change inherent in postmodern philosophy to criminological theorizing, and to issues of crime control.

Postmodern social thought, which developed primarily in Europe after World War II, represents "a rejection of the enlightenment belief in scientific rationality as the main vehicle to knowledge and progress . . ."[21] Postmodernism epitomizes those societies that have entered a new age characterized less by an emphasis on industrialization and material production, and more by a concern with ideas, information, and individual needs. Hence, the new American "information society" with its drift toward quasisocialism—which is so characteristic of postindustrial societies, rampant mass consumption, and overall technological sophistication—is one of the first truly postmodern societies to emerge in the world.

This book, at least in part, is a postmodernist work in that it describes not only historical criminology, but focuses in some detail on new forms of crime brought about by social changes which occurred following World War II. In particular, Chapter 12 with its detailed descriptions of high-technology crime and this chapter's futurist orientation both provide a postmodernist focus.

Postmodern criminology is not a single theory, but rather a group of new and emerging criminological perspectives that are all informed by the tone of postmodernism. At the cutting edge of postmodern criminology can be found novel paradigms with such intriguing titles as chaos theory, discourse analysis, topology theory, critical theory, feminist theory, peacemaking criminology, realist criminology, constitutive theory, and anarchic criminology.[22]

All postmodern criminologies build on the feeling that past criminological approaches have failed to realistically assess the true causes of crime and have therefore failed to offer workable solutions for crime control—or if they have, that such theories and solutions may have been appropriate at one time, but that they are no longer applicable to the postmodern era. Hence, much postmodern criminology is deconstructionist, and such theories are sometimes called deconstructionist theories.

Deconstructionist
theories emerging approaches which challenge existing criminological perspectives to debunk them, and which work toward replacing them with concepts more applicable to the postmodern era.

Deconstructionist theories are approaches that challenge—often quite effectively—existing criminological perspectives to debunk them and to work toward replacing them with approaches more relevant to the postmodern era. Bruce Di-Cristina,[23] for example, proposes one form of postmodern criminology that he calls "anarchic criminology." Anarchic criminology is "a criminology which embraces alternative methods and epistemologies, encourages imaginative solutions to social and criminal problems, and in the process continually undermines encrusted hierarchies of certainty, truth, and power."[24]

Two especially notable authors in the field of postmodern criminology are **Stuart Henry** and **Dragan Milovanovic,**[25] whose constitutive criminology was discussed briefly in Chapter 8. Constitutive criminology, which is rooted in phenomenological criminology, claims that crime and crime control are not "object-like entities," but rather constructions produced through a social process in which offender, victim, and society are all involved.[26]

A central feature of constitutive criminology is its assertion that individuals shape their world while also being shaped by it. Hence, the behaviors of those who offend and victimize others cannot be understood in isolation from the society of which they are a part. Individuals, however, tend to remain unaware of the role they play in the social construction of their subjective worlds, and fail to realize that, at least to some degree, they are able to create new meanings while freeing themselves from old biases.

One area that well demonstrates constructionist notions is the sociology of law—which highlights the inherent interrelatedness between law and social structure. Milovanovic, for example, suggests the application of semiotics to the study of law.[27] *Semiotics* is a term akin to *semantics,* and both words derive from the Greek word *sêma,* meaning "sign." Milovanovic sees semiotics as especially useful in the study of law and criminology because everything we know, say, do, think, and feel is mediated through signs—a sign being anything that stands for something else. Hence, language, gestures, sensations, objects, and events are all interpreted by the human mind through the use of signs. A semiotic criminology is concerned, therefore, with identifying how language systems (e.g., those of medicine, law, education, gangs, sports, prison communities, criminal justice practitioners, and criminologists) communicate uniquely encoded values. Such values are said to "oppress those who do not communicate meaning from within the particular language system in use" because they may prevent effective discourse with those in power.

The application of semiotics to the study of law can be illustrated by the phrase "mental illness." As a sign, this phrase is imbued with multiple—perhaps even contradictory—meanings. Two possible interpretations for what this sign represents would include a disease in need of treatment, and a person needing psychiatric services. Moreover, mental illness means something different in the law (wherein the proper phrase is "legal insanity") than it does in medicine or in the community. Different interpretations reflect different values, and these values can be traced to divergent interest groups. Moreover, as Milovanovic notes, the meaning of mental illness has changed over time—and continues to change.

Semiotics can also be applied directly to the notion of crime, as crime itself is a "socially constructed category," or sign. In the words of Henry and Milovanovic, crime "is a categorization of the diversity of human conflicts and transgressions into a single category 'crime,' as though these were somehow all the same. It is a melting of differences reflecting the multitude of variously motivated acts of personal injury into a single entity."[28] Such a statement, to the minds of constitutive criminologists, lays bare the true meaning of the word *crime*—effectively "deconstructing" it.

Crime should be understood, say Henry and Milovanovic, as an integral part of society—not something separate and apart from it. From this perspective, a kind of false consciousness, or lack of awareness, gives rise to criminal activity. "[C]rime is seen to be the culmination of certain processes that allow persons to believe that they are somehow not connected to other humans and society. These processes place others into categories or stereotypes and make them different or alien, denying them their humanity. These processes result in the denial of responsibility for other people and to other people."[29] Hence, from a constitutive point of view, crime is simply "the power to deny others," and crime is caused by "the structure, ideology and invocation of discursive practices that divide human relations into categories, that divide responsibility from others and to others into hierarchy and authority relations."

RATIONAL CHOICE THEORY

Strictly speaking, rational choice theory is not a postmodern approach, because it is primarily a modern version of classical deterrence theories which were discussed in Chapter 4. Nonetheless, rational choice theory, a product of the 1980s, contains a number of seminal new ideas. Proponents of the theory claim that it was a natural outgrowth of the realization that no existing criminological theory "contained an assumption of a rational, thinking individual."[30] **Rational choice theory** is built upon the assumptions of economists, many of whom view human behavior—including that which is criminal—as the result of conscious choice. Rational choice theory is noteworthy for its emphasis on the rational and adaptive aspects of criminal offending, rather than on what other approaches might view as pathological aspects of the criminal event. Rational choice theory "predicts that individuals choose to commit crime when the benefits outweigh the costs of disobeying the law. Crime will decrease," according to such theories, "when opportunities are limited, benefits are reduced, and costs are increased."[31]

Two varieties of rational choice theory can be identified. One, which builds on an emerging emphasis on victimization, is called lifestyle theory or routine activities theory. A second, which is largely an extension of the rational choice perspective, is called situational choice theory.

Routine activities theory (also called **lifestyle theory**) was proposed by **Lawrence Cohen** and **Marcus Felson** in 1979.[32] Cohen and Felson suggested that lifestyles contribute significantly to both the volume and type of crime found in any society. The two believed that changes in the nature of American society during the 1960s and 1970s—specifically increased personal affluence and greater involvement in social activities outside the home—brought about increased rates of household theft and personal victimization by strangers. Central to the routine activities approach is the claim that crime is likely to occur when a motivated offender and a suitable victim come together in the absence of preventative measures (which were sometimes termed "capable guardians"). Hence, "the risk of criminal victimization varies dramatically among the circumstances and locations in which people place themselves and their property."[33] For example, a person who routinely uses an automated teller machine late at night in an isolated location is far more likely to be preyed upon by robbers than is someone who stays home after dark. Lifestyles that contribute to criminal opportunities are likely to result in crime because they increase the risk of potential victimization.[34] Although noncriminal lifestyles at a given point in the life course are partly the result of unavoidable social roles and assigned social positions, those who participate in a given lifestyle generally make rational decisions about specific behaviors (such as going to a given automatic teller machine at a certain time). The same is true of criminal lifestyles. Hence, the meshing of choices made by both victims and criminals contributes significantly to both the frequency and type of criminal activity observed in society.

Rational choice theory a perspective which holds that criminality is the result of conscious choice, and which predicts that individuals choose to commit crime when the benefits outweigh the costs of disobeying the law.

Routine activities theory (or lifestyle theory) a brand of rational choice theory which suggests that lifestyles contribute significantly to both the volume and type of crime found in any society.

In a later work,[35] Felson suggested that a number of "situational insights" might combine to elicit a criminal response from individual actors enmeshed in a highly varied social world. Felson pointed out that "individuals vary greatly in their behavior from one situation to another" and said that criminality might flow from temptation, bad company, idleness, or provocation. Convenience stores, for example, create temptations toward theft when they display their merchandise within easy reach of customers. Other authors[36] have defined the term *situation* to mean "the perceptive field of the individual at a given point in time" and have suggested that it "can be described in terms of who is there, what is going on, and where it is taking place."

Situational choice theory views criminal behavior "as a function of choices and decisions made within a context of situational constraints and opportunities."[37] It suggests that the probability of criminal activity can be reduced by changing the features of a given social situation. **Ronald Clarke** and **Derek Cornish,** collaborators in the development of the situational choice perspective, analyze the choice-structuring properties of a potentially criminal situation. They define *choice-structuring properties* as "the constellation of opportunities, costs, and benefits attaching to particular kinds of crime."[38] Clarke and Cornish suggest the use of situational strategies such as "cheque guarantee cards, the control of alcohol sales at football matches, supervision of children's play on public housing estates, vandal resistant materials and designs, 'defensible space' architecture, improved lighting, closed-circuit television surveillance,"[39] and the like, as effective crime-preventative additions to specific situations—all of which might lower the likelihood of criminal victimization in given instances.

In brief, rational choice theorists concentrate on "the decision-making process of offenders confronted with specific contexts" and have shifted "the focus of the effort to prevent crime . . . from broad social programs to target hardening, environmental design or any impediment that would [dissuade] a motivated offender from offending."[40]

As mentioned earlier, rational choice theory is a modern version of classical deterrence theory. Earlier approaches, however, focused largely on the balance between pleasure and pain as the primary determinant or preventative of criminal behavior. Rational choice theory tends to place less emphasis on pleasure and emotionality, and more upon rationality and cognition. Some rational choice theorists have gone so far as to distinguish among the types of choices offenders make as they move toward criminal involvement. Involvement decisions have been described as "multistage" and are said to "include the initial decision to engage in criminal activity as well as subsequent decisions to continue one's involvement or to desist."[41] Event decisions, on the other hand, relate to particular instances of criminal opportunity such as the decision to rob a particular person or to let them pass. Event decisions, in contrast to involvement decisions which may take months or even years to reach, are usually made quickly.

In a recent study, Laura J. Moriarty and James E. Williams found that the routine activities approach explained 28 percent of property crimes committed in socially disorganized (high-crime) areas of a small Virginia city, and explained only 11 percent of offenses committed in low-crime areas.[42] In the words of the authors: "this research demonstrates more support for routine activities theory in

Situational choice theory a brand of rational choice theory which views criminal behavior as a function of choices and decisions made within a context of situational constraints and opportunities.

socially disorganized areas than in socially organized areas." Hence, although one could argue that the kinds of routine activities supportive of criminal activity are more likely to occur in socially disorganized areas, it is also true that the presence (or absence) of certain ecological characteristics (i.e., the level of social disorganization), may either enhance (or reduce) the likelihood of criminal victimization. As the authors state, "those areas characterized by low socioeconomic status will have higher unemployment rates, thus creating a larger pool of motivated offenders. Family disruption characterized by more divorced or separated families will result in more unguarded living structures, thus making suitable targets more available. Increased residential mobility will result in more non-occupied housing, which creates a lack of guardianship over the property and increases the number of suitable targets."[43]

Situational Crime Control Policy

Building upon the work of rational and situational choice theorists, Israeli criminologist David Weisburd describes the advantages of a situational approach to crime prevention. Weisburd points out that: "Crime prevention research and policy have traditionally been concerned with offenders or potential offenders. Researchers have looked to define strategies that would deter individuals from involvement in crime or rehabilitate them so they would no longer want to commit criminal acts. In recent years crime prevention efforts have often focused on the incapacitation of high-rate or dangerous offenders so they are not free to victimize law-abiding citizens. In the public debate over crime prevention policies, these strategies are usually defined as competing approaches. However, they have in common a central assumption about crime prevention research and policy: that efforts to understand and control crime must begin with the offender. In all of these approaches, the focus of crime prevention is on people and their involvement in criminality."[44]

"Although this assumption continues to dominate crime prevention research and policy," says Weisburd, "it has begun to be challenged by a very different approach that seeks to shift the focus of crime prevention efforts." The new approach developed in large part as a response to the failures of traditional theories and programs. The 1970s, in particular, saw a shattering of traditional assumptions about the effectiveness of crime prevention efforts, and led to a reevaluation of research and policy about crime prevention. For many scholars and policymakers, this meant having to rethink assumptions about criminality and how offenders might be prevented from participating in crime. Others suggested that a more radical reorientation of crime prevention efforts was warranted. They argued that the shift must come not in terms of the specific strategies or theories that were used, but in terms of the unit of analysis that formed the basis of crime prevention efforts. This new crime prevention effort called for a focus not on people who commit crime but on the context in which crime occurs.[45]

Situational crime prevention a social policy approach that looks to develop greater understanding of crime and more effective crime prevention strategies through concern with the physical, organizational, and social environments that make crime possible.

This approach, which is often called **situational crime prevention,** looks to develop greater understanding of crime and more effective crime prevention strategies through concern with the physical, organizational, and social environments that make crime possible.[46] The situational approach does not ignore offenders; it merely places them as one part of a broader crime prevention equation that is centered on the context of crime. It demands a shift in the approach to crime prevention, however, from one that is concerned primarily with why people commit crime to one that looks primarily at why crime occurs in specific settings. It moves the context of crime into central focus and sees the offender as but one of a number of factors that affect it. Situational crime prevention is closely associated with the idea of a "criminology of place," discussed in a box in Chapter 7.

Weisburd suggests that a "reorientation of crime prevention research and policy from the causes of criminality to the context of crime provides much promise." Says Weisburd: "At the core of situational prevention is the concept of opportunity . . ." In contrast to offender-based approaches to crime prevention that usually focus on the dispositions of criminals, situational crime prevention begins with the opportunity structure of the crime situation. By opportunity structure, advocates of this perspective are not referring to sociological concepts such as differential opportunity or anomie, but rather to the immediate situational and environmental components of the context of crime. Their approach to crime prevention is to try to reduce the opportunities for crime in specific situations. This may involve efforts as simple and straightforward as **target hardening** or access control.[47]

The value of a situational approach lies in the fact that criminologists have found it difficult to identify who is likely to become a serious offender, or to predict the timing and types of future offenses that repeat offenders are likely to commit. And, as Weisburd says, "legal and ethical dilemmas make it difficult to base criminal justice policies on models that still include a substantial degree of statistical error." Moreover, Weisburd adds: "If traditional approaches worked well, of course, there would be little pressure to find new forms of crime prevention. If traditional approaches worked well, few people would possess criminal motivation and fewer still would actually commit crimes."

Situational prevention advocates argue that the context of crime provides a promising alternative to traditional offender-based crime prevention policies.[48] They assume that situations provide a more stable and predictable focus for crime prevention efforts than do persons. In part, this assumption develops from commonsense notions of the relationship between opportunities and crime. Shoplifting, for example, is by definition clustered in stores and not residences, and family disputes are unlikely to be a problem outside of the home. High-crime places, in contrast to high-crime people, cannot flee to avoid criminal justice intervention; and crime that develops from the specific characteristics of certain places cannot be easily transferred to other contexts.

Another example can be had in robberies, which are seen as most likely to be found in places where many pedestrians stroll (such as bus stops and business districts), where there are few police or informal guardians (e.g., doormen), and where a supply of motivated offenders can be found nearby or at least within easy public transportation access.[49] Similarly, such places are not likely to be centers for prostitution, which would favor easy access of cars (and little interference by shopkeepers who are likely to object to the obvious nature of street solicitations), nor flashing, which is more likely to be found in the more anonymous environments of public parks.

Situational crime-control policy suggests twelve ways in which environments and situations can be changed to reduce crime. They are:[50]

Target hardening the reduction in criminal opportunity, generally through the use of physical barriers, architectural design, and enhanced security measures, of a particular location.

1. target hardening
2. access control
3. offender deflection (e.g., through physical barriers)
4. facilitator control (e.g., gun controls)
5. entry/exit screening (e.g. metal detectors)
6. formal surveillance (e.g., security guards or television monitoring)
7. employee surveillance (e.g., doormen, clerks)
8. natural surveillance (e.g., street lighting)
9. target removal (e.g., removing cash from registers after business hours)
10. property identification (e.g., etching, tagging)
11. inducement removal (e.g., rapid repair of disabled vehicles left by the road-side)
12. rule setting (e.g., "no one allowed beyond this point," etc.)

Critique of Rational Choice Theory

Rational and situational choice theories have been criticized for their overemphasis on individual choice and their relative disregard for the social and economic inequality of persons and groups. Likewise, rational choice theory seems to assume that everyone is equally capable of making rational decisions when, in fact, such is probably not the case. Some individuals are more logical than others by virtue of temperament, personality, or socialization, whereas others are emotional, hotheaded, and unthinking. Empirical studies of rational choice theory have added scant support for the perspective's underlying assumptions, tending to show instead that criminal offenders are often unrealistic in their appraisals of the relative risks and rewards facing them.[51] Similarly, rational and situational choice theories seem to disregard individual psychology and morality by their emphasis on external situations. Moral individuals, say critics, when faced with easy criminal opportunities, may rein in their desires and turn their backs on temptation.

The emphasis of rational and situational choice theories upon changing aspects of the immediate situation to reduce crime has been criticized for resulting in the **displacement** of crime from one area to another.[52] Target hardening,[53] a key crime-prevention strategy among such theorists, has sometimes caused criminals to find new targets of opportunity in other areas.[54]

Displacement a shift of criminal activity from one spatial location to another.

FEMINIST THEORY

As some have observed, "women have been virtually invisible in criminological analysis until recently and much theorizing has proceeded as though criminality is restricted to men."[55] Others put it this way: "criminological theory assumes a woman is like a man."[56] Recently, however, advances in feminist theory have been applied to criminology, resulting in what some have called a **feminist criminology.**

Early works in the field included **Freda Adler's** *Sisters in Crime*[57] and **Rita J. Simon's** *Women and Crime.*[58] Both books were published in 1975, and in them the authors attempted to explain existing divergences in crime rates between men and

Feminist criminology a developing intellectual approach which emphasizes gender issues in the subject matter of criminology.

women as due primarily to socialization rather than biology. Women, claimed these authors, were taught to believe in personal limitations, faced reduced socioeconomic opportunities, and as a result, suffered from lowered aspirations. As gender equality increased, they said, it could be expected that male and female criminality would take on similar characteristics. As Chapter 2 points out, however, such has not been the case to date, and the approach of Adler and Simon has not been validated by observations surrounding increased gender equality over the past few decades.

Although early feminist theorizing may not have borne the fruit that some researchers anticipated, it has led to a heightened awareness of gender issues within criminology. Two of the most insightful contemporary proponents of the usefulness of applying feminist thinking to criminological analysis are **Kathleen Daly** and **Meda Chesney-Lind.** Daly and Chesney-Lind have identified the following five elements of feminist thought that "distinguish it from other types of social and political thought."[59]

1. Gender is not a natural fact but a complex social, historical, and cultural product; it is related to, but not simply derived from, biological sex difference and reproductive capacities.
2. Gender and gender relations order social life and social institutions in fundamental ways.
3. Gender relations and constructs of masculinity and femininity are not symmetrical but are based on an organizing principle of men's superiority and social and political-economic dominance over women.
4. Systems of knowledge reflect men's views of the natural and social world; the production of knowledge is gendered.
5. Women should be at the center of intellectual inquiry, not peripheral, invisible, or appendages to men.

In a similar, but more recent, analysis of feminist criminology, Susan Caulfield and Nancy Wonders describe "five major contributions that have been made by feminist scholarship and practice"[60] to criminological thinking: (1) a focus on gender as a central organizing principle of contemporary life; (2) the importance of power in shaping social relationships; (3) a heightened sensitivity to the way in which social context helps shape human relationships; (4) the recognition that social reality must be understood as a process, and the development of research methods which take this into account; and (5) a commitment to social change as a crucial part of feminist scholarship and practice. As is the case with most feminist writing in the area of criminology today, Caulfield and Wonders hold that these five contributions of feminist scholarship "can help to guide research and practice within criminology...."

Feminism is a way of seeing the world—it is not strictly a sexual orientation. To be a feminist is to "combine a female mental perspective with a sensitivity for those social issues that influence primarily women."[61] Central to understanding feminist thought in both its historical and its contemporary modes is the realization that feminism views gender in terms of power relationships. In other words, according to feminist approaches, men have traditionally held much more power in society than have women. Male dominance has long been reflected in the patriarchal structure of Western society, a structure which has excluded women from much decision making in socially significant areas. Sexist attitudes—deeply ingrained notions of male superiority—have perpetuated inequality between the sexes. The consequences of sexism and of the unequal gender-based distribution of power have been far reaching, affecting fundamental aspects of social roles and personal expectation at all levels.

Various schools of feminist thought exist, with liberal and radical feminism envisioning a power-based and traditional domination of women's bodies and minds by men throughout history. Radical feminism depicts men as fundamentally brutish, aggressive, and violent and sees men as controlling women through sexuality by taking advantage of women's biological dependency during child-bearing years and their inherent lack of physical strength relative to men. Liberal feminists, although they want the same gender equality as other feminists, lay the blame for present inequalities on the development within culture and society of "separate and distinct spheres of influence and traditional attitudes about the appropriate role of men and women. . . ."[62] A recent book by Alida V. Merlo and Joycelyn M. Pollock,[63] for example, points out that feminists are often blamed in today's political atmosphere for the recent upsurge in crime because many, by entering or creating innovative family structures, have lowered what might otherwise be the positive effect of traditional family values on crime control. Socialist feminists, who provide a third perspective, see gender oppression as a consequence of the economic structure of society and as a natural outgrowth of capitalist forms of social organization. Egalitarian societies, from the socialist point of view, would be built around socialist or Marxist principles. A fourth and complementary feminist perspective has been identified by Sally Simpson who refers to it as an alternative framework developed by "women of color."[64] In Simpson's words, "[t]he alternative frameworks developed by women of color heighten feminism's sensitivity to the complex interplay of gender, class, and race oppression."

John Hagan built upon defining features of power relationships in his book *Structural Criminology*,[65] in which he explained that power relationships existing in the wider society are effectively "brought home" to domestic settings and are reflected in everyday relationships between men, women, and children within the context of family life. Hagan writes: "work relations structure family relations, particularly relations between fathers and mothers and, in turn, relations between parents and their children, especially mothers and their daughters."[66] Hagan's approach has been termed **power-control theory,** and it is one which suggests that "family class structure shapes the social reproduction of gender relations, and in turn the social distribution of delinquency."[67] In most middle- and upper-middle-class families, says Hagan, a paternalistic model, in which the father works and the mother supervises the children, is the norm. Under the paternalistic model girls are controlled by both parents—through male domination and by female role modeling. Boys, however, are less closely controlled and are relatively free to deviate from social norms, resulting in higher levels of delinquency among males. In lower-middle- and lower-class families, however, the paternalistic model is frequently absent. Hence, in such families there is less "gender socialization and less maternal supervision of girls," resulting in higher levels of female delinquency.

In a work supportive of Hagan's thesis, Evelyn K. Sommers[68] recently conducted a series of four hour-long interviews with fourteen female inmates in a Canadian

Power-control theory a perspective which holds that the distribution of crime and delinquency within society is to some degree founded upon the consequences which power relationships within the wider society hold for domestic settings, and for the everyday relationships between men, women, and children within the context of family life.

medium-security prison. Focusing on what led to violations of the criminal law, Sommers identified four common themes to explain the criminality of the women she interviewed: (1) economic and financial need, (2) drug involvement, (3) personal anger rooted in sexual and physical abuse or a sense of loss, and (4) fear. Because "need" was identified as the cause of lawbreaking behavior by four of five women interviewed, Sommers concluded that women's criminality is based on two underlying issues: the effort to maintain connection within relationships (such as between mother and child), and a personal quest for empowerment (as single mothers are expected to be independent and capable of providing for themselves and their children).

In a cogent analysis which encompasses much of contemporary feminist theory, Daly and Chesney-Lind suggest that feminist thought is more important for the way it informs and challenges existing criminology than for the new theories it offers. Much current feminist thought within criminology emphasizes the need for gender awareness. Theories of crime causation and prevention, it is suggested, must include women, and more research on gender-related issues in the field is badly needed. Additionally, say Daly and Chesney-Lind, "criminologists should begin to appreciate that their discipline and its questions are a product of white, economically privileged men's experiences"[69] and that rates of female criminality, which are lower than those of males, may highlight the fact that criminal behavior is not as "normal" as once thought. Because modern-day criminological perspectives were mostly developed by white middle-class men, the propositions and theories they advance fail to take into consideration women's "ways of knowing."[70] Hence, the fundamental challenge poised by feminist criminology is: Do existing theories of crime causation apply as well to women as they do to men? Or, as Daly and Chesney-Lind ask, given the current situation in theory development, "do theories of men's crime apply to women?"[71]

Other feminists have analyzed the process by which laws are created and legislation passed, and have concluded that modern-day statutes frequently represent characteristically masculine modes of thought. Such analysts have concluded that existing criminal laws are overly rational and hierarchically structured, reflecting traditionally male ways of organizing the social world.[72] Such statutes, some analysts suggest, need to be replaced by, or complemented with, "a system of justice based upon what are the specifically feminine principles of care, connection and community."[73]

In the area of social policy, feminist thinkers have pointed to the need for increased controls over men's violence toward women, the creation of alternatives (to supplement the home and traditional family structures) for women facing abuse, and the protection of children. They have also questioned the role of government, culture, and the mass media in promulgating pornography, prostitution, and rape and have generally portrayed ongoing crimes against women as characteristic of continuing traditions in which women are undervalued and controlled. Many radical feminists have suggested the replacement of men with women in positions of power, especially within justice system and government organizations, while others have noted that replacement still would not address needed changes in the structure of the system itself which is gender biased due to years of male domination. Centrists, on the other hand, suggest a more balanced approach, believing that individuals of both genders have much to contribute to a workable justice system.[74]

Aileen Wuornos, accused female serial killer. Although some women are moving into areas of traditional male criminality, the number of women committing most forms of crime is still far lower than that of men. How does the criminality of women appear to differ from that of men? *Daytona Beach News/Sygma.*

Critique of Feminist Theory

In the area of theoretical development, feminist criminology has yet to live up to its promise. Throughout the late 1970s and 1980s few comprehensive feminist theories of crime were proposed as feminist criminology focused instead on descriptive studies of female involvement in crime.[75] Although such data gathering may have laid the groundwork for theory building which is yet to come, few descriptive studies attempted to link their findings to existing feminist theory in any comprehensive way. Theory development suffered again in the late 1980s and early 1990s as an increased concern with women's victimization, especially the victimization of women at the hands of men, led to further descriptive studies with a somewhat different focus. Male violence against women was seen as adding support to the central tenet of feminist criminology that the relationship between the sexes is primarily characterized by the exercise of power (or lack thereof). Such singularity of focus, however, did not make for broad theory building. As one writer explains the current state of feminist criminology, "[f]eminist theory is a theory in formation."[76] To date, feminist researchers have continued to amass descriptive studies, while feminist analysis has hardly advanced beyond a framework for the "deconstruction"[77] of existing theories—that is, for their reevaluation in light of feminist insights. A fair assessment of the current situation would probably conclude that the greatest contributions of feminist thought to criminological theory building are yet to come.

Feminist criminology has faced criticism from many other directions. As mentioned previously, predicted increases in female crime rates have failed to materialize as social opportunities available to both genders have become more balanced.

Similarly, other thinkers have pointed to fundamental flaws in feminist thought, asking questions such as, "If men have more power than women, then why are so many more men arrested?"[78] Where studies do exist,[79] gender disparities in arrest are rarely found, nor do sentencing practices seem to favor women.[80] The chivalry hypothesis of many years ago, under which it was proposed that women are apt to be treated more leniently by the justice system because of their gender, appears no longer operative today.[81]

Some critics even argue that a feminist criminology is impossible. Daly and Chesney-Lind, for example, agree that although feminist thought may inform criminology, "a feminist criminology cannot exist because neither feminism nor criminology is a unified set of principles and practices."[82] In other words, according to these authors, a criminology built solely on feminist principles is unlikely because neither feminist thought nor criminology meets the strict requirements of formal theory building. Even with such a caveat in mind, however, it should still be possible to construct a gender-aware criminology, that is, one which is informed by issues of gender and that takes into consideration the concerns of feminist writers. A "feminist-oriented criminology," say Caulfield and Wonders, is one that will transgress traditional criminology. "This transgression, or 'going beyond boundaries,'" they write, "must occur at a number of levels across a number of areas covered within criminology"[83] and will eventually move us toward a more just world.

PEACEMAKING CRIMINOLOGY

Throughout much of history formal agencies of social control, especially the police, officials of the courts, and correctional personnel, have been seen as pitted against criminal perpetrators and would-be wrongdoers. Crime control has been traditionally depicted in terms of a kind of epic struggle in which diametrically opposed antagonists continuously engage one another, but in which only one side can emerge as victorious. Recently, however, a new point of view, **peacemaking criminology,** has come to the fore. Criminology as peacemaking has its roots in Christian and Eastern philosophies, and advances the notion that social control agencies and the citizens they serve should work together to alleviate social problems and human suffering and thus reduce crime.[84] Peacemaking criminology, which includes the notion of service, has also been called "compassionate criminology" and suggests that "[c]ompassion, wisdom, and love are essential for understanding the suffering of which we are all a part and for practicing a criminology of nonviolence."[85]

Peacemaking criminology is a new undertaking, popularized by the works of **Harold E. Pepinsky**[86] and **Richard Quinney**[87] beginning in 1986. Both Pepinsky and Quinney restate the problem of crime control from one of "how to stop crime" to one of "how to make peace" within society and between citizens and criminal justice agencies. Peacemaking criminology draws attention to many issues, among them (1) the perpetuation of violence through the continuation of social policies based on dominant forms of criminological theory, (2) the role of education in peacemaking, (3) "commonsense theories of crime," (4) crime control as human rights enforcement, and (5) conflict resolution within community settings.[88]

Peacemaking criminology a perspective which holds that crime-control agencies and the citizens they serve should work together to alleviate social problems and human suffering and thus reduce crime.

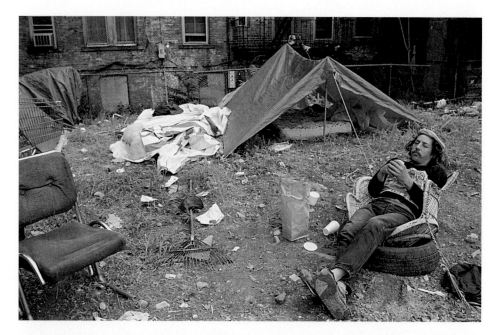

A homeless man in New York City. Peacemaking criminology holds that the alleviation of social problems and the reduction of human suffering will lead to a truly just world, and thus reduce crime. What do you think? *Susan Tannenbaum/Impact Visuals Photo & Graphics, Inc.*

Commonsense theories of crime are derived from everyday experience and beliefs and are characteristic of the person-in-the-street. Unfortunately, say peacemaking criminologists, fanciful commonsense theories all too often provide the basis for criminological investigations, which in turn offer support for the naive theories themselves. One commonsense theory criticized by peacemaking criminologists is the "black-male-as-savage theory,"[89] which holds that African-American men are far more crime prone than their white counterparts. Such a perspective, frequently given added credence by official interpretations of criminal incidence data, only increases the crime-control problem by further distancing black Americans from government-sponsored crime-control policies. A genuine concern for the problems facing all citizens, say peacemaking criminologists, would more effectively serve the ends of crime control.

Richard Quinney and John Wildeman well summarize the underpinnings of peacemaking criminology with these words: "(1) thought of the Western rational mode is conditional, limiting knowledge primarily to what is already known; (2) each life is a spiritual journey into the unknown and the unknowable, beyond the ego-centered self; (3) human existence is characterized by suffering; crime is suffering; and the sources of suffering are within each of us; (4) through love and compassion, beyond the ego-centered self, we can end suffering and live in peace, personally and collectively; (5) crime can be ended only with the ending of suffering, only when there is peace and social justice; and (6) understanding, service, justice—all these—flow naturally from love and compassion, from mindful attention to the reality of all that is, here and now. A criminology of peacemaking—a nonviolent criminology of compassion and service—seeks to end suffering and thereby eliminate crime."[90]

Elsewhere Quinney writes: "A society of meanness, competition, greed, and injustice is created by minds that are greedy, selfish, fearful, hateful, and crave power over others. Suffering on the social level can be ended only with the ending of suffering on the personal level. Wisdom brings the awareness that divisions between people and groups are not between the bad and the good or between the criminal and the noncriminal. Wisdom teaches interbeing. We must become one with all who suffer from lives of crime and from the sources that produce crime. Public policy must then flow from this wisdom."[91]

Other recent contributors to the peacemaking movement include Bo Lozoff, Michael Braswell, and Clemmons Bartollas. In *Inner Corrections,*[92] Lozoff and Braswell claim that "[w]e are fully aware by now that the criminal justice system in this country is founded on violence. It is a system which assumes that violence can be overcome by violence, evil by evil. Criminal justice at home and warfare abroad are of the same principle of violence. This principle sadly dominates much of our criminology." *Inner Corrections,* which is primarily a compilation of previous works on compassion and prison experience, provides meditative techniques and prayers for those seeking to become more compassionate, and includes a number of letters from convicts who demonstrate the book's philosophy.

In another recent work entitled "Correctional Treatment, Peacemaking, and the New Age Movement,"[93] Bartollas and Braswell apply New Age principles to correctional treatment. "Most offenders suffered abusive and deprived childhoods," they write. "Treatment that focuses on the inner child and such qualities as forgiveness and self-esteem could benefit offenders. Some New Age teachings tempered by the ancient spiritual traditions may offer offenders the hope they can create a future that brings greater fulfillment than their past. This changed future may include growing out of the fear of victimization, becoming more positive and open to possibilities, viewing one's self with more confidence and humility, understanding the futility of violence, and attaining emotional and financial sufficiency."[94]

In a fundamental sense, peacemaking criminologists exhort their colleagues to transcend personal dichotomies to end the political and ideological divisiveness that separates people. "If we ourselves cannot know peace . . . how will our acts disarm hatred and violence?"[95] they ask. Lozoff and Braswell express the same sentiments this way: "Human transformation takes place as we change our social, economic and political structure. And the message is clear: without peace within us and in our actions, there can be no peace in our results. Peace is the way."[96]

Critique of Peacemaking Criminology

Peacemaking criminology has been criticized as being naive and utopian, as well as for failing to recognize the realities of crime control and law enforcement. Few victims, for example, would expect to gain much during the victimization process from attempting to make peace with their victimizers (although such strategies do occasionally work). Such criticisms, however, may be improperly directed at a level of analysis which peacemaking criminologists have not assumed. In other words, peacemaking criminology, while it involves work with individual offenders, envisions positive change on the societal and institutional level and does not suggest to victims that they attempt to effect personal changes in offenders.

REALIST CRIMINOLOGY

Realist criminology an emerging perspective that insists on a pragmatic assessment of crime and its associated problems.

Realist criminology, another recent addition to the criminological landscape, is a natural outgrowth of practical concerns with street crime, the fear of crime, and everyday victimization. **Realist criminology** insists on a pragmatic assessment of crime and its associated problems in everyday terms—that is, terms understandable to those people most often affected by crime: victims and their families, offenders, and criminal justice personnel. The test insisted upon by realist criminology is not whether a particular perspective on crime control or an explanation of crime causation complies with rigorous academic criteria, but whether the perspective speaks meaningfully to those faced with crime on a daily basis. As one contemporary source states, "for realists crime is no less harmful to its victims because of its socially constructed origins."[97]

Realist criminology takes two forms: left realism and right realism. Left realism, also called radical realism or critical realism, builds on many of the concepts inherent in radical and Marxist criminology, while simultaneously claiming greater relevancy than either of its two parent perspectives. Left realism also tends to distance itself from some of the more visionary claims of early radical and Marxist theory. Left realism appears to have developed simultaneously in the United States and England.[98] Daniel J. Curran and Claire M. Renzetti portray left realism as a natural consequence of increasingly conservative attitudes toward crime and criminals in both Europe and North America. "Though not successful in converting many radicals to the right," they write, "this new conservatism did lead a number of radical criminologists to temper their views a bit and to take what some might call a less romanticized look at street crime."[99]

Some authors credit **Walter DeKeseredy**[100] with popularizing left realist notions in North America, and **Jock Young**[101] is identified as a major source of left realist writings in England. Prior to the writings of DeKeseredy and Young, radical criminology, with its emphasis upon the crime-inducing consequences of existing power structures, tended to portray the ruling class as the "real criminals" and saw street criminals as social rebels who were acting out of felt deprivation. In contrast, DeKeseredy and Young were successful in refocusing leftist theories onto the serious consequences of street crime and upon the crimes of the lower classes. A central tenet of left realism is the claim that radical ideas must be translated into realistic social policies if contemporary criminology is to have any practical relevance. The major goal of left realism is to achieve "a fair and orderly society" through a practical emphasis on social justice.[102]

Right realism, on the other hand, appeals to those committed to existing power relationships within society. According to criminologist David Nelken, "[r]ight realism arose in the United States as a political strategy for addressing the urban decay and underclass produced by the very conservative forces with which it identifies."[103] It is a way of thinking "oriented to all right-thinking people who believe that the criminal law institution is there to protect their persons and property through strong measures of general deterrence, specific deterrence and incapacitation."[104] In other words, right realism is a criminological perspective that appeals to conservative, propertied, and powerful segments of the population.

Critique of Realist Criminology

Realist criminology has been convincingly criticized for representing more of an ideological emphasis than a theory. As Don C. Gibbons explains, "left realism can best be described as a general perspective centered on injunctions to 'take crime seriously' and to 'take crime control seriously' rather than as a well-developed criminological perspective."[105] Realist criminologists appear to build upon preexisting theoretical frameworks, but rarely offer new propositions or hypotheses that are testable. They do, however, frequently suggest crime-control approaches which are in keeping with the needs of the victimized. Policies promulgated by left realists understandably include an emphasis on community policing, neighborhood justice centers, and dispute resolution mechanisms, whereas right realists are more punitive in their policy suggestions. Beirne and Messerschmidt summarize the situation this way: "What left realists have essentially accomplished is an attempt to theorize about conventional crime realistically while simultaneously developing a 'radical law and order' program for curbing such behavior."[106]

THEORY INTEGRATION

The field of criminology today is rife with various theoretical explanations. Some are old, others are new. Many are complex, while a few are straightforward. Each theoretical approach is limited, although it may provide part of the explanation for why crime occurs or may offer a portion of the answer to the question of how to control crime. It may apply to only a certain type of offender, it may explain only a particular form of crime, or it may derive from only one philosophical or theoretical base.

Some have called the contemporary situation an embarrassment of riches, whereas others have compared it with the old fable of many blind men trying to understand an elephant—each "sees" only a small part of the overall picture. As a consequence, an emphasis on theory integration, with the ultimate goal of developing a unified theory of crime causation and prevention, began to emerge in the 1980s. Advocates of theory integration suggest that initial attempts at blending the propositions of different perspectives should begin at the level characteristic of those theories. In other words, theoretical approaches concerned with analyzing crime at the individual level (often called microlevel theories) might be integrated at the same time that sociological, political, and economic explanations (called macrolevel theories) are woven together. Finally, cross-level integration might be attempted.[107]

Other criminologists have developed rudimentary metatheories or theories about theories and the theorizing process, which they suggest may help to meld existing theories. Some metatheoreticians, however, have expressed the concern that we may integrate theories without first properly examining their worth and that, as a consequence, we may be left with highly elaborate integrated theories that are worthless.[108]

Unfortunately for advocates of integration, however, there seems "to be a consensus that there are too many problems for successful integration to take place. . . ."[109] The reasons why successful integration can never occur, say Frank P. Williams and Marilyn McShane,[110] are (1) "crime is a very complex phenomenon," often determined and defined by whimsical legislative action and powerful interests; (2) "theories attempt to explain different pieces of the crime puzzle" and cannot be made to address all of its aspects; and (3) theories are "embedded in the assumptions we make about human nature and the way the world functions," and we all make different assumptions.

Einstadter and Henry summarize efforts at theoretical integration in criminology with these words: "The plain fact is that integrated theorizing does not lead to a more comprehensive understanding of crime or criminal etiology. Not only does the approach leave gaps between integrated theories, through which vital nuggets of the total reality of criminological explanation slip, but by presenting a range of theories as an integrated package, it tricks us into believing that a comprehensive coverage of criminological theory has been achieved."[111]

"Vital nuggets" of the reality of crime and justice can be found in such approaches as feminist criminology and black criminology, and advocates of theoretical integration are hard put to counter the ongoing development of such focused approaches. Some forms of feminist criminology, for example, even though they offer instructive insights, represent exclusive viewpoints which actively seek dismissal of much existing criminological thought—not integration with it. Similarly, other authors have advocated development of a black criminology to represent the experiences and felt needs of African-Americans and black criminologists.[112] Facing these developments, some feel that fragmentation of criminological theory, not integration, is the rule today.

Such critiques, however, may be overly harsh. One mistake made by advocates of theoretical integration is to assume that *all* existing theories must somehow be embraced and subsumed under *one* encompassing theoretical umbrella. A better strategy may be to work toward a multiple-theory approach that seeks the integration of only a few theories at a time. Multiple-theory formulations may provide the building blocks of larger and more comprehensive integrated theories of the future.

Sometimes a single organizing concept can help blend multiple perspectives. Less than a year ago, for example, Francis T. Cullen, in an incoming presidential address to the Academy of Criminal Justice Sciences, identified the concept of social support as a potential "organizing concept for criminology."[113] "In short," said Cullen, "my thesis is that both across nations and across communities, crime rates vary inversely with the level of social support. America," he said, "has higher rates of serious crime than other industrialized nations because it is a less supportive society." The idea of social support, said Cullen, is inherent in many criminological perspectives even though few theorists use the term directly. Cullen pointed to the ecological theories of the Chicago school, in which gangs were said to replace ineffectual families, as early examples of the social support thesis. Other research, including that on child abuse,[114] ethnographic studies of the "truly disadvantaged," and studies of welfare which show that "governmental assistance to the poor tends to lessen violent crime," adds credence to the social support thesis, said Cullen. Because the concept of social support is capable of linking so many studies and so many other perspectives, it may truly hold value as an organizing or integrative concept in the field of criminology.

Cullen suggested that a "social support paradigm"—one which holds that "social support [whether] delivered through government social programs, communities, social networks, families, interpersonal relations, or agents of the criminal justice system . . . reduces criminal involvement"—can serve not only as a useful integrative tool, but also "can provide grounds for creating a more supportive 'Good Society.'" Specifically, Cullen maintained, "the provision of social supports reduces criminogenic strains, fosters effective parenting and a nurturing family life, supplies the human and social capital needed to desist from crime, creates opportunities for prosocial modeling, strengthens efforts at informal and formal control, and reduces opportunities for victimization." Nonetheless, Cullen admits that an integrative theory of social support is a long way off. "Research must discern which of these hunches have merit," he says, "and to what degree."

Although we may not yet be able to see the practical promise of theoretical integration, work in the area has just begun. The door to this area will doubtlessly remain open a while longer.

■ POLICIES OF THE FUTURE

In a recent article, the eminent writer George F. Cole raised the question: "How can lawmakers, police, courts, and corrections begin to plan for the eventualities that lie ahead?" Cole concluded that "[i]t is essential that policy makers be given the best evidence as to prospects for future developments pertaining to the justice system and the broader socioeconomic and political context within which it will operate. Not all uncertainties about the future can be removed, but systematic and insightful exploration of the range of possibilities can provide a sounder basis for planning and a useful perspective on priorities for innovation."[115] Cole identified a number of "drivers," or significant changes likely to occur over the next twenty-five years, which he says "are likely to impact the crime and justice environment by the year 2010." The list he created is shown in Table 14.1.

The significance of many of the factors listed in Table 14.1 for crime-control planners can be clearly seen in the writings of **Gene Stephens.** Stephens, one of the best known futurists to focus on crime in the past decade, observes that "[c]rime is increasing worldwide, and there is every reason to believe the trend will continue through the 1990s and into the early years of the twenty-first century."[116] In particular, observes Stephens, street crimes are escalating in formerly communist countries throughout Eastern Europe, and in other European nations such as those in Scandinavia and the United Kingdom. According to Stephens, the United States was one of the first nations to experience a rapid rise in criminality because, in many ways, it was the most advanced nation on the globe. The United States is a highly diverse, multicultural, industrialized, and democratic society which strongly supports individual freedoms and has fostered a strong sense of personal independence among its citizens.

❖

TABLE 14.1

LIST OF DRIVERS LIKELY TO IMPACT THE CRIME AND JUSTICE ENVIRONMENT BY THE YEAR 2010

Demography

1. Overall U.S. population increases to 300,000,000.
2. Proportion of Americans older than age 40 grows from 37% to 45%.
3. Minorities increase to 26% of the population.
4. The flow of legal immigrants, increasingly from Latin America and Asia, continues at a rate of about 750,000 per year.
5. Advancing technology and a changing economy result in a disproportionate impact on less skilled, lower socioeconomic groups.

Economics

1. Restructuring of the economy continues with disruptions in some mature industrial sectors, rapid growth in the high-technology and service fields, and some outflow of jobs and capital to other nations.
2. The federal budget deficit improves, but only slowly, so funding for domestic programs remains tight.
3. Economies of the nations of the former Soviet Union remain unstable.
4. Checks and credit cards assume a larger portion of consumer monetary transactions.
5. Real growth in output and income generally is slow but steady.

Technology

1. Copying technologies advance rapidly.
2. Automation of financial transactions increases.
3. Miniaturization of computers gives patrol officers instant access to crime information files.
4. Scientists discover a chemical that has the ability to break the physical dependence on drugs from which addicts suffer.
5. Gains in laser and fiber-optic technologies revolutionize organizations.

Crime Factors

1. The war on drugs of the 1990s has been cut back as cocaine use declines and law enforcement proves costly.
2. Participation of women in criminal activity increases as their societal role is redefined.
3. Handguns continue to be owned by a significant portion of the population.
4. Incarceration rates stabilize as construction of costly new prisons declines. There is an expansion of the use of probation and intermediate sanctions.
5. Disposal of nuclear and toxic wastes becomes a major organized crime activity.

Source: George F. Cole, "Criminal Justice in the Twenty-First Century: The Role of Futures Research," in John Klofas and Stan Stojkovic, eds., *Crime and Justice in the Year 2010* (Belmont, Calif.: Wadsworth, 1995), pp. 4–5. Copyright © Wadsworth Publishing Company, 1995. Reprinted with permission.

Multiculturalism and heterogeneity, says Stephens, increase anomie, and previously isolated and homogeneous societies such as Japan, Denmark, China, and Greece are now facing a growing cultural diversity due to international migration, the expansion of new social ideals, and an increase in foreign commerce. "Heterogeneity in societies will be the rule in the twenty-first century," says Stephens, "and failure to recognize and plan for such diversity can lead to serious crime problems, especially in emerging multicultural societies."[117] Stephens's thesis is best summarized in this passage from his work: "The connection between crime and culture cannot be overemphasized: There are high-crime and low-crime cultures around the world. In the years ahead, many low-crime cultures may become high-crime cultures because of changing world demographics and politicoeconomic systems. In general, heterogeneous populations in which people have lots of political freedom (democracy) and lots of economic choice (capitalism) are prime candidates for crime unless a good socialization system is created and maintained."[118]

Homogeneous nations—in which citizens share similar backgrounds, life experiences, and values—produce citizens who are generally capable of complying with the wishes of the majority and who can legislate controls over behavior, which are not difficult for most citizens to respect. In such societies a tradition of discipline, a belief in the laws, and acceptance of personal responsibility are typically the norm.

Diverse societies, on the other hand, suffer from constant internal conflict, with much of that conflict focused on acceptable ways of living and working. Heterogeneous societies tend to place a strong emphasis on individualism, and disagreement about the law and social norms is rife. Characteristic of such cultures is the fact that lawbreakers tend to deny responsibility, "and violators go to great lengths to avoid capture and conviction." To highlight the difference between homogeneous and heterogeneous societies, Stephens points to the fact that in some highly homogeneous cultures, such as Japan, those who break norms will often punish themselves, even if their transgressions are not publicly discovered. Such self-punishing behavior would be almost unthinkable in an advanced heterogeneous society such as the United States. As Stephens explains, "Some nations, such as the United States, face pervasive *anomie* due to their lack of restraints on human desires."[119]

Heterogeneity can arise in numerous ways, even within a society that had previously been relatively homogenous. One source of increasing and important differences in American society today, for example, has been the growth of a technological culture which has produced two separate and distinct groups—the technologically capable and those who are incapable of utilizing modern technology. To these two groups we might add a third: the technologically aware, or those who realize the importance of technology but who, for whatever reason—be it age, lack of education, poverty, or other life circumstances—have not yet acquired the skills necessary to participate fully in what our highly technological society has to offer. In Stephens's words: "More people are turning to street crime and violence because they find themselves unprepared, educationally or emotionally, to cope with the requirements for success in the new era."[120]

Another reason why crime rates are high—and growing—in increasingly heterogeneous societies, according to Stephens, is that such societies often display a lack of consistent childcare philosophies and child-rearing methods. "In some societies," says Stephens, "parents are seen as primarily responsible for their children, but all citizens share in that responsibility, since everyone's welfare is affected by the proper socialization of each child." In others, children are viewed as the parents' property, and little is expected of parents other than that they be biologically capable of reproducing. No requirements are set in such societies for parental knowledge, skills, income, education, and so on. Stephens describes child-rearing practices in such societies as "helter-skelter, catch-as-catch-can child care. . . ." Lacking child-rearing standards in which the majority of members of society can meaningfully participate, heterogeneous societies tend to produce adults who are irresponsible and who do not adhere to legal or other standards of behavior.

According to Stephens, future crimes will be plentiful, with countries around the world experiencing explosive growth in their crime rates. "The United States," he says, "was the first industrialized, democratic, heterogeneous nation and thus the first to face the crime problems associated with *anomie*."[121] Now, however, other nations are undergoing increased modernization, with many entering the postmodern era previously occupied solely by the United States. "[W]e can theorize," says Stephens, "that crime will be a growth industry in many countries as they find themselves gripped by the same social forces that have long affected the United States."[122]

Other authors have similarly attempted to describe crime-control issues that may face future policymakers.[123] Richter H. Moore, Jr., for example, identifies the following seven issues that are likely to concern crime-control planners in the near future.[124]

- *New Criminal Groups:* According to Moore, "groups such as Colombian drug cartels, Jamaican posses, Vietnamese gangs, various Chinese groups, and Los Angeles black street gangs are now a much bigger concern than the Mafia," and the criminal activity and influence of these new groups are growing rapidly. Traditional law enforcement responses, such as those developed to deal with Italian-American "Mafia" organizations, may be inappropriate in the face of the new challenges these groups represent.
- *Language Barriers:* According to Moore, "U.S. law-enforcement officials now find themselves hampered by a lack of understanding about the language and culture of some of the new criminal groups" operating in America. Cuban, Mexican, Colombian, Japanese, and Chinese criminals and criminal organizations are becoming commonplace, and such groups are increasingly involved in international communications and travel.
- *Distrust by Ethnic Communities:* Recent immigrant groups have been slow to assimilate into American culture and society. As a consequence, many of these groups hold strongly to native identities, distancing themselves from formal agencies of social control such as the police. As Moore points out, "[i]n many of their countries of origin, new immigrants see police as corrupt, self-serving individuals, a viewpoint often not without foundation." A distrust of police and government representatives is nearly instinctual for members of such groups, making the work of law enforcement within the context of immigrant communities challenging and often difficult.
- *Greater Reliance on Community Involvement:* Moore observes that "[d]ue to the increasing costs of electronic surveillance, informant programs, undercover operations, and witness-protection programs, police are now encour-

aging community members to become more involved in their own security." The involvement of private citizens in the battle against crime may be the only realistic solution to the problem. Neighborhood watch groups, the use of community volunteers within criminal justice organizations, along with other neighborhood self-help programs such as school and church-based education, all suggest the future of neighborhood-based crime-control policy.

- *Regulating the Marketplace:* Moore advises that decriminalization and legalization will become of increasingly greater concern to future legislators who will focus on "regulating the marketplace" for criminal activities such as gambling, drug trafficking, and prostitution.
- *Reducing Public Demand:* Similarly, according to Moore, future crime-control policies will aim to reduce involvement in criminal activity "through better education" and other policies that will, over the long term, lower the demand for drugs and other illegal services.
- *Increased Treatment:* Although in contrast with many of today's get-tough policies, Moore sees a greater emphasis in the future on the treatment of all forms of criminality, including drug abuse, gambling, rape, and other law-breaking behaviors.

Postmodernism suggests that effective crime control in any future heterogeneous society can best be achieved by the adoption of a peace model based on cooperation rather than retribution. The **peace model** of crime control, having emerged largely from the themes embodied in peacemaking criminology, focuses on effective ways for developing a shared consensus on critical issues that have the potential to seriously affect the quality of life. These issues include major crimes such as murder and rape, but in future societies will also extend to property rights, rights to the use of new technologies, the ownership of information, and so on. Relatively minor issues, including sexual preference, nonviolent sexual deviance, gambling, drug use, noise, simple child custody claims, and publicly offensive behavior, will be dealt with fairly, but in ways that require few resources beyond those immediately available in the community.

Peace model an approach to crime control which focuses on effective ways for developing a shared consensus on critical issues which have the potential to seriously affect the quality of life.

Alternative dispute resolution mechanisms will be necessary in any future heterogeneous society because burgeoning disagreements about everyday issues will overwhelm the ability of existing resources such as the courts and police to deal with them.[125] Mediation programs, such as modern-day dispute resolution centers and neighborhood justice centers, can be expected to expand in number, and to be characterized by cooperative efforts to reach dispute resolution, rather than by adversarial-like proceedings now characteristic of most American courts. Dispute resolution programs are based on the principle of **participatory justice**, in which all parties to a dispute accept a kind of binding arbitration by neutral parties. Now operating in over 200 areas throughout the country, dispute resolution centers often utilize administrative hearings and ombudsmen and are staffed by volunteers who work to resolve disputes without assigning blame.

Participatory justice a relatively informal type of criminal justice case processing which makes use of local community resources rather than requiring traditional forms of official intervention.

The Community Dispute Settlement Program which began in Philadelphia in the 1970s was one of the earliest of modern-day community mediation programs in the country and has been well studied.[126] Mediation in America, however, has a long and varied history. For many years Native American tribes have routinely employed dispute resolution mechanisms in dealing with behavioral problems and

Restorative justice a
postmodern perspective
which stresses remedies
and restoration rather
than prison, punishment,
and victim neglect.

even crime. Perhaps the best known dispute settlement mechanism among Native Americans today is the Navajo Peacemaker Court, which serves as an adjunct to the tribal court.[127]

Miami's "drug court," a local-area judicial initiative, provides an example of another kind of dispute resolution program. The drug court program, which began in 1989, diverts nonviolent drug users from the traditional path of streets to court to jail, and is one of the first of its kind in the nation. Officially called the Dade County Diversion and Treatment Program, the drug court "channels almost all nonviolent defendants arrested on drug possession charges into an innovative court-operated rehabilitation program as an alternative to prosecution.... [T]he program expands on the traditional concept of diversion to provide a year or more of treatment and case management services that include counseling, acupuncture, fellowship meetings, education courses, and vocational services along with strict monitoring through periodic urine tests and court appearances. Defendants who succeed in the program have their criminal cases dismissed."[128] Drug court processing appears to be successful at reducing the incidence of repeat offenses, does not result in a criminal record for those who complete the program, and offers drug-dependent offenders a second chance at gaining control over substance abuse problems.

Many alternative dispute resolution strategies are really a form of restorative justice. Postmodern writers describe **restorative justice** as "a new system based on remedies and restoration rather than on prison, punishment and victim neglect."[129] They see it as "a system rooted in the concept of a caring community" and hope that it will lead to social and economic justice and increased concern and respect for both victims and victimizers in the not too distant future.

Alternative dispute resolution strategies are not without their critics who charge that such programs are often staffed by poorly qualified individuals who are ill prepared to mediate disputes effectively. Nonetheless, as case processing expenses continue to rise, and as minor cases continue to flood justice system agencies, we can expect that an emphasis on alternative means of dispute resolution will continue.

SUMMARY

For all but the most astute, the future is difficult to presage. It is safe to assume, however, that the future will differ from the past, and that important differences in any future criminology will involve issues of theory formulation and crime-control policy. We can get some hint of what is to come by examining postmodern approaches. Although tending toward increased realism in their view of crime and criminal behavior, these approaches generally advocate humane alternatives to traditional crime-control agendas. Some have termed such postmodern policies "restorative justice" and have suggested that crime-control programs of the near future must take into account both the suffering of victims and the inequities within society that promulgate criminality. Others, however, have complained that "postmodernism does not provide any practical guidance on policy. At most," such critics say, "it offers a basis for exposing possible pretenses and illusions in the pursuit of a just policy."[130] Postmodern criminology, because of its emphasis on deconstructionism, has also been criticized "for not valuing anything, and for a belief that 'anything goes.'"[131]

But those who perceive postmodern criminology as shortsighted fail to recognize that a new social order requires a new way of understanding it. Dragan Milovanovic, one writer whose work in the area is becoming increasingly important, believes that "[a]ffirmative postmodern criminology has emerged in the 1990s as a paradigm not only for deconstructing oppressive forms, but also for affirmatively reconstructing the new order."[132] Others point out: "It is still too early to evaluate the impact of postmodernism on criminology. Yet its influence is being felt in the increased questioning of traditional criminological concepts."[133] If early signs are any indication, postmodern criminology combined with the traditional approaches of the past appear to offer the best hope for coping with crime and for developing a truly just society in the twenty-first century.

WEB WATCH

Access the *Criminology Today* home page on the World Wide Web by pointing your browser at www.prenhall.com/cjcentral. Once there, click on *Criminology Today* to access the wealth of electronic resources supporting this text.

Onsite resources include (1) "Chapter Links," which provides succinct overviews of critical ideas from the textbook and links selected materials from around the Web to concepts found in the text; (2) "General Reference—Law and Justice Links." Organized by chapter, these links lead to other useful resources on the World Wide Web such as libraries, electronic discussion lists, and electronic journals; (3) "Criminology Sites on the Web," which lists links to organizations such as the American Society of Criminology and the National Organization for Victims Assistance (NOVA), as well as crime prevention links and statistics on crime and justice. Many other Web-based resources can be accessed via the *Criminology Today* site, including the federal Justice Information Center, the Bureau of Justice Statistics, the FBI, the RAND Corporation, the Vera Institute of Justice, PAVNET (an online "Partnership Against Violence," run by seven different federal agencies), and the National White Collar Crime Center.

Still another feature of the *Criminology Today* Web site is e-mail homework. Homework can be composed onsite and submitted to instructors using the instructor's e-mail address. To use the e-mail homework feature, click on "E-Mail Homework" on the opening page, and then type answers to the questions that appear in the spaces provided. Use your instructor's e-mail address to submit homework answers. The *Criminology Today* Web site also provides links to powerful Web-based search engines that can help you find topics of interest to you as you progress through your course of study. Search engines can be found under the home page heading "Criminology Sites on the Web."

DISCUSSION QUESTIONS

▪▪

1. This book emphasizes a social problems versus social responsibility theme. Which perspective do you think will be dominant in the twenty-first century? Why?

2. Do you believe it is possible to know the future? What techniques are identified in this chapter for assessing possible futures? Which do you think holds the most promise? Why?

3. How does the situational approach to crime control differ from more traditional "offender-centered" approaches? Which, in your opinion, is more likely to deter crime? Why?

4. What have been the major contributions of feminist thinking to the field of criminology? Do you believe that a feminist criminology is possible? Why or why not?

5. What do we mean by the word *deconstructionist* in the context of new criminological approaches to crime explanation? Why do some authors say that feminist criminology is deconstructionist?

6. Describe the emerging theoretical approaches outlined in this chapter. Which appeals the most to you? Why?

7. Describe *peacemaking criminology*. What are its central tenets? Do you believe that peacemaking criminology is realistic? Why or why not?

8. What is *postmodernism?* How has postmodernism affected criminology? What predictions for the future can we make based on an understanding of postmodernist approaches?

NOTES

▪▪

[1] James Q. Wilson, "Crime and Public Policy," in James Q. Wilson and Joan Petersilia, *Crime* (San Francisco: Institute for Contemporary Studies, 1995), p. 507.

[2] Cynthia Manson and Charles Ardai, eds., *Future Crimes* (New York: Donald I. Fine, 1992), p. x.

[3] Joseph F. Coates, "The Highly Probable Future: 83 Assumptions About the Year 2025," *The Futurist,* vol. 28, no. 4 (July/August 1994), p. 51.

[4] Alvin Toffler, *Future Shock* (New York: Random House, 1970).

[5] Alvin Toffler, *Powershift: Knowledge, Wealth, and Violence at the Edge of the 21st Century* (New York: Bantam Books, 1990).

[6] Alvin Toffler, *The Third Wave* (New York: Bantam Books, 1981).

[7] John Naisbitt, *Megatrends: Ten New Directions Transforming Our Lives* (New York: Warner Books, 1982).

[8] Although this chapter cannot cover all future aspects of the criminal justice system, readers are referred to C. J. Swank, "Police in the 21st Century: Hypotheses for the Future," *International Journal of Comparative and Applied Criminal Justice,* vol. 17, nos. 1 and 2 (Spring/Fall 1993), pp. 107–120, for an excellent analysis of policing in the future.

[9] Society of Police Futurists International, "PFI: The Future of Policing" (brochure), no date.

[10] William L. Tafoya, "Futures Research: Implications for Criminal Investigations," in James N. Gilbert, ed., *Criminal Investigation: Essays and Cases* (Columbus, Ohio: Charles E. Merrill, 1990), p. 214.

[11] As identified by George F. Cole, "Criminal Justice in the Twenty-First Century: The Role of Futures Research," in John Klofas and Stan Stojkovic, eds., *Crime and Justice in*

the Year 2010 (Belmont, Calif.: Wadsworth, 1995).

[12] Ibid.

[13] Ibid.

[14] Richter H. Moore, Jr., "Wiseguys: Smarter Criminals and Smarter Crime in the 21st Century," The Futurist, vol. 28, no. 5 (September/October 1994), p. 33.

[15] Ibid.

[16] Georgette Bennett, Crimewarps: The Future of Crime in America (Garden City, N.Y.: Anchor/Doubleday, 1987).

[17] L. Edward Wells, "Explaining Crime in the Year 2010," in Klofas and Stojkovic, Crime and Justice in the Year 2010, pp. 36–61.

[18] Ibid., pp. 48–49.

[19] Ibid., pp. 54–57.

[20] Frank P. Williams III and Marilyn D. McShane, Criminological Theory, 2nd ed. (Englewood Cliffs, N.J.: Prentice Hall, 1994), p. 257.

[21] Gregg Barak, "Introduction: Criminological Theory in the 'Postmodernist' Era," in Gregg Barak, ed., Varieties of Criminology: Readings from a Dynamic Discipline (Westport, Conn.: Praeger, 1994), pp. 1–11.

[22] For an excellent and detailed discussion of many of these approaches, see Dragan Milovanovic, Postmodern Criminology (Hamden, Conn.: Garland, 1997).

[23] Bruce DiCristina, Methods in Criminology: A Philosophical Primer (New York: Harrow and Heston, 1995).

[24] Jeff Ferrell, "Anarchy Against the Discipline," a review of Bruce DiCristina's Methods in Criminology: A Philosophical Primer (New York: Harrow and Heston, 1995), in the Journal of Criminal Justice and Popular Culture, vol. 3, no. 4 (August 15, 1995).

[25] See, for example, Stuart Henry and Dragan Milovanovic, Constitutive Criminology: Beyond Postmodernism (London: Sage, 1995); and Dragan Milovanovic, Postmodern Criminology (Hamden, Conn.: Garland, 1997).

[26] Postmodern Criminology.

[27] Dragan Milovanovic, Primer in the Sociology of Law, 2nd ed. (New York: Harrow and Heston, 1994).

[28] Stuart Henry and Dragan Milovanovic, Constitutive Criminology: Beyond Postmodernism (London: Sage, 1995), p. 118.

[29] Werner Einstadter and Stuart Henry, Criminological Theory: An Analysis of Its Underlying Assumptions (Fort Worth: Harcourt Brace, 1995), p. 291.

[30] Frank P. Williams III and Marilyn D. McShane, Criminological Theory, 2nd ed. (Englewood Cliffs, N.J.: Prentice Hall, 1994), p. 221.

[31] Felton M. Earls and Albert J. Reiss, Breaking the Cycle: Predicting and Preventing Crime (Washington, D.C.: National Institute of Justice, 1994), p. 49.

[32] L. E. Cohen and Marcus Felson, "Social Change and Crime Rate Trends: A Routine Activity Approach," American Sociological Review, vol. 44, no. 4 (August 1979), pp. 588–608. Also, see Marcus Felson and L. E. Cohen, "Human Ecology and Crime: A Routine Activity Approach," Human Ecology, vol. 8, no. 4 (1980), pp. 389–406; Marcus Felson, "Linking Criminal Choices, Routine Activities, Informal Control, and Criminal Outcomes," in Derek B. Cornish and Ronald V. Clarke, eds., The Reasoning Criminal: Rational Choice Perspectives on Offending (New York: Springer-Verlag, 1986), pp. 119–128; and Ronald V. Clarke and Marcus Felson, eds., Advances in Criminological Theory: Routine Activity and Rational Choice (New Brunswick, N.J.: Transaction, 1993).

[33] Lawrence E. Cohen and Marcus Felson, "Social Change and Crime Rate Trends: A Routine Activities Approach," American Sociological Review, vol. 44, no. 4 (1979), p. 595.

[34] For a test of routine activities theory as an explanation for victimization in the workplace, see John D. Wooldredge, Francis T. Cullen, and Edward J. Latessa, "Victimization in the Workplace: A Test of Routine Activities Theory," Justice Quarterly, vol. 9, no. 2 (June 1992), pp. 325–335.

[35] Marcus Felson, Crime and Everyday Life: Insight and Implications for Society (Thousand Oaks, Calif.: Pine Forge Press, 1994).

[36] Gary LaFree and Christopher Birkbeck, "The Neglected Situation: A Cross-National Study of the Situational Characteristics of Crime," Criminology, vol. 29, no. 1 (February 1991), p. 75.

[37] Ronald V. Clarke and Derek B. Cornish, eds., Crime Control in Britain: A Review of Police and Research (Albany: State University of New York Press), p. 8.

[38] See Derek B. Cornish and Ronald V. Clarke, "Understanding Crime Displacement: An Application of Rational Choice Theory," Criminology, vol. 25, no. 4 (November 1987), p. 933.

[39]Clarke and Cornish, *Crime Control in Britain: A Review of Police and Research*, p. 48.

[40]Werner Einstadter and Stuart Henry, *Criminological Theory: An Analysis of Its Underlying Assumptions* (Fort Worth: Harcourt Brace, 1995), p. 70.

[41]Daniel J. Curran and Claire M. Renzetti, *Theories of Crime* (Boston: Allyn & Bacon, 1994), p. 18.

[42]Laura J. Moriarty and James E. Williams, "Examining the Relationship Between Routine Activities Theory and Social Disorganization: An Analysis of Property Crime Victimization," *American Journal of Criminal Justice,* vol. 21, no. 1, 1996, pp. 43–59.

[43]Ibid., p. 46.

[44]David Weisburd, "Reorienting Crime Prevention Research and Policy: From the Causes of Criminality to the Context of Crime," *NIJ Research Report* (Washington, D.C.: NIJ, June 1997).

[45]Material in this section comes from Weisburd, "Reorienting Crime Prevention Research and Policy."

[46]See P.J. Brantingham and P. L. Brantingham, "Situational Crime Prevention in Practice," *Canadian Journal of Criminology,* January 1990, pp. 17–40; and R. V. Clarke, "Situational Crime Prevention: Achievements and Challenges," in M. Tonry and D. Farrington, eds., *Building a Safer Society: Strategic Approaches to Crime Prevention, Crime and Justice: A Review of Research,* vol. 19 (Chicago: University of Chicago Press, 1995).

[47]Weisburd, op. cit.

[48]See, for example, J.E. Eck and D. Weisburd, eds., *Crime and Place: Crime Prevention Studies,* vol. 4 (Monsey, N.Y.: Willow Tree Press, 1995).

[49]See L. Sherman, "Hot Spots of Crime and Criminal Careers of Places," in J.E. Eck and D. Weisburd, eds., *Crime and Place: Crime Prevention Studies,* vol. 4 (Monsey, N.Y.: Willow Tree Press, 1995); and L. Sherman, P. R. Gartin, and M.E. Buerger, "Hot Spots of Predatory Crime: Routine Activities and the Criminology of Place," *Criminology,* vol. 27, no. 1 (1989), pp. 27–56.

[50]Weisburd, op. cit.

[51]Kenneth D. Tunnell, "Choosing Crime: Close Your Eyes and Take Your Chances," *Justice Quarterly,* vol. 7 (1990), pp. 673–690.

[52]See R. Barr and K. Pease, "Crime Placement, Displacement and Deflection, in M. Tonry and N. Morris, eds., *Crime and Justice: A Review of Research,* vol. 12 (Chicago: University of Chicago Press, 1990).

[53]For a good summation of target hardening, see Ronald V. Clarke, *Situational Crime Prevention* (New York: Harrow and Heston, 1992).

[54]For a good summation of studies on displacement, see R. Hesseling, "Displacement: A Review of the Empirical Literature," in R. V. Clarke, ed., *Crime Prevention Studies,* vol. 3 (Monsey, N.Y.: Willow Tree Press, 1994).

[55]Don C. Gibbons, *Talking About Crime and Criminals: Problems and Issues in Theory Development in Criminology* (Englewood Cliffs, N.J.: Prentice Hall, 1994), p. 165, citing Loraine Gelsthorpe and Alison Morris, "Feminism and Criminology in Britain," *British Journal of Criminology* (Spring 1988), pp. 93–110.

[56]Sally S. Simpson, "Feminist Theory, Crime and Justice," *Criminology,* vol. 27, no. 4 (1989), p. 605.

[57]Freda Adler, *Sisters in Crime: The Rise of the New Female Criminal* (New York: McGraw-Hill, 1975).

[58]Rita J. Simon, *Women and Crime* (Lexington, Mass.: Lexington Books, 1975).

[59]Kathleen Daly and Meda Chesney-Lind, "Feminism and Criminology," *Justice Quarterly,* vol. 5, no. 5 (December 1988), pp. 497–535.

[60]Susan Caulfield and Nancy Wonders, "Gender and Justice: Feminist Contributions to Criminology," in Gregg Barak, ed., *Varieties of Criminology: Readings from a Dynamic Discipline* (Westport, Conn.: Praeger, 1994), pp. 213–229.

[61]Roslyn Muraskin and Ted Alleman, *It's a Crime: Women and Justice* (Englewood Cliffs, N.J.: Prentice Hall, 1993), p. 1.

[62]Carol Pateman, "Feminist Critiques of the Public/Private Dichotomy," in Anne Phillips, ed., *Feminism and Equality* (Oxford: Basil Blackwell, 1987).

[63]Alida V. Merlo and Joycelyn M. Pollock, eds., *Women, Law and Social Control* (Needham Heights, Mass.: Allyn and Bacon, 1995).

[64]Simpson, "Feminist Theory, Crime and Justice."

[65]John Hagan, *Structural Criminology* (New Brunswick, N.J.: Rutgers University Press, 1989), p. 130.

[66] Ibid., p. 13.

[67] Ibid.

[68] Evelyn K. Sommers, *Voices from Within: Women Who Have Broken the Law* (Toronto: University of Toronto Press, 1995).

[69] Daly and Chesney-Lind, "Feminism and Criminology," p. 506.

[70] Ibid.

[71] Ibid., p. 514.

[72] For an intriguing analysis of how existing laws tend to criminalize women and their reproductive activities, see Susan O. Reed, "The Criminalization of Pregnancy: Drugs, Alcohol, and AIDS," in Muraskin and Alleman, *It's a Crime: Women and Justice,* pp. 92–117; and Drew Humphries, "Mothers and Children, Drugs and Crack: Reactions to Maternal Drug Dependency," in Muraskin and Alleman, *It's a Crime: Women and Justice,* pp. 131–145.

[73] Dawn H. Currie, "Feminist Encounters with Postmodernism: Exploring the Impasse of the Debates on Patriarchy and Law," *Canadian Journal of Women and the Law,* vol. 5, no. 1 (1992), p. 10.

[74] For an excellent overview of feminist theory in criminology, and for a comprehensive review of research regarding female offenders, see Joanne Belknap, *The Invisible Woman: Gender Crime and Justice* (Belmont, Calif.: Wadsworth, 1996).

[75] Such studies are still ongoing and continue to add to the descriptive literature of feminist criminology. See, for example, Deborah R. Baskin and Ira Sommers, "Female Initiation into Violent Street Crime," *Justice Quarterly,* vol. 10, no. 4 (December 1993), pp. 559–583; Scott Decker, Richard Wright, Allison Redfern, and Dietrich Smith, "A Woman's Place Is in the Home: Females and Residential Burglary," *Justice Quarterly,* vol. 10, no. 1 (March 1993), pp. 143–162; and Jill L. Rosenbaum, "The Female Delinquent: Another Look at the Role of the Family," in Muraskin and Alleman, *It's a Crime: Women and Justice,* pp. 399–420.

[76] Ronald L. Akers, *Criminological Theories: Introduction and Evaluation* (Los Angeles: Roxbury, 1994), p. 39.

[77] For additional insight into the notion of "deconstruction" as it applies to feminist thought within criminology, see Carol Smart, *Feminism and the Power of Law* (New York: Routledge, 1989).

[78] Daly and Chesney-Lind, "Feminism and Criminology," p. 512.

[79] See, for example, Darrell J. Steffensmeier and Emile Andersen Allan, "Sex Disparities in Arrests by Residence, Race, and Age: An Assessment of the Gender Convergence/Crime Hypothesis," *Justice Quarterly,* vol. 5, no. 1 (March 1988), pp. 53–80.

[80] Darrell Steffensmeier, John Kramer, and Cathy Streifel, "Gender and Imprisonment Decisions," *Criminology,* vol. 31, no. 3 (August 1993), pp. 411–446. Gender-based differences, however, have been discovered in some instances of probation-and parole-related decision making. See Edna Erez, "Gender, Rehabilitation, and Probation Decisions," *Criminology,* vol. 27, no. 2 (1989), pp. 307–327; and Edna Erez, "Dangerous Men, Evil Women: Gender and Parole Decision-Making," *Justice Quarterly,* vol. 9, no. 1 (March 1992), pp. 106–126.

[81] See, for example, Kathleen Daly, "Neither Conflict nor Labeling nor Paternalism Will Suffice: Intersections of Race, Ethnicity, Gender, and Family in Criminal Court Decisions," *Crime and Delinquency,* vol. 35, no. 1 (January 1989), pp. 136–168.

[82] Citing Allison Morris, *Women, Crime and Criminal Justice* (New York: Blackwell, 1987).

[83] Caulfield and Wonders, "Gender and Justice: Feminist Contributions to Criminology," p. 229.

[84] For examples of how this might be accomplished, see F. H. Knopp, "Community Solutions to Sexual Violence: Feminist/Abolitionist Perspectives," in *Criminology as Peacemaking* (Bloomington: Indiana University Press), pp. 181–193; and S. Caringella-MacDonald and D. Humphries, "Sexual Assault, Women, and the Community: Organizing to Prevent Sexual Violence," *Criminology as Peacemaking,* pp. 98–113.

[85] Richard Quinney, "Life of Crime: Criminology and Public Policy as Peacemaking," *Journal of Crime and Justice,* vol. 16, no. 2 (1993), pp. 3–9.

[86] See, for example, Harold E. Pepinsky, "This Can't Be Peace: A Pessimist Looks at Punishment," in W. B. Groves and G. Newman, eds., *Punishment and Privilege* (Albany: Harrow

and Heston, 1986); Harold E. Pepinsky, "Violence as Unresponsiveness: Toward a New Conception of Crime," *Justice Quarterly,* vol. 5 (1988), pp. 539–563; and Pepinsky and Quinney, *Criminology as Peacemaking.*

[87]See, for example, Richard Quinney, "Crime, Suffering, Service: Toward a Criminology of Peacemaking," *Quest,* vol. 1 (1988), pp. 66–75; Richard Quinney, "The Theory and Practice of Peacemaking in the Development of Radical Criminology," *Critical Criminologist,* vol. 1, no. 5 (1989), p. 5; and Richard Quinney and John Wildeman, *The Problem of Crime: A Peace and Social Justice Perspective,* 3rd ed. (Mayfield, Calif.: Mountain View Press, 1991)—originally published as *The Problem of Crime: A Critical Introduction to Criminology* (New York: Bantam, 1977).

[88]All these themes are addressed, for example, in Pepinsky and Quinney, *Criminology as Peacemaking.*

[89]For a good discussion of this "theory," see John F. Galliher, "Willie Horton: Fact, Faith, and Commonsense Theory of Crime," in ibid., pp. 245–250.

[90]Quinney and Wildeman, *The Problem of Crime: A Peace and Social Justice Perspective,* pp. vii–viii.

[91]Richard Quinney, "Life of Crime: Criminology and Public Policy as Peacemaking," *Journal of Crime and Justice,* vol. 16, no. 2 (1993), abstract.

[92]Bo Lozoff and Michael Braswell, *Inner Corrections: Finding Peace and Peace Making* (Cincinnati: Anderson, 1989).

[93]Clemmons Bartollas and Michael Braswell, "Correctional Treatment, Peacemaking, and the New Age Movement," *Journal of Crime and Justice,* vol. 16, no. 2 (1993), pp. 43–58.

[94]Ibid.

[95]Ram Dass and P. Gorman, *How Can I Help? Stories and Reflections on Service* (New York: Alfred A. Knopf, 1985), p. 165; as cited in *The Problem of Crime: A Peace and Social Justice Perspective,* 3rd ed., p. 116.

[96]Lozoff and Braswell, *Inner Corrections,* p. vii.

[97]Einstadter and Henry, *Criminological Theory: An Analysis of Its Underlying Assumptions,* p. 233.

[98]For an excellent review of critical realism within a Canadian context, see John Lowman

and Brian D. MacLean, eds., *Realist Criminology: Crime Control and Policing in the 1990s* (Toronto: University of Toronto Press, 1994).

[99]Daniel J. Curran and Claire M. Renzetti, *Theories of Crime* (Boston: Allyn & Bacon, 1994), p. 283.

[100]See M. D. Schwartz and W. S. DeKeseredy, "Left Realist Criminology: Strengths, Weaknesses, and the Feminist Critique," *Crime, Law, and Social Change,* vol. 15, no. 1 (January 1991), pp. 51–72; W. S. DeKeseredy and B. D. MacLean, "Exploring the Gender, Race, and Class Dimensions of Victimization: A Left Realist Critique of the Canadian Urban Victimization Survey," *International Journal of Offender Therapy and Comparative Criminology,* vol. 35, no. 2 (Summer 1991), pp. 143–161; and W. S. DeKeseredy and M. D. Schwartz, "British and U.S. Left Realism: A Critical Comparison," *International Journal of Offender Therapy and Comparative Criminology,* vol. 35, no. 3 (Fall 1991), pp. 248–262.

[101]See Jock Young, "The Failure of Criminology: The Need for a Radical Realism," in R. Matthews and J. Young, eds., *Confronting Crime* (Beverly Hills: Sage, 1986), pp. 4–30; Jock Young, "The Tasks of a Realist Criminology," *Contemporary Crisis,* vol. 11, no. 4 (1987) pp. 337–356; and "Radical Criminology in Britain: The Emergence of a Competing Paradigm," *British Journal of Criminology,* vol. 28 (1988), pp. 159–183.

[102]Roger Matthews and Jock Young, "Reflections on Realism," in Jock Young and Roger Matthews, eds., *Rethinking Criminology: The Realist Debate* (Newbury Park, Calif.: Sage, 1992).

[103]David Nelken, ed., *The Futures of Criminology* (Thousand Oaks, Calif.: Sage, 1994), p. 91.

[104]Ibid.

[105]Don C. Gibbons, *Talking About Crime and Criminals: Problems and Issues in Theory Development in Criminology,* (Englewood Cliffs, N.J.: Prentice Hall, 1994), p. 170.

[106]Piers Bierne and James W. Messerschmidt, *Criminology* (New York: Harcourt Brace Jovanovich, 1991), p. 501.

[107]For a more detailed discussion of theory integration, see Stephen F. Messner, Marvin D. Krohn, and Allan A. Liska, eds., *Theoretical Integration in the Study of Deviance and Crime:*

Problems and Prospects (Albany: State University of New York Press), p. 1989.

[108] Joan McCord, "Theory, Pseudotheory, and Metatheory," in W. S. Laufer and F. Adler, eds., *Advances in Criminological Theory*, vol. 1 (New Brunswick, N.J.: Transaction, 1989), pp. 127–145.

[109] Williams and McShane, *Criminological Theory*, p. 265.

[110] Ibid., pp. 266–267.

[111] Einstadter and Henry, *Criminological Theory: An Analysis of Its Underlying Assumptions*, p. 309.

[112] See, for example, Katheryn K. Russell, "Development of a Black Criminology and the Role of the Black Criminologist," *Justice Quarterly*, vol. 9, no. 4 (December 1992), pp. 668–683.

[113] Francis T. Cullen, "Social Support as an Organizing Concept for Criminology: Presidential Address to the Academy of Criminal Justice Sciences," *Justice Quarterly*, vol. 11, no. 4 (December 1994), pp. 527–559.

[114] See, for example, Carolyn Smith and Terence P. Thornberry, "The Relationship Between Childhood Maltreatment and Adolescent Involvement in Delinquency," *Criminology*, vol. 33, no. 4 (1995), pp. 451–477.

[115] Cole, "Criminal Justice in the Twenty-First Century: The Role of Futures Research," pp. 4–5.

[116] Gene Stephens, "The Global Crime Wave," *The Futurist*, vol. 28, no. 4 (July/August 1994), pp. 22–29.

[117] Ibid.

[118] Ibid.

[119] Ibid.

[120] Ibid.

[121] Ibid.

[122] Ibid.

[123] For an interesting and alternative view of the future—one that evaluates what might happen if the insight provided by feminist perspectives on crime were implemented—see M. Kay Harris, "Moving Into the New Millennium: Toward a Feminist Vision of Justice," in Pepinsky and Quinney, *Criminology as Peacemaking*.

[124] Richter H. Moore, Jr., "Wiseguys: Smarter Criminals and Smarter Crime in the 21st Century," *The Futurist*, vol. 28, no. 5 (Sept.-Oct. 1994), p. 33.

[125] For a good overview of such programs, see Thomas E. Carbonneau, *Alternative Dispute Resolution: Melting the Lances and Dismounting the Steeds* (Chicago: University of Illinois Press, 1989).

[126] See, for example, J. E. Beer, *Peacemaking in Your Neighborhood: Reflections on an Experiment in Community Mediation* (Philadelphia: New Society Publishers, 1986); and J. Beer, E. Steif, and C. Walker, *Peacemaking in Your Neighborhood: Mediator's Handbook* (Philadelphia: Friends Mediation Service, 1987).

[127] For an excellent review of alternative dispute mechanisms among Native American groups, see D. LeResche, "Native American Perspectives on Peacemaking," *Mediation Quarterly*, vol. 10, no. 4 (Summer 1993).

[128] Peter Finn and Andrea K. Newlyn, "Miami's 'Drug Court': A Different Approach" (Washington, D.C.: National Institute of Justice, June 1993), p. 2.

[129] Fay Honey Knopp, "Community Solutions to Sexual Violence: Feminist-Abolitionist Perspectives," in Pepinsky and Quinney, *Criminology as Peacemaking*, p. 183.

[130] Martin D. Schwartz and David O. Friedrichs, "Postmodern Thought and Criminological Discontent: New Metaphors for Understanding Violence," *Criminology*, vol. 32, no. 2 (1994), p. 237.

[131] Williams and McShane, *Criminological Theory*, p. 280.

[132] Dragan Milovanovic, "Postmodern Criminology: Mapping the Terrain," *Justice Quarterly*, vol. 13, no. 4 (December 1996), pp. 567–610.

[133] Williams and McShane, *Criminological Theory*, p. 297.

GLOSSARY

Administrative law regulates many daily business activities, and violations of such regulations generally result in warnings or fines, depending on their adjudged severity.

Age of Reason. See **Enlightenment.**

Aggravated assault (UCR) the unlawful attack by one person upon another for the purpose of inflicting severe or aggravated bodily injury. See also **simple assault.**

Alloplastic adaptation that form of adjustment which results from changes in the environment surrounding an individual.

Anomie a social condition in which norms are uncertain or lacking. Also see **strain theory.**

Antisocial or **asocial personality** refers to individuals who are basically unsocialized and whose behavior pattern brings them repeatedly into conflict with society.

Applied research scientific inquiry that is designed and carried out with practical application in mind.

Arson any willful or malicious burning or attempt to burn, with or without intent to defraud, a dwelling house, public building, motor vehicle or aircraft, personal property of another, etc.

Asocial personality. See **antisocial personality.**

Assault. See **aggravated assault** or **simple assault.**

Asset forfeiture the authorized seizure of money, negotiable instruments, securities, or other things of value. In federal antidrug laws: the authorization of judicial representatives to seize all monies, negotiable instruments, securities, or other things of value furnished or intended to be furnished by any person in exchange for a controlled substance, and all proceeds traceable to such an exchange.

Atavism a concept used by Cesare Lombroso to suggest that criminals are physiological throwbacks to earlier stages of human evolution. The term is derived from the Latin term *atavus,* which means "ancestor."

Audit trail a sequential record of computer system activities that enables auditors to reconstruct, review, and examine the sequence of states and activities surrounding each event in one or more related transactions from inception to output of final results back to inception.

Autoplastic adaptation that form of adjustment which results from changes within an individual.

Behavior theory a psychological perspective which posits that individual behavior which is rewarded will increase in frequency, while that which is punished will decrease.

Biological theories (of criminology) maintain that the basic determinants of human behavior, including criminality, are constitutionally or physiologically based and often inherited.

Born criminals individuals who are born with a genetic predilection toward criminality.

Bourgeoisie in Marxian theory, the class of people which owns the means of production.

Broken windows thesis a perspective on crime causation which holds that physical deterioration in an area leads to increased concerns for personal safety among area residents, and to higher crime rates in that area.

Bulletin board system (BBS) a computer accessible by telephone used like a bulletin board to leave messages and files for other users.

Burglary 1. By the narrowest and oldest definition: the trespassory breaking and entering of the dwelling house of another in the nighttime with the intent to commit a felony. 2. The unlawful entry of any fixed structure, vehicle or vessel used for regular residence, industry or business, with or without force, with intent to commit a felony or larceny.

Burglary (UCR) the unlawful entry of a structure to commit a felony or a theft.

Capital punishment the legal imposition of a sentence of death upon a convicted offender. Another term for the death penalty.

Carjacking the stealing of a car while it is occupied.

Chicago school. See **ecological theory.**

Civil law body of law that regulates arrangements between individuals, such as contracts and claims to property.

Classical school a criminological perspective operative in the late 1700s and early 1800s which had its roots in the Enlightenment, and which held that men and women are rational beings, that crime is the result of the exercise of free will, and that punishment can be effective in re-

ducing the incidence of crime, as it negates the pleasure to be derived from crime commission.

Clearance rate the proportion of reported or discovered crimes within a given offense category that are solved.

Code of Hammurabi an early set of laws established by the Babylonian King Hammurabi, who ruled the ancient city from 1792 to 1750 B.C.

Cohort a group of individuals sharing certain significant social characteristics in common, such as gender, time, and place of birth.

Cohort analysis a social scientific technique which studies a population that shares common characteristics over time. Cohort analysis usually begins at birth and traces the development of cohort members until they reach a certain age.

Common law law originating from usage and custom rather than from written statutes. The term refers to nonstatutory customs, traditions, and precedents that help guide judicial decision making.

Computer abuse any incident without color of right associated with computer technology in which a victim suffered or could have suffered loss, and/or a perpetrator by intention made or could have made gain.[1]

Computer bulletin board. See **bulletin board system (BBS).**

Computer crime any violation of a federal or state computer crime statute.

Computer-related crime any illegal act for which knowledge of computer technology is involved for its investigation, perpetration, or prosecution.

Computer virus a set of computer instructions that propagates copies or versions of itself into computer programs or data when it is executed.

Conditioning a psychological principle which holds that the frequency of any behavior can be increased or decreased through reward, punishment, and/or association with other stimuli.

Conduct norms the shared expectations of a social group relative to personal conduct.

Confidentiality. See **data confidentiality.**

Conflict perspective an analytical perspective on social organization which holds that conflict is a fundamental aspect of social life itself and can never be fully resolved.

Confounding effects rival explanations, also called competing hypotheses, which are threats to the internal or external validity of any research design.

Consensus model an analytical perspective on social organization which holds that most members of society agree as to what is right and what is wrong, and that the various elements of society work together in unison toward a common and shared vision of the greater good.

Constitutional theories those which explain criminality by reference to offenders' body types, inheritance, genetics, and/or external observable physical characteristics.

Constitutive criminology the study of the process by which human beings create an ideology of crime that sustains it (the notion of crime) as a concrete reality.

Containment those aspects of the social bond which act to prevent individuals from committing crimes and keep them from engaging in deviance.

Containment theory a form of control theory which suggests that a series of both internal and external factors contributes to law-abiding behavior.

Control group a group of experimental subjects which, although the subject of measurement and observation, is not exposed to the experimental intervention.

Control theory. See **social control theory.**

Controlled experiments those that attempt to hold conditions (other than the intentionally introduced experimental intervention) constant.

Corporate crime a violation of a criminal statute either by a corporate entity or by its executives, employees, or agents acting on behalf of and for the benefit of the corporation, partnership, or other form of business entity.[2]

Correctional psychology that aspect of forensic psychology which is concerned with the diagnosis and classification of offenders, the treatment of correctional populations, and the rehabilitation of inmates and other law violators.

Correlation a causal, complementary, or reciprocal relationship between two measurable variables. See also **statistical correlation.**

Cosa Nostra (literally, "our thing") or **Mafia** a term signifying organized crime, and one of a variety of names for the Outfit, the Mob, the syndicate, or simply, the organization.

Crime human conduct in violation of the criminal laws of a state, the federal government, or a local jurisdiction that has the power to make such laws.

Criminal anthropology the scientific study of the relationship between human physical characteristics and criminality.

Criminal homicide the causing of the death of another person without legal justification or excuse. Also, the illegal killing of one human being by another.

Criminal homicide (UCR) the name of the UCR category which includes and is limited to all offenses of causing the death of another person without justification or excuse.

Criminal justice the scientific study of crime, the criminal law, and components of the criminal justice system, including the police, courts, and corrections.

Criminal justice system the various agencies of justice, especially police, courts, and corrections, whose goal it is to apprehend, convict, punish, and rehabilitate law violators.

Criminal law that body of law that regulates actions which have the potential to harm interests of the state or the federal government.

Criminality a behavioral predisposition that disproportionately favors criminal activity.

Criminalize to make illegal.

Criminaloids a term used by Cesare Lombroso to describe occasional criminals who were pulled into criminality primarily by environmental influences.

Criminologist one who is trained in the field of criminology; also, one who studies crime, criminals, and criminal behavior.

Criminology an interdisciplinary profession built around the scientific study of crime and criminal behavior, including their form, causes, legal aspects, and control.

Criminology of place. See **environmental criminology.**

Critical criminology. See **radical criminology.**

Culture conflict a sociological perspective on crime which suggests that the root cause of criminality can be found in a clash of values between variously socialized groups over what is acceptable or proper behavior.

Cybercrime crime committed with the use of computers, or via the manipulation of digital forms of data. Another term for computer crime.

Cyberspace the computer-created matrix of virtual possibilities, including online services, wherein human beings interact with each other and with technology itself.

Cycloid a term developed by Ernst Kretschmer to describe a particular relationship between body build and personality type. The cycloid personality, which was associated with a heavyset, soft type of body, was said to vacillate between normality and abnormality.

Dangerous drugs a term used by the Drug Enforcement Administration (DEA) to refer to "broad categories or classes of controlled substances other than cocaine, opiates, and cannabis products." Amphetamines, methamphetamines, PCP (phencyclidine), LSD, methcathinone, and "designer drugs" are all considered dangerous drugs.

Dangerousness the likelihood that a given individual will later harm society or others; it is often measured in terms of **recidivism,** or as the likelihood of new crime commission or rearrest for a new crime within a five-year period following arrest or release from confinement.

Data confidentiality an ethical requirement of social scientific research which stipulates that research data not be shared outside of the research environment.

Data encryption the process by which information is encoded, making it unreadable to all but its intended recipients.

Date rape unlawful forced sexual intercourse with a woman against her will which occurs within the context of a dating relationship.

Daubert *standard* a test of scientific acceptability applicable to the gathering of evidence in criminal cases.

Deconstructionist theories emerging approaches which challenge existing criminological perspectives to debunk them, and which work toward replacing them with concepts more applicable to the postmodern era. Deconstructionist theories are generally postmodernist approaches, none of which have yet developed fully enough to actually deserve the name "theory."

Decriminalization (of drugs) reduces criminal penalties associated with the personal possession of a controlled substance.

Defensible space the range of mechanisms that combine to bring an environment under the control of its residents.

Demography the study of the characteristics of population groups (**demographics** the characteristics of such groups usually expressed in statistical fashion).

Descriptive statistics describe, summarize, or highlight the relationships within data which have been gathered.

Designer drugs "new substances designed by slightly altering the chemical makeup of other illegal or tightly controlled drugs."[3]

Deterrence the prevention of crime. See also **general deterrence** and **specific deterrence.**

Deterrence strategy a crime-control strategy that attempts "to diminish motivation for crime by increasing the perceived certainty, severity, or celerity of penalties."[4]

Deviance behavior that violates social norms or is statistically different from the "average."

Differential association the sociological thesis that criminality, like any other form of behavior, is learned through a process of association with others who communicate criminal values.

Discrediting information information that is inconsistent with the managed impressions being communicated in a given situation.

Displacement a shift of criminal activity from one spatial location to another.

DNA fingerprinting (or **profiling**) the use of biological residue found at the scene of a crime for genetic comparisons in aiding the identification of criminal suspects.

Dramaturgical perspective (also **dramaturgy**) a theoretical point of view which depicts human behavior as centered around the purposeful management of interpersonal impressions.

Drug-defined crimes violations of laws prohibiting or regulating the possession, use, or distribution of illegal drugs.

Drug-related crimes crimes in which drugs contribute to the offense (excluding violations of drug laws).

Drug trafficking. See **trafficking.**

Durham rule a standard for judging legal insanity which holds that "an accused is not criminally responsible if his unlawful act was the product of mental disease or mental defect."

Ecological theory, also commonly called the **Chicago school of criminology.** A type of sociological approach which emphasizes demographics (the characteristics of population groups) and geographics (the mapped location of such groups relative to one another) and sees the social disorganization that characterizes delinquency areas as a major cause of criminality and victimization.

Ectomorph a body type originally described as thin and fragile, with long, slender, poorly muscled extremities and delicate bones.

Ego the reality-testing part of the personality; also referred to as the reality principle. More formally, the personality component that is conscious, most immediately controls behavior, and is most in touch with external reality.[5]

Electroencephalogram (EEG) electrical measurements of brain wave activity.

Encryption. See **data encryption.**

Endomorph a body type originally described as soft and round, or overweight.

Enlightenment, (the) also known as the Age of Reason. A social movement that arose during the eighteenth century, and built upon ideas such as empiricism, rationality, free will, humanism, and natural law.

Environmental crimes violations of the criminal law which, although typically committed by businesses or by business officials, may also be committed by other persons or organizational entities, and which damage some protected or otherwise significant aspect of the natural environment.

Environmental criminology an emerging perspective which emphasizes the importance of geographic location and architectural features as they are associated with the prevalence of criminal victimization. (Note: as the term has been understood to date, environmental criminology is *not* the study of environmental crime, but rather a perspective that stresses how crime varies from place to place.)

Environmental scanning "a systematic effort to identify in an elemental way future developments (trends or events) that could plausibly occur over the time horizon of interest,"[6] and that might impact one's area of concern.

Ethnic succession the continuing process whereby one immigrant or ethnic group succeeds another through assumption of a particular position in society.

Eugenics the study of hereditary improvement by genetic control.

Evolutionary ecology an approach to understanding crime that draws attention to the ways people develop over the course of their lives.

Experiment. See **controlled experiments** or **quasi-experimental design.**

Expert systems computer hardware and software that attempt to duplicate the decision-making processes used by skilled investigators in the analysis of evidence and in the recognition of patterns which such evidence might represent.

External validity   the ability to generalize research findings to other settings.

Federal interest computers   those that are the property of the federal government, that belong to financial institutions, or are accessed across state lines without authorization.

Felony   a serious criminal offense; specifically one punishable by death or by incarceration in a prison facility for a year or more.

Felony murder   a special class of criminal homicide whereby an offender may be charged with first-degree murder when that person's criminal activity results in another person's death.

Feminist criminology   a developing intellectual approach which emphasizes gender issues in the subject matter of criminology.

First-degree murder   criminal homicide that is planned or involves premeditation.

Focal concerns   the key values of any culture, and especially the key values of a delinquent subculture.

Folkways   time-honored customs. Although folkways carry the force of tradition, their violation is unlikely to threaten the survival of the group. See also **mores.**

Forcible rape   as defined in the UCR Program, is the carnal knowledge of a female forcibly and against her will. Assaults or attempts to commit rape by force or threat of force are also included in the UCR definition; however, statutory rape (without force) and other sex offenses are excluded.

Forensic psychiatry   that branch of psychiatry having to do with the study of crime and criminality.

Forfeiture.   See **asset forfeiture.**

Frustration-aggression theory   holds that frustration, which is a natural consequence of living, is a root cause of crime. Criminal behavior can be a form of adaptation when it results in stress reduction.

Future criminology   the study of likely futures as they impinge on crime and its control.

Futures research   "a multidisciplinary branch of operations research" whose principal aim "is to facilitate long-range planning based on (1) forecasting from the past supported by mathematical models, (2) cross-disciplinary treatment of its subject matter, (3) systematic use of expert judgment, and (4) a systems-analytical approach to its problems."[7]

Futurist   one who studies the future.

General deterrence   a goal of criminal sentencing which seeks to prevent others from committing crimes similar to the one for which a particular offender is being sentenced.

General theory   one that attempts to explain all (or at least most) forms of criminal conduct through a single, overarching approach.

Guilty but mentally ill (GBMI)   a finding that offenders are guilty of the criminal offense with which they are charged but, because of their prevailing mental condition, they are generally sent to psychiatric hospitals for treatment rather than to prison. Once they have been declared "cured," however, such offenders can be transferred to correctional facilities to serve out their sentences.

Habitual offender statutes   laws intended to keep repeat criminal offenders behind bars. These laws sometimes come under the rubric of "three strikes and you're out."

Hacker   a person who views and uses computers as objects for exploration and exploitation.

Hedonistic calculus or **utilitarianism**   the belief, first proposed by Jeremy Bentham, that behavior holds value to any individual undertaking it according to the amount of pleasure or pain that it can be expected to produce for that person.

Heroin signature program (HSP)   a DEA program that identifies the geographic source area of a heroin sample through the detection of specific chemical characteristics in the sample peculiar to the source area.

Homicide. See **criminal homicide.**

Household crimes (NCVS) attempted and completed crimes that do not involve confrontation (such as burglary, motor vehicle theft, and household larceny).

Hypoglycemia a condition characterized by low blood sugar.

Hypothesis 1. [a]n explanation that accounts for a set of facts and that can be tested by further investigation . . . 2. [s]omething that is taken to be true for the purpose of argument or investigation.[8]

Id the aspect of the personality from which drives, wishes, urges, and desires emanate. More formally, the division of the psyche associated with instinctual impulses and demands for immediate satisfaction of primitive needs.[9]

Illegitimate opportunity structure subcultural pathways to success which are disapproved of by the wider society.

Impression management the intentional enactment of practiced behavior which is intended to convey to others one's desirable personal characteristics and social qualities.

Incapacitation the use of imprisonment or other means to reduce the likelihood that an offender will be capable of committing future offenses.

Individual rights advocates those who seek to protect personal freedoms in the face of criminal prosecution.

Inferential statistics specify how likely findings are to be true for other populations, or in other locales.

Informed consent an ethical requirement of social scientific research which specifies that research subjects will be informed as to the nature of the research about to be conducted, their anticipated role in it, and the uses to which the data they provide will be put.

Insanity (law) a legally established inability to understand right from wrong, or to conform one's behavior to the requirements of the law.

Insanity (psychological) persistent mental disorder or derangement.[10] Also, a defense allowable in criminal courts.

Integrated theory an explanatory perspective that merges (or attempts to merge) concepts drawn from different sources.

Interactionist perspectives. See **social process theories.**

Interdiction an international drug control policy that aims to stop drugs from entering the country illegally.

Internal validity the certainty that experimental interventions did indeed cause the changes observed in the study group; also the control over confounding factors which tend to invalidate the results of an experiment.

Internet the world's largest computer network.

Intersubjectivity a scientific principle which requires that independent observers see the same thing under the same circumstances for observations to be regarded as valid.

Irresistible impulse test a standard for judging legal insanity which holds that a defendant is not guilty of a criminal offense if the person, by virtue of their mental state or psychological condition, was not able to resist committing the action in question.

Juke family a well-known "criminal family" studied by Richard L. Dugdale.

Just deserts model the notion that criminal offenders deserve the punishment they receive at the hands of the law, and that punishments should be appropriate to the type and severity of crime committed.

Kallikak family a well-known "criminal family" studied by Henry H. Goddard.

Kefauver Committee formed in 1951, was the better known name for the federal Special Committee to investigate Originated Crime in Interstate Commerce.

Kriminalpolitik the political handling of crime, or a criminology-based social policy.

Labeling an interactionist perspective which sees continued crime as a consequence of limited opportunities for acceptable behavior which follow from the negative responses of society to those defined as offenders.

Larceny   the unlawful taking or attempted taking of property other than a motor vehicle from the possession of another, by stealth, without force and without deceit, with intent to permanently deprive the owner of the property.

Larceny-theft (UCR)   the unlawful taking, carrying, leading, or riding away by stealth of property, other than a motor vehicle, from the possession or constructive possession of another, including attempts.

Law and order advocates   those who suggest that, under certain circumstances involving criminal threats to public safety, the interests of society should take precedence over individual rights.

Law Enforcement Assistance Administration (LEAA)   A federal program established under Title 1 of the Omnibus Crime Control and Safe Streets Act of 1967, designed to provide assistance to police agencies.

Learning theory   the general notion that crime is an acquired form of behavior.

Legalization   (of drugs) eliminates the laws and associated criminal penalties that prohibit the production, sale, distribution, and possession of a controlled substance.

Life course theories   explanations for criminality that recognize that criminogenic influences have their greatest impact during the early stages of life, and hold that experiences which children have shape them for the rest of their lives.

Lifestyle theory.   See **routine activities theory.**

Mafia.   See *Cosa Nostra*.

Mala in se   acts that are thought to be wrong in and of themselves.

Mala prohibita   acts that are wrong only because they are prohibited.

Marxist criminology.   See **radical criminology.**

Mass murder   the illegal killing of four or more victims at one location, within one event.

McNaughten *rule*   a standard for judging legal insanity which requires that offenders not know what they were doing, or if they did, that they not know it was wrong.

Mesomorph   a body type described as athletic and muscular.

Meta-analysis   a study of other studies about a particular topic of interest.

Misdemeanor   a criminal offense which is less serious than a felony; one punishable by incarceration, usually in a local confinement facility, typically for a year or less.

Money laundering   the process of converting illegally earned assets, originating as cash, to one or more alternative forms to conceal such incriminating factors as illegal origin and true ownership.[11]

Monozyotic (or MZ) twins,   as opposed to dizygotic (or DZ) twins, develop from the same egg, and carry virtually the same genetic material.

Moral enterprise   a term which encompasses all the efforts a particular interest group makes to have its sense of propriety enacted into law.

Mores   behavioral proscriptions covering potentially serious violations of a group's values. Examples might include strictures against murder, rape, and robbery. See also **folkways.**

Motor vehicle theft (UCR)   the theft or attempted theft of a motor vehicle. According to the FBI, this offense category includes the stealing of automobiles, trucks, buses, motorcycles, motorscooters, snowmobiles, etc.

National Crime Victimization Survey (NCVS)   conducted annually by the Bureau of Justice Statistics (BJS); provides data on surveyed households that report they were affected by crime.

National Incident-Based Reporting System (NIBRS)   a new form of the UCR that will collect data on each single incident and arrest within twenty-two crime categories.

Natural law   the philosophical perspective that certain immutable laws are fundamental to human nature and can be readily ascertained through reason. Manmade laws, in contrast, are said to derive from human experience and history—

both of which are subject to continual change.

Natural rights the rights which, according to natural law theorists, individuals retain in the face of government action and interests.

Negligent homicide in Uniform Crime Reports (UCR) terminology causing death of another by recklessness or gross negligence.

Neoclassical criminology a contemporary version of classical criminology which emphasizes deterrence and retribution with reduced emphasis on rehabilitation.

Neurosis functional disorders of the mind or of the emotions involving anxiety, phobia, or other abnormal behavior.

Nurturant strategy a crime-control strategy that attempts "to forestall development of criminality by improving early life experiences and channeling child and adolescent development"[12] into desirable directions.

Occupational crime any act punishable by law which is committed through opportunity created in the course of an occupation that is legal.[13]

Offense (1) a violation of the criminal law or, in some jurisdictions, (2) a minor crime, such as jaywalking, sometimes described as "ticketable."

Office of Juvenile Justice and Delinquency Prevention (OJJDP) a national program that develops monetary and direct victim service programs for juvenile courts.

Omerta the informal, unwritten code of organized crime which demands silence and loyalty, among other things, of family members.

Operant behavior behavior that affects the environment in such a way as to produce responses or further behavioral cues.

Operationalization the process by which concepts are made measurable.

Opportunity structure a path to success. Opportunity structures may be of two types: legitimate and illegitimate.

Organized crime the unlawful activities of the members of a highly organized, disciplined association engaged in supplying illegal goods and services, including but not limited to gambling, prostitution, loansharking, narcotics, labor racketeering, and other unlawful activities of members of such organizations.[14]

Panopticon a prison designed by Jeremy Bentham which was to be a circular building with cells along the circumference, each clearly visible from a central location staffed by guards.

Paradigm an example, model, or theory.

Paranoid schizophrenics schizophrenic individuals who suffer from delusions and hallucinations.

Part I offenses that group of offenses, also called "major offenses" or "index offenses," for which the UCR publishes counts of reported instances, and which consist of murder, rape, robbery, aggravated assault, burglary, larceny, auto theft, and arson.

Participant observation a variety of strategies in data gathering in which the researcher observes a group by participating, to varying degrees, in the activities of the group.[15]

Participatory justice a relatively informal type of criminal justice case processing which makes use of local community resources rather than requiring traditional forms of official intervention.

Peace model an approach to crime control which focuses on effective ways for developing a shared consensus on critical issues which have the potential to seriously affect the quality of life.

Peacemaking criminology a perspective which holds that crime-control agencies and the citizens they serve should work together to alleviate social problems and human suffering and thus reduce crime.

Penal couple a term that describes the relationship between victim and criminal. Also, the two individuals most involved in the criminal act—the offender and the victim.

Pharmaceutical diversion the process by which legitimately manufactured controlled substances are diverted for illicit use.

Phenomenological criminology the study of crime as a social phenomenon that is created through a process of social interaction.

Phenomenology the study of the contents of human consciousness without regard to external conventions or prior assumptions.

Phone phreak a person who uses switched, dialed-access telephone services as objects for exploration and exploitation.

Phrenology the study of the shape of the head to determine anatomical correlates of human behavior.

Piracy. See **software piracy.**

Pluralistic perspective an analytical approach to social organization which holds that a multiplicity of values and beliefs exist in any complex society, but that most social actors agree on the usefulness of law as a formal means of dispute resolution.

Positivism the application of scientific techniques to the study of crime and criminals.

Postcrime victimization or **secondary victimization** refers to problems in living which tend to follow from initial victimization.

Postmodern criminology a brand of criminology that developed following World War II, and that builds on the tenets inherent in postmodern social thought.

Power-control theory a perspective which holds that the distribution of crime and delinquency within society is to some degree founded upon the consequences which power relationships within the wider society hold for domestic settings, and for the everyday relationships between men, women, and children within the context of family life.

Primary deviance initial deviance often undertaken to deal with transient problems in living.

Primary research research characterized by original and direct investigation.

Proletariat in Marxian theory, the working class.

Protection/avoidance strategy a crime-control strategy that attempts to reduce criminal opportunities by changing peo-

ple's routine activities, increasing guardianship, or by incapacitating convicted offenders.[16]

Psychiatric criminology theories derived from the medical sciences, including neurology, and which, like other psychological theories, focus on the individual as the unit of analysis. Psychiatric theories form the basis of psychiatric criminology. See **forensic psychiatry.**

Psychiatric theories those derived from the medical sciences, including neurology, and which, like other psychological theories, focus on the individual as the unit of analysis.

Psychoactive substances those substances that affect the mind, mental processes, or emotions.

Psychoanalysis the theory of human psychology founded by Freud on the concepts of the unconscious, resistance, repression, sexuality, and the Oedipus complex.[17]

Psychoanalytic criminology a psychiatric approach developed by the Austrian psychiatrist Sigmund Freud which emphasizes the role of personality in human behavior, and which sees deviant behavior as the result of dysfunctional personalities.

Psychological profiling the attempt to categorize, understand, and predict the behavior of certain types of offenders based on behavioral clues they provide.

Psychological theories those derived from the behavioral sciences and which focus on the individual as the unit of analysis. Psychological theories place the locus of crime causation within the personality of the individual offender.

Psychopath or **sociopath** a person with a personality disorder, especially one manifested in aggressively antisocial behavior, which is often said to be the result of a poorly developed superego.

Psychopathology the study of pathological mental conditions, that is, mental illness.

Psychosis a form of mental illness in which sufferers are said to be out of touch with reality.

Psychotherapy a form of psychiatric treatment based on psychoanalytical principles and techniques.

Public policy a course of action that government takes in an effort to solve a problem or to achieve an end.

Punishments undesirable behavioral consequences likely to decrease the frequency of occurrence of that behavior.

Pure research research undertaken simply for the sake of advancing scientific knowledge.

Qualitative methods research techniques that produce subjective results or results that are difficult to quantify.

Quantitative methods research techniques that produce measurable results.

Quasi-experimental designs approaches to research which, although less powerful than experimental designs, are deemed worthy of use when better designs are not feasible.

Radical criminology a perspective which holds that the causes of crime are rooted in social conditions which empower the wealthy and the politically well organized, but disenfranchise those less fortunate. Also called **Marxist** or **critical criminology.**

Randomization the process whereby individuals are assigned to study groups without biases or differences resulting from selection.

Rape (NCVS) carnal knowledge through the use of force or the threat of force, including attempts. Statutory rape (without force) is excluded. Both heterosexual and homosexual rape are included.

Rape (UCR). See **forcible rape.**

Rational choice theory a perspective which holds that criminality is the result of conscious choice, and which predicts that individuals choose to commit crime when the benefits outweigh the costs of disobeying the law.

Reaction formation the process in which a person openly rejects that which he or she wants, or aspires to, but cannot obtain or achieve.

Realist criminology an emerging perspective that insists on a pragmatic assessment of crime and its associated problems.

Recidivism the repetition of criminal behavior.

Recidivism rate the percentage of convicted offenders who have been released from prison and who are later rearrested for a new crime, generally within five years following release. Also see **dangerousness.**

Reintegrative shaming that form of shaming, imposed as a sanction by the criminal justice system, that is thought to strengthen the moral bond between the offender and the community.

Replicability (experimental) a scientific principle which holds that the same observations made at one time can be had again at a later time if all other conditions are the same.

Research the use of standardized, systematic procedures in the search for knowledge.[18]

Research design the logic and structure inherent in an approach to data gathering.

Restitution a criminal sanction, in particular the payment of compensation by the offender to the victim.

Restorative justice a postmodern perspective which stresses "remedies and restoration rather than prison, punishment and victim neglect."[19]

Retribution the act of taking revenge upon a criminal perpetrator.

Rewards desirable behavioral consequences likely to increase the frequency of occurrence of that behavior.

RICO an acronym for the Racketeer Influenced and Corrupt Organization statute, which was part of the federal Organized Crime Control Act of 1970.

Robbery (UCR) the unlawful taking or attempted taking of property that is in the immediate possession of another by force or threat of force or violence and/or by putting the victim in fear.

Routine activities theory (or **lifestyle theory**) a brand of rational choice theory which suggests that lifestyles contribute significantly to both the volume and type of crime found in any society.

Scenario writing a technique intended to predict future outcomes, and builds upon environmental scanning by attempting to assess the likelihood of a variety of possible outcomes once important trends have been identified.

Schizophrenics mentally ill individuals who are out of touch with reality and suffer from disjointed thinking.

Second-degree murder criminal homicide that is unplanned and is often described as a "crime of passion."

Secondary analysis the reanalysis of existing data.

Secondary deviance that which results from official labeling and from association with others who have been so labeled.

Secondary research new evaluations of existing information which has already been collected by other researchers.

Selective incapacitation a social policy which seeks to protect society by incarcerating those individuals deemed to be the most dangerous.

Serial murder criminal homicide which involves the killing of several victims in three or more separate events.

Simple assault (NCVS) an attack without a weapon resulting either in minor injury or in undetermined injury requiring less than two days of hospitalization.

Situational choice theory a brand of rational choice theory which views criminal behavior "as a function of choices and decisions made within a context of situational constraints and opportunities."[20]

Situational crime prevention a social policy approach that looks to develop greater understanding of crime and more effective crime prevention strategies through concern with the physical, organizational, and social environments that make crime possible.[21]

Social bond the rather intangible link between individuals and the society of which they are a part; created through the process of socialization.

Social capital the degree of positive relationships with other persons and with social institutions, that individuals build up over the course of their lives.

Social class distinctions made between individuals on the basis of important defining social characteristics.

Social contract the Enlightenment-era concept that human beings abandon their natural state of individual freedom to join together and form society. Although, in the process of forming a social contract, individuals surrender some freedoms to society as a whole, government, once formed, is obligated to assume responsibilities toward its citizens and to provide for their protection and welfare.

Social control theory a perspective which predicts that when social constraints on antisocial behavior are weakened or absent, delinquent behavior emerges. Rather than stressing causative factors in criminal behavior, control theory asks why people actually obey rules instead of breaking them.

Social disorganization a condition said to exist when a group is faced with social change, uneven development of culture, maladaptiveness, disharmony, conflict, and lack of consensus.

Social ecology an approach to criminological theorizing that attempts to link the structure and organization of human community to interactions with its localized environment.

Social epidemiology the study of social epidemics and diseases of the social order.

Social learning theory a psychological perspective that says people learn how to behave by modeling themselves after others whom they have the opportunity to observe.

Social pathology a concept that compares society to a physical organism and sees criminality as an illness.

Social policies government initiatives, programs, and plans intended to address problems in society. The "War on Crime," for example, is a kind of generic (large-scale) social policy—one consisting of many smaller programs.

Social problems perspective the belief that crime is a manifestation of underlying social problems such as poverty, discrimination, pervasive family violence, inadequate socialization practices, and the breakdown of traditional social institutions.

Social process theories, also known as **interactionist perspectives** emphasize the give-and-take which occurs between offender, victim, and society—and specifically between the offender and agents of formal social control such as the police, courts, and correctional organizations.

Social relativity the notion that social events are differently interpreted according to the cultural experiences and personal interests of the initiator, the observer, or the recipient of that behavior.

Social responsibility perspective the belief that individuals are fundamentally responsible for their own behavior and that they choose crime over other, more law-abiding, courses of action.

Social-structural theories explain crime by reference to various aspects of the social fabric. They emphasize relationships between social institutions and describe the types of behavior which tend to characterize *groups* of people as opposed to *individuals.*

Social structure the pattern of social organization and the interrelationships between institutions characteristic of a society.

Socialization the lifelong process of social experience whereby individuals acquire the cultural patterns of their society.

Sociobiology "the systematic study of the biological basis of all social behavior."[22]

Sociopath. See **psychopath.**

Software piracy the unauthorized and illegal copying of software programs.

Somatotyping the classification of human beings into types according to body build and other physical characteristics.

Specific deterrence a goal of criminal sentencing which seeks to prevent a particular offender from engaging in repeat criminality.

State-organized crime acts defined by law as criminal and committed by state offi-cials in the pursuit of their job as representatives of the state.[23]

Statistical correlation the simultaneous increase or decrease in value of two numerically valued random variables.[24]

Statistical school a criminological perspective with roots in the early 1800s which seeks to uncover correlations between crime rates and other types of demographic data.

Statute a formal written enactment of a legislative body.[25]

Statutory law law in the form of statutes or formal written strictures, made by a legislature or governing body with the power to make law.

Stigmatic shaming that form of shaming, imposed as a sanction by the criminal justice system, that is thought to destroy the moral bond between the offender and the community.

Strain theory or **anomie theory** a sociological approach which posits a disjuncture between socially and subculturally sanctioned means and goals as the cause of criminal behavior.

Strategic assessment a technique that assesses the risks and opportunities facing those who plan for the future.

Subcultural theory a sociological perspective that emphasizes the contribution made by variously socialized cultural groups to the phenomenon of crime.

Subculture a collection of values and preferences which is communicated to subcultural participants through a process of socialization.

Sublimation the psychological process whereby one aspect of consciousness comes to be symbolically substituted for another.

Substantial capacity test a standard for judging legal insanity which requires that a person lack "the mental capacity needed to understand the wrongfulness of his act, or to conform his behavior to the requirements of the law."

Superego the moral aspect of the personality; much like the conscience. More formally, the division of the psyche that develops by the incorporation of the perceived moral standards of the community, is mainly unconscious, and includes the conscience.[26]

Supermale   a male individual displaying the XYY chromosome structure.

Superpredators   a new generation of juveniles "who are coming of age in actual and 'moral poverty' without the benefits of parents, teachers, coaches and clergy to teach them right from wrong and show them 'unconditional love.' "[27] The term is often applied to those inner-city youths who meet the criteria it sets forth.

Survey research   a social science data-gathering technique which involves the use of questionnaires.

Tagging   like **labeling,** the process whereby an individual is negatively defined by agencies of justice.

Target hardening   the reduction in criminal opportunity, generally through the use of physical barriers, architectural design, and enhanced security measures, of a particular location.

Techniques of neutralization   culturally available justifications which can provide criminal offenders with the means to disavow responsibility for their behavior.

TEMPEST   a standard developed by the U.S. government that requires that electromagnetic emanations from computers designated as "secure" be below levels that would allow radio receiving equipment to "read" the data being computed.

Terrorism   a violent act or an act dangerous to human life in violation of the criminal laws of the United States or of any state to intimidate or coerce a government, the civilian population, or any segment thereof, in furtherance of political or social objectives.[28]

Testosterone   the primary male sex hormone; produced in the testes, its function is to control secondary sex characteristics and sexual drive.

Tests of significance   statistical techniques intended to provide researchers with confidence that their results are in fact true, and not the result of sampling error.

Thanatos   a death wish.

Theory   a series of interrelated propositions that attempt to describe, explain, predict, and ultimately to control some class of events. A theory gains explanatory power from inherent logical consistency and is "tested" by how well it describes and predicts reality.

Threat analysis (or **risk analysis**)   involves a complete and thorough assessment of the kinds of perils facing an organization.

Three-strikes   a provision of some criminal statutes which mandates life imprisonment for criminals convicted of three violent felonies or serious drug offenses.

Total institutions   facilities from which individuals can rarely come and go, and in which communal life is intense and circumscribed. Individuals in total institutions tend to eat, sleep, play, learn, and worship (if at all) together.

Trafficking   includes manufacturing, distributing, dispensing, importing, and exporting (or possession with intent to do the same) a controlled substance or a counterfeit substance.[29]

Trephination   a form of surgery, typically involving bone and especially the skull. Early instances of cranial trephination have been taken as evidence for primitive beliefs in spirit possession.

Twelve Tables   early Roman laws written circa 450 B.C. which regulated family, religious, and economic life.

Unicausal   having one cause. Unicausal theories posit only one source for all that they attempt to explain.

Uniform Crime Report (UCR)   a summation of crime statistics tallied annually by the Federal Bureau of Investigation (FBI) and consisting primarily of data on crimes reported to the police and of arrests.

Utilitarianism.   See **hedonistic calculus.**

Variable   a concept that can undergo measurable changes.

Verstehen   the kind of subjective understanding that can be achieved by criminologists who immerse themselves into the everyday world of the criminals they study.

Victim impact statement   a written document which describes the losses, suffering, and trauma experienced by the crime victim or by the victim's survivors. In jurisdictions where victim impact statements are used, judges are expected to consider them in arriving at an appropriate sentence for the offender.

Victim-precipitated homicide killing in which the "victim" was the first to commence the interaction or was the first to resort to physical violence.

Victim-proneness the degree of an individual's likelihood of victimization.

Victim–witness assistance programs counsel victims, orient them to the justice process, and provide a variety of other services such as transportation to court, child care during court appearances, and referrals to social service agencies.

Victimization rate (NCVS) a measure of the occurrence of victimizations among a specified population group. For personal crimes, this is based on the number of victimizations per 1,000 residents age 12 or older. For household crimes, the victimization rates are calculated using the number of incidents per 1,000 households.

Victimogenesis the contributory background of a victim as a result of which he or she becomes prone to victimization.

Victimology the study of victims and their contributory role, if any, in crime causation.

Victims of Crime Act (VOCA) passed by the U.S. Congress in 1984, it helps support local and state victim assistance programs.

Virus (computer) a set of computer instructions that propagates copies or versions of itself into computer programs or data when it is executed.

White-collar crime violations of the criminal law committed by a person of respectability and high social status in the course of his or her occupation.

NOTES

⚏

[1] This and other computer crime–related terms are generally adapted from Donn B. Parker, *Computer Crime: Criminal Justice Resource Manual* (Washington, D.C.: National Institute of Justice, 1989).

[2] Michael L. Benson, Francis T. Cullen, and William J. Maakestad, *Local Prosecutors and Corporate Crime* (Washington, D.C.: National Institute of Justice, 1993).

[3] James A. Inciardi, *The War On Drugs II* (Mountain View, Calif.: Mayfield), 1992, p. 79.

[4] Bryan Vila, "A General Paradigm for Understanding Criminal Behavior: Extending Evolutionary Ecological Theory," *Criminology,* vol. 32, no. 3 (August 1994), pp. 311–359.

[5] *American Heritage Dictionary and Electronic Thesaurus* (Boston: Houghton Mifflin, 1987).

[6] George F. Cole, "Criminal Justice in the Twenty-First Century: The Role of Futures Research," in John Klofas and Stan Stojkovic, eds., *Crime and Justice in the Year 2010* (Belmont, Calif.: Wadsworth, 1995).

[7] Society of Police Futurists International, *PFI: The Future of Policing* (brochure), no date.

[8] *American Heritage Dictionary and Electronic Thesaurus* on CD-ROM (text copyrighted 1987 by the Houghton Mifflin Company).

[9] Ibid.

[10] Ibid.

[11] Clifford Karchmer and Douglas Ruch, "State and Local Money Laundering Control Strategies," *NIJ Research in Brief* (Washington, D.C.: NIJ, 1992), p. 1.

[12] Bryan Vila, "A General Paradigm for Understanding Criminal Behavior: Extending Evolutionary Ecological Theory."

[13] Gary S. Green, *Occupational Crime* (Chicago: Nelson-Hall, 1990), p. 12.

[14] The Omnibus Crime Control Act of 1970.

[15] Frank E. Hagan, *Research Methods in Criminal Justice and Criminology* (New York: Macmillan, 1993), p. 103.

[16] Bryan Vila, "Human Nature and Crime Control: Improving the Feasibility of Nurturant

Strategies," *Politics and the Life Sciences,* March 1997, pp. 3–21.

[17]*American Heritage Dictionary and Electronic Thesaurus.*

[18]Abraham Kaplan, *The Conduct of Inquiry: Methodology for Behavioral Science* (San Francisco: Chandler, 1964), p. 71.

[19]Fay Honey Knopp, "Community Solutions to Sexual Violence: Feminist-Abolitionist Perspectives," in Harold Pepinsky and Richard Quinney, eds., *Criminology as Peacemaking* (Bloomington: Indiana University Press, 1991), p. 183.

[20]Ronald V. Clarke and Derek B. Cornish, eds., *Crime Control in Britain: A Review of Police and Research* (Albany: SUNY Press), p. 8.

[21]David Weisburd, "Reorienting Crime Prevention Research and Policy: From the Causes of Criminality to the Context of Crime," *NIJ Research Report* (Washington, D.C.: NIJ, June 1997).

[22]Edward O. Wilson, *Sociobiology: The New Synthesis* (Cambridge: The Belknap Press of Harvard University Press, 1975).

[23]William J. Chambliss, "State-Organized Crime—The American Society of Criminology, 1988 Presidential Address," *Criminology,* vol. 27, no. 2 (1989), pp. 183–208.

[24]*American Heritage Dictionary and Electronic Thesaurus.*

[25]Henry Campbell Black, *Black's Law Dictionary,* 6th ed. (St. Paul: West Publishing Co., 1990), p. 1410.

[26]Ibid.

[27]The term *superpredator* is generally attributed to John J. DiIulio, Jr. See John J. DiIulio, Jr., "The Question of Black Crime," *The Public Interest,* Fall 1994, pp. 3–12.

[28]Federal Bureau of Investigation, Counterterrorism Section, *Terrorism in the United States, 1987* (Washington, D.C.: FBI, December 1987).

[29]Bureau of Justice Statistics, *Drugs, Crime and the Justice System* (Washington, D.C.: U.S. Department of Justice, December 1992), p. 181.

INDEXES

SUBJECT INDEX

NAME INDEX